Ideas
in
Cultural Perspective

Journal of the history of ideas.

Ideas in Cultural Perspective

edited by

Philip P. Wiener and Aaron Noland

RUTGERS UNIVERSITY PRESS

New Brunswick, New Jersey

Copyright © 1962 by Rutgers, The State University
Library of Congress Catalogue Card Number: 62-13766
Printed in the United States of America

Rutgers University Press is grateful for permission to reprint these articles which first appeared in the following issues of the Journal of the History of Ideas:

"The Mona Lisa in the History of Taste," by GEORGE BOAS (I, 2, pp. 207–224, 1940); "Religion and Modern Individualism," by HERBERT BUTTERFIELD (XXII, 1, pp. 33–46, 1961); "The Historical Background of Maritain's Humanism," by G. G. COULTON (V. 4, pp. 415–433, 1944); "Jane Addams on Human Nature," by MERLE CURTI (XXII, 2, pp. 240–253, 1961); "James Marsh and American Philosophy," by JOHN DEWEY (II, 2, pp. 131–150, 1941); "Intellectual History and Its Neighbors," by JOHN HIGHAM (XV, 3, pp. 339–347, 1954); "History and the Humanities," by HAJO HOLBORN (IX, 1. pp. 65–69, 1948); "Goethe and the History of Ideas," by WALTER A. KAUFMANN (X, 4, pp. 503–516, 1949); "The Idea of God in Elizabethan Medicine," by PAUL H. KOCHER (XI, 1. pp. 3–29, 1950); "The Genesis and Character of English Nationalism," by HANS KOHN (I, 1, pp. 69–94, 1940); "Lotze's Influence on the Pragmatism and Practical Philosophy of William James," by OTTO F. KRAUSHAAR (I, 4, pp. 439–458, 1940); "The Modern System of the Arts: A Study in the History of Aesthetics," by PAUL OSKAR KRISTELLER (XII, 4, pp. 496–527 and XIII, 1, pp. 17–46, 1951–52); "Reflections on the History of Ideas," by ARTHUR O. LOVEJOY (I, 1, pp. 3–23, 1940); "Recent Trends in the Theory of Historiography," by MAURICE MANDELBAUM (XVI, 4, pp. 506–517, 1955); "'Preparation for Salvation' in XVIIth-Century New England," by PERRY MILLER (IV, 3, pp. 253–286, 1943); "St. Augustine and the Christian Idea of Progress," by THEODOR E. MOMMSEN (XII, 3, pp. 346–374, 1951); "Individualism in Jean Jaurès' Socialist Thought," by AARON NOLAND (XXII, 1, pp. 63–80, 1961); "The Theoretical Development of the Sociology of Religion," by TALCOTT PARSONS (V, 2, pp. 176–190, 1944); "The Influence of XVIII-Century Ideas on the French Revolution," by HENRI PEYRE (X, 1, 63–87, 1949); "Timelessness and Romanticism," by GEORGES POULET (XV, 1, pp. 3–22, 1954); "Leonardo and Freud. An Art-Historical Study," by MEYER SCHAPIRO (XVII, 2, pp. 147–178, 1956; "Bach: The Conflict Between the Sacred and the Secular," by LEO SCHRADE (VII, 2, pp. 151–194, 1946); "Rembrandt and His Contemporary Critics," by SEYMOUR SLIVE (XIV, 2, pp. 203–220, 1953); "Political Philosophy and History," by LEO STRAUSS (X, 1, pp. 30–50, 1949); "Symposium on 'Causation in History,'" by FREDERICK J. TEGGART and MORRIS R. COHEN (III, 1, pp. 3–29, 1942); "The Double Standard," by KEITH THOMAS (XX, 2, pp. 195–216, 1959); "Existential Philosophy," by PAUL TILLICH (V, 1, pp. 44–70, 1944); "Some Methods and Problems in the History of Ideas," by PHILIP P. WIENER (XXII, 4, pp. 531–548, 1961); "Christian Myth and Christian History," by LYNN WHITE, Jr. (III, 2, pp. 145–158, 1942); "The Social Background of Taine's Philosophy of Art," by MARTHA WOLFENSTEIN (V, 3, pp. 332–358, 1944); "Extradeical and Intradeical Interpretations of Platonic Ideas," by HARRY A. WOLFSON (XXII, 1, pp. 3–32, 1961); "Chinese Civilization," by ARTHUR F. WRIGHT (XXI, 2, pp. 233–255, 1960).

Preface

Professor Arthur O. Lovejoy, father of the XXth-century study of the history of ideas, has indicated certain general features of that study, illustrated by this volume of essays selected from the *Journal of the History of Ideas,* of which he was the first Editor:

(1) the presence and influence of the same presuppositions or other operative "ideas" in very diverse provinces of thought in different periods;

(2) the rôle of semantic transitions and confusions, of shifts and ambiguities in the meanings of terms in the history of thought and taste;

(3) the internal tensions or waverings in the mind of almost every individual—sometimes discernible even in a single writing or on a single page—arising from conflicting ideas or incongruous propensities of feeling or taste to which he is susceptible, and

(4) implicit or incompletely explicit *assumptions,* or more or less *unconscious mental habits,* operating in the thought of an individual or a generation.

The articles presented here serve to illustrate the *range* of the history of ideas and some of its methods and problems.

Part I of this volume contains articles on the methodology of the history of ideas and on the relation of this discipline to other areas of intellectual history. Part II contains articles which explore the history of ideas in literature and art. Part III is devoted to articles examining the ideas in social and political thought. Part IV is composed of studies in philosophical and religious thought.

Philip P. Wiener
Aaron Noland

The City College, New York
February, 1962

Contents

Preface

I. METHODOLOGY IN THE HISTORY OF IDEAS

1. Reflections on the History of Ideas (I, 1, pp. 3–23)
   Arthur O. Lovejoy   3
2. Some Problems and Methods in the History of Ideas (XXII, 4, pp. 531–48) .... *Philip P. Wiener*   24
3. Symposium on "Causation in History" (III, 1, pp. 3–29)
   Frederick J. Teggart and Morris R. Cohen   42
4. Concerning Recent Trends in the Theory of Historiography (XVI, 4, pp. 506–517) .... *Maurice Mandelbaum*   69
5. Intellectual History and Its Neighbors (XV, 3, pp. 339–347)
   John Higham   81

II. HISTORY OF IDEAS IN LITERATURE AND ART

1. Leonardo and Freud: An Art-Historical Study (XVII, 2, pp. 147–178) .... *Meyer Schapiro*   93
2. The Mona Lisa in the History of Taste (I, 2, pp. 207–224)
   George Boas   127
3. The Modern System of the Arts: A Study in the History of Aesthetics (XII, 4, pp. 496–527; XIII, 1, pp. 17–46)
   Paul Oskar Kristeller   145
4. Rembrandt and His Contemporary Critics (XIV, 2, pp. 203–220) .... *Seymour Slive*   207
5. Bach: The Conflict Between the Sacred and the Secular (VII, 2, pp. 151–194) .... *Leo Schrade*   225
6. Goethe and the History of Ideas (X, 4, pp. 503–516)
   Walter A. Kaufmann   269
7. The Social Background of Taine's Philosophy of Art (V, 3, pp. 332–358) .... *Martha Wolfenstein*   283

III. SOCIAL AND POLITICAL THOUGHT

1. History and the Humanities (IX, 1, pp. 65–69)
   Hajo Holborn   313
2. The Theoretical Development of the Sociology of Religion (V, 2, pp. 176–190) .... *Talcott Parsons*   318
3. Political Philosophy and History (X, 1, pp. 30–50)
   Leo Strauss   333
4. The Study of Chinese Civilization (XXI, 2, pp. 233–255)
   Arthur F. Wright   354

5. The Genesis and Character of English Nationalism
     (I, 1, pp. 69–94) . . . . *Hans Kohn* 377
6. The Influence of XVIIIth-Century Ideas on the French
     Revolution (X, 1, pp. 63–87) . . . . *Henri Peyre* 403
7. Individualism in Jean Jaurès' Socialist Thought
     (XXII, 1, pp. 63–80) . . . . *Aaron Noland* 428
8. The Double Standard (XX, 2, pp. 195–216)
                                                                         Keith Thomas 446
9. Jane Addams on Human Nature (XXII, 2, pp. 240–253)
                                                                           Merle Curti 468

IV. PHILOSOPHICAL AND RELIGIOUS THOUGHT

1. Extradeical and Intradeical Interpretations of Platonic
     Ideas (XXII, 1, pp. 3–32) . . . . *Harry A. Wolfson* 485
2. St. Augustine and the Christian Idea of Progress
     (XII, 3, pp. 346–374) . . . . *Theodor E. Mommsen* 515
3. Christian Myth and Christian History (III, 2, pp. 145–158)
                                                                       Lynn White, Jr. 544
4. The Historical Background of Maritain's Humanism
     (V, 4, pp. 415–433) . . . . *G. G. Coulton* 558
5. The Idea of God in Elizabethan Medicine (XI, 1, pp. 3–29)
                                                                        Paul H. Kocher 577
6. "Preparation for Salvation" in XVIIth-Century New
     England (IV, 3, pp. 253–286) . . . . *Perry Miller* 604
7. Lotze's Influence on the Pragmatism and Practical
     Philosophy of William James (I, 4, pp. 439–458)
                                                                    Otto F. Kraushaar 638
8. Timelessness and Romanticism (XV, 1, pp. 3–22)
                                                                       Georges Poulet 658
9. James Marsh and American Philosophy (II, 2, pp. 131–150)
                                                                           John Dewey 678
10. Existential Philosophy (V, 1, pp. 44–70)
                                                                          Paul Tillich 698
11. Religion and Modern Individualism (XXII, 1, pp. 33–46)
                                                                   Herbert Butterfield 725

Index   739

I

METHODOLOGY IN THE HISTORY OF IDEAS

Reflections on the History of Ideas[1]

by ARTHUR O. LOVEJOY

Reprinted from the *Journal of the History of Ideas*—Vol I, No. 1, pp. 3-23

I

Whatever other definitions of man be true or false, it is generally admitted that he is distinguished among the creatures by the habit of entertaining general ideas. Like Br'er Rabbit he has always kept up a heap o' thinking; and it has usually been assumed—though the assumption has been nominally disputed by some schools of philosophers—that his thoughts have at all times had a good deal to do with his behavior, his institutions, his material achievements in technology and the arts, and his fortunes. Every branch of historical inquiry, consequently, may be said to include within its scope some portion of the history of ideas. But as a result of the subdivision and specialization increasingly characteristic of historical as of other studies during the last two centuries, the portions of that history which are pertinent to separate historical disciplines came to be treated usually in relative, though seldom in complete, isolation. The history of political events and social movements, of economic changes, of religion, of philosophy, of science, of literature and the other arts, of education, have been investigated by distinct groups of specialists, many of them little acquainted with the subjects and the researches of the others. The specialization which—the limitations of the individual mind being what they are—had this as its natural consequence was indispensable for the progress of historical knowledge; yet the consequence proved also, in the end,

[1] It has been thought desirable by the Board of Editors that the first number of the *Journal of the History of Ideas* should contain some prefatory observations on the nature and aims of the studies which the journal is designed to promote, and for some of the fruits of which it may provide a suitable vehicle of publication. The Editor to whom the task has been assigned has, however, already written somewhat lengthily elsewhere on the general subject (in *The Great Chain of Being*, 1936, Lecture I and in *Proc. of the Amer. Philos. Soc.*, vol. 78, pp. 529-543), and some repetition, in substance if not in phraseology, of these previous disquisitions on the same topic has been unavoidable. Some aspects of it, on the other hand, which have been there dealt with, have been here passed over, in order to have space for comments on certain relevant but currently controverted questions. For the opinions expressed on these questions the writer alone is responsible.

an impediment to such progress. For the departmentalization—
whether by subjects, periods, nationalities, or languages—of the
study of the history of thought corresponds, for the most part, to
no real cleavages among the phenomena studied. The processes of
the human mind, in the individual or the group, which manifest
themselves in history, do not run in enclosed channels corresponding to the officially established divisions of university faculties; even
where these processes, or their modes of expression, or the objects
to which they are applied, are logically discriminable into fairly
distinct types, they are in perpetual interplay. And ideas are the
most migratory things in the world. A preconception, category,
postulate, dialectical motive, pregnant metaphor or analogy, "sacred
word," mood of thought, or explicit doctrine, which makes its first
appearance upon the scene in one of the conventionally distinguished provinces of history (most often, perhaps, in philosophy)
may, and frequently does, cross over into a dozen others. To be
acquainted only with its manifestation in one of these is, in many
cases, to understand its nature and affinities, its inner logic and
psychological operation, so inadequately that even *that* manifestation remains opaque and unintelligible. All historians—even, in
their actual practice, those who in theory disclaim any such pretension—seek in some sense and to some degree to discern causal
relations between events; but there is, unhappily, no law of nature
which specifies that all, or even the most important, antecedents of
a given historic effect, or all or the most important consequents of a
given cause, will lie within any one of the accepted subdivisions
of history. In so far as the endeavor to trace such relations stops
at the boundaries of one or another of these divisions, there is
always a high probability that some of the most significant—that is,
the most illuminating and explanatory—relations will be missed.
It has even sometimes happened that a conception of major historic
influence and importance has long gone unrecognized, because its
various manifestations, the parts which make up the whole story,
are so widely dispersed among different fields of historical study,
that no specialist in any one of these fields became distinctly aware
of it at all. Historiography, in short, for excellent practical reasons,
is divided, but the historic process is not; and this discrepancy
between the procedure and the subject-matter has tended, at best,
to produce serious lacunae in the study of the history of man, and
at worst, sheer errors and distortions.

Of such considerations as these, scholars in many branches of historical inquiry have in recent years become increasingly sensible. None, certainly, questions the indispensability of specialization; but more and more have come to see that specialization is not enough. In practice this sometimes manifests itself in a crossing-over of individual specialists into other fields than those to which they had originally devoted themselves and for which they have been trained. Administrative officers of educational institutions have sometimes been known to complain, with a certain puzzlement, of teachers and investigators who will not "stick to their subjects." But in most cases this propensity to disregard academic fences is not to be attributed to a wandering disposition or a coveting of neighbors' vineyards; it is, on the contrary, usually the inevitable consequence of tenacity and thoroughness in the cultivation of one's own. For— to repeat an observation which the present writer has already made elsewhere, with primary reference to literary history—"the quest of a historical understanding even of single passages in literature often drives the student into fields which at first seem remote enough from his original topic of investigation. The more you press in towards the heart of a narrowly bounded historical problem, the more likely you are to encounter in the problem itself a pressure which drives you outward beyond those bounds." To give specific illustrations of this fact would unduly lengthen these prelusive remarks;[2] examples will doubtless appear in abundance in subsequent pages of this journal. It is sufficient here to note, as a highly characteristic feature of contemporary work in many of the branches of historiography that are in any way concerned with the thoughts of men (and their related emotions, modes of expression, and actions), that the fences are—not, indeed, generally breaking down— but, at a hundred specific points, being broken through; and that the reason for this is that, at least at those points, the fences have been found to be obstacles to the proper comprehension of what lies on either side of them.

There is, unquestionably, some danger to historical scholarship in this newer tendency. It is the danger already intimated, that scholars soundly trained in the methods and widely acquainted with the literature of one limited—even though it be an arbitrarily limited—field may prove inadequately equipped for exploring other

[2] Some have been adduced by the writer in a paper above mentioned, *Proc. of the Amer. Philos. Soc.*, Vol. 78, pp. 532–535.

provinces into which they have, nevertheless, been naturally and legitimately led by the intrinsic connections of the subjects that they are investigating. Most contemporary historians of any national literature, for example, or of science or a particular science, recognize in principle—though many still recognize too little—that ideas derived from philosophical systems have had a wide, and sometimes a profound and decisive, influence upon the minds and the writings of the authors whose works they study; and they are constrained, therefore, to deal with these systems and to expound these ideas for their readers. But they do not—it is perhaps not too unmannerly to say—always do it very well. When this is the case, the fault, no doubt, often lies partly with the existing histories of philosophy, which frequently fail to give the non-philosopher what he most needs for his special historical inquiry; but they are, in any case, unsatisfying to the scholar who has learned from experience in his own specialty the risks of too implicit reliance upon secondary or tertiary sources. Even more, however, than an extensive reading of philosophical texts is needed for the accurate and sufficient understanding of the working of philosophical ideas in literature or in science—a certain aptitude for the discrimination and analysis of concepts, and an eye for not immediately obvious logical relations or quasi-logical affinities between ideas. These powers are, by a happy gift of nature, sometimes found in historical writers who would deprecate the title of "philosophers"; but in most cases, when they are attained at all, they owe much, also, to a persistent cultivation and training, of which the student of philosophy naturally gets more than specialists in the history of literature or science—and for lack of which the latter sometimes seem to the philosopher to go more or less widely astray in their necessary divagations into philosophy. They, in turn—especially the historian of science—could doubtless not infrequently respond with a *tu quoque* to the historian of philosophy; if so, the present point is the better illustrated; and many other illustrations of it might all too easily be found.

The remedy for the effects defective of specialization in historical inquiry, then, does not lie in a general practice, on the part of specialists, of simply invading one another's territories or taking over one another's jobs. It lies in closer coöperation among them at all those points where their provinces overlap, the establishment of more and better facilities for communication, mutual criticism and mutual aid—the focussing upon what are, in their nature, common problems, of all the special knowledges that are pertinent to them. It is one of the purposes of this journal to contribute, so far as its resources permit, towards such a more effective *liaison* among those whose studies have to do with the diverse but interrelated parts of history, in so far as history is concerned with the activities of man's mind and the effects of these upon what he has been and has done—or (to change the metaphor) to assist towards more cross-fertilization among the several fields of intellectual historiography. It is hoped that the journal will serve—among other things—as a useful medium for the publication of researches which traverse the customary boundary-lines, or are likely to be of interest and value to students in other fields than those in which they primarily lie. Its prospectus has already indicated, by way of illustration, some topics concerning which its editors believe further investigation to be potentially profitable, and on which contributions will be especially welcome:

1. The influence of classical on modern thought, and of European traditions and writings on American literature, arts, philosophy, and social movements.
2. The influence of philosophical ideas in literature, the arts, religion, and social thought, including the impact of pervasive general conceptions upon standards of taste and morality and educational theories and methods.
3. The influence of scientific discoveries and theories in the same provinces of thought, and in philosophy; the cultural effects of the applications of science.
4. The history of the development and the effects of individual pervasive and widely ramifying ideas or doctrines, such as evolution, progress, primitivism, diverse theories of human motivation and appraisals of human nature, mechanismic and organismic conceptions of nature and society, metaphysical and historical determinism and indeterminism, individualism and collectivism, nationalism and racialism.

But the function of this journal is not solely to help to bring about a fruitful correlation between older and more specialized disciplines. For the study of the history of ideas does not need to justify itself by its potential services—however great—to historical studies bearing other names. It has its own reason for being. It is not merely ancillary to the others; it is rather they that are, in great part, ancillary to it. To know, so far as may be known, the thoughts that have been widely held among men on matters of common human concernment, to determine how these thoughts have arisen, combined, interacted with, or counteracted, one another, and how they have severally been related to the imagination and emotions and behavior of those who have held them—this, though not, indeed, the whole of that branch of knowledge which we call history, is a distinct and essential part of it, and its central and most vital part. For, while the fixed or changing environmental conditions of human life, individual and collective, and conjunctions of circumstance which arise from no man's thinking or premeditation, are factors in the historic process never to be disregarded, the actor in the piece, its hero—some would in these days say, its villain—is still *homo sapiens;* and the general task of intellectual historiography is to exhibit, so far as may be, the thinking animal engaged—sometimes fortunately, sometimes disastrously—in his most characteristic occupation. If—as some would be content to say—the justification of *any* study of history is simply the human interestingness both of its episodes and of the moving drama of the life of our race as a whole, then this study has that justification in the highest degree. Or if historical inquiry in general is defended on the ground—which some contemporary historians appear to reject— that the knowledge which it yields is "instructive," that it provides material towards possible general conclusions—conclusions which do not relate merely to the occurrence and successions of past and particular events—then no part of historiography seems to offer a better promise of this sort of serviceableness than a duly analytical and critical inquiry into the nature, genesis, development, diffusion, interplay and effects of the ideas which the generations of men have cherished, quarreled over, and apparently been moved by. That the knowledge which man needs most is knowledge of himself is a sufficiently old and respectable opinion; and intellectual history manifestly constitutes an indispensable, and the most considerable, part of such knowledge, in so far as any study of the past may contribute to it. At no moment, indeed, in the life of the race has the pertinency of the Delphian imperative been more tragically apparent; for it must now be plain to everyone that the problem of human nature is the gravest and most fundamental of our problems, that the question which more than any others demands answer is the question, "What's the matter with man?"

II

The general observation that knowledge concerning the history of ideas has an independent value, and is not merely instrumental to other studies, might well seem too obvious to require emphasis, were it not that it has consequences, not always clearly realized, with respect to the methods and aims of literary history. The thoughts of men of past generations have had their most extensive, and often their most adequate and psychologically illuminating, expression in those writings which are commonly differentiated from other writings—though by criteria not usually very clear—as "literature." Wherever the line of division be drawn, it would generally be agreed that literature is, at least among other things, an art. Since there is no universal consensus as to the meaning of "art," this classification does not, of itself, greatly clarify the subject; but one may perhaps say, without too much risk of dissent, that a work of "art" is such by virtue of its relation either to an artist who produces it or to a potential reader, hearer or beholder of it (or to both). And, considered solely in the second relation, the work of art may be said to be differentiated from other visible or audible artificial objects by its capacity to produce in the perceiver a distinctive something called an "aesthetic enjoyment," or at least an "aesthetic experience," which (though definition of it is here judiciously avoided) is at all events not simply identical either with cognitive experience or with a recognition of a possible ulterior utility which the object may serve. Works of art, further, are usually held to differ widely in respect of their aesthetic values—however these are to be measured. Now it has, especially by some recent writers, been maintained that a work of art, so conceived, must contain its aesthetic value, that is, the sources of the aesthetic experience it evokes, in itself, and not in anything extraneous to itself. It makes no difference, so far as the aesthetic quality and efficacy of a poem are concerned, who wrote it, or when, or what sort of person he was, or from what motive he wrote it, or even what he meant to convey by it; and if the reader permits his mind to be occupied with such questions as these, he weakens or wholly loses the experience which it is the function of the poem, as a work of art, to afford. And it is consequently argued, by some who are preoccupied with this aspect of literature, that the study of literary history results chiefly in the accumulation of collateral information *about*, e.g., poems, which adds nothing to the aesthetic experience as such, but, on the contrary, impedes or annuls it, by interposing what is aesthetically irrelevant between the poem and the reader. Thus Mr. C. S. Lewis observes that "any and every result which may follow from my reading of a poem cannot be included in my poetical apprehension of it, and cannot, therefore, belong to the poem as a poem," and, starting from this (in itself undisputable) premise, he attacks, with an argumentative verve and skill which has itself a good deal of art in it, the notion that "poetry is to be regarded as an 'expression of personality,'" and laments "the steadily increasing role of biography in our literary studies." "When we read poetry as it ought to be read, we have before us no representation which claims to be the poet, and frequently no representation of a *man*, a *character*, or a *personality* at all." There can, in fact, be "poems without a poet"—i.e., writings which (like passages in the English Bible) have in the course of time acquired a poetic value which is not due to anything that anyone ever *put* into them.[3] (Any essential distinction between the experience of beauty in natural objects and in works of art is here apparently obliterated.) If knowledge about the poet's "personality" is thus foreign to the "poetical apprehension" of the poem, still more foreign must be the other sorts of knowledge which the literary historians so busily pursue, about his experiences, education, associations, "background," sources, philosophical opinions, contemporary reputation, later influence, and the like.

These views are not cited here principally for the purpose of discussing the issues of aesthetic theory which they raise; yet one of these issues has some pertinency to the present subject, and is worth brief consideration before passing to the main point. It is the general question whether information about, say, a poem, not contained in it, is necessarily incapable of enhancing the aesthetic experience, or "poetical apprehension," of the reader; and I suggest that the answer must be in the negative. One may, of course, so *define* the terms "aesthetic" or "poetical apprehension" that an affirmative answer to the question necessarily follows; but the con-

[3] *The Personal Heresy: A Controversy.* By E. M. W. Tillyard and C. S. Lewis, 1939, pp. 1, 4, 5, 16.

sequence is then a purely verbal one, having nothing to do with any matter of psychological fact. But it is hard to see how anyone can, except through such verbal inference, find plausibility in the thesis that the sources of what would commonly be recognized as the aesthetic enjoyment of a poem, or of any work of art, must consist wholly in its own literal and explicit content.[4] For—upon the very view which has been illustrated by some sentences of Mr. Lewis's—the aesthetic value of the poem depends upon its effect on the reader; and this in turn, surely, depends much upon the reader—upon what the psychologists once liked to call "the mass of apperception" which he brings to the reading. The external stimulus giving rise to the experience consists, it is true, in the actual words of the poem; but the capacity, even of the separate words, to suggest imagery or to arouse emotion, not to say to convey ideas, is due to the associations which they already possess in the reader's mind, and these may be, and often are, the products of other reading. Any allusive word or passage illustrates this.

> Perhaps the self-same song that found a path
> Through the sad heart of Ruth, when, sick for home,
> She stood in tears amid the alien corn.

The poem does not tell you who Ruth was, nor where she is elsewhere mentioned in literature; *that* is a piece of extraneous historical information—though one, fortunately, familiar to all Occidental readers. Will anyone venture to assert that, for most of them, the aesthetic enjoyment of the lines is diminished, and not, rather, heightened, by their possession of this knowledge? And is there any reason to suppose that knowledge of a similar kind, even though less generally possessed, may not similarly enrich—for those who have it—the aesthetic value of many other passages? Instances in which it quite certainly does so might be adduced by the hundred, if there were space for them. The historical perspectives which a word or a poem may bring, clearly or dimly, to mind are often (given the necessary acquaintance with history) a great part of the aesthetic experience which it evokes—an augmentation of its imaginative voluminosity. Nor are the possible contributions of the his-

---

[4] The subject has been dealt with illuminatingly, and more adequately than is possible here, by Louis Teeter in an essay ("Scholarship and the Art of Criticism," *ELH* September, 1938) which should be required reading for any who concern themselves with this question.

torian to the "poetical apprehension" of the reader limited to obviously allusive or evocative single passages. It is he, often, who enables the reader to recapture, in writings of earlier times, aesthetic values which had been lost because the frame of reference, the preconceptions, the mood, which once gave them such value for their contemporaries were no longer current. How meager would be the aesthetic content of the *Divine Comedy* as a whole, or of most of its parts, to a modern reader—especially a non-Catholic reader—wholly ignorant of medieval ideas and feelings and pieties, or incapable, while reading it, of making these in some degree his own, by an effort of the imagination! Indeed, the exercise of the historical imagination, even apart from its function in the revitalizing of this or other masterpieces, has itself been, since Western men became historically-minded, one of the chief sources of aesthetic experience—though that is another story. Obviously, not all historical or other knowledge pertinent to, but derived from sources extrinsic to, a given work of art thus adds to its potency. Some does and some does not; no general rule can be laid down on the subject in advance. But it is by no means evident that even knowledge from external sources about the *artist,* his "personality" or his life, is one of the sorts of collateral information which necessarily do *not* have this effect, and that biographical studies consequently cannot contribute to the enjoyment of literature. The aesthetic irrelevance of a considerable part of the chronicles, scandalous or edifying, of the lives of authors, can hardly be denied. Whether any of the discoveries about Shakespeare heighten the effect of the plays is at least debatable; and it is more than dubious whether an acquaintance with the private life of the Reverend C. L. Dodgson makes *Alice in Wonderland* more enjoyable. But there are many instances on the other side of the account. Doubtless there would be a touching pathos in "All, all are gone, the old familiar faces," if the poem were anonymous, but there is much more when I know that it was written by Charles Lamb—a fact which is no part of the poem—and know something of the tragic circumstances in his life. Or consider Coleridge's "Dejection, an Ode": our present knowledge (which we owe to his biographers and the collectors of his letters) of the experiences out of which it arose, and of the fact that it marked the end of his great creative period as a poet, makes the poem far more moving than it can have been to the generality of the readers of the *Morning Post* in 1802. Such knowledge adds what may be called a new dimension to a work of art, the dramatic dimension—as, in a play, a single poetic passage, though it may have beauty in isolation, owes its full effect to the reader's knowledge of the fictitious personality of the speaker and of the situation which evokes it and makes it dramatically apposite.

> For God's sake, let us sit upon the ground
> And tell sad stories of the death of kings. . . .

The whole passage might be taken out of its context and given a place in an anthology; but would one who had known it only as a detached fragment find his "imaginative apprehension" of it diminished upon learning that it is, in the play, spoken by a king, and that king, Richard II, and at a crisis in his fortunes calling for resolute action rather than self-pitying musings on the ironies of royal state? The increment of aesthetic content which the lines gain from such knowledge of their dramatic setting is essentially similar to that which a poem or other writing may sometimes gain from the reader's knowledge of its authorship, its place in the author's life and its relation to his character. This is not, to be sure, an element in the art, *i.e.*, the design, of the creator of the work; but it is not the less on that account an enrichment of aesthetic experience on the side of the reader—which is presumably one of the purposes of the "teaching of literature."[5] And if the work be considered with respect to the skill, or "artistry," of its creator, the "aesthetic appreciation" of this is least of all possible without going beyond the work itself. For it is dependent upon a knowledge—or an assumption—about what he was trying to do,

[5] In the debate of Lewis and Tillyard, to which reference has been made, two "personal heresies," not sufficiently discriminated, seem to be at issue. One is the assumption that a poem (and a single poem is usually meant) *necessarily* tells us anything about the "personality" of the poet. In maintaining the negative on this issue, Mr. Lewis seems to me to have the better of the argument. But the correct answer, I suggest, is that no generalization on the point is legitimate; some poems do, and some don't. The more serious question concerns Mr. Lewis's view that, when "we read a poem as it ought to be read," we *ought not* to know, or want to know, anything about the poet, since this interferes with the "imaginative experience." And this is a part of the larger question, above discussed, whether *any* extrinsic knowledge about a poem can contribute to the aesthetic experience generated by reading it. This more general and fundamental issue, however, is not very definitely considered by either contributor to this, in many respects, brilliant example of the gentle art of controversy.

which can by no means always be safely or fully inferred from the obvious content of the work; and it is also dependent upon an acquaintance with other extrinsic matters, such as his subject (if or in so far as his purpose is assumed to be descriptive or realistic), the limitations of his medium, other examples of the treatment of the same subject or of essays in the same *genre,* and (when they can be certainly determined) the sources of which he made use. This element in the appreciation of (for example) "Kubla Khan" has, surely, not been decreased by the publication of *The Road to Xanadu.*

The very notion, then, of a work of art as a self-contained kind of thing is a psychological absurdity. It *functions* as art through what it does for the experiencer of it; nothing in it has aesthetic efficacy except through its power to evoke certain responses in him; so that one may say that, except in a physical sense, its content is as much in him as in itself. And this general consideration alone, even apart from the citation of particular examples, seems to establish a sufficient presumption against the doctrine, now somewhat fashionable in various quarters, that, in the reading of literature, ignorance is always bliss, that the best reader is the one who has least in his mind, and that, consequently, the sort of knowledge which may result from the historical study of literature is never serviceable to the aesthetic purposes of that art. But though many and notable services of this kind can be and have been rendered by such study, it is still needful to insist—and this is the point chiefly pertinent to the present theme—that that is not its only, or even its principal, function. "Literary history," as the late Edwin Greenlaw wrote, "looks on literature as one phase of that history of the human spirit which is one of the chief learnings, is humanism itself."[6] It is, in short, a part, and a major part, of the quest of that knowledge of the workings of man's mind in history which, having its own excuse for being, is not subservient even to ends so valuable as the aesthetic appreciation or the criticism of individual works of art. But so conceived, the province and the methods of literary history must be determined by its own historical-psychological purpose, and not by contemporary critical appraisals either of the aesthetic excellence or the philosophical validity of the writings of men of former times. Evident as this may appear, some confusion of ideas with respect to the matter still seems common, not only in

[6] *The Province of Literary History,* 1931, p. 38.

the public mind, and among literary critics, but also among students and teachers of literature. Because, *as* an art, it exists to be "enjoyed" (in the wider sense of the term), it is sometimes, tacitly if not explicitly, assumed that the purpose of studying or teaching it is exclusively to increase or communicate that enjoyment; and, in so far as this assumption prevails, the natural result is the limitation of the study to what is now regarded as "good" literature—the writings which still have (or are, often somewhat naïvely, taken by academic teachers to have) a high aesthetic value for most readers of our own time. Thus a distinguished English scholar who has recently rediscovered an almost forgotten but admirable English prose writer of the seventeenth century (Peter Sterry), and has edited selections from his works, explains that his (the editor's) "aim has been to exhibit not so much those aspects of Sterry's work that probably made the greatest impression on his contemporaries as those elements which appear to me to have the universal and enduring qualities of great literature." Here, obviously, the part of the contents of this author's writings which is of greater historical value—the part which throws most light upon what was distinctive of the thoughts, the moods, the taste, of his age and group—is treated as more or less negligible, because it has (or, *for that very reason,* is presumed to have) less "literary" value. Now, to make available to the contemporary reader a forgotten piece of "great"— or at all events, still enjoyable—literature, is assuredly a laudable thing. But it is a strange thing to disregard, in such a writing, what is most pertinent to that "one of the chief learnings"—that essential portion of the "history of the human spirit"—to which it is the prime office of the literary historian, *quâ* historian, to contribute. It is not now in general true that those who devote themselves to this study neglect their function as historians of ideas (including artistic methods and aesthetic valuations and tastes); but, because of the confusion of the two aims, they are sometimes subject to reproach for occupying themselves so much with what is *not* "good literature," perhaps not even "literature" at all; and they themselves often seem a little apologetic about it. Something like a declaration of independence for the genuinely historical study of literature, in itself and in its relations to other phases of the history of man thinking, feeling, imagining and evaluating, is even now not wholly superfluous. In this journal, the independence (which does not imply the indifference) of the historiography of literature with respect to all non-historical criteria of relevance and importance, and also its inseparable connection with most of the other parts of that total history, are assumed *ab initio*. As a source of delight and a means to the widening and deepening of inner experience, literature has one value; as "criticism of life" it has another (for the appraisal of which a knowledge of its history is one of the necessary means); and it has a third as an indispensable body of documents for the study of man and of what he has done with ideas and what diverse ideas have done for and to him.

III

To avert possible misunderstanding, let it be said that the terms "ideas" and "intellectual" are not here used in a sense implying any assumption of the solely or chiefly logical determination of opinions and behavior and of the historical movement of thought. There is now widely current even among the general public a doctrine that the beliefs, and professed grounds of belief, as well as the acts, of individuals and of social groups are not shaped by "intellectual" processes, but by unavowed or "subconscious" non-rational desires, passions or interests. This "discovery of the irrational," a recent writer has declared, "makes the genius of our age. . . . The intellectual revolution of the twentieth century is likely to prove the charting of the *terra incognita* of the irrational and the extraction of its implications for every area of human thought." It is "nothing short of a Copernican revolution in ideas," since it means that "the rational, right-thinking man has as surely ceased to be considered the center of our intellectual system as the earth has ceased to be the center of our planetary system."[7] The discovery is not so new as it is commonly supposed to be, and it is questionable whether exploration of the *"terra incognita* of the irrational" was not attempted with as much diligence and subtlety in the seventeenth century as in the twentieth. But at all events it is little likely to be unduly neglected by contemporary students of the history of thought. Few of them are accustomed to look upon man as a highly rational animal, in the laudatory sense, or to deny that alogical factors play a great part in most of the phenomena which they investigate; and it would be a misconception to suppose

[7] Max Lerner in *The Nation,* Oct. 21, 1939. The term "rational," of course, needs definition, and the assumption of the equivalence of "non-rational" and "irrational" requires examination; but into these topics it is impossible to enter here.

that the intellectual historian is concerned solely with the history of intellection.

Perhaps the greater danger at present lies upon the other side. One of the safest (and most useful) generalizations resulting from a study of the history of ideas is that every age tends to exaggerate the scope or finality of its own discoveries, or re-discoveries, to be so dazzled by them that it fails to discern clearly their limitations and forgets aspects of truth against prior exaggerations of which it has revolted. Now, that the doctrine of the non-rational determination of men's judgments and ideologies is not true without exceptions is the obvious assumption of all who enunciate opinions and publish ostensibly reasoned arguments for them—and therefore, the assumption of the authors of the doctrine, and of all who seek to justify by evidence any historical proposition whatever. It is true that some representatives of the theory known as "the sociology of knowledge" (*Wissenssoziologie*), holding that the "modes of thought" of all individuals are determined by, and therefore relative to, the nature of the social groups to which the individuals belong—not merely economic classes but also "generations, status groups, sects, occupational groups, schools, etc."—deduce from this psychological hypothesis a sort of generalized relativistic (or, as they prefer to call it, "relational") logic or epistemology. Upon the set of presuppositions characteristic of a given group, some conclusions are valid, some invalid—but (apparently) each group has its own "thought-model," its distinctive standards of what is true or false, which do not hold good for others. And certain adherents of this form of the general doctrine seem willing to have this relativism applied to their own contentions; thus Mr. Karl Mannheim writes that "even one's own point of view may always be expected to be peculiar to one's [social] position."[8] Yet the ingenious and often suggestive interpretations of history put forth by members of this school do not, in fact, have the air of being presented as valid for the reader in one of his capacities, say that of a professor of sociology, and invalid for him in another capacity, say that of a man over forty years of age, or an income-tax payer in one of the lower brackets; nor are these reasonings presented (as might

[8] Karl Mannheim: *Ideology and Utopia*, 1936, p. 269; *cf*. the whole section "The Sociology of Knowledge," pp. 236–280. See also Robert K. Merton's excellent brief review of this movement, "The Sociology of Knowledge," in *Isis*, XXVII, 3, November, 1937, pp. 493–503.

be expected) as valid only for readers belonging to precisely the same economic class and generation and status-group and occupational group and sect as their authors. If they were so presented, their claims to consideration would obviously be extremely restricted. The spokesmen of this sort of sociological relativism, in short, patently give *some* place to common criteria of factual truth and of legitimacy in inference, which their theory, in its extreme interpretation, would exclude. They do not, it is clear, really believe that the proposition that George Washington was a great landed proprietor is true for a Virginia Episcopalian but false for a Chicago Baptist—nor that their own thesis that opinions and "thought-models," outside of pure science, are shown by historical evidence to be correlated with social status or position, ought to be accepted only by persons of a particular status or position. Even they, then, necessarily presuppose possible limitations or exceptions to their generalization, in the act of defending it.

But if there *are* limitations or exceptions to the truth of the doctrine of the non-rational determination of men's judgments, it follows that two types of factor are at work in the history of thought; and it is the business of the historian—if he can—at once to discriminate and to correlate them, and perhaps, in the long run, to arrive at some rough quantitative estimate of the relative part played by each. But to make this discrimination in particular instances—which must be done *before* any general conclusions can be regarded as established—is unquestionably a hazardous and uncertain business; and the more weight you initially give to the rôle of the non-rational in these matters, the more hazardous and uncertain the appraisal of that rôle must itself appear. It is perilously easy to find more or less plausible explanations, in terms of non-rational motives, for other mens' reasonings, opinions or tastes—to "unmask ideologies" which you happen to dislike—and, in the nature of the case, it is exceedingly difficult to demonstrate the correctness or adequacy of such specific explanations, unless by deduction from *a priori* general premises dogmatically assumed at the outset—a type of question-begging exemplified in our own time on a huge scale. Nevertheless, given a sufficient degree of caution as well as of acumen on the part of the historian (including the biographer), some success in this delicate task of distinguishing the two components in the formation of men's judgments is, doubtless, not past hoping for.

Meanwhile, the usual ambition of the contemporary historiographer to find conjectural "affective" or "sociological" explanations for the explicit facts of the history of ideas obviously cannot justify—though it sometimes tends to result in—a neglect to observe with as much adequacy, accuracy and judicial-mindedness as may be, the facts to be explained—to investigate widely and to analyze searchingly, through their expression in words, the kinds of ideas that have actually appealed to men, to note upon what grounds beliefs have seemed to those who held them to have been based, how they have changed from generation to generation, and under what conditions these changes have taken place. Even if most or all expressed judgments and reasonings were but "rationalizations" of blind emotions or cravings, the nature of the cravings must be chiefly inferred from the content of the rationalizations; the need to rationalize is, upon the same hypothesis, not less imperative than the cravings; and once a rationalization has been formed, it is antecedently improbable—and could be shown by historical evidence to be untrue—that it will remain otiose and inert, having no repercussions upon the affective side of consciousness out of which it may have arisen. When a man has given a reason for his belief, his moral approbation or disapprobation, his aesthetic preference, he is—happily or otherwise—caught in a trap; for the reason is likely to entail, or to seem to entail, consequences far beyond and, it may be, contrary to, the desire which generated it, or, not less awkwardly, contrary to undeniable matters of fact; even if he seeks to evade those consequences, he will suffer the embarrassment of appearing to his fellows irrational because arbitrary and inconsistent; and an aversion from manifest and admitted irrationality is, after all, by no means the least pervasive or least powerful of emotions in the creature that has long, and with evident gratification, been accustomed to define himself as the rational animal. Man, moreover, is not only an incurably inquisitive but an incurably ratiocinative being, and the exercise of this function, as of others, carries its own pleasure with it. To recognize a nice distinction, to discover a new truth, or what appears to be such, to feel that one is reasoning well and coercively, to triumph over an at first baffling problem—these are all accompanied by a sense of power and therefore by lively satisfactions. And the satisfactions cannot be enjoyed without the presupposition of rules of procedure and of criteria of success not peculiar to oneself, but inherent in the nature of the subject-matter.

For these reasons, if there were no others, the intellectual historiographer will still do well to entertain the hypothesis that logic is one of the important operative factors in the history of thought, even though he cannot accept this assumption in the extreme form in which it was once widely held. According to that older but now evanescent view, what we chiefly witness, in the temporal sequence of beliefs, doctrines and reasonings, is the working of an immanent dialectic whereby ideas are progressively clarified and problems consecutively get themselves solved, or at least advanced towards less erroneous or inadequate "solutions." Perhaps the strongest reason why we no longer find this picture of a majestic logical forward movement in history convincing is that we have become increasingly aware of the oscillatory character of much of the history of thought, at least of Western thought, outside the domain of strictly experimental science. On any intelligibly formulable general question, there are usually two not entirely unplausible extreme positions, with a number of intermediate ones; and much of the historic spectacle, so far as the dominant tendencies of successive periods are concerned, seems to consist in alternate shifts from one extreme to the other, either abruptly or gradually through the intermediate stages. This phenomenon is, of course, especially conspicuous in political and social history, and in the history of taste and of the arts. A tendency to radical innovation flourishes for a time and perhaps eventuates in a revolution, which is followed by a reaction, more or less extreme, and a period of dominant conservatism. Democracy, or some measure of it, through a long struggle, replaces absolute monarchy, to be succeeded suddenly by dictatorship. This seems to be the all-but universal pattern of the sequences of politico-social history—excepting those contemporary revolutions of which the end is not yet. There is little in such history thus far to encourage the belief that it moves continuously in any particular direction; it has, in the long view, as Polybius long since observed, much more the look of a series of periodic recurrences, though the periods are of very unequal length. So in matters of taste and aesthetic fashions: the majority of connoisseurs in one period care, for example, only for Gothic architecture, then they despise it, then they admire it again, then they once more revolt against it; now fixed "form" is the criterion of excellence, now "irregularity" and freedom of expression; once the "picturesque" was all the go, now it is belittled. "Romanticism," in some sense of the vague term, displaces "classicism" in literature, and gives place to it again. If you wish to prophesy about the future, in any of these matters, the actuarially safest working rule would seem to be to take what are now venerated idols and predict that they will sooner or later become hobgoblins—and still later, idols once more.

And no honest observer even of the history of philosophical opinion can deny that a similar phenomenon of oscillation is to be found in it. Moods of radical intellectualism are followed by anti-intellectualisms, of one or another variety. In recent American and British philosophy, after the dominance of idealism for a generation, realism, as we all know, came flooding back,—and there are now some indications that its tide is receding. (These oscillations, it should hardly need saying, have no relevance to the question of the validity of any of the views which succeed one another; there is nothing more naïve, or more indicative of a failure to learn one of the real lessons of the history of thought, than the tendency of some, even among philosophers, to take the bare fact that a way of thinking is now *démodé* as indicative either that it is false or that it will not come back.) The history of philosophy assuredly is not, in the successions of the ideas and systems which it presents, an exclusively logical process, in which objective truth progressively unfolds itself in a rational order; its course is shaped and diverted by the intrusion of many factors which belong to the domain of the psychologist or the sociologist, and have nothing to do with philosophy as a would-be science. But since this aspect of the matter is now in so little danger of being disregarded, it is more to the purpose to dwell upon the residuum of truth in the older view. It must still be admitted that philosophers (and even plain men) *do* reason, that the temporal sequence of their reasonings, as one thinker follows another, is usually in some considerable degree a logically motivated and logically instructive sequence. For a very familiar example that will hardly be disputed, both Berkeley and Hume did, plainly, bring to notice implications of Locke's premises which Locke had not seen—implications that were actually *there*, waiting, as it were, to be brought to light. In both cases, perhaps—certainly in Berkeley's—extra-logical motives help to explain why the later philosophers *noticed* these implications; the idealism which Berkeley thought it possible to deduce, in part, by combining the simple Lockian thesis that "the mind hath no immediate objects but its own ideas" with the principle of parsimony was a consequence manifestly welcome for religious reasons: it dished the materialists completely, it provided a new argument for the existence of God, it seemed to imply a more direct and intimate relation, even in the common business of sense-perception, between the human and the divine mind. In Hume's case, at least in his non-political works, it is hard to see any extra-logical motivation, except a certain pleasure in horripilating the orthodox and an intense ambition for a reputation as an original writer; it seems questionable whether his sceptical conclusions themselves were really emotionally welcome to him. And even when alogical motives may seem to explain psychologically the readiness of one philosopher to observe a *non-sequitur,* or an unexamined presupposition, or an undeveloped implication, in a doctrine of his predecessor, it frequently, and perhaps usually, remains the case that it is such actual logical facts that he observes—as a review of the entire history of philosophy would easily show. In their criticisms of other people's ways of thinking men inevitably appeal largely to common rational principles, or what at the time are accepted as such, however partially they may follow such principles in arriving at their own beliefs or valuations. On the offensive, many a thinker little capable of self-criticism has shown himself an acute and cogent reasoner; so that, somewhat paradoxically, it is through their quarrels that philosophers have most illuminated the logic of their problems, and it is in the polemical part of the history of reflective thought that the cool white light of reason may most often be seen emerging.

The study of the history of thought, then, must still be pursued with an open and alert eye for the action of "intellectual" processes in the narrower sense, processes in which—along with all the emotive factors, the blank, quasi-aesthetic likings for one or another type of concept or imagery or "metaphysical pathos," and the biases due to personal or group interests—ideas manifest their own natural logic. By natural logic I do not mean necessarily good logic. It sometimes may and sometimes may not be that; and the question how far it can be would involve a digression into logical theory itself, which would be out of place here. But it will hardly be denied that numerous ideas have, if not necessary connections, at least elective affinities, with various other ideas, and incongruities with yet others, and that most propositions, taken in conjunction with others which are usually assumed though they may be unexpressed, have implications not always evident or welcome to those who affirm them. An idea, in short, is after all not only a potent but a stubborn thing; it commonly has its own "particular go;" and the history of thought is a bilateral affair—the story of the traffic and interaction between human nature, amid the exigencies and vicissitudes of physical experience, on the one hand, and on the other, the specific natures and pressures of the ideas which men have, from very various promptings, admitted to their minds.

(b) whatever confronts the mind when it perceives or thinks—sensations of qualities, feelings, impressions, memory images, or compounds of these—the meaning of "ideas" in British terminism or nominalism. The "plain historical method" for Locke meant taking stock introspectively of the various kinds of such ideas "of sensation and reflection, simple and complex, etc.";

(c) "ideal"—the question in the *Parmenides* whether dirt, hair, etc. have ideas suggests that the distinction between a logically coherent "idea" and a humanly desirable "ideal" often disappears in Platonism;

(d) beliefs or judgments—e.g. the idea of the primitive goodness of man before he was spoiled by civilization, the idea that progress is inevitable, or that all history is class struggle.

Senses (c) and (d) of "idea" as ideal and as belief are opposed to senses (a) and (b) of ideas epistemologically, because (a) and (b), intuitions and images, refer to immediate experience whereas (c) and (d), the desired ideal and the hypothetical belief, are more mediated by abstract symbols or concepts. The historian of ideas can find and must seek not only written documents for the ideals and beliefs of an age but will seek also the iconographic evidence of the arts. For example, paintings of consumptives in the XIXth century show how literary men and the public for whom they were writing reacted to medical theories of Pasteur and Koch, undoubtedly without understanding them.

Now the history of ideas is not a pure or original discipline but a compositive or derivative one, because it is dependent on other disciplines whose borders it penetrates. We assume that men first have to think and talk about the world in which they have to survive and find ways of creating or modifying the social and artistic forms they pass on to the next generation. So far as recorded history goes, there are always symbols (whether gestural, pictorial, verbal, or abstract forms) expressing the life of ideas before men take notice of the changes in these ideas as worthy of separate telling.

Aristotle's first book of his so-called *Metaphysics* is a classic example of the history of philosophic ideas. It is not only the richest source of our knowledge of pre-Socratic cosmologies—man's first scientific guesses at the riddle of the universe—but is also an excellent illustration of the derivative nature and of some of the problems of the history of ideas.[3] We all know that Aristotle, like his teacher Plato, traced the genetic growth of the more general ideas that enter into knowledge from the individual's sense-experiences and memories, fused in *techne* and *episteme,* so that knowledge of the universal comes after knowing how individual things behave in our experience.

[3] Cf. H. Cherniss, "The History of Ideas and Ancient Greek Philosophy" in *Studies in Intellectual History* (Baltimore, 1953), 39–42.

All theories of knowledge recognize the basic Aristotelian distinction between what is first in the order of nature, "first in itself," and what is first in the order of knowing, "first for us." Well, the history of ideas is faced with the problem of noting which ideas have been taken as "first" in the two orders.

Any comparative study of different conceptions of "firstness" in the thought of various periods reveals how such ideas, employed often as unconscious axioms, vary in different contexts. Was this not the sort of question Aristotle asked himself about the pre-Socratics, namely, why did such eminent minds, in fact, whole schools of serious thinkers, arrive at such diverse conceptions of the first principles of the universe as Water, Air, Fire, the Indefinite, the One, Unchanging Being, Becoming, Number, Atoms, Chance, Purposive Mind, etc.?

One of the marvellous achievements of the study of the history of ideas is that it makes it possible to reconstruct part of the thinking of minds that lived over twenty centuries ago. That achievement is as great a tribute to the mind of *homo sapiens* as his fathoming of the stars and atoms; it is even more difficult, since the stars and atoms are still here to be consulted, but the thoughts of Aristotle and of his colleagues can only be pieced together from fragments, too often mutilated by the ravages of time and editors. Here again the problem of critical examination of the texts is fundamental. Documents like Aristotle's edited *Metaphysics* or logical treatises require the knowledge of a Greek scholar, a philosopher, and a historian. For example, it is an amazing fact that only recently the distinguished Polish logician and philosopher Lukaciewicz discovered, after a critical, historical investigation of the texts of Aristotle's logical writings, that for over 2000 years Aristotle's theory of the syllogism has been misrepresented in the textbooks from which philosophers have studied logic since ancient times. To recover Aristotle's original ideas, when all we have are edited versions of students' notes of Aristotle's "golden stream of discourse," means critical study of editors' arrangements of the texts, Syriac, Hebrew, Arabic, and Latin translations, scholastic commentaries, and modernized versions. The problem of individualism might find a nice example here of the difficulty of reconstructing the individual Aristotle, *maestro di color che sanno,* pupil and friend of Plato but a greater friend of truth, tutor of Alexander the Great, the man who left provisions in his will for his second wife, uncle of the great botanist Theophrastus, etc. The problem of the individual was formulated in Aristotle's theory of the union of form and matter, soul and body, and in his epistemology. We can *know* only universals, but all our knowledge begins with individual experiences. The infant knows all men as "Father," Aristotle remarked in order to illustrate the sense in which universals shape knowledge from the start.

Individuum est ineffabile, qua individuum but not *qua* the universal qualities which must be present in individuals if they are to be known and talked about or recorded in history. The problem of universals acquires a particular importance for the historian of ideas. In order to write a history of an idea, must not the historian assume that there is an invariant universal idea which undergoes transformation in various historical contexts? So Aristotle traced the idea of material Substance or prime matter in the pre-Socratics from Thales to Empedocles, as though he was simply reporting what he had discovered. But it is also clear that Aristotle had designs on his predecessors, that he wished to use them to illustrate his own doctrine of four causes, or that he honestly believed his doctrine was implicit in the pre-Socratic philosophies of nature. The material cause was exemplified in Thales' Water, Anaximander's seeds and Anaximenes' Air, the formal cause by the Eleatics' Being and Pythagorean Number, the efficient cause by the motions of Democritean atoms, and the final cause by Anaxagoras' Mind. Then the critical historians' problem is typically illustrated by the effort to discover to what extent Aristotle was imputing to his predecessors his own ideas or really making articulate and developing further the intrinsic structure of the whole truth implicit in his predecessors' ideas. The tendency to find a continuity between our own ideas and those of past thinkers is both a necessary methodological concept and yet also a possible pitfall. We must assume that the minds of past generations were not absolutely different from our own, or else all communication and understanding between ourselves and our predecessors are impossible. Solipsism and mysticism are not possible methods for the historian of ideas.

On the other hand, we must always face the problem of avoiding the error of substituting our own attitudes and beliefs for those of the past, even when or especially when we admire and emulate them. Love can be blind in intellectual matters. The appeal of historical novels raises the problem of the relation of literary form and historical truth. Again, in Aristotle, this problem was posed by his dictum that poetry is more universal than history.

Why are literature and the arts less continuous in their historical development than the sciences and our forms of law and government? Perhaps the answer lies in the predominance of the individual qualities of unique historical events or experiences symbolized in works of art; but there are historical fashions and schools of art as there are historical tendencies and philosophies of science.

The continuity *and* uniqueness of the music of Bach, Haydn, and Mozart are as discernible to the trained ear as the logical similarities *and* differences of Descartes', Spinoza's, and Leibniz's philosophies or of Locke's, Berkeley's, and Hume's.

The discoveries in the history of science of once unobservable entities like microbes, electrical charges, Neptune, or Mendeleyev's predicted elements (gallium and germanium) are undeniably wonderful evidence of the powers of the mind and its cumulative growth, attracting more people every year to the sciences. Derek Price has calculated that the rate of growth of the scientific population is so much greater than that of the world's population, that extrapolation of these growth-curves would yield the startling result of more scientists in the world than people after a certain time! The causes for the accelerated tempo of scientific progress need investigation, and the history of ideas can here make use of statistical and other such methods of sociological and historical inquiry without sacrificing its fundamental insights into the humanistic aspects of scientific interest and developments; I mean the aesthetic, speculative, and moral aspects of science and the historical relations of science to literature and the arts, religion, education, and politics.

As wonderful as the scientific exploration of the atom and of galaxies, more remote from us in space and time than our imagination can picture, is the exploration of the minute facts of the history of the mind and the reconstruction of its aspirations, motivations, failures, and achievements. The recapture of the vision of the world as seen by minds long gone is the marvellous feat of the historian of ideas. What the Emperor Constantine probably thought and felt like, as he surveyed the site of the future city he wished to build as the Rome of the Eastern Empire, Gibbon has depicted so convincingly that we feel in reading Gibbon as if we were transported to the IVth century and reliving the Emperor's feelings and thoughts. The unique irrecoverable individual event, particular feelings, and peculiar associations of ideas that surged through the Emperor's mind we cannot know, but their universal features we can know, and if we have the magical literary gifts of a Gibbon, we can almost reenact the experience, always vicariously, as in any dramatic performance. The history of ideas can and should be dramatic and its method of presenting the findings can look to the drama for a model: unity of plot or structure in an idea, its transformations under the stress and strain of conflicting circumstances, and its happy fulfillment when the idea contributes to future progress or its tragic death when the idea fails to meet the intellectual needs of a changing world, and passes into oblivion, perhaps deservedly, should we not point out?

We don't know whether Galileo muttered under his breath "Eppur se muove" but we do know that those are exactly the words he could and should have uttered and must have felt like uttering, and some day there may be absolute documentary proof of it, though that seems unlikely at present. Also Ernst Mach's reconstruction of the sort of experiment Galileo *might* have done in arriving at his law of inertia is a *Gedankexperiment,* but so convincing is it, that the historian of other than scientific ideas can well profit methodologically from Mach's example. Galileo himself used a thought experiment in refuting Aristotle's law of falling bodies. I recall Galileo's argument because my point is that the method of the thought experiment is indispensable for the historian of ideas. By asking whether Newton could have discovered the law of universal gravitation without Kepler's and Galileo's laws, we learn how scientific thought historically depends on a cumulative continuity of mental effort and criticism through the ages. The story of the apple is not merely legendary but misleading when it gives people the idea that science occurs to an empty mind by a sudden intuition unrelated to traditional thoughts on the same problem.

The problem of "influences" in the history of ideas is another perpetual problem. "Action at a distance" seems to be admissible in the field of intellectual influences. The ideas of Plato still have their influence on students separated by more than two millenia from his writings. Direct contact with even the writings of a thinker is not always necessary for it is possible to find that there are other persons whose minds and talk or writings form a chain of influence traceable, however, by some historian or recorder of the ideas. Mersenne "was in fact an influential exponent of mechanism"[4] because he served as "the letter-box" ("la poste") of scientific and philosophic XVIIth-century Europe. On the negative side, not all pupils are disciples: Aristotle was not merely a pupil of Plato. The great individual thinkers not only show great capacity for learning from their teachers and predecessors, but also the original power to supersede them by critical dissatisfaction with their ideas. What are the climacteric conditions most favorable to new ideas, and in what sense is a mind *influenced* by "the climate of opinion"? More precise definitions and specification of causal conditions are needed. It will not do to say "X influenced Y because what is true of X is true of Y, and X preceded Y." The fallacy of *post hoc, ergo propter hoc* and the possibility that X and Y have a common source in Z or derive from a common tradition must not be forgotten.[5]

---

[4] C. C. Gillispie, *The Edge of Objectivity, an Essay in the History of Scientific Ideas* (Princeton, 1960), 111.

[5] R. Mondolfo, "Nota sobre los 'Antecedentes' en la Historia de la Filosofia," *Philosophia,* 22 (1959), 5–9; Mondolfo properly suggests that influences depend negatively on the intellectual tradition against which an idea reacts.

II

No discussion of problems and methods can mean much apart from the subject-matter, interests, and general basic assumptions of the investigators. A distinctive feature of our subject-matter is its breadth with respect to the regional and temporal span of ideas which permeate cultures as well as disciplines. We note the local and epochal tinge given to ideas but only to compare or contrast such regional and temporal characteristics with other appearances of the ideas under different historical conditions. Or we note how an idea in a poem like Pope's *Essay on Man* expressed an old philosophical problem, the idea of the great chain of being. We leave to the specialist the details of a single thinker's biography but we are interested in the influence of that thinker's ideas on his and later generations.

For the sake of discussion we present very briefly some problems of method in each of the following types of intellectual historiography:—(1) biographical and autobiographical; (2) sociological; (3) philological; (4) metaphysical and theological; (5) scientific. Of course, they overlap considerably.

(1) The *biographical* and *autobiographical* method, e.g. Plato's Socratic dialogues, Plutarch's *Lives,* Augustine's *Confessions,* Descartes' *Discourse on Method,* is especially valuable for the historian of ideas when accompanied by the impersonal analyses of abstract ideas and contemporary philosophical writings. Though we learn much of the individual Socrates and his ideas in the *Apology, Crito, Phaedo,* and the later dialogues, especially when Xenophon's account agrees with Plato's, Socrates must still be distinguished from Plato's admiring portrayal. Plato's silence about Democritus speaks well for the laughing philosopher; what is *not* said by X of a contemporary thinker Y known to X has its historical significance and suggests conflicts of ideas at the basis of conflicts of strong personalities. Proclus' Introduction to Euclid's *Elements* gives us our knowledge of Pythagorean ideas which made geometry an essential part of the liberal education of Western man. Diogenes' *Lives of the Philosophers* is notoriously gossipy and unreliable. Saint Augustine's *Confessions* set the model for Pascal and Rousseau and the whole tradition of soul-searching analyses in Christian ethics. Descartes' *Discours de la Méthode* and Spinoza's *De emendatione intellectu* contain autobiographical pages which throw an essential light on the ideas of their times. The *Selbst-Darstellung* series of German philosophers and the Schilpp *Library of Living Philosophers* have made excellent use of the method of starting with an intellectual autobiography, and then having the writer face his contemporary critics. By contrast, Hegel's *History of Philosophy* scarcely mentions individual philosophers: they are merely chips of his Absolute, and express its "cunning."

Certain problems posed by the biographical method arise from the fact that Peter's opinions of Paul very often tell us more about Peter than about Paul. Leibniz's monadology would deduce this psychological fact from his metaphysical doctrine of internal relations. Bertrand Russell's works on *Leibniz* and on the *History of Western Philosophy* tell us more about Russell than about Leibniz and the history of philosophy. But then we have a method suggested here of learning about a person's ideas, namely, find out what his opinions are of other persons' ideas!

The method of comparative biography was instituted by Plutarch's parallel *Lives* and corresponding insights into the comparative merits of Greek and Roman civilizations. Yet even here as the disciple of the neoplatonist Ammonius, Plutarch in his account of Archimedes seems to be exhibiting his neoplatonic commitment to the superiority of theory to sense-experience in underscoring the alleged contempt of the great Syracusan mathematician for experiment. The question here is whether Plutarch is not simply stereotyping Archimedes' own utterances intended for aristocratic ears about the meniality of experiments. The fact is that Archimedes was the greatest applied mathematician and experimental physicist of antiquity, so that he was either far ahead of his speculative audience or unaware himself of his own true powers. To what extent a great mind knows or does not know its own powers is a nice question for psychology. In any case, the intellectual historian is faced with the problem of comparing the statements of a thinker about himself and his methods with his actual attainments and methods. The historian of the mind is in a better position, from the standpoint of his ability to trace an individual's influence on later ages, to judge the attainments of an individual than the individual's own autobiographical claims. *Ipse dixit* is not an indubitable criterion of truth in intellectual autobiography. A case in point is Newton's method and his professed indebtedness to his teacher Henry More and the ideas of the Cambridge neo-Platonists. We have an interesting methodological problem here, viz. to what extent even great thinkers fail to understand their own methods and sources, but in so failing reveal something of the *Zeitgeist* as well as of themselves. Croce's and Collingwood's curious monadistic view that the ultimate aim of all historiography is increased self-awareness on the part of the historian, also rests on the questionable assumption that the historian's subject-matter must ultimately be autobiographical. A more prudent view would regard the historian's statements about the past or about himself as *hypotheses* requiring documentation to test introspective methods of verification.

Another problematic feature of the biographical method is the vexatious question of judging the evidential weight of unpublished papers and correspondence. The dilemma here arises when the historian is also asked to edit a selection of such MSS. He must determine which of these MSS are or are not worthy of publication or were not intended for publication. The editorial problem is further aggravated when the author has left several drafts, e.g. in the case of Charles S. Peirce's *Collected Papers*. Also, biographers often find more information about a man's life just prior to the time he achieves recognition; but then the formative years, the heart-rending struggles of his youth, are not so truly known or are gladly forgotten.

Finally, a central problem of method—touching the heart of the present conference theme of individualism—is the relative significance of the intellectual biographies or autobiographies of so-called "minor" and "major" thinkers. The very distinction of "minor" and "major" may reflect popular prejudice, but even so is worth historical notice. The intellectual biographer of an unknown or neglected minor figure may properly claim to find in his subject a revealing key to the opinions of a larger cross-section of the contemporary population than the more advanced thinkers of the same era. Which is the more significant for the historian of ideas, the minor or major figure?[6] The Hegelian takes the latter "great-man" view on the ground that the metaphysical "spirit of the times" is best expressed by the "world-historical" great man. When and why the working-class man became a fit subject for literature, history, or philosophy is a question that calls for a sociological analysis.

(2) The *sociology* of knowledge is a second approach, brought to the fore by Comte and Hegel and central to Marx's class-analysis, partly in continuation of the social philosophies of Locke, Montesquieu, Voltaire, and the other French encyclopedists. The problem of Marxists and Mannheim's school of sociological historians of ideology is that of the universality of the idea of truth. There are logical confusions here which Morris R. Cohen and Karl Popper have penetratingly exposed in their critiques of sociologism and psychologism. Of course, the historian of ideas is not called upon to judge whether the ideas he is tracing are true or simply beliefs held to be true. However, when we know that the ideas are false, then the historian has to inquire whether it was known at the time that the ideas believed were false. Minds like Aristotle and and Ptolemy who believed the earth had a central, stationary place in the universe cannot be described as being as ignorant or as prejudiced as those who opposed Copernicus and Galileo.

[6] On the value-judgments implied in the terms "minor" and "major," cf. M. R. Cohen, *The Meaning of Human History* (La Salle, Ill., 1950), Ch. 7. Minor figures reflect popular ideas of their time, whereas the major ones represent new path-breaking movements of thought.

The logical impasse of the sociology of knowledge is the endless regress of referring all ideas to the group presuppositions of the persons who hold the ideas, including the group of sociological analysts of these persons, the group of critics of this second group, *etc., ad infinitum.*

There are social aspects of ideas and criteria for appraising ideas of tremendous weight in the history of thought for explaining the domination of some ideas, the less persistent tenure of others, and the near extinction of some species of ideas like those of racial superiority. I say "near extinction" since false ideas persist long after they have been disproved by scientists or scholars. Such "cultural lags" are important for the historian of social thought and institutions. Also, social considerations alone explain why the written language differs from the oral and why the polite oral speech differs from the slang or argot of the street. That class-affiliations affect linguistic structure is a still defensible Marxian view despite Stalin's dictatorial decree against Professor Marr.

However, we must draw the line against the sociological approach when it produces such contradictory monstrosities as "Bourgeois *vs.* Soviet" science. That the best language of all science is mathematical, and its best method is experimental is the great logical lesson to be learnt from the internal history of scientific ideas, even after various external social contexts have been studied. The difference between the internal and external history of science raises the problem of the historical relationships of the community of savants to the larger community of the world. Similar problems appear for the history of other disciplines.

Philosophical historians have spoken of the material and economic forces that move men and explain all social history. But the very insistence of such historians on the political importance of all men becoming conscious of this philosophy of history, so that to join the Party was almost a logically inevitable corollary, shows that implicitly another force, "the bond of common ideas,"[7] is implicitly invoked. Now, the problem for the historian of ideas is to discover such common intellectual bonds underneath the complex events of history, as Trevor-Roper does when he finds in Francis Bacon's philosophy, as espoused and presented by three foreign visitors to England (the Poles Samuel Hartlib and John Dury and the Bohemian Comenius), the key to the new philosophy of the English nation that emerged in the decade 1620–1630 as the New Deal philosophy in America emerged out of the depression of 1929. How absurd for the nominalist to deny the common morbid effects of the economic and social tragedies we

---

[7] H. R. Trevor-Roper "Three Foreigners and the Philosophy of the English Revolution," [Samuel Hartlib, John Dury, Jan A. Komensky (Comenius)], *Encounter* (Feb. 1960), 9.

saw with so much sorrow in 1930 that the partly psychopathological word "depression" was most appropriately adopted to designate the era.[8] The commonly felt idea that something must be done to avoid repetitions of such tragic collapse of man's social intelligence surely was a universally pervasive idea of the decade 1930–40, and the idea for which millions have died, viz. that the fascist and Nazi retreat from reason was not the solution—both of these ideas surely cannot be easily dismissed from consideration as essential intellectual elements that contribute to an understanding of the terrible events of World War II and the crisis of liberalism which has still not subsided.

The rôle of utopias in the history of political ideas needs more study, for utopias are hypotheses created by the mind of man in social desperation and in aspiration for a better society. Logically, an ideal utopia, by supplying what is missing, should reveal what was needed at the time when the Utopia was conceived.

Leonard Krieger in his article on "History and Law in the XVIIth Century: Pufendorf,"[9] shows how XVIIth-century historiography grew out of political and legal interests when the prevailing philosophy of history was rationalistic (in the Cartesian sense), so that while Francis Bacon, Hobbes, Spinoza, and Leibniz refer to history, they tend to subordinate it to universal principles of the mind, mechanical forces, natural law, or theodicy, respectively. It is important to note that the naturalism of the XIXth and early XXth centuries would not subordinate the historical element, but elevated it into an evolutionistic philosophy. If the individual was reduced to a mere mode or monad in the XVIIth century dynamics of eternal nature, he was also engulfed in the waves of XIXth century evolutionism.[10] I agree with Mr. Simon that "it is more fruitful to acknowledge and to analyze the inconsistencies even of eminent thinkers than to try to torture them into consistency" (*loc. cit.*, 299, f.n. 36).

(3) A third method is the *philological* one of tracing ideas and their transmutations through key-words or expressions and their change in time. The meanings of "physis," "nomos," "logos," "arete," "techne," "episteme," etc. are keys to the Hellenic legacy to philosophy; that "virtue" meant "manliness" in Rome, and "cunning" in Machiavelli suggests diverse ideals of individuality. How important it

[8] Historians of ideas must distinguish names they give to past periods, e.g. the Middle Ages or Red Decade, from the names consciously used during the period, e.g. Renaissance, Enlightenment, Depression.

[9] *J.H.I.*, XXI, 2 (April 1960), 198f.

[10] "The development of society as well as the development of man and the development of life generally, may be described as a tendency to individuate—*to become a thing* (acquire a personality)." H. Spencer, *Social Studies*, 408, quoted by Walter M. Simon in his "Herbert Spencer and the 'Social Organism,'" *J.H.I.* (April 1960), 296.

is for students of Plato to learn that Jowett's translation of Plato's dialogues is influenced by the XIXth-century terminology of German-inspired idealistic metaphysics, so that "Absolute Beauty" was Jowett's forced reading of Plato's *kalos autos,* simply "beauty itself." Plato gave the terms "Sophist" and "sensuous" a bad odor, and "psyche" and "ideas" an honorific aura of transcendence.

As a precursor of the "higher criticism" of the Bible Spinoza consciously advocated the philological method of determining the meaning of terms in Scripture by comparing the various contexts in which the same Hebrew word is used. By calling Moses' story of his Mt. Sinai interview "a pious fable," Spinoza showed his understanding of historical method and art.

A word is equivalent to a personality, Charles S. Peirce once pointed out,[11] for a word like a person experiences changes, that is, both are influenced by the external cultural environment of other persons; words are judged good or bad as persons are according to conventions; the meaning of a word is distinguished from the spoken sounds or written marks though inseparable from them, as the personality is distinguishable but inseparable from the body of the person.

Why are etymologies unreliable guides to meanings of words? Because words like all human beings change their associations in time. Habits of speech change, so that we do not know too exactly how the words of Shakespeare's plays were pronounced in his day or exactly what overtones these words elicited. Still we can make astoundingly good guesses as to the ideas expressed. Our tape-recording machines today will facilitate the problem for future historians of our spoken language today. Here again, the unique features of our culture will yield the right of way to the universal transmissible features. It is altogether likely that the spoken language in its rich slang and racy obscenities will express ideas which no respectable writer will dare to put into writing, but the philological approach to the history of ideas can scarcely neglect the unwritten language. Another limitation of the philological method is the fact that many ideas are expressed in non-verbal signs, especially in the arts of architecture, sculpture, painting, the dance, dress, etc. Iconology necessarily predominates in cultures where illiteracy was the rule for the majority of people. The cinema and television of today are materials for future iconologic analysis of our culture.

Just as there are concrete words and abstract words, so there appear to be minds of the same two sorts of emphasis, or perhaps mood. However, Duhem was hardly accurate in distinguishing along national lines the ample concrete mind from the more narrow, abstract

---

[11] *Collected Papers of Charles Sanders Peirce,* vol. 7, ed. A. W. Burks (Cambridge, Mass., 1958), paragr. 584ff.

analytical mind, *l'esprit de géomètre* from *l'esprit de finesse*.[12] Duhem erred by introducing extra-scientific nationalistic and nominalistic concepts to explain differences of theories and styles of thought internal to the history of a science or of literature.

The philological method can serve as an instrument of criticism. As an example, an article in *Isis* (Dec. 1959), p. 459f., "On the Presumed Darwinism of Alberuni Eight Hundred Years Before Darwin" by Jan Z. Wilczynski (Beirut, Lebanese State University) properly criticizes what I take to be a typical Soviet nationalistic article by a Turkestan author T. I. Rainow on "The Great Scholars of Uzbekistan (IXth to XIth centuries)."[13]

Rainow's paper claimed to see in Alberuni a precursor of Darwin:

Thus, in modern language we could express this thought of Alberuni as follows: Nature performs natural selection of the most adequate, well-adapted beings through the extermination of others, and in this case, it proceeds in the same way as farmers and gardeners. We see, therefore, that Darwin's great idea of natural selection through the struggle for life and survival of the fittest was already reached by Alberuni approximately 800 years before Darwin. It is true that he seized it in the most general outlines only, but curiously enough, even the very meaning and the way in which he came to it were the same as Darwin's. The latter, as we know, discovered natural selection by observation of the methods of artificial selection, as applied by animal breeders.

Now Rainow used an English translation (London, 1887) of Alberuni's Arabic work on *India:* "An account of the religion, philosophy, literature, geography, chronology, astronomy, customs, laws and astrology of India about A.D. 1030." Wilczynski correctly observes that "in Alberuni's *India,* in itself an outstanding work, some views resembling the basic principles of Darwin's future doctrine are undeniably to be found. They are, however, vague and accidental; at any rate they do not form a coherent theory, nor did Alberuni himself realize or pretend to ascribe to them any possible significance as far as their biological meaning might be concerned" (*Isis, loc. cit.,* p. 466).

My point is that greater emphasis could have been put by Rainow's critic on the philological fact that the translator used Darwinian terms; in 1887 they meant much more than in 1030!

It is beyond my competence to discuss the complex relations of

---

[12] Cf. P. Duhem, *La Théorie physique* (Paris, 1906) and the more pertinent references to Rankine's "abstractive" vs. "hypothetical" methods in the construction of scientific ideas. Also, cf. C. P. Snow, *The Search* (New York, 1934[1], 1958[2]), 258–260.

[13] *Wielikije Uczenyje Uzbecistana (IX-XI bb),* Tashkent: Edition Ousphan, 1943, p. 62f.

philology to literary criticism and cultural history.[14] However, I do know that the editors of the *Journal of the History of Ideas* do not find the aesthetic appreciation of literary or artistic works incompatible with the historical analysis of ideas embodied in these works. It is a mistake to believe that the historian of ideas aims to reduce works of literature and art to mere anthropological documents or objects of historical curiosity. I should agree with John Dewey (*Art as Experience*) that knowledge of the historical context of a literary or artistic work may well enhance one's appreciation of it. Some literatures and arts become extinct and can be enjoyed only through philological and historical research, e.g. Old English illuminated MSS.

(4) By the *metaphysical* and *theological* approach to the history of ideas I mean the method of fitting all ideas and history into an allegedly eternal framework or philosophy of history which determines not only the structure but also the occasions for the appearance of ideas and their careers. So Plato in *Timaeus* regarded the creation of the cosmos as predetermined by moral causes as much as the cyclical succession of forms of government are. Aristotle's teleological metaphysics of history predetermined the governance of physical and biological changes by purposive or final causes, and so political constitutions also would necessarily reflect the almost biologically predetermined character of people. The Hebrew-Christian philosophy of history continued to emphasize the moral factor at first in dramatic mythology and then in metaphysical rationalizations like Augustine's theodicy, revived by Bossuet's *Discours universelle* in the XVIIth century. When Voltaire wished to attack the scholastic metaphysics of history, he attacked the Hebrews as the original sponsors of the mythical idea of heaven and hell, of the Garden of Eden, of man's disobedience and necessary fall, of the Messianic coming and redemption of man. The influence of this theodicic method of historical thinking appears in Butterfield's view that since we are all sinners we should abstain from passing moral judgment on historical figures, even when dealing with Hitler. But the problem still remains whether it is feasible or desirable for historians to remain or try to be morally aloof in their professional work as historians. In any case, historians of thought have always been moral partisans of some ideas and condemned other ideas on variously professed grounds: the love of truth and beauty, of country and God, of one's own people or culture against barbarians and Gentiles, of freedom *versus* tyranny, of democratic leaders *versus* dictators, etc. It is seriously questionable whether

---

[14] Cf. Erich Auerbach, *Mimesis: the Representation of Reality in Western Literature* (Princeton, 1953) and other writings reviewed by Charles F. Breslin in "Philosophy or Philology: Auerbach and Aesthetic Historicism," *J.H.I.*, XXII, 3 (July–Sept. 1961), 369–81.

any history of any idea would ever be written or read if there were no strong moral passions aroused in the historian or the reader by the cold recital of that idea's effects on human affairs. Of course, we must agree that objective truth in history as well as in any honest search for truth requires our not permitting *our* moral feelings to determine the facts or intrude into the order of the intellectual events recounted. But, as I understand Butterfield, he does not wish to exclude from historiography a vivid account of the moral passions and high feelings or dramatic tensions that the documentary evidence objectively indicates as an essential part of the human events reported. Where mankind universally condemns unnecessary infliction of pain and wholesale slaughter as wanton immorality, do not such events become objectively subject-matter for historical description in moral terms? Should we not, for example, describe as morally great some historical individuals like Socrates, the Buddha, Confucius, Lao-Tze, Moses, Christ, Lincoln, Ghandi, and as morally bad historical individuals like those who conspired against Socrates, the Neros and Caligulas, the Hitlers, or are we to abstain from all such moral judgment? Does not the biographer have to assume some moral value for some of his subject's actions as his legacy to posterity, as even the autobiographer does for his own life?

(5) The "scientific" approach.—The Polish historian of philosophy W. Tatarkiewicz has made a useful distinction for the so-called "humanistic scientist":

We should keep in mind that the *humanistic sciences* are *not* sciences about *psychic phenomena* as against the natural sciences which deal with physical phenomena. The history of art, ethnography, linguistics, and other typically humanistic sciences do not deal with psychical but with psychophysical phenomena. The humanistic sciences are those that inquire into the *creations of man*—as against the natural sciences that inquire into creations of nature; this is the real difference between them.[15]

In the history of a physical science like astronomy, in addition to the advances due to instruments, students forget the historical rôle of theories, so that Copernicus like Aristarchus and Ptolemy were great astronomers precisely because they created a systematic view of the heavens *without* telescopes or cameras.

Tatarkiewicz's distinction does not call for a unique intuitive or super-empirical method of "understanding" for the *Geisteswissenschaften* against the method of the *Naturwissenschaften*.

"Scientific historiography" has various meanings which are often confounded: (a) the search for diverse physical and biological factors

[15] W. Tatarkiewicz, "Nomological and Typological Sciences," from *Reports of the Polish Academy of Sciences*, vol. 46 (1945), 28ff.; translated by Dr. Max Reiser, *Journal of Philosophy* (March 31, 1960), 239.

said to "determine" thought—geography, climate, Buckle's "aspect of nature," racialism, Malthusianism, Social Darwinism, correlation of skeletal structure and ways of life, etc.; (b) the subsumption of all intellectual and cultural changes under "pattern of events" or "laws" of history—Auguste Comte's three stages, Hegel's dialectic unfolding of the *Weltgeist* through the *Volksgeist* in the deeds and thoughts of the "world-historical" individual or "great-man," Marxian class-struggle theory, Henry Adams "phase-rule" applied to history, Spengler's and Toynbee's organicistic determinism, etc.; (c) the search for probable causes and empirical correlations of culturally concomitant developments in the history of arts, languages and literatures, natural and social sciences, religions and philosophies.

The basic concept or problem in all three of these diverse conceptions of the scientific way to study the history of ideas is the nature of causation.[16]

Can we not proceed to investigate probable causes for intellectual developments without committing ourselves to a philosophy of "historical inevitability"? David Hume was able to write good history and assign psychological causes to England's political life without abandoning his scepticism about the demonstrability of "necessary connection" in causality. An interesting linguistic fact here is that Hume used everyday words to express causal relations in history.[17]

Marxists do not confine themselves to dialectics or economic factors when they interpret history for political purposes, so that there is the problem of the difference between *professed* theories of historical causation and the beliefs implicit in the Marxists' intellectual activities.

Our problem is to be as empirical as any natural scientist and yet do justice to the organic inter-relatedness of the various aspects of cultural history. It does not seem to me necessary to resort to a transempirical or private intuitionist method simply because we are dealing with the human mind and its complex historical patterns of thought.

I conclude these very brief remarks on methodology with some further questions for discussion and research.

1. To what extent must the internal history of ideas in the Arts and Sciences be studied apart from external causes?

---

[16] Cf. "Symposium on Causation," M. R. Cohen and F. J. E. Teggart, *J.H.I.* (1942). See *infra*, 42–68.

[17] Hume says, for example, that Julius Caesar, after invading Great Britain in 55 B.C., "was constrained, by the necessity of his affairs and the approach of winter, to withdraw his forces into Gaul." *History of England*, vol. I, ch. 1, p. 4. Or, the barons who opposed King John (in 1215) easily saw from Pope Innocent's letters "that they must reckon on having the Pope, as well as the king, for their adversary." *Ibid.*, p. 426.

2. Do great periods of art and literature generally precede these of science and philosophy? This suggestive problem was posed by Charles S. Peirce as a rhetorical question and hypothesis.

3. To what extent does the self-image of an individual or a whole group of individuals within a culture enter as a causal factor in the history of that culture?

4. Is the consistency or lack of consistency in a thinker's work, the morality or immorality of his conduct, the beauty or lack of it in his living, a part of his thought and life that needs to be included in the historian's account of the ideas of that individual thinker?

5. Are all ideas dated, or must some ideas like the idea of God, of human nature, of the opposition of good and evil, of truth and error, of immortality and freedom, and of the mystery of the individual [18] be regarded as eternal?

6. Is there any clear idea or criterion of progress in human thought, and if so, how specifically has that idea manifested itself in the various arts and sciences? What relation did such an idea of progress for mankind have on the development and education of the individual?

7. Does the originality or priority-claims of an individual thinker proceed from his initial statement or from the manner in which he develops the ideas?

8. Where does an individual's own ideas begin or end, and his debt to his predecessors or his influence on his successors begin and end?

9. As individual efforts in the arts and sciences become more dependent on organizational and state support, how are original creativity and independent research affected?

10. How will the population explosion, the new Afro-Asiatic states, and the increasing life-span affect the study of the history of ideas?

[18] "In that new way of living and new form of society, which is born of the heart, and which is called the Kingdom of Heaven, there are no nations, there are only individuals. . . . Christianity, the mystery of the individual is precisely what must be put into the facts to make them meaningful." Boris Pasternak, *Dr. Zhivago*, Pt. I, Ch. 4, sec. 12.

Symposium on "Causation in History"

by FREDERICK J. TEGGART AND MORRIS R. COHEN

Reprinted from the *Journal of the History of Ideas*—Vol. III, No. 1, pp. 3-29

1. The situation in the world today presents difficulties which challenge our intellectual capabilities and resources. The guidance of the affairs of nations in terms of political, economic, and humanitarian theories has led to conditions in which our mode of life is directly threatened. The defense of our own position, in opposition to "realistic" policies based on ideologies and the worship of the State, calls for new knowledge, and one possibility for acquiring such knowledge would seem to lie in the investigation of "Causation in Historical Events."[1]

When as students of history we approach the subject of "causation," we find ourselves in difficulties, for the problem is not one that has received sustained consideration. In accounting for historical events every historian has been a law to himself.

As a problem, "causation in historical events" has been discussed primarily by philosophers who frankly disavow any interest in historical research. The arguments which they advance with respect to historical knowledge are based upon the common practice of historical writers, but what they discover in the procedure of historians is dictated by their own interests. Philosophy has no guidance to offer historical students. The historian must face his own problems without aid from philosophers, mathematicians, physicists, or biologists.

2. As commonly stated, the objective of historical inquiry is to tell "what it was that actually took place." In theory this end is to be attained by utilizing approved documentary sources of information. It is recognized, however, that the sources enable us only to establish specific and isolated facts, whereas it is taken for granted that mere assemblages of particular facts are not history. "The historian," we are told, "will not write mere annals." The historian, it is said, must give something more than a record of events, he must discover the connection between one event and another. Further, it is understood that "history needs the idea of

[1] This paper was read at the meeting of the American Historical Association on December 28, 1940. The subject was set by the Committee on Program, which also imposed a strict time limit on the contributors.

cause to make it intelligible and comprehensible." "Every narrative, even the most simple one, involves an explanation of causes."

It is accepted, then, that the historian must go beyond the documents and the facts established by critical analysis. In this situation it becomes of primary importance to know how the historian is to proceed so that he may introduce into his narrative the required explanation or interpretation of the facts, and may discover the causal linkage or relation between the events he describes.

3. In the first place, the historian endeavors to make what has happened intelligible through emphasis on human agency. It is assumed that, for the historian, "the individual is always the principle of explanation"; that for him "the only concrete cause is the individual human will."

Since, then, the historian is concerned with the activities of individuals as causal agents, it is inevitable that he should dwell upon the part played by great men. Even the exponents of this view, however, come down step by step to the activities of less important individuals and, in the end, to the influence of insignificant happenings and to Voltaire's theory of "Cleopatra's nose." The great-man theory leads ultimately to the view that chance is the dominant factor in history.

(As a contribution to the study of "causation," we need investigations, based upon comparison of instances, of the conditions under which Caesars, Bonapartes, and Hitlers arise.)

4. From a different point of view, it is argued that the historian makes the known occurrences of the past intelligible, and reveals causation, by the creation of a synthesis (Henri Berr). A writer of the moment tries to make this contention clearer by saying that "historical facts are arranged by historians in a frame of reference, the frame supplying causal connections."

The causal element in historical synthesis is conceived to lie in the movement of advance or decline, of success or failure, which the particular historian discovers in the history of a given country. Consequently we are left with as many patterns of causation as there are narratives of the same series of events, and it is difficult to see how the idea which any particular historian employs to give life and unity to his "story" of a nation is to be regarded as contributory to our knowledge of "that which always precedes a given effect."

5. When we extend our view to the rise and fall of empires, the

general thought which first presents itself, as Hegel remarked, is that of change. So in recent literature we find it said that "historical explanation is an explanation of the world in terms of change," that "the term 'history' implies a process of significant change," that, as Professor Bury thought, "every historical event is a moment in a continuous process of change."

The influence of the word "change" on the thought of scholars engaged in the investigation of what has happened in the past is unfortunate. It suggests the necessity for detecting or discovering some pattern in a postulated continuous movement, and, as a consequence, tends to direct the efforts of historians to search for evidence, on the one hand, of "cycles," on the other, of the "development," "growth," or "evolution" of culture or of mankind. We are instructed, indeed, that men and their actions form part of a whole, and that the historian is to imagine a process of evolution in which, as a framework, he may dispose the elements furnished by the documents (Langlois & Seignobos, *Introduction to the Study of History*, 224). Attention is thus transferred from the examination of actual changes to the task of formulating a philosophy of life (Professor Fling), or of deciding upon our personal adherence to naturalism or idealism (Professor Bury). It is not to be wondered at that in these circumstances so many questions of history "remain insoluble by historical methods" (Langlois & Seignobos, 295).

6. The ideas, first, of cycles, and second, of a unilinear development of mankind are contributions to modern thought made respectively by Greek philosophy and Christian theology. From the Greeks we have inherited also an idea which has an immediate bearing upon the problem of causation.

Observation of what was going on around him suggested to Heraclitus of Ephesus the conception of a process through the operation of which the actual conditions in his time had been brought about. Thus, in his opinion, it was a result of the way things work in political society that "some are bond and some free." Since the observed condition was produced by war, the generalization followed that war, actual or metaphorical, was "father" and "king" of all, and that "all things come into being through strife." Attention to affairs in a given present, then, led Heraclitus to infer that the conditions perceived were the outcome of the continuous operation of observable processes, and so to the opinion that present processes might be taken as explanatory of what had happened in the past.

I cannot here take time to trace the long history of the procedure initiated by Heraclitus. It is significant for the question under consideration, however, that the idea of a process which, through its continuous operation, has brought about change in the course of time has been utilized in History, no less than in the sciences of Geology and Evolutionary Biology. It is, indeed, the principle of explanation employed in those various "interpretations" of history which rely upon some economic, racial, or other "struggle" to account for present conditions in the world. In modern times the idea of "struggle" has been employed as a substitute for the directive agency of Providence.

7. The essential difficulty in the study of causation in historical events lies in the fact that the recognized objectives of historical explanation leave no place for the investigation of causes as a specific undertaking. If, however, in opposition to established usage we set ourselves to this effort, it at once appears that we are not without resources.

What we are given in experience is not one history, but a great number of histories. History is not unitary, but pluralistic. Every region and area has its own history, and the investigation of causation becomes possible when it is seen that the activities of men under different conditions may be compared.

Again, what we are given in experience is not change, but evidence of changes, and changes may be investigated and compared. Further, what we are given in experience is not a series of events said to be "unique," but an infinite number of occurrences at different times and in different places. It is true that, in pursuit of their special interests, some philosophers stress the aspect of uniqueness in events (indicated by names and dates), and seem to imply that there is no possibility of events having features in common. Nevertheless, when you personally speak of the attempted invasion of England in 1940, you inevitably bring in some reference to the other attempted invasions by Philip II and Napoleon Bonaparte. Your action in this respect is simply that of adding a new member to an already recognized class of events.

If we are to inquire into causation, it will be necessary to become familiar with the idea that there are classes of events, for where there are two or more occurrences which have features in common, these occurrences may be compared, and the possibility of comparison opens the way to induction. Historians who may concern themselves with the events of the twentieth century will always be forced to give attention to the rise of dictators, a class of events. You, I think, will admit it to be a matter of urgency that we should leave no means untried to enlarge our understanding of this menacing phenomenon.

8. A class of events, once recognized, sets a problem for investigation, and every such problem calls for solution in terms of causation. But here, instead of further generalities, I invite your consideration of an instance in which historians uniformly (1) have accepted the existence of a class of events, and (2) have proceeded, without demur, to account for the facts by an exposition of causes. I refer to the barbarian invasions of the Roman empire. If the subject should seem to you remote, it at least has the merit that it admits of methodical examination without admixture of disturbing emotions.

As a preliminary step, let me say that it is often taken for granted that "science always chooses some phase or aspect of the existing world for detailed examination" (S. P. Lamprecht). The statement is inaccurate. Actual inquiry begins when an individual encounters some specific difficulty in experience, as when he finds that the accepted account of some phenomenon is at variance with the facts. Every advance in knowledge, from the time of Thales or of Copernicus, has been made by some one who has resolutely faced a difficulty in thought.

Now Professor Bury, an authority on the barbarian invasions, says that the German tribes were driven by the urgency of the food question to seek new abodes and were attracted by the rich provinces of Rome (*Selected Essays*, 62). The historian recognized explicitly the existence of a class of events, and responded to the need of offering an explanation of the occurrences. The explanation given was not, however, the result of his own researches; he took it over unquestioned from his predecessors, without scrutiny of its relation to the facts and without inquiry as to the source from which it had been derived. In other words, Professor Bury ignored a difficulty which had an important bearing upon a subject which he treated regularly in lectures. He consulted the sources for his facts; it did not occur to him to scrutinize the authorities for his explanation of the facts.

Every difficulty in thought which is neglected or slurred over is a failure of duty in scholarship and constitutes a serious obstacle to the advancement of knowledge.

9. We begin, then, with the fact that for centuries the northern frontiers of the Roman empire were subject to the invasions of Germanic and other peoples. The frequent recurrence of these invasions has set a problem to which every scholar who has concerned himself with ancient or medieval history has responded by advancing some explanatory theory. Now, in making this response to a recognized problem, historians have, as a matter of fact, admitted the applicability of the "method of science" to historical inquiry. Consequently it is of importance to note that, though they have unhesitatingly offered explanations of these phenomena, they have done this without awareness of their own procedure, and hence without taking into account the steps which must necessarily lie between the statement of a problem and the presentation of a solution.

In an investigation of the barbarian invasions the procedure found necessary (see my *Rome and China*, 1939) has been as follows: first, to recognize the existence of a class of events, and hence of a problem for investigation; second, to examine the theories or explanations heretofore put forward to account for the occurrences; third, when these theories were found to be at variance with the facts, to assemble all data which might be regarded as pertinent to the subject. With this object in view, the procedure adopted was to set down, in chronological order, all known events, wars, and disturbances in each separate kingdom or region of the Eurasian continent for a period of five hundred years. The next step was to compare occurrences in each of the many areas for which it was possible to find evidence either in European or Asiatic sources. When the work of comparison had been carried out, it was discovered that (during the period from 58 B.C. to A.D. 107, the period covered in *Rome and China*) every uprising on the European borders of the Roman empire had been preceded by the outbreak of war either on the eastern frontiers of the empire or in the "Western Regions" of the Chinese. Moreover, the correspondence in events was discovered to be so precise that, whereas wars in the Roman East were followed uniformly and always by disturbances on the lower Danube and the Rhine, wars in the eastern

T'ien Shan were followed uniformly and always by disturbances on the Danube between Vienna and Budapest.

Systematic inquiry was rewarded, then, by the discovery, for the first time, of correlations in historical events. I use the word "correlation" because it has been found, in all cases, that when the first event occurred (in the T'ien Shan or the Roman East), the second occurred (on the Pannonian Danube or the lower Danube and the Rhine), and, further, that when the first event did not occur, the second did not occur. The discovery that certain sets of events—wars in Asia and barbarian invasions in Europe—are correlated is a matter of unusual importance, for it demonstrates the existence of a type or order of historical facts which has not hitherto received attention.

10. The correspondences or correlations in events to which I have called your attention may appear to accord with the formula, "The same cause always has the same effect," but you will already have asked yourself how these correspondences are to be accounted for. Karl Pearson, the eminent authority on scientific method, remarks that "the conception of correlation between two occurrences . . . is the wider category by which we have to replace the old idea of causation." Again, he says, "The aim of science ceases to be the discovery of 'cause' and 'effect' . . . it seeks out the phenomena which are most highly correlated." We are now in a position to see, however, that the discovery of correlations does not replace and is not a substitute for the investigation of causation. We have found that, in a certain class of events, "when this happens, that happens," and that the second event appears only on the occurrence of the first, but this result does not afford even a momentary stopping place for our intellectual interest; conversely, indeed, it brings up the original question in a more explicit and more urgent form. Thus we are forced to ask how the correspondences or correlations discovered are to be accounted for. Without further elaboration, I may say that as the outcome of this long and difficult phase of the investigation I reached the conclusion that the correspondence of wars in the East and invasions in the West had been due to interruptions of trade.[2]

[2] The "conclusion" referred to is, in fact, an hypothesis, and as such is open to revision. On the other hand, the various statements concerning occurrences are based upon the evidence of historical documents, and are not hypothetical, though in the few cases where he has ventured to disagree with the views of modern authorities the

11. The Romans should have been able, one would think, to discern that wars on the eastern frontiers of the empire were invariably followed by outbreaks on the lower Danube and the Rhine. Nevertheless, even though time after time disturbances in the East and attacks by the northern barbarians are mentioned in the same context by historians, and even by poets, there is no indication in the sources that the conjunction ever provoked comment or inspired reflection. Certainly Augustus persisted in his attempts to dominate Armenia, though the actual results on the Danube and the Rhine might have been unerringly predicted. I am, however, convinced, from circumstantial evidence, that the relation of events in the Near East and in Europe was known to and acted upon both by Tiberius and Trajan. Yet any assured inference from correspondences in events which may have been made by Roman authorities was subject to the doubt cast by the invasions of Pannonia, which we now know were linked with wars in Mongolia and were independent of events in Armenia or Syria. Specifically, the Romans were debarred from positive knowledge of the relation of events by reason of the attenuated character of the information which reached them from the world east of the Caspian Sea. Even so, the poet Horace gives expression to the opinion that disturbances among the Seres, the Bactrians, and the tribes on the Jaxartes were worth watching.

The world has changed since the first and second centuries, for then there were but three "great powers" in Eurasia: Rome, Parthia, and China. The basic change, however, has been created by the emergence of sea-power into prominence since the circumnavigation of Africa and the discovery of the Cape route to India. In the period after 1498 the relations of peoples have evidently become more intricate and involved, but it is not on this account to be assumed that correspondences in events are no longer discoverable—especially since no one has looked for them. I am disposed to believe that interruptions of trade still continue to be a most important factor in creating disturbances throughout the world. But I recommend, as the part of wisdom, that before embarking on deep-sea voyages we should familiarize ourselves with the rela-

---

judgment of the investigator may be at fault. The essential feature of the argument is that comparison of histories on a world basis leads to observation of correspondences in events, and these correspondences invite revision of inherited ideas concerning causation in history.

tions in events during what I may designate loosely as the "land-route period."

12. Let us now look the problem of causation in the face. "The search for causes is ultimately derived from the search for means to the practical realisation of results in which we are interested" (A. E. Taylor). We are today in difficulties of the most practical character, and we are in urgent need of new knowledge. The knowledge we require can be derived only from the close investigation of human experience on a world basis. Historians have stood aloof from the urgencies of life, and have declaimed against any aim for their subject beyond the "objective" statement of facts. But they have been willing to go beyond the facts, in compliance with the conventions of literature. Let us admit that historians alone are equipped to undertake the study of causation in historical events—are they to continue to refuse their aid in presence of the emergency which now presses upon our civilization?

It is useless to say we can do nothing, as long as we attempt nothing. Men sought for the "cause" of malaria simply in the belief that it could be discovered. They found that "chills and fever" could be overcome, not by some elaboration of conventional dosage, but by the application of kerosene to stagnant pools. No theorizing could possibly have led to this result. Similarly, they set to work to discover some means of preventing recurrences of the "Black Death" or bubonic plague; as a result of the study of causation, we now employ rat catchers. Scientists work on the principle and in the belief that the investigation of causation will ultimately lead to the alleviation of human misery and suffering. It is useless to speculate whether and how this alleviation may in any instance be accomplished—until investigation has been carried out. We cannot master the intricacies of historical events all at once, and with our eyes fixed upon the production of traditional histories. We must undertake the investigation of some problem, however limited in scope it may at first sight appear to be. Galileo established a new science by investigating the rate of falling bodies.

I noticed not long ago, in an important journal, the confident statement that "the excursions of literary men into politics" were a hopeful sign for the future. It would be a hopeful sign were historians to concern themselves with the extraordinarily difficult task of investigating "causation in historical events."

CAUSATION IN HISTORICAL EVENTS

MORRIS R. COHEN

In the controversies as to the methodology of history the question of causation has occupied a central place. The defense of human autonomy or free will has led many to such a sharp separation between mind and nature as to deny any application of natural causation to human affairs. On the other hand, naturalists have taken it as axiomatic that historiography can become scientific, i.e., give us verifiable knowledge free from bias or superstition, only if it submits to the methods of natural science which operate with causal laws.

A generation ago the naturalists seemed to be carrying the day in the social sciences and thus in the theory of history. But recent idealists have used the extreme empiricism of anti-metaphysical positivists to argue that the laws of physics are purely statistical and thus not different in kind from the constant correlations that we find in public or national affairs. Quetelet's and Buckle's use of statistics to prove the reign of iron laws of causality in human affairs is thus reversed into a denial that such laws can be found in physics. This positivism seems to have been recently reinforced by a vague rumor that Heisenberg and others have swept away the concept of determinism from physical science.

That the arguments on both sides are carried on with more sweeping enthusiasm than discrimination, is seen in the fact that both positivists and Hegelian idealists come to the same fatalistic conclusion that man cannot change the course of history; and from the determinist dogma quite opposing conclusions are drawn. Thus some hold that not only is history subject to laws but that only the superstition of free-will has prevented us from discovering them; while others argue that since the whole temporal system of events is determined, it is vain to pick out any one element in the world and say it is the cause of any particular event that follows it.

In such a situation a review of elementary considerations seems worth while.

The original sense of the word history, which still survives in the term natural history, included any description of the nature of anything, e.g., Aristotle's *History of Animals* or Theophrastus's

History of Plants. And though our word used *simpliciter* is today restricted to accounts of past happenings it still includes purely physical and biological as well as human events. Thus we have histories of our terrestrial globe or of parts of it as well as of various biologic species. Opponents of naturalism, such as Croce, may insist on restricting the word history not only to human affairs, but even to some particular phase of political life in which they happen to be interested or to some special way of dealing with it. But no arbitrary definition or resolution to use a word in a peculiar sense can well deny that biographies such as Plutarch's Life of Caesar and Tacitus's Life of Agricola are substantially histories of Rome or that Herodotus was justified in including the development of the Nile, its delta, and the soil of Egypt, in the magnificent book which has given him the title, The Father of History. There are doubtless distinctive elements in human affairs which give distinctive form to the causal relation that is applicable to them. But since men are born, live, and die on this earth, and their activities are conditioned by the presence or absence of food, water, and other physical and biological factors, the meaning of causality in history cannot be altogether unrelated to its meaning in the natural sciences. It is well, therefore, to consider first the general nature of causation before dealing with the special features which it assumes in human history.

I

It is interesting to note in passing that the word cause, from the Latin *causa*, corresponding to the Greek αἰτία, is originally a social and more specifically a legal term. This sense continues in the phrase "cause of action" or "legal case." It came into natural philosophy through the analogy of nature to a well ordered realm ruled by law. The Greek as well as the modern historians used a variety of expressions for the causal relation, e.g., an antecedent led to, gave rise to, brought about, made, produced, created, or influenced a certain consequent, or the latter was due to, resulted from, came as a consequence of, or was conditioned by the former. Polybius[1] drew explicit distinctions between αἰτία πρόφασις and ἀρχή i.e., the motive force, the excuse or reason, and the beginning or origin, in German *Ursache*. Aristotle's famous doctrine of the four causes: the material, the form, the efficient cause, and the pur-

[1] *Histories*, III cc 6–7, 31.

CAUSATION IN HISTORICAL EVENTS 53

pose or end, deal with what we would call today the grounds or reasons why anything whatsoever takes place in the way it does. It is thus not much different from the modern principle of sufficient reason except that in the interest of clarity we restrict the causal relation to changes or phenomena in time and space.

In general we all believe that human, like other events, are in some way connected, and that there is always a reason or ground why anything happens. Only that which has nothing beside or outside of itself to change it in any way can be causeless or *causa sui*, e.g., Spinoza's Substance or Hegel's Absolute Idea. This cannot be said of anything which is a part of the temporal stream. That is why we ask such questions as what brought about the present war, the depression of 1929, or any other event in which we are at all interested. But it is obviously not enough to say that events are in some way connected. The significant question is what is the nature of this connection.

Since history deals with occurrences in time, the element of temporal sequence must enter into causality and distinguish it from the relation between whole and part, form and content, or any other abstract, purely logical or mathematical, condition. It also seems wise at the outset to be cautioned against the ancient fallacy of *post hoc ergo propter hoc*. Whatever causality may be it is more than mere succession in time. All sorts of superstitions and absurdities result from ignorng this, for instance, arguing that because the introduction of a new game of cards preceded a given event such as an epidemic of dysentery, the former was the cause of the latter. However, though this is elementary, an influential philosophic doctrine urges that causality is nothing but repeated succession. And under the name of correlation this has become a canon of scientific procedure among recent "research" workers in psychology, sociology and education.

This doctrine began with Hume's attempt to eliminate necessity from the causal relation by an argument similar to that by which Zeno seemed to disprove the possibility of motion.

Having as a follower of Locke and Berkeley, reduced everything to a discrete series of successive "impressions" or "ideas" as "states of mind," he naturally could not find that any consequent "state" was contained in any antecedent one, and this seemed to rule out any real or necessary connection between things.

Not only as a historian and in his more mature *Essays,* but even in his youthful *Treatise,* Hume himself was candid enough to recognize the untenability of the completely sceptical or nihilistic results of his basic assumptions. He admitted that in practice we must continue to believe that things are really or necessarily connected. Nor does it require much acumen to see the inconsistency of reducing all causality to mere succession and then explaining the belief in, or habitual expectation of, necessary connection as *caused* by the repetition of the same sequence of events. In the first place, it is not true that the repetition of any succession has always been followed by the expectation of its invariant recurrence. The fact that some people rightly or wrongly see causal relations where others have for ages failed to suspect their existence, suggests that the issue is not so simple. Moreover the expectation that the future *will be* like the past assumes a certain inherent and invariant constancy in the order of nature which no number of past observations can by themselves prove. The fact that for twenty-five thousand days in succession a man has taken a walk before breakfast will not prevent his failure to do so tomorrow.

Despite its logical frailties, however, the Humean doctrine has found powerful support not only in the forces which have made for modern subjectivism or extreme psychologic individualism, but curiously enough in the modern effort to eliminate all occult qualities and anthropomorphism from the field of physics. As the popular notion of cause involves some analogy to human action in which purpose and effort enter, physicists have sought to purify their science from all such implications by reducing their descriptions to mathematical relations between observable elements or operations. It is this which led Karl Pearson, whose special field of competence was in the mathematics of statistics, to the attempt to make correlation take the place of causation.

But the fact that many have uncritically accepted Pearson as an authority on scientific method generally, cannot wipe out a logical difference in the nature of things. A correlation is an empirical or historical statement that in a certain proportion of instances two elements *have* occurred simultaneously or successively. A causal relation asserts more than mere past coincidence. It affirms that there is some reason or ground why, whenever the antecedent occurs, the consequent must follow. The assertion of a causal relation may be false in fact, or not supported by adequate evidence, but the element of necessity, the exclusion of a contrary possibility, is an essential part of its meaning. Even if it were true that every time we observed a uniform succession we inferred a causal relation, the content of the proposition inferred would still be logically different from that which led to it.

The foregoing does not deny that the observation of a correlation frequently suggests or leads us to discover a causal relation. What we have insisted on is that correlations are often mere coincidences that do not indicate any significant connection, or any reason for expecting such correlation to continue. I have on several occasions referred to the high correlation of 87% for 13 years between the death-rate in the State of Hyderabad and the membership in the International (American) Machinists Union. If there are not many instances of this sort, it is because we do not, as a rule, look for them. We generally begin with a hunch or a suspicion of a causal relation between certain facts and seek for correlation to confirm it. But to regard such confirmation as proof is to commit the fallacy of arguing from the affirmation of the consequent. A number of diverse hypotheses, notably theologic ones, find their teachings confirmed by everything that happens, but this will not verify any one of them. For verification involves not only confirmation but the exclusion or disproof of alternative hypotheses.

Suppose it were established that between 58 B.C. and 107 A.D. every invasion of or rebellion in the Roman Empire was preceded by a "disturbance" in the trade routes between China and Rome. Clearly that would not be sufficient to prove a causal relation. For if previous or subsequent invasions or rebellions had no such antecedents, or if "disturbances" of these trade routes were not at other times followed by wars of this kind, the assertion that the correlation for the limited period was more than a series of coincidences would be definitely disproved. Nor would the existence of such correlation exclude the possibility that even in the given cases such factors as love of independence, irritations at Roman oppression, the attraction of richer lands, or the ambition of kings or powerful leaders, were the direct or immediate causes. To maintain the thesis in question we should have to prove that such a rebellion as that of Judea in 68 B.C. was not caused by religious differences or anything other than a disturbance in the trade routes between China and Rome.

Suppose that our meteorologic records showed that the average rainfall in our states was for a number of years higher under Republican than under Democratic governors, should we hold that a causal relation was thus established? The objection might at once be raised that no one supposes that a natural phenomenon such as rain could be influenced by any purely political event. But if we ignore the fact that many *have* attributed the absence of rain to the moral or religious sins of governors or their people, and have sought to bring about a greater rainfall by prayer, the foregoing objection only confirms the necessity for distinguishing between correlation and causation. For it admits that the causal relation holds only between the members of certain classes of phenomena. Now it is most important to be on guard against the fallacy of selection, of generalizing about any group which we have selected as a class. Thus if a number of Chinese merchants fail to pay their bills promptly, I may readily be led to regard their failure as connected with their being Chinese, whereas it may be due to quite different conditions, such as the fact that they are all, like others not known to me, connected with a certain bank, that they are all among those who sold goods to a certain bankrupt firm or to a depressed economic class, or because of some other unknown reason.

Historical phenomena do not come to us already properly classified. It is we who classify them in diverse ways according to the purposes of our inquiry. The category of "trade disturbance" may thus include diverse phenomena some of which may and some of which may not be relevant to the invasions of the Roman Empire or to rebellions within it.[2]

It is true that two phenomena between which there is no direct causal relation may, if they vary concomitantly, be the effects of a common cause. Thus, suppose we find that states with a high degree of literacy excel in crime. It will not necessarily be true that either crime is the cause of literacy or *vice versa,* but both may be

[2] Even the terms invasion, rebellion and war denote things so heterogeneous that discrimination leading to the recognition of different kinds or sub-classes is necessary before we can expect to find a common cause. Villa's invasion of the United States was quite a different affair from Burgoyne's, and an American Indian rebellion or war a quite different sort of event from the World War. Similarly raids of Kurdish tribes were different kinds of affairs than the invasion of Rome by Hannibal or of Illyria by Rome. In the present state of our knowledge, it is futile to ask the cause of disease. We must in our aetiology first deal with different kinds of diseases; and much more is this the case with wars.

consequences of a relatively larger proportion of urban population. "The Island of St. Kilda is not rich enough to support a single pickpocket." But that only pushes back the problem how to determine that any circumstance such as city life is the cause of such phenomena as greater literacy and greater criminality.

Thus, despite some amateurish philosophizing on the part of some physicists or biologists when they take a vacation from the field of their special competence, the fact is that natural science is never satisfied with empirical statistical correlation but ever seeks to formulate universal laws that assert not that A has followed B a number of times but that there is an intimate connection between the two such that whenever A occurs B must follow, i.e., the possibility of B not following A is ruled out. In putting its laws in the form of equations science always seeks to eliminate as far as possible all arbitrary constants.

When the inadequacy of mere correlation between two terms is recognized we try to establish the causal relation by interpolating a middle term. The ancients found a correlation between exposure to damp air, especially at night, and malaria. It was an essential task of biology and medical science to ask why these two should be thus connected. An intermediate term was found in the bite of certain mosquitoes. But why should the bite of the mosquito produce the given result? Again an intermediate term is found in the virus that is injected into the organism by the bite. But why should that virus destroy the red blood corpuscles? It is obvious that no matter how many middle terms are thus interpolated we still have a discrete series and the question why two terms should be causally connected remains. This is, of course, no objection to a process which extends our knowledge even though it never can be absolutely completed. The prolongation of life may be desirable though the hour of death is only postponed thereby. Natural science, however, sets before itself a definite ideal of transforming the discrete series into a continuous one by finding an element of identity between antecedent and consequent and thus justifying the judgment of necessary connection. We approximate to that ideal in the laws of conservation of mass and energy, and indeed, in all the formulae of mathematical physics in which certain relations remain invariant. Assuming some identity throughout all the physical processes, the connection between any two states can become a necessary one. We explain why water and sunshine are necessary for plants if we show the identity of the water and the plant tissue or the identity of the energy in the sun's rays and that by which the chlorophyl transforms inorganic into organic compounds. In that phase of their being in which things are identical they cannot be different, though they must be different in other respects in order to be at all distinguishable and thus form a plurality of things.

The prejudice against admitting the element of necessity in our world has been largely supported by the reaction against those metaphysical theories which try to put customary or cherished but questionable opinions beyond attack by enthroning them as necessary truths. But it is really impossible to get along in our daily life or in scientific investigation without the idea of necessity. Every day we recognize that certain acts are necessary, i.e., that we have no alternative. In mathematics we prove that the Pythagorean theorem necessarily follows from Euclidean axioms by showing that it is impossible for the latter to be true and the former to be false. Similarly we prove that it is impossible for physical things to have certain properties without having others that are logically or mathematically connected with them. Thus we prove that if the earth, sun and moon are in a given position and their motions conform to the law of gravitation, an eclipse must necessarily follow at a certain time.

It will be seen that the necessity of physical happenings is thus conditional, i.e., no event is necessary absolutely or by itself but only if it is connected with other events and is thus part of a system. To this human events are clearly no exception.

We may now sum up our discussion thus far by saying that in its most rigorous form causality denotes the sum of the necessary and sufficient conditions for the occurrence of any event. A circumstance that is not necessary for a given event, i.e., if the event can take place without it, cannot be the cause. And similarly if a circumstance is not sufficient to bring about the given event, i.e., if the former can occur without the latter, it cannot be the cause. We must, however, recognize that popular discourse and thought do not always conform to this definite test of causality. This shows itself in the view that there can be a plurality of causes. Thus it is said that a headache may be due to noxious vapors, to eye strain, to indigestion, or to various other antecedents. Similarly it is said that wars can be caused by the ambition of rulers, or be forced on them by all sorts of circumstances. It has, however, been readily shown that the appearance of a plurality of causes is merely the failure to refine the classification of antecedents and consequence to the same extent. Different organic conditions produce different sorts of headaches; and what is common to all of the latter corresponds to what is common to eye strain, indigestion, etc. So likewise are there various kinds of wars and the courses they take are not independent of the specific conditions which lead to them.

The rigorous test of causality is professed by the conscientious historical investigator and often applied by the critic of proposed causes for known events. When sober students of history deny that the Battle of Tours was the cause of the check to Arab power in the West, or that Waterloo was the decisive cause of the elimination of Napoleon, they show that these battles were unnecessary for the occurrence of the given results, that the latter would in all probability have occurred even if these battles had not taken place. Similarly we reject oppression of the masses as a sufficient cause for a revolution by showing that oppressed people sometimes become weak, apathetic and lack the power to organize successful revolutions. But the historian as a narrator of what happens is under pressure to tell a coherent story and this does not permit him to stop to indicate ever so often the inadequacy or inconclusiveness of his evidence. Hence most historians adopt much looser conceptions of causality.

One of the serious obstacles to a rigorous consideration of the evidence necessary to establish causal relation in history is the wide acceptance of the positivistic and narrowly empiricist dogma, professed even by such idealists as Croce, that history is not at all concerned with what might or could have happened. It is curious that those most concerned with the close relation between history and practice should hold this dogma, when it is so obvious that all practical activity involves weighing the consequences of alternatives only one of which is realized. Indeed we cannot grasp the full significance of what happened unless we have some idea of what the situation would have been otherwise. Nor is there much logical force in the argument that all our evidence bears on what did happen and not at all on what might have happened. There is considerable evidence that if Alexander had been drowned crossing the Granicus none of his generals could have accomplished what he did. For in fact the events after his death showed that no one of them could sufficiently control the others. Similarly it can be hardly be questioned that if Lincoln had not been murdered, his national prestige, his influence in the Republican party, and his political tact and experience would have enabled him to guide the Reconstruction of the South more successfully in a humane direction than was possible for a southern Democrat as inadaptable to the actual situation as was Andrew Johnson.

The objection, however, has been raised that histories deal with individual unrepeatable events, that causal efficacy holds only between them, and that the introduction of laws is at best a purely verbal device which may help to describe multitudes of facts but does not add to our knowledge of any particular occurrence. To explain the fall of an apple by the law of gravitation seems like explaining why I feel hungry by the fact that many others also do.

This objection oversimplifies the uniqueness of historic events and misses the true rôle of laws as universal propositions.

The absolutely unique, that which has no element in common with anything else, is indescribable—since all description and all analysis are in terms of predicates, class concepts or repeatable relations. Let us take a unique event, for example, that King John signed the Magna Charta at Runnymede on June 6th, 1415 A.D. Neither the individual John, the date, nor the specific act will occur again. Yet our statement identifies John as one of a class, the kings of England, who are defined as the occupants of certain offices or as bearing certain relations to the various elements of the people of England. Magna Charta is significant as one of a number of political documents; and not only is the physical act of signing repeatable but the motives which we assume compelled John to do it are recurrent ones in human experience. The date itself denotes a unique or unrepeatable state of the world. But note that it is defined in terms of a number of repeatable intervals, namely, years. Although language can never be self-sufficient and ultimately always depends upon a demonstrative element, i.e., a pointing to something which must be experienced, yet that to which the demonstrative points has its character determined by its abstract or repeatable traits.

The nominalist misses the practical and theoretic significance of universal laws as hypotheses in regard to what are the invariant connections between abstract phases of particular events or existences. Common experience only roughly blocks out, from the big blooming confusion that nature presents to the undeveloped intelligence, such objects and sequences as more or less immediately serve organic or practical needs. To obtain more accurate knowledge of nature we need more refined analysis than is possible with the less discriminately used categories of common sense. Unsupported objects such as apples and feathers fall with varying velocities, but others such as smoke or balloons go up, and the planets move in peculiarly tortuous ways in relation to the fixed stars or our earth. Can we formulate an accurate universal proposition (i.e., one without any exception) that will enable us to tell what is relevant and what is irrelevant to all these motions? The law of gravitation does precisely this. It not only widens our horizon and integrates diverse realms, but apparent exceptions are explained by seeking and finding other laws such as those of electricity and magnetism.

This picking out of the elements which are relevant or causally related to a given phenomenon is the essence of the service which science renders in making the world intelligible and manageable. It may well be argued that the physical laws which thus connect phenomena in necessary relations are themselves contingent, that is, they are either generalizations from empirically observed phenomena or they are derived from wider generalizations of the way things have happened to appear. Since all proof of existence rests on assumptions, it is not possible to prove everything, and contingency cannot thus ever be entirely removed. Note, however, that while a law such as Newton's in regard to gravitation cannot be proved by the consequences which it explains, it cannot be utterly or entirely false so far as it describes what has actually been observed to happen on such a large scale. Another law such as Einstein's may replace it as a more accurate description. But such other law will have to include the truth of the older one under restricted conditions. And this the general theory of relativity indeed does, just as the modern electro-magnetic theory of light includes both the older wave and the corpuscular theories to the extent that they actually described optical phenomena.

It has been suggested by Poincaré and Peirce that the laws of uniformity of nature which in our present era seem to hold true may really be changing slowly so that in the remote future gravitation may vary not as at present, according to the inverse square, but according to some higher or lower power. Though there is no positive evidence for this it must be admitted that we know nothing that makes this impossible. But even if the laws now assumed are found to be changing, science will have to seek a law or formula for their variation, however difficult it might be to discover it.

Thus while it is possible to question any particular law it is neither practically nor theoretically feasible to believe that there are no laws whatsoever in the world of existence. It is not practically possible because all rational or deliberative conduct is based upon the assumption of some fixed order or mechanism by which our objectives can be realized. Nor could any account or description be given of any natural realm if there were no identity of anything at different moments. Science and sanity postulate a world in which there are certain fixed characters. A world in which nothing was impossible, in which a smile could become a forest fire or the clothes on my back a highroad or river, would be a chaos beyond anything in the most insane mind, and there could be no investigation in such a world, since nothing could be determined about anything in it.

Confusion on this point has resulted from the failure to discriminate between two kinds of determinism which may be respectively called absolute and qualified. The former is characteristic of philosophies which, like that of Spinoza or Hegel, allow for no genuine alternatives in the absolute reality. Contrary to the general impression, the system of laws which is the object of science does allow for contingency and irrelevance in the world. The difference between the two kinds of determinism may be represented by the following image.

Let us take some complicated modern drawing or painting that has no symmetry or repetitions in it. Let us cut it up into a number of small pieces, no two of which have the same shape, shuffle them up, and then try to rearrange them so as to recreate the original. The solution of the problem is absolutely determinate in that each fragment has one and only one place where it can fit. Every piece has a unique relation to every other piece, and if only one is missing the original design of the whole cannot be grasped, since the parts already known will not supply us with any analogies whereby we can fill in what is missing.

For a model of a limited determinist system let us take a picture that has a good deal of symmetry and repetition. Cut it up so that many pieces are like others and a number of smaller pieces can be combined to fill the place of a larger one. Since the original design is a definite one the problem of reconstructing it is also determinate. But in solving it analogies or laws may be discovered as to how various fragments should be put together; and when we come to a gap, we can on the basis of analogies to other parts form reasonable hypotheses as to how to fill it.

Now in an absolutely determinate system such as Spinoza's Substance, Hegel's Absolute, Mill's total state of the universe which is the cause of any particular change,—all of which are popularly expressed in Tennyson's "Flower in the crannied wall,"—there is no room for repetitions or laws. For every event in it is absolutely unique and connected with everything else in a unique or unrepeatable manner. But in the world of practice and science there are fungible or replaceable things, and it is the fact of similarity or repeatability of patterns that makes possible the laws of natural science.

Consider a homely example. The water-pipe in my cellar bursts. On the previous day a woman with an envious disposition passed my house. Since the latter was undoubtedly a part of the total world of events, the "organic" view must regard it as part of the cause. But according to this mode of reasoning every other past event was a part of the cause, and there is no reason for picking out the frost and the character of the pipes. We should thus have no guidance in trying to prevent the recurrence of the unfortunate event, nor would there be any point in saying that the freezing and expansion of water depends upon temperature if it also depends on everything else. Science and practice assume a world in which not everything, but only certain things or factors are relevant to a given event.

This realization that there are irrelevancies in the world enables us to see how one-sided or superficial is the view that there are no accidental or fortuitous coincidences in nature or history. If causation takes place only along certain lines, then the coincidence or crossing of two such lines is an accidental event in each, since it is not determined by the nature of either alone. Accidents, like necessity, are relative to our system. Now it may well be argued that if one knows the time and place at which two apparently independent systems or bodies start, and the directions and velocities at which they travel, one can predict where and when their paths will cross, just as we can tell when the two hands of a clock will cross. But, from this argument it does not follow that there is no contingency in nature. We can predict when the hour and hands will cross only on the assumption that our clock will always keep perfect time which unfortunately no actual instrument ever does. We cannot tell when it will slow down or stop altogether. The Laplacian intelligence that can predict every natural event can deal only with a world in which every particle moves according to a formula that does not change with time. But even in such a world such an intelligence would have to know the actual coordinates of all the (finite or infinite) particles that constitute the world at any one moment, and these would be contingent (or derived from a previous contingent state). Even the ultimate formula according to which all motion is to take place would be contingent in the sense that it would at best be a statement that we have found the world to behave in accordance with it. We could not prove the impossibility of the world behaving according to some other formula. Contingency cannot therefore be entirely eliminated. But neither can we get rid of relative necessity. When the proper discrimination is made, there is no contradiction between the two—certainly not so long as we restrict ourselves to finite or limited systems.

II

We may now consider some of the distinctive traits of causal laws in human history.

(1) In doing so we must be especially on guard against the complementary fallacies of pan-logism and nominalism. Though history must implicitly or explicitly involve laws if we are to pass from present data to past facts, the search for the latter as they actually occurred distinguishes truthful history from works of fiction. And it is a demonstrable error to suppose that anything in regard to specific existence can be deduced from purely logical considerations. In this respect history is like geology or any branch of applied rather than theoretic physics.

On the other hand to assign a cause for that which is unique in a given event is to indulge in unverifiable guess-work—since verification involves deduction from hypothesis and repetition of experimental conditions. Biology does not pretend to be able to explain "sports" or extreme variations and the historian or social scientist cannot explain what it was that enabled men of genius to do the unprecedented things which they did, as in the case of Homer, Amos, Buddha, Irnerius, or Shakespeare. Climate, race, epoch, or the class struggle will not explain the *difference* between Bacon and Coke, Jesus and Judas, Thomas Jefferson and John Marshall. And so the historian cannot really explain why in a little backward corner of the world there should arise the remarkable group of Hebrew prophets, why within such a short period the city of Athens should have produced Socrates and Plato, Aeschylus, Sophocles, Euripides, and Aristophanes, Thucydides and Xenophon, or why Germany should within 100 years have brougth forth Lessing, Kant, Fichte, Schelling, Hegel, and Schopenhauer. We can, however, say that there can be no writers in a community where writing is unknown, and that these men could not have done what they did if there were not conditions which made it possible for them to undertake what they did and find some support from others for carrying on their work.

(2) While there is nothing to indicate that the events of human history may not be connected according to some laws or invariant order, we must not jump to the uncritical assumption that these laws must have as simple a form as those of mechanics, astronomy, or other branch of physics. Let us note, to begin with, that the phenomena of civilization are infinitely more complex, since they include biologic and mental as well as inorganic factors. And when situations depend upon too large a number of factors, or when these factors do not form a linear series, but modify each other in complex ways, we may not ever be able to discover the laws or to formulate manageable equations for dealing with the phenomena. We make progress in natural science, when we can vary one factor and keep every other constant. Such experimental conditions are not generally available in the human or even always in the purely biologic field.

(3) Time enters into human history, as in the organic realm generally, in a way that it does not in the inorganic realm. We may pass over the significant question as to whether new elements do not develop in the course of time as distinctive individuals or unprecedented social institutions enter the social arena. For even in the purely inorganic realm there are genuine novelties when new combinations are formed, e.g., when fluorine is combined with oxygen. (It is an error to assume that *all* the properties of a compound can be deduced from the nature of its elements.) But past

events have a more persistent and uneliminable influence in the organic and human than in the inorganic realms. If we have the mechanical or electrical coordinates of a body or physical system, we do not need to inquire into its past history to determine its future course. To put it in other terms, physical systems can generally be restored to previous conditions and the effects of intervening history thus eliminated. This cannot be done in the organic and human realm where the effect of age and experience cannot be wiped out. When sociologists, economists and other students of human affairs speak of social dynamics, social forces, or conditions of equilibrium, they obviously have physics before them as the model science. Now the laws of physics are formulated as equations in which there enter indefinitely repeatable time and space intervals but no dates or locations. The latter are essential ingredients in history.

(4) The laws peculiar to history proposed by Plato, Aristotle, Vico, Hegel, Comte, Marx, Spencer, Spengler and others, take the form of a series of stages, like the stages in the growth of an organism, which, it is claimed, necessarily succeed each other in an invariant order. Such laws cannot be reduced to differential equations which assume a continuity holding in the most minute intervals. History takes a macroscopic or mesoscopic rather than a microscopic view of events. Historic events may in part be explained by laws expressing what goes on in the microscopic realm. But human intelligence has met with such difficulty in thus explaining the most elementary phases of our history that a complete explanation would be beyond our hopes, even if it were not logically impossible to a finite mind that is dependent on temporal experience.

(5) One of the complexities which distinguish causation in human history is the fact that our ability to foresee part of the future modifies our conduct in the present. Some of those who believe in free will have used this as an argument against any application of ordinary causality to human affairs. But this is by no means a necessary consequence of recognizing that intelligent volition is a factor in our history. We may for our present limited purpose ignore the strictly metaphysical or supernatural aspect of the question, since ordinary history can restrict itself to the ascertainable manifestations of human will in the world of time and space. The issue thus reduces itself to two questions: (a) Is

human volition a verifiable causal element in history, and (b) are there ascertainable causes for the ways in which human beings exercise the volition that history can recognize?

(a) That men often deliberate and make up their minds to do certain things rather than others is an undeniable fact in history. And we generally regard it as a cause or part of the cause for the building or destroying of churches, houses, bridges, writing or publishing books, or engaging in any of the arts. There seems little doubt that people who have certain ideas on religion or politics will in many respects act differently from those who hold opposing convictions. Sometimes we actually see persons changing their courses of conduct when they become converted to a new creed. This, however, does not mean that pure or disembodied thought is known to be a cause for any event in nature. For we do not know of any human volition apart from a physical organism. We cannot by mere thinking or willing add a cubit unto our stature or even make an automobile go. We can express ourselves and modify the physical world only by some physical act of our organism, such as to make sounds, gestures, marks on paper, or the like.

(b) In our daily judgments of people and events, few of us doubt that what men and women will to do depends on all sorts of physical, physiological, and social conditions. This does not mean that under the same socio-historic circumstances all men and women will act in the same way. Different individuals approach the same or similar situations with different attitudes and much depends on what we call their character. But in the formation of these characters, early training and socio-historic environment are not irrelevant. This is shown by the fact that the more we know of the past of individuals or groups the better we can predict how they will act. Far from believing that any of us are free to will anything at all, we resent the suggestion that we are capable of desiring or willing to bring about things that are atrocious, dishonorable, or insane. There are doubtless insuperable difficulties in finding out in advance, with any high degree of rigor and accuracy, what people will want to do under given conditions. But to deny the possibility of any prediction at all is inconsistent with practice and the postulates of rational science or history. There is a difference between difficulties and impossibilities.

We may conclude by noting some consequences of the conception of causation as equivalent to the sum of necessary and sufficient conditions. The application of this concept to the events which constitute human history is both a necessary ideal and yet inherently difficult of attainment. The best we can achieve by rigorous scientific procedure is some progress in the approximation to this ideal. The number of circumstances or factors involved in the cause of any specific event may be far in excess of those that are humanly ascertainable. But we can say with a great deal of confidence that some things are altogether irrelevant and some conditions are more directly involved than others in bringing about certain events. Our most serious difficulties arise from the fact that the terms between which social or historical causation holds are not generally clearly defined as they are in the physical sciences. As was indicated before, any two terms must have a certain homogeneity if the causal relation is to hold between them. Wisdom here as elsewhere consists in analyzing our questions before we attempt to answer them. Thus when anyone asks whether it is religion or economics that is the cause of a given event, it is helpful to remember that such elements as religion and economics are not necessarily mutually exclusive, and that to answer the question which is more important we must have some definite measure of importance. Above all, we must beware of the popular fallacy which assumes that all social elements or institutions form a linear series, so that between any two one can always say which is prior to the other. For obviously many institutions are co-existent and continue to modify each other. Thus ignorance and poverty may each be said to be the cause of the other, and that the state brings law into being is as true as that law shapes and brings the state into being. But the detailed analysis of the relations between the different factors in historical causation is not the object of this paper. The reflections here offered are intended as an aid in such analysis.

Concerning Recent Trends in the Theory of Historiography[1]

by Maurice Mandelbaum

Reprinted from the *Journal of the History of Ideas*—Vol. XVI, No. 4, pp. 506-517

Thirty years ago, in a presidential address to the American Historical Association,[2] Charles M. Andrews surveyed the changes which had occurred in American historiography since the founding of the Association. Looking back upon that survey of the period between 1884 and 1924, I think one must say that the changes which he noted in historiographical methods and practices were far more profound than any changes which have since occurred, or which seem at the moment to be looming on the horizon. In almost all respects the methods and practices of historians remain essentially what Andrews regarded them as properly being,[3] and many of his prophecies have been fulfilled.

However, in the last thirty years the *theory* of historiography, as distinguished from its practice, has undergone a series of changes which were not anticipated by Andrews, and with which (so far as I know) he himself did not subsequently deal. The theory of historiography which was implicit in his address was more nearly akin to that of most of his predecessors than it was to that of many of his most noted successors. And what is true with reference to Andrews' presidential address is, I believe, quite generally true in this country: by the end of the first quarter of this century the methods and practices of historians had become stabilized into the form in which we now find them, but in the second quarter of the century major controversies arose among historians concerning the theory of historiography. It is to certain aspects of the latter controversies that this paper is addressed.

One can, I believe, say that the theory of historiography—or what is sometimes known as the formal or critical philosophy of history—embraces three major types of problem. One concerns the "objectivity" of historical knowledge; that is, it is concerned with what constitutes valid knowledge of the historical process, and with estimating the extent to which we may be said to possess such knowledge. The second branch involves a consideration of the relations between historical knowledge and other forms of knowledge or of

---

[1] Based on a paper read at the meetings of the American Historical Association held in New York, December 28-30, 1954.

[2] "These Forty Years," *American Historical Review*, XXX (Jan. 1925), 225-50.

[3] Perhaps the most important exception is his view of the relations between the discipline of history and the disciplines of government, economics, sociology, law, etc. (Cf. *loc. cit.*, 233.)

pseudo-knowledge; for example, it is concerned with the relations between history and memory, between history and myth, and (more especially) between history and scientific generalization. The third branch deals with what might be termed the pragmatics of history; that is, it attempts to assess the practical uses of a study of the past, relating the discipline of history to the political, moral, and intellectual ends which it can or should serve. In the present note I shall only deal with the first two of these branches of the theory of historiography; I shall not discuss questions which turn about the pragmatics of history, since any discussion of these questions leads far afield. Not only do such discussions presuppose the acceptance of views regarding the other two problems, but they also involve such more general considerations as those concerning the duties of any intellectual to the society of which he is a part. Because there are a limited number of positions which can be adopted regarding the latter types of question, there have not been any decisively new views regarding the uses to which the study of history should be put.[4] Such changes as one can note among discussions of the pragmatics of history are primarily reflections of changes in views regarding the possibility of objective historical knowledge and regarding the relations between history and other modes of knowledge. It is to a consideration of these latter changes that I shall now turn.

1. CHANGING VIEWS REGARDING THE OBJECTIVITY OF HISTORICAL KNOWLEDGE

In tracing the views which have recently been held regarding the problem of the adequacy of the historian's knowledge of that with which his inquiries purportedly deal, one must distinguish between those articles and books which have been written by historians and those written by philosophers. I believe it fair to say that among historians the presidential addresses of Becker and of Beard constituted the first major challenges to the previously accepted idea that the historian was able to grasp and to delineate the nature of history-as-actuality.[5] Thus, it was not until the thirties that the

---

[4] This topic has been a perennial theme of the presidential addresses of the American Historical Association. Cf. H. Ausubel: *Historians and Their Craft: A Study of the Presidential Addresses of the American Historical Association, 1884–1945* (New York, 1950).

[5] C. L. Becker: "Everyman His Own Historian," *Am. Hist. Rev.*, XXXVII (Jan., 1932), 221–236; C. A. Beard: "Written History as an Act of Faith," *Am. Hist. Rev.*, XXXIX (Jan., 1934), 219–231. Cf. the wide-ranging citations in C. M. Destler: "Some Observations on Contemporary Historical Theory," *Am. Hist. Rev.*, LV (April, 1950), 503–529.

controversies regarding the possibility of objective historical knowledge which had previously occupied Continental philosophers exerted any appreciable impact on American thought.[6] Since that time, as the members of this Association are aware, this problem has been much discussed. It seems to me that one or another form of the position which can be characterized as "relativism" has not only grown in influence among historians, but must be characterized as the dominant position of those practicing American historians who have written on the problem.[7]

However, it can scarcely be said that contemporary philosophers have followed the same trend. To be sure, the later works of Croce and Collingwood, of Cassirer, and of Dewey, carry out the implications of their earlier writings and foster the conviction that one or another form of relativism is still the dominant mode of thought among philosophers who deal with the problem. Yet one can cite a host of discussions in which the basic theses of relativism are rejected.[8] In short, so far as philosophy is concerned, those who have

[6] Cf. W. S. Holt: "The Idea of Scientific History in America," the *Journal of the History of Ideas,* I (June, 1940), 361, n. 26.

[7] E.g., the position adopted by the Committee on Historiography of the Social Science Research Council can best be characterized as "objective relativism" (*Theory and Practice in Historical Study: A Report of the Committee on Historiography,* Social Science Research Council, Bulletin 54. New York, 1946). Cf. also the articles cited in the bibliography of the foregoing report and by Destler (*loc. cit.*). Cf. also Bull. 64 of the Social Science Research Council, 4–13, 15f.

[8] For example, all three symposiasts who discussed historical explanation before the Aristotelian Society in 1947 rejected the theory of relativism, although each represented a different point of view on other topics. A. M. MacIver and M. Ginsberg hold to a position which I have attempted to defend, and which, I believe, is again becoming more widely held, as the succeeding references will show; W. H. Walsh's position is more nearly akin to the neo-Kantian position of Windelband and Rickert. (Cf. *Aristotelian Society,* Supp. Vol. XXI [London, 1947], 45ff., 74f., 65–67, and W. H. Walsh: *An Introduction to Philosophy of History* [London, 1951], 116–118.)

Other references (arranged in alphabetical order) are: A. C. Danto: "Mere Chronicle and History Proper," *Journ. of Phil.,* L (March 12, 1953), 173–182, and "On Historical Questioning," *Journ. of Phil.,* LI (Feb., 4, 1954), 89–99; G. C. Field: "Some Problems of the Philosophy of History," *Proc. of the British Academy,* XXIV (1938), 55–83; A. O. Lovejoy: "Present Standpoints and Past History," *Journ. of Phil.* XXXVI (August 31, 1939), 477–489 (for a more extended survey of Lovejoy's thought, cf. my "A. O. Lovejoy and the Theory of Historiography," in the *Journal of the History of Ideas,* IX [October, 1948], 412–423); A. I. Melden: "Historical Objectivity, A 'Noble Dream'?" *Journ. of General Educ.,* VII (Oct. 1952), 17–24; E. Nagel: "Some Issues in the Logic of Historical Analysis," *Scientific Monthly,* LXXIV (March, 1952), 162–169; K. Popper: *The Open Society and Its Enemies* (London, 1945), vol. II, 246–248, et pass.; L. Reis and P. O. Kristeller:

recently written on the question seem far less impressed by the philosophic arguments for the relativity of historical knowledge than were philosophers of the last generation. Yet it would certainly be unfair to say that any reasonably complete consensus of opinion has developed among philosophers on this topic. This, unfortunately, will surprise no one. However, the lack of consensus and the increasing tendency to oppose the earlier theories of relativism is a fact which should be borne in mind more often than it sometimes has been by those historians who cite philosophic authority to buttress their theories of historiography.

The difficulty with most philosophic discussions of the problem of historical knowledge (and here I include my own work in this field) is that they have usually attempted to deal with the issues in terms of a general theory of knowledge.[9] They have been inclined to concentrate on those aspects of historiographical method which have been treated in manuals of historiography, attempting to show, in terms of a general theory of knowledge, whether activities such as selecting among facts and synthesizing these facts render suspect any claim that the historian can apprehend what actually occurred in the past. One major difficulty in this procedure is that the general theory of knowledge which one holds will antecedently determine the type of conclusion which one reaches.[10] While I believe it to have been

---

"Some Remarks on the Method of History," *Journ. of Phil.*, XL (April 29, 1943), 225–245; M. C. Swabey: *The Judgment of History* (New York, 1954), Ch. 1; M. G. White: "Toward an Analytic Philosophy of History," in M. Farber: *Philosophic Thought in France and the United States* (Buffalo, 1950), 717ff.; P. P. Wiener: "On Methodology in the Philosophy of History," *Journ. of Phil.*, XXXVIII (June 5, 1941), 309–324. I should also be inclined to include M. R. Cohen in this list, although his position as stated in *The Meaning of Human History* (LaSalle, Illinois, 1947) is not unambiguous. In addition, all of the works referred to in footnote 11 seem to me to entail the acceptance of a non-relativistic position.

[9] E. W. Strong has attempted to avoid this error. If I understand his position aright, I should be inclined to class his work among those works cited in note 8. Cf. "Fact and Understanding in History," *Journ. of Phil.*, XLIV (Nov. 6, 1947), 637–644; "How Is Practice of History Tied to Theory?" *ibid.*, XLVI (September 29, 1949), 637–644; "Criteria of Explanation in History," *ibid.*, XLIX (January 31, 1952), 57–67; "The Materials of Historical Knowledge," in Y. H. Krikorian: *Naturalism and the Human Spirit* (New York, 1944), 154–182; "Reason in History," in *Univ. of California Publications in Philosophy*, XXI (1939), 125–150.

[10] Another difficulty, which is now coming to be more widely recognized, is that the conventional distinction between analysis and synthesis, as described in manuals of historiography, is in many respects misleading. Cf. the cited papers of E. W. Strong, Danto, and Reis and Kristeller; also Mandelbaum: *The Problem of Historical Knowledge* (New York, 1938), 293–297 *et pass.* and "Causal Analysis in History," in the *Journal of the History of Ideas*, III (Jan. 1942), 35–37.

useful to demonstrate that the activities of selection and synthesis are compatible with alternative views regarding the objectivity of historical knowledge, a continuation of the discussion along these lines does not, at present, seem profitable.

2. THE PROBLEM OF THE PLACE OF HISTORIOGRAPHY IN THE ECONOMY OF KNOWLEDGE

As is well known, there were many attempts in the nineteenth century to assimilate history into the body of the sciences by means of a merger between history and sociology. At the end of the century this tendency called forth a reaction which is associated with the names of Dilthey, Windelband, Rickert, and Croce, and which has been continued in the thought of Collingwood and Cassirer. The original root of the reaction was the idea that the method and aims of the historian are different from those of the scientist: the historian is interested in understanding the particular, the concrete, the unique, while the scientist is interested in understanding the general, the repetitive, the abstract. Thus the historical and scientific ideals of understanding are different, and the modes of explanation which are appropriate in the two fields are also different. This dichotomy has recently come under severe criticism by a number of philosophers,[11] and I believe that it can fairly be said that the distinction which was drawn by, say, Dilthey and Rickert can no longer be maintained in its original form.[12] However, a new influence has been

[11] Cf. P. Gardiner: *The Nature of Historical Explanation* (London, 1952); J. W. N. Watkins: "Ideal Types and Historical Explanation," *British Journ. for the Phil. of Science*, III (May, 1952), 22–43; C. G. Hempel: "The Function of General Laws in History," *Journ. of Phil.*, XXXIX (January 15, 1942), 35–48; and "Problems of Concept and Theory Formation in the Social Sciences," in *Science, Language, and Human Rights* (Philadelphia, 1952), 65–86; A. Hofstadter: "Generality and Singularity in Historical Judgment," *Journ. of Phil.*, XLII (February 1, 1945), 57–65; E. Nagel: *op. cit.*, and "Problems of Concept and Theory Formation in the Social Sciences," in *Science, Language and Human Rights* (Philadelphia, 1952), 43–64; K. Popper: *op. cit.*, and "The Poverty of Historicism," *Economica*, N.S., XI (1944), 86–103, 119–137; E. W. Strong (cf. note 9); M. G. White: *op. cit.*, and "Historical Explanation," *Mind*, N.S., LII (July, 1943), 212–229, and "A Note on the Method of History," *Journ. of Phil.*, XL (June 10, 1943), 317–319; P. P. Wiener, *op. cit.*

Since there has been some misunderstanding of my position (cf. the criticism made by Gardiner, *op. cit.*, pp. 83ff.) I should like to call attention to my article "Causal Analysis in History" (*loc. cit.*).

[12] Even the paper of Reis and Kristeller and the book by Walsh (both of which are inclined to maintain more of a distinction between history and science than the articles cited in the preceding note) are willing to concede a larger place (though still a subsidiary one) to the rôle played by generalizations in the actual practices of historians.

added to the previous forms of the argument, and this influence has not been countered by those who have sought to undermine the dichotomy between historical and scientific modes of explanation. It consists in the increasing stress which has been placed on the concept of "memory": history is being defined as a form of memory.

This tendency to identify history and memory has two confluent philosophic sources in contemporary theories of historiography: on the one hand it springs from the metaphysics of idealism, as in Croce and Collingwood; on the other, it springs from existentialism.[13] In both cases the historian is viewed as dealing with data which only have meaning in so far as they reverberate within him, that is, in so far as he rethinks or relives them, or is able, in other ways, to build them into his own individual or social experience. In short, the past with which the historian actually deals is a living memory which is found in the present and is capable of moulding the future; it is not independent of the historian's own thoughts or of his own existential problems. Since the data with which scientists deal, and the tasks of understanding which they set themselves, are not generally interpreted as occupying a similar status, those who follow either the idealist or the existentialist traditions will insist that the historian's activity cannot be, and should not be, assimilated to the current conception of scientific understanding.[14] In fact, within both the idealist and the existentialist camps there is a tendency to limit the place which science plays in the total economy to knowledge—a limitation more severe than that previously placed upon it by, say, Rickert. To this, of course, those who follow what is usually termed a "naturalistic" (or "empirical," or "positivistic") philosophy take strenuous exception. Thus, once again, it may be said that general philosophic considerations enter the debate concerning the theory of historiography, and play a major rôle in determining which of the alternative positions is to be accepted by a given theorist.

While it is almost surely true that disagreements springing from ultimate philosophic convictions will always bedevil the theory of

---

[13] Cf. R. Niebuhr: *Faith and History* (New York, 1949); K. Jaspers: *The Origin and Goal of History* (New Haven, 1953); E. Rosenstock-Huessy: "The Predicament of History," *Journ. of Phil.*, XXXII (February 14, 1935), 93–100.

I should also be inclined to interpret Cassirer's position on this point as being closely affiliated with existentialist modes of thought. Cf. his *Essay on Man* (New Haven, 1944), Ch. 10.

The clearest expression of this point of view, as espoused by an historian, is to be found in G. J. Renier: *History, Its Purpose and Method* (Boston, 1950).

[14] For a recent treatment of the problem in an existentialist manner, cf. Fritz Kaufmann: "Reality and Truth in History," in *Perspectives in Philosophy* (Ohio State Univ., 1953), 43–54.

historiography, I think that both historians and philosophers would be well served if the theory of historiography were to have a greater variety of concrete problems to discuss than has previously been the case. This would not in itself overcome those ultimate disagreements which spring from divergences in general philosophic positions, but it would have the advantage of forcing us to face a greater number of specific problems against which our theories could be tested. In philosophic theory, as in science, a theory is regarded as being more adequate if it has been reached after examining its fruitfulness as a means of dealing with a variety of instances, rather than having been accepted after examining only a few of those instances which are relevant to its conclusions. In my opinion there is a problem which has been unduly neglected by both philosophers and historians, although it is relevant to any theory of the objectivity of historical knowledge or to any theory of the relations between history and science (or between history and literature, or history and myth). Strangely enough, this neglected problem is "What constitutes the subject-matter of the discipline of history?".

3. THE SUBJECT-MATTER OF THE DISCIPLINE OF HISTORY

In the recent literature which is concerned with the theory of historiography, little attention has been focussed on the question of what actually does, or what ideally should, constitute the subject-matter of the discipline of history. It is not, I believe, difficult to understand why this has been the case. In the first place, the late nineteenth century controversy over the relative merits of "political" and "cultural" history merged with the discussion of numerous other topics, such as the relation of history to sociology and group psychology, and the problem of contingency vs. determinism in the historical process; as a consequence the issues between the two theories were never sharply defined and were rarely debated in terms of their own merits. In the second place, historians broadened the scope of the subject-matters with which they were concerned, and broadened them to include so many factors in the social life of man that no common thread was easily discernible in all of their studies. As a consequence of this we find that the dictum that " history is simply what historians do " (a dictum which has its analogues in many other fields) is interpreted to mean that there is no specific, delimited subject-matter which it is the task of historians to explore. Instead of having led to inquiries concerning what it is that historians actually *do* do, the dictum seems to have provided a justification for abandoning any attempt to define the province of history.

Still, it is not easy to write a manual of historiography, nor to discuss the theory of historiography, without making some attempt to state, however generally and loosely, what it is that characterizes the subject-matter of the discipline of history. In so far as one can find any consensus of opinion among recent works, it appears to be the case that the discipline of history is now being defined either in terms of special mode of inquiry, or in terms of that discipline which seeks to discover and depict all that has occurred during the course of human existence.[15] Both of these definitions appear to me to be inadequate, and I shall attempt to suggest their weaknesses.

A) It seems to me that the attempt to define the province of the discipline of history by means of its method of inquiry is clearly inadequate if one wishes to do justice to what historians actually do, and *what they do not do*. If such a definition were to be accepted, whatever could be investigated by the modes of inquiry used by historians would constitute a subject-matter with which the historian could legitimately be concerned. Thus (to use an illustration of Collingwood's) if the question of who played centre-forward on a village soccer team could be investigated by the procedures of the historian

---

[15] Because most theorists of historiography do not take the problem of defining the subject-matter of history as constituting a serious and consequential problem, their statements concerning the topic are less clear and consistent than one would wish them to be. Therefore, I shall not attempt to classify the materials upon which the following discussion is based. I merely append an alphabetical list of references to materials published since 1930:

C. A. Beard: *The Discussion of Human Affairs* (New York, 1936), Ch. 8, 9; C. L. Becker: "Everyman His Own Historian," *loc. cit.*; M. Bloch: *The Historian's Craft* (New York, 1953), 20–29, 194f., *et pass.*; E. Cassirer: *Essay on Man* (New Haven, 1944), 174–177; R. G. Collingwood: *The Idea of History* (Oxford, 1946), 7–10; P. Gardiner, *op. cit.*, Part II; G. J. Garraghan: *A Guide to Historical Method* (New York, 1946), 4–10; L. Gottschalk: *Understanding History* (New York, 1950), Ch. 2, 3; F. A. Hayek: *The Counterrevolution of Science* (Glencoe, Ill., 1952), 70–73; S. Kent: *Writing History* (New York, 1941), 1–3; J. Huizinga: "A Definition of the Concept of History," in R. Klibansky and H. J. Paton: *Philosophy and History* (Oxford, 1936), 1–10; E. M. Hulme: *History and Its Neighbors* (New York, 1942), Part I, Ch. 2, and Part II, *pass.*; H. D. Oakeley: *History and the Self* (London, 1934), Ch. 1, *et pass.*; C. Oman: *On the Writing of History* (New York, 1939), Ch. 1; G. J. Renier, *op. cit.*, Ch. 1, 2; G. Salvemini: *Historian and Scientist* (Cambridge, Mass., 1939), Ch. 1, *et pass.*; E. W. Strong: *op. cit.*, in Krikorian: *Naturalism and the Human Spirit* (New York, 1944), 154–157; *Theory and Practice in Historical Study* (Soc. Sci. Res. Council, Bull. 54), Ch. 1, 5; J. M. Vincent: *Aids to Historical Research* (New York, 1934), Ch. 1; W. H. Walsh: *op. cit.*, Ch. 2; M. G. White: *op. cit.*, in Farber: *Philosophic Thought in France and the United States*.

The extent to which the neglect of this problem persists can be seen in Bulletin 64 of the Social Science Research Council. The definition of the specific subject-matter of history is there scrupulously avoided (cf. pp. 22, 24f., and 106).

(as indeed it can), then it would be as truly an historical question as is the question of who won the battle of Cannae.[16] This, I submit, is an arbitrary and misleading view of what constitutes the subject-matter of the discipline of history.

B) It is also misleading to hold the allied view that the subject-matter of history embraces all that has been said or done by men. Historians have been interested in many things: in the growth and decline of nations, in the modes of life characteristic of a given place and time, in economic and intellectual changes, in the rôle which specific institutions or individuals have played in preserving or changing the life of a society, and so on indefinitely. Yet even this variety of topics does not signify that historians, either individually or collectively, have been engaged in the hopeless enterprise of reconstructing all that has ever occurred in the life of men. While it is impossible to say in advance of any specific thought or action that it will not form part of some historian's account, we can attempt to state the conditions which must be fulfilled if it is to be an integral part of that account. These conditions are that it must be regarded in relation to the nature of a specific society, or to changes which have taken place, or are taking place, within that society. Thus, a physical event or the thoughts or actions of a specific individual are of significance to the historian under some circumstances, but not under all circumstances; in so far as such a physical event influenced life in a specific society, it is an occurrence of historical importance; in so far as it did not—and most of the events in physical nature do not—it does not belong within the purview of the historian. Similarly, and more importantly, in so far as the specific thoughts or actions of an individual influence the society of which he is a part, or are viewed as expressions of the life of that society, such thoughts and actions belong within the scope of the discipline of history. Yet, most actions of most individuals do not have any demonstrable significance for the nature of the societies to which they belong (nor to the nature of any other society), and unless they happen to be investigated as symptoms of the modes of life present in their society, they are not, as we say, " of historical significance." In short, they do not belong to the subject-matter of the discipline of history.

4. THE IMPORTANCE OF DEFINING THE SUBJECT-MATTER OF HISTORY

It is unnecessary to point out that the foregoing attempt to circumscribe the boundaries of the discipline of history is by no means novel.

[16] Collingwood believes that it is. Cf. *The Philosophy of History*, an Historical Association Leaflet, No. 79 (1930). (Quoted by Renier, *op, cit.*, p. 37.)

Even today, when the broader definitions of "history" have received such wide currency, the term "social" frequently crops up in these definitions. What I should, however, like to stress is the theoretical importance which attaches to any definition of the subject-matter of the discipline of history. I shall now briefly indicate how the two broader definitions of the field necessarily lead to the theory of historical relativism and to certain implications regarding the relations between history and other forms of knowledge.

Take the view that the province of history is to be defined not in terms of a special subject-matter, but as a special method of inquiry. Such a definition either presupposes or entails the view that the procedures which an historian follows are unique, and it thereby prejudges one of the two major problems of the theory of historiography: what relations exist between history and science and between history and other modes of knowledge or pseudo-knowledge. Less obviously, but no less importantly, it has implications for the question of the objectivity of historical knowledge. For if one holds that any subject-matter which is investigated by the methods of history is as truly a subject belonging within that discipline as is any other subject-matter, then how can one explain why the historian should sometimes seek out the identity of a particular soccer player, at other times seek out information about the battle of Cannae? The only reasonable answer which could be given to this question would be that in some cases he is interested in the identity of a given soccer player, but in most cases he is not. Thus, the importance of the fact to be established rests on its *importance to the historian;* it is not important because it is a fact which must be known if one wishes to establish what occurred within an objectively defined context of historical events.

Similarly, a definition of the subject-matter of the discipline of history which states that the goal of the historian is to reconstruct all that has occurred in the human past, leads to a relativistic position. Such a definition makes the historian's subject-matter inexhaustible, and the gap between history-as-written and history-as-actuality becomes immeasurably large. As Louis Gottschalk says: "The reconstruction of the total past of mankind, although it is the goal of historians, thus becomes a goal they know full well is unattainable." [17] In other words, this definition of the subject-matter of history makes some form of relativism inescapable. Further, it carries implications for the other major problem of the theory of historiography, viz., the place which the discipline of history occupies in the total economy of knowledge. If the subject-matter of history embraces all that has

[17] *Op. cit.*, p. 42.

ever been thought, felt, said, or done by man (and all that has ever influenced this inexhaustible material), then there are only two possible relations between history and those other disciplines which also are concerned with man: either the latter are merely subdivisions of historical knowledge, or they are differentiated not by their subject-matter but by their methods. Both alternatives have in fact been held. On the one hand, the discipline of history has been interpreted as embracing all of the veridical self-knowledge of man; on the other hand, it has been viewed as a discipline which employs its own methods, which are different from the methods of the sciences, and thus is able to yield another "dimension" to the kind of knowledge of man which is given by the sciences. Historians may not be averse to having either rôle assigned to their discipline, but I submit that the question of the relation between history and other disciplines should not be prejudged by the definition of the subject-matter of history, *unless* one is willing to defend such a definition by showing that it conforms to the subject-matter with which those whom we are ready to acknowledge as historians actually deal. I find it difficult to believe that an analysis of historical works will show that any historian has actually taken his subject-matter to be all that had been thought, felt, said, or done by every individual who lived at the time and in the place with which his account deals. On the contrary, as I have suggested, it appears to be the case that those works which we regard as being unquestionable examples of historical inquiry show that historians are concerned with understanding and delineating the nature of specific societies and the changes which have taken place within these societies.

I shall not attempt to justify this contention here. I wish only to point out that it provides an alternative to the two most prevalent contemporary views of what constitutes the subject-matter of the discipline of history. And I should like to suggest that just as these two alternative views have implications both for the problem of the objectivity of historical knowledge and for the problem of the place of history as a discipline in the economy of our knowledge, so too does this definition of the subject-matter of history.

First, our definition sets the question of historical relativism in a wider framework than is usually the case. If this definition is accepted, one cannot confine attention to those features of the historian's task which may appear to methodologists to be particularly troublesome, or particularly easy of fulfillment: one would have to consider how, if at all, objectivity may be attained in *any* of the disciplines which are concerned with understanding the nature of specific societies. Such an enlargement of the problem would, I believe, tend to eliminate too sweeping assertions. Further, it would tend to mitigate the danger of answering the question concerning the objectivity of historical knowledge merely in terms of a general theory of knowledge: our general theory would have to be shown to be compatible with what we are willing to accept concerning other social disciplines, and not merely with what we antecedently believe concerning the objectivity of historiographical practices.[18]

Second, the view of the subject-matter of history that I have proposed also has implications for the problem of what place the discipline of history occupies in the total economy of our knowledge. It sharpens the nature of this question by focussing attention on the relations between history and social theory, rather than allowing the debate to proceed in terms of such general questions as whether history and science are differing ways of viewing reality. The actual relations between historical writing and social theories would then provide a field for empirical investigations. Such investigations, I submit, would be more likely to illuminate the relations between history and other forms of knowledge than would any answers which could be reached by discussions of the nature of Time, of Memory, of Freedom, or of Uniqueness.

---

[18] One notes, for example, that in Caroline F. Ware's introduction to *The Cultural Approach to History* (New York, 1940) almost all of the theses of historical relativism are accepted, and it is then held that the historian can profitably learn from the approach used by anthropologists. If it is true that the subject-matter of history is what I take it to be, relativism would either have to be said to characterize the work of anthropologists, or the thesis of relativism would have to be modified or abandoned with respect to historical investigations.

Intellectual History and Its Neighbors

by JOHN HIGHAM*

Reprinted from the *Journal of the History of Ideas*—Vol. XV, No. 3, pp. 339-347

The writing of intellectual history has been the work of many hands, and we have come to do it from all the points of the academic compass. Philosophers, literary scholars, historians and others have converged upon one another, bringing their various interests, backgrounds and methods to a common task for which they were not initially trained. It is, then, an interdisciplinary enterprise on which they have entered, and intellectual history exhibits the marks of any such enterprise in our day: the blessings of effervescence and the curse of confusion. Along with an exhilirating sense of pioneering and the joy of smashing through conventional walls come the perplexities of understanding just what is going on.

In studying intellectual history, as in conducting a foreign policy, one may adopt a variation on one of three attitudes. The expansionist point of view, extending over new terrain the claims of the academic homeland, may breed a good deal of jostling and rivalry as representatives of established disciplines claim competing spheres of influence over intellectual history. Isolationists may venture abroad without realizing that they have done so—and pursue their separate ways through the tumult while steadfastly ignoring it. Proponents of collective security may inspire one another and borrow from one another, sometimes to the extent of entering into formally cooperative arrangements as in the American Studies programs. The dangers of academic isolation or expansion are evident enough. Those of cooperation should not get out of sight. In trying to fuse insights and procedures derived from unlike disciplines, intellectual historians may lose a sense of direction; they may exchange customary means of analysis for formulas of the lowest common denominator which answer all questions and clarify none. At the risk of imposing my own kind of imperialism on intellectual history I want to suggest that until it assumes another name or character it forms a branch of history. Whatever else it involves, it deserves from students of every academic persuasion a central allegiance to the aims and methods of historical study. I propose, at any rate, to appraise the dimensions of intellectual history and its relations to other disciplines from the vantage-point of its historical foundations.

I assume that history characteristically reports particular and unique human experiences in an attempt to elucidate their connections through time. Above all the historian wants to know why a sequence of happenings took place as it did. To find out, he links those specific experiences one to the other with the aid of appropriate

---

* This paper was read to the Pacific Coast Branch of the American Historical Association in December, 1952.

generalizations. He does not, like the scientist, move away from particulars toward a system of general, verifiable concepts; nor does he, like the artist, move into particulars to disclose the values inherent in them. The historian moves between particular experiences to learn how one begot another. But to establish these relationships he employs both the values of the artist and the inclusive propositions of the scientist; in his hands tested constructs and untestable values become functional to a narrative task.

Intellectual history differs from other varieties simply because it has a distinctive subject-matter. In concentrates on experiences occurring inside men's heads. It centers on man's inner experiences, the experiences which he has in thinking. Many other disciplines, of course, share an interest in man as a thinking being, but they concern themselves either with one kind of thinking or with thinking in general. Intellectual history is unlimited in scope, but it should respect the historian's method. It deals with all sorts of thoughts but deals with them discretely, in terms of their genetic relations in time and place.

The historian's concern with ideas in all their specific variety compels a close and precise attention to the documents which reveal them; and this practical condition in turn has often encouraged misunderstanding of the permissible range of intellectual history. Partly because the most discriminating and readily available documents are produced by highly articulate people, intellectual historians have tended to write mostly about the thoughts which circulate among intellectuals. Meanwhile a substantial, perhaps a preponderant part of the academic world relegates to social history the study of the moods and beliefs of the man in the street, reserving for intellectual history the study of high-level ideas.[1] To define the field in this limited sense is to miss much of its complexity and significance. At least by construing it narrowly we run the risk of pre-judging its affiliations and character. Intellectual history may (though it need not in any single instance) embrace simple attitudes in simple or complicated people as well as systematic knowledge and speculation. It includes Little Orphan Annie as well as Adam Smith. I am not of course proposing our absorption in men's trivial reactions to the passing scene. History is selective; it looks for the bolder contours on the landscape of the past. In examining the mental landscape the intellectual historian selects the relatively enduring ideas which sway

---

[1] Evidence of the vogue of this distinction among professional historians is in T. C. Cochran, "A Decade of American Histories," *Pennsylvania Magazine of History and Biography*, 73 (1949), 154–55; W. T. Hutchinson in *American Historical Review*, 58 (1952), 126.

a considerable number of people over a period of some time; but he may select them from the comics as well as from the philosophers.

Whether he deals in popular myths or in metaphysics, the intellectual historian must perform the historian's task of relating the particular inner happenings which interest him to a context of other happenings which explain them. Here a quest for definition grows more difficult. What kind of other happenings? What type of context? Where should the connective generalizations serviceable to intellectual history lead? These questions have given rise to two rather distinct answers which amount almost to two different conceptions of the discipline. In one view the connections lead outward to an external context of events and behavior. Intellectual history becomes an investigation of the connections between thought and deed. Crane Brinton expressed a version of this approach in emphasizing as intellectual history's primary task the uncovering of relations between what a few men write or say and what many men actually do.[2] On the other hand a second school has insisted principally on establishing the internal relationships between what some men write or say and what other men write or say. This kind of intellectual history directs attention away from the context of events in order to enlarge and systematize the context of ideas. It seeks the connections between thought and thought.

The distinction between an internal and an external history of thinking is, I believe, widely appreciated, although the proponents of each have seldom ventured into explicit controversy beyond an appeal for emphasis.[3] Having had little debate, we have only begun to assess the respective ramifications and consequences of each approach. Yet such assessment must precede an adequate understanding of the nature of intellectual history and its place in the spectrum of knowledge, for the two approaches contain their own underlying assumptions, lead to different disciplinary affiliations, and suggest contrasting objectives.

Hardly anyone today would argue the total wrong-headedness of either the internal or the external view of intellectual history. Indeed many scholars seem increasingly concerned with combining the two. The difficulties involved in any real merging of them, however, are far

[2] Crane Brinton, *Ideas & Men: The Story of Western Thought* (New York, 1950), 7.
[3] Merle Curti's *The Growth of American Thought* (New York, 1942) brought the distinction I am making clearly into view; see p. vi. Arthur O. Lovejoy has ably defended his own internal approach in "Reflections on the History of Ideas," the Journal of the History of Ideas, I (1940), 3–23. I have also profited from the attack on this position in Bert J. Loewenberg, *The History of Ideas: 1935–1945; Retrospect and Prospect* (New York, 1947), 13–18. And I am especially indebted to the stimulus of Professor Curti's interest in this whole issue.

more than technical. At bottom each approach expresses a fundamental philosophical commitment. Often accepted implicitly, one commitment or the other directs scholarship more than scholars realize. They may refuse a categorical choice; they may work under the tensions of a divided allegiance. But they can hardly serve two masters with equal loyalty. The issue lies between two ways of conceiving the human mind; and entangled in each is a divergent view of human nature.

A primary interest in the outward links between thought and deed presupposes the notion that mind at its best or most characteristic is functional. Mind makes its mark by serving the practical needs of the workaday world. The relations between thinking and the concrete circumstances of life acquire importance in the light of the functionalist's respect for the utility of the mind as an instrument of survival. At the same time a functional orientation supplies a rough yardstick for measuring the historical significance of ideas. The test is action, and the importance of an idea approximates that of the deeds associated with it. By this criterion, for example, a persuasive propagandist like Tom Paine might loom larger in history than a frustrated genius like Henry Adams.

On the other hand the internal approach to intellectual history rests upon quite different assumptions. A concern with the inner affinities and structures among ideas neglects functional criteria. Instead, the historian assumes that mind at its best or most characteristic reaches beyond practical needs to create a world of values and achievements which have their own excuse for being. The mind pursues objectives somehow "higher" (or at least more noteworthy) than survival, and in place of the yardstick of action one must apply some internal standard to measure its most significant output. The logical consistency of a sequence of thought, the elaboration of a world view, the achievement of a reverberating insight, or the power of an idea to bear further intellectual fruit—these become the norms of an intellectual history pledged to the sheer creative vitality of the human mind.

Parenthetically it is worth noting that the theories of the intellectual process at issue here point toward even vaster alternatives. A view of the mind calls forth a view of human nature. If the mind creates in ways that are neither bound by nor referable to the demands of an external environment—if ideas have a life of their own—then human nature bursts and transcends the patterns of the natural world around it. If, on the other hand, mind interests us as an agent of bio-social adaptation, we tend to assimilate human nature to an encompassing system of nature.

Without venturing to cope with the whole problem of the nature of man, it is easy to see objections to either conception of the mind as a controlling principle in historiography. Functional presuppositions are chargeable with devaluing mind. By reducing thought to a series of responses to situations, the functionalist treats it as merely auxiliary to the main business of life. He tends to neglect what his standards cannot appraise—the inner " go," the spontaneity, or the qualitative richness of mental phenomena. He can tell us little about the persistence of an intellectual heritage after the environment has grown hostile to it; still less can he account for the quite impractical ways in which the mind seems to pour forth religious and artistic symbols.[4]

The dualistic assumptions behind the internal history of thought create contrary difficulties. These assumptions tend to divorce thinking from doing and to confine it within categories that have no reference to the world of material circumstance. A separation from events forces an increased degree of subjectivity on intellectual history, since all the elements in the story are then intangibles. With the aid of publishers' records we can trace the circulation of books, but we can never with the same precision trace the circulation of ideas. We can observe the meeting of two armies and know that the destiny of an idea hangs upon their encounter, but we can never quite so clearly see the meeting of two ideas. Furthermore the notion that mind has its own distinctive and superior goals involves an intellectualistic bias. Ideas capable of the most subtle or systematic articulation become the center of attention and are endowed with special potency. Intellectual history narrows to the history of intellectuals, and among the products of thought literature and philosophy assume a privileged status. Carried far enough, the same bias leads to a sweeping assertion of the primacy of ideas in history, just as a functionalist bias ultimately debases ideas into passive echoes of events.

If no student of ideas can escape some preference for one or the other of these two positions, surely all can profit from the fullest understanding of the possibilities as well as the limitations inherent in each. For such understanding the professional historian has a strategic location. His discipline lies between and to some extent bridges the gulf separating the humanities from the social sciences. Now the intellectualism of the internal approach appears most typically and completely in humanistic scholarship, while the functionalism of the external view is characteristic of the social sciences. The distinction certainly is not sharp nor is the correspondence exact, for too many cross-currents have blown between them to permit the humanities or

[4] S. K. Langer, *Philosophy in a New Key* (New York, 1948), 24-33.

social sciences to follow entirely separate ways. Literary scholars like Vernon L. Parrington, deriving stimulus from social scientists, have weighted intellectual history with a functional emphasis, while an occasional writer on the other side of the fence—like the psychoanalyst Erich Fromm—has made fruitful use of humanistic insights.[5] Still, in their main thrust the humanities and social sciences have diverged.[6] The former look toward the qualitative exploration of an inner world of values and imagination. The latter, seeking quantitative measurements of human phenomena, tend to objectify ideas and values into forms of behavior. And the internal study of intellectual history has developed particularly within the value-oriented humanities, just as the external history of thinking has benefited especially from the behavioral emphasis of the social sciences. Perhaps historians—without final allegiance to either domain—can see further into the opportunities of intellectual history by learning from the example of each.

Among the branches of history the intellectual one lies closest to the humanities and has received the most encouragement from them. (On the other hand, economic history with its wealth of measurable data has probably felt the impact of the social sciences more than any other branch, while having the least contact with the humanities.) Certainly the humanities have influenced the writing of intellectual history far more directly than have the social sciences. Perhaps the most central contribution has come from philosophy, which is the critic of abstractions. In its rôle as one of the humanities, philosophy seeks to harmonize and clarify the most basic and general propositions involved in value judgments. It is hard to see how an internal analysis of thought can proceed without some philosophical training. From it we receive skill in definition, in discriminating meanings, in detecting assumptions, in formulating issues. These abilities come into constant play in intellectual history because the factual units with which it principally deals are not events which we can observe directly but rather ideas and sentiments which we must define in order to know. An internal history of the connections between ideas obviously calls for especially close philosophical scrutiny. A few philosophers such as Arthur O. Lovejoy have made important advances in the writing of intellectual history by demonstrating ways of grasping

---

[5] Vernon L. Parrington, *Main Currents in American Thought*, 3 vols. (New York, 1927-30); Erich Fromm, *Escape from Freedom* (New York, 1941).   [6] I refer to American scholarship, the divergence being much more noticeable here than in Europe, where a positivistic tradition has not had so commanding an influence over the social sciences. See E. K. Francis, " History and the Social Sciences: Some Reflections on the Re-integration of Social Science," *Review of Politics*, XIII (1951), 354-74.

the underlying unities which run through many diverse provinces of thought. Other philosophers have worked in the history of philosophy, which differs from intellectual history by interesting itself more in the logical implications of doctrines than in their genetic relationships. By and large the philosophers' overriding interest in abstractions has kept them from contributing as much in substance as in method. Relatively few philosophical scholars do justice to history's concrete particularity. It is significant that a philosopher's proposal to trace the history of liberal social thought in modern America should turn out instead as an analytical critique of five men.[7]

Literary scholars have more than made up for the aloofness of most philosophers. Intellectual history, written chiefly from an internal point of view, has become a leading concern in departments of literature. Relying heavily on philosophy and history, these scholars have resurrected many of the movements of thought which have supported and pervaded literary achievements. The distinctive contribution which the best students of literature make is not, I think, the analytical precision characteristic of the best philosophical inquiry. Rather it is a sense of the imaginative and emotional overtones in the history of thought. The literary scholar should have an ear sensitive to the resonance of ideas. If he has, he can communicate the passions and aspirations woven through them. He can add an internal dimension to intellectual history by capturing the fusion of thought and feeling. His studies, however, often leave historians unsatisfied by adapting intellectual history to the purposes of literary criticism. One who feels a primary obligation to sharpen aesthetic judgments will naturally employ intellectual history as a means of vivifying literary documents instead of using all documents as means of understanding why men thought and felt the way they did.

The humanities, then, tend to celebrate the finer products of mind, and in doing so they bring to a focus all of the characteristic consequences of an internal approach: a sensitivity to qualitative distinctions, an exaltation of creative thought, an appreciation of subjective criteria for judging it, a restricted sphere of interest and a limited body of materials. How different the prevailing temper in the social sciences! There an attempt to describe the uniformities in human affairs leads to an ideal of quantitative measurement. There the subjective categories appropriate to value judgments are rejected for principles derived from observations of how men behave.[8] There a

[7] M. G. White, *Social Thought in America: The Revolt Against Formalism* (New York, 1949).

[8] Humanists, of course, vigorously dispute the claim of many social scientists to the possession of a more objective kind of knowledge. Quite possibly the conclusions

respect for the molding force of social controls replaces the humanistic emphasis on creative thinkers. There scholars struggle with massive data to interpret the life of the mass of mankind. In so far as he studies ideas, therefore, the social scientist wants to learn how numbers of people put them to work within a larger pattern of living. His stress on quantity, objectivity, and behavior will lead to external analysis.

Few social scientists take much interest in the past, and fewer have contributed directly to intellectual history, though we should remember such notable exceptions as Tawney and Weber. The ideals of social science have, however, gradually filtered into the historical profession and there have exerted a somewhat roundabout influence on intellectual studies. Although each of the social disciplines deserves separate appraisal, I want simply to mention three general ways in which we can profit from more direct contact with them.

First, the social sciences may yet teach us something about how to count. Certainly statistical analyses are much more difficult with historical than with contemporary data, and the difficulty increases the further into the past one goes. Even with voluminous records we can probably never count ideas but only certain outward tokens of intellectual life. But any advance toward mathematical precision should clearly seem desirable to those who value exact knowledge. Who knows, for example, what new light a statistical historian might cast on changing attitudes by counting the appearance of certain "loaded" words or phrases in nineteenth-century magazines?

Quantification works better for large aggregations than for small ones, and the social scientist typically deals with large ones—with crowds and classes and age groups and cultures. We need to study his procedures if we are going to fulfill the whole range of intellectual history. The internal analysis of the humanist applies chiefly to the intellectual elite; it has not reached very far into the broad field of popular thought. The blunter, external approach of the social sciences leads us closer to the collective loyalties and aspirations of the bulk of humanity.

Finally the social sciences offer us a multitude of tentative generalizations and classifications which can enrich our interpretative schemes if we use them cautiously. Very likely few principles of human affairs are exactly applicable outside of the historical epoch which conceived

---

attainable in the humanities are no less objective than those reached in the social sciences, but the latter have been more insistent on developing techniques of objective analysis. The humanities must employ such subjective concepts as evil, will, etc., and do not shrink from doing so.

them, but since we bring our own notions and hunches to the past in any case, we may well find, in social science, hypotheses which discipline the historical imagination. These fields can guide us especially in formulating generalizations which connect thought and behavior, for the social sciences—in contrast to the humanities—have lavished attention on functional problems. For example, one of the shrewdest definitions of an intellectual has been provided by an economist in behavioral terms.[9]

So far I have tried to show how two types of intellectual history, each shaped by a characteristic assumption about the mind, draw aid and stimulus from the two realms of knowledge in which those assumptions find a natural locus. But this is not an end to the matter. For all of its interdisciplinary affiliations intellectual history, like any historical enterprise, must fulfill its own objectives and move toward its own goals. Here the internal-external dichotomy presents a final face. In my view intellectual history confronts within the field of history two different tasks, each related to one of the two approaches in question. On the one hand, intellectual history needs to develop a viable degree of autonomy as a branch of history. It needs a more coherent form and structure of its own in order to escape subordination to other disciplines and a subordinate place among the fields of history. This self-fulfillment must come largely through clarification of the causal connections between ideas. It depends, therefore, principally on internal analysis.

Intellectual history has a second task exactly the reverse of autonomy: a task of synthesis. The history of thought must contribute what it can to the organization and understanding of history as a whole. In some sense all human activity has a mental component, and intellectual history is displaying increasing usefulness as an integrative tool. This synthetic objective is approachable by studying the causal linkage of ideas with political, social, and economic events. It depends ultimately on external analysis.

Now that my argument is complete I fear that I have made too much of it. In the practice of historians the line of cleavage is hardly ever absolute. Most historians take some account of both perspectives and of both objectives. Their work gains subtlety through a skillful blend, just as the two types of intellectual history advance through mutual interaction. The difference, then, is one of emphasis. But the emphasis is basic. At some point in his thinking or research each scholar must choose. He can choose with sophistication if he appreciates the values sacrificed no less than the advantages gained.

[9] J. Schumpeter, *Capitalism, Socialism and Democracy* (New York, 1942), 147.

II

HISTORY OF IDEAS IN LITERATURE AND ART

Leonardo and Freud: An Art-Historical Study*

by MEYER SCHAPIRO

Reprinted, with revisions, from the *Journal of the History of Ideas*—Vol. XVII, No. 2, pp. 147-178

In the literature on art, Freud's little book on Leonardo—*Eine Kindheitserinnerung des Leonardo da Vinci* (A Childhood Reminiscence of Leonardo da Vinci) [1]—has been the prime example of divination of an artist's personality through psychoanalytic concepts. Whatever one may think of Freud's conclusions, an unprejudiced reader will recognize the hand of a master in his powerful theory which is expounded there with a beautiful simplicity and vigor. Ingenious in probing hitherto unnoticed avowals of the artist, the book also commands admiration for its noble image of Leonardo's mind and character. But most students of art who have written on Leonardo since this work appeared have ignored it, although they are concerned like Freud with the artist's psychology in accounting for singular features of his art.[2] Only lately, Sir Kenneth Clark, in one of the best recent books on Leonardo, has paid homage to Freud in accepting as a deep insight Freud's explanation of the painting of St. Anne, the Virgin and Child;[3] but he has not followed Freud in the more essential matter of characterizing the painter's personality.[4] What has been lacking— after forty-five years—is an evaluation of Freud's book from the point of view of the history of art. The results of such a study are presented here not in order to criticize psychoanalytic theory, but rather to judge its application to a problem in which the data, it must be said, are extremely sparse.[5]

* This article is the substance of a lecture given at the William Alanson White Institute, New York City, on January 12, 1955.

[1] In the series: *Schriften zur angewandten Seelenkunde*, Heft VII (Leipzig, Vienna, 1910). English translation by A. A. Brill, with the title: *Leonardo da Vinci* (New York, 1916), now reprinted in Anchor Books. Important for the notes by Marie Bonaparte, the translator and editor, is the French edition: *Un souvenir d'enfance de Léonard de Vinci* (Paris, 1927). All our quotations are from the German edition of the collected works: Sigmund Freud, *Gesammelte Werke* (London, 1943), VIII, 127-211, referred to hereafter as *GW*.

[2] E.g., L. H. Heydenreich, *Leonardo da Vinci* (London, New York, Basel, 1954), who includes a special bibliography on "Personality and Appearance."

[3] Sir Kenneth Clark, *Leonardo da Vinci*, 1940 (2nd ed., Cambridge, 1952), especially 4, 151, 169n.   [4] Marcel Brion, *Léonard de Vinci* (Paris, 1952), 13, follows Freud's point on this picture without acknowledging Freud's authorship; where he does refer to him by name, as on p. 130, he misrepresents him seriously. He also speaks of the episode of the bird as capital for Leonardo's life (on 12, 216, 217) without citing Freud. Monsieur Brion attributes to psychoanalysis the view that Leonardo was deprived of maternal love and therefore developed various complexes (454).

[5] The article of Erwin O. Christensen, "Freud on Leonardo da Vinci," *Psychoanalytic Review*, XXXI (1944), 153-64, is completely uncritical.

I

In reading Leonardo's notebooks, Freud was especially struck by the following passage which I quote from his own text: " This writing distinctly about the vulture seems to be my destiny, because among the first recollections of my infancy it seemed to me that as I lay in my cradle a vulture came to me and opened my mouth with its tail and struck me many times with its tail inside my lips." [6]

That memory of Leonardo's interested no one who had previously written on the artist, although it is the only reference to his childhood in the immense mass of notes. From experience with patients, Freud had come to believe that such recollections do not concern real episodes but are adult fantasies which are referred back to childhood because of a related experience and owe their meaning to the latter. He observed that among his patients dreams or fantasies of this kind are sexual images; they pertain to a wish that is common in passive homosexuals who have transposed to the adult sexual sphere an experience of their infancy. The vulture's phallic tail in the child's mouth replaces the mother's breast.

Why did Leonardo substitute a vulture for the mother? Here Freud's great curiosity about philology, folklore and archaeology—studies which, like psychoanalysis, uncover and decipher a hidden past—came into play. He recalled that in Egyptian writing the hieroglyph for " mother " is a vulture and that the vulture-headed goddess Mut is sometimes represented with a phallus. The resemblance of " Mut " and " Mutter " is one that Freud could not regard as accidental.

The vulture, he supposed, was identified with the mother in Leonardo's fantasy not only because the latter knew the equivalence of mother and vulture in Egyptian writing—Egyptian ideas were available to the Italians of the Renaissance through a Hellenistic author, Horapollo—but also because of the belief, held by the Egyptians, the Greeks and the Romans, that the vulture exists only in the female sex. This strange bird conceived through the wind, and was therefore cited by the Church fathers as a natural prototype of the Virgin birth. If a vulture could be fecundated by the wind, then Mary could conceive through the Holy Spirit. Although Freud knew no Renaissance text of this belief and referred to older writers like St. Augustine, the idea was current in Leonardo's time. In a treatise by Pierio Valeriano, dedicated to Cosimo di Medici, the vulture is mentioned as a natural analogue of the Virgin Mary because of its marvellous fecundation by the wind.[7]

---

[6] *GW*, VIII, 156ff.

[7] Ioannis Pierii Valeriani *Hieroglyphica, sive de sacris Aegyptiorum aliarumque gentium litteris commentariorum libri LVIII* (Cologne, 1631), lib. xviii, cap. 4, pp. 217, 218. The original edition dates from 1556.

FIGURE 1. The Virgin and Child with St. Anne and St. John Baptist.
Burlington House, London.

(Reproduced by courtesy of the Royal Academy of Arts, London)

FIGURE 2. The Virgin and Child with St. Anne.

Louvre, Paris.

(Reproduced with the permission of Fratelli Alinari, Firenze)

Reading such an ancient text, Leonardo could associate the vulture with his mother because, as an illegitimate child brought up without the father, he knew her as a virgin parent. Freud assumes that in her abandonment and loneliness, she lavished upon the child all the love that would otherwise have gone to the father; her passionate kisses stimulated Leonardo to a precocious sexuality and fixation upon herself. He remained attached thereafter to the image of his mother and could only be attracted by boys like the one she had loved. On that infantile situation depended not only Leonardo's passive homosexuality, but also the course of his artistic career, with its strange inhibitions, and the outcome of his scientific bent. His normal infantile inquisitiveness, stimulated by the absence of the father, was unconstrained by parental authority, so that his instinct of investigation could later develop freely and venture beyond the boundaries of contemporary beliefs.

It should be said that Freud regards these early experiences as a necessary but not sufficient condition of Leonardo's growth. Why there took place a partial repression together with an unusually intense sublimation of the unrepressed libido (or sexual energy) in the artistic and scientific spheres—in accordance with Freud's theory of the convertibility of psychic forces—he admits he does not know. Biological make-up determines in some individuals a reaction of strong repression; in others, sublimation. The organic bases of character lie outside the domain of psychoanalytic research. "The artistic gift and the capacity for work, being intimately bound up with sublimation, we must admit that the essence of the artistic function also remains inaccessible to psychoanalysis."

When Leonardo was less than five years old, perhaps when he was three (Freud supposes), his father, who had married shortly after Leonardo's birth and had no children by this marriage, took the little boy to his home as an adopted son. The child thus enjoyed the affection of two mothers, the natural mother, Caterina, a peasant girl in the town of Vinci, and the stepmother, Albiera, the first wife of Piero da Vinci. Years later, in painting the group of Saint Anne with Mary and the infant Christ, Freud continues, Leonardo remembered his two mothers. In both versions—the cartoon in the Royal Academy in London (fig. 1) and the painting in the Louvre (fig. 2)—Mary looks only slightly younger than her mother, contrary to the apocryphal legend according to which Anne was childless and beyond the age of bearing when, through a divine miracle, Mary was born. This image of the two young mothers of equal grace and charm was explained by Freud as an invention of Leonardo's, which only an artist with his childhood experience could have devised. The appeal of the Mona Lisa had a similar origin in Leonardo's early life, as Walter Pater had already divined. This smiling woman whose face, through Leonardo's portrait, has haunted the Western world ever since, attracted the painter precisely because she touched his childhood memory; it was after portraying Mona Lisa that he painted Saint Anne with the Virgin and infant Christ, endowing the faces of the women with the same smile. The conception of the smiling woman is itself a re-animated memory of the tenderness of his devoted mother. In the account of Leonardo, written about thirty years after the artist's death, Vasari describes as his first works some plaster sculptures of smiling women and of children. Leonardo's art begins then with the kind of image that dominates his mature years—the smiling maternal woman and her child.

Not long after Freud's first publication of his work on Leonardo, an analyst-disciple, Oskar Pfister, discerned in the painting at the Louvre the form of a vulture in the blue robe of Mary, enveloping her waist and the lower part of her body.[8] The bird's head, with its marked beak, appears at the left; on the other side, the robe is prolonged like a vulture's tail, ending in the child's mouth. This discovery was accepted by Freud as an unexpected confirmation of his decipherment of the infantile memory. " The key to all of Leonardo's accomplishments and misfortunes lies hidden in the infantile fantasy about the vulture."[9]

In presenting the argument, I have not achieved the persuasiveness of Freud, whose reconstruction of the artist's personality is a moving and coherent account of the psychological fortunes of a man of genius. I have omitted much of the theoretical matter on which Freud builds his interpretation. But I believe I have given the essential points of his speculation and theory, so far as they concern Leonardo's art. Freud was aware that much of his book rested on uncertain assumptions about the artist's life and that his method was risky; he was convinced, however, that with the available facts a better explanation would require the further development of psychoanalytic concepts.

II

Let us consider first the text about the vulture. It was objected in 1923 by Eric Maclagan, an English student of Renaissance art, that Freud, relying on a German translation, had misread Leonardo.[10] The bird which the artist remembered as having inserted its tail in his

[8] Oskar Pfister, "Kryptolalie, Kryptographie und unbewusster Vexierbild bei Normalen," *Jahrbuch für psychoanalytische und psychopathologische Forschungen*, V (1913), 146–151, quoted by Freud and illustrated, *GW*, VIII, 187, 188. Pfister repeats the observation in his article, "Psychoanalyse und bildende Kunst," in E. Federn and H. Meng, *Das psychoanalytische Volksbuch* (Bern, 1939), 610.   [9] *GW*, VIII, 210.

mouth was not a vulture, but a kite—the Italian word is "nibbio." A kite is also a rapacious bird, but no eater of carrion and looks quite different from the vulture. More important, it is not the bird represented by the Egyptians in the hieroglyph for "mother," to which folklore attributes only a female sex; nor is it the bird which is cited by the Church fathers in connection with the Virgin Birth.[11]

Yet although the passage concerns a kite rather than a vulture, Freud's question about the origin of Leonardo's fantasy remains. I do not propose to investigate its psychoanalytic meaning—this would be beyond my power—but something can be learned about its manifest content by ordinary textual study.

Re-reading the passage, it is clear to us that Leonardo was reflecting on how he came to write about the kite.[12] It occurs on the back of a sheet on which he has noted various observations on the flight of birds.[13] In his writings on flight several birds are mentioned, but the kite is named more often than any other; it is for Leonardo the bird in which he can best observe the natural mechanisms of flight. The movements of the tail in particular offer some hints for the design of a flying machine.

"When the kite in descending turns itself right over and pierces the air head downwards, it is forced to bend the tail as far as it can in the opposite direction to that which it desires to follow; and then again bending the tail swiftly, according to the direction in which it wishes to turn, the change in the bird's course corresponds to the turn of the tail, like the rudder of a ship which when turned turns the ship, but in the opposite direction."[14]

"Many are the times when the bird beats the corner of its tail in order to steer itself, and in this action the wings are used sometimes very little, sometimes not at all."[15]

"At the tail of the kite there is the stroke of the air which presses

[10] Eric Maclagan, "Leonardo in the Consulting Room," *Burlington Magazine*, XLII (1923), 54–57.   [11] Maclagan observed, too, that the entry in Leonardo's notes about the funeral of a Caterina did not concern Leonardo's mother, as Freud had thought, but more probably a servant, considering the context and the small expenditure for the burial.

[12] The passage reads: "Questo scriversi distintamente del nibbio par che sia mio destino, perchè nella prima ricordatione della mia infantia e' mi parea che, essendo io in culla, che un nibbio venisse a me e mi aprisse la bocca colla sua coda, e molte volte mi percuotesse con tal coda dentro alle labra." For the Italian text and the translation, see J. P. Richter, *The Literary Works of Leonardo da Vinci*, 2nd ed. (London, New York, Toronto, 1939), II, 342, no. 1363. Leonardo's writings are available in a more complete English translation: *The Notebooks of Leonardo da Vinci*, by Ed. MacCurdy (New York, 1939). For the passage on the kite, see p. 1122.

[13] MacCurdy, 422, 423 (Codex Atlanticus, f. 66r).

[14] *Ibid.*, 489.   [15] *Ibid.*, 484; the next passage (485) mentions the kite's tail.

with fury closing up the void which the movement of the bird leaves of itself, and this occurs at each side of the void so created."

On the same page, Leonardo writes: "We may say the same of the rudder placed behind the movement of the ship, imitated from the tails of birds; as to which experience teaches us how much more readily this small rudder is turning during the rapid movements of great ships than the whole ship itself."[16]

Leonardo's idea that the kite's tail can serve as a model for a rudder, he owes to a classical author, Pliny, whom he quotes in other places. From a list of books that Leonardo jotted down in his papers, we know that he possessed the *Natural History* of Pliny, probably in the Italian translation.[17]

In his account of the kite ("milvus"), Pliny wrote: "It seems that this bird by the movements of its tail taught the art of steersmanship, nature demonstrating in the sky what was required in the deep."[18] This passage was quoted by the same Valeriano whom I have cited above on the vulture. In the chapter on the kite, in his book on emblems and symbols, we read: "The kite is the symbol of the art of steering," and, quoting Pliny: "the example of the kite taught men how to steer boats; the rudder is derived from the kite's tail."[19]

According to Valeriano, the kite is an emblem for the pilot.[20] Leonardo's choice of the kite as the bird of his destiny has apparently more to do with his scientific problem than Freud supposed. If in Leonardo's fantasy the kite beats its tail in the child's mouth, one may see there an allusion to the characteristic movement of the tail against the wind and the currents of air of which the breath is a counterpart.

Although hardly a complete explanation, this brings us a little closer to Leonardo's thought. Why, it will be asked, does he locate the episode in his childhood? Why the strange association of the kite with the infant's mouth?

Here again a philological approach is helpful. This fantasy about an incident of childhood as an omen of adult fortune or genius is no unique form, but an established literary pattern. Cicero, in his book *On Divination*, writes: "When Midas, the famous king of Phrygia, was a child, ants filled his mouth with grains of wheat as he slept.

---

[16] *Ibid.*, 469; note also the chapter heading: How the tail of the bird is used as a rudder (453). [17] *Ibid.*, 1163.

[18] *Naturalis Historia*, lib. X, cap. 12: "iam videntur artem gubernandi docuisse caudae flexibus, in caelo monstrante natura quod opus esset in profundo."

[19] *Hieroglyphica*, lib. XVII, cap. 40, pp. 213, 214. [20] *Ibid.*, 214. The same text of Pliny was quoted in 1499 by Polydore Vergil, *De rerum inventoribus libri octo*, (Basel, 1575), 229, cap. 15.

It was predicted that he would be a very wealthy man, and so it turned out." In the next line, Cicero adds: " While Plato was an infant asleep in his cradle, bees settled on his lips and this was interpreted to mean he would have a rare sweetness of speech." [21] His future eloquence was foreseen in his infancy. These texts were copied by a Roman writer, Valerius Maximus, whose treatise on heroes and exemplary individuals was one of the most widely read books in Leonardo's time.[22]

What is interesting in these examples is not simply the foretelling of a child's future through a small animal, but the characteristic investment of the mouth with a symbol of that future. Pliny, for instance, writes that a " nightingale alighted on the mouth of the sleeping infant Stesichorus " who became a great lyric poet.[23] According to Pausanias, " the young Pindar fell asleep in the mid-day heat. Bees flew over him and deposited wax on his lips, giving him the gift of song." [24] In all these classical legends, the omen is located in the mouth, the place of speech and more particularly of the breath or spirit. This common *topos* was adopted by the Christians for their own heroes. In the life of Saint Ambrose in the *Golden Legend,* by Jacobus Voragine (c. 1228/30–1298) a popular book during the Renaissance, we read: " While he lay asleep in his crib, a swarm of bees descended upon him, and the bees went into his mouth as into a hive, and then they flew away so high that the eye could not follow them. Then the child's father, greatly frightened, exclaimed: ' This child, if he lives, will surely be a man of great deeds.' " [25]

We have then a series of traditional tales, known in Leonardo's time, which resemble his memory of the kite; they foretell a hero's future from an episode of his infancy—a small creature, generally a bird or bee, alights upon the child's mouth or enters it as an omen of future greatness.

In another place in the same work on flight—a note written on the cover—Leonardo resorts to the image of a bird to express his hopes for successful flight: " The great bird [that is, his flying machine] will take its first flight upon the back of the great swan, filling the whole world with amazement and filling all records with its fame and it will

[21] *De Divinatione*, I, xxxvi, 78, translated by Falconer, Loeb Library, 309.
[22] *Moralium Exemplorum libri novem* (Venice, 1546), 20, lib. I, cap. 6. The same stories are told by a Greek writer, Aelian, *Variae Historiae*, lib. XII, 45.
[23] Pliny, *op. cit.*, lib. X, 43.
[24] *Description of Greece*, IX, 23, 2, translated by W. H. S. Jones, Loeb Library, IV, 268, 269. The same story is told about the infant Pindar by Philostratus (*Imagines*, lib. II, 12) and Aelian (*Variae Historiae*) lib. XII, 45).
[25] Jacobus de Voragine, *The Golden Legend*, tr. and adapted from the Latin by Granger Ryan and Helmut Ripperger (2 vols., New York, 1941), I, 25.

bring eternal glory to the nest where it was born."[26] The "great swan" (*ciceri*) is a pun on the name of the mountain, *Monte Ceceri*, from which he hoped to launch the plane.

An Excursus on the fantasy of the bird in the child's mouth

The connection of the bird with genius or inspiration is very old. Psychoanalysis explains it by the dependence of all creativeness on sexuality, both in its sublimated and actualized forms, and by the symbolic equivalence of flying and coitus in dream fantasy, folklore, and language. The bird in Semitic and Greek literature is the carrier of heavenly gifts, the mediating source of genius and greatness. Thus the child brought up by birds is destined for power; the ancient Oriental monarchs, Semiramis, Achamanes, are nurslings of doves and eagles.[27] These examples confirm the sense of Leonardo's fantasy as an omen of future achievement, but they lack the specific element of the bird's tail in the child's mouth.

The mouth, as the region of speech, breath, and nourishment, is significant for poetic inspiration, wisdom, and prophecy. Inspiration is the introjection of a powerful external force, often identified with the father. Prophecy is, in a literal sense, "divination." In the Bible, God touches the prophet's mouth: "The Lord put forth his hand and touched my mouth. And the Lord said to me, Behold, I have put my words into thy mouth" (Jeremiah I, 9).

In Celtic and Scandinavian tradition, eating the flesh of a bird or other creature (snake, salmon) inspired poetry or gave wisdom and the gift of prophecy. A frequent theme in those literatures is the acquisition of poetic or mantic power by putting the crushed or burnt thumb into the mouth (Finn, Sigurd, Taliesin).[28]

Another possible connection of Leonardo's fantasy is with the image of the Holy Spirit. The Trinity is often represented in the Middle Ages with the dove's tail in God's mouth.[29] In Leonardo's time occurs a variant based on the *filioque* of the Western doctrine of the procession of the Holy Spirit in which the wings of the descending bird reach from the lips of God the Father to those of Christ the Son.[30] Leonardo's fantasy could be interpreted accordingly as an analogous identification with the father.

The psychoanalyst, Dr. Ernest Jones, has published a text which offers some resemblance to Leonardo's fantasy, but he has not connected the two documents. The poet Henry Vaughan, in a letter of 1694, told of "a young lad father and motherless, and soe very poor that he was forced to beg; butt

---

[26] MacCurdy, 420, 421 and note.

[27] For these and other examples, see Alfred Jeremias, *Das alte Testament im Lichte des alten Orients* (2nd ed. Leipzig, 1906), 411, 412.

[28] Robert D. Scott, *The Thumb of Knowledge in Legends of Finn, Sigurd and Taliesin* (New York, 1930).

[29] See Wolfgang Braunfels, *Die heilige Dreifaltigkeit* (Düsseldorf, 1954), fig. 37 (portable altar from Hildesheim); A. N. Didron, *Christian Iconography*, (London, 1886), II, fig. 144. The theme occurs in a relief by Verrocchio, Leonardo's teacher, in the Bargello Museum in Florence.   [30] Didron, *op. cit.*, II, fig. 143.

att last was taken up by a rich man, that kept a great stock of sheep upon the mountains not far from the place where I now dwell, who clothed him and sent him into the mountains to keep his sheep. There in summertime following the sheep and looking to their lambs, he fell into a deep sleep; In which he dreamt, that he saw a beautifull young man with a garland of green leafs upon his head, and an hawk upon his fist; with a quiver full of Arrows att his back, coming towards him (whistling several measures or tunes all the way) and att last lett the hawk fly att him, which (he dreamt) gott into his mouth and inward parts, and suddenly awaked in a great fear and consternation: but possessed with such a vein, or gift of poetrie, that he left the sheep and went about the Countrey, making songs upon all occasions, and came to be the most famous Bard in all the Countrey in his time." [31]

The story seems to combine pagan Celtic, Greek and Christian Renaissance elements. Vaughan tells it à propos the vein of inspired rhapsodic poetry called *Awen* by the later Welsh bards. It is a tale about inspiration, and in the discovery or awakening of the poetic gift of a poor shepherd is like the story of the herdsman Caedmon. The beautiful young man is evidently Apollo, the god of poetry, whose messenger to men is the hawk. According to the neo-Platonist, Porphyry (233–c. 304), an author read in the Renaissance, eating the heart of a hawk is the ingestion of the divine spirit and will give power of prophecy.[32] Interesting for Freud's account of Leonardo is the fact that the boy is homeless and without parents, and is finally adopted. The hawk entering his mouth and touching his inward parts suggests not only the Celtic legend of the poet eating a bird that gives inspiration, but also a Renaissance theme: God as a hawk which feeds on the soul and the heart.[33]

All these parallels indicate the general field of ideas to which Leonardo's fantasy belongs; they do not account for the more specific features of the kite and the tail in the infant's mouth. Here the context of the notes on flight supplies, I think, the essential manifest meaning.

The psychoanalyst will ask: Though Freud was mistaken in reading " vulture " for " kite," and his evidence from Egyptian and Christian folklore concerning the vulture is irrelevant, does not the fantasy about a kite inserting its tail in the infant's mouth retain the homosexual meaning that Freud discerned and permit his inferences about Leonardo's childhood?

[31] See Ernest Jones, " The Madonna's Conception Through the Ear," *Jahrbuch der Psychoanalyse*, VI (1914), reprinted in *Essays in Applied Psychoanalysis* (London, 1923), 338, 339; *Vaughan's Works*, edited by L. C. Martin (Oxford, 1914), II, 675, 676, letter of October 9, 1694.

[32] *De Abstinentia ab Esu Animalium*, lib. II, 48.

[33] Cf. the poem of Alonso de Ledesma, *El Nebli de Amor Divino:* The hawk of divine love / Which has the soul for its prey / Feeds on hearts. From Otho Vaenius, *Amoris Divini Emblemata* (Antwerp, 1615), quoted by Mario Praz, *Studies in 17th Century Imagery* (London, 1939), I, 128.

The careful reading of Freud's book will show that he built upon the unique, legendary characteristics of the vulture a positive account of Leonardo's infancy to fill the gaps in the documents; such details as the solitude and abandonment of the mother and her passionate love of the child and even the circumstances favorable to Leonardo's fruitful sublimation to science, are constructed in part from the equivalence of the vulture and the Virgin. From his theory of the infantile origins of homosexuality, Freud could infer only that Leonardo had a fixation upon his mother, but not the specific relationships and events on which his account of Leonardo's personality and art depend. One can plausibly imagine, contrary to Freud, that from the beginning this young Italian mother was no outcast from her family, and that in the absence of the child's father her brothers and her own father assumed in the child's feelings and thoughts the rôle of his father. We can imagine, too, that he might have been brought up by a mother hostile to the illegitimate child whose existence disgraced her. If Caterina was already married when the boy was adopted by his natural father, we can suppose that the birth of a half-brother changed the little Leonardo's situation in his home and made the return to his true father attractive. A recently discovered document indicates how far Freud was misled in his reconstruction. Antonio, the paternal grandfather of Leonardo, in recording the child's birth and baptism in the family diary, has named ten godparents, mostly neighbors whose presence at the ceremony strongly suggests that the child was born in the paternal home and accepted there from the beginning.[34]

All these possibilities were ignored by Freud because of his certitude about the vulture and its legend; this, together with the theorems of infantile sexual development and of the origins of homosexuality in the fixation upon an over-affectionate mother (Leonardo's inversion was known through a document recording his arrest at twenty-four on a charge of sodomy [35]) compelled the inference that Freud presents in his book. That is why the vulture is so necessary to Freud and why the book is called: A Childhood Reminiscence of Leonardo da Vinci.

The kite is another story, and where Leonardo speaks of it as a parent, his comment is still less favorable to Freud's interpretation of the childhood memory. In a collection of fables about the passions in his Notebooks, one called "Envy" concerns the kite: "Of the kite we read that when it sees that its children are too fat, it pecks their

[34] See Emil Möller, "Der Geburtstag des Lionardo da Vinci," *Jahrbuch der preussischen Kunstsammlungen*, 60 (1939), 71-75.

[35] Luca Beltrami, *Documenti e memorie riguardanti la vita e le opere di Leonardo da Vinci* (Milan, 1919), 4, 5.

sides out of envy and keeps them without food." [36] The kite here is not the model of the good mother who wishes to have her child her own forever; she is the opposite of the vulture which, according to a tradition (ignored by Leonardo) is the best of all mothers, protecting her young for a hundred and twenty days and scratching herself to give her blood to her young—an emblem of compassion like the pelican which symbolizes Christ's sacrifice.[37]

Freud might have read the fable of *Envy* in the Notebooks; but the father of psychoanalysis dismissed this part of Leonardo's writings as " allegorical natural history, animal fables, jokes and prophecies, trivialities unworthy of so great a genius." [38]

The fable of the kite is not an original work of Leonardo, but was probably excerpted from an older collection. A psychologist could infer from his interest in this bit of natural history that Leonardo did not forgive Caterina his illegitimacy and her willingness to abandon him to a step-mother.[39]

If I have discussed at so great length what analysts call the manifest content of Leonardo's fantasy, it is because this aspect has not only been insufficiently considered by Freud, but has even been distorted in his reconstruction of the occasion and process of Leonardo's conscious thought. Building upon the unfortunate vulture, he has imagined Leonardo reading a church father and coming upon a reference to the vulture as a prototype of the Virgin birth; this, according to Freud, recalled to the artist his own mother and infancy; he could feel then his identity with the Christ child whom he had so often represented, and his own great destiny as a man of science, the first to fly.[40]

III

Freud's account of the painting of Saint Anne, the Virgin and the infant Christ (fig. 2) raises questions of another order. Here he attacks one of the most elusive problems in the psychology of artists: how a new conception is born.

It is true that in Freud's explanation, the originality concerns a theme rather than the invention of a form; but a later analyst, we shall see, has drawn from Freud's work a corollary about the creation of a new form as well.

[36] MacCurdy, 1074; Richter, 261. The harshness of the hawk to its young is noted, after Cassiodorus, by the Welsh writer, Giraldus Cambrensis (*Topography of Ireland*, chap. VIII), who recommends it as a model for the training of human infants and children.

[37] Valerianus, *Hieroglyphica*, lib. XVIII, cap. 4, p. 217.   [38] *GW*, VIII, 136.

[39] In another fable, The Ape and the Bird, Leonardo tells of an ape who in his uncontrollable affection for a fledgling bird, kissed it and " squeezed it until he killed it." It is a lesson, he wrote, " for those who, by not punishing their children, let them come to mischief " (MacCurdy, 1062, Richter, II, 278).   [40] *GW*, VIII, 159.

The first requirement of such an attempt to account for a new image in art is that the investigator establish its priority. It would be futile to credit to the peculiarity of a single mind what was already a common possession of artists. At this point the psychoanalyst must rely on the discipline of the history of art, and to some extent on the neighboring cultural fields—the history of religion and social life—to which belong certain of the elements represented in Renaissance pictures.

The historians of these fields will tell us, if their investigations have touched upon them, to what extent a new image has been prepared by others or pertains to a common tendency of feeling and thought, and how far an artist has modified the inherited matter in realizing his personal conceptions.

But although Freud, in his ethnological papers, was deeply aware of the collective patterns in culture and referred them to some universal psychic process or mechanism, in writing on Leonardo he ignored the social and the historical where they are most pertinent to his task. Where he does allude to them, we are surprised by what he takes to be general conditions of Renaissance art. Thus he supposes that since the men of the Renaissance were aggressive, Leonardo's gentleness must be interpreted as an exceptional and therefore significant individual peculiarity.[41] Freud sees it as an abreaction against an early sadistic impulse, or as a fixation upon the mother and his own infantile stage; and since all great artists paint some erotic pictures, the absence of such themes from Leonardo's work indicates to Freud the strength of his sexual repression.[42] But those features of the culture of the time which bear more directly on the painting of Saint Anne, Freud disregards. He does not ask, for example, what was thought of Saint Anne during that period, or how common was her image. It is this side of Leonardo's work that I shall consider now.

In a sermon of 1539 Martin Luther said: " All the fuss about Saint Anne began when I was a boy of fifteen; before that she was unknown."[43] The cult of Anne dates then, in Luther's memory, from his fifteenth year, which fell in 1498. Now the first picture by Leonardo of *Saint Anne, the Virgin and Child*—the cartoon in London (fig. 1)—is generally placed in 1498 or 1499.[44] This may be regarded as a chance coincidence, one of the hundreds of striking synchronisms of unconnected events with which history is filled; but we learn from

---

[41] *Ibid.*, 134, 135, 204.   [42] *Ibid.*, 136.

[43] Quoted by E. Schaumkell, *Der Kultus der heiligen Anna am Ausgange des Mittelalters* (Freiburg i. Br. and Leipzig, 1893), 12.

[44] This is the opinion of Clark and Heydenreich, but H. Bodmer, *Leonardo, des Meisters Gemälde und Zeichnungen* (Klassiker der Kunst, Stuttgart and Berlin, 1931), 408, places it in 1500 in Florence.

the historians of the Church that the cult of Saint Anne, which had a long past, became widespread and reached its culmination in the years between 1485 and 1510.[45] During that twenty-five-year period Anne was so fashionable a saint that a writer could say in 1506 that Anne was "overshadowing the fame and glory of her daughter."[46] More new pictures and sculptures, as well as lives and legends, of Anne seem to have been produced in those decades than in the preceding or following centuries. Numerous chapels and religious brotherhoods were founded in her name. The German emperor Maximilian was a member of a confraternity of Saint Anne and inscribed his standard to Anna Selbdritt on one side and to the Virgin on the other.[47]

The growth of the cult of Saint Anne was undoubtedly connected with the interest in the doctrine of the Immaculate Conception, although other factors were present. Often debated since the twelfth century, the Immaculate Conception became a central controversial issue in the later fifteenth.[48] Just as the Virgin Mary had conceived Christ without sin, so it was held that Mary was conceived immaculately by her mother Anne and had therefore not inherited the sin of Adam and Eve. Churchmen of great authority, like Bernard of Clairvaux and Thomas Aquinas, had opposed that doctrine because it implied that Mary had no need to be redeemed by Christ, though Christ came to save all mankind. In 1475 a Milanese Dominican, Vincenzo Bandelli, objected to the doctrine of the Immaculate Conception that it assimilated Anne to Mary, making Anne a virgin in conceiving Mary—*eius mater in concipiendo virgo fuisset*. Popular belief tended, in fact, to imagine Anne's conception of Mary as a miraculous event without the intercourse or concupiscence which constituted original sin *materialiter;* the way was open to a series of supernatural conceptions of the ancestors of the Virgin, all free from original sin. Some theologians tried to save the theory by distinguishing between the act of conception and the moment of endowment of the embryo with a soul, when original sin was supposedly transmitted; it was at that latter moment that by special grace Mary was freed from original sin. The argument did not convince everyone and the controversy continued until 1854 when the Immaculate Conception of Mary by Saint Anne became officially a dogma of the Roman Catholic Church.

[45] Schaumkell, *op. cit.;* and Beda Kleinschmidt, *Die heilige Anna, Ihre Verehrung in Geschichte, Kunst und Volkstum* (Düsseldorf, 1930), 160ff.; Yrjö Hirn, *The Sacred Shrine, a Study in the Poetry and Art of the Catholic Church* (London, 1912), 214–249.

[46] Jakob Wimpfeling, quoted by Kleinschmidt, *op. cit.,* 138, n. 1.

[47] Schaumkell, *op. cit.,* 16.

[48] For this whole paragraph, see *Dictionnaire de Théologie Catholique,* VII, 1120–1126.

For centuries the doctrine had been supported mainly by the Franciscan order. The Carmelites and Augustinians then took it over, but against the strong objections of the Dominicans who were powerful in the Church. During that time, the cult of Saint Anne, which had been restricted to a few localities, became more general. But it was not until 1481 that the feast of Anne (July 26) was made obligatory by Pope Sixtus IV, a former Franciscan.[49] A few years before, in 1476, the same pope had granted an indulgence for the recitation of an office of the Immaculate Conception. And in 1477 and 1483, Sixtus issued bulls forbidding theologians to treat the doctrine of the Immaculate Conception as heretical, although the other view was permitted. His chapel in the Vatican, the famous Sistine Chapel, was dedicated to the Immaculately Conceived Virgin.

In 1494, shortly before Leonardo drew his cartoon of Saint Anne, her cult received a new stimulus from a book, *Tractatus de Laudibus Sanctissimae Annae*, by a German abbot, John Tritenheim (Trithemius). This little work, written in praise of Anne, holding her up as a model of Christian womanhood and defending her cult and the doctrine of the Immaculate Conception against the doubting Dominicans, was printed in several editions and seems to have been widely read.

That same year, Pope Alexander VI issued an indulgence for those who recited a prayer to Anne and Mary which was printed on the indulgence ticket. A believer who recited that prayer, affirming the Immaculate Conception, before an image of Anne, Mary and the Christ Child—the so-called Anna Metterza or Anna Selbdritt—was relieved of 10,000 years of punishment in purgatory for mortal sins and 20,000 years for venial ones.[50] The prayer was often printed on single sheets with a woodcut of Anna, Mary and the Child, which were pasted on doors and walls. Images of the three holy persons were produced in great numbers then; they often show Mary sitting on the lap of Anne with the Christ Child on Mary's lap, an object of the tender attentions of the two women.[51]

This type of image was hardly an invention of Leonardo, as Freud has supposed, nor was his cartoon or painting " almost the first " example as Ernst Kris has written.[52] Far from originating in the unique constellation of Leonardo's personality, the theme of *Anna Metterza* was traditional and had acquired a new vogue throughout

---

[49] Kleinschmidt, *op. cit.*, 134.

[50] *Ibid.*, 163, and Schaumkell, *op. cit.*, 22, n. 1.

[51] W. L. Schreiber, *Handbuch der Holz- und Metalschnitte des XV. Jahrhunderts* (Leipzig, 1927), III, no. 1191, 1195.

[52] *Psychoanalytic Explorations in Art* (New York, 1952), 19.

Catholic Europe during his lifetime—a vogue which depended not only on theological doctrine, but on more earthly needs. A chapter of Trithemius' book is devoted to explaining and justifying the expansion of the cult of Saint Anne. In the critical state of contemporary Christendom, when the Western nations had been defeated by the Turkish fleets, when faith was in decline and society disintegrating, it was necessary, he believed, to strengthen the family and to promote a more intimate spiritual life through the cult of this maternal saint; the founding of numerous confraternities devoted to Anne helped to unite the members who came from different professions and walks of life.[53] "Through Anne's patronage," he wrote, "we can escape all the ills of the tottering world."[54] She is more generous than Mary and grants to the faithful what her daughter refuses; she performs miracles, even raising the dead.

A modern student of her cult has pointed to the role of Anne as the protector of pregnant women and the patron of the family during a time when families were extraordinarily large, with as many as twenty children.[55] According to the legend, Anne was a model of fertility, marrying three times. She is often represented as Anna Trinuba et Tripara, surrounded by the offspring of her three marriages. In a portrait of the Emperor Maximilian and his family, each figure was inscribed with a name from the family of Anne.[56]

Behind Leonardo's picture, then, was the widespread contemporary cult of Saint Anne and the new interest in the holy family. Anne, Mary and Christ were worshipped as a trinity, a "*humanissima trinitas*" more accessible than the "*divinissima trinitas*" of the Father, Son and Holy Ghost. When the Pope Sixtus IV made the feast of Anne obligatory, he imposed in the same decree the feast of another family saint, Joseph, the foster-father of Christ and husband of Mary.

Is not Leonardo's painting unique, however, in showing Anne and Mary as women of nearly equal age—a feature that Freud explained by the artist's unconscious memory of his childhood under the care of two mothers? Contrary to Freud's belief, Anne and Mary had been represented together as young saints long before Leonardo. The originality of his conception lies elsewhere, as we shall soon see. Anne's youthfulness in certain images may be explained by the theological idealization of Anne as the double of her daughter Mary and by a general tendency in the art of the Middle Ages and the Renaissance to picture female saints as beautiful, virginal figures. In popular accounts of Anne's miracles, in the Legends and exempla around 1500,

[53] *Op. cit.* (Mainz, 1494), cap. XV.   [54] "Per cuius patrocinium omnis mundi labentis mala securi possumus evadere," *op. cit.*, cap. XI.
[55] Kleinschmidt, *op. cit.*, 164ff.   [56] *Ibid.*, 158 and figs. 94, 95 (by B. Striegel).

she appears to the faithful as a "beautiful" or "pretty" woman ("wunderbarlich gezieret hüpsch und schone").[57] It should be observed, too, that in Roman and in mediaeval Christian literature, the type of the old-young woman is not at all uncommon. Ideal female figures, especially personifications (Rome, Nature, the World, the Church, Philosophy and even Old Age), are pictured in visionary and poetic writings as old women who are rejuvenated and beautiful.[58]

In the projection of the theological pattern of the Virgin upon Saint Anne, the latter acquired her daughter's virtues and powers. Trithemius described with feeling the perfect maternal tenderness and grace of Anne, which were the necessary source of the qualities of Mary. She had been chosen by God, already before the creation of the world, to be Mary's mother. Her own birth became a subject of extraordinary fantasy in the Middle Ages. In an old French poem she was said to have issued from her father Phanuel's thigh, which he touched with a knife after cutting an apple, thus causing it to conceive.[59] In this strange medley of pagan and Jewish legend, Anne is born like Dionysus from a divine thigh ("Phanuel" comes from the Hebrew for "the face of God"), but is connected indirectly with the apple that occasioned original sin—Phanuel cut the apple from the tree of knowledge without eating it, just as Mary, born of a mother who was not virgin, remained untouched by original sin. By the thirteenth century, the simple people—naïve, unintellectual worshippers, unconstrained by theology and science—had come to believe that Anne, too, conceived miraculously through the Holy Ghost. In the account of Mary's birth in the *Golden Legend* by Jacobus de Voragine, an angel tells Anne's husband, Joachim, that it often happens, when God has closed a womb, that he has done it in order to open it afterwards miraculously, so that it may be known that the child to be born is not an issue of lust; such were the miraculous births of Isaac and Joseph and Samson from old and barren mothers.[60] Anne had been cursed by sterility and was childless after twenty years of marriage; her husband's offering was rejected in the temple because he had no offspring. The legend, which is based on very old apocryphal writings,[61] goes on to relate how an angel appeared to Joachim and told

[57] Schaumkell, *op. cit.*, 46, 56.

[58] Ernst Robert Curtius, *European Literature and the Latin Middle Ages* (Bollingen Series, XXXVI, New York, 1953), 101–105.

[59] C. Chabaneau, *Le Romanz de Saint Fanuel et de Sainte Anne* (Paris, 1889), 11ff., lines 435ff.; Hirn, *op. cit.*, 231ff.

[60] *Op. cit.*, at September 8.

[61] For the older sources in the proto-evangile of James, the gospel of the pseudo-Matthew and the gospel of the Birth of Mary, see *The Apocryphal New Testament*, translated by M. R. James (Oxford, 1926), 39, 73, 79.

him to meet Anne at the Golden Gate, where an angel had bidden Anne to go; they kissed on meeting, and at that instant, according to popular belief, was conceived the child that the angel had promised. In the paintings of this scene, an angel above the couple recalls the Annunciation to Mary and the Incarnation of Christ. The Meeting of Joachim and Anne illustrates the Immaculate Conception.[62]

In Leonardo's time there were three common types of images of *Anna Metterza*. Of one, the best known example is Masaccio's painting in the Accademia in Florence (c. 1425); here the family trinity forms a great pyramid, austere and powerful, with an old Anne enthroned above and Mary at her feet, holding the child in her lap. In the second type, already well established in the middle or third quarter of the fourteenth century, Mary sits on her mother's knee and plays with the child on her own lap, often in affectionate embrace. This is the basis of Leonardo's picture. In a third variant, the child is placed on Anne's other knee or Anne holds Christ and Mary separately in each arm. The odd conception of a mature woman sitting like a child on another's knee was not at all disturbing or unnatural to mediaeval minds, which employed representation as a means of symbolizing religious ideas and could express by this grouping of three figures their essential character as a mystic family line. Common to all the types was the hieratic note in the scale and rigidity of the figures; Anne is the tallest and dominates the group. The relative ages and the order of generations, corresponding to the order of authority in the family, are symbolized by the varying size and level of the figures.[63]

In the late fifteenth century, we observe a new tendency to loosen the form and to envision this family group in a more human and natural way: Anne and Mary are of the same height and both play with the child. In an engraving made before 1500, Dürer represents Anne and Mary as equally tall, standing figures fondling the child in their arms.[64] In Cranach's altarpiece from Torgau, in the Frankfurt Museum, completed in 1509—perhaps before Leonardo's painting in the Louvre—Anne and Mary sit on the same bench both playing with the child. Here Anne has a young face, in some respects younger than Mary's.[65]

[62] Hirn, *op. cit.*, 238.

[63] For the types of Anna Metterza, see Kleinschmidt, *op. cit.*, 217ff., with numerous illustrations, and L. H. Heydenreich, " La Sainte Anne de Léonard de Vinci," *Gazette des Beaux-Arts* (1933), 205ff.

[64] *Dürer, des Meisters Gemälde, Kupferstiche und Holzschnitte*, Klassiker der Kunst (Stuttgart, Leipzig, 1908), pl. 108.

[65] Kleinschmidt, *op. cit.*, 274, fig. 195; for the youthful Anne and Mary repeated on the wings of the same altarpiece, see Curt Glaser, *Lukas Cranach* (Leip-

But the two women had already been represented alike in Italian art over a hundred years before. In a work painted in 1367 by the Sienese Luca di Tomé, the Virgin holding the child sits on the knee of Anne who is simply an enlarged replica of her daughter.[66] The whole is still subject to the hierarchical conception of the Middle Ages in the distinctions of size and level. By 1500, a common scale applies to everyone, in accord with the search for a natural, though idealized, human form in the art of the High Renaissance.

Yet Leonardo, the most advanced artist of his age, while removing all supernatural attributes like the haloes and humanizing the figures more completely, preserves the old iconic type of *Anna Metterza,* with its artificial symbolic structure, at a time when Northern art separates the two figures and places the child between them in a natural familial relationship. If he ventures to draw the heads of Anne and Mary on the same level in the London cartoon (fig. 1), he returns in later versions to the old conception, with Anne's head above Mary's. In the final painting in the Louvre (fig. 2), this difference of level is made to appear, however, as the natural result of a spontaneous movement of the Virgin who bends forward in playing with the child. The new equality of the women, their common humanity, is thus reconciled with their inequality as mother and daughter. By placing the child on the ground to the side, Leonardo overcomes also the static symmetry in the older relationships of child and mother, in which Mary is to Anne as Christ to Mary.

In Freud's reconstruction of the inner history of the Saint Anne painting, it was Leonardo's meeting with Mona Lisa that reawakened his unconscious memory of Caterina and inspired him to picture Anne and Mary as his two mothers, just as they had appeared to him in his childhood. This interpretation rests on a general schema that Freud had devised some years before to describe the process of poetic creation: an actual experience revives an old memory which is then elaborated as a wish fulfillment in artistic form.[67] In applying this

---

zig, 1921), 66, 67. The type of Anne and Mary sitting on a broad throne, with the child standing between them, already occurs in Italy in the 14th century—see the altarpiece in the Boston Museum by Barna da Siena (George Kaftal, *Iconography of the Saints in Tuscan Art* [Florence, 1952], 230, fig. 247). For other examples of the youthful Anne, cf. a Bohemian painting of the late 14th century in Breslau (Kleinschmidt, *op. cit.,* fig. 154), a painting by Lochner in Breslau (*ibid.,* pl. 12), Ghirlandaio's fresco of the Marriage of the Virgin (*ibid.,* fig. 110), Carpaccio's *Meeting at the Golden Gate* (*ibid.,* fig. 114), Filippino Lippi, Meeting of Joachim and Anna (1497), in Copenhagen (K. B. Neilson, *Filippino Lippi,* Cambridge, Mass., 1938, fig. 65), etc.

[66] Kleinschmidt, *op. cit.,* fig. 147. Cf. also fig. 146 for a 13th century German sculpture with youthful Anne and Mary.

[67] See his article of 1908, " Der Dichter und das Phantasieren," *GW,* VII, 217, 221.

schema to the *Saint Anne,* Freud has forgotten the early date of the London cartoon. As he himself correctly maintained, in opposition to certain writers,[68] the cartoon was done just before 1500 in Milan, and thus precedes by several years the portrait of Mona Lisa. Significant, too, for Leonardo's process is the fact that in the preparatory sketches he drew for different projects of a painting of *Anna Metterza,* the type of Saint Anne is not fixed. The dates of these drawings are still debated but, according to excellent judges, a drawing of his in the Louvre which shows Anne as an old woman,[69] post-dates the London cartoon. Leonardo's vacillation between the young and the old Anne recalls the uncertainty of the doctrine of the Immaculate Conception during this time. Supported and opposed by various groups, the doctrine won a momentary tolerance by the papacy, only to lose it in the following years.

The smiles of the women, which owe their charm to the infinite delicacy of Leonardo's art, are not so clear an evidence as Freud assumed of the painter's fixation upon his mother. He was aware of the weakness of his reasoning on this point and remarked in a note that " connoisseurs of art will think of the peculiar rigid smile of archaic Greek statues, e.g., those from Aegina, and will also perhaps discover something similar in the figures of Leonardo's teacher, Verrocchio, and will therefore not be inclined to follow my deductions." [70]

They will not only think of Verrocchio's smiling faces, they will remember, too, that Leonardo was brought to this master as a child by his father who was a friend of the artist and that the young student collaborated with his teacher and repeated certain of Verrocchio's themes. The plaster sculptures of smiling women and of children which Vasari mentions among Leonardo's first works have disappeared, but several such pieces by Verrocchio and his shop survive; it is possible that Vasari had these in mind when he wrote of the beginnings of Leonardo's art. Among Verrocchio's works are several smiling faces of a subtlety of expression approaching the later pictures of Leonardo.[71] The face of Saint Anne in the Louvre reminds us of his master's bronze *David,* triumphant also, with smiling face and delicate modeling around the lips and chin. Leonardo's training as a sculptor in Verrocchio's shop, where nicety of modeling was in honor, perhaps suggested to him the new possibilities of refined, elusive play

[68] *GW*, VIII, 186, n. 1.

[69] K. Clark, *Leonardo da Vinci,* pl. 51. Clark dates it c. 1508–1510; Anny E. Popp (*Leonardo-Zeichnungen* [Munich, 1928], 9) places it c. 1501; A. E. Popham, *The Drawings of Leonardo da Vinci* (New York, 1945), pl. 174 B, 1498–1499.

[70] *Op. cit.,* p. 179, n. 1.

[71] E.g., the Bargello Museum relief of the Virgin and Child, and an angel on the tomb of Forteguerri (1474) in the cathedral of Pistoia.

of light and shadow in the painting of his faces. Since the young Leonardo was already a member of the artist's guild while employed by Verrocchio and had collaborated with his master on important commissions, it has been conjectured that the older man was influenced by his more gifted pupil in the 1470s.[72] There is no reason, however, to assume Verrocchio's indebtedness to the younger artist for the motif of the smile.

Not only the fact that the early Greek sculptors, searching for a more natural form, represented the smile as a fixed attribute of the face—a generalized first expression of the subjective and physiognomic (as the advanced leg in both Egyptian and archaic Greek statues was a generalized expression of the body's mobility)[73]—but also the recurrence of the smile in Florentine art in the works of Donatello and Desiderio da Settignano, several decades before Leonardo, make it difficult to accept Freud's explanation of this widespread conventional motif in Leonardo's art by the peculiarity of his childhood. Only his personal rendering of the inherited smile, its singular qualities which depend on the artist's style in a broader sense and on his matured perception of the human face, may be referred to Leonardo's character. It would be a question then not simply of the smile as an element occasioned by a memory or experience, but of the expressive nuance which it owes to the pervasive tendency of the artist in treating all his feminine and youthful themes. He endows them with a mysterious passage of light and dark that he has described in his notes as the grace and softness of faces at dusk and in bad weather. By the indefiniteness and subtlety of the modelled forms, by light and shadow and other devices, he opens the way for the observer's revery.

This complex quality of the whole may well depend on structures of Leonardo's character disclosed by Freud. It may be, too, that the artist adopted and developed the existing theme of the smile with a special ardor because of the fixation upon his mother. But Freud's theory provides no bridge from the infantile experience and the mechanisms of psychic development to the style of Leonardo's art. In Freud's book the original elements of the work of art are simply representations of childhood memories and wishes; the style itself belongs to another—perhaps biological—domain of the individual, untouched by his concepts. An artist's impressions, and especially those of his childhood, must undergo, he thought, far-reaching changes before they could be embodied in a work of art; yet in writing of the smile, Freud does not hesitate to infer an exact accord of the painting

---

[72] See W. R. Valentiner, "Leonardo as Verrocchio's Co-worker," *Art Bulletin*, XII (1930), 43–89.

[73] I have proposed this explanation of the "archaic smile" in *Art Bulletin*, XIII, 1931, 485, 486.

and the infantile impression underneath all the modalities of the smile in different pictures. The smile of Mona Lisa, which attracts Leonardo because it recalls his mother, Freud describes as ambiguous, a duality of the reserved and sensual, the tender and menacing; his mother's smile in the picture of Saint Anne, which Freud sees as " the same, without question, as La Gioconda's," has lost the " enigmatic and disquieting character ... and expresses only intimacy and a tranquil felicity." [74] Yet in rendering in Mona Lisa's face the double sense of her smile, Leonardo remained faithful to the deeper content of his first memories, " for his mother's excessive tenderness was fatal to him." [75] Finally, in his later pictures of the androgynous Saint John and Bacchus, the same smile conveys a secret of love, the consciousness of unavowable pleasures.[76]

If Freud was mistaken in supposing that Leonardo invented the pictorial type of *Anna Metterza*, with Mary sitting on her mother's knee and holding the Christ child, or that the smiling, youthful Anne was an idea of Leonardo's arising from an unconscious early memory revived by the meeting with Mona Lisa, there are, however, truly original features in the painting. But these have been ignored by Freud, although they have psychological interest and perhaps require for their explanation the use of Freud's concepts.

Exceptional in the images of the subject is the presence of Saint John the Baptist as the friend of the infant Christ (fig. 1). It is an apocryphal motif that Leonardo had already used in the painting of the *Virgin of the Rocks*.[77] The two children, who were cousins, had often appeared together in Florentine art of an earlier generation and were to become a favored theme of Raphael. Like Anne a patron saint of Florence, John enjoyed a privileged place in Florentine art. His baptistery was the building to which the city was most attached and on which were spent the greatest resources of its art. Saint Anne was John's great-aunt, and since his birth from an aged and barren mother, Elizabeth, was regarded as miraculous and somehow exempt from original sin—a parallel to Anne's conception of Mary [78]—his presence in the image of *Anna Metterza* affirmed both the familial and supernatural sense of the theme. In the London cartoon the pairing of the figures effects a correspondence of old and young, as if Anne were the mother of John. Her finger pointing upward, perhaps to indicate the divine origin of Christ, is also a traditional gesture of the Baptist proclaiming the greater one who is to come; it is repeated by Leonardo in a later image of Saint John.[79]

[74] *Op. cit.*, 184.   [75] *Ibid.*, 186.   [76] *Ibid.*, 189.
[77] Cf. R. Eisler, in *Burlington Magazine*, XC (1948), 239.
[78] Hirn, *op. cit.*, 215, 218.
[79] Clark, *op. cit.*, plate 66.

In the course of work on the *Saint Anne*, Leonardo replaced the figure of John by a lamb (fig. 2). Freud sees the change as an artistic necessity, the result of the painter's desire to repair a defect of form in the London cartoon. Even in the final picture in the Louvre, the two women " are fused with one another like badly condensed figures in a dream; it is sometimes difficult to say where Anne ends and Mary begins .... But what seems a fault of composition from the critic's point of view, is justified for the analyst by reference to its hidden sense. The two mothers of his childhood had to fuse for the artist into a single figure." In the London cartoon, " the two maternal figures are even more intimately fused, their outlines are still more uncertain, so that critics, far removed from any concern with interpretation, could say that ' both heads seem to grow from a single trunk '."

After having done the cartoon, Leonardo " felt the need to overcome this dream-like fusion of the two women which corresponded to his childhood memory and to separate the two heads from each other. This he accomplished by detaching Mary's head and upper body from her mother and by having her bend forward. To motivate this shift, the infant Christ had to be moved from his mother's lap to the ground; there was no room then for the little John, who was replaced by the lamb." [80]

It is remarkable that Freud, who is so attentive to details of expression as significant marks of the personality, should explain these striking changes in the family image as purely aesthetic decisions. To Leonardo's contemporaries, the new version appeared as a distinct religious conception. This we know from their comments on another picture of the maternal group in which the changes in question were already largely achieved.

Between the London cartoon and the painting in the Louvre, Leonardo undertook in 1501 an *Anna Metterza* for the altarpiece of the church of the Annunciation in Florence, a house of the Servites— a religious order related to the Franciscans and like them devoted to the doctrine of the Immaculate Conception. Leonardo seems not to have carried out the painting, but he produced, beside some drawings that have survived, a cartoon which is known through a description and a painted copy by Brescianino.[81] When exhibited unfinished to the Florentine public, this cartoon attracted crowds of admiring visitors for two days.

The description, which is the main source of our knowledge of the cartoon, is part of a letter by a vice-general of the Carmelite order, Pietro da Novellara, addressed to Isabella d'Este, who had asked him to obtain for her, while in Florence, a picture by Leonardo. He replied that Leonardo, a slow and unwilling artist, was unlikely to

[80] *Op. cit.*, 186, n. 1.
[81] W. Suida, *Leonardo und sein Kreis* (Munich, 1929), fig. 131.

satisfy her request; but he went on to describe a work of Leonardo's that he had just seen: " a marvellous cartoon of the Christ child about a year old who, as if about to slip out of his mother's arm, grasps a lamb and seems to hold it fast. The mother, half-rising from Saint Anne's lap, is taking the child to draw it from the lamb—that sacrificial animal which signifies the passion of Christ is a lamb which has taken on the sins of the world—while Saint Anne, rising slightly from her seat, seems as if she would hold back her daughter so that she would not separate the child from the lamb; this would perhaps signify that the Church did not want to prevent the passion of Christ since mankind's fate depended upon it." [82]

What the Carmelite (and no doubt other religious observers) interpreted as a theological idea, has for us today a more purely human aspect. We cannot help but see it as an image with deeper psychological meanings. What strikes us is not only the substitution of the lamb for John, but the resulting tension between the figures. In the first cartoon (fig. 1), a stable symmetry rules all the postures and movements; the two children are in a friendly rapport and correspond to the two women, who might be their respective mothers. The picture is a " sacred conversation " in an atmosphere of perfect harmony. In the lost Servite cartoon and in the Louvre painting which is built upon it,[83] the lamb resists the Christ child who mounts it and hugs its sides with both legs. The child looks back to his mother; she restrains him, bending far forward in the effort to hold him; Anne, on whose lap the Virgin sits, looks on in smiling approval. I do not know of an earlier example of the *Anna Metterza* with this complex interplay of the figures or with the motif of the child and the lamb.[84]

In substituting a lamb for John, Leonardo has brought an ambiguity into both the theological and human meanings of the scene. The lamb is a symbol of Christ, the sacrificial host and redeemer, as the Carmelite explained; but it is also the symbol of John who foretells the coming of Christ. In mounting and hugging the lamb, the

[82] For this letter, see John Shapley, " A Lost Cartoon for Leonardo's Madonna with Saint Anne," *Art Bulletin*, VII (1924), 98, 99, and Clark, *op. cit.*, 108. There is also a contemporary poem by Girolamo Casio to the same effect; for the text and translation, see Shapley, *op. cit.*, 100.

[83] Among other changes, the painting reverses the positions of the figures in the cartoon, to judge by the description, the copy and a drawing for the head of Saint Anne (Popham, *op. cit.*, plate 183). It should be said that neither the Carmelite's description nor the copy nor the painting in the Louvre agrees entirely with the account of the Servite cartoon by Vasari who mentions a figure of the infant John playing with the lamb.

[84] In Raphael's adaptation of the Servite cartoon in his painting of the Holy Family (1505) in the Prado Museum, the Virgin helps the child to sit on the lamb, and Joseph, at the side, replaces Anne.

child expresses his "passion" both as the accepted self-sacrifice and as the love of the creature that stands for his cousin John.

Here, following Freud's analysis of Leonardo's personality, one may ask whether in this image of the fatherless Holy Family, Leonardo does not project (and conceal) a narcissistic and homosexual wish in replacing the figure of Christ's playmate John—an ascetic and the victim of an incestuous woman—by the lamb which stands for both John and himself.

The history of the formation of the *Saint Anne* is more complex, and though it may reenforce some of Freud's ideas, it does not support altogether his view of the genesis of the image. In a sketch in Venice, probably earlier than the Servite cartoon, the lamb is drawn at the feet of Anne and Mary who holds the child in her lap—he plays with the lamb's mouth or jaw.[85] The lamb's position is like that of the unicorn at the feet of a seated young woman in a much older drawing by Leonardo—a mediaeval symbol of chastity.[86] On the back of this drawing are several sketches for a composition of the Madonna with the child hugging a cat.[87] It is evident that the elements which make up the original features of the *Saint Anne* in the Louvre—particularly the child with the lamb—had occupied Leonardo's thought for many years before the meeting with Mona Lisa and some of them independently of the theme of Saint Anne.[88]

IV

A disciple of Freud, Dr. Ernst Kris, who brings to psychoanalysis a training and experience as an historian of art, has tried to complete Freud's interpretation by discerning in the hidden emotional grounds of the image the sources of the artistic invention as well. Where Freud saw a defect of composition, Kris assumes a new creative form. "Unity between the three figures was established not only by gestures; they seem to merge into each other since they are inscribed into a pyramidal configuration. By similar devices Leonardo created in several of his paintings compositions which exercised considerable influence on the development of the art of his time."[89] It is not clear whether Dr. Kris is summarizing Freud or drawing from the latter a new consequence for the explanation of Leonardo's style. He is himself aware of the great difficulties in relating "form and content"

[85] Popham, *op. cit.*, pl. 174 A.   [86] *Ibid.*, pl. 27 (British Museum).   [87] *Ibid.*, pl. 11.

[88] Interesting for the Louvre picture is a painting from Botticelli's workshop in the Pitti Palace in Florence: the standing Virgin, with head inclined, holds the nude Christ child who bends far over to embrace the little standing John, clad in what appears to be a sheepskin—Jacques Mesnil, *Sandro Botticelli* (Paris, 1938), pl. XCI and p. 161.

[89] Kris, *Psychoanalytic Explorations in Art* (New York, 1952), 19, 22.

through a theory of their common psychological roots, and he is sceptical of the vulture discovered in Mary's robe. But what seems here to be an advance in the psychoanalytic study of art—which has until now paid little attention to style—is a lapse in historical and aesthetic understanding. The pyramidal form as such is no invention of Leonardo's; what is distinctive in his formal composition lies elsewhere and is the result of a development in the course of his life rather than the outcome of work on a single theme like the Saint Anne.

The older Italian images of *Anna Metterza* show, since the fourteenth century, a compact pyramidal grouping. In these versions all the figures are submitted more or less to the axis of the pyramid; they form a static symmetrical whole, as in Masaccio's great painting; all face the observer, or each has a dominant plane distinct from that of the neighboring figure. Compared with the old types, the novelty of Leonardo's form, later carried further by Michelangelo and Raphael, lies rather in the fact that within the conventional pyramid of three or four figures, each has a complex asymmetry of contrasted forms in depth, often in a foreshortened S, and each person responds actively to another. In older art, a single limb may be moved without affecting the rest of the body; for Leonardo, the body is a self-adjusting system, with an easy flow and cohesion of forms, in which the movement of any part entails the response of all the others. From this comes the charm of a unity which comprises within a stable enclosing form so much play and lability of the parts. (This is not the sum of Leonardo's great originality as a painter; he contributed, besides, a new fullness and subtlety of modelling, a palpable atmosphere, a mysterious light and shadow which point to later art, and the infinitely extended landscape background as a lyrical revelation of mood in counterpoint to the figures.)

In the Louvre painting, the child, looking up at his mother, moves away from her to play with the lamb, at the same time constraining the little beast; Mary pulls the child back to her and in doing so, turns away from Anne; Anne, her lower body directed to the left, looks back to the child at the lower right. In this overlapping and interlocking of bodies, with the progression from the most stable figure of Anne to the most active and divided figure of Christ through Mary's mediating posture, every movement is counterposed to contrasting movements, whether of the figure itself or the neighboring bodies; but together they form a compact unit of a higher order, a family.

It was Leonardo who first developed the exemplary forms of such dynamically balanced composition. Composition here means something imaginative and ideal, one of those fundamental structures or modes of grouping that mark an epoch and become canonical, like an architectural order or poetic form.[90]

Its stages can be followed in Leonardo's successive works. He does not possess it from the beginning of his career. It is rudimentary in the Virgin of the Rocks painted in 1483; it is not yet clearly developed in the first cartoon of Saint Anne; nor is it fully realized in the other drawings of this subject. But it appears with great force in a work which has nothing to do with the maternal theme; the Last Supper, painted in Milan in 1495 to 1497. In this composition, dominated by the central figure of Christ, the twelve apostles are broken up into four groups of three; in each group we see different reactions and inter-relations of three figures who are confronted by the same unspoken question posed by the disturbing words of Christ: One of you shall betray me. It is a work that combines a highly concentrated form—the central Christ, the symmetrical table and architecture in a converging perspective rhythm—with the extraordinarily varied movements of the enclosed figures aroused by the central force, each figure subject to his distinct emotion expressed in gesture and pose, yet clearly a member of a group of three with its own unity of contrasted reactions.

This distinction of character is a Renaissance achievement. It is not only a new approach to the theme of the Last Supper—in spirit more dramatic than liturgical or theological—but a far-reaching conception of collective behavior in which the individual is revealed.

Leonardo's study of the grouping of the apostles was a preparation for the *Saint Anne*. In the London cartoon, the gesture of Anne pointing upward is like the gesture of the first apostle at Christ's left in the Last Supper (although the meaning is different). In the Louvre painting, the overlapping of the bodies, the varied directions and levels of the heads within a group of three figures, recall the three apostles at Christ's right hand.

If one wishes to relate the new form to the psychological content of the *Saint Anne*, the connection will be found, I think, not so much in the process of fusing into a stable pyramid the two mothers who haunted Leonardo's memory since childhood, but rather in the opposite process of giving to the traditional closed group of child and parents an articulation of contrasts which could render the spontaneity and conflicting impulses of the individuals while retaining the family attachment. Whether smoothly harmonized or left in an unresolved state of tortuous involvement, these opposed movements within the idealized individual are a characteristic of High and Late Renaissance art; in the first case they form a classical canon in which

[90] For an excellent account of Leonardo as a composer, see H. Wölfflin, *Die klassische Kunst, Eine Einführung in die italienische Renaissance* (7th ed., Munich, 1924), 20–43.

the body is stable, though active, and relaxed, though confined; in the other case, they anticipate the Mannerist style of the mid-sixteenth century, where the classical form appears strained or affected, the result of an effort that deforms and depresses the individual, who is an increasingly introverted or tragic figure.

In spite of Leonardo's refinement of drawing and search for graceful forms, I do not believe that the new classical ideal is perfectly realized in the *Saint Anne*. There remains an aspect of the rigid and artificial in the group, most evident in the abrupt pairing of Anne and Mary, with the sharp contrast of their profile and frontal forms. It may be explained, perhaps, by Leonardo's commitment to the traditional mediaeval type of *Anna Metterza*, in conflict with his own tendency towards variation, distinctness and movement. Throughout his life, he conceived his more iconic compositions around a dominant, isolated, central figure—as in the *Adoration of the Magi*, the *Virgin of the Rocks*, and the *Last Supper*—and therefore found in the *Saint Anne*, with its two mothers of equal weight, an especially refractory theme. He could not adopt the solution of Northern artists who placed the two women side by side, with a little Christ between them. It is this discrepancy between the inherited type and the mature goals of Leonardo's art that accounts in part for the suggestion of later Mannerist art in the *Saint Anne*.

V

In a general article that Freud wrote not long after his study of Leonardo, speaking of the significance of his researches for various fields, he remarked that " the intimate personality of the artist which lies hidden behind his work can be divined from this work with more or less accuracy." [91] It is obvious that for this purpose all the available works of an artist must be considered. In interpreting Leonardo's art, Freud examines, however, mainly pictures that represent women. The *Adoration of the Magi* is mentioned as an example of his neurotic difficulty in finishing a picture, and the *Last Supper* as a painting executed with a characteristic slowness and destined to ruin by his experimentation with technique. The content of these great pictures is nowhere taken into account. We have the impression in reading Freud that Leonardo's fantasy as a painter was bounded by soft images of women and children and effeminate youths. Another side of Leonardo, evident in his virile images of men, is ignored. There we see him as an artist with a singular vision of force.

For the townhall of Florence, Leonardo painted in 1504–1505 a mural picture of the Battle of Anghiari, a Florentine victory over the

[91] " Das Interesse an der Psychoanalyse (1913)," *GW*, VIII, 407.

Pisans, which has come down to us only in descriptions, sketches and copies.[92] Before the most important copy, done by Rubens,[93] we are astonished by Leonardo's love of violence, his ferocious power in rendering the impact of savagely fighting figures. Only a part of the work is preserved in Rubens' copy—a struggle between opposed horsemen; few Renaissance artists have represented the terrible fury of hand-to-hand combat as vividly as Leonardo. Vasari noted before the original that "rage, hatred and revenge are no less visible in the men than in the horses."

From the beginning of his career, Leonardo was passionately interested in the horse. (For the Duke of Milan he made a silver lyre in the form of a horse's head, a reconciliation of the strong and the sweet.) The background of the early, unfinished painting of the *Adoration of the Magi* contains wonderful rearing horses, ridden and constrained by pagan, athletic figures of proud young men—a beautiful contrast to the venerable types in the foreground, humble and passive, adoring the infant Christ.[94]

Important for this side of his art was the association with Verrocchio which I have mentioned before. Leonardo's versatility as artist and technician owes much, it has been surmised, to his early apprenticeship to Verrocchio; this master was sculptor, painter, goldsmith, architect and engineer, and at home in other crafts as well. The emulation of his teacher appears above all in Leonardo's tragic attempts to produce an equestrian statue in bronze. Verrocchio had created in the 1480s a grandiose bronze horseman, the famous *Colleoni* in Venice. It was a work carried out stubbornly; he had to fight the decision of the Venetians that he should make only the horse and another artist, the man. In the end Verrocchio did both. Twice in Milan Leonardo undertook to carry out equestrian monuments in bronze, one of Prince Trivulzio and the other of Duke Francesco Sforza. Only some drawings have survived; but from these we can judge Leonardo's passionate feeling for the heroic.[95]

In his old age, Leonardo produced furious drawings of cataclysms, overwhelming forces unleashed upon mankind, a mountain falling upon a village, the world coming to an end with enormous turbulence— works of an impassioned, destructive imagination, employing a knowledge of science to express a titanic revulsion against humanity.[96] Drawing them, he seems like the old, despairing Lear invoking the elements of the storm.

Freud has in fact remarked in Leonardo the traces of a converted sadistic impulse.[97] He refers to his known vegetarianism and Vasari's

---

[92] Popham, *op. cit.*, pl. 191–201.   [93] Clark, *op. cit.*, pl. 44.
[94] *Ibid.*, pl. 13, 14, 16, and Popham, *op. cit.*, pl. 30–37.   [95] Popham, *op. cit.*, pl. 91–102.
[96] *Ibid.*, pl. 292–296; Clark, *op. cit.*, pl. 62–65.   [97] *Op. cit.*, 134, 135, 204.

engaging picture of the young genius walking through the marketplace of Florence, buying caged birds in order to release them, as evidences of a hidden childhood sadism. Of the abundant overt examples of his love of violence, Freud mentions only his drawing of hanged men and his interest in military engineering. But is Leonardo's kindness to animals so surely a sign of repressed sadistic feeling? The story of his freeing caged birds may be explained differently. In folklore and in folk custom, the release of a captive bird is believed to bring good luck. As late as the 1860's, people of all classes in Paris came to the market to buy birds and free them, a magic sacrifice that promised success, whether in love or business or examinations.[98] The scientific bent of Leonardo and his intellectual independence did not free him from popular beliefs; his note-books record without criticism some odd superstitions. But the episode described by Vasari had possibly to do with his study of flight. One may note too that on a sheet covered with scientific observations about the atmosphere and body surfaces, he has drawn a bird sitting in a cage, with the inscription: "the thoughts turn towards hope."[99]

Leonardo's abstention from animal flesh may be regarded as a medical belief, sustained by philosophical conviction; it was inspired perhaps by ancient authors in vogue among the Florentine NeoPlatonists. He might have read in Porphyry's treatise *De Abstinentia ab Esu Animalium* (IV, 16) that the wisest of the Persian magi abstained from meat.

The aggressive feelings of Leonardo are better illustrated by the unconstrained fantasies of violence in both his writings and pictures and by his misanthropic taste for the ugly, the deformed and caricatural in the human face than by his vegetarianism and his release of captive birds. From the beginning of his career as an artist, Leonardo produced beside the tender images others of a violent and threatening character. Vasari records among his early works the painting of a hybrid monster, like a Medusa's head, compounded of the forms of insects and reptiles, and secretly designed to terrify his father.

A more complete psychoanalytic study of Leonardo would have to take into account two other pictures ignored by Freud. One is the *Leda and the Swan* (known only through copies and some original drawings)[100] which contradicts Freud's statement that Leonardo betrays an extreme repression in his total avoidance of erotic subjects.[101]

---

[98] Cf. Paul Sébillot, *Le Folk-lore de France*, III, *La Faune et le Flore* (Paris, 1906), 190.

[99] *Notebooks*, ed. MacCurdy, 61 and note 1, 372, 373.

[100] Clark, *op. cit.*, pl. 41; Heydenreich, *op. cit.*, pl. 68; Popham, *op. cit.*, pl. 208.

[101] *Op. cit.*, 136. Lomazzo, a 16th century theoretician and critic of art, speaks of Leonardo's "composizioni lascive" (Beltrami, *Documenti*, 196, no. 21).

The other is the great unfinished *Jerome* in the Vatican,[102] a powerful image of masculine ascetic feeling. It is not, like Botticelli's *Jerome*, the scholarly saint in his study, but the tormented, penitent hermit in the wilderness, beating his bared breast with a stone, while the lion before him roars with pain from the thorn in his foot.

There is in Freud's account an intimation of the masculine side of Leonardo, but he does not attempt to investigate it seriously. To explain why his art is so uneven and why he cannot finish his work, Freud points to the relations with his father. Since Leonardo identified with him at a certain age, he had to treat his own children—his paintings and sculptures—as his father had treated him, by abandoning his work.[103] This analogy will convince few readers. However, Freud observes too that in identifying with his father, the young Leonardo strove to copy and excel him; he passed then through a period of intense creativeness which was renewed later when he enjoyed the support of a substitute father, his patron Sforza, the Duke of Milan. His great works were produced in those two periods of fatherly attachment. But since his sublimation to art, the argument continues, was unaccompanied by real sexual activity, which is the pattern of all creativeness, Leonardo could not sustain his work for long.[104] In the late 1490's and towards 1500, it deteriorates more and more.

At the age of fifty, through some obscure biological process, there takes place, according to Freud, a reactivation of the erotic energies. In Leonardo, this change coincided with his meeting with Mona Lisa whose personality, concentrated outwardly in her smile, revived the artist's childhood memories. Through the re-erotizing of his imagination, he was again able to produce masterpieces. But since he was still sexually repressed, and had lost the support of both the Duke and his father (who died in 1504), the reawakening was short-lived. He turned to science, an interest compatible with sexual repression and depending on a sublimation that belongs to an earlier period of infancy than the sublimation to art.[106]

[102] Clark, *op. cit.*, pl. 18.

[103] *Op. cit.*, 192, 193. On Leonardo's relation to his father, see my note "Two Slips of Leonardo and a Slip of Freud," *Psychoanalysis* (Feb. 1956).

[104] *Op. cit.*, 206. The reader interested in the problem of the effect of repression on the artist will find a strong statement of a view contrary to Freud's in Van Gogh's letter of August 1888 to the painter Emile Bernard (Vincent Van Gogh, *Letters to Emile Bernard*, edited and translated by Douglas Lord (Cooper), New York, 1938, 70ff.). [105] *Op. cit.*, 207.

[106] For Freud's account of Leonardo's sublimation to science, there is a parallel in the life of Newton, a posthumous child whose mother married again when he was three; after that he was brought up by his maternal grandmother. For a survey and criticism of psychoanalytic ideas concerning sublimation, see H. B. Levey (Lee), "A Critique of the Theory of Sublimation," *Psychiatry*, II, 1939.

More than once in his study of Leonardo, Freud has warned the reader that psychoanalysis does not pretend to explain genius or the grounds of excellence in art. But he believed, as he said elsewhere, that psychoanalysis "could reveal the factors which awaken genius and the sort of subject-matter it is fated to choose." [107] He cannot assert this, however, without risking some judgments about the quality of single works of art, apart from the accepted estimations of the artist as a whole. For how can he speak otherwise of the early experiences as factors that facilitate or block the action of an organically rooted power? To construct his picture of Leonardo's spiritual fortunes, Freud, we have seen, must become a critic of art and commit himself to judgments about the better and worse in the painter's career, his good and bad periods, and he must venture, too, some opinions about the dates of works which professional historians were still unable to decide.[108]

From all this the reader can judge the difficulties of a psychoanalytic approach to an artist, which seeks to explain the content of his art, his qualities of style, and the vicissitudes of his work, as well as to infer from the paintings the personality and early life of the artist. Nevertheless, Freud was able, thanks to his theory and method, and perhaps even more to his deep sympathy for the tragic and problematic in Leonardo, to pose altogether new and important questions about his personality, questions which were unsuspected by earlier writers and to which no better answers than Freud's have yet been given.

I believe this study of Freud's book points to weaknesses which will be found in other works by psychoanalysts in the cultural fields: the habit of building explanations of complex phenomena on a single datum and the too little attention given to history and the social situation in dealing with individuals and even with the origin of customs, beliefs, and institutions.

In appealing so often to history in this paper, I do not mean to oppose historical or sociological explanations to psychological ones. The former, too, are in part psychological; the terms used in describing social behavior sum up what we know of individuals, although historians make little use of Freud's psychology of the unconscious. But if all historical explanations depended on psychology, we could

[107] Freud's foreword to Marie Bonaparte, *Edgar Poe* (Paris, 1933).
[108] Freud's judgment of Leonardo's productivity and quality should be compared with that of Clark (*op. cit.*, 107); speaking of the admiration of the Florentines for Leonardo's Servite cartoon of *Anna Metterza*, he says: "Such popular enthusiasm would hardly have been possible in Milan, and helps us to understand why the five years he spent in Florence were more productive than the preceding eighteen years spent in the north of Italy."

not correctly apply the psychological concepts, whether psychoanalytic or those of behavioral psychology or of the everyday commonsense understanding of human nature, unless we knew the state of the individual and his human environment—data that cannot be supplied without historical study. Where Freud has misinterpreted Leonardo, and he admits more than once in his book how speculative his attempt is, it was in part because he ignored or misread certain facts. His false conclusions do not imply that psychoanalytic theory is wrong; the book on Leonardo, a brilliant *jeu d'esprit*, is no real test of this theory, which here has been faultily applied. Just as a theory of physics would not be disproved by an experiment with incomplete or incorrectly recorded data, so Freud's general account of psychological development and the unconscious processes is untouched by the possible misapplications to Leonardo. His principles may for other reasons turn out to be inadequate and then be replaced by better ones; these will be usable, even if incomplete, in a new psychological study of Leonardo. But to apply them fruitfully, the analyst will need a fuller knowledge of Leonardo's life and art and of the culture of his time.[109]

---

[109] Since this was written there has appeared the article by R. Richard Wohl and Harry Trosman, " A Retrospect of Freud's Leonardo, an Assessment of a Psychoanalytic Classic," *Psychiatry*, XVIII (1955), 27–39. The authors correct Freud's mistranslation of the text concerning the kite, but are unaware of Maclagan's article of 1923 (see note 10 above); they propose no fresh interpretation of the reminiscence, but criticize Freud's theory of the genesis of homosexuality in the light of more recent psychoanalytic studies. Freud's error about the vulture has also been noted by Ernest Jones in the second volume of his biography of Freud (New York, 1955), after a personal communication from James Strachey (348), but he does not evaluate the consequences of the correction for the book as a whole. It seems that Jung, too, had discovered the outlines of a vulture in the painting of Saint Anne (348). Finally, of great interest for the personal significance of Leonardo to Freud, whose combination of scientific and artistic gifts has often been noted, is the fact, reported by Jones, that the Leonardo book was Freud's favorite among his own works.

I must mention also the book by Giuseppina Fumagalli, *Eros di Leonardo* (Milan, 1952), which I could not consult until now. The author wishes to demonstrate, against Freud, Leonardo's sexual normality and the rich erotic content of his art. She observes, after " Havelock " (a confusion of Havelock Ellis and Maclagan?—Ellis, in reviewing Freud's book in the *Journal of Mental Science* in 1910 did not catch the error), that the bird of Leonardo's memory was no vulture. She argues at length that Leonardo was not homosexual, explaining the episode of 1476 by the customs of the time and by Leonardo's universal curiosity and desire for all experience.

The Mona Lisa in the History of Taste

by GEORGE BOAS

Reprinted from the *Journal of the History of Ideas*—Vol. I, No. 2, pp. 207-224

The search for aesthetic standards by means of which any work of art can be finally judged would seem to presuppose either that every such work is an unchanging entity, or that, regardless of whether it changes or not, it should always be judged in the same way. Neither of these presuppositions appears tenable to the writer of this paper, who holds, on the contrary, that works of art are not the locus of one value, known as "beauty" or something similar, but are rather multivalent, that certain of their values are experienced by some persons, others by others, and that there is no *a priori* method—except that of fiat—of determining which of the many values are properly "aesthetic." One objection usually raised against this position is that there happen to be some works of art which "the judgment of posterity" has always held to be admirable or "great," and that one has only to examine their characteristics to discover what the distinguishing marks of great works of art are. The Parthenon, the *Aeneid, Hamlet,* and so on, it is maintained, have always enjoyed a high reputation. They are great by almost universal consent; or, if there have been periods when they were not highly esteemed, that is because the people of those periods had poor taste.

It cannot be denied that there are works of art which have almost always been greatly admired. (For the sake of the argument one may neglect those times when they were not discussed at all, having been overlooked for some reason or other.) But having admitted that, one faces the question whether the name, *Hamlet,* or the Parthenon, or the *Aeneid,* has always meant the same thing. Physically, the words or the shapes of stone in which they are embodied have changed little, though the little is not without some importance; but the physical basis of these and other works of art is only a small part of them. More important is what people have looked for in them and either found or not found. Thus the *Aeneid* as a Roman epic differs from the *Aeneid* as an instrument of magic, and *Hamlet* as a chivalric tragedy of revenge differs from *Hamlet* as a Freudian drama. It may be argued that the work of art as the artist intended it is the real work of art, and that we should suspend judgment until we have recaptured it in its primitive state. In most cases such a quest is probably futile, for we often have no way of knowing what an artist intended, and in any event we can, for the most part, only reconstruct what he intended from what we ourselves find. And that is to no small extent dependent upon our education and our original nature. Moreover, to recapture through study an artist's intention is different from reacting directly to a work of art; and the professor of English literature who, having studied Elizabethan language and customs and theatrical practice and the biography of Shakespeare, reads *Hamlet,* is not psychologically identical with the Elizabethan spectator who went to the theater and saw *Hamlet* during what may be called its lifetime. Whatever else Shakespeare may have been up to, he was certainly not producing plays for professors of English to study three hundred years after his death. We may reasonably conclude that to define the work of art as the work intended by the artist gives us only the slenderest clues to appropriate standards for judging it.

The purpose of this paper is to take one of the works of art which have been most admired until recent times, and to examine briefly what critics or commentators of different periods have said about it. From what they said we hope to be able to infer what they were looking for. We are not so much interested in knowing why they admired the work of art as in knowing what they saw in it. It will be found that in at least this one case the work of art was identical with itself throughout history in name only. We have chosen as our example Leonardo's *Mona Lisa.*

I

The *Mona Lisa,* it should be recalled, is usually considered to be a portrait of the wife of Francesco del Giocondo, painted between 1503 and 1506. There is no conclusive evidence that it was intended as an allegory, though the background does not put that beyond the bounds of possibility.[1] No mention is made of it in the artist's literary remains, so that we do not know at what the artist himself was aiming. We do, however, know what he thought the proper fashion of representing women was, and that will be pointed out later.

[1] Everything about this famous picture has been disputed. We have accepted the traditional name of the sitter, but A. Venturi in the *Enciclopedia Italiana* maintains that she was Costanza d'Avalos and that the misty background did have allegorical significance. See his section in the article on Leonardo. L. Roger-Milès, in his *Léonard de Vinci et les Jocondes,* 1923, pp. 68 ff., maintains that it is not even a portrait.

Leonardo's contemporaries apparently did not consider the *Mona Lisa* his most important work. Several accounts of Italian painting, written during Leonardo's life or a little later, fail even to mention it. This is true of *Il Libro di Antonio Billi*[2] and of an anonymous work written during the forties of the sixteenth century.[3] Paolo Giovio, writing after Leonardo's death, says simply that he painted the portrait of Mona Lisa, "wife of Francesco del Giocondo, which was bought by King Francis I, it is said, for 4000 *scudi*."[4] In the short *Vita* he mentions the *Last Supper* and tells the story of Louis XII's desire to cut it out of the wall on which it was painted, and the *Virgin and Saint Anne*, but does not mention the *Mona Lisa*. There is nothing here, except the unusually high price, which is of interest. The same may be said of the comment of Raffaelo Borghini, made in 1584, that the portrait was such *che non puo l'arte far davantaggio*.[5] More to the point is the criticism of Lomazzo, who praises it along with portraits by Raphael and Andrea del Sarto as peculiarly adapted to its subject.[6]

The most influential of the earlier comments on the *Mona Lisa* is that of Vasari, which established a tradition. This paragraph is the best known of the classical statements, and it was apparently the source of most of the anecdotes repeated in later times about the picture. It was first published in 1550, some forty-odd years after the portrait was painted. The passage runs as follows:

> Whoever shall desire to see how far art can imitate nature, may do so to perfection in this head, wherein every peculiarity that could be depicted by the utmost subtlety of the pencil has been faithfully reproduced. The eyes have the lustrous brightness and moisture which is seen in life, and around them are those pale, red, and slightly livid circles, also proper to nature, with the lashes, which can only be copied as they are with the greatest difficulty; the eyebrows also are represented with the closest exactitude, where fuller and where more thinly set, with the separate hairs delineated as they issue from the skin, every turn being followed, and all the pores exhibited in a manner that could not be more natural than it is: the nose, with its beautiful and delicately roseate nostrils, might be easily believed to be alive; the mouth, admirable in its outline, has the lips uniting the rose-tints of

[2] See de Fabriczy, *Arch. Stor. Ital.*, ser. V, tom. 7.

[3] *Ibid.*

[4] See Tiraboschi. *Stor. della lett. Ital.*, T. VI, p. iv, lib. iii, c. 7, xxxii (Venice, 1823, VI, 4–5, p. 1602).

[5] See *Il Riposo*, Florence, 1584, p. 370 f.

[6] G. P. Lomazzo, *Trattato dell' arte della pittura*, etc., Milan, 1584–85, p. 434.

their colour with that of the face, in the utmost perfection, and the carnation of the cheek does not appear to be painted, but truly of flesh and blood: he who looks earnestly at the pit of the throat cannot but believe that he sees the beating of the pulses, and it may be truly said that this work is painted in a manner well calculated to make the boldest master tremble, and astonishes all who behold it, however well accustomed to the marvels of art. Mona Lisa was exceedingly beautiful, and while Leonardo was painting her portrait, he took the precaution of keeping some one constantly near her, to sing or play on instruments, or to jest and otherwise amuse her, to the end that she might continue cheerful, and so that her face might not exhibit the melancholy expression often imparted by painters to the likenesses they take. In this portrait of Leonardo's on the contrary there is so pleasing an expression, and a smile so sweet, that while looking at it one thinks it rather divine than human, and it has ever been esteemed a wonderful work, since life itself could exhibit no other appearance.[7]

There are two important features in this criticism: first, it is Leonardo's skill that is the subject of admiration, rather than the effect of the picture upon the observer, or the "self-expression" of the artist, or a symbol of something called "the times"; second, the painter's skill is supposed to be directed towards reproducing a natural object as faithfully as possible.

To think of the artist as a craftsman who learns and applies a technique is, of course, not unusual in the history of criticism. Even the most fervent admirer of Croce would admit that some artists are more skillful technicians than others. But to focus one's appreciation upon this has been by no means a universal practice among critics. Forgetting, for the purposes of this paper, the past history of such an attitude, as seen, for instance, in the elder Pliny, it is not improbable that technical skill became particularly interesting in the Renaissance, when *homo faber* began experimenting and inventing as he had not done since Alexandrian days.

But one may praise an artist's skill and yet not believe that it was oriented towards a reproduction of "nature." One may admire the exquisite technique of an Odilon Redon, for instance, or a Braque, and say nothing whatsoever about the likeness of its result to anything natural. One may admire the technique of a Byzantine fresco

[7] Giorgio Vasari, *Lives of the Most Eminent Painters, Sculptors, and Architects*, tr. by Mrs. Jonathan Foster, London, 1876, II, p. 384 f. It is perhaps worth noting that in the eighteenth century Leonardo was to be blamed by at least one writer for too great fidelity to nature, uncorrected by a study of the antique. See [Dezallier d'Argenville,] *Abrégé de la Vie des plus Fameux Peintres*, 1745, p. 74.

in which the "natural" is almost completely recreated and transformed. The idea that "nature" was of interest and importance in her own right belongs to a period in which men seek to observe facts and record them, and think that observation and record are good in themselves. Vasari, who was himself a painter, is perhaps more sensitive to technical excellence than a critic who has no experience in producing works of art. His own paintings are, like those of most of his contemporaries, admirably skillful in perspective and other tricks of illusion. It is therefore possible, though not probable, that he was simply erecting his own type of skill into a standard for all artists.

It would, however, be sheer pedantry to attempt to prove what everyone knows, namely, that the Renaissance in Italy was marked by an almost religious regard for what later became natural science, and by a delight in the arts which helped man understand the things of nature.[8] The whole matter has been clearly and succinctly told by Burckhardt in his *The Civilization of the Renaissance in Italy*, and requires no retelling. But it may be said that the Italians of this period were the first men to rediscover natural beauty, to write biographies again, as the Alexandrians did, to describe in detail the human face and form, to collect strange animals and even strange people. It is in keeping with this taste that the sketch-books of Jacopo Bellini, of Leonardo, of Pisanello, and of their contemporaries are filled with drawings of animals, flowers, clouds, mountains, and other natural things.

But "fidelity to nature" is a notoriously equivocal formula. The multiple meanings of "nature" and its derivatives have been discriminated by A. O. Lovejoy and we shall not attempt to expand upon his treatment of the subject.[9] But we must notice what the phrase meant to Vasari and earlier to Leonardo. In the passage

[8] As early as 1493 Bellincioni had written a sonnet on another portrait by Leonardo, that of Cecilia Gallerani, the mistress of Ludovico Sforza. The sonnet plays upon the rivalry between art and nature and begins,

Di chi ti adiri? A chi invidia Natura?
Al Vinci che ha ritratto une tua stella . . .

(For the whole sonnet, see *Le Rime di Bernardo Bellincioni*, ed. by Pietro Fanfani, Bologna, 1878.) The idea is, of course, a literary commonplace and for that very reason of peculiar interest. The portrait, it may be added, seems to have disappeared. A similar idea is found in the Latin verses on a portrait of Lucrezia Crivelli in *The Notebooks of Leonardo da Vinci*, 1938, II, 394.

[9] See *Primitivism in Antiquity*, pp. 447 ff., and "Nature as Aesthetic Norm," *Mod. Lang. Notes*, XLII (1927), pp. 444 ff.

quoted from the biographer and critic, one observes that the artist is praised for reproducing the likeness of his sitter as Apelles is said to have reproduced the likeness of his grapes. Just as the birds in the classical instance pecked at the painted grapes, so the observer of the *Mona Lisa* believes the original to be before him, with beating pulses and living eyes. But before the passage is over one finds that Leonardo is praised also for painting the woman with a pleasant and smiling expression, as she appeared when listening to cheerful music or jesting talk; so that "while looking at it one thinks it rather divine than human."

How much literary exaggeration is expressed in these last words and how much they echo a Neoplatonic strain is hard to tell. Even in Leonardo, whose interest in reproducing natural objects led to those amazing anatomical and botanical and geological drawings, there are Neoplatonic elements. If he says, on the one hand, "Wisdom is the daughter of experience," and backs it up with minutely detailed studies of what he observes, he says on the other, "Nature is full of infinite causes which were never set forth in experience."[10] If he says, "O marvellous Necessity, thou with supreme reason constrainest all effects to be the direct result of their causes, and by a supreme and irrevocable law every natural action obeys thee by the shortest possible process," he also says, "Nature being capricious and taking pleasure in creating and producing a continuous succession of lives and forms . . . ."[11] Which of these Natures he saw as he drew his sketches, there is now no saying. But the probability is that most of his contemporaries saw in the sketches after they were drawn the capriciously creative and fertile Nature rather than the mechanistic and purely geometrical.

For a hundred or more years after Vasari there is little or no mention of the *Mona Lisa*. According to the French historian, Lemonnier,[12] Leonardo and his Italian *confrères* who were called to France by Francis I "furent traités avec toutes sortes d'égards et reçurent des appointements en rapport avec leur réputation." There was even circulated the old story that Leonardo died in the King's arms, a story now discredited.[13] But although more of his

[10] *Notebooks*, I, 85 and 77, respectively.

[11] *Ibid.*, I, 253 and 80 respectively. For a denial of the presence of Neoplatonism in Leonardo, see E. Panofsky, *Studies in Iconology*, 1939, p. 182. The writer of this paper is preparing a study of "nature" and allied terms in Leonardo.

[12] In Lavisse's *Histoire de France*, V, i, 316.

[13] See L. Roger-Milès, *op. cit.*, pp. 15 f. The story, as is well known, dates from the time of Vasari.

authentic pictures belonged to the crown—and now to the French Republic—than to any other single collector, most French writings of the sixteenth, seventeenth, and even eighteenth centuries are silent about him.[14] He is not mentioned in the letters of Marguerite d'Angoulême,[15] in the works of Rabelais, Montaigne—not even in his *Journal de Voyage*—nor the Pleiade; the courtiers, who might have seen at least the *Mona Lisa,* say nothing that we have been able to discover of either the picture or its author; even Louis Leroy, whose *De la Vicissitude ou variété des choses de l'univers* (1579) lists the painters whose works have raised his times to eminence, omits Leonardo's name. One possible reason for this is that the *Mona Lisa* belonged to the King and therefore not many people had the chance to see it. But the most famous pictures and sculptures of the time were made familiar to the interested public by engravings, and if Leonardo had captured the imagination of Frenchmen, his works would doubtless have been both known and spoken of, as those of Raphael were.[16]

In the middle of the seventeenth century, Leonardo's name and the *Mona Lisa* emerge once more. Père Dan, who made a catalogue of the works of art at Fontainebleau, calls it the *premier en estime, comme une merveille de la peinture.*[17] In whose estimation it ranked first and why it was considered a marvel are not revealed. Félibien, somewhat later, continues the Vasari tradition.

> This is one of the most finished of his works. It is said that he took so much pleasure in working on it that he spent four months on it, and that

[14] Though Poussin drew the illustrations for the edition of the *Trattato* which appeared in the middle of the seventeenth century, Leonardo was not so highly esteemed as Raphael, for instance, or even some of the lesser painters. *Cf.* A. Fontaine, *Les doctrines d'art en France*, 1909, p. 3.

[15] The sister of his great French patron, who, according to Roger-Milès, *op. cit.,* p. 65, is portrayed in Leonardo's (?) *Marriage of Saint Catherine.*

[16] The portrait could only have been seen by persons admitted to the "gilt cabinet" at Fontainebleau, which would have required special permission. It was removed to Versailles by Louis XIV, probably after 1694, the last date on which it appears in the inventories of Fontainebleau (See *La Grande Encyclopédie,* XVIII, p. 950). It was not exhibited in the Louvre until after the Revolution. It does not appear to have been engraved until the nineteenth century. For its history in France, see the catalogue of the Louvre by Georges Lafenestre and Eugène Richtenberger, tr. by B. H. Dausseron, p. 56.

[17] *Trésor des Merveilles de Fontainbleau* (1642), quoted by Rigollot, *Cat. de l'oeuvre de Léonard de Vinci,* 1849, pp. 65 ff. Cassiano del Pozzo in 1625 saw the painting and commented on its bad condition. See Müntz, *Léonard de Vinci,* 1899, p. 421.

while he was painting this lady there was always someone near her who sang or played some musical instrument, so as to keep her joyful and prevent her from assuming that melancholy air which comes over one easily when one is inactive and motionless.

Truly, said Pymandre, if I may give my opinion, the time which he put into it was well spent, for I have never seen anything more finished or more expressive. There is so much grace and so much sweetness in the eyes and features of this face, that it appears to be alive. When one looks at this portrait, one would say it was a real woman who takes pleasure in being seen.

It is true, I replied, that Leonardo appears to have taken particular care to finish it well. And Francis I considered this picture to be one of the most finished products of this painter, wished to own it, and paid four thousand *écus* for it.[18]

The excellence of Leonardo's artistry is judged in this passage by its "finish" in the representation of a gentle and sweet woman's face. The time given to the work, four months, becomes a matter of the greatest interest to subsequent critics, who vary it as they will. Vasari had said that Leonardo "loitered" over it for four years—not months—and then had left it unfinished. Lanzi, pointing out the unfinished state of most of Leonardo's pictures, continues by saying that the impression of lack of finish is attributable to the artist's having left certain portions of his pictures less perfectly finished than others. This deficiency, he says, cannot be detected always by the best judges. "The portrait, for instance, of Mona Lisa Gioconda, . . . was minutely examined by Mariette in the collection of the king of France, and was declared to be carried to so high a degree of finish that it was impossible to surpass it."[19] Stendhal passes on the story, saying that the artist "never considered it finished."[20] Delecluze reduces the time to three years.[21] The story continues to our own day through Houssaye, the American Moses F. Sweetser,

[18] André Félibien, *Entretiens sur les vies et sur les ouvrages des plus excellens Peintres anciens et modernes*, 2d ed., 1685–1688, I, 193 f.

[19] Luigi Lanzi, *The History of Painting in Italy*, tr. by Thomas Roscoe, new ed. rev., 1853. The history was first published in 1789 and was considered for many years authoritative. It was translated and revised by the Reverend G. W. D. Evans in 1848. In translation the passage appears, "the labor of four years, and, after all, left unfinished." Mariette was the author of the *Abecedario de Pierre Jean Mariette*, which I have not seen.

[20] *Hist. de la Peinture en Italie*, 1817, I, 223 f.

[21] *Léonard de Vinci*, 1841, p. 29.

his contemporary, Mrs. Charles W. Heaton, Gabriel Séailles, Mantz, Edward McCurdy, E. V. Lucas, and even Elbert Hubbard.[22]

II

For some three hundred years no one appears to have seen anything mysterious about this painting. It was the portrait of a certain merchant's wife in a cheerful mood, and what was found extraordinary in it was its fidelity to nature. But a merchant's wife is still a woman, and women began to occupy a curious position in many early nineteenth-century minds. They had previously been cruel, coquettish, vain, deceitful, gentle, fickle, tender, weak, but they had rarely been enigmatic. On the contrary, men knew them only too well. But the early nineteenth century introduced a new woman into the history of ideas—*la femme fatale*.[23]

The *femme fatale* emerged with Romanticism. She was all sensation and feeling, as against masculine rationality. She captured men by her apparent passivity, lying in wait like a fascinating serpent for the flitting bird who was the male. Whether the Romanticists knew it or not, she could trace her ancestry back to the Eve of Philo Judaeus. The Romantic critics, whether they were engaged in interpreting paintings or poetry, treated their works of art as if they were hieroglyphs. Each had a hidden "meaning" which only the initiated could uncover. To be one of the initiated, one must have a peculiar kind of sensitivity, an eye that not merely saw the perceptual screen of things but penetrated to something called the reality behind it. Such metaphors in practice meant that the critic was not to record what he saw, but to let his imagination freely play about the work of art and to report what it constructed.

What Vasari was for the pre-nineteenth century critic, Théophile Gautier and Walter Pater became for their contemporaries and successors. Both started a tradition—in apparent independence of

[22] See respectively, *Hist. de Léonard de Vinci*, pp. 439 f; *Leonardo da Vinci*, Boston, 1879, p. 59; *Leonardo da Vinci and his Works*, 1874, p. 51 f; *Léonard de Vinci*, 1892, p. 140; *Leonardo da Vinci*, 1898, II, 158; *Leonardo da Vinci*, 1904, p. 113; *Leonardo da Vinci*, 1926, p. 9; *Little Journeys to the Homes of Eminent Artists*, 1902, X, ii, p. 46. Elbert Hubbard translated the sum of 4000 *scudi* into eighty thousand dollars. Stendhal had been content with forty five thousand francs.

[23] This is, of course, a commonplace, but see Mario Praz, *The Romantic Agony*, 1933, ch. IV, esp. pp. 243 ff. The reader also would do well to complete what follows in our text by pursuing Mr. Berenson's suggestion of the influence of Lavater and the other physiognomists. See his *The Study and Criticism of Italian Art*, 1916, p. 24.

each other—which has not died even to-day. Gautier's paragraph was the earlier published.

Leonardo da Vinci retained the finesse of the Gothic period while animating it with a spirit entirely modern. . . . The faces of Vinci seem to come from the upper spheres to be reflected in a glass or rather in a mirror of tarnished steel, where their image remains eternally fixed by a secret similar to that of the daguerreotype. We have seen these faces before, but not upon this earth: in some previous existence perhaps, which they recall to us vaguely. How explain otherwise the strange, almost magic charm which the portrait of Mona Lisa has for even the least enthusiastic natures? Is it her beauty? Many faces by Raphael and other painters are more correct. She is no longer even young; her age must be that loved by Balzac, thirty years; through the subtle modelling we divine the beginnings of fatigue, and life's finger has left its imprint on this peachlike cheek. Her costume, because of the darkening of the pigments, has become almost that of a widow; a crêpe veil falls with the hair along her face; but the expression, wise, deep, velvety, full of promise, attracts you irresistibly and intoxicates you, while the sinuous, serpentine mouth, turned up at the corners, in the violet shadows, mocks you with so much gentleness, grace, and superiority, that you feel suddenly intimidated, like a schoolboy before a duchess. The head with its violet shadows, seen as through black gauze, arrests one's dreams as one leans on the museum railing before her, haunts one's memory like a symphonic theme. Beneath the form *expressed,* one feels a thought which is vague, infinite, *inexpressible,* like a musical idea. One is moved, troubled, images *already seen* pass before one's eyes, voices whose note seems familiar whisper languorous secrets in one's ears; repressed desires, hopes which drive one to despair stir painfully in the shadow shot with sunbeams; and you discover that your melancholy arises from the fact that la Joconde three hundred years ago greeted your avowal of love with this same mocking smile which she retains even to-day on her lips.[24]

Here simple fidelity to nature has completely disappeared; the eternal feminine has taken its place. The *Mona Lisa* is not the portrait of a young woman; she has ripened through experience. She recalls past lives, stirs up repressed desires, mocks you with her smile. At once a new strain enters into French criticism. Whereas the earlier critics had seen sweetness and gentleness, the later began to see something more troubling. Even Taine, who was scarcely a

[24] Théophile Gautier *et al., Les Dieux et les demi-dieux de la peinture,* [1863], p. 24 f. The article on Leonardo first appeared in 1858. For further information about it, see Spoelberch de Lovenjoul, *Hist. des oeuvres de Théophile Gautier,* pp. 160, 262 ff.

victim of "the Romantic agony," found the famous smile "doubting, licentious, Epicurean, deliciously tender, ardent, sad," and united it to the smiles of the Saint John, the Saint Anne, and other Vincian smiles.[25] Houssaye, one of the co-authors of Gautier's book, who was interested enough in facts to write a life of Leonardo, also is captivated by the new mystery. He feels it his duty to bring in her "charm, provocative and ineffable, cruel and divine, sybilline and voluptuous."[26] This diabolical charm appears also, somewhat intensified, in Charles Blanc and Paul Mantz.

Before a painting so wonderful and so admired, the time which was consumed in painting it is explained either by the fact that the artist experienced the fascination which he has so well expressed, and prolonged as far as possible the sweets of conversation with this charming woman, or that he had difficulty in expressing the proud serenity and restrained provocation of this face whose smile, at certain moments, seems satanic and still magnetises us by its long and voluptuous glances. It seems that after having carried the modelling to the point of the most delicate shading, to imperceptible accents, and thus brought it close to us by palpitating truth, the artist may have desired then to withdraw it into the mystery of half-light, to hold it remote from our gaze by shrouding it in a gauze and to make it appear as a dream amid a wild landscape, against an unbelievable background of little mountains, blue, rocky, pointed, cut from crystal, and like stalactites turned upwards towards the skies."[27]

All that was lacking now was an explanation of the mysterious charm of this face. The explanation must lie, according to romantic procedure, in the life of the painter, and it was not hard to find reasons for believing that the original Lisa was the mistress of the painter.[28] Charles Clément told the extraordinary story in full. He noticed, he says, that whereas the men's heads by Leonardo were all individualized, those of the women were all identical. On a panel belonging to the Orleans family was discovered a reclining female whose features were those of *La Gioconda*. In the Fesch Collection and in the Hermitage are two half-length nudes with the same face.

[25] H. Taine, *Voyage en Italie*, 1902 (1st ed. 1865), II, 409.
[26] Arsène Houssaye, *Op. cit.*, p. 125.
[27] *Hist. des peintres de toutes les écoles*. Ecole Florentine, 1879. See p. 27 f. for the full account. It is typical of writers of this school that they will say, "stalactites turned upwards towards the skies" rather than "stalagmites."
[28] *Michelangelo, Leonardo da Vinci and Raphael*, tr. by Louisa Corhan, (n.d.), pp. 201 ff.; French ed. 1861. A poem on the same theme was produced by M. A. Dollfus and may be found in Houssaye, *op. cit.*, pp. 335 f.

The original Lisa was the third wife of Giocondo—so that her husband must have been much older than she. Leonardo was young, witty and handsome when he painted her. The portrait at which "he worked or pretended to work" for four years never became the property of her husband. Finally, it is from the time when he painted the *Mona Lisa* that the other female heads begin to resemble hers.

As a matter of cold fact it requires no deep observation of Leonardo's portrait to see how little it resembles the Saint Anne and the Saint John and the various Madonnas. The one common character is the smile, but the series of thirty or more archaic maidens in the Acropolis museum in Athens have an identical smile, which they share with many other archaic statues of both men and women. Are we to conclude from this anything except that such smiles were the fashion of the times? Leonardo's saints and other supernatural beings do resemble one another; he gave them a certain "ideal" head. But the portraits attributed to him are individualized. The face of the *Mona Lisa* cannot be said to resemble the face of *La Belle Ferronière*, if that portrait be indeed by him. And neither of them closely resembles his saints.

Pater's famous passage on our painting is of course better known to English readers than Gautier's, and was perhaps the source of most later American and English interpretations of it. Pater suggests more than he states, whether from timidity, ignorance, or critical principle, but one may vaguely discern through his poetic prose that, like Clément, he finds a disconcerting similarity running through all the female heads and, like Gautier, a symbol of metempsychosis. The symbolism, he maintains, is not "crude," but the picture has "a subdued and graceful mystery." He believes that the "unfathomable smile, always with a touch of something sinister in it," plays over all of Leonardo's work. "From childhood we see this image defining itself on the fabric of his dreams; and but for express historical testimony, we might fancy that this was but his ideal lady, embodied and beheld at last." He suggests a fusion of his dream and the real Mona Lisa. And then follows the purple passage which has been reprinted even in anthologies of poetry. In that face "strange thoughts and fantastic reveries and exquisite passions" are "deposited cell by cell" upon the flesh. "All the thoughts and experiences of the world have been etched and moulded there, in that they have of power to refine and make expressive the outward form, the animalism of Greece, the lust of Rome, the reverie of the middle age with its spiritual ambition and imaginative loves, the return of the Pagan world, the sins of the Borgias." Mona Lisa becomes the "fancy of perpetual life," a reincarnation of Leda, Helen, Saint Anne.[29]

Few art critics of the nineteenth century, capable of reading Pater, resisted his musical style, and we find dozens of imitators of him in the years that followed the publication of *The Renaissance*. Mrs. Charles W. Heaton, for instance, saw in the portrait, "a sweet but perplexing poem," and a visible embodiment of "the words of the preacher, 'vanitas vanitatum.' "[30] Mr. Frank Preston Stearns, after a passage on the "meaning" of the smile, dwells upon the sense of mystery in Leonardo's character, which is "expressed without reservation" in this picture.[31] Elbert Hubbard, in one of his *Little Journeys*, brought in the words of the Preacher, as well as those of Walter Pater, added Cleopatra to Leda, Helen, and Saint Anne, and filled three pages with an eloquent description of a smile which he called "ineffable."[32] Mr. George B. Rose expressed the usual thoughts about the "inscrutability" of the smile, "a smile that is only on the lips, while in the eyes there are unsounded depths. Vainly we question her; like the Sphinx her riddle eludes us still."[33] Mr. Edward McCurdy, after an analysis of the details of the portrait, concludes, "Thus, on the very confines of fantasy, and girt

[29] Walter Pater, *The Renaissance*, 1st ed., 1873. The essay itself was first published in the *Fortnightly Review*, Nov. 1869, pp. 494 ff. Donald A. Stauffer, in an interesting article, *Monna Melancholia* (*Sewanee Review*, XL, 89 ff.) gives reasons for believing that Pater had never seen the original of the *Mona Lisa* and had superimposed Dürer's *Melancholy I* upon it in his memory. For intimations of an influence of Gautier on Pater through Swinburne, called to my attention by Professor Meyer Schapiro, see Louise Rosenblatt, *L'Idée de l'art pour l'art etc.*, 1931, p. 195.

[30] *Leonardo da Vinci and his Works*, 1874, p. 52.

[31] *The Midsummer of Italian Art*, 1895, p. 60. Though the Notebooks had not as yet been published when Mr. Stearns's book appeared, the *Treatise on Painting* alone might have shown him that Leonardo was enamored more of precision and clarity than of mystery.

[32] *Little Journeys to the Homes of Eminent Artists*, X, no. 2, pp. 46–50, (Feb. 1902). Hubbard's opinion of the picture may not seem important; but he was considered a great authority on "culture" by the general public of his day. The circulation of his *Little Journeys* was always large and his writings must have been the source of the aesthetic ideas of many unschooled Americans.

[33] *The World's Leading Painters*, 1912, p. 50. In a similar vein Laura Spencer Porter conveyed to the ladies of America the "meaning" of the *Mona Lisa* in the *Woman's Home Companion*, April, 1914, (XLI, p. 54.)

about with suggestions of strange lights and furtive shadows, he has created in this portrait of Madonna Lisa, third wife of a Florentine official, a myth of the embodiment of which men dream as of the eternal enigma of womanhood."[34]

III

From Gautier and Pater, as is clear, runs a tradition which is the very opposite of that started by Vasari. Whereas the Italian biographer and critic chiefly saw in the *Mona Lisa* a wonderful technical feat, the reproduction of a natural object, the French and English "aesthetes" saw it as a hieroglyph which required not simply contemplation but deciphering. It would appear to have become second nature to think of a picture—at least of this picture—as something of a rebus, a symbol whose meaning could be discovered only by a critic's intuition. That this school of writers attributed their theory of artistry to the artists whose works interested them need surprise no one. Critics are in the habit of reading an artist's mind.

This habit became strengthened when the psychology of Sigmund Freud achieved popularity. The nineteenth and twentieth centuries have been noteworthy, among other things, for a peculiar paradox: a combination of great scientific accomplishment with anti-intellectualism. Early in the former century, Schopenhauer began to argue that the understanding was created by the will to serve its own ends, an argument which he sought to deduce from Kantian principles. These ends, however, were not those of Kant's Practical Reason; they were, on the contrary, purely biological; and it was easy for Schopenhauer's successors to identify them with sexual ends. An artist, according to Freud, is a man whose sexual frustrations are released symbolically in pictures or statues or other works of art. Appetites which would never pass the Censor if expressed in their true nature, are permitted to appear in disguise.

As is well known, according to this theory the fundamental appetite of the human male is his love for his mother, known as the Oedipus Complex. Since incest in most Occidental society is not encouraged, the Oedipus Complex can only be released through art,

[34] *Leonardo da Vinci*, 1904, pp. 115 f. It is interesting to observe that James Jackson Jarves, the American collector and critic, who alone of the writers cited— and many others not cited—knew the Italian painters of the Renaissance intimately, was almost unique in his time in continuing the Vasari tradition rather than what we have called the Romantic. See his *Art Studies of the Old Masters of Italy*, 1861, I, p. 400.

and hence a Freudian critic will be likely to see in a picture a symbol of the artist's passion for his mother. Here, it will be observed, the critic assumes that the artist is not communicating something to the observer—he is really concealing something from the observer—but unconsciously expressing something of himself. When this something is revealed, it does not mean that the picture will be liked any the more; no standard of aesthetic judgment is implied in the psychoanalysis of a work of art. But it is clear that what mainly interests a Freudian, in any such work, will be the discovery of the unconscious motive. Freud's interpretation follows.

It was quite possible that Leonardo was fascinated by the smile of Mona Lisa because it had awakened something in him which had slumbered in his soul for a long time, in all probability an old memory.[35] This memory was of sufficient importance to stick to him once it had been aroused; he was forced continually to provide it with new expression. The assurance of Pater that we can see an image like that of Mona Lisa defining itself from Leonardo's childhood on the fabric of his dreams, seems worthy of belief and deserves to be taken literally.

Vasari mentions as Leonardo's first artistic endeavors, "heads of women who laugh." The passage, which is beyond suspicion, as it is not meant to prove anything, reads more precisely as follows: "He formed in his youth some laughing feminine heads out of lime, which have been reproduced in plaster, and some heads of children, which were as beautiful as if modeled by the hands of a master. . . ."

Thus we discover that his practice of art began with the representation of two kinds of objects, which would perforce remind us of the two kinds of sexual objects which we have inferred from the analysis of his vulture phantasy. If the beautiful children's heads were reproductions of his own childish person, then the laughing women were nothing else but reproductions of Caterina, his mother, and we are beginning to have an inkling of the possibility that his mother possessed that mysterious smile which he lost, and which fascinated him so much when he found it again in the Florentine lady. . . .[36]

Not only is Freud able to construct a part of the hidden life of Leonardo from the *Mona Lisa,* he is also able to build up the life of the artist's mother. Since she was not married to Piero da Vinci, she was forced to "compensate herself for not having a husband."

[35] According to Vasari, the smile had to be artificially produced and preserved.
[36] Sigmund Freud, *Leonardo da Vinci*, 1916, pp. 85 ff. There is no objective evidence that Caterina resembled Lisa, in smile or otherwise.

In the manner of all ungratified mothers she thus took her little son in place of her husband, and robbed him of a part of his virility by the too early maturing of his eroticism. . . . When in the prime of his life Leonardo re-encountered that blissful and ecstatic smile as it had once encircled his mother's mouth in caressing, he had long been under the ban of an inhibition forbidding him ever again to desire such tenderness from women's lips. But as he had become a painter he endeavored to reproduce this smile with his brush and burnish all his pictures with it, whether he executed them himself or whether they were done by his pupils under his directions, as in Leda, John, and Bacchus.[37]

The way was now open for further embroidering on this psychological background, and critics were not slow to follow it. Pictures became clues to the subconscious labyrinths of an artist's mind. Regardless of the fact that this particular picture seemed to have been painted as a portrait, which might lead one to suppose that its appearance was to a large extent determined by the attributes of the woman who sat for it, its main interest was now held to lie in what it could tell us about the man who made it. This shift in critical attention was the kind of reversal of opinion best illustrated in the Hegelian dialectic. Whereas in Vasari the picture was considered with reference to its closeness to the objective world of nature, in Freud it is considered as a disclosure of the most intimately subjective world, the so-called Unconscious. But since the world which it reveals can be known only by means of a theory which is applied to the particular object, rather than one which has been deduced from it, the critic has only to make up his mind what was in the artist's Unconscious and then discover it spread out before him in the picture.

One finds a still more remarkable example of this in the volume written on our artist by Rachel Annand Taylor, *Leonardo the Florentine*. For her the *Mona Lisa* is a phase in Leonardo's transition from concealment to avowal of his homosexuality. It is, she says,[38] "as if he were afraid to see his Narcissus except in a disguise." Presumably when he painted his Saint John, he was no longer ashamed to see his Narcissus. But even if he were not, it is hardly likely that he painted the picture in order to inform the world that he had conquered his shame. This becomes doubly true if one accepts the Freudian theory that art is always a symbolical rather than a literal satisfaction of repressions.

[37] *Ibid.*, p. 91 ff.

[38] Rachel Annand Taylor, *Leonardo the Florentine*, 1927, esp. pp. 350–354. Only one who has gone through the whole of this book can get its full flavor.

Happily, we are not engaged in an examination of Freudianism. Our purpose is simply to indicate how it reoriented aesthetic comment on this picture in the twentieth century. A writer now feels it possible to assume that a painter is painting for himself rather than for an observer, and that, if an observer should present himself before a picture, he should find in it what the artist himself concealed in it. But since only initiated Freudians know what is concealed in pictures, the uninitiated observer fails to see what the picture really is, or "means." He is in the position of a European ignorant of Chinese looking at Chinese characters and thinking they are merely patterns.

If the *Mona Lisa* at the present time is considered old-fashioned, that is probably to be attributed more to the writings of the Gautier-Pater school than to those of the psycho-analysts. Leonardo himself is far from old-fashioned; but it is now the scientific and philosophical Leonardo rather than the artistic. This paper is not concerned with the decline of interest in the painting, but we may be permitted to suggest that M. Paul Valéry is probably right in saying that the association of "mystery" with the picture has had more influence than any other one thing in disgusting people with it.[39]

The tendency in the criticism of painting from about 1910 to the beginning of sur-realism has been technical. It has consisted largely in studies of form, color, drawing. Only since Marxian criticism became fashionable has there been much attention paid to subject-matter. But in such criticism little is said of adequacy of representation—fidelity to "nature"; the critic is concerned only with the "social significance" of the work of art. Hence to such critics, the *Mona Lisa* would have no great interest, unless, perhaps, as an illustration of the rise of the middle class, for the lady so carefully portrayed was probably a *bourgeoise*.

It may not be inappropriate to terminate with a celebrated passage from the artist's note-books about the portraiture of women.

[39] See his *Leonardo da Vinci*, 1929, p. 58. For other hostile criticisms of this celebrated picture, see Berenson's *The Study and Criticism of Italian Art*, pp. 3 f.; A. C. Barnes, *The Art in Painting*, 1925, p. 368; P. Dearmer, "Leonardo da Vinci, a Criticism," *Contemporary Review*, Vol. 135 (1929), p. 217. The Italian Futurists, in their campaign to liberate Italian art from the museum-pieces, quite naturally attacked it. A good example may be found in Soffici's *Giornale di Bordo*, 1915, p. 147: "In tram.—Vedo scritto su un muro a grandi lettere bianche su fondo blu: GIOCONDA: ACQUA PURGATIVA ITALIANA. E piu giù la faccia melensa di Monna Lisa. Finalmente. Ecco che si comincia anche da noi a far della buona critica artistica."

"Women," Leonardo says, "should be represented in modest attitudes with legs close together, arms folded, and their heads low and bending sideways."[40] The head of La Gioconda is not bending sideways, but otherwise the precept appears to be carried out in the painting. Add to it the memorandum on the importance of painting faces in a nebulous light, and you begin to have a clue to his method of portraiture. This will throw no light on what is "expressed" by the picture, nor is that, fortunately, our affair. We know that Leonardo was attracted by chiaroscuro and busy with the means of utilizing it. We may fittingly leave to psychiatrists the problem why such things interested him.

Our purpose in this paper has been merely to show how a given work of art may in different periods have essentially different content—and therefore be admired for different, if not for contradictory, reasons. If this instance is typical, it would appear that works of art which "withstand the test of time" change their natures as the times change. The work of art becomes thus the locus of a new set of values determined by the preconceptions or the predominant interest of the new critic or observer.

---

[40] *The Notebooks of Leonardo da Vinci,* p. 240.

The Modern System of the Arts

by PAUL OSKAR KRISTELLER

Reprinted from the *Journal of the History of Ideas*—Vol. XII, No. 4, pp. 496-527 and Vol. XIII, No. 1, pp. 17-46

Dedicated to Professor Hans Tietze on his 70th birthday

I

The fundamental importance of the eighteenth century in the history of aesthetics and of art criticism is generally recognized. To be sure, there has been a great variety of theories and currents within the last two hundred years that cannot be easily brought under one common denominator. Yet all the changes and controversies of the more recent past presuppose certain fundamental notions which go back to that classical century of modern aesthetics. It is known that the very term " Aesthetics " was coined at that time, and, at least in the opinion of some historians, the subject matter itself, the " philosophy of art," was invented in that comparatively recent period and can be applied to earlier phases of Western thought only with reservation.[1] It is also generally agreed that such dominating concepts of

* I am indebted for several suggestions and references to Professors Julius S. Held, Rensselaer Lee, Philip Merlan, Ernest Moody, Erwin Panofsky, Meyer Schapiro, and Norman Torrey.

[1] B. Croce, *Estetica come scienza dell'espressione e linguistica generale: Teoria e storia*, 5th ed. (Bari, 1922; first ed., 1901); *Problemi di estetica*, 2nd ed. (Bari, 1923); *Storia dell'estetica per saggi* (Bari, 1942). Katharine E. Gilbert and Helmut Kuhn, *A History of Esthetics* (New York, 1939). See also: J. Koller, *Entwurf zur Geschichte und Literatur der Aesthetik von Baumgarten bis auf die neueste Zeit* (Regensburg, 1799). R. Zimmermann, *Aesthetik*, pt. I: *Geschichte der Aesthetik als philosophischer Wissenschaft* (Vienna, 1858). M. Schasler, *Kritische Geschichte der Aesthetik* (Berlin, 1872). K. Heinrich von Stein, *Die Entstehung der neueren Aesthetik* (Stuttgart, 1886). William Knight, *The Philosophy of the Beautiful*, vol. I (*Being Outlines of the History of Aesthetics*) (London, 1891). B. Bosanquet, *A History of Aesthetic*, 3rd ed. (London, 1910). Max Dessoir, *Aesthetik und allgemeine Kunstwissenschaft* (Stuttgart, 1906). Ernest Bergmann, *Geschichte der Aesthetik und Kunstphilosophie: Ein Forschungsbericht* (Leipzig, 1914). Frank P. Chambers, *Cycles of Taste* (Cambridge, Mass., 1928); *The History of Taste* (New York, 1932). A. Baeumler, *Aesthetik* (*Handbuch der Philosophie*, I, C; Munich-Berlin, 1934). For poetry and literature: G. Saintsbury, *A History of Criticism and Literary Taste in Europe*, 3 vols. (Edinburgh, 1900-04; extremely weak on the theoretical side). For music: H. Sahlender, *Die Bewertung der Musik im System der Kuenste: Eine historisch-systematische Untersuchung* (thes. Jena, 1929). For the visual arts: A. Dresdner, *Die Kunstkritik: Ihre Geschichte und Theorie*, vol. I (Munich, 1915). Julius Schlosser, *Die Kunstliteratur* (Vienna, 1924). Lionello

modern aesthetics as taste and sentiment, genius, originality and creative imagination did not assume their definite modern meaning before the eighteenth century. Some scholars have rightly noticed that only the eighteenth century produced a type of literature in which the various arts were compared with each other and discussed on the basis of common principles, whereas up to that period treatises on poetics and rhetoric, on painting and architecture, and on music had represented quite distinct branches of writing and were primarily concerned with technical precepts rather than with general ideas.[2] Finally, at least a few scholars have noticed that the term "Art," with a capital A and in its modern sense, and the related term "Fine Arts" (Beaux Arts) originated in all probability in the eighteenth century.[3]

In this paper, I shall take all these facts for granted, and shall concentrate instead on a much simpler and in a sense more fundamental point that is closely related to the problems so far mentioned, but does not seem to have received sufficient attention in its own right. Although the terms "Art," "Fine Arts" or "Beaux Arts" are often identified with the visual arts alone, they are also quite commonly understood in a broader sense. In this broader meaning, the term "Art" comprises above all the five major arts of painting, sculpture, architecture, music and poetry. These five constitute the irreducible nucleus of the modern system of the arts, on which all writers and thinkers seem to agree.[4] On the other hand, certain additional arts are sometimes added to the scheme, but with less regularity, depending on the different views and interests of the authors concerned: gardening, engraving and the decorative arts, the dance and the theatre, sometimes the opera, and finally eloquence and prose literature.[5]

Venturi, *History of Art Criticism* (New York, 1936); *Storia della critica d'arte* (Rome, 1945). R. Wittkower, "The Artist and the Liberal Arts," *Eidos* I (1950), 11-17. More special studies will be quoted in the course of this paper.

[2] M. Menendez y Pelayo, *Historia de las Ideas estéticas en España* III (Buenos Aires, 1943). E. Cassirer, *Die Philosophie der Aufklärung* (Tübingen, 1932), 368ff. T. M. Mustoxidi, *Histoire de l'Ēsthétique française* (Paris, 1920).

[3] L. Venturi, "Per il nome di 'Arte,'" *La Cultura*, N.S. I (1929), 385-88. R. G. Collingwood, *The Principles of Art* (Oxford, 1938), 5-7. See also the books of Parker and McMahon, cited below.

[4] Theodore M. Greene, *The Arts and the Art of Criticism* (Princeton, 1940), 35ff. P. Frankl, *Das System der Kunstwissenschaft* (Brünn-Leipzig, 1938), 501ff.

[5] See the works of Zimmermann and Schasler, cited above, note 1.

The basic notion that the five "major arts" constitute an area all by themselves, clearly separated by common characteristics from the crafts, the sciences and other human activities, has been taken for granted by most writers on aesthetics from Kant to the present day. It is freely employed even by those critics of art and literature who profess not to believe in "aesthetics"; and it is accepted as a matter of course by the general public of amateurs who assign to "Art" with a capital A that ever narrowing area of modern life which is not occupied by science, religion, or practical pursuits.

It is my purpose here to show that this system of the five major arts, which underlies all modern aesthetics and is so familiar to us all, is of comparatively recent origin and did not assume definite shape before the eighteenth century, although it has many ingredients which go back to classical, medieval and Renaissance thought. I shall not try to discuss any metaphysical theories of beauty or any particular theories concerning one or more of the arts, let alone their actual history, but only the systematic grouping together of the five major arts. This question does not directly concern any specific changes or achievements in the various arts, but primarily their relations to each other and their place in the general framework of Western culture. Since the subject has been overlooked by most historians of aesthetics and of literary, musical or artistic theories,[6] it is hoped that a brief and quite tentative study may throw light on some of the problems with which modern aesthetics and its historiography have been concerned.

II

The Greek term for Art ($\tau\acute{\epsilon}\chi\nu\eta$) and its Latin equivalent (ars) do not specifically denote the "fine arts" in the modern sense, but were applied to all kinds of human activities which we would call crafts or sciences. Moreover, whereas modern aesthetics stresses the fact that Art cannot be learned, and thus often becomes involved in the curious endeavor to teach the unteachable, the ancients always understood by Art something that can be taught and learned. Ancient statements about Art and the arts have often been read and understood as if they were meant in the modern sense of the fine arts. This may in some

[6] I have come across only two authors who saw the problem quite clearly: H. Parker, *The Nature of the Fine Arts* (London, 1885), esp. 1-30. A. Philip McMahon, *Preface to an American Philosophy of Art* (Chicago, 1945). The latter study is better documented but marred by polemical intentions. I hope to add to their material and conclusions.

cases have led to fruitful errors, but it does not do justice to the original intention of the ancient writers. When the Greek authors began to oppose Art to Nature, they thought of human activity in general. When Hippocrates contrasts Art with Life, he is thinking of medicine, and when his comparison is repeated by Goethe or Schiller with reference to poetry, this merely shows the long way of change which the term Art had traversed by 1800 from its original meaning.[7] Plato puts art above mere routine because it proceeds by rational principles and rules,[8] and Aristotle, who lists Art among the so-called intellectual virtues, characterizes it as a kind of activity based on knowledge, in a definition whose influence was felt through many centuries.[9] The Stoics also defined Art as a system of cognitions,[10] and it was in this sense that they considered moral virtue as an art of living.[11]

The other central concept of modern aesthetics also, beauty, does not appear in ancient thought or literature with its specific modern connotations. The Greek term καλόν and its Latin equivalent (*pulchrum*) were never neatly or consistently distinguished from the moral good.[12] When Plato discusses beauty in the *Symposium* and the *Phaedrus,* he is speaking not merely of the physical beauty of human persons, but also of beautiful habits of the soul and of beautiful cognitions, whereas he fails completely to mention works of art in this connection.[13] An incidental remark made in the *Phaedrus*[14] and elaborated by Proclus[15] was certainly not meant to express the modern triad of Truth, Goodness and Beauty. When the Stoics in one of their famous statements connected Beauty and Goodness,[16] the context as well as Cicero's Latin rendering[17] suggest that they meant by

[7] ὁ βίος βραχύς, ἡ δὲ τέχνη μακρή. Hippocrates, *Aphorisms*, 1. Seneca, *De brevitate vitae*, 1. Schiller, *Wallensteins Lager, Prolog*, 138. Goethe, *Faust I*, Studierzimmer 2, 1787.

[8] *Gorgias*, 462 b ff.   [9] *Nicomachean Ethics*, VI 4, 1140 a 10.

[10] *Stoicorum Veterum Fragmenta*, ed. H. von Arnim, I, p. 21; II, p. 23 and 30; III, p. 51.   [11] *Ibid.*, III, pp. 49 and 148f.

[12] R. G. Collingwood, "Plato's Philosophy of Art," *Mind*, N.S. 34 (1925), 154-72, esp. 161f.   [13] *Symposium*, 210 a ff. *Phaedrus*, 249 d.

[14] τὸ δὲ θεῖον καλόν, σοφόν, ἀγαθόν, καὶ πᾶν ὅτι τοιοῦτον. 246 d–e.

[15] *Commentary on Plato's Alcibiades* I (ed. Cousin, 356–57). I am indebted for this reference to Dr. Laurence Rosán. The καλόν does not denote aesthetic beauty in this passage any more than in Plato, and to interpret the σοφόν as Truth seems arbitrary. Yet the passage may have influenced its editor, Cousin.

[16] *Stoicorum Veterum Fragmenta* III, p. 9ff. (μόνον τὸ καλὸν ἀγαθόν).

[17] *Ibid.*, III, p. 10f., and I, pp. 47 and 84. Cicero, *De finibus* III, 26 (quod honestum sit id solum bonum).

"Beauty" nothing but moral goodness, and in turn understood by "good" nothing but the useful. Only in later thinkers does the speculation about "beauty" assume an increasingly "aesthetic" significance, but without ever leading to a separate system of aesthetics in the modern sense. Panaetius identifies moral beauty with decorum,[18] a term he borrows from Aristotle's *Rhetoric*,[19] and consequently likes to compare the various arts with each other and with the moral life. His doctrine is known chiefly through Cicero, but it may also have influenced Horace. Plotinus in his famous treatises on beauty is concerned primarily with metaphysical and ethical problems, but he does include in his treatment of sensuous beauty the visible beauty of works of sculpture and architecture, and the audible beauty of music.[20] Likewise, in the speculations on beauty scattered through the works of Augustine there are references to the various arts, yet the doctrine was not primarily designed for an interpretation of the "fine arts."[21] Whether we can speak of aesthetics in the case of Plato, Plotinus or Augustine will depend on our definition of that term, but we should certainly realize that in the theory of beauty a consideration of the arts is quite absent in Plato and secondary in Plotinus and Augustine.

Let us now turn to the individual arts and to the manner in which they were evaluated and grouped by the ancients. Poetry was always most highly respected, and the notion that the poet is inspired by the Muses goes back to Homer and Hesiod. The Latin term (*vates*) also suggests an old link between poetry and religious prophecy, and Plato is hence drawing upon an early notion when in the *Phaedrus* he considers poetry one of the forms of divine madness.[22] However, we should also remember that the same conception of poetry is expressed with a certain irony in the *Ion*[23] and the *Apology*,[24] and that even in

---

[18] Cicero, *De officiis* I 27, 93ff. R. Philippson, "Das Sittlichschoene bei Panaitios," *Philologus* 85 (N.F. 39, 1930), 357–413. Lotte Labowsky, *Die Ethik des Panaitios* (Leipzig, 1934). [19] III 7, 1408 a 10ff.

[20] *Enn.* V 8, 1. I 6, 1–3. See also I 3, 1. There is no evidence that Plotinus intended to apply his remarks on music to all the other fine arts, as E. Krakowski believes (*Une philosophie de l'amour et de la beauté: L'esthétique de Plotin et son influence* [Paris, 1929], 112ff.). The triad of Goodness, Truth and Beauty is made a basis of his interpretation by Dean William R. Inge (*The Philosophy of Plotinus* II [London, 1918], 74ff. and 104) but does not occur in the works of Plotinus.

[21] K. Svoboda, *L'esthétique de Saint Augustin et ses sources* (Brno, 1933). E. Chapman, *Saint Augustine's Philosophy of Beauty* (New York, 1939). E. Gilson, *Introduction à l'étude de Saint Augustin*, 3rd ed. (Paris, 1949), 279f.

[22] 245 a.   [23] 533 e ff.   [24] 22 a ff.

the *Phaedrus* the divine madness of the poet is compared with that of the lover and of the religious prophet.[25] There is no mention of the "fine arts" in this passage, and it was left to the late sophist Callistratus[26] to transfer Plato's concept of inspiration to the art of sculpture.

Among all the "fine arts" it was certainly poetry about which Plato had most to say, especially in the *Republic,* but the treatment given to it is neither systematic nor friendly, but suspiciously similar to the one he gives to rhetoric in some of his other writings. Aristotle, on the other hand, dedicated a whole treatise to the theory of poetry and deals with it in a thoroughly systematic and constructive fashion. The *Poetics* not only contains a great number of specific ideas which exercised a lasting influence upon later criticism; it also established a permanent place for the theory of poetry in the philosophical encyclopaedia of knowledge. The mutual influence of poetry and eloquence had been a permanent feature of ancient literature ever since the time of the Sophists, and the close relationship between these two branches of literature received a theoretical foundation through the proximity of the *Rhetoric* and the *Poetics* in the corpus of Aristotle's works. Moreover, since the order of the writings in the Aristotelian Corpus was interpreted as early as the commentators of late antiquity as a scheme of classification for the philosophical disciplines, the place of the *Rhetoric* and the *Poetics* after the logical writings of the *Organon* established a link between logic, rhetoric and poetics that was emphasized by some of the Arabic commentators, the effects of which were felt down to the Renaissance.[27]

Music also held a high place in ancient thought; yet it should be remembered that the Greek term μουσική, which is derived from the Muses, originally comprised much more than we understand by music. Musical education, as we can still see in Plato's *Republic,* included not only music, but also poetry and the dance.[28] Plato and Aristotle, who also employ the term music in the more specific sense familiar to us, do not treat music or the dance as separate arts but rather as

---

[25] 244 a ff.   [26] *Descriptiones*, 2.

[27] L. Baur, "Die philosophische Einleitungslitteratur bis zum Ende der Scholastik," in: Dominicus Gundissalinus, *De divisione philosophiae,* ed. L. Baur (*Beiträge zur Geschichte der Philosophie des Mittelalters,* IV, 2-3, Muenster, 1903), 316ff. See also J. Mariétan, *Problème de la classification des sciences d'Aristote à St. Thomas* (thes. Fribourg, 1901).

[28] *Republic* II, 376 e ff.

elements of certain types of poetry, especially of lyric and dramatic poetry.[29] There is reason to believe that they were thus clinging to an older tradition which was actually disappearing in their own time through the emancipation of instrumental music from poetry. On the other hand, the Pythagorean discovery of the numerical proportions underlying the musical intervals led to a theoretical treatment of music on a mathematical basis, and consequently musical theory entered into an alliance with the mathematical sciences which is already apparent in Plato's *Republic*,[30] and was to last far down into early modern times.

When we consider the visual arts of painting, sculpture and architecture, it appears that their social and intellectual prestige in antiquity was much lower than one might expect from their actual achievements or from occasional enthusiastic remarks which date for the most part from the later centuries.[31] It is true that painting was compared to poetry by Simonides[32] and Plato,[33] by Aristotle[34] and Horace,[35] as it was compared to rhetoric by Cicero,[36] Dionysius of Halicarnassus[37] and other writers.[38] It is also true that architecture was included among the liberal arts by Varro[39] and Vitruvius,[40] and

[29] *Poetics* 1, 1447 a 23ff. *Laws* II, 669 e f.   [30] VII, 531 a ff.

[31] Dresdner, *l.c.*, 19ff. E. Zilsel, *Die Entstehung des Geniebegriffs* (Tübingen, 1926), 22ff. B. Schweitzer, " Der bildende Künstler und der Begriff des Künstlerischen in der Antike," *Neue Heidelberger Jahrbücher*, N.F. (1925), 28–132. Hans Jucker, *Vom Verhältnis der Römer zur bildenden Kunst der Griechen* (Frankfurt, 1950). For ancient art theories in general: Eduard Mueller, *Geschichte der Theorie der Kunst bei den Alten*, 2 vols. (Breslau, 1834–37). Julius Walter, *Die Geschichte der Aesthetik im Altertum* (Leipzig, 1893). For Plato and Aristotle: G. Finsler, *Platon und die Aristotelische Poetik* (Leipzig, 1900). S. H. Butcher, *Aristotle's Theory of Poetry and Fine Art*, 4th ed. (London, 1911). A. Rostagni, " Aristotele e Aristotelismo nella storia dell'estetica antica," *Studi italiani di filologia classica*, N.S. 2 (1922), 1–147. U. Galli, " La mimesi artistica secondo Aristotele," *ibid.*, N.S. 4 (1927), 281–390. E. Cassirer, " Eidos und Eidolon: Das Problem des Schönen und der Kunst in Platons Dialogen," *Vorträge der Bibliothek Warburg*, II: Vorträge 1922–23, I (Leipzig-Berlin, 1924), 1–27. R. G. Collingwood, " Plato's Philosophy of Art," *Mind*, N.S. 34 (1925), 154–72. E. Bignami, *La Poetica di Aristotele e il concetto dell'arte presso gli antichi* (Florence, 1932). P.-M. Schuhl, *Platon et l'art de son temps* (*Arts plastiques;* Paris, 1933). R. McKeon, " Literary Criticism and the Concept of Imitation in Antiquity," *Modern Philology*, 34 (1936–37), 1–35.

[32] Plutarch, *De gloria Atheniensium* 3, 346 F ff.   [33] *Republic* X, 605 a ff.
[34] *Poetics* 1, 1447 a 19ff.; 2, 1448 a 4ff.   [35] *De arte poetica* 1ff.; 361ff.
[36] *De inventione* II, 1.   [37] *De veteribus scriptoribus* 1.
[38] Quintilian, *Institutio Oratoria* XII, 10, 3ff.
[39] F. Ritschl, " De M. Terentii Varronis disciplinarum libris commentarius," in his *Kleine philologische Schriften* III (Leipzig, 1877), 352–402.
[40] Cf. *De architectura* I, 1, 3ff.

painting by Pliny [41] and Galen,[42] that Dio Chrysostom compared the art of the sculptor with that of the poet,[43] and that Philostratus and Callistratus wrote enthusiastically about painting and sculpture.[44] Yet the place of painting among the liberal arts was explicitly denied by Seneca [45] and ignored by most other writers, and the statement of Lucian that everybody admires the works of the great sculptors but would not want to be a sculptor oneself, seems to reflect the prevalent view among writers and thinkers.[46] The term δημιουργός, commonly applied to painters and sculptors, reflects their low social standing, which was related to the ancient contempt for manual work. When Plato compares the description of his ideal state to a painting [47] and even calls his world-shaping god a demiurge,[48] he no more enhances the importance of the artist than does Aristotle when he uses the statue as the standard example for a product of human art.[49] When Cicero, probably reflecting Panaetius, speaks of the ideal notions in the mind of the sculptor,[50] and when the Middle Platonists and Plotinus compare the ideas in the mind of God with the concepts of the visual artist they go one step further.[51] Yet no ancient philosopher, as far as I know, wrote a separate systematic treatise on the visual arts or assigned to them a prominent place in his scheme of knowledge.[52]

[41] *Natural History* XXXV, 76f.

[42] *Protrepticus* (*Opera*, ed. C. G. Kuehn, I [Leipzig, 1821], 39).

[43] *Oratio* XII. Cf. S. Ferri, " Il discorso di Fidia in Dione Crisostomo," *Annali della R. Scuola Normale Superiore di Pisa, Lettere, Storia e Filosofia*, Ser. II, vol. V (1936), 237–66.

[44] Philostratus, *Imagines*. Callistratus, *Descriptiones*. Ella Birmelin, " Die Kunsttheoretischen Gedanken in Philostrats Apollonios," *Philologus* 88, N.F. 42 (1933), 149–80; 392–414.

[45] *Epistolae Morales* 88, 18.

[46] *Somnium* 14. Cf. Plutarch, *Pericles* 1–2.

[47] *Republic* V, 472 d. Cf. VI, 501 a ff.   [48] *Timaeus* 29 a.

[49] *Physics* II 3, 194 b 24f. and 195 a 5f. *Metaphysics* IV 2, 1013 a 25f. and b 6f.

[50] *Orator* 8f.

[51] W. Theiler, *Die Vorbereitung des Neuplatonismus* (Berlin, 1930), 1ff. Birmelin, *l.c.*, p. 402ff. Plotinus, *Enn.* I 6, 3; V 8, 1. E. Panofsky, *Idea* (Leipzig-Berlin), 1924. The ancient comparison of God with the craftsman was reversed by the modern aestheticians who compared the " creative " artist with God. Cf. Milton C. Nahm, " The Theological Background of the Theory of the Artist as Creator," the *Journal of the History of Ideas*, 8 (1947), 363–72. E. Kris and O. Kurz, *Die Legende vom Künstler* (Vienna, 1934), 47ff.

[52] The opinion of S. Haupt (" Die zwei Bücher des Aristoteles περὶ ποιητικῆς τέχνης, *Philologus* 69, N.F. 23 [1910], 252–63) that a lost section of Aristotle's *Poetics* dealt with the visual arts, as well as with lyrical poetry, must be rejected.

If we want to find in classical philosophy a link between poetry, music and the fine arts, it is provided primarily by the concept of imitation (μίμησις). Passages have been collected from the writings of Plato and Aristotle from which it appears quite clearly that they considered poetry, music, the dance, painting and sculpture as different forms of imitation.[53] This fact is significant so far as it goes, and it has influenced many later authors, even in the eighteenth century.[54] But aside from the fact that none of the passages has a systematic character or even enumerates all of the "fine arts" together, it should be noted that the scheme excludes architecture,[55] that music and the dance are treated as parts of poetry and not as separate arts,[56] and that on the other hand the individual branches or subdivisions of poetry and of music seem to be put on a par with painting or sculpture.[57] Finally, imitation is anything but a laudatory category, at least for Plato, and wherever Plato and Aristotle treat the "imitative arts" as a distinct group within the larger class of "arts," this group seems to include, besides the "fine arts" in which we are interested, other activities that are less "fine," such as sophistry,[58] or the use of the mirror,[59] of magic tricks,[60] or the imitation of animal voices.[61] Moreover, Aristotle's distinction between the arts of necessity and the arts of pleasure [62] is quite incidental and does not identify the arts of pleasure with the "fine" or even the imitative arts, and when it is emphasized that he includes music and drawing in his scheme of education in the *Politics*,[63] it should be added that they share this place with grammar (writing) and arithmetic.

[53] See above, note 31. Cf. esp. Plato, *Republic* II, 373 b; X, 595 a ff. *Laws* II, 668 b f. Aristotle, *Poetics* 1, 1447 a 19ff. *Rhetoric* I 11, 1371 b 6ff. *Politics* VIII 5, 1340 a 38f.

[54] It seems clear, at least for Plato (*Republic* X and *Sophist* 234 a ff.) that he arrived at his distinction between the productive and imitative arts without any exclusive concern for the "fine arts," since imitation is for him a basic metaphysical concept which he uses to describe the relation between things and Ideas.

[55] Perhaps lyrical poetry is also excluded. It is not discussed by Aristotle, except for certain special kinds, and there are passages in Plato's *Republic* (X, 595 a) that imply that only certain kinds of poetry are imitative.

[56] See above, note 29. [57] Aristotle, *Poetics* 1, 1447 a 24ff.
[58] Plato, *Sophist* 234 e f. [59] *Republic* X, 596 d f.
[60] *Ibid.*, 602 d. Cf. *Sophist*, 235 a.
[61] Plato, *Cratylus*, 423 c. Cf. Aristotle, *Poetics* 1, 1447 a 21 (a controversial passage). See also *Rhetoric* III 2, 1404 a 20ff. for the imitative character of words and language. [62] *Metaphysics* I 1, 981 b 17ff. [63] VIII 3, 1337 b 23ff.

The final ancient attempts at a classification of the more important human arts and sciences were made after the time of Plato and Aristotle. They were due partly to the endeavors of rival schools of philosophy and rhetoric to organize secondary or preparatory education into a system of elementary disciplines (τὰ ἐγκύκλια). This system of the so-called "liberal arts" was subject to a number of changes and fluctuations, and its development is not known in all of its earlier phases.[64] Cicero often speaks of the liberal arts and of their mutual connection,[65] though he does not give a precise list of these arts, but we may be sure that he did not think of the "fine arts" as was so often believed in modern times. The definitive scheme of the seven liberal arts is found only in Martianus Capella: grammar, rhetoric, dialectic, arithmetic, geometry, astronomy, and music. Other schemes which are similar but not quite identical are found in many Greek and Latin authors before Capella. Very close to Capella's scheme, and probably its source, was that of Varro, which included medicine and architecture, in addition to Capella's seven arts.[66] Quite similar also is the scheme underlying the work of Sextus Empiricus. It contains only six arts, omitting logic, which is treated as one of the three parts of philosophy. The Greek author, Sextus, was conscious of the difference between the preliminary disciplines and the parts of philosophy, whereas the Latin authors who had no native tradition of philosophical instruction were ready to disregard that distinction. If we compare Capella's scheme of the seven liberal arts with the modern system of the "fine arts," the differences are obvious. Of the fine arts only music, understood as musical theory, appears among the liberal arts. Poetry is not listed among them, yet we know from other sources that it was closely linked with grammar and rhetoric.[67] The visual arts have no place in the scheme, except for occasional attempts at inserting them, of which we have spoken above. On the other hand, the liberal arts include grammar and logic, mathematics and astronomy,

---

[64] Moritz Guggenheim, *Die Stellung der liberalen Künste oder encyklischen Wissenschaften im Altertum* (progr. Zürich, 1893). E. Norden, *Die antike Kunstprosa* II, 4th ed. (Leipzig-Berlin, 1923), 670ff. H.-J. Marrou, *Histoire de l'éducation dans l'antiquité* (Paris, 1948), 244f. and 523f.; also *Saint Augustin et la fin de la culture classique* (Paris, 1938), 187ff. and 211ff.

[65] *Pro Archia poeta* 1, 2: "etenim omnes artes quae ad humanitatem pertinent habent quoddam commune vinculum."   [66] See above, note 39.

[67] Charles S. Baldwin, *Ancient Rhetoric and Poetic* (New York, 1924), esp. 1ff., 63ff., 226ff.

that is, disciplines we should classify as sciences.

The same picture is gained from the distribution of the arts among the nine Muses. It should be noted that the number of the Muses was not fixed before a comparatively late period, and that the attempt to assign particular arts to individual Muses is still later and not at all uniform. However, the arts listed in these late schemes are the various branches of poetry and of music, with eloquence, history, the dance, grammar, geometry and astronomy.[68] In other words, just as in the schemes of the liberal arts, so in the schemes for the Muses poetry and music are grouped with some of the sciences, whereas the visual arts are omitted. Antiquity knew no Muse of painting or of sculpture; they had to be invented by the allegorists of the early modern centuries. And the five fine arts which constitute the modern system were not grouped together in antiquity, but kept quite different company: poetry stays usually with grammar and rhetoric; music is as close to mathematics and astronomy as it is to the dance, and poetry;[69] and the visual arts, excluded from the realm of the Muses and of the liberal arts by most authors, must be satisfied with the modest company of the other manual crafts.

Thus classical antiquity left no systems or elaborate concepts of an aesthetic nature,[70] but merely a number of scattered notions and suggestions that exercised a lasting influence down to modern times but had to be carefully selected, taken out of their context, rearranged, reemphasized and reinterpreted or misinterpreted before they could be utilized as building materials for aesthetic systems. We have to admit the conclusion, distasteful to many historians of aesthetics but grudgingly admitted by most of them, that ancient writers and thinkers, though confronted with excellent works of art and quite susceptible to their charm, were neither able nor eager to detach the aesthetic quality of these works of art from their intellectual, moral, religious and practical function or content, or to use such an aesthetic quality as a standard for grouping the fine arts together or for making them the subject of a comprehensive philosophical interpretation.

[68] J. von Schlosser, " Giusto's Fresken in Padua und die Vorläufer der Stanza della Segnatura," *Jahrbuch der Kunsthistorischen Sammlungen des Allerhöchsten Kaiserhauses* XVII, pt. 1 (1896), 13–100, esp. 36. Pauly-Wissowa, *Real-Encyclopaedie der classischen Altertumswissenschaft* 16 (1935), 680ff., esp. 685f. and 725ff.

[69] Carolus Schmidt, *Quaestiones de musicis scriptoribus Romanis* . . . (thes. Giessen, Darmstadt, 1899).

[70] Schlosser, *Kunstliteratur*, 46ff.

III

The early Middle Ages inherited from late antiquity the scheme of the seven liberal arts that served not only for a comprehensive classification of human knowledge but also for the curriculum of the monastic and cathedral schools down to the twelfth century.[71] The subdivision of the seven arts into the Trivium (grammar, rhetoric, dialectic) and Quadrivium (arithmetic, geometry, astronomy and music) seems to have been emphasized since Carolingian times.[72] This classification became inadequate after the growth of learning in the twelfth and thirteenth centuries. The classification schemes of the twelfth century reflect different attempts to combine the traditional system of the liberal arts with the threefold division of philosophy (logic, ethics and physics) known through Isidore, and with the divisions of knowledge made by Aristotle or based on the order of his writings, which then began to become known through Latin translations from the Greek and Arabic.[73] The rise of the universities also established philosophy, medicine, jurisprudence and theology as new and distinct subjects outside the liberal arts, and the latter were again reduced from the status of an encyclopaedia of secular knowledge they had held in the earlier Middle Ages to that of preliminary disciplines they had held originally in late antiquity. On the other hand, Hugo of St. Victor was probably the first to formulate a scheme of seven mechanical arts corresponding to the seven liberal arts, and this scheme influenced many important authors of the subsequent period, such as Vincent of Beauvais and Thomas Aquinas. The seven mechanical arts, like the seven liberal arts earlier, also appeared in artistic representations, and they are worth listing: *lanificium, armatura, navigatio, agricultura, venatio, medicina, theatrica*.[74] Architecture as

---

[71] P. Gabriel Meier, *Die sieben freien Künste im Mittelalter* (progr. Einsiedeln, 1886–87). Norden, *l.c.* A. Appuhn, *Das Trivium und Quadrivium in Theorie und Praxis* (thes. Erlangen, 1900). P. Abelson, *The Seven Liberal Arts* (thes. Columbia University, New York, 1906). For artistic representations of this scheme, see P. d'Ancona, "Le rappresentazioni allegoriche delle arti liberali nel medio evo e nel rinascimento," *L'Arte* 5 (1902), 137–55; 211–28; 269–89; 370–85. E. Mâle, *L'art religieux du XIIIe siècle en France*, 4th ed. (Paris, 1919), 97ff.

[72] P. Rajna, "Le denominazioni Trivium e Quadrivium," *Studi Medievali*, N.S. 1 (1928), 4–36.

[73] Besides the works of Baur and Mariétan, cited above (note 27), see M. Grabmann, *Die Geschichte der scholastischen Methode* II (Freiburg, 1911), 28ff.

[74] Hugonis de Sancto Victore *Didascalicon*, ed. Ch. H. Buttimer (Washington, 1939), bk. II, ch. 20ff.

well as various branches of sculpture and of painting are listed, along with several other crafts, as subdivisions of *armatura*, and thus occupy a quite subordinate place even among the mechanical arts.[75] Music appears in all these schemes in the company of the mathematical disciplines,[76] whereas poetry, when mentioned, is closely linked to grammar, rhetoric and logic.[77] The fine arts are not grouped together or singled out in any of these schemes, but scattered among various sciences, crafts, and other human activities of a quite disparate nature.[78] Different as are these schemes from each other in detail, they show a persistent general pattern and continued to influence later thought.

If we compare these theoretical systems with the reality of the same period, we find poetry and music among the subjects taught in many schools and universities, whereas the visual arts were confined to the artisans' guilds, in which the painters were sometimes associated with the druggists who prepared their paints, the sculptors with the goldsmiths, and the architects with the masons and carpenters.[79] The treatises also that were written, on poetry and rhetoric, on music, and on some of the arts and crafts, the latter not too numerous, have all a strictly technical and professional character and show no tendency to link any of these arts with the others or with philosophy.

The very concept of "art" retained the same comprehensive meaning it had possessed in antiquity, and the same connotation that it was teachable.[80] And the term *artista* coined in the Middle Ages indicated either the craftsman or the student of the liberal arts.[81] Neither for Dante[82] nor for Aquinas has the term Art the meaning

[75] *Ibid.*, ch. 22. For the position of the architect in particular, see N. Pevsner, "The Term 'Architect' in the Middle Ages," *Speculum* XVII (1942), 549-62.

[76] Cf. G. Pietzsch, *Die Klassifikation der Musik von Boetius bis Ugolino von Orvieto* (thes. Freiburg, 1929).

[77] Ch. S. Baldwin, *Medieval Rhetoric and Poetic* (New York, 1928). E. Faral, *Les arts poétiques du XIIe et du XIIIe siècle* (Paris, 1924). R. McKeon, "Poetry and Philosophy in the Twelfth Century," *Modern Philology* 43 (1946), 217-34.

[78] E. De Bruyne, *Études d'Esthétique médiévale* II (Bruges, 1946), 371ff., and III, 326ff.

[79] Schlosser, *Kunstliteratur*, 65. N. Pevsner, *Academies of Art, Past and Present* (Cambridge, 1940), 43ff. M. Wackernagel, *Der Lebensraum des Künstlers in der Florentinischen Renaissance* (Leipzig, 1938), 306ff.   [80] De Bruyne, *l.c.*

[81] C. Du Cange, *Glossarium Mediae et Infimae Latinitatis* I (Paris, 1937), 413.

[82] D. Bigongiari, "Notes on the Text of Dante," *Romanic Review* 41 (1950), 81f.

we associate with it, and it has been emphasized or admitted that for Aquinas shoemaking, cooking and juggling, grammar and arithmetic are no less and in no other sense *artes* than painting and sculpture, poetry and music, which latter are never grouped together, not even as imitative arts.[83]

On the other hand, the concept of beauty that is occasionally discussed by Aquinas [84] and somewhat more emphatically by a few other medieval philosophers [85] is not linked with the arts, fine or otherwise, but treated primarily as a metaphysical attribute of God and of his creation, starting from Augustine and from Dionysius the Areopagite. Among the transcendentals or most general attributes of being, *pulchrum* does not appear in thirteenth-century philosophy, although it is considered as a general concept and treated in close connection with *bonum*. The question whether Beauty is one of the transcendentals has become a subject of controversy among Neo-Thomists.[86] This is an interesting sign of their varying attitude toward modern aesthetics, which some of them would like to incorporate in a philosophical system based on Thomist principles. For Aquinas himself,

[83] L. Schuetz, *Thomas-Lexikon*, 2nd ed. (Paderborn, 1908), 65–68. A. Dyroff, " Zur allgemeinen Kunstlehre des hl. Thomas," *Abhandlungen zur Geschichte der Philosophie des Mittelalters, Festgabe Clemens Bäumker* . . . (Beiträge zur Geschichte der Philosophie des Mittelalters, Supplementband II, Münster, 1923), 197–219. De Bruyne, *l.c.*, III, 316ff. J. Maritain, *Art et Scolastique* (Paris, 1920), 1f. and 28f. G. G. Coulton, *Art and the Reformation* (Oxford, 1928), 559ff.

[84] M. De Wulf, " Les théories esthétiques propres à Saint Thomas," *Revue Neo-Scolastique* 2 (1895), 188–205; 341–57; 3 (1896), 117–42. M. Grabmann, *Die Kulturphilosophie des Hl. Thomas von Aquin* (Augsburg, 1925), 148ff. I. Chapman, " The Perennial Theme of Beauty," in *Essays in Thomism* (New York, 1942), 333–46 and 417–19. E. Gilson, *Le Thomisme*, 5th ed. (Paris, 1945), 382–83.

[85] M. Grabmann, " Des Ulrich Engelberti von Strassburg O.P. (+ 1277) Abhandlung De pulchro," *Sitzungsberichte der Bayerischen Akademie der Wissenschaften, Philosophisch-Philologische und Historische Klasse (Jahrgang 1925)*, no. 5. Cf. H. Pouillon, " Le premier Traité des propriétés transcendentales, La Summa de bono du Chancelier Philippe," *Revue Néoscolastique de Philosophie* 42 (1939), 40–77. A. K. Coomaraswamy, " Medieval Aesthetic," *The Art Bulletin* 17 (1935), 31–47; 20 (1938), 66–77 (reprinted in his *Figures of Speech or Figures of Thought* [London, 1946], 44–84. I am indebted for this reference to John Cuddihy). E. Lutz ," Die Ästhetik Bonaventuras," *Studien zur Geschichte der Philosophie: Festgabe . . . Clemens Bäumker gewidmet* (Beiträge zur Geschichte der Philosophie des Mittelalters, Supplementband, Münster, 1913), 195–215.

[86] Maritain, *l.c.*, p. 31ff., esp. 40. Chapman, *l.c.* L. Wencelius, *La philosophie de l'art chez les Néo-Scolastiques de langue française* (Paris, 1932), esp. 93ff.

or for other medieval philosophers, the question is meaningless, for even if they had posited *pulchrum* as a transcendental concept, which they did not, its meaning would have been different from the modern notion of artistic beauty in which the Neo-Thomists are interested. Thus it is obvious that there was artistic production as well as artistic appreciation in the Middle Ages,[87] and this could not fail to find occasional expression in literature and philosophy. Yet there is no medieval concept or system of the Fine Arts, and if we want to keep speaking of medieval aesthetics, we must admit that its concept and subject matter are, for better or for worse, quite different from the modern philosophical discipline.

IV

The period of the Renaissance brought about many important changes in the social and cultural position of the various arts and thus prepared the ground for the later development of aesthetic theory. But, contrary to a widespread opinion, the Renaissance did not formulate a system of the fine arts or a comprehensive theory of aesthetics.

Early Italian humanism, which in many respects continued the grammatical and rhetorical traditions of the Middle Ages, not merely provided the old Trivium with a new and more ambitious name (*Studia humanitatis*) but also increased its actual scope, content and significance in the curriculum of the schools and universities and in its own extensive literary production. The *Studia humanitatis* excluded logic, but they added to the traditional grammar and rhetoric not only history, Greek and moral philosophy, but also made poetry, once a sequel of grammar and rhetoric, the most important member of the whole group.[88] It is true that in the fourteenth and fifteenth centuries poetry was understood as the ability to write Latin verse and to interpret the ancient poets, and that the poetry which the humanists defended against some of their theological contemporaries or for which they were crowned by popes and emperors was a quite different thing from what we understand by that name.[89] Yet the name poetry, meaning at first Latin poetry, received much honor and

---

[87] M. Schapiro, " On the Aesthetic Attitude in Romanesque Art," in *Art and Thought, Essays in Honor of A. K. Coomaraswamy* (London, 1947), 130–50.

[88] See my article, " Humanism and Scholasticism in the Italian Renaissance," *Byzantion* 17 (1944–45), 346–47, esp. 364–65.

[89] K. Vossler, *Poetische Theorien in der italienischen Frührenaissance* (Berlin, 1900).

glamor through the early humanists, and by the sixteenth century vernacular poetry and prose began to share in the prestige of Latin literature. It was the various branches of Latin and vernacular poetry and literature which constituted the main pursuit of the numerous "Academies" founded in Italy during that period and imitated later in the other European countries.[90] The revival of Platonism also helped to spread the notion of the divine madness of the poet, a notion that by the second half of the sixteenth century began to be extended to the visual arts and became one of the ingredients of the modern concept of genius.[91]

With the second third of the sixteenth century, Aristotle's *Poetics*, along with his *Rhetoric*, began to exercise increasing influence, not only through translations and commentaries, but also through a rising number of treatises on Poetics in which the notions of Aristotle constituted one of the dominant features.[92] Poetic imitation is regularly

[90] M. Maylender, *Storia delle Accademie d'Italia*, 5 vols. (Bologna, 1926–30). See also Pevsner, *l.c.*, 1ff.   [91] Zilsel, *l.c.*, 293ff.

[92] J. E. Spingarn, *A History of Literary Criticism in the Renaissance*, 6th ed. (New York, 1930). G. Toffanin, *La fine dell'umanesimo* (Turin, 1920). Donald L. Clark, *Rhetoric and Poetry in the Renaissance* (New York, 1922). Charles S. Baldwin, *Renaissance Literary Theory and Practice* (New York, 1939). Among the commentators, Franciscus Robortellus groups poetry with rhetoric and various parts of logic (*In librum Aristotelis de arte poetica explicationes* [Florence, 1548], p. 1) and takes *Poetics* 1447 a 18ff. to refer to painting, sculpture and acting (p. 10f.: "sequitur similitudo quaedam ducta a pictura, sculptura et histrionica"). Vincentius Madius and Bartholomaeus Lombardus also group poetry with logic and rhetoric (*In Aristotelis librum de poetica communes explanationes* [Venice, 1550], p. 8) but interpret the same passage in terms of painting and music (p. 40–41): "aemulantium coloribus et figuris alios, pictores inquam, voce autem alios, phonascos scilicet (music teachers), aemulari, quorum pictores quidem arte, phonasci autem consuetudine tantum imitationem efficiunt." Petrus Victorius states that Aristotle does not list all the imitative arts in the beginning of the *Poetics* (*Commentarii in primum librum Aristotelis de arte poetarum*, 2nd ed. [Florence, 1573], p. 4) and refers the imitation through voice not to music, but to the copying of the song of birds (p. 6: "cum non extet ars ulla qua tradantur praecepta imitandi cantum avis aut aliam rem voce") and of other animals (p. 7). Lodovico Castelvetro repeatedly compares poetry to painting and sculpture as to other imitative arts (*Poetica d'Aristotele volgarizzata et sposta* [Basel, 1576], p. 14ff.; 581) but recognizes music and the dance as parts of poetry (p. 13: "la poesia di parole, di ballo e di suono"). Significant is his attempt to relate poetry to the realm of the soul as opposed to the body (p. 342: "il dipintore rappresenta la bonta del corpo, cio è la bellezza, e'l poeta rappresenta la bonta dell'animo, cio è i buoni costumi"; Cf. H. B. Charlton, *Castelvetro's Theory of Poetry* [Manchester, 1913], 39). Fran-

THE MODERN SYSTEM OF THE ARTS 161

discussed along Aristotelian lines, and some authors also notice and stress the analogies between poetry, painting, sculpture and music as forms of imitation. However, most of them know that music for Aristotle was a part of poetry, and that he knew other forms of imitation outside of the "fine arts," and hardly anyone among them is trying to establish the "imitative arts" as a separate class.

Musical theory retained during the Renaissance its status as one of the liberal arts,[93] and the author of an early treatise on the dance tries to dignify his subject by the claim that his art, being a part of music, must be considered as a liberal art.[94] It seems that the prac-

cesco Patrici, anti-Aristotelian in poetics as well as in philosophy, rejects the principle of imitation altogether and calls it a term with many meanings, unfit to serve as a genus for several arts (*Della Poetica, La Deca disputata* [Ferrara, 1586], p. 63): "Perciò che così in confuso presa (*i.e.*, imitation), non pare potere essere genere univoco nè analogo a Pittori, a Scoltori, a Poeti e ad Istrioni, artefici cotanto tra loro differenti"; p. 68: "essendo adunque la imitazione della favola stata commune a scrittori, istorici, a filosofi, a sofisti, a dialogisti, ad istoriali e a novellatori." Bernardino Daniello (*Della poetica* [Venice, 1536], p. 69f.) compares the poet not only to the painter but also to the sculptor. Antonius Minturnus compares poets, musicians and painters as imitators (*De poeta* [Venice, 1559], p. 22: "Videbam enim ut pictorum musicorumque ita poetarum esse imitari") but stresses repeatedly that music in ancient times was joined to poetry (p. 49; 60; 91: "eosdem poetas ac musicos fuisse"; 391) and compares poetry also with history and other sciences (p. 76; 87ff.; 440f.). In another work, the same author, echoing Aristotle's *Poetics*, compares poetry to painting and acting (*L'arte poetica* [Naples, 1725], p. 3: "i pittori con li colori e co' lineamenti la facciano, i parasiti e gl'istrioni con la voce e con gli atti, i poeti . . . con le parole, con l'armonia, con i tempi") and treats music and dance as parts of poetry (*ibid.*). Johannes Antonius Viperanus defines poetry as imitation through verse and thus differentiates it from other forms of imitation. Lucian can be called a poet, "sed ea dumtaxat ratione qua pictores, mimi et imitatores alii propter nominis generalem quandam lateque diffusam significationem nominari possunt et nominantur etiam poetae" (*De poetica libri tres* [Antwerp, 1579], p. 10). Giovanni Pietro Capriano divides the imitative arts into two classes, the noble and the ignoble. The former appeal to the noble senses of seeing and hearing and have durable products, such as poetry, painting and sculpture, the latter for which no examples are given appeal to the three lower senses and produce no lasting works (*Della vera poetica* [Venice, 1555], fol. A 3–A 3v. Cf. Spingarn, p. 42). Music is treated as a part of poetry (*ibid.*). Other writers on poetics whom I have examined, such as Fracastoro or Scaliger, have nothing to say on the other "fine arts," except for occasional comparisons between poetry and painting. B. Varchi also groups poetry with logic, rhetoric, history and grammar (*Opere*, ed. A. Racheli, II [Trieste, 1859], p. 684). Cf. Spingarn, 25.

[93] A. Pellizzari, *Il Quadrivio nel Rinascimento* (Naples, 1924), 63ff.

[94] Guglielmo Ebreo Pesarese, *Trattato dell'arte del ballo* (*Scelta di curiosità letterarie*, 131, Bologna, 1873), p. 3 and 6–7.

tice of the Improvvisatori as well as the reading of classical sources suggested to some humanists a closer link between music and poetry than had been customary in the preceding period.[95] This tendency received a new impetus by the end of the sixteenth century, when the program of the Camerata and the creation of the opera brought about a reunion of the two arts. It would even seem that some of the features of Marinismo and baroque poetry that were so repulsive to classicist critics were due to the fact that this poetry was written with the intention of being set to music and sung.[96]

Still more characteristic of the Renaissance is the steady rise of painting and of the other visual arts that began in Italy with Cimabue and Giotto and reached its climax in the sixteenth century. An early expression of the increasing prestige of the visual arts is found on the Campanile of Florence, where painting, sculpture, and architecture appear as a separate group between the liberal and the mechanical arts.[97] What characterizes the period is not only the quality of the works of art but also the close links that were established between the visual arts, the sciences and literature.[98] The appearance of a distinguished artist who also was a humanist and writer of merit, such as Alberti, was no coincidence in a period in which literary and classical learning began, in addition to religion, to provide the subject matter for painters and sculptors. When a knowledge of perspective, anatomy, and geometrical proportions was considered necessary for the painter and sculptor, it was no wonder that several artists should have made important contributions to the various sciences. On the other hand, ever since Filippo Villani, the humanists, and their journalist successors in the sixteenth century looked with favor upon the work of contemporary artists and would lend their pen to its praise. From the end of the fourteenth century through the sixteenth the writings of the artists and of authors sympathetic to the visual arts

[95] Raphael Brandolini, *De musica et poetica opusculum* (ms. Casanatense C V 3, quoted by Adrien de La Fage, *Essais de diphthérographie musicale* . . . [Paris, 1864], 61ff.).

[96] Lodovico Zuccolo, *Discorso delle ragioni del numero del verso italiano* (Venice, 1623), 65ff. ("mentre si addatta non la musica a i versi, ma questi si accommodano a quella contro ogni dovere," p. 65).

[97] Schlosser, "Giusto's Fresken," 70ff.; *Kunstliteratur*, 66.

[98] Dresdner, 77ff. L. Olschki, *Geschichte der neusprachlichen wissenschaftlichen Literatur*, I: *Die Literatur der Technik und der angewandten Wissenschaften vom Mittelalter bis zur Renaissance* (Heidelberg, 1919), 31ff.

repeat the claim that painting should be considered as one of the liberal, not of the mechanical arts.[99] It has been rightly noted that the classical testimonies in favor of painting, mainly from Pliny, Galen and Philostratus, were not as authoritative and strong as the Renaissance authors who quoted them in support of their claim believed or pretended to believe. Yet the claim of Renaissance writers on painting to have their art recognized as liberal, however weakly supported by classical authority, was significant as an attempt to enhance the social and cultural position of painting and of the other visual arts, and to obtain for them the same prestige that music, rhetoric, and poetry had long enjoyed. And since it was still apparent that the liberal arts were primarily sciences or teachable knowledge, we may well understand why Leonardo tried to define painting as a science and to emphasize its close relationship with mathematics.[100]

The rising social and cultural claims of the visual arts led in the sixteenth century in Italy to an important new development that occurred in the other European countries somewhat later: the three visual arts, painting, sculpture and architecture, were for the first time clearly separated from the crafts with which they had been associated in the preceding period. The term *Arti del disegno,* upon which "Beaux Arts" was probably based, was coined by Vasari, who used it as the guiding concept for his famous collection of biographies. And this change in theory found its institutional expression in 1563 when in Florence, again under the personal influence of Vasari, the painters, sculptors and architects cut their previous connections with the craftsmen's guilds and formed an Academy of Art (*Accademia del Disegno*), the first of its kind that served as a model for later similar institutions in Italy and other countries.[101] The Art Academies followed the pattern of the literary Academies that had been in existence for some time, and they replaced the older workshop tradition with a regular kind of instruction that included such scientific subjects as geometry and anatomy.[102]

---

[99] Schlosser, *Kunstliteratur,* 50; 79f.; 98; 136; 138; 385. Anthony Blunt, *Artistic Theory in Italy 1450–1600* (Oxford, 1940), 48ff. K. Birch-Hirschfeld, *Die Lehre von der Malerei* (thes. Leipzig, 1911), 25. For a French example of 1542, see F. Brunot, *Histoire de la langue française* . . . VI, 1 (1930), 680.

[100] *The Literary Works of Leonardo da Vinci,* ed. Jean Paul Richter, I, 2nd ed. (London, 1939), 31ff.

[101] Schlosser, *Kunstliteratur,* 385ff. Olschki, II (*Bildung und Wissenschaft im Zeitalter der Renaissance in Italien,* Leipzig, 1922), 188ff. Blunt, 55ff. Pevsner, 42ff.

[102] Pevsner, 48.

The ambition of painting to share in the traditional prestige of literature also accounts for the popularity of a notion that appears prominently for the first time in the treatises on painting of the sixteenth century and was to retain its appeal down to the eighteenth: the parallel between painting and poetry. Its basis was the *Ut pictura poesis* of Horace, as well as the saying of Simonides reported by Plutarch, along with some other passages in Plato, Aristotle and Horace. The history of this notion from the sixteenth to the eighteenth century has been carefully studied,[103] and it has been justly pointed out that the use then made of the comparison exceeded anything done or intended by the ancients. Actually, the meaning of the comparison was reversed, since the ancients had compared poetry with painting when they were writing about poetry, whereas the modern authors more often compared painting with poetry while writing about painting. How seriously the comparison was taken we can see from the fact that Horace's *Ars poetica* was taken as a literary model for some treatises on painting and that many poetical theories and concepts were applied to painting by these authors in a more or less artificial manner. The persistent comparison between poetry and painting went a long way, as did the emancipation of the three visual arts from the crafts, to prepare the ground for the later system of the five fine arts, but it obviously does not yet presuppose or constitute such a system. Even the few treatises written in the late sixteenth and early seventeenth century that dealt with both poetry and painting do not seem to have gone beyond more or less external comparisons into an analysis of common principles.[104]

[103] Rensselaer W. Lee, "Ut pictura poesis: The Humanistic Theory of Painting," *The Art Bulletin* 22 (1940), 197-269. See also W. G. Howard, "Ut pictura poesis," *Publications of the Modern Language Association* 24 (1909), 40-123. Lessing, *Laokoon*, ed. William G. Howard (New York, 1910), p. L ff. Denis Mahon, *Studies in Seicento Art and Theory* (London, 1947).

[104] *Due dialoghi* di M. Giovanni Andrea Gilio da Fabriano, *Nel primo de' quali si ragiona de le parti morali, e civili appertenenti a Letterati Cortigiani, et ad ogni gentil'huomo, e l'utile, che i Prencipi cavano da i Letterati. Nel secondo si cagiona de gli errori de Pittori circa l'historie* . . . (Camerino, 1564). Antonius Possevinus, *De poesi et pictura ethnica humana et fabulosa collata cum vera honesta et sacra* (1595), in his *Bibliotheca selecta de ratione studiorum* II (Cologne, 1607), 407ff. (this treatise is based on an explicit comparison between the two arts, cf. 470: "quae poeticae eadem picturae conveniunt monita et leges"). Filippo Nuñes, *Arte poetica, e da pintura e symmetria, com principios de perspectiva* (Lisbon, 1615; not seen; the *Arte de pintura* was reprinted separately in 1767; cf. Innocenzo Francisco da Silva, *Diccionario Bibliographico Portuguez* II [Lisbon, 1859], 303-04).

The sixteenth century formulated still other ideas that pointed in the direction of later developments in the field of aesthetics. Just as the period attached great importance to questions of " precedence " at courts and in public ceremonies, so the Academies and educated circles inherited from the medieval schools and universities the fancy for arguing the relative merits and superiority of the various sciences, arts or other human activities. This type of debate was by no means limited to the arts, as appears from the old rivalry between medicine and jurisprudence,[105] or from the new contest between " arms and letters." Yet this kind of discussion was also applied to the arts and thus helped to strengthen the sense of their affinity. The parallel between painting and poetry, in so far as it often leads to a plea for the superiority of painting over poetry, shows the same general pattern.[106] No less popular was the contest between painting and sculpture, on which Benedetto Varchi in 1546 held a regular inquiry among contemporary artists, whose answers are extant and constitute interesting documents for the artistic theories of the time.[107] The question was still of interest to Galileo.[108] The most important text of this type is Leonardo's *Paragone,* which argues for the superiority of painting over poetry, music, and sculpture.[109] In a sense, this tract contains the most complete system of the fine arts that has come down to us from the Renaissance period. However, the text was not composed by Leonardo in its present form, but put together from his scattered notes by one of his pupils, and again rearranged by most of the modern editors. In any case, architecture is omitted, the separation between poetry and music is not consistently maintained, and the comparison seems to be extended to the mathematical disciplines

[105] E. Garin, *La disputa delle Arti nel Quattrocento* (Florence, 1947).

[106] Schlosser, *Kunstliteratur,* 154ff.

[107] G. G. Bottari, *Raccolta di lettere sulla pittura scultura ed architectura* I (Rome, 1754), 12ff. Cf. Schlosser, *Kunstliteratur,* 200ff. See also Varchi's own lecture on this subject (*Opere,* ed. A. Racheli, II [Trieste, 1859], 627ff.).

[108] Letter to Lodovico Cardi da Cigoli (1612), in his *Opere, Edizione Nazionale* XI (Florence, 1901), 340-43. On the authenticity of this letter, see Margherita Margani, " Sull'autenticità di una lettera attribuita a G. Galilei," *Atti della Reale Accademia delle Scienze di Torino* 57 (1921-22), 556-68. I am indebted for this reference to Edward Rosen.

[109] *The Literary Works, l.c. Paragone: A Comparison of the Arts by Leonardo da Vinci,* ed. Irma A. Richter (London, 1949). Lionardo da Vinci, *Das Buch von der Malerei,* ed. H. Ludwig, I (Vienna, 1882). Miss Richter changes the arrangement of the manuscript, which in its turn is not due to Leonardo himself.

with which painting, as a science, is closely linked for Leonardo.

Another line of thinking which might be called the amateur tradition appears in several writers of the sixteenth and seventeenth centuries, probably first in Castiglione's *Courtier*.[110] The exercise, as well as the appreciation of poetry, music and painting are grouped together as pursuits appropriate for the courtier, the gentleman, or the prince. Again, the occupation with these "fine arts" is not clearly marked off from fencing, horseriding, classical learning, the collecting of coins and medals and of natural curiosities or other equally worthy activities. But there seems to be a sense of the affinity between the various arts in their effect upon the amateur, and by the first half of the seventeenth century, the taste and pleasure produced by painting, music and poetry is felt by several authors to be of a similar nature.[111] It does not seem that Plotinus' view that beauty resides in the objects of sight, hearing, and thought exercised any particular influence at that time.[112]

The most explicit comparison between poetry, painting, and music that I have been able to discover in Renaissance literature is the appendix which the Bohemian Jesuit, Jacobus Pontanus, added to the third edition of his treatise on poetics.[113] In stressing the affinity

[110] B. Castiglione, *Il Cortegiano*, Bk. I. Giovanni Battista Pigna, *Il Principe* (Venice, 1561), fol. 4 v–5. Peachham's *Compleat Gentleman* (1622), ed. G. S. Gordon (Oxford, 1916), chs. 10–13.

[111] Lodovico Zuccolo (*Discorso delle ragioni del numero del verso Italiano*, Venice, 1623), speaking of our judgment concerning verse and rhythm in poetry, refers for a comparison to painting and music (p. 8: "onde habbiamo in costume di dire, che l'occhio discerne la bellezza della Pittura, e l'orecchio apprende l'armonia della Musica; ... quel gusto della Pittura e della Musica che sentiamo noi ..."; cf. B. Croce, *Storia dell'estetica per saggi* [Bari, 1942], 44f.). A comparison between painting and music is made also by Richard Asheley in the preface of his translation of Louis Le Roy (1594); cf. H. V. S. Ogden, "The Principles of Variety and Contrast in Seventeenth Century Aesthetics and Milton's Poetry," the *Journal of the History of Ideas*, 10 (1949), 168.

[112] *Enn.* I 6, 1. Marsilius Ficinus, *Commentarium in Convivium Platonis de amore*, Oratio 5, cap. 2 (*Marsilio Ficino's Commentary on Plato's Symposium*, ed. Sears R. Jayne, *The University of Missouri Studies* XIX, 1 [Columbia, 1944], 65–66). Cf. his *Theologia Platonica*, Bk. XII, chs. 5–7 (*Opera* [Basel, 1576], I, 275ff.). See also St. Thomas, *Summa Theologiae* II, I, 27, 1.

[113] Jacobi Pontani de Societate Jesu *Poeticarum Institutionum libri III*. Editio tertia cum auctario ... (Ingolstadt, 1600), 239–50: "Auctarium. Collatio Poetices cum pictura, et musica" (I have used the copy of Georgetown University; the passage is lacking in the first edition of 1594, of which Columbia University has a

between the three arts as forms of imitation aiming at pleasure, the author goes beyond his classical sources.[114] He argues for the status of painting as a liberal art, as many others had done before, but also places musical composition (not musical theory) as a separate art on the same plane with poetry and painting. The passage is quite remarkable, and I should like to think that it was influential, since the work was often reprinted, in France also, where much of the later discussion on these topics took place.[115]

Renaissance speculation on beauty was still unrelated to the arts and apparently influenced by ancient models. Nifo's treatise *de pulchro*, still quoted in the eighteenth century, dealt exclusively with personal beauty.[116] Francesco da Diacceto's main philosophical work, which carries the same title, continues the metaphysical speculations of Plotinus and of his teacher Ficino and does not seem to have exercised any lasting influence.[117]

That the Renaissance, in spite of these notable changes, was still far from establishing the modern system of the fine arts appears most clearly from the classifications of the arts and sciences that were pro-

---

copy, and in the second edition of 1597 owned by the Newberry Library and kindly examined for me by Hans Baron; my attention was drawn to it by K. Borinski, *Die Antike in Poetik und Kunsttheorie* II [Leipzig, 1924], 37ff. and 328ff.

[114] "Scriptores antiqui Poeticem cum pictura et musica componere soliti, plurimam utique illius cum hisce duabus artibus affinitatem cognationemque magnam et omnino ingenium eius ac proprietatem declarare voluerunt" (239–40). "Omnium insuper commune est delectationem gignere, siquidem ad honestam animi voluptatem potius quam ad singularem aliquam utilitatem repertae . . . videntur. Porro poetica et musica . . . auditum permulcent . . . pictura oculis blanditur" (242). Sculpture is also once brought in: "fas sit sculptores, caelatores, fictores propter similitudinem quandam pictoribus sociare" (244).

[115] A. de Backer and Ch. Sommervogel, *Bibliothèque des écrivains de la Compagnie de Jésus*, new ed., II (Liége-Lyon, 1872), 2075–81, list several French printings of the work, of which at least one is clearly based on the third edition. See also the catalogue of the Bibliothèque Nationale, which lists a 3rd ed. issued in Avignon, 1600.

[116] Augustinus Niphus, *de pulchro, de amore* (Lyons, 1549). The work is quoted by J. P. de Crousaz, *Traité du Beau*, 2nd ed. (Amsterdam, 1724), I, 190. I have not seen Marcus Antonius Natta, *De pulcro* (Pavia, 1553; cf. *Catalogo ragionato dei libri d'arte e d'antichità posseduti dal Conte Cicognara* I [Pisa, 1821], 188f.).

[117] See my article, "Francesco da Diacceto and Florentine Platonism in the Sixteenth Century," *Miscellanea Giovanni Mercati* IV (Studi e Testi 124, Vatican City, 1946), 260–304, esp. 279ff.

posed during that period. These schemes continued in part the traditions of the Middle Ages, as is clear in the case of such Thomists as S. Antonino or Savonarola.[118] On the whole, however, there is a greater variety of ideas than in the preceding period, and some of the thinkers concerned were neither backward nor unrepresentative. Vives, Ramus, and Gesner largely follow the old scheme of the liberal arts and the university curriculum of their time.[119] Neither Agrippa of Nettesheim [120] nor Scaliger,[121] nor in the seventeenth century Alsted [122] or Vossius,[123] shows any attempt to separate the fine arts

[118] Baur, *l.c.*, 391ff. Spingarn, 24.

[119] Johannes Ludovicus Vives, *De disciplinis*, in his *Opera omnia* VI (Valencia, 1785). Petrus Ramus, *Collectaneae, Praefationes, Epistolae, Orationes* (Marburg, 1599). Conrad Gesner (*Bibliotheca Universalis* II, Zürich, 1548) places poetry between rhetoric and arithmetic; music between geometry and astronomy; and lists architecture, sculpture and painting scattered among the mechanical arts such as transportation, clothmaking, alchemy, trade, agriculture and the like. Gesner is important as the author of a classification scheme designed for bibliographical purposes. The later history of such schemes has been studied, and it appears that the arts, meaning the visual arts and music, did not attain a distinct place in them before the eighteenth century, whereas up to the present day poetry, for obvious reasons, has never been combined with the other arts in these bibliographical schemes. Cf. Edward Edwards, *Memoirs of Libraries* (London, 1859), 747ff. W. C. Berwick Sayers, *An Introduction to Library Classification*, 7th ed. (London, 1946), 74ff. My attention was drawn to this material by Prof. Thomas P. Fleming.

[120] Henricus Cornelius Agrippa ab Nettesheim, *De incertitudine et vanitate scientiarum* (no place, 1537), gives a random list of arts and sciences, in which poetry appears between grammar and history, music between gambling and the dance, painting and sculpture between perspective and glassmaking (specularia), architecture between geography and metal work. In his *De occulta philosophia* (*Opera* I [Lyons, s.a.], bk. I, ch. 60; cf. E. Panofsky, *Albrecht Dürer* I [Princeton, 1943], 168ff.), Agrippa distinguishes three kinds of melancholy and inspiration which he assigns, respectively, to the manual artists such as painters and architects, to the philosophers, physicians and orators, and to the theologians. It is significant that he has the manual artists share in inspiration, but does not link them with the poets mentioned in the same chapter, and he clearly places them on the lowest of the three levels.

[121] In a rather incidental passage, he groups architecture with cooking and agriculture; singing and the dance with wrestling; speech with navigation (Julius Caesar Scaliger, *Poetices libri septem* [no place, 1594], bk. III, ch. 1, p. 206). Varchi has several random groupings of the arts and finally gives the prize to medicine and next to architecture (*Opere* II, 631ff.). Nizolius classes poetry with grammar, rhetoric and history (Robert Flint, *Philosophy as Scientia Scientiarum and a History of Classifications of the Sciences* [New York, 1904], 98f.).

[122] He includes poetry under philology, and music under theoretical philosophy (*Ibid.*, 113–15).

from the sciences; they list them scattered among all kinds of sciences and professions, and the same is still true of the eighteenth-century *Cyclopaedia* of E. Chambers.[124] Francis Bacon connects poetry with the faculty of imagination,[125] but does not mention the other arts, and the same is true of Vico,[126] whom Croce considers the founder of modern aesthetics.[127] Bonifacio stresses the link between poetry and painting, but otherwise does not separate the fine arts from the sciences,[128] and the same is true of Tassoni.[129] Even Muratori, who again stresses imagination in poetry and at times compares poetry and painting, when he speaks of the *arti* connected with poetry means eloquence and history, in other words, the *studia humanitatis*.[129a] The

---

[123] Gerardus Johannes Vossius, *De artium et scientiarum natura ac constitutione libri quinque* (in his *Opera* III, Amsterdam, 1697). He lists four groups of arts: The vulgar arts such as tailoring and shoemaking; the four popular arts of reading and writing, of sports, of singing and of painting (this group is borrowed from Aristotle's *Politics* VIII 3, 1337 b 23ff.); the seven liberal arts; the main sciences of philosophy (with eloquence), jurisprudence, medicine and theology.

[124] 5th ed. (London, 1741), III (first published in 1727). He classes painting with optics under mixed mathematics, music again under mixed mathematics, architecture and sculpture with the trades also under mixed mathematics, gardening with agriculture, and poetry with rhetoric, grammar and heraldry.

[125] *Of the Advancement of Learning* (*The Philosophical Works of Francis Bacon*, ed. John M. Robertson [London, 1905], 79 and 87ff.). Cf. F. H. Anderson, *The Philosophy of Francis Bacon* (Chicago, 1948), 149.

[126] Vico's theory of phantasy refers to poetry only. In an incidental passage he lists two groups of arts: the visual arts, and oratory, politics, medicine (*De antiquissima Italorum sapientia*, ch. 2, in *Le orazioni inaugurali* . . . , ed. G. Gentile and F. Nicolini [Bari, 1914], 144).   [127] *Estetica*, l.c., 243ff.

[128] Giovanni Bonifacio, *L'Arte de' Cenni* . . . (Vicenza, 1616). He combines painting with poetry on account of their similarity, but places them between rhetoric and history (553ff.). Music appears between astrology and arithmetic (517ff.), architecture with sculpture between navigation and woolmaking (614ff.).

[129] Alessandro Tassoni, *Dieci libri di pensieri diversi*, 4th ed. (Venice, 1627). He places poetry between history and oratory (597ff.), puts architecture after agriculture and before decoration, sculpture, painting and clothing (609ff.), whereas music appears between arithmetic and astronomy (657ff.). Benedetto Accolti, another forerunner of the *Querelle des anciens et modernes* who lived in the fifteenth century, discusses only military art and politics, philosophy, oratory, jurisprudence, poetry, mathematics and theology (*Dialogus de praestantia virorum sui aevi*, in Philippi Villani *liber de civitatis Florentiae famosis civibus*, ed. G. C. Galletti [Florence, 1847], 106–07 and 110–28).

[129a] Lodovico Antonio Muratori, *Della perfetta poesia italiana*, ch. 6: " quelle arti nobili che parlano all'intelletto, come sono la Rettorica, la Storica, la Poetica " (in his *Opere* IX, pt. I [Arezzo, 1769], 56). These three arts are called " figliuole o ministre della filosofia morale " (*ibid.*), and the analogy with painting, based on the concept of imitation, is applied to all three of them (*ibid.*, 59).

modern system of the fine arts does not appear in Italy before the second half of the eighteenth century, when such writers as Bettinelli began to follow the lead of contemporary French, English and German authors.[130]

V

During the seventeenth century the cultural leadership of Europe passed from Italy to France, and many characteristic ideas and tendencies of the Italian Renaissance were continued and transformed by French classicism and the French Enlightenment before they became a part of later European thought and culture. Literary criticism and poetic theory, so prominent in the French classical period, seem to have taken little notice of the other fine arts.[131] Only La Mesnardière in his *Poetics* has an introductory remark on the similarity between poetry, painting and music, a point he calls a commonplace in Latin and Italian treatises on poetics,[132] which is but vaguely reminiscent of such writers as Madius, Minturno, and Zuccolo, but for which we can indicate no specific source unless we assume the author's familiarity with the appendix of Jacobus Pontanus.[133]

[130] *Dell'Entusiasmo delle Belle Arti* (1769). The author lists as Belle Arti: poetry, eloquence, painting, sculpture, architecture, music and the dance (Saverio Bettinelli, *Opere* II [Venice, 1780], 36ff.). In the preface, apparently added in 1780, he cites the *Encyclopédie*, André, Batteux, Schatfibury (*sic*), Sulzer and others (11).

[131] F. Brunetière, *L'évolution des genres dans l'histoire de la littérature*, 5th ed. (Paris, 1910). A. Soreil, *Introduction à l'histoire de l'Esthétique française: Contribution à l'étude des théories littéraires et plastiques en France de la Pléiade au XVIIIe siècle* (thes. Liége, Brussels, 1930).

[132] " Mais entre les plus agréables (*i.e.*, arts and sciences), dont le principal objet est de plaire à la phantasie, on sçait bien que la peinture, la musique et la poësie sont sa plus douce nourriture " (Jules de La Mesnardiere, *La poétique* I [Paris, 1639], 3). " Plusieurs livres sont remplis de la grande conformité qui est entre ces trois Arts. C'est pourquoy, sans m'arrester à des redites importunes, dont les Traittez de Poësie Latins et Italiens ne sont desia que trop chargez . . . " (*ibid.*, 4). Cf. Soreil, 48. Helen R. Reese, *La Mesnardière's Poetique* (1639): *Sources and Dramatic Theories* (Baltimore, 1937), 59.

[133] See above, notes 92, 111, 113–15. It is also instructive to compare the subtitles in the Italian and French editions of Cesare Ripa's famous *Iconologia*. In Italian (Padua, 1618): *Opera utile ad Oratori, Predicatori, Poeti, Pittori, Scultori, Disegnatori, e ad ogni studioso, per inventar concetti, emblemi ed imprese, per divisare qualsivoglia apparato Nuttiale, Funerale, Trionfale*. In French (Paris, 1644): *Oeuvre . . . nécessaire à toute sorte d'esprits, et particulièrement à ceux qui aspirent à estre, ou qui sont en effet orateurs, poëtes, sculpteurs, peintres, ingenieurs, autheurs de medailles, de devises, de ballets, et de poëmes dramatiques.*

Yet the *Siècle de Louis XIV* was not limited in its achievements to poetry and literature. Painting and the other visual arts began to flourish, and with Poussin France produced a painter of European fame. Later in the century Lulli, although of Italian birth, developed a distinctive French style in music, and his great success with the Parisian public went a long way to win for his art the same popularity in France it had long possessed in Italy.[134]

This rise of the various arts was accompanied by an institutional development which followed in many respects the earlier Italian model, but was guided by a conscious governmental policy and hence more centralized and consistent than had been the case in Italy.[135] The Académie Française was organized in 1635 by Richelieu for the cultivation of the French language, poetry, and literature after the model of the Accademia della Crusca.[136] Several years later, in 1648, the Académie Royale de Peinture et de Sculpture was founded under Mazarin after the model of the Accademia di S. Luca in Rome, and tended to detach French artists from the artisans' guilds to which they had previously belonged.[137] Many more Academies were founded by Colbert between 1660 and 1680. They included provincial academies of painting and sculpture,[138] the French Academy in Rome, dedicated to the three visual arts,[139] as well as Academies of Architecture,[140] of Music,[141] and of the Dance.[142] However, the system of

[134] J. Écorcheville, *De Lulli à Rameau, 1690-1730: L'Esthétique musicale* (Paris, 1906).

[135] My attention was called to this problem by Dr. Else Hofmann. Cf. Pevsner, 84ff. *La Grande Encyclopédie* I, 184ff. *L'Institut de France: Lois, Statuts et Réglements concernant les anciennes Académies et l'Institut, de 1635 à 1889*, ed. L. Aucoc (Paris, 1889). *Lettres, Instructions et Mémoires de Colbert*, ed. P. Clement, V (Paris, 1868), LIII ff. and 444ff. [136] Aucoc, p. XXI–XLIII.

[137] Aucoc, p. CIV ff. Pevsner, 84ff.

[138] Founded in 1676. Aucoc, CXXXVIII ff.

[139] Founded in 1666. *Lettres . . . de Colbert*, p. LVIII ff. and 510f.

[140] Founded in 1671. Aucoc, CLXVI ff. *Lettres . . . de Colbert*, LXXII.

[141] This Academy, which was nothing else but the Paris Opera, can be traced back to a privilege granted to Pierre Perrin in 1669; cf. *La Grande Encyclopédie* I, 224f. The Opera was definitely established in 1672 when a similar privilege was granted to Lulli, authorizing him "d'establir une académie royale de musique dans nostre bonne ville de Paris . . . pour faire des représentations devant nous . . . des pièces de musique qui seront composées tant en vers français qu'autres langues estrangères, pareille et semblable aux académies d'Italie" (*Lettres . . . de Colbert*, 535f.). [142] Founded in 1661. *La Grande Encyclopédie* I, 227.

the arts that would seem to underly these foundations is more apparent than real. The Academies were founded at different times, and even if we limit ourselves only to the period of Colbert, we should note that there were also the Académie des Sciences [143] and the Académie des Inscriptions et Médailles,[144] which have no relation to the "Fine Arts"; that there was at least a project for an Académie de Spectacles to be devoted to circus performances and other public shows; [145] and that the Académie de Musique and the Académie de Danse, like this projected Académie de Spectacles, were not organizations of distinguished professional artists or scientists, like the other Academies, but merely licensed establishments for the regular preparation of public performances.[146] Moreover, an extant paper from the time of Colbert that proposed to consolidate all Academies in a single institution makes no clear distinction between the arts and the sciences [147] and lends additional though indirect support to the view that Colbert's Academies reflect a comprehensive system of cultural disciplines and professions, but not a clear conception of the Fine Arts in particular.

Along with the founding of the Academies, and partly in close connection with their activities, there developed an important and extensive theoretical and critical literature on the visual arts.[148] The Conférences held at the Académie de Peinture et Sculpture are full of

[143] Founded in 1666. Aucoc, IV. *Lettres . . . de Colbert,* LXII ff.

[144] Founded in 1663. It changed its name to Académie Royale des Inscriptions et belles-lettres in 1716. Aucoc, IV and LI ff.

[145] The privilege granted to Henri Guichard in 1674 but not ratified authorizes him " de faire construire des cirques et des amphithéâtres pour y faire des carrousels, des tournois, des courses, des joustes, des luttes, des combats d'animaux, des illuminations, des feux d'artifice et généralement tout ce qui peut imiter les anciens jeux des Grecs et des Romains," and also " d'establir en nostre bonne ville de Paris des cirques et des amphithéâtres pour y faire lesdites représentations, sous le titre de l'Académie Royale de spectacles" (*Lettres . . . de Colbert,* 551f.).

[146] This appears clearly from the charters, cited or referred to above.

[147] A note prepared by Charles Perrault for Colbert in 1666 proposes an Académie générale comprising four sections: belles-lettres (grammaire, éloquence, poésie); histoire (histoire, chronologie, géographie); philosophie (chimie, simples, anatomie, physique experimentale); mathématiques (géometrie, astronomie, algèbre). *Lettres . . . de Colbert,* 512f. Poetry appears thus among *belles-lettres* with grammar and eloquence, and the other fine arts are not mentioned.

[148] Lee, *l.c.* Soreil, *l.c.* A. Fontaine, *Les doctrines d'art en France . . . De Poussin à Diderot* (Paris, 1909).

interesting critical views,[149] and separate treatises were composed by Du Fresnoy, De Piles, Fréart de Chambray, and Félibien.[150] Du Fresnoy's Latin poem *De arte graphica,* which was translated into French and English and made the subject of notes and commentaries, was in its form a conscious imitation of Horace's *Ars poetica,* and it begins characteristically by quoting Horace's *Ut pictura poesis* and then reversing the comparison.[151] The parallel between painting and poetry, as well as the contest between the two arts, were important to these authors, as to their predecessors in Renaissance Italy, because they were anxious to acquire for painting a standing equal to that of poetry and literature. This notion, which has been fully studied,[152] remained alive until the early eighteenth century,[153] and it is significant that the honor painting derives from its similarity to poetry is sometimes extended, as occasionally in the Italian Renaissance, to sculpture, architecture and even engraving as related arts.[154] Even the term *Beaux Arts,* which seems to have been intended at first for the visual arts alone, corresponding to *Arti del Disegno,* seems sometimes for these authors to include also music or poetry.[155] The comparison between painting and music is also made a few times,[156] and Poussin himself, who lived in Italy, tried to transfer the theory of the Greek musical modes to poetry and especially to painting.[157]

[149] *Conférences de l'Académie Royale de Peinture et de Sculpture,* ed. Félibien (London, 1705). *Conférences de l'Académie Royale de Peinture et de Sculpture,* ed. H. Jouin (Paris, 1883). *Conférences inédites de l'Académie Royale de Peinture et de Sculpture,* ed. A. Fontaine (Paris, n.d.).

[150] Cf. Lee, *l.c.,* and Schlosser, *l.c.*

[151] "Ut pictura poesis erit; similisque poesi sit pictura . . ." (C. A. Du Fresnoy, *De arte graphica* [London, 1695], 2).

[152] Fontaine, *l.c.;* Lee, *l.c.*

[153] P. Marcel, "Un débat entre les Peintres et les Poètes au début du XVIIIe siècle," *Chronique des Arts* (1905), 182-83; 206-07.

[154] Cf. *L'Art de Peinture* de C. A. Du Fresnoy, ed. R. de Piles, 4th ed. (Paris, 1751), 100. Félibien, *Entretiens sur les vies* . . . 4 (Paris, 1685), 155.

[155] *Conférences,* ed. Jouin, 240. R. de Piles, *Abrégé de la vie des Peintres* . . . (Paris, 1699), 23. Cf. Brunot, *Histoire de la langue française,* 6, 1, 681.

[156] *Conférences,* ed. Félibien, preface ("dans la musique et dans la poësie qui conviennent le plus avec la Peinture"). Félibien, *Entretiens sur les vies et sur les ouvrages des plus excellens peintres anciens et modernes,* pt. IV (Paris, 1685), 155. R. de Piles, *Cours de Peinture par principes* (Paris, 1708), 9. *Conférences,* ed. Jouin, 240; 277-78; 328.

[157] N. Poussin, *Traité des modes,* in his *Correspondance,* ed. Ch. Jouanny (Paris, 1911), 370ff. Cf. *Conférences,* ed. Jouin, 94. Soreil, 27.

One of the great changes that occurred during the seventeenth century was the rise and emancipation of the natural sciences. By the second half of the century, after the work of Galileo and Descartes had been completed and the Académie des Sciences and the Royal Society had begun their activities, this development could not fail to impress the literati and the general public. It has been rightly observed that the famous *Querelle des Anciens et Modernes,* which stirred many scholars in France and also in England during the last quarter of the century, was due largely to the recent discoveries in the natural sciences.[158] The Moderns, conscious of these achievements, definitely shook off the authority of classical antiquity that had weighed on the Renaissance no less than on the Middle Ages, and went a long ways toward formulating the concept of human progress. Yet this is only one side of the Querelle.

The Querelle as it went on had two important consequences which have not been sufficiently appreciated. First, the Moderns broadened the literary controversy into a systematic comparison between the achievements of antiquity and of modern times in the various fields of human endeavor, thus developing a classification of knowledge and culture that was in many respects novel, or more specific than previous systems.[159] Secondly, a point by point examination of the claims of the ancients and moderns in the various fields led to the insight that in certain fields, where everything depends on mathematical calculation and the accumulation of knowledge, the progress of the moderns over the ancients can be clearly demonstrated, whereas in certain other fields, which depend on individual talent and on the taste of the critic, the relative merits of the ancients and moderns cannot be so clearly established but may be subject to controversy.[160]

[158] This aspect has been studied especially by Richard F. Jones (*Ancients and Moderns,* St. Louis, 1936). For a broader treatment of the *Querelle:* H. Rigault, *Histoire de la querelle des Anciens et des Modernes,* in his *Oeuvres complètes* I [Paris, 1859]. H. Gillot, *La Querelle des anciens et des modernes en France* [Paris, 1914]. O. Diede, *Der Streit der Alten und Modernen in der englischen Literaturgeschichte des XVI. und XVII. Jahrhunderts* (thes. Greifswald, 1912). J. Delvaille, *Essai sur l'histoire de l'idée de progrès jusqu'à la fin du XVIIIe siècle* (Paris, 1910), 203ff. J. B. Bury, *The Idea of Progress* (London, 1920), 78ff.

[159] Brunetière (120) emphasizes that Perrault extended the discussion from literary criticism toward a general aesthetics, by drawing upon the other arts and even the sciences. The Italian forerunners of the *Querelle* had no system of the arts and sciences comparable to that of Perrault or Wotton, see above, note 128.

[160] Rigault (323f.) recognizes this distinction in Wotton, and Bury (104f. and 121ff.) attributes it to Fontenelle and Wotton. We shall see that it is also present in Perrault. For Wotton, see below.

Thus the ground is prepared for the first time for a clear distinction between the arts and the sciences, a distinction absent from ancient, medieval or Renaissance discussions of such subjects even though the same words were used. In other words, the separation between the arts and the sciences in the modern sense presupposes not only the actual progress of the sciences in the seventeenth century but also the reflection upon the reasons why some other human intellectual activities which we now call the Fine Arts did not or could not participate in the same kind of progress. To be sure, the writings of the *Querelle* do not yet attain a complete clarity on these points, and this fact in itself definitely confirms our contention that the separation between the arts and the sciences and the modern system of the fine arts were just in the making at that time. Fontenelle, as some scholars have noticed, indicates in an occasional statement of his *Digression* that he was aware of the distinction between the arts and the sciences.[161]

Much more important and explicit is the work of Charles Perrault. His famous *Parallèle des Anciens et des Modernes* discusses the various fields in separate sections which reflect a system: the second dialogue is dedicated to the three visual arts, the third to eloquence, the fourth to poetry, and the fifth to the sciences.[162] The separation of the fine arts from the sciences is almost complete, thought not yet entirely, since music is treated in the last book among the sciences, whereas in his poem, *Le Siècle de Louis le Grand,* which gave rise to the whole controversy, Perrault seems to connect music with the other arts.[163] Moreover, in his prefaces Perrault states explicitly that at

---

[161] Fontenelle (*Digression sur les Anciens et les Modernes,* 1688, in his *Oeuvres* IV [Amsterdam, 1764], 114–31, esp. 120–22) admits the superiority of the ancients in poetry and eloquence, but stresses the superiority of the moderns in physics, medicine and mathematics. Significant is the emphasis on the more rigorous method introduced by Descartes.

[162] Charles Perrault, *Parallèle des Anciens et des Modernes,* 4 vols. (Paris, 1688–96). These are the subjects treated in the fifth dialogue (vol. 4, 1696): astronomie, géographie, navigation, mathématiques (geometry, algebra, and arithmetic), art militaire, philosophie (logique, morale, physique, métaphysique), médecine, musique, jardinage, art de la cuisine, véhicles, imprimerie, artillerie, estampes, feux d'artifice.

[163] This is the grouping in the poem (*Parallèle,* vol. I (Paris, 1693), 173ff.): oratory, poetry, painting, sculpture, architecture, gardening, music. In the second dialogue also Perrault compares the visual arts repeatedly with music which he calls a *bel art* (146 and 149). Another work connected with the Querelle, François de Callière's *Histoire poëtique de la guerre nouvellement déclarée entre les anciens et les modernes* (Amsterdam, 1688; first ed., Paris, 1687) deals primarily with poetry and eloquence, but gives one section (Book 11, p. 213ff.) to painting, sculpture and

least in the case of poetry and eloquence, where everything depends on talent and taste, progress cannot be asserted with the same confidence as in the case of the sciences which depend on measurement.[164] Equally interesting, though unrelated to the *Querelle,* is another writing of Perrault, *Le Cabinet des Beaux Arts* (1690). This is a description and explanation of eight allegorical paintings found in the studio of a French gentleman to whom the work is dedicated. In the preface, Perrault opposes the concept *Beaux Arts* to the traditional *Arts Libéraux,* which he rejects,[165] and then lists and describes the eight "Fine Arts" which the gentleman had represented to suit his taste and interests: Éloquence, Poésie, Musique, Architecture, Peinture, Sculpture, Optique, Méchanique.[166] Thus on the threshold of the eighteenth century we are very close to the modern system of the Fine Arts, but we have not yet quite reached it, as the inclusion of Optics and Mechanics clearly shows. The fluctuations of the scheme show how slowly emerged the notion which to us seems so thoroughly obvious.

---

music. This is brought out in the title of the anonymous English translation: *Characters and Criticisms, upon the Ancient and Modern Orators, Poets, Painters, Musicians, Statuaries, and other Arts and Sciences* (London, 1705). Cf. A. C. Guthkelch, *The Library,* 3rd ser., vol. 4 (1913), 270–84.

[164] "Si nous avons un avantage visible dans les Arts dont les secrets se peuvent calculer et mesurer, il n'y a que la seule impossibilité de convaincre les gens dans les choses de goût et de fantaisie, comme sont les beautez de la Poësie et de l'Eloquence qui empesche que nous ne soyons reconnus les maîtres dans ces deux Arts comme dans tous les autres" (*Parallèle* I [Paris, 1693], preface). "Les Peintres, les Sculpteurs, les Chantres, les Poëtes / Tous ces hommes enfin en qui l'on voit regner / Un merveilleux sçavoir qu'on ne peut enseigner" (*Le génie,* verse epistle to Fontenelle, *ibid.,* 195f.). "Si j'avois bien prouvé, comme il est facile de le faire, que dans toutes les Sciences et dans tous les Arts dont les secrets se peuvent mesurer et calculer, nous l'emportons visiblement sur les Anciens; il n'y auroit que l'impossibilité de convaincre les esprits opiniastres dans les choses de goust et de fantaisie, comme sont la plupart des beautez de l'Eloquence et de la Poësie, qui pust empescher que les Modernes ne fussent reconnus les maistres dans ces deux arts comme dans tous les autres" (*ibid.,* 202). Cf also vol. III, preface. In his general conclusion also (IV, 292f.) Perrault excepts poetry and eloquence from his proof for the superiority of the Moderns.

[165] "Apres avoir abandonné cette division (of the seven liberal arts), on a choisi entre les Arts qui méritent d'être aimés et cultivés par un honnête homme ceux qui se sont trouvées être davantage du goût et du genie de celui qui les a fait peindre dans son cabinet" (p. 1f.).

[166] Eloquence, poetry, and music are put together in one group, as are the three visual arts (p. 2).

VI

During the first half of the eighteenth century the interest of amateurs, writers and philosophers in the visual arts and in music increased. The age produced not only critical writings on these arts composed by and for laymen,[167] but also treatises in which the arts were compared with each other and with poetry, and thus finally arrived at the fixation of the modern system of the fine arts.[168] Since this system seems to emerge gradually and after many fluctuations in the writings of authors who were in part of but secondary importance, though influential, it would appear that the notion and system of the fine arts may have grown and crystallized in the conversations and discussions of cultured circles in Paris and in London, and that the formal writings and treatises merely reflect a climate of opinion resulting from such conversations.[169] A further study of letters, diaries and articles in elegant journals may indeed supplement our brief survey, which we must limit to the better known sources.

The treatise on Beauty by J. P. de Crousaz, which first appeared in 1714 and exercised a good deal of influence, is usually considered as the earliest French treatise on aesthetics.[170] It has indeed something to say on the visual arts and on poetry, and devotes a whole section to music. Moreover, it is an important attempt to give a philosophical analysis of beauty as distinct from goodness, thus restating and developing the notions of ancient and Renaissance Platonists. Yet the author has no system of the arts, and applies his notion of beauty without any marked distinction to the mathematical sciences and to the moral virtues and actions as well as to the arts, and

---

[167] Dresdner, 103ff.

[168] Fontaine, *Les doctrines d'art*. Soreil, *l.c.* W. Folkierski, *Entre le classicisme et le romantisme: Étude sur l'esthétique et les l'esthéticiens du XVIIIe siècle* (Cracow-Paris, 1925). T. M. Mustoxidi, *Histoire de l'Esthétique française, 1700–1900* (Paris, 1920). For music, see also Écorcheville, *l.c.* Hugo Goldschmidt, *Die Musikaesthetik des 18. Jahrhunderts und ihre Beziehungen zu seinem Kunstschaffen* (Zürich-Leipzig, 1915). While these scholars discuss most of the relevant sources, none of them focuses on the problem which concerns us.

[169] " Tel livre qui marque une date n'apporte, à vrai dire, rien de nouveau sur le marché des idées, mais dit tout haut et avec ordre ce que beaucoup de gens pensent en détail et disent tout bas, sans s'arrêter à ce qu'ils disent " (Soreil, 146).

[170] *Traité du Beau*, 2 vols. (Amsterdam, 1724).

the fluidity of his "aesthetic" thought is shown by the fact that in his second edition he substituted a chapter on the beauty of religion for the one dealing with music.[171]

During the following years, the problem of the arts seems to have dominated the discussions of the Académie des Inscriptions, and several of its lectures which were printed somewhat later and exercised a good deal of influence stress the affinity between poetry, the visual arts and music.[172] These discussions no doubt influenced the important work of the Abbé Dubos that appeared first in 1719 and was reprinted many times in the original and in translations far into the second half of the century.[173] Dubos' merits in the history of aesthetic or artistic thought are generally recognized. It is apparent that he discusses not only the analogies between poetry and painting but also their differences, and that he is not interested in the superiority of one art over the others, as so many previous authors had been. His work is also significant as an early, though not the first, treatment of painting by an amateur writer, and his claim that the educated public rather than the professional artist is the best judge in matters of painting as well as of poetry is quite characteristic.[174] He did not

[171] "Le dernier chapitre où j'avois entrepris d'établir sur mes principes les fondemens de ce que la musique a de beau . . . on y en a substitué un autre . . . . C'est celui de la beauté de la religion" (preface of the second edition). On the treatment of music in the first edition, which I have not seen, cf. H. Goldschmidt, 35–37.

[172] In a lecture given in 1709, Abbé Fraguier describes poetry and painting as arts that have only pleasure for their end (*Histoire de l'Académie Royale des Inscriptions et Belles Lettres* . . . I (1736), 75ff.). In a *Deffense de la Poësie*, presented before 1710, Abbé Massieu distinguishes "ceux [arts] qui tendent à polir l'esprit" (eloquence, poetry, history, grammar); "ceux qui ont pour but un délassement et un plaisir honneste" (painting, sculpture, music, dance); and "ceux qui sont les plus nécessaires à la vie" (agriculture, navigation, architecture) (*Mémoires de littérature tirez de l'Académie Royale des Inscriptions* II (1736), 185f.). In a lecture of 1721, Louis Racine links poetry with the other *beaux arts* (*ibid.*, V (1729), 326). In a lecture of 1719, Fraguier treats painting, music, and poetry as different forms of imitation (*ibid.*, VI (1729), 265ff.). There are many more papers on related subjects.

[173] *Réflexions critiques sur la poësie et sur la peinture*, 4th ed., 3 vols. (Paris, 1740). A. Lombard, *L'Abbé Du Bos: Un initiateur de la pensée moderne (1670–1742)* (thes. Paris, 1913). Id., *La Querelle des anciens et des modernes; l'abbé du Bos* (Neuchatel, 1908). Aug. Morel, *Étude sur l'Abbé Dubos* (Paris, 1850). Marcel Braunschvig, *L'Abbé DuBos renovateur de la critique au XVIIIe siècle* (thes. Paris, Toulouse, 1904). P. Peteut, *Jean-Baptiste Dubos* (thes. Bern, 1902). E. Teuber, "Die Kunstphilosophie des Abbé Dubos" *Zeitschrift für Aesthetik und allgemeine Kunstwissenschaft* 17 (1924), 361–410. H. Trouchon, *Romantisme et Préromantisme* (Paris, 1930), 128ff.   [174] II, 323ff.

THE MODERN SYSTEM OF THE ARTS

invent the term *beaux-arts*, nor was he the first to apply it to other than the visual arts, but he certainly popularized the notion that poetry was one of the *beaux-arts*.[175] He also has a fairly clear notion of the difference between the arts that depend on "genius" or talent and the sciences based on accumulated knowledge,[176] and it has been rightly observed that in this he continues the work of the "Moderns" in the *Querelle des Anciens et des Modernes*, especially of Perrault.[177] Significant also is his acquaintance with English authors such as Wotton and Addison.[178] Finally, although the title of his work refers only to poetry and painting, he repeatedly has occasion to speak also of the other visual arts as linked with painting, especially of sculpture and engraving,[179] and he discusses music so frequently [180] that his English translator chose to mention this art in the very title of the book.[181] However, Dubos is as unsystematic in his presentation and arrangement as he is interesting for the variety of his ideas, and he fails to give anywhere a precise list of the arts other than poetry and painting or to separate them consistently from other fields of professions.[182]

Voltaire also in his *Temple du Goût* (1733) seems to link together several of the fine arts, but in an informal and rather elusive fashion which shows that he was unable or unwilling to present a clear

[175] I, 4; II, 131.

[176] "Qu'il est des professions où le succès dépend plus du génie que du secours que l'art peut donner, et d'autres où le succès dépend plus du secours qu'on tire de l'art que du génie. On ne doit pas inferer qu'un siècle surpasse un autre siècle dans les professions du premier genre, parce qu'il le surpasse dans les professions du second genre." The ancients are supreme in poetry, history and eloquence, but have been surpassed in the sciences such as physics, botany, geography, and astronomy, anatomy, navigation. Among the fields where progress depends "plus du talent d'inventer et du génie naturel de celui qui les exerce que de l'état de perfection où ces professions se trouvent, lorsque l'homme qui les exerce fournit sa carrière," Dubos lists painting, poetry, military strategy, music, oratory, and medicine (II, 558ff.).

[177] Lombard, *La querelle. Id.*, L'Abbé Du Bos, 183ff.

[178] Lombard, *L'Abbé Du Bos*, 189f. and 212.

[179] I, 393; 481. II, 157f.; 177; 195; 224; 226; 228ff.

[180] I, 435ff.; 451 ("Les premiers principes de la musique sont donc les mêmes que ceux de la poesie et de la peinture. Ainsi que la poësie et la peinture, la musique est une imitation"). The third volume, which deals with the ancient theatre, contains an extensive treatment of music and the dance.

[181] *Critical Reflections on Poetry, Painting and Music*, translated by Thomas Nugent (London, 1748).

[182] Thus he once groups together grammarians, painters, sculptors, poets, historians, orators (II, 235). For another example, see above, note 176.

scheme.[183] More important for the history of our problem is the Essay on Beauty of Père André (1741), which exercised a good deal of influence.[184] His Cartesian background is worth noticing, although it is not enough to ascribe an aesthetics to Descartes.[185] The major sections of the work discuss visible beauty, which includes nature and the visual arts, the beauty of morals, the beauty of the works of the spirit, by which he means poetry and eloquence, and finally the beauty of music.[186] André thus moves much closer to the system of the arts than either Crousaz or Dubos had done, but in his treatise the arts are still combined with morality, and subordinated to the problem of beauty in a broader sense.

The decisive step toward a system of the fine arts was taken by the Abbé Batteux in his famous and influential treatise, *Les beaux arts réduits à un même principe* (1746).[187] It is true that many elements of his system were derived from previous authors, but at the same time it should not be overlooked that he was the first to set forth a clearcut system of the fine arts in a treatise devoted exclusively to this subject. This alone may account for his claim to originality as well as for the enormous influence he exercised both in France and abroad, especially in Germany.[188] Batteux codified the modern system of the fine arts almost in its final form, whereas all previous authors had merely prepared it. He started from the poetic theories of Aristotle and Horace, as he states in his preface, and tried to extend their principles from poetry and painting to the other arts.[189] In his first chapter, Batteux gives a clear division of the arts.

[183] " Nous trouvâmes un homme entouré de peintres, d'architectes, de sculpteurs, de doreurs, de faux connoisseurs, de flateurs " (Voltaire, *Le temple du goût*, ed. E. Carcassonne [Paris, 1938], 66). " On y passe facilement, / De la musique à la peinture, / De la physique au sentiment, / Du tragique au simple agrément, / De la danse à l'architecture " (*ibid.*, 84).

[184] *Essai sur le Beau* (Amsterdam, 1759; first ed. 1741). Cf. E. Krantz, *Essai sur l'esthétique de Descartes* . . . (Paris, 1882), 311ff.   [185] Krantz, *l.c.*

[186] " Beau visible; beau dans les moeurs; beau dans les pièces de l'esprit; beau musical " (cf. p. 1).

[187] *Les beaux arts réduits à un même principe*, new ed. (Paris, 1747; first ed., 1746). Cf. M. Schenker, *Charles Batteux und seine Nachahmungstheorie in Deutschland* (Leipzig, 1909). Eberhard Freiherr von Danckelman, *Charles Batteux* (thes. Rostock, 1902).

[188] Trouchon, *l.c.* Schenker, *l.c.* For an English treatise based on Batteux, see below.

[189] " Le principe de l'imitation que le philosophe grec (Aristotle) établit pour les beaux arts, m'avoit frappé. J'en avois senti la justesse pour la peinture qui est une poesie muette . . . " (p. VIII). " J'allai plus loin: j'essayai d'appliquer le même principe à la musique et à l'art de geste " (VIII f.). He also quotes Cicero, *Pro Archia*, for the unity of the fine arts (p. X).

He separates the fine arts which have pleasure for their end from the mechanical arts, and lists the fine arts as follows: music, poetry, painting, sculpture and the dance.[190] He adds a third group which combines pleasure and usefulness and puts eloquence and architecture in this category. In the central part of his treatise, Batteux tries to show that the "imitation of beautiful nature" is the principle common to all the arts, and he concludes with a discussion of the theatre as a combination of all the other arts. The German critics of the later eighteenth century, and their recent historians, criticized Batteux for his theory of imitation and often failed to recognize that he formulated the system of the arts which they took for granted and for which they were merely trying to find different principles. They also overlooked the fact that the much maligned principle of imitation was the only one a classicist critic such as Batteux could use when he wanted to group the fine arts together with even an appearance of ancient authority. For the "imitative" arts were the only authentic ancient precedent for the "fine arts," and the principle of imitation could be replaced only after the system of the latter had been so firmly established as no longer to need the ancient principle of imitation to link them together. Diderot's criticism of Batteux has been emphasized too much, for it concerned only the manner in which Batteux defined and applied his principle, but neither the principle itself, nor the system of the arts for which it had been designed.

As a matter of fact, Diderot and the other authors of the *Encyclopédie* not only followed Batteux's system of the fine arts, but also furnished the final touch and thus helped to give it a general currency not only in France but also in the other European countries. Montesquieu in his essay on taste written for the *Encyclopédie* takes the fine arts for granted.[191] Diderot, whose interests included music and the visual arts and who was also acquainted with such English authors as Shaftesbury, Addison and Hutcheson, criticizes Batteux in his *Lettre sur les Sourds et Muets* (1751), in which he demands a better and more detailed comparison between poetry, painting and music that would take into account the different modes of expression of those arts as they would affect their treatment of even the same subject

[190] " Les autres ont pour objet le plaisir . . . on les appelle les beaux arts par excellence. Tels sont la musique, poésie, la peinture, la sculpture et l'art du geste ou la danse " (p. 6).

[191] *Essai sur le goût* (*Oeuvres complètes de Montesquieu*, ed. E. Laboulaye, VII [Paris, 1879], 116): " La poésie, la peinture, la sculpture, l'architecture, la musique, la danse, les différentes sortes de jeux, enfin les ouvrages de la nature et de l'art peuvent lui [to the soul] donner du plaisir . . . ." Cf. Edwin P. Dargan, *The Aesthetic Doctrine of Montesquieu* (thes. Johns Hopkins University, Baltimore, 1907), 21.

matter.[192] In the article on the Arts for the *Encyclopédie*, Diderot does not discuss the fine arts, but uses the old distinction between the liberal and mechanical arts and stresses the importance of the latter.[193] Yet in his article on beauty, he does discuss the fine arts, mentions Crousaz and Hutcheson and gives qualified approval to both André and Batteux, calling each of these two good works the best in its category and criticizing Batteux merely for his failure to define his concept of " beautiful nature " more clearly and explicitly.[194]

Still more interesting is D'Alembert's famous *Discours préliminaire*. In his division of knowledge, purportedly based on Francis Bacon, D'Alembert makes a clear distinction between philosophy, which comprises both the natural sciences and such fields as grammar, eloquence, and history, and " those cognitions which consist of imitation," listing among the latter painting, sculpture, architecture, poetry and music.[195] He criticizes the old distinction between the liberal and mechanical arts, and then subdivides the liberal arts into the fine arts which have pleasure for their end, and the more necessary or useful liberal arts such as grammar, logic and morals.[196] He concludes with

[192] *Oeuvres complètes de Diderot*, ed. J. Assézat, 1 (1875), 343ff. The preface is addressed to Batteux (*Lettre à l'auteur des Beaux-arts réduits à un même principe*, 347). Towards the end of his treatise, Diderot summarizes his criticism as follows: " Mais rassembler les beautés communes de la poésie, de la peinture et de la musique; en montrer les analogies; expliquer comment le poète, le peintre et le musicien rendent le même image . . . c'est ce qui reste à faire, et ce que je vous conseille d'ajouter à vos Beaux-arts réduits à un même principe. Ne manquez pas non plus de mettre à la tête de cet ouvrage un chapître sur ce que c'est que la belle nature, car je trouve des gens qui me soutiennent que, faute de l'une de ces choses, votre traité reste sans fondement; et que, faute de l'autre, il manque d'application" (385). On Diderot's aesthetic doctrines, see: Werner Leo, *Diderot als Kunstphilosoph* (thes. Erlangen, 1918). R. Loyalty Cru, *Diderot as a Disciple of English Thought* (New York, 1913), 395ff.

[193] *Encyclopédie ou Dictionnaire Raisonné des sciences, des arts et des métiers* I (Paris, 1751), 713ff.

[194] " Son Essai sur le beau [*i.e.*, of Père André] est le système le plus suivi, le plus étendu et le mieux lié que je connaisse. J'oserais assurer qu'il est dans son genre ce que le Traité des Beaux-Arts réduits à un seul principe est dans le sien. Ce sont deux bons ouvrages auxquelles il n'a manqué qu'un chapître pour être excellents . . . M. l'abbé Batteux rappelle tous les principes des beaux-arts à l'imitation de la belle nature; mais il ne nous apprend point ce que c'est que la belle nature" (Diderot, Oeuvres 10 [1876], 17. *Encyclopédie* 2 [1751], 169ff.). For the same criticism of Batteux, see also the *Lettre sur les sourds*, above, note 192.

[195] " Des connaissances qui consistent dans l'imitation " (D'Alembert, *Oeuvres* [Paris, 1853], 99f. Cf. *Encyclopédie* I (1751), p. I ff.).

[196] " Parmi les arts libéraux qu' on a réduit à des principes, ceux qui se proposent l'imitation de la nature ont été appelés beaux-arts, parce qu'ils ont princi-

a main division of knowledge into philosophy, history and the fine arts.[197] This treatment shows still a few signs of fluctuation and of older notions, but it sets forth the modern system of the fine arts in its final form, and at the same time reflects its genesis. The threefold division of knowledge follows Francis Bacon, but significantly d'Alembert speaks of the five fine arts where Bacon had mentioned only poetry. D'Alembert is aware that the new concept of the fine arts is taking the place of the older concept of the liberal arts, which he criticizes, and he tries to compromise by treating the fine arts as a subdivision of the liberal arts, thus leaving a last trace of the liberal arts that was soon to disappear. Finally, he reveals his dependence on Batteux in certain phrases and in the principle of imitation, but against Batteux and the classical tradition he now includes architecture among the imitative arts, thus removing the last irregularity which had separated Batteux's system from the modern scheme of the fine arts. Thus we may conclude that the *Encyclopédie,* and especially its famous introduction, codified the system of the fine arts after and beyond Batteux and through its prestige and authority gave it the widest possible currency all over Europe.

After the middle of the century and after the publication of the *Encyclopédie,* speculation on the fine arts in France does not seem to have undergone any basic changes for some time. The notion was popularized and stabilized through such works as Lacombe's portable dictionary of the Fine Arts, which covered architecture, sculpture, painting, engraving, poetry and music, and through other similar works.[198] The term Beaux Arts, and " Art," in the new sense, found its way into the dictionaries of the French language that had ignored it before. And the Revolution gave the novel term a new institu-

---

palement l'agrément pour objet. Mais ce n'est pas la seule chose qui les distingue des arts libéraux plus nécessaires ou plus utiles, comme la grammaire, la logique ou la morale " (105)

[197] " La peinture, la sculpture, l'architecture, la poésie, la musique et leurs différentes divisions composent la troisième distribution générale, qui naît de l'imagination, et dont les parties sont comprises sous le nom de beaux-arts " (117).

[198] Jacques Lacombe, *Dictionnaire portatif des Beaux-Arts ou Abrégé de ce qui concerne l'architecture, la sculpture, la peinture, la gravure, la poésie et la musique, avec la définition de ces arts, l'explication des termes et des choses qui leur appartiennent,* new ed. (Paris, 1753; first ed. 1752). The preface refers to " Le goût que le public témoigne pour les Beaux-Arts " and to " la nécessité d'un livre qui renferme les Recherches et les Connoissances d'un amateur " (p. III). Pierre Estève, *L'esprit des Beaux Arts,* 2 vols. (Paris, 1753). P.-J.-B. Nougaret, *Anecdotes des Beaux Arts, contenant tout ce que la Peinture, la Sculpture, la Gravure, l'Architecture, la Littérature, la Musique etc. et la vie des artistes offrent de plus curieux et de plus piquant,* 3 vols. (Paris, 1776-80; the work actually covers only the visual arts).

tional expression when it merged several of the older Academies into the Académie des Beaux Arts.[199] Gradually, the further developments of aesthetics in Germany began to affect French philosophy and literature. The second edition of the *Encyclopédie,* published in Switzerland in 1781, has additions by Sulzer, including an article on aesthetics [200] and a section on Fine Arts appended to the article on Art that had not appeared in the first edition.[201] Early in the nineteenth century, the philosopher Victor Cousin, following Kant and the Scottish thinkers of the eighteenth century, as well as what he believed he found in Plato, Proclus and other classical sources, centered his philosophical system on the three concepts of the Good, the True and the Beautiful, understanding by the latter the realm of art and aesthetics.[202] Cousin's wide influence in the later nineteenth century went a long ways toward establishing this triad in modern value theory and toward fortifying the place of aesthetics in the system of philosophical disciplines. It also induced many thinkers and historians to interpret in terms of this scheme a number of ancient and medieval notions that resembled it superficially but had in reality a very different meaning and context. Meanwhile, as Cousin's doctrine was spreading among philosophers and historians, French literature and criticism had long been feeling the impact of Romanticism. They were beginning to develop modern problems and theories concerning the arts and their interpretation, no longer related to the discussions of the eighteenth century, and were laying the ground for more recent present-day tendencies.

VII

Having followed the French development through the eighteenth

[199] Aucoc, 6–7. The section for literature and the fine arts of the *Institut,* created in 1795, comprised: grammaire, langues anciennes, poésie, antiquité et monuments, peinture, sculpture, architecture, musique, déclamation.

[200] *Encyclopédie* 13 (Berne and Lausanne, 1781), 84–86: " Esthétique ... terme nouveau, inventé pour désigner une science qui n'a été réduite en forme que depuis peu d'années. C'est la philosophie des beaux-arts." [Aristotle did not have such a theory.] " M. Dubos est, si je ne me trompe, le premier d'entre les modernes qui ait entrepris de déduire d'un principe général la théorie des beaux-arts, et d'en démontrer les règles.... Feu M. Baumgarten ... est le premier qui ait hasardé de créer sur des principes philosophiques la science générale des beaux-arts, à laquelle il a donné le nom d'esthétique." [201] *Ibid.* 3 (1781), 484ff.

[202] V. Cousin, *Du Vrai, du Beau et du Bien,* 29th ed. (Paris, 1904; first ed., 1836, based on lectures delivered in 1817–18). Cf. P. Janet, *Victor Cousin et son oeuvre* (Paris, 1885). E. Krantz (*Essai sur l'esthétique de Descartes* [Paris, 1882], 312f.) emphasizes that Cousin was the first French thinker who gave a separate place to aesthetics and to beauty in his philosophical system.

century, we must discuss the history of artistic thought in England.[203] The English writers were strongly influenced by the French down to the end of the seventeenth century and later, but during the eighteenth century they made important contributions of their own and in turn influenced continental thought, especially in France and Germany. Interest in the arts other than poetry began to rise slowly in the English literature of the seventeenth century. Works of an encyclopedic nature show little awareness of the separate function of the fine arts,[204] whereas an author such as Henry Peacham, who continued the amateur tradition of the Renaissance, would not only write a treatise on drawing, but also recommend the cultivation of painting, music and poetry, of classical studies and the collecting of coins and other antiquities and of natural curiosities, for the education of a perfect gentleman.[205] John Evelyn, who was the model of a *virtuoso*, included artistic and scientific interests,[206] but the work of the *virtuosi* of the Royal Society soon led to a separation between the arts and the sciences.[207] The *Querelle*, which was at least partly caused by the emancipation of the natural sciences in the seventeenth century, spread from France to England. The most important treatise in England representing the views of the Moderns, that of Wotton, tried to cover systematically all the human arts and activities, just as Perrault

[203] James E. Tobin, *Eighteenth Century English Literature and Its Cultural Background: A Bibliography* (New York, 1939), 11–16; 27–33. John W. Draper, *Eighteenth Century English Aesthetics: A Bibliography* (Heidelberg, 1931). B. Sprague Allen, *Tides of English Taste (1619–1800)*, 2 vols. (Cambridge, Mass., 1937). F. Mirabent, *La estética inglesa del siglo XVIII* (Barcelona, 1927). Karl L. F. Thielke, *Literatur- und Kunstkritik in ihren Wechselbeziehungen: Ein Beitrag zur englischen Aesthetik des 18. Jahrhunderts* (Halle, 1935). John W. Draper, "Aristotelian 'Mimesis' in Eighteenth Century England," *PMLA* 36 (1921), 372–400. Id., "Poetry and Music in Eighteenth Century Aesthetics," *Englische Studien* 67 (1932–33), 70–85. J. G. Robertson, *Studies in the Genesis of Romantic Theory in the Eighteenth Century* (Cambridge, 1923), 235ff. Elizabeth W. Manwaring, *Italian Landscape in Eighteenth Century England* (New York, 1925), 14ff. Herbert M. Schueller, "Literature and Music as Sister Arts: An Aspect of Aesthetic Theory in Eighteenth-Century Britain," *Philological Quarterly* 26 (1947), 193–205.

[204] George Hakewill (*An Apologie or Declaration of the Power and Providence of God in the Government of the World* . . . , 3rd ed., Oxford, 1635), who compares the ancients and moderns in the arts and sciences (Bury, 89), puts poetry between history and the art military (278ff.), architecture and painting between philosophy and navigation (303ff.), whereas sculpture and music receive no separate treatment in his work. [205] See above, note 110.

[206] *The Literary Remains of John Evelyn*, ed. W. Upcott (London, 1834).

[207] James A. H. Murray, *A New English Dictionary on Historical Principles*, vol. 10, pt. 2 (Oxford, 1928), 240f. Several of the seventeenth-century passages given for "virtuoso" include a scientific interest. The limitation of the term to a taste for the arts is clear in Shaftesbury, see below. Cf. Manwaring, *l.c.*, 25.

had done, and emphasized like Perrault the fundamental difference between the sciences that had made progress since antiquity, and the arts that had not.[208] A translation of one of the French works related to the *Querelle*, Callière's *History of the War of the Ancients and Moderns*, was published as late as 1705, and reveals in its very title the growing sense of the affinity of the fine arts.[209] Even before the end of the seventeenth century, Dryden had translated Du Fresnoy's poem on painting with De Piles' commentary and had added his famous introduction on the Parallel of Painting and Poetry which popularized the notion in England.[210] This translation was still of interest to Sir Joshua Reynolds, who wrote some notes on it.[211] Early in the eighteenth century, Jonathan Richardson was praising painting as a liberal art,[212] and John Dennis in some of his critical treatises on

[208] William Wotton, *Reflections upon Ancient and Modern Learning*, 3rd ed. (London, 1705). " . . . of these particulars there are two sorts: one, of those wherein the greatest part of those learned men who have compared Ancient and Modern Performances, either give up the cause to the Ancients quite, or think, at least, that the Moderns have not gone beyond them. The other of those, where the Advocates for the Moderns think the case so clear on their side, that they wonder how any man can dispute it with them. Poesie, Oratory, Architecture, Painting, and Statuary, are of the first sort; Natural History, Physiology, and Mathematics, with all their Dependencies, are of the second" (p. 18, end of ch. 2). "The generality of the learned have given the Ancients the preference in those arts and sciences which have hitherto been considered: but for the precedency in those parts of learning which still remain to be enquired into, the Moderns have put in their claim, with great briskness. Among this sort, I reckon mathematical and physical sciences, in their largest extent" (p. 74f., ch. 7). In the first group, Wotton discusses Moral and Political knowledge, Eloquence and Poesie, grammar, architecture, statuary and painting. The second group includes, besides the sciences, philology and theology, also gardening which is treated with agriculture (ch. 22, p. 272) and music which is placed between optics and medicine (ch. 25, p. 307). The chapter on gardening is lacking in the first edition (London, 1694). Wotton does once compare music with painting ("For, in making a Judgment of Music, it is much the same thing as it is in making a judgment of Pictures," 311), but he treats music as a "physico-mathematical science, built upon fixed rules, and stated proportions" (309f.), and also in other respects his two groups do not coincide with the modern distinction between fine arts and sciences. Wotton is obviously moving towards that distinction, but I do not see that he goes beyond Perrault in this respect, as stated by Rigault (323f.) and Bury (121f.). No distinction between the arts and sciences is made by Sir William Temple, "An Essay upon the Ancient and Modern Learning" (1690), in *Critical Essays of the Seventeenth Century*, ed. J. E. Spingarn, vol. 3 (Oxford, 1909), 32–72.   [209] See above, note 163.

[210] C. A. Du Fresnoy, *De arte graphica*, tr. J. Dryden (London, 1695), p. I–LVIII: "Preface of the Translator, with a Parallel of Poetry and Painting." *The Critical and Miscellaneous Prose of John Dryden*, ed. E. Malone, vol. III (London, 1800), 291ff.

[211] Sir Joshua Reynolds, *The Literary Works* II (London, 1835), 297–358 (first ed., 1783).

[212] Jonathan Richardson, *The Theory of Painting* (first published in 1715), in his *Works* (London, 1792), 5ff.

poetics stressed the affinity between poetry, painting and music.[213]

Of greater importance were the writings of Anthony, Earl of Shaftesbury, one of the most influential thinkers of the eighteenth century, not only in England but also on the continent.[214] His interest and taste for literature and the arts are well known, and his writings are full of references to the various arts and to the beauty of their works. The ideal of the *virtuoso* which he embodied and advocated no longer included the sciences, as in the seventeenth century, but had its center in the arts and in the moral life.[215] Since Shaftesbury was the first major philosopher in modern Europe in whose writings the discussion of the arts occupied a prominent place, there is some reason for considering him as the founder of modern aesthetics.[216] Yet Shaftesbury was influenced primarily by Plato and Plotinus, as well as by Cicero, and he consequently did not make a clear distinction between artistic and moral beauty.[217] His moral sense still includes both ethical and aesthetic objects.[218] Moreover, although references to the particular arts are frequent in his writings, and some of his works are even entirely devoted to the subjects of painting [219] or of poetry,[220] the passages in which he mentions poetry, the visual arts and music together are not too frequent, and do not contain any more specific notions than may be found in earlier authors.[221] Poetry, especially, appears still in the company not only

[213] *The Critical Works of John Dennis*, ed. Edward N. Hooker, vol. I (Baltimore, 1939), 201f. ("The Advancement and Reformation of Modern Poetry," 1701); 336 ("The Ground of Criticism in Poetry," 1704).

[214] His importance is stressed by all historians of aesthetics. See also E. Cassirer, *Die platonische Renaissance in England und die Schule von Cambridge* (Leipzig, 1932), 115; 138ff. G. Spicker, *Die Philosophie des Grafen von Shaftesbury* (Freiburg, 1872), 196ff. Christian Friedrich Weiser, *Shaftesbury und das deutsche Geistesleben* (Leipzig-Berlin, 1916). L. Stuermer, *Der Begriff "moral sense" in der Philosophie Shaftesbury's* (thes. Königsberg, 1928).

[215] Anthony, Earl of Shaftesbury, *Characteristics*, ed. John M. Robertson (London, 1900), vol. I, 214f.; II, 252f. *The Life, Unpublished Letters, and Philosophical Regimen of Anthony, Earl of Shaftesbury*, ed. B. Rand (London, 1900), 249 ("A virtuoso to propose poetry, music, dance, picture, architecture, garden, and so on"); 416f. ("Had Mr. Locke been a virtuoso, he would not have philosophized thus"); 478; 484; 496; 506.   [216] See Cassirer, *l.c.*, above, note 214.

[217] *Characteristics* II, 128; 138.   [218] *Characteristics* I, 262; II, 136f.

[219] Anthony, Earl of Shaftesbury, *Second Characters*, ed. B. Rand (Cambridge, 1914).   [220] *Characteristics* I, 101ff.

[221] "From music, poetry, rhetoric, down to the simple prose of history, through all the plastic arts of sculpture, statuary, painting, architecture, and the rest; everything muse-like, graceful, and exquisite was rewarded with the highest honours..." (*i.e.*, by the Greeks). *Characteristics* II, 242. Cf. *ibid.*, II, 330, where criticism of poetry is compared to the judgment of music or painting. I, 94 (beauty in architecture, music, poetry); II, 129; 252f.

of eloquence but also of history, thus reflecting the Renaissance tradition of the *Studia humanitatis*.[222] Almost equally influential in England as well as on the continent, at least in literary circles, was Joseph Addison. His famous essays on imagination, which appeared in the *Spectator* in 1712, are remarkable not merely for their early emphasis on that faculty, but also for the manner in which he attributes the pleasures of the imagination to the various arts as well as to natural sights. Without ever giving a definite system, he constantly refers to gardening and architecture, painting and sculpture, poetry and music, and makes it quite clear that the pleasures of the imagination are to be found in their works and products.[223]

The philosophical implications of Shaftesbury's doctrine were further developed by a group of Scottish thinkers. Francis Hutcheson, who considered himself Shaftesbury's pupil, modified his doctrine by distinguishing between the moral sense and the sense of beauty.[224] This distinction, which was adopted by Hume[225] and quoted by Diderot, went a long ways to prepare the separation of ethics and aesthetics, although Hutcheson still assigned the taste of poetry to the moral sense.[226] A later philosopher of the Scottish school, Thomas

---

[222] II, 242. There seems to be a tendency in Shaftesbury to associate not only the beauty of the senses with the visual arts and music, but also the beauty of character and virtue, or moral beauty, with poetry. I, 136 ("moral artist"); 216 ("poetical and moral truth, the beauty of sentiments, the sublime of characters . . ."); II, 318 ("to morals, and the knowledge of what is called poetic manners and truth"); 331f. ("a sense of that moral truth on which . . . poetic truth and beauty must naturally depend"). This is not merely a residue of the old moralistic interpretation of poetry, but an attempt to correlate the emerging system of the fine arts with Plato's ladder of beauty. Cf. the statement of Castelvetro, above, note 92.

[223] Joseph Addison, *Works*, ed. Tickell, II (London, 1804), 354ff. (*Spectator*, no. 411ff.). Addison includes architecture, and perhaps gardening, along with natural sights, among the primary pleasures, whereas he lists as secondary pleasures the "arts of mimicry," i.e., "statue, picture, description, or sound" (376). Significant also is a sentence from an earlier essay, published in the *Spectator*, no. 29, on April 3, 1711: "that music, architecture, and painting, as well as poetry and oratory, are to deduce their laws and rules from the general sense and taste of mankind . . ." (*ibid.*, I, 78).

[224] Francis Hutcheson, *An Inquiry into the Original of our Ideas of Beauty and Virtue* (Glasgow, 1772; first ed., 1725), p. XI; 8; 100. Cf. Thomas Fowler, *Shaftesbury and Hutcheson* (New York, 1883). William Robert Scott, *Francis Hutcheson* (Cambridge, 1900). John J. Martin, *Shaftesbury's und Hutcheson's Verhältnis zu Hume* (thes. Halle, 1905).

[225] D. Hume, *An Enquiry concerning the Principles of Morals* (1751), Appendix I: "Concerning Moral Sentiment." Cf. *A Treatise of Human Nature* (1739-40), Book III, Part I, Section II.

[226] *L.c.*, 239 ("We shall find this sense to be the foundation also of the chief pleasures of poetry"). For the root of this idea in Shaftesbury, see above, note 222.

Reid, introduced common sense as a direct criterion of truth, and although he was no doubt influenced by Aristotle's notion of common sense and the Stoic and modern views on "common notions," it has been suggested that his common sense was conceived as a counterpart to Hutcheson's two senses.[227] Thus the psychology of the Scottish school led the way for the doctrine of the three faculties of the soul, which found its final development in Kant and its application in Cousin.

Other English authors, motivated by critical rather than philosophical interests and probably influenced by French authors, popularized the notion of the affinity between poetry, painting, and music, —e.g., Charles Lamotte [228] and Hildebrand Jacobs.[229] More philosophical are the essays of James Harris, who continued Shaftesbury and had some influence on German writers. In the first of his three essays, which are written in an elegant dialogue form but heavily annotated with references to classical authors, Harris expounds the concept of art on the basis of Aristotle and with its older comprehensive meaning. In the second essay, he distinguishes between the necessary arts and the arts of elegance, putting under the latter category especially music, painting and poetry, and comparing these three arts with each other according to their relative merits. The third essay deals with happiness as the art of human conduct.[230] About

[227] Thomas Reid, *Works*, 4th ed. (Edinburgh, 1854). Matthias Keppes, *Der Common Sense als Princip der gewissheit in der Philosophie des Schotten Thomas Reid* (Munich, 1890), 15. Cf. F. Ueberweg, *Grundriss der Geschichte der Philosophie*, III, 12th ed. (Berlin, 1924), 416. O. Robbins, "The Aesthetics of Thomas Reid," *The Journal of Aesthetics and Art Criticism* 5 (1942), 30–41.

[228] Charles Lamotte, *An Essay upon Poetry and Painting* . . . (Dublin, 1745; first ed., 1730).

[229] Hildebrand Jacobs, *Of the Sister Arts; an Essay*, in his *Works* (London, 1735), 379–419 (first ed., 1734). "If it be allow'd with Cicero that all Arts are related, we may safely conclude, that Poetry, Painting, and Music are closely ally'd" (379). "Poetry is much nearer ally'd to Painting, than to Music. Lyric Poetry approaches more to Music than any other Species of it, as Dramatic, and Pastoral Poetry do to Painting" (380). "The same Rules which Aristotle lays down as necessary for the Poets to observe in the Formation of he (*sic*) Manners, or Characters, are equally instructive to the Painters" (401). "That the Ancients were more excellent than we in most Parts of these Arts of Ornament, is as manifest, as that latter Ages have invented many useful Things entirely unknown to them" (412). However, the moderns are said to be superior in music (392). These statements are so explicit and interesting that it would be worth while to explore the influence of this author in France and Germany.

[230] J(ames) H(arris), *Three Treatises, the first concerning art, the second concerning music, painting, and poetry, the third concerning happiness* (London, 1744). "All arts have this in common that they respect human life. Some contribute to

the same time, the poet Akenside continued the work of Addison;[231] and before the middle of the century the important French works of Dubos and Batteux were presented to English readers, the former in a translation,[232] the latter in an anonymous version or summary, entitled *The Polite Arts*.[233]

During the second half of the eighteenth century, English writers continued to discuss the various arts. But they were not so much interested in expounding and developing a system of the fine arts, which they took pretty much for granted, as in discussing general concepts and principles concerning the arts; e.g., Home, Burke, and Gerard; or else the relations between the particular arts; e.g., Daniel Webb or John Brown, to mention only some of the more influential

---

its necessities, as medicine and agriculture; others to its elegance, as music, painting, and poetry" (53). These three arts are called mimetic (65; 94).

[231] Mark Akenside, *The Pleasures of Imagination*, in his *Poetical Works*, ed. G. Gilfillan (Edinburgh, 1857), 1ff. In the preface of 1744, painting and sculpture, music and poetry are listed as imitative arts, and the poem is said to cover " all the various entertainment we meet with, either in poetry, painting, music, or any of the elegant arts" (p. 1). In the general argument added to the edition of 1757, the pleasures of imagination are said to proceed from natural objects or "from works of art, such as a noble edifice, a musical tune, a statue, a picture, a poem," and music, sculpture, painting and poetry are called "elegant arts" (77).

[232] See above, note 181.

[233] *The Polite Arts, or, a Dissertation on Poetry, Painting, Musick, Architecture, and Eloquence* (London, 1749). The work is anonymous, and dedicated to William Cheselden. In the copy of the Yale University Library I have used, a contemporary manuscript note at the end of the preface identifies the author as follows: " Hippesley, son of the player, & bred under Mr. Cheselden & now surgeon abroad to the African company, 1753" (p. IX). This is obviously John Hippisley (d. 1767) son of the actor (d. 1748), to whom the following anonymous writings have been attributed: Dissertation on Comedy . . . (London, 1750); Essays, 1. On the Populousness of Africa, 2. On the Trade at the Forts on the Gold Coast, 3. On the Necessity of erecting a Fort at Cape Appollonia (London, 1764). Cf. *Dictionary of National Biography* IX, 903. The essay on *The Polite Arts* appears to depend closely on Batteux. This is the division of the arts given in ch. 2: "Arts may be divided into three kinds. The first have the Necessities of Mankind for their Object . . . . From this the Mechanick Arts arose. The next kind have Pleasure for their Object . . . They are called Polite Arts by way of Excellency, such are Musick, Poetry, Painting, Sculpture, and the Art of Gesture or Dancing. The third kind are those which have usefulness and Pleasure at the same time for their Object: such are Eloquence and Architecture" (5-6). A close comparison between the anonymous English essay and Batteux's treatise shows that the former follows the latter verbatim for large sections of the text, but alters its model through numerous transpositions, omissions and additions. The most important among the latter are two chapters on Eloquence and Architecture at the end of the English essay.

writers.[234] All these English and Scottish writers show a strong preoccupation with psychology, as might be expected from the general trend of English thought in that century. They exercised considerable influence on the continent, especially in Germany, where many of their works appeared in translations. It has been noted that the emphasis of writers and literary critics on the affinity between poetry and painting was followed after the middle of the century by an increasing insistence on the links between poetry and music.[235] One reason for this may have been the public attention which music received in London after the appearance of Handel,[236] just as had been the case in Paris after the success of Lulli. On the other hand, if poetry really tended to exchange the company of painting for that of music, this merely reflects a change in style and taste from descriptive to emotional poetry that corresponds to the transition from classicism to romanticism. A new epoch in English critical and artistic theory begins toward the very end of the century with Coleridge, who imported from Germany some of the aesthetic notions of Kant and of the early Romanticists. The further development these ideas received through Coleridge and his English successors in the nineteenth century is beyond the scope of this paper.

[234] Henry Home, Lord Kames, *Elements of Criticism* (New York, 1830; first ed., 1762). He lists poetry, painting, sculpture, music, gardening and architecture as "fine arts" (11). E. Burke, *A Philosophical Enquiry into the Origin of our Ideas of the Sublime and Beautiful* (London, 1770; first ed., 1757). Alexander Gerard, *An Essay on Taste* (London, 1759). He lists as the "finer arts": music, painting, statuary, architecture, poetry and eloquence (189). Daniel Webb, *Observations on the Correspondence between Poetry and Music* (London, 1769; cf. Hans Hecht, *Daniel Webb*, Hamburg, 1920). Dr. (John) Brown, *A Dissertation on the Rise, Union, and Power, the Progressions, Separations, and Corruptions, of Poetry and Musick* (London, 1763; cf. Hermann M. Flasdieck, *John Brown (1715-66) und seine Dissertation on Poetry and Music*, Halle, 1924). Thomas Robertson, *An Inquiry into the Fine Arts* (London, 1784; he quotes Batteux and Bettinelli, and lists as fine arts: music, speech, architecture, painting, sculpture, gardening, dance, eloquence, poetry and also history, cf. 14–17). Sir William Jones, *Essay II. on the Arts, commonly called Imitative*, in his *Poems*, 2nd ed. (London, 1777), 191ff. (he also quotes Batteux and discusses especially poetry, music and painting. James Beattie, *An Essay on Poetry and Music, as they affect the Mind*, 3rd ed. (London, 1779; written in 1762). Hugh Blair, *Lectures on Rhetoric and Belles Lettres* (London, 1787; first ed., 1783).

[235] John W. Draper, "Poetry and Music in Eighteenth Century Aesthetics," *Englische Studien* 67 (1932–33), 70–85. Herbert M. Schueller, "Literature and Music as Sister Arts . . . ," *Philological Quarterly* 26 (1947), 193–205.

[236] Cf. H. Parker, *The Nature of the Fine Arts* (London, 1885), 18ff.

VIII

Discussion of the arts does not seem to have occupied many German writers in the seventeenth century, which was on the whole a period of cultural decline.[237] The poet Opitz showed familiarity with the parallel of poetry and painting,[238] but otherwise the Germans did not take part in the development we are trying to describe before the eighteenth century. During the first part of that century interest in literature and literary criticism began to rise, but did not yet lead to a detailed or comparative treatment of the other arts. However, some of the French and English writers we have mentioned were widely read and also translated into German during the course of the century, such as Dubos and Batteux, Shaftesbury and Harris. The critical writings of the Swiss authors, Bodmer and Breitinger, focus from the very beginning on the parallel between painting and poetry, and reflect the influence of Addison and perhaps of Dubos.[239] Even their classicist opponent, Gottsched, mentions occasionally the affinity between poetry, painting, music, and the other arts,[240] as does Johann

---

[237] For German aesthetics in the eighteenth century, see, besides the general histories of aesthetics: F. Braitmaier, *Geschichte der poetischen Theorie von den Diskursen der Maler bis auf Lessing*, 2 pts. (Frauenfeld, 1888–89). E. Gurcker, *Histoire des doctrines littéraires et esthétiques en Allemagne*, 2 vols. (Paris, 1883–96). Robert Sommer, *Grundzüge einer Geschichte der deutschen Psychologie und Aesthetik von Wolff-Baumgarten bis Kant-Schiller* (Würzburg, 1892). M. Dessoir, *Geschichte der neueren deutschen Psychologie*, 2nd ed. (Berlin, 1902). H. Goldschmidt, *Die Musikaesthetik des 18. Jahrhunderts* . . . (Zürich and Leipzig, 1915). W. Dilthey, *Das Erlebnis und die Dichtung*, 4th ed (Leipzig, 1913), 42ff. E. Cassirer, *Freiheit und Form*, 2nd ed. (Berlin, 1918), 97ff. Herman Wolf, *Versuch einer Geschichte des Geniebegriffs in der deutschen Aesthetik des 18. Jahrhunderts* (Heidelberg, 1923). K. Bauerhorst, *Der Geniebegriff* . . . (thes. Breslau, 1930). B. Rosenthal, *Der Geniebegriff des Aufklärungszeitalters* (Berlin, 1933).

[238] C. Borinski, *Die Kunstlehre der Renaissance in Opitz' Buch von der deutschen Poeterey* (thes. Munich, 1883), 44f.

[239] *Die Discourse der Mahlern* (1721–22), ed. Th. Vetter (Frauenfeld, 1891). The analogy between poetry and painting is stressed in discourse no. 19 (p. 91) and extended to sculpture in discourse no. 20 (97ff.). The same analogy is stressed in the later works of Bodmer and Breitinger. See Johann Jacob Bodmer, *Critische Betrachtungen ueber die Poetischen Gemälde der Dichter* (Zürich, 1741), 27ff. Johann Jacob Breitinger, *Critische Dichtkunst* (Zürich, 1740), 3ff. and 29ff. (where the comparison with painting is extended to history and eloquence). Cf. R. De Reynold, *Histoire littéraire de la Suisse au XVIIIe siècle*, II (Lousanne, 1912): *Bodmer et l'École Suisse*. R. Verosta, *Der Phantasiebegriff bei den Schweizern Bodmer und Breitinger* (progr. Vienna, 1908). F. Braitmaier, *Die poetische Theorie Gottsched's und der Schweizer* (progr. Tübingen, 1879). F. Servaes, *Die Poetik Gottscheds und der Schweizer* (Strassburg, 1887).

[240] Johann Christoph Gottsched, *Versuch einer Critischen Dichtkunst*, 3rd ed. (Leipzig, 1742), 98 (where poetry is compared with painting, sculpture, music and dance).

Elias Schlegel, who is said to have been influenced by the lectures of Fraguier and other authors published in the Memoirs of the Académie des Inscriptions.[241] His brother Johann Adolf Schlegel, who was one of the translators of Batteux, added to his version several original essays in which he criticizes the theory of imitation and also presents a modified system of the fine arts.[242] Yet all these writers were primarily interested in poetics and literary criticism and drew upon the other arts only for occasional analogies.

These critical discussions among poets and literati constitute the general background for the important work of the philosopher Alexander Gottlieb Baumgarten and of his pupil Georg Friedrich Meier.[243]

[241] Johann Elias Schlegels *Aesthetische und dramaturgische Schriften*, ed. J. von Antoniewicz (Heilbronn, 1887). In an essay composed in 1745, Schlegel compares poetry with architecture, painting and sculpture (97), in another essay dated 1742–43 with painting, sculpture and music (107ff.). On his French sources, see the introduction, p. XXXVI ff. and XCV ff.

[242] Herrn Abt Batteux . . . . *Einschränkung der Schönen Künste auf einen einzigen Grundsatz*, tr. Johann Adolf Schlegel, 3rd ed. (Leipzig, 1770; first ed., 1751), II, 155ff.: "Abhandlung no. 5. Von der Eintheilung der schönen Künste nach ihrer verschiednen Absicht." Schlegel summarizes Batteux but insists that eloquence and architecture should be included among the fine arts (157) and also adds prose poetry as well as drawing and engraving to the list (180–81). Cf. Hugo Bieber, *Johann Adolf Schlegels poetische Theorie in ihrem historischen Zusammenhange untersucht* (Berlin, 1912).

[243] Alexander Gottlieb Baumgarten, *Aesthetica*, ed. B. Croce (Bari, 1936; first ed., 1750–58). This edition also contains (1–45) his *Meditationes Philosophicae de nonnullis ad poema pertinentibus* (1735). B. Poppe, *Alexander Gottlieb Baumgarten* (thes. Münster, Borna-Leipzig, 1907), who publishes from a Berlin manuscript the text of Baumgarten's course on Aesthetics, delivered in German, probably in 1750–51 (65ff.). Georg Friedrich Meier, *Abbildung eines Kunstrichters* (Halle, 1745). *Id.*, *Anfangsgründe aller schönen Wissenschaften*, 2nd ed. (Halle, 1754–59; first ed., 1748–50). Thomas Abbt, *Alexander Gottlieb Baumgartens Leben und Character* (Halle, 1765). Georg Friedrich Meier, *Alexander Gottlieb Baumgartens Leben* (Halle, 1763). Th. W. Dannel, *Gottsched und seine Zeit*, 2nd ed. (Leipzig, 1855), 211ff. Carolus Raabe, *A. G. Baumgarten aestheticae in disciplinae formam redactae parens et auctor* (thes. Rostock, 1873). Hans Georg Meyer, *Leibniz und Baumgarten als Begründer der deutschen Aesthetik* (thes. Halle, 1874). Johannes Schmidt, *Leibnitz und Baumgarten, ein Beitrag zur Geschichte der deutschen Aesthetik* (thes. Halle, 1875). E. Prieger, *Anregung und metaphysische Grundlagen der Aesthetik von Alexander Gottlieb Baumgarten* (thes. Berlin, 1875). M. Bojanowski, *Literarische Einflüsse bei der Entstehung von Baumgartens Aesthetik* (thes. Breslau, 1910). Ernst Bergmann, *Die Begründung der deutschen Aesthetik durch Alexander Gottlieb Baumgarten und Georg Friedrich Meier* (Leipzig, 1911). A. Riemann, *Die Aesthetik Alexander Gottlieb Baumgartens* (Halle, 1928). Hans Georg Peters, *Die Aesthetik Alexander Gottlieb Baumgartens und ihre Beziehungen zum Ethischen* (Berlin, 1934).

Baumgarten is famous for having coined the term aesthetics, but opinions differ as to whether he must be considered the founder of that discipline or what place he occupies in its history and development. The original meaning of the term aesthetics as coined by Baumgarten, which has been well nigh forgotten by now, is the theory of sensuous knowledge, as a counterpart to logic as a theory of intellectual knowledge.[244] The definitions Baumgarten gives of aesthetics show that he is concerned with the arts and with beauty as one of their main attributes, but he still uses the old term liberal arts, and he considers them as forms of knowledge.[245] The question whether Baumgarten really gave a theory of all the fine arts, or merely a poetics and rhetoric with a new name, has been debated but can be answered easily. In his earlier work, in which he first coined the term aesthetics, Baumgarten was exclusively concerned with poetics and rhetoric.[246] In his later, unfinished work, to which he gave the title *Aesthetica*, Baumgarten states in his introduction that he intends to give a theory of all the arts,[247] and actually makes occasional references to the visual arts and to music.[248] This impression is confirmed by the text of Baumgarten's lectures published only recently,[249] and

[244] "Sint ergo νοητά cognoscenda facultate superiore objectum logices; αἰσθητά, ἐπιστήμης αἰσθητικῆς sive aestheticae" (*Meditationes*, ed. Croce, #116, p. 44). The distinction is reminiscent of the one made by Speusippus and related by Sextus Empiricus (*Adversus Mathematicos* VII, 145: Σπεύσιππος δέ ἐπεὶ τῶν πραγμάτων τὰ μὲν αἰσθητὰ τὰ δὲ νοητά, τῶν μὲν νοητῶν κριτήριόν ἔλεξεν εἶναι τὸν ἐπιστημονικὸν λόγον, τῶν δὲ αἰσθητῶν τὴν ἐπιστημονικὴν αἴσθησιν). *Aesthetica*, #1 (ed. Croce, p. 55): "Aesthetica theoria liberalium artium, gnoseologia inferior, ars pulcre cogitandi ... est scientia cognitionis sensitivae."

[245] *Ibid.* See also #3 (p. 55) where the usefulness of aesthetics is thus described: "bona principia studiis omnibus artibusque liberalibus subministrare."

[246] In the *Meditationes* (#117, ed. Croce, p. 44–45), *rhetorica generalis* and *poetica generalis* are introduced as the main parts of *aesthetica*.

[247] In #5 (ed. Croce, p. 56) he raises this objection against himself: "eam eandem esse cum rhetorica et poetica," and answers thus: "latius patet ... complectitur has cum aliis artibus ac inter se communia."

[248] #4, p. 55 (musicus); #69, p. 76 (musici); #780, p. 461–62 (music, painting); #83, p. 82–83 (music, the dance, painting, where painting is also assigned to one of the Muses).

[249] "Die ganze Geschichte der Maler, Bildhauer, Musikverständigen, Dichter, Redner wird hierher gehören, denn alle diese verschiedenen Teile haben ihre allgemeinen Regeln in der Aesthetik" (ed. Poppe, 67). "Er [Aristotle] teilt seine Philosophie, wodurch die menschliche Kenntnis verbessert werden soll, in die Logik, Rhetorik und Poetik, die er zuerst als Wissenschaften vorträgt. Die Einteilung selbst ist unvollkommen. Wenn ich sinnlich schön denken will, warum soll ich bloss in Prosa oder in Versen denken? Wo bleibt der Maler und Musikus?" (69).

by the writings of his pupil Meier.[250] On the other hand, it is quite obvious, and was noted by contemporary critics, that Baumgarten and Meier develop their actual theories only in terms of poetry and eloquence and take nearly all their examples from literature.[251] Baumgarten is the founder of aesthetics in so far as he first conceived a general theory of the arts as a separate philosophical discipline with a distinctive and well-defined place in the system of philosophy. He failed to develop his doctrine with reference to the arts other than poetry and eloquence, or even to propose a systematic list and division of these other arts. In this latter respect, he was preceded and surpassed by the French writers, especially by Batteux and the Encyclopaedists, whereas the latter failed to develop a theory of the arts as part of a philosophical system. It was the result of German thought and criticism during the second half of the eighteenth century that the more concrete French conception of the fine arts was utilized in a philosophical theory of aesthetics for which Baumgarten had formulated the general scope and program.

When Meier tried to answer the critics of his teacher Baumgarten, he stated that Baumgarten and himself had spoken only about literature, since they did not know enough about the other arts.[252] The broadening scope of German aesthetics after Baumgarten, which we must now try to trace, was due not only to the influence of Batteux, of the Encyclopaedists, and of other French and English writers, but also to the increasing interest taken by writers, philosophers, and the lay public in the visual arts and in music. Winckelmann's studies of

"... da die Erklärung auch auf Musik und Malerei gehen muss" (71). "... alle Künste, die man schön nennet, werden von der Kenntnis dieser Regeln den grössten Nutzen haben" (75). "Die Aesthetik geht viel weiter als die Rhetorik und Poetik" (76). These lectures are also notable for the more frequent references to French and English authors.

[250] "So lange es Maler, Dichter, Redner, Musickverständige und so weiter gegeben hat, so lange ist Aesthetik ausgeübt worden" (*Anfangsgründe*, vol. I, #6, p. 10). He then lists as liberal arts and "fine sciences": "die Redekunst, die Dichtkunst, die Music, die Historie, die Malerkunst und wie sie alle heissen" (#16, p. 27). Cf. p. 21; 581, etc.

[251] "Wir werden in den Exempeln immer bei der Rede stehen bleiben ..." (Baumgarten, ed. Poppe, #20, p. 82). "Ob nun gleich die Aesthetick auch die Gründe zu den übrigen schönen Künsten enthält, so werde ich doch meine allermeisten Exempel aus den Rednern und Dichtern nehmen" (Meier, *Anfangsgründe*, pt. 1, #19, p. 31).

[252] "Und wenn philosophische Köpfe, welche die Music, Malerkunst, und alle übrige schöne Künste ausser der Rede und Dichtkunst, verstehen, die aesthetischen Grundsätze auf dieselben werden anwenden: so wird der einzige Einwurf, der bisher mit Artigkeit und vielem Scheine wider die Aesthetic gemacht worden, gänzlich wegfallen" (*Alexander Gottlieb Baumgartens Leben*, 43f.).

classical art are important for the history of our problem for the enthusiasm which he stimulated among his German readers for ancient sculpture and architecture, but not for any opinion he may have expressed on the relation between the visual arts and literature.[253] Lessing's *Laokoon* (1766), too, has a notable importance, not only for its particular theories on matters of poetry and of the visual arts, but also for the very attention given to the latter by one of the most brilliant and most respected German writers of the time.[254] Yet the place of the *Laokoon* in the history of our problem has been misjudged. To say that the *Laokoon* put an end to the age-old tradition of the parallel between painting and poetry that had its ultimate roots in classical antiquity and found its greatest development in the writers of the sixteenth, seventeenth, and early eighteenth century, and thus freed poetry from the emphasis on description, is to give only one side of the picture. It is to forget that the parallel between painting and poetry was one of the most important elements that preceded the formation of the modern system of the fine arts, though it had lost this function as a link between two different arts by the time of Lessing, when the more comprehensive system of the fine arts had been firmly established. In so far as Lessing paid no attention to the broader system of the fine arts, especially to music, his *Laokoon* constituted a detour or a dead end in terms of the development leading to a comprehensive system of the fine arts. It is significant that the *Laokoon* was criticized for this very reason by two prominent contemporary critics, and that Lessing in the posthumous notes for the second part of the work gave some consideration to this criticism, though we have no evidence that he actually planned to extend his analysis to music and to a coherent system of the arts.[255]

The greatest contributions to the history of our problem in the interval between Baumgarten and Kant came from Mendelssohn, Sulzer, and Herder. Mendelssohn, who was well acquainted with French and English writings on the subject, demanded in a famous article that the fine arts (painting, sculpture, music, the dance, and architecture) and belles lettres (poetry and eloquence) should be re-

[253] G. Baumecker, *Winckelmann in seinen Dresdner Schriften* (Berlin, 1933). Henry C. Hatfield, *Winckelmann and his German Critics* (New York, 1943).

[254] Lessings *Laokoon*, ed. H. Bluemner, 2nd ed. (Berlin, 1880). *Loakoon*, ed. William G. Howard (New York, 1910). Howard, " Ut pictura poesis," *l.c.* R. Lee, " Ut pictura poesis," *l.c.* Croce, *Estetica, l.c.*, 505ff. K. Leysaht, *Dubos et Lessing* (thes. Rostock, Greifswald, 1874).

[255] Several passages in Lessing's notes for a continuation of the *Laokoon* refer to music and the dance and to their connection with poetry (ed. Bluemner, *l.c.*, 397; 434ff.).

duced to some common principle better than imitation,[256] and thus was the first among the Germans to formulate a system of the fine arts. Shortly afterwards, in a book review, he criticized Baumgarten and Meier for not having carried out the program of their new science, aesthetics. They wrote as if they had been thinking exclusively in terms of poetry and literature, whereas aesthetic principles should be formulated in such a way as to apply to the visual arts and to music as well.[257] In his annotations to Lessing's *Laokoon*, published long after his death, Mendelssohn persistently criticizes Lessing for not giving any consideration to music and to the system of the arts as a whole;[258] we have seen how Lessing, in the fragmentary notes for a continuation of the *Laokoon*, tried to meet this criticism. Mendelssohn also formulated a doctrine of the three faculties of the soul corresponding to the three basic realms of goodness, truth and beauty, thus continuing the work of the Scottish philosophers.[259] He did not work

[256] Moses Mendelssohn, " Betrachtungen über die Quellen und die Verbindungen der schönen Künste und Wissenschaften" (1757), in his *Gesammelte Schriften (Jubiläumsausgabe)* 1 (Berlin, 1929), 165–90. Cf. G. Kannegiesser, *Die Stellung Moses Mendelssohn's in der Geschichte der Aesthetik* (thes. Marburg, 1868). Ludwig Goldstein, *Moses Mendelssohn und die deutsche Aesthetik* (Königsberg, 1904).

[257] Review of G. F. Meier's *Auszug aus den Anfangsgründen aller schönen Künste und Wissenschaften* (1758), in his *Gesammelte Schriften*, vol. 4, pt. 1, Leipzig, 1844, 313–18. " Allein uns dünkt, dass der Erfinder dieser Wissenschaft der Welt nicht alles geliefert habe, was seine Erklärung des Wortes Aesthetik verspricht. Die Aesthetik soll eigentlich die Wissenschaft der schönen Erkenntnis überhaupt, die Theorie aller schönen Wissenschaften und Künste enthalten; alle Erklärungen und Lehrsätze müssen daher so allgemein seyn, dass sie ohne Zwang auf jede schöne Kunst insbesondere angewendet werden können. Wenn man z.B. in der allgemeinen Aesthetik erklärt, was erhaben sei, so muss sich die Erklärung sowohl auf die erhabene Schreibart, als auf den erhabenen Contour in der Malerei und Bildhauergunst, auf die erhabenen Gänge in der Musik, und auf die erhabene Bauart anwenden lassen . . . " (314). Baumgarten and Meier give the impression, " als wenn man bei der ganzen einrichtung des Werks bloss die schönen Wissenschaften, d.i. die Poesie und Beredsamkeit, zum Augenmerk gehabt hätte . . . " (315). " Eine Aesthetik aber, deren Grundsätze bloss entweder a priori geschlossen, oder bloss von der Poesie und Beredsamkeit abstrahirt worden sind, muss in Ansehung dessen, was sie hätte werden können, wenn man die Geheimnisse aller Künste zu Rathe gezogen hätte, ziemlich eingeschränkt und unfruchtbar seyn. Dass aber die Baumgarten'sche Aesthetik wirklich diese eingeschränkte Gränzen hat, ist gar nicht zu läugnen " (316).

[258] *Laokoon*, ed. Bluemner, *l.c.*, 359; 376; 384; 386 (Dichtkunst, Malerey, Baukunst, Musik, Tanzkunst, Farbenkunst, Bildhauerkunst). Mendelssohn, *Gesammelte Schriften* 2 (1931), 231ff.

[259] " Man pflegt gemeiniglich das Vermögen der Seele in Erkenntnissvermögen und Begehrungsvermögen einzutheilen, und die Empfindung der Lust und Unlust schon mit zum Begehrungsvermögen zu rechnen. Allein mich dünkt, zwischen dem

out an explicit theory of aesthetics, but under the impact of French and English authors he indicated the direction in which German aesthetics was to develop from Baumgarten to Kant.

What Mendelssohn had merely set forth in a general outline and program, the Swiss thinker Sulzer, who was well versed in French literature but spent the greater part of his life in Northern Germany, was able to develop in a more systematic and elaborate fashion. Sulzer began his literary activity with a few short philosophical articles in which his interest for aesthetics was already apparent, and in which he also leaned toward the conception of an aesthetic faculty of the soul separate from the intellectual and moral faculties,[260] a conception in whose development Mendelssohn and the philosopher Tetens also took their part.[261] Some years later, he was prompted by the example of Lacombe's little dictionary of the fine arts to compile a similar

---

Erkennen und Begehren liege das Billigen, der Beyfall, das Wohlgefallen der Seele, welches noch eigentlich von Begierde weit entfernt ist. Wir betrachten die Schönheit der Natur und der Kunst, ohne die mindeste Regung von Begierde, mit Vergnügen und Wohlefallen . . . . Ich werde es in der Folge Billigungsvermögen nennen, um es dadurch sowohl von der Erkenntniss der Wahrheit, als von dem Verlangen nach dem Guten abzusondern" (*Morgenstunden*, ch. 7 (Frankfurt-Leipzig, 1786), 118–19 (first ed. 1785). See also the fragment of 1776, *Gesammelte Schriften*, vol. 4, pt. 1 (1844), 122f. L. Goldstein, *l.c.*, 228–29. A similar distinction appears already in an article of 1763 ("Abhandlung über die Evidenz in metaphysischen Wissenschaften," *Gesammelte Schriften* 2 (1931), 325; cf. K. F. Wize, *Friedrich Justus Riedel und seine Aesthetik* (Berlin, 1907), 19–20): "Das Gewissen ist eine Fertigkeit, das Gute vom Bösen, und der Warheitssinn, eine Fertigkeit, das Wahre vom Falschen durch undeutliche Schlüsse richtig zu unterscheiden. Sie sind in ihrem Bezirke das, was der Geschmack in dem Gebiete des Schönen und Hässlichen ist."

[260] Johann Georg Sulzer, *Vermischte Philosophische Schriften*, 2 vols. (Leipzig, 1773–81). In an article of 1751–52, he distinguishes between *Sinne, Herz, Einbildungskraft* and *Verstand*, relating the second faculty to moral sentiments and the third to the fine arts (vol. 1, pp. 24 and 43; see also vol. 2, p. 113; A. Palme, *J. G. Sulzers Psychologie und die Anfänge der Dreivermögenslehre*, Berlin, 1905). Otherwise, the distinction of the three faculties of the soul does not yet appear clearly or consistently in these early writings, but only in his *Allgemeine Theorie der Schönen Künste*, 2nd ed., II (Leipzig, 1778), 240, art. Geschmak): "Der Geschmak ist im Grunde nichts anders, als das Vermögen das Schöne zu empfinden, so wie die Vernunft das Vermögen ist, das Wahre, Vollkommene und Richtige zu erkennen; das sittliche Gefühl, die Fähigkeit, das Gute zu fühlen" (cf. Wize, *l.c.*, 24).

[261] Johann Nicolas Tetens, *Philosophische Versuche ueber die menschliche Natur und ihre Entwickelung*, 2 vols. (Leipzig, 1777). He distinguishes three faculties: *Verstand, Wille*, and *Empfindsamkeit* or *Gefühl* (I, 619ff.). Cf. J. Lorsch, *Die Lehre vom Gefühl bei Johann Nicolas Tetens* (thes. Giessen, 1906). W. Uebele, *Johann Nicolaus Tetens* (Berlin, 1911), 113ff. A. Seidel, *Tetens' Einfluss auf die kritische Philosophie Kants* (thes. Leipzig, Würzburg, 1932), 17ff.

dictionary in German on a much larger scale.[262] This General Theory of the Fine arts, which appeared in several editions, has been disparaged on account of its pedantic arrangement, for it is clear, comprehensive and learned, and had a considerable importance in its time. The work covers all the fine arts, not only poetry and eloquence, but also music and the visual arts, and thus represents the first attempt to carry out on a large scale the program formulated by Baumgarten and Mendelssohn. Thanks to its wide diffusion, Sulzer's work went a long way to acquaint the German public with the idea that all the fine arts are related and connected with each other. Sulzer's influence extended also to France, for when the great *Encyclopédie* was published in Switzerland in a second edition, many additions were based on his General Theory, including the article on aesthetics and the section on the Fine Arts.[263]

In the decades after 1760, the interest in the new field of aesthetics spread rapidly in Germany. Courses on aesthetics were offered at a number of universities after the example set by Baumgarten and Meier, and new tracts and textbooks, partly based on these courses, appeared almost every year.[264] These authors have been listed, but their individual contributions remain to be investigated. The influence of the great *Encyclopédie* is attested by a curious engraving printed in Weimar in 1769 and attached to a famous copy of the *Encyclopédie*.[265] It represents the tree of the arts and sciences as

[262] *Allgemeine Theorie der Schönen Künste*, 2nd ed., 4 vols. (Leipzig, 1777–78; first ed., 1771–74; new ed., 4 vols., 1792–99). For his dependence on Lacombe, see his *Vermischte Philosophische Schriften* 2, p. 70 ("In diesem Jahre [1756] erhielt er durch ein französisches Werkchen, das Dictionaire des beaux Arts vom Herrn La Combe, nach des Herrn Hirzel Erzählung, die Veranlassung zu seiner allgemeinen Theorie, oder vielmehr zu seinem Wörterbuch der schönen Künste"). Johannes Leo, *Zur Entstehungsgeschichte der "Allgemeinen Theorie der Schönen Künste" J. G. Sulzers* (thes. Heidelberg, Berlin, 1906), 31ff. and 57. See also: Ludwig M. Heym, *Darstellung und Kritik der aesthetischen Ansichten Johann Georg Sulzers* (thes. Leipzig, 1894). Karl J. Gross, *Sulzers Allgemeine Theorie der Schönen Künste* (thes. Berlin, 1905). [263] See above, note 200–201.

[264] Sulzer, *Allgemeine Theorie*, new ed., I (1792), 47ff. I. Koller, *Entwurf zur Geschichte und Literatur der Aesthetik* . . . (Regensburg, 1799). E. Bergmann, *Geschichte der Aesthetik und Kunstphilosophie* (Leipzig, 1914), 15ff.

[265] This copy was exhibited in New York by the Services Culturels de l'Ambassade de France in January, 1951. The engraving has the title: " Essai d'une distribution généalogique des sciences et des arts principaux. Selon l'explication détaillée du Système des connoissances humaines dans le Discours préliminaire des Éditeurs de l'encyclopédie, publiée par M. Diderot et M. d'Alembert, à Paris en 1751. Reduit en cette forme pour découvrir la connoissance humaine d'un coup d'oeuil. Par Chrétien Guillaume Roth. À Weimar, 1769." The section corresponding to imagination contains poetry, painting, engraving, sculpture, music and architecture with their respective subdivisions.

given in the text of D'Alembert's *Discours,* putting the visual arts, poetry and music with their subdivisions under the general branch of imagination. Among the minor aesthetic writers of this period, Riedel has attracted some scholarly attention, probably because he was the target of Herder's criticism.[266] In his treatise on aesthetics, based on university lectures, Riedel gives a full discussion of all the fine arts, and also sets out with a general division of philosophical subjects into the True, the Good and the Beautiful.[267]

It is interesting to note the reaction to this aesthetic literature of the leaders of the younger generation, especially of Goethe and of Herder. Goethe in his early years published a review of Sulzer which was quite unfavorable. Noticing the French background of Sulzer's conception, Goethe ridicules the grouping together of all the arts which are so different from each other in their aims and means of expression, a system which reminds him of the old-fashioned system of the seven liberal arts, and adds that this system may be useful to the amateur but certainly not to the artist.[268] This reaction shows

[266] Friedrich Just Riedel, *Theorie der schönen Künste und Wissenschaften* (Jena, 1767). Kasimir Filip Wize, *Friedrich Justus Riedel und seine Aesthetik* (thes. Leipzig, Berlin, 1907). Richard Wilhelm, *Friedrich Justus Riedel und die Aesthetik der Aufklärung* (Heidelberg, 1933).

[267] " Der Mensch hat dreyerley Endzwecke, die seiner geistigen Vollkommenheit untergeordnet sind, das Wahre, das Gute und das Schöne; für jeden hat ihm die Natur eine besondere Grundkraft verliehen: für das Wahre den sensus communis, für das Gute das Gewissen, und für das Schöne den Geschmack . . ." (*Theorie,* 6). Johann Georg Heinrich Feder in his *Oratio de sensu interno* (1768) quotes Riedel and lists: veritas, pulchritudo (bonitas idealis), honestas (pulchritudo moralis); sensus veri sensusque communis, sensus pulchri sive gustus, sensus iusti et honesti seu conscientiae moralis (Wize, 21-22). On Platner's unpublished aesthetics of 1777-78, see E. Bergmann, *Ernst Platner und die Kunstphilosophie des 18. Jahrhunderts* (Leipzig, 1913).

[268] J. W. Goethe, review of Sulzer's *Die schönen Künste in ihrem Ursprung* (1772). " Sehr bequem in's Französische zu übersetzen, könnte auch wohl aus dem Französischen übersetzt sein." " Hier sei für niemanden nichts gethan als für den Schüler, der Elemente sucht, und für den ganz leichten Dilettanten nach der Mode." " Da sind sie denn (the fine arts) . . . wieder alle beisammen, verwandt oder nicht. Was steht im Lexikon nicht alles hintereinander? Was lässt sich durch solche Philosophie nicht verbinden? Mahlerei und Tanzkunst, Beredsamkeit und Baukunst, Dichtkunst und Bildhauerei, alle aus einem Loche, durch das magische Licht eines philosophischen Lämpchens auf die weisse Wand gezaubert . . . ." " Dass einer, der ziemlich schlecht räsonnierte, sich einfallen liess, gewisse Beschäftigungen und Freuden der Menschen, die bei ungenialischen gezwungenen Nachahmern Arbeit und Mühseligkeit wurden, liessen sich unter die Rubrik Künste, schöne Künste klassifizieren zum Behuf theoretischer Gaukelei, das ist denn der Bequemlichkeit wegen Leitfaden geblieben zur Philosophie darüber, da sie doch nicht verwandter sind, als septem artes liberales der alten Pfaffenschulen." " Denn um den Künstler allein ist es zu thun . . . . Am gaffenden Publikum, ob das, wenn's ausgafft hat, sich Rechenschaft geben kann, warum es gaffte oder nicht, was liegt an dem? " (*Goethes Werke, Sophien-Ausgabe,* 37 (Weimar, 1896), 206ff.).

that the system of the fine arts was something novel and not yet firmly established, and that Goethe, just like Lessing, did not take an active part in developing the notion that was to become generally accepted. Toward the very end of his life, in the *Wanderjahre*, Goethe shows that he had by then accepted the system of the fine arts, for he assigns a place to each of them in his pedagogical province.[269] Yet his awareness of the older meaning of art is apparent when in a group of aphorisms originally appended to the same work he defines art as knowledge and concludes that poetry, being based on genius, should not be called an art.[270]

Herder, on the other hand, took an active part in the development of the system of the fine arts and used the weight of his literary authority to have it generally accepted. In an early but important critical work (*Kritische Waelder, 1769*), he dedicates the entire first section to a critique of Lessing's *Laokoon*. Lessing shows merely, he argues, what poetry is not, by comparing it with painting. In order to see what its essence is, we should compare it with all its sister arts, such as music, the dance, and eloquence. Quoting Aristotle and Harris, Herder stresses the comparison between poetry and music, and concludes that this problem would require another Lessing.[271] In the fourth section, he quotes Mendelssohn as well as the more important English and French authors, and presents his own system of the fine arts, which includes all the essential elements though it differs from previous authors in some detail.[272] Herder's later contributions

[269] *Wilhelm Meisters Wanderjahre*, Bk. II, ch. 8 (*Sophien-Ausgabe*, 25 (1895), 1ff.) where music, poetry and the visual arts are treated as sisters. See also Bk. III, ch. 12 (*ibid.*, 216ff.).

[270] "Künste und Wissenschaften erreicht man durch Denken, Poesie nicht; denn diese ist Eingebung . . . . Man sollte sei weder Kunst noch Wissenschaft nennen, sondern Genius" (*Aus Makariens Archiv*, in *Goethe's Werke, Vollständige Ausgabe letzter Hand*, vol. 23 (Stuttgart-Tübingen, 1829), 277-78. *Sophien-Ausgabe*, 42, pt. 2 (1907), 200).

[271] "Hr.L. zeigt, was die Dichtkunst gegen Malerei gehalten nicht sey; um aber zu sehen, was sie denn an sich in ihrem ganzen Wesen völlig sey, müsste sie mit allen schwesterlichen Künsten und Wissenschaften, z.E. Musik, Tanzkunst und Redekunst verglischen, und philosophisch unterschieden werden" (*Herders Sämmtliche Werke*, ed. B. Suphan, 3 (Berlin, 1878), 133). "Hier (on the distinction of poetry and music) wunsche ich der Dichtkunst noch einen Lessing" (161). David Bloch, *Herders als Aesthetiker* (thes. Würzburg, Berlin, 1896). Guenther Jacoby, *Herders und Kants Aesthetik* (Leipzig, 1907). Kurt May, *Lessings und Herders kunsttheoretische Gedanken in ihrem Zusammenhang* (Berlin, 1923). Emilie Lutz, *Herders Anschauungen vom Wesen des Dichters und der Dichtkunst in der ersten Hälfte seines Schaffens* (thes. Erlangen, 1925). Wolfgang Nufer, *Herders Ideen zur Verbindung von Poesie, Musik und Tanz* (Berlin, 1929).

[272] *Sämmtliche Werke*, ed. Suphan, 4 (1878), 3ff. Malcolm H. Dewey, *Herder's Relation to the Aesthetic Theory of his Time* (thes. Chicago, 1920).

to aesthetics are beyond the scope of this paper.

I should like to conclude this survey with Kant, since he was the first major philosopher who included aesthetics and the philosophical theory of the arts as an integral part of his system. Kant's interest in aesthetic problems appears already in his early writing on the beautiful and sublime, which was influenced in its general conception by Burke.[273] He also had occasion to discuss aesthetic problems in several of his courses. Notes based on these courses extant in manuscript have not been published, but have been utilized by a student of Kant's aesthetics. It appears that Kant cited in these lectures many authors he does not mention in his published works, and that he was thoroughly familiar with most of the French, English and German writers on aesthetics.[274] At the time when he published the *Critique of Pure Reason,* he still used the term aesthetics in a sense different from the common one, and explains in an interesting footnote, that he does not follow Baumgarten's terminology since he does not believe in the possibility of a philosophical theory of the arts.[275] In the following years, however, he changed his view, and in his *Critique of Judgment,* which constitutes the third and concluding part of his philosophical system, the larger of its two major divisions is dedicated to aesthetics, whereas the other section deals with teleology. The system of the three *Critiques* as presented in this last volume is based on a threefold division of the faculties of the mind, which adds the faculty of judgment, aesthetic and teleological, to pure and practical reason. Aesthetics, as the philosophical theory of beauty and the arts, acquires equal standing with the theory of truth (metaphysics or epistemology) and the theory of goodness (ethics).[276]

[273] *Beobachtungen über das Gefühl des Schönen und Erhabenen* (1764), in *Immanuel Kants Werke,* ed. E. Cassirer, 2 (Berlin, 1922), 243–300.

[274] O. Schlapp, *Kants Lehre vom Genie und die Entstehung der Kritik der Urteilskraft* (Göttingen, 1901).

[275] " Die Deutschen sind die einzigen, welche sich jetzt des Worts Aesthetik bedienen, um dadurch das zu bezeichnen, was andere Kritik des Geschmacks heissen. Es liegt hier eine verfehlte Hoffnung zum Grunde, die der vortreffliche Analyst Baumgarten fasste, die kritische Beurtheilung des Schönen unter Vernunftprincipien zu bringen, und die Regeln derselben zur Wissenschaft zu erheben. Allein diese Bemühung ist vergeblich." He then states that he will use the term aesthetics for the critical analysis of perception (*Kritik der Reinen Vernunft, Transszendentale Aesthetik* #1, ed. Cassirer, 3 (1923), 56f.).

[276] *Kritik der Urteilskraft* (1790). Juergen Bona Meyer, *Kant's Psychologie* (Berlin, 1870). Carl Theodor Michaelis, *Zur Entstehung von Kants Kritik der Urteilskraft* (progr. Berlin, 1892). A. Apitzsch, *Die psychologischen Voraussetzungen der Erkenntniskritik Kants* (thes. Halle, 1897). A. Bäumker, *Kants Kritik*

In the tradition of systematic philosophy this was an important innovation, for neither Descartes nor Spinoza nor Leibniz nor any of their ancient or medieval predecessors had found a separate or independent place in their system for the theory of the arts and of beauty, though they had expressed occasional opinions on these subjects. If Kant took this decisive step after some hesitation, he was obviously influenced by the example of Baumgarten and by the rich French, English, and German literature on the arts his century had produced, with which he was well acquainted. In his critique of aesthetic judgment, Kant discusses also the concepts of the sublime and of natural beauty, but his major emphasis is on beauty in the arts, and he discusses many concepts and principles common to all the arts. In section 51 he also gives a division of the fine arts: speaking arts (poetry, eloquence); plastic arts (sculpture, architecture, painting, and gardening); arts of the beautiful play of sentiments (music, and the art of color).[277] This scheme contains a few ephemeral details that were not retained by Kant's successors.[278] However, since Kant aesthetics has occupied a permanent place among the major philosophical disciplines, and the core of the system of the fine arts fixed in the eighteenth century has been generally accepted as a matter of course by most later writers on the subject, except for variations of detail or of explanation.

IX

We shall not attempt to discuss the later history of our problem after Kant, but shall rather draw a few general conclusions from the development so far as we have been able to follow it. The grouping together of the visual arts with poetry and music into the system of the fine arts with which we are familiar did not exist in classical antiquity, in the Middle Ages or in the Renaissance. However, the ancients contributed to the modern system the comparison between poetry and painting, and the theory of imitation that established a

---

der Urteilskraft (Halle, 1923). W. Bröcker, *Kants Kritik der aesthetischen Urteilskraft* (thes. Marburg, 1928). H. W. Cassirer, *A Commentary on Kant's Critique of Judgment* (London, 1938), 97ff.

[277] #51. "Von der Einteilung der schönen Künste" (ed. Cassirer, 5 (1922), 395ff.).

[278] The *Farbenkunst*, mentioned also by Herder and by Mendelssohn in his notes on Lessing's *Laokoon* (ed. Bluemner, 386) refers to the color piano invented by Abbé Castel, which was expected to produce a new art of color combinations. Cf. Bluemner, *l.c.*, 596–97. L. Goldstein, *Moses Mendelssohn*, 92–93. The commentators of the *Critique of Judgment* (J. H. v. Kirchmann, J. C. Meredith, J. H. Bernard, H. W. Cassirer) fail to explain this detail.

kind of link between painting and sculpture, poetry and music. The Renaissance brought about the emancipation of the three major visual arts from the crafts, it multiplied the comparisons between the various arts, especially between painting and poetry, and it laid the ground for an amateur interest in the different arts that tended to bring them together from the point of view of the reader, spectator and listener rather than of the artist. The seventeenth century witnessed the emancipation of the natural sciences and thus prepared the way for a clearer separation between the arts and the sciences. Only the early eighteenth century, especially in England and France, produced elaborate treatises written by and for amateurs in which the various fine arts were grouped together, compared with each other and combined in a systematic scheme based on common principles. The second half of the century, especially in Germany, took the additional step of incorporating the comparative and theoretical treatment of the fine arts as a separate discipline into the system of philosophy. The modern system of the fine arts is thus pre-romantic in its origin, although all romantic as well as later aesthetics takes this system as its necessary basis.

It is not easy to indicate the causes for the genesis of the system in the eighteenth century. The rise of painting and of music since the Renaissance, not so much in their actual achievements as in their prestige and appeal, the rise of literary and art criticism, and above all the rise of an amateur public to which art collections and exhibitions, concerts as well as opera and theatre performances were addressed, must be considered as important factors. The fact that the affinity between the various fine arts is more plausible to the amateur, who feels a comparable kind of enjoyment, than to the artist himself, who is concerned with the peculiar aims and techniques of his art, is obvious in itself and is confirmed by Goethe's reaction. The origin of modern aesthetics in amateur criticism would go a long way to explain why works of art have until recently been analyzed by aestheticians from the point of view of the spectator, reader and listener rather than of the producing artist.

The development we have been trying to understand also provides an interesting object lesson for the historian of philosophy and of ideas in general. We are accustomed to the process by which notions first formulated by great and influential thinkers are gradually diffused among secondary writers and finally become the common property of the general public. Such seems to have been the development of aesthetics from Kant to the present. Its history before Kant is of a very different kind. The basic questions and conceptions underlying modern aesthetics seem to have originated quite apart from the traditions of systematic philosophy or from the writings of important original authors. They had their inconspicuous beginnings in secondary authors, now almost forgotten though influential in their own time, and perhaps in the discussions and conversations of educated laymen reflected in their writings. These notions had a tendency to fluctuate and to grow slowly, but only after they had crystallized into a pattern that seemed generally plausible did they find acceptance among the greater authors and the systematic philosophers. Baumgarten's aesthetics was but a program, and Kant's aesthetics the philosophical elaboration of a body of ideas that had had almost a century of informal and non-philosophical growth. If the absence of the scheme of the fine arts before the eighteenth century and its fluctuations in that century have escaped the attention of most historians, this merely proves how thoroughly and irresistibly plausible the scheme has become to modern thinkers and writers.

Another observation seems to impose itself as a result of our study. The various arts are certainly as old as human civilization, but the manner in which we are accustomed to group them and to assign them a place in our scheme of life and of culture is comparatively recent. This fact is not as strange as may appear on the surface. In the course of history, the various arts change not only their content and style, but also their relations to each other, and their place in the general system of culture, as do religion, philosophy or science. Our familiar system of the five fine arts not merely originated in the eighteenth century, but it also reflects the particular cultural and social conditions of that time. If we consider other times and places, the status of the various arts, their associations and their subdivisions appear very different. There were important periods in cultural history when the novel, instrumental music, or canvas painting did not exist or have any importance. On the other hand, the sonnet and the epic poem, stained glass and mosaic, fresco painting and book illumination, vase painting and tapestry, bas relief and pottery have all been " major " arts at various times and in a way they no longer are now. Gardening has lost its standing as a fine art since the eighteenth century. On the other hand, the moving picture is a good example of how new techniques may lead to modes of artistic expression for which the aestheticians of the eighteenth and nineteenth century had no place in their systems. The branches of the arts all have their rise and decline, and even their birth and death, and the distinction between " major " arts and their subdivisions is arbitrary and subject to change. There is hardly any ground but critical tradition or philosophical preference for deciding whether engraving is a separate art (as most of the eighteenth-century authors believed) or a subdivision of painting, or whether poetry and prose, dramatic and epic poetry, instrumental and vocal music are separate arts or subdivisions of one major art.

As a result of such changes, both in modern artistic production and in the study of other phases of cultural history, the traditional system of the fine arts begins to show signs of disintegration. Since the latter part of the nineteenth century, painting has moved further away from literature than at any previous time, whereas music has at times moved closer to it, and the crafts have taken great strides to recover their earlier standing as decorative arts. A greater awareness of the different techniques of the various arts has produced dissatisfaction among artists and critics with the conventions of an aesthetic system based on a situation no longer existing, an aesthetics that is trying in vain to hide the fact that its underlying system of the fine arts is hardly more than a postulate and that most of its theories are abstracted from particular arts, usually poetry, and more or less inapplicable to the others. The excesses of aestheticism have led to a healthy reaction which is yet far from universal. The tendency among some contemporary philosophers to consider Art and the aesthetic realm as a pervasive aspect of human experience rather than as the specific domain of the conventional fine arts also goes a long way to weaken the latter notion in its traditional form.[279] All these ideas are still fluid and ill defined, and it is difficult to see how far they will go in modifying or undermining the traditional status of the fine arts and of aesthetics. In any case, these contemporary changes may help to open our eyes to an understanding of the historical origins and limitations of the modern system of the fine arts. Conversely, such historical understanding might help to free us from certain conventional preconceptions and to clarify our ideas on the present status and future prospects of the arts and of aesthetics.

[279] John Dewey, *Art as Experience* (New York, 1934).

Rembrandt and His Contemporary Critics[1]

by SEYMOUR SLIVE

Reprinted from the *Journal of the History of Ideas*—Vol. XIV, No. 2, pp. 203-220

I

The Dutch have a quality which, according to an axiom of the atelier, makes them the ideal audience for the painter: they enjoy paintings with their eyes, not with their ears. They prefer to look at pictures rather than to write, read or talk about them.

J. Huizinga, the Dutch historian of culture, views his countrymen as nominalists engaged in speechless, sceptical contemplation. This accounts, he adds, for their predilection for the picture as a means of expression as opposed to the word and explains the relative absence of drama, novels, memoirs and good personal letters in Holland. The Dutch seem to feel little need to put their personal experiences into closed intellectual or literary forms; they care little for ceremony or the formal compliment.

These national characteristics, if one is permitted today to speak of national characteristics, certainly help to explain part of the joy which the seventeenth-century Netherlander must have received from the numerous still lifes of every description, from the landscapes, seascapes, town views, genre scenes and portraits which he painted or saw and bought, but about which he seldom wrote or theorized. He was satisfied simply to paint a picture or to look at one; he felt no urge to use it as a point of departure for refined theoretical speculation. Moreover, we shall see that the kind of painting in which most Dutch artists excelled—still lifes, landscapes, genre scenes—did not lend itself to pre-eighteenth-century general discussions on painting.

Frits Lugt, the Dutch connoisseur and art historian, gives additional evidence for the Dutch antipathy toward closed systems in the field of art. He points out that in spite of Ploos van Amstel's advocacy in the eighteenth century of a Dutch equivalent for *Kunstwissenschaft*, not even the word ever took hold. The word *Kunstgelehrter*, so popular in neighboring Germany, has no Dutch equivalent. The Dutch use only the nouns *kunsthistoricus*, art historian, and *kunstkenner*, connoisseur. And Mr. Lugt, the Netherlander, does not attempt to generalize on his observations. He merely says, "This is very significant."

[1] Material used in this essay has been included in a study of *Rembrandt and His Critics: 1630-1730* submitted to the University of Chicago as a doctoral dissertation, which will be published in *Kunsthistorische Bijdragen* of the Utrecht University Institute of Art History. The author gratefully acknowledges the invaluable assistance he received from Prof. Ulrich Middeldorf, Prof. J. E. van Gelder, Prof. Wolfgang Stechow and Mr. K. G. Boon.

At any rate, there can be no doubt that the people of the Netherlands were unusually inarticulate during their Golden Age of painting. Houbraken, the Dutch Vasari, did not publish his lives of the Dutch painters until 1718, almost half a century after the death of most of his country's great masters. No Dutch Leonardo left copious notes on his works and thoughts. More than a century's diligent research has not turned up a note written by Hals, Steen, Ruisdael or Vermeer. How different this period is from the twentieth century, when the manifesto of many contemporary artists is as important in a gallery as a scorecard is at a ball game.

No libretto was needed for most seventeenth-century Dutch painting, and although all painting is mute it is possible to speak of the unique silence of Dutch painting. One need only recall that seventeenth-century Dutch painters developed the first great school of still life painting, the most silent of all genres of painting. Dutch landscapes are hushed, too. It is impossible to acknowledge tremendous skies or vast vistas if there is chatter Silence reigns everywhere. Emanuel de Witte found it in church interiors; genre painters in kitchens, bed rooms or drawing rooms. Occasionally a lute or a spinet is heard; but much more often we are in a silent interior watching an old woman praying, a servant girl peeling apples, a physician taking the pulse of a young girl, or a lace maker busy at her pillow. The children painted by these artists show all the qualities which make them children except that of making noise. Their deportment, like their clothing, is a replica of that of their parents. However, the greatest master of silence, Vermeer, as the father of eleven children, apparently had little faith in the talent of children for silence; none appear in any of his genre scenes. Only Steen's children howl; they compensate for the reserve of their numerous peers.

A relative silence is found even in Dutch taverns and bordellos. Ostade, in his youth, had his Brouweresque moments; but in his middle and late works he tempered his initial noise and wildness. When we leave the carousers and drinkers for the streets and town views of a Berckheyde or Van der Heyden we find them full of space, light and air; we then encounter a few scattered pedestrians, but never clamorous crowds. The marine painters prefer quiet, or at most moderate seas to gales. Only a few represented battles at sea. Among the thousands of painters, and there were thousands, who worked in Holland during the seventeenth century, only a handful depicted clashing armies. The horrors of a bloody war of independence just won or of an insurrection just quelled did not attract the quiet brush of the painter nor the contemplative eye of the patron.

As striking as the silence in seventeenth-century Dutch painting is the reticence of the huge public which bought and hung pictures in Holland during the seventeenth century. This must be borne in mind when the criticism of Rembrandt by his Dutch contemporaries is examined. However, the small number of references to art by seventeenth-century Dutch writers, artists and patrons must not be dismissed as merely an inherent cultural inhibition. There were a great many reasons for the numerous fifteenth- and sixteenth-century Italian and seventeenth-century French discussions on art. One of them was certainly the struggle of the artist to prove that he was engaged in a liberal, not in a manual, art. These discussions were part of the artist's struggle for status. But the Dutch seventeenth-century artist who made revolutionary strides in the use of tonal painting and who dismissed the pomp and rhetoric of traditional history painting still worked within the medieval framework of the guild. Even in Utrecht, the Dutch town which was closest to Italy from the point of view of religion and style, it was not until 1644 that the painters' guild of St. Luke petitioned to have its name changed to *Schilders-College* because this name was more noble. This was only a request for the change of a name. The first group of Dutch artists to show dissatisfaction with the old guild organization did so only fourteen years before Rembrandt died, when a group of artists in the Hague in 1655 petitioned for exemption from the guild of St. Luke, in order to form an Academy. Before this time the Dutch artist, who was also frequently a stocking salesman, tavern keeper or tulip bulb specialist, was content with his membership in the guild which also protected the embroiderer and wood carver. He was more interested in protecting his traditional rights and privileges than in theoretical discussions about the nature of art.

II

The relative reticence of both artist and patron in seventeenth-century Holland is the main cause for the difficulty of arriving at definitive conclusions about what Rembrandt's contemporaries thought of his work.

One might ask: does it matter to us if Rembrandt was praised or pooh-poohed by his contemporaries? Is the question a relevant one? Is not the important question: what does Rembrandt mean to us today? After all we have his works and it is through the study of them that we must find the formal qualities which are the basis for our understanding of any work of art as an aesthetic object. The conditions under which an art object came to be, its history, its effect upon the generation for which it was produced or upon succeeding generations are outside of the work of art *qua* work of art. Agreed. However, even the formal qualities which are distilled out of a work of art must be interpreted, and an analysis of what Rembrandt's contemporaries saw in his work will help us see it against the organic whole of the culture in which it was produced. Without attempting this task we run the danger of not seeing the work of art at all.

Although a formidable army of scholars and archivists has been busy for more than a century correcting the errors made by seventeenth-, eighteenth- and early nineteenth-century biographers of Rembrandt, there is still great confusion about the work, life and character of Holland's greatest artist. To be sure, we no longer find it necessary to debate whether or not Rembrandt van Rijn was ever christened Paul. We can also categorically assert that Rembrandt was not in Venice in 1638; and, thanks to the recent research of Rembrandt students who have proved that he was never in England, we can even cautiously state, that as far as we know, Rembrandt never left his homeland.

Public museums and private collections opened to the public have made amateurs as well as specialists familiar with all phases of his work. Although there is no consensus on all aspects of his stylistic development, there is certainly general agreement on its direction, from his early carefully finished works to his deeply moving and personalized paintings of the late fifties and sixties. With our highly refined historical sense we have no difficulty comparing him with Caravaggio, Rubens, Poussin or his Dutch peers, in order to set off the nature of his achievement. The literature devoted to Rembrandt would fill a good-sized library. But the monumental catalogues raisonnés written on his paintings, etchings and drawings, the monographs devoted to his iconography as well as to his style, and the careful studies which have been made of the composition of the paint and types of varnishes he used have done little to explode the legends which surround Rembrandt and his work.

The Ur-myth on Rembrandt states that Rembrandt was a howling success and amassed a tremendous fortune in Leiden and Amsterdam until 1642, when he painted the *Night Watch*, a group portrait of the civic guards who served under Captain Cocq. All Amsterdam was shocked, runs the tale, when Rembrandt delivered this painting. Such audacity! Rembrandt dared attempt to change the traditional Dutch group portrait! The men who had commissioned the painting were outraged by this unseemly hoax. Had they each paid Rembrandt one hundred guilders to be depicted as a dim piece of animated shade? No, this picture was unacceptable. The honest Dutchmen demanded that Rembrandt change the picture, or paint a new one, or refund their money. Stubborn Rembrandt refused to listen to any of the complaints or suggestions of his patrons. He was satisfied with his painting. He knew it was great. Of course, there was a tremendous scandal; therefore, from 1642 until his death in 1669 Rembrandt received few if any commissions. The *Night Watch* was cut down and hung on some obscure wall. This did not induce Rembrandt to change his way of painting. He realized that he was a misunderstood genius and refused to prostitute his art by catering to the tastes of the stupid backward public. He spent his last years in the same fashion as Van Gogh, that other great Dutch master, spent his life—misunderstood, without a friend or a guilder, or even a good piece of herring.

This biography makes a wonderfully romantic story and perhaps it finds wide acceptance today because of the current belief that it is in the nature of things that any artist worth his salt must be misunderstood by his contemporaries. There are good reasons for believing that the artist of today is suspect if he is popular. But is it impossible for us to imagine that there were periods in history when there was not an unbridgeable chasm between the artist and his public?

It is true that Rembrandt's *Night Watch* broke many traditions of sixteenth- and seventeenth-century Dutch group portrait painting; but there is absolutely no evidence to support the assumption that his patrons were dissatisfied with the picture, and that it caused a tremendous shift in his fortune and social life.

Julius Held called attention to this fact in the February, 1950, issue of *Art News*. However, the art world does not like such news. When the Cleveland and St. Louis museums bought late Rembrandt canvasses in Autumn, 1950, *Time Magazine* of course referred to them as products of Rembrandt's dirt-poor, friendless last years. Do away with the Rembrandt myths and he is no longer excellent copy.

At this point it is worth noting that the *Night Watch* did not receive its title until late in the eighteenth century. Before that time it was simply referred to as the portrait of Captain Cocq and his civic guards. When in 1947 it was cleaned and stripped of its dark varnish and dirt it was promptly baptized the Day Watch. Seventeenth-century writers called it neither the Night or the Day Watch, for a very good reason: the men portrayed in the picture did not go out on night or day watches. They were members of a militia who were supposed to be ready to defend Amsterdam if the city was attacked. Dutch militia groups saw action during the fifteenth and sixteenth centuries. During the seventeenth they were seldom needed for defense purposes. However, they did not dissolve, but continued as social organizations, and their time seems to have been divided between target practice and activities around a festive board.

None of the meagre evidence we have regarding the opinions of Captain Cocq and his guards on their group portrait indicates that they were displeased with their picture. Cocq had a water color made of the painting for his family album around 1653. No adverse comment was entered in the album; the picture was merely described. Another small contemporary copy of the picture was made, which is now in the National Gallery in London. Copies are usually an indication of a work's popularity. However, more substantial evidence can be submitted to demonstrate that the romanticized Rembrandt biography which uses the so-called *Night Watch* as its keystone is apocryphal.

In 1658 or 1659 Bronchorst and Cruysbergen, two men portrayed in the painting, testified before a notary that each man who figured in the composition had paid Rembrandt about a hundred guilders—depending upon his position in the picture. Their testimony was given in order to support Rembrandt's contention that an assessment he had made of his estate was fair and just and not too high. Their testimony makes three points clear. Rembrandt was well paid for this group portrait—about 1600 guilders. Secondly, those who were in the picture knew what place they were going to occupy because they paid according to their position in the picture. There was, and is, nothing unusual about the subject of a portrait paying the artist according to whether a head, bust, half length or full length portrait has been executed. And finally, if Bronchorst and Cruysbergen were dissatisfied with their portraits, or if the members of their militia group were unhappy with the picture, they would not have testified for Rembrandt.

We also know that the painting was not hidden on some obscure wall. It was in a large new guild hall made for the civic guardsmen, with five other group portraits made by popular painters of the period, from the time it was finished in 1642 until it was moved in 1715 to the Town Hall of Amsterdam. No wall in either building can be considered obscure.

Although not all late seventeenth-century critics applaud the *Night Watch* without reservation, available evidence proves that it received more praise than condemnation. No evidence proves that it was responsible for a great shift in Rembrandt's popularity in 1642.

Then we may ask, just what did Rembrandt's contemporaries think of his work? Fortunately, there are some data which indicate how this question should be answered.

III

The man who has the honor of having written the first extensive account of Rembrandt as a painter is Constantin Huygens, the famous Dutch diplomat, poet, musician, athlete and dilettante of the arts. He began an autobiography around 1630, when he was 34 years old, and in it discussed painting. As young artists worthy of special attention he singles out Rembrandt and Jan Lievens, who worked together in Leiden until 1631, when Rembrandt left for Amsterdam. What did the young polished diplomat who was at home in the courts of Europe think of the miller's son, Rembrandt, and the embroiderer's son, Lievens?

Huygens wrote that the two artists were already on a par with the most famous painters and would soon surpass them. High praise for the two young painters who were not yet 25 years old. This commendation becomes even more impressive when one learns how familiar Huygens was with the painters of his time and how conscious he was of the great change which took place in Netherlandish painting during the first decades of the seventeenth century. He wrote that late sixteenth-century and early seventeenth-century Dutch mannerists depicted clearly outlined subjects, while the new generation of painters could render movement and the transitory quality of appearance. The young painters can even introduce the impression of the warmth of the sun and moving air into their pictures. It is obvious that Huygens recognized the possibilities of tonal painting and was not appalled by the change from a linear to a painterly style.

This shift in the style of Dutch painting had its complicated roots in Italy, where a similar change had taken place two or three decades before Huygens wrote his autobiography.

Italian Seicento writers on painting also recognized this change in discussing the relative merits of the Carracci group as opposed to the followers of Caravaggio. But no Seicento author, not even the most balanced amongst them, could admit that the followers of Caravaggio could possibly surpass the Carracci. Of course, when *Caravaggismo* was differentiated from *Carraccismo* in seventeenth-century Italian texts, it was not done on the basis of mere stylistic analysis. All seventeenth-century writers on art accepted implicitly or explicitly a hierarchy of kinds of painting: biblical and historical subjects crowned this hierarchy. The Italian critics insisted that a particular style of painting, that of the Carracci, was most suitable for rendering serious, imaginative historical compositions, while the other style, that of Caravaggesque painters, was more suitable for unpretentious genre pieces.

Huygens also accepted the hierarchy of subjects in painting; but what is singular in his account is that he does not demand a certain *style* for historical pictures. Although Rembrandt and Lievens used a Dutch version of *Caravaggismo* in their early history paintings Huygens did not condemn the young artists. In fact, he applauded their style.

Huygens makes much of the humble origins of both painters. He feels their low birth is superb proof against the argument that "noble blood " is superior to " ordinary blood." He adds that a group of doctors dissected the corpse of a nobleman in order to examine his blood and discovered it did not differ from that of an ordinary farmer. He also insists that the artists are not indebted to their parents for their talent. It would be a mistake to conclude that Huygens underlined their humble origins because of unique democratic currents in seventeenth-century Dutch thought. Biographers of artists have been content to accept the fact that nature can distribute artistic gifts without checking the income or social status of the recipient, at least since Ghiberti wrote that Cimabue discovered Giotto drawing the sheep he was tending for his poor father. Huygens adds that Rembrandt and Lievens owe nothing to their teachers. They would have gone far and achieved as much if they had had no teachers. They owe everything to their natural talent. Huygens considered this high praise. Fifty years later Rembrandt critics will argue that because Rembrandt did not have professors of art to give him the essential rules he failed to reach the summit of painting.

Huygens considered Rembrandt's early work superior to that of Lievens in judgment and in the representation of lively emotional expression. Although he has great praise for Lievens, he singles out a painting by Rembrandt for analysis: *Judas Returning the Pieces of Silver*. This picture shows, writes Huygens, Rembrandt's superior ability to convey the expression of emotion in a small carefully worked out painting. Huygens is generous with his compliments: the picture can stand comparison with any Italian or ancient picture; in it the beardless son of a Dutch miller has surpassed Protogenes, Apelles and Parrhasius. Even if we discount the propensity of a man with Huygens' humanistic background to summon the name of the ancient painters at the drop of a brush, there can be no doubt that he admired this painting. Huygens congratulated Rembrandt for his treatment of expression, gesture and movement—all indispensable talents for a history painter. He wrote that the central figure of Judas is beside himself, bewailing his crime, imploring the pardon he dares not hope for, his face a vision of horror, his hair in wild disorder, his clothes rent, his arms contorted, his hands pressed fiercely together. Prostrate on his knees, his whole body seems ravaged and convulsed by his hideous despair.

Thus Rembrandt won his first recognition as a painter of history pictures—the most important type of painting to seventeenth-century man. Before the turn of the eighteenth century some Rembrandt critics will conclude that this is his weakest genre.

The great praise and respect which Huygens, the man of the world and the man of means, had for the self-made artist who was made of different flour than his father, was not limited to the written word.

He also helped Rembrandt get commissions. Rembrandt made portraits of members of his family, and it is difficult to imagine that Huygens, who was the secretary of Stadholder Prince Frederick Henry of Orange, did not have something to do with the portraits Rembrandt made of the Prince and his wife around 1632. However, the faith which Huygens expressed in Rembrandt's future development was not based on the artist's ability as a face painter. Huygens' faith in the young artist as a great painter of historical compositions turned into a choice commission in the 1630's: a Passion series of five pictures painted for the Prince of Orange.

From seven letters which Rembrandt sent to Huygens, we learn that he also acted as the artist's agent for this commission. From the same letters we also learn that Rembrandt rewarded Huygens with his painting of the *Blinding of Samson* for services rendered.

The Passion series has been severely criticized by some twentieth-century Rembrandt students for its crude pathos and gruesome design; but it is significant to learn that the series pleased one of Holland's most important patrons—the Prince of Orange. He ordered an *Entombment, Resurrection* and *Ascension* after the first two, the *Elevation* and *Descent from the Cross,* had been delivered. If the Prince was not satisfied with the *Elevation* and *Descent* he would not have ordered the other three pictures. Huygens, who considered the *Judas* a work which could stand comparison with any picture, must have applauded the obvious depiction of expression, dramatic action and lighting in the five scenes. Would Rembrandt have rewarded Huygens with his *Blinding of Samson,* his most gruesome and most violent picture, if he did not think there were qualities in it which would please him? It is an error to think that Rembrandt never considered the tastes of his patrons. During the thirties he showed no sign of the insolent independence and deliberate disregard of his patrons' wishes so often associated with his approach to his work. He, himself, in a letter to Huygens dated January 12, 1639, wrote that in the *Entombment* and *Resurrection,* in order to please his Excellency the Prince, he concentrated upon expressing the greatest amount of inward emotion (*die meeste ende die naetuereelste beweechgelickheyt*).[2]

---

[2] The letter is transcribed in C. Hofstede de Groot, *Die Urkunden über Rembrandt* (The Hague, 1906), No. 65. The interpretation of the phrase *die meeste ende die naetuereelste beweechgelickheyt* has been the cause of discussion among Rembrandt scholars. H. E. van Gelder, " Marginalia bij Rembrandt—De natureelste beweechgelickheyt," *Oud Holland,* LX (1943), 148–151, suggests that Rembrandt referred to " inner " not " outer " movement when he used the word *beweechgelickheyt,* because that was the sense of the word during the sixteenth and seventeenth centuries. Therefore, when Rembrandt wrote that he gave special attention to *die meeste ende die naetuereelste beweechgelickheyt* he had in mind " the greatest inward emotion." [*Note 2 continued at foot of next page*]

We can infer that the inward emotion Rembrandt strove for would win approval from his patron. It was part of the current idiom of the high Baroque, which depicted dramatic events with an intensification of movement, expression and the effects of light.

By the time the Passion series was completed in 1639 Rembrandt's reputation as a successful and popular painter was well established. His portrait commissions were legion and he already had a considerable reputation as a teacher. His fame also extended beyond the borders of Holland. Two of his paintings were already in England around 1640, in the collection of Charles I. His early etchings of old men, Jews, Orientals and beggars were an immediate success. Soon after they were printed they found their way into the studios of publishers who issued sheets bearing portraits of famous and infamous men and women. Rembrandt's anonymous character studies were baptized with the names of popular emperors, kings, philosophers, soldiers, and villains. François Langlois, a Parisian print publisher, employed engravers in the thirties to make copies after Rembrandt's etchings. Interesting transformations took place. A copy of a laughing man after an etching of Rembrandt became Democritus; Judas was turned into Heraclitus; two Orientals became Mohammed and Philo Judaeus. Sometimes the same head was used for more than one character. Langlois turned Rembrandt's *Old Man with a Flowing Beard and a Fur Cap,* dated 1630, into Plato; Moncornet, another Parisian print publisher, used the same old man for his portrait of Marcus Agrippa. The possibilities of these transformations were infinite and were exploited by German as well as French publishers.

By the early forties artistic circles in France were familiar with more than Rembrandt's etchings and coarse copies of them. When the French painter, Claude Vignon, wrote to the above-mentioned Langlois from Paris, in November, 1641, he told him to give his best regards to Van Dyck when in London. He also asked him to give his best wishes to Rembrandt when in Amsterdam and to be sure to buy some of his work. Vignon also asked Langlois to tell the Dutch

---

Jakob Rosenberg interprets the phrase quite differently in his *Rembrandt* (Cambridge, 1948), I, 116; 226, note 29. He writes that it means " the greatest and most natural movement " of the figures, and rejects Professor van Gelder's interpretation as unconvincing because it " seems to be contradicted by the pictures themselves, in which outer movement in the Baroque sense still dominates, and by the aesthetics of the period." Professor Rosenberg is correct when he maintains that Professor van Gelder's interpretation seems to be contradicted by the *Entombment* and *Resurrection;* however, the author believes that Baroque art theory confirms rather than contradicts Professor van Gelder's interpretation. The principle that the bodily movement of the figures in a painting should express human emotions and passions was articulated as early as the fifteenth century, and no seventeenth century theorist or painter would have thought of denying this notion. This interpretation of the phrase is expanded in the study cited in note 1 above.

painter that Signor Lopez had bought his painting of *Bilaam's Ass*, painted in 1626. He added that this picture would be sold with Lopez' collection in December. Thus here in 1641 we find Rembrandt's name in excellent company. He is mentioned by a Frenchman in the same breath with Van Dyck, and we learn that Alphonso Lopez, Richelieu's colorful agent and a shrewd collector, who owned Raphael's *Castiglione* and Titian's so-called *Ariosto* and *Flora*, also bought Rembrandt's work.

If Langlois did see Rembrandt when he arrived in Amsterdam in 1641 or 1642, he saw Rembrandt working on pictures quite different from *Bilaam's Ass*. In 1642, it will be recalled, the *Night Watch* was delivered.

Rembrandt's merits did not go unsung in his homeland in the forties. In 1641, J. Orlers, the burgomaster of Leiden, took pleasure in pointing with pride to Leiden's illustrious son. In his biography of the artist, which was the first written, he called him "one of the most famous painters of our century."

Philips Angel in the same year and in the same town gave an address on St. Luke's Day in Praise of Painting. He summoned Rembrandt's name and his painting of *Samson's Wedding Feast*, painted in 1638, to demonstrate that painting can and should teach. This idea was a hoary old commonplace; its ancient and respectable lineage can be traced back at least to Horace's simile *ut pictura poesis*. It had been found in books on painting since the fifteenth century, when Leone Battista Alberti wrote his *Della Pictura*, the first Renaissance treatise on painting. Since it was assumed that any painter worthy of the name must depict subjects taken from Biblical or ancient history, it is not surprising to find writers frequently reminding painters that if they want to attain perfection in their art they must have more than a nodding acquaintance with the Scriptures, ancient history, poetry and fables.

Angel pointed to the *wijt beruchten* Rembrandt as a shining example of a painter who makes excellent use of the study of history. His *Wedding Feast of Samson* reveals his diligent spirit and the careful thought which he has given to the passage in *Judges*. This is first of all apparent in the way he has depicted the guests at the table. They are reclining, not seated. This is the way the ancients conducted themselves at table and the way the Turks still do. Angel's aside about the Turks shows his own preoccupation with learning; it must be remembered he gave his address in Leiden, an university town.

In order to show that this is no ordinary feast, Rembrandt has placed long-haired Samson in the foreground posing his riddle to some of the Philistines. His gesture is a very natural one and proves that he is posing a riddle. In short, Rembrandt has accomplished two things in this painting: he has shown us how wedding feasts were once celebrated and that this a unique wedding. He has achieved this, Angel concluded, by a precise reading of the Bible and by carefully thinking about what he has read.

Angel's praise was not simply a eulogy of a renowned son of Leiden given to a Leiden audience on the day of the patron saint of painters. His praise was based on a logically constructed argument, not rhetoric.

Many late seventeenth-, eighteenth-, and early nineteenth-century critics will continue to believe that history painting is the noblest occupation of an artist and that a knowledge of the appropriate gestures, manners and customs of the people depicted is an indispensable branch of painting; but they will not award Rembrandt the palm for his accomplishment in this field. Some will even claim he was illiterate and thus could not even pretend to wear the mantle of a history painter. But all the critics who discussed his work before 1642 applauded him exactly for his work as a history painter. And there does not seem to have been a shift in Rembrandt's reputation after he completed the *Night Watch*.

Constantin Huygens' remarkable sons, for example, when still at a tender age followed in the footsteps of their father in their admiration for Rembrandt. Christian Huygens, when but 16, wrote to his brother Lodewijk in 1645 that he had made a copy in oil of a head of an old man by Rembrandt that is so good that it is difficult to distinguish it from the original. In the same letter he writes that he and his brother Constantin are currently working with pastels and if Lodewijk saw the results obtained by stumping with this medium he would no longer use graphite. It is not too far-fetched to assume that Christian's letter is an indication that Dutch amateurs and dilettantes around the middle of the seventeenth century were still pleased with the tonal and painterly effects which the elder Huygens had praised twenty years earlier. Rembrandt's style, his use of broken and lost outlines and his exploitation of tone rather than line, and the potentialities of pastels are closely related. Young Christian was enthusiastic about both Rembrandt and pastels. A preference for pastels meant a predilection for Rembrandt. One can also invert the proposition.

The two brothers who discovered the wonders of pastels when students continued to show an interest in the arts when they reached maturity. Constantin wrote to his brother Christian in Paris, in 1633, to sketch a Carracci drawing in Jabach's famous collection in Paris, because he wanted to compare the disposition of the figures in Jabach's sheet with one owned by Rembrandt, which he also believed was by Carracci because of *l'hardiesse de la plume*.

This letter shows that Rembrandt was in good relations with members of the distinguished Huygens family from the beginning until the end of his career. It is also of interest to know that Christian could be called upon the year he was elected to the Royal Society—and after he had already discovered a satellite to Saturn and perfected the pendulum clock—to make a sketch of a Carracci drawing. Here is proof that at least a fraction of the audience acquainted with Rembrandt during his last years was sensitive and cultivated. It is not difficult to imagine Constantin and Rembrandt discussing "l'hardiesse de la plume" of a drawing; not in French to be sure, but certainly the cautious connoisseur and the artist were able to communicate and understand each other.

However, proof that Rembrandt did not fall into oblivion or was looked upon only with contempt after he painted the *Night Watch* does not rest merely upon letters written by school boys and sons of an old friend.

Rembrandt not only continued to receive portrait commissions in Amsterdam during the forties, fifties and sixties; there is ample evidence that important collectors outside of Holland were interested in his work. In Italy Don Antonio Ruffo, the great Sicilian collector, began ordering portraits of ancient heroes from Rembrandt in 1652. In 1654 Rembrandt sent his *Aristotle* to Ruffo in Sicily. The Italian also gave Rembrandt commissions in the sixties, when he ordered an *Alexander,* now lost, and a *Homer.* In 1669, the year Rembrandt died, Ruffo asked the artist to send him some of his etchings. 189 Rembrandt prints were sent to the fortunate collector! Cosimo de' Medici, later Cosimo III, was in Rembrandt's studio December 29, 1667. Certainly not an indication of oblivion. Cosimo probably bought the self-portrait of Rembrandt, dated around 1655, which was in the Medici collection and is now in the Uffizi, when he was in Holland. It would be tedious to list all the prominent European collectors who owned Rembrandt's works before he died; let us return to comments his countrymen made on his work after he painted the *Night Watch.*

Poems and epigrams praising Rembrandt's paintings, etchings and drawings began to appear in Holland during the forties and continued to be published until his death. Poetic references come easily to the Dutch; chambers of rhetoricians were organized in the Netherlands as early as the fifteenth century by burghers and artisans. They flourished during the sixteenth and seventeenth centuries and in the course of the eighteenth were gradually superseded by baroque grand opera and drama. They were composed of artistically minded members of a number of different craft guilds, just as in Shakespeare's *Midsummer Night's Dream* a tailor, a joiner, a carpenter and other artisans perform a play together. The artistic merits of much of what the rhetoricians wrote is questionable. Most of them should have been content with being contemplative nominalists; however, if nothing else, they did develop a facility in composing verse for their own meetings and for all kinds of festive occasions. In fact they placed a premium upon facility. The kneeling man with a bald head in Jan Steen's painting of the important patriotic festival, *Prince's Day,* in the Rijksmuseum, Amsterdam, is a rhetorician. He is not kneeling because he is doing homage to the prince; he is merely lifting his glass to his lips after having recited a poem which, in accordance with a custom of the rhetoricians, he has composed on his knees as proof of his facility in improvisation.

All the seventeenth-century Dutch strophes which were dedicated to Rembrandt may not have been composed while the poet was on his knees; but even if they were composed in a sitting or standing position their depth and insight are not extraordinary. We must not look for a Baudelarian sensitivity among seventeenth-century Dutch rhetoricians.

Four lines of a poem by Lambert van den Bos published in 1650 in praise of Martin Kretzer's collection, which contained paintings by Titian, Bassano and Rubens as well as by Rembrandt, give us an idea of the tenor of this poetry:

> I will not attempt your fame
> O Rembrandt, with my pen to scrawl
> For the esteem you receive in every hall
> Is known when I merely mention your name.

It is safe to assert that this is not great poetry. Nor does Van den Bos attempt to articulate what Rembrandt's great fame rests upon. He mouths what can be taken for granted: the mere mention of the painter's name in 1650 is sufficient to bring to mind the honor the painter has received. Since the poem is written in praise of Kretzer's cabinet we can infer that the poet considered the possession of a work by Rembrandt proof of the collector's good judgment.

During the sixties Dutch poets continued to eulogize him. Jan Vos, in a poem praising Amsterdam, printed in 1662, listed Amsterdam's leading painters: Rembrandt, Flinck, De Wit, Van der Helst and others. He wrote that these painters spread Amsterdam's fame as far and wide as her ships sail the seas. The metaphor is a favorite one of Dutch poets of the time. Rembrandt heads the list of Amsterdam's great painters; he is the flagship.

Jeremias de Decker in 1667 dedicated a poem to the painter in appreciation of a portrait Rembrandt had made of him. He is pleased that the Apelles of his time has painted him and would like to put into words Rembrandt's art and spirit, but alas he lacks the wisdom of a Vasari or Van Mander, he writes. The poet consoles himself with the thought that it is really not necessary to versify the nature of Rembrandt's greatness, for it is known wherever Dutch ships sail. And it is even known in Rome, where it equals the art of Raphael and Michelangelo. This poem, published two years before Rembrandt died, repeats some of the ideas Huygens had expressed thirty years earlier in his autobiography. De Decker also wrote a poem praising a painting by Rembrandt of *Christ and Mary Magdalene*. He praises what earlier critics found laudable, Rembrandt's ability to translate the Biblical text accurately into paint and his ability to create an illusion. It seems, he writes, as if Christ is speaking to Mary. He adds a most significant comment: the shadow of the rocks, which Rembrandt painted very high for artistic reasons, enhances the picture and gives it majesty. Thus not all of Rembrandt's late contemporary critics disapproved of his use of shadows, nor were late nineteenth-century critics the first to discover the poetry of his chiaroscuro.

We have briefly traced Rembrandt's reputation from the beginning to the end of his career and have not yet cited a contemporary word of censure of his work. However, it would be a mistake to conclude that all of the artist's contemporaries were sensitive Rembrandt connoisseurs. For example, J. Boogaard in 1660 and Jan Vos in 1662 dedicated lines to Rembrandt's portrait of Coppenol, the master calligrapher of Amsterdam, and concluded that Coppenol's calligraphy was more worthy of praise than the artist's depiction of the writing master.

One may very well ask, and should ask, what did Joost van den Vondel, generally recognized as the greatest poet of seventeenth-century Holland, have to say about Rembrandt? He only mentioned him in two of his poems, once in four lines he wrote on a portrait Rembrandt had done of Anslo, the Mennonite preacher, in which the poet admonishes Rembrandt to paint Anslo's *voice,* for he who wants to see Anslo must hear him (this poem was published in 1644 and probably refers to a double portrait of Anslo and his wife or to an etching of Anslo, both dated 1641), and again in a poem which praises Coppenol. Vondel also wrote a verse on a portrait Rembrandt had painted of Jan Six's mother; in these lines his name is not even mentioned. Vondel was a friend of many of Rembrandt's patrons and friends—he knew Huygens and Jan Six—and yet he never had the painter do his portrait. Nor did Vondel, who wrote memorial poems for many of his friends and for many of Amsterdam's leading citizens, write a memorial poem to Rembrandt when the artist died.

There are good reasons for the silent treatment Vondel gave Rembrandt during the last three decades of his career. The poet's tastes, as Schmidt-Degener has pointed out, tended toward the polished pomp and rhetoric of the official Flemish and Italianate Dutch painters rather than the personal style worked out by the late Rembrandt. Govaert Flinck was Vondel's favorite painter. To be sure Flinck was a Rembrandt pupil; but after he left Rembrandt's studio he acquired an elegance and finish which Rembrandt never achieved. In 1653 he painted Vondel's portrait. When the authorities of Amsterdam decided to decorate their new classicistic town hall in the late fifties with a series of eight historical paintings depicting events in Holland's early history, Flinck, not Rembrandt, was given the commission. Flinck made studies for the series which showed the uprising of the Batavians under Julius Civilis against their Roman rulers; but Flinck died in 1660 before he could execute his sketches. The commission was then distributed among a number of artists. Rembrandt was asked to paint a picture for this series: a scene taken from Tacitus depicting the *Conspiracy of Julius Civilis*. The painting was executed and put in place in 1662. For reasons which Rembrandt specialists are still debating the painting was removed. Because the Julius Civilis painting was never returned it has been frequently assumed that the authorities were not pleased with the manner in which Rembrandt achieved an unprecedented monumentality based upon a unique use of chiaroscuro. However, there is no concrete proof that the painting was rejected because the municipal authorities had a different conception of what the style of an official historical painting should be.

If we examine the work of Rembrandt pupils such as Flinck, Maes, Bol and Hoogstraten we can find indications of what can be considered a change in taste suggesting that Rembrandt's work was not considered *à la mode* in all circles. Their early works used Rembrandt's chiaroscuro and subjects, and they were concerned with translating the work of their master into their own idiom. In the fifties and sixties they attempted to translate a mélange of Italian, Flemish and French into Dutch. But the change in attitude toward Rembrandt first finds written form in a biography of the artist written in 1675, six years after his death, by Joachim von Sandrart, a German painter and prolific writer on art and artists. He had been in Amsterdam from 1637 until 1645, and he must have known Rembrandt, for he painted one of the militia pieces which decorated the guild hall where Rembrandt's *Night Watch* hung. As early as the thirties Sandrart was in Italy, and by the time he writes his lines on Rembrandt he has the glibness and aplomb of an academic doctrinaire. He writes that Rembrandt missed true greatness because he never visited Italy where the ancients and the theory of art may be studied. It is worth noting that none of Holland's great masters of her golden age of painting—Hals, Van Goyen, Ruisdael, Steen, Vermeer or Rembrandt—made the trip across the Alps. This defect was all the more serious, continues Sandrart, because Rembrandt could hardly read. This remark would have puzzled Philips Angel, who in 1641 praised Rembrandt for his careful study of the Bible and historical texts. Rembrandt's cardinal sin, according to Sandrart, was that he opposed and contradicted the rules of art, such as anatomy, proportion, the study of classical statues and Raphael's drawing. He was guided by nature, not by rules. Andries Pels, a countryman of Rembrandt's, took up this theme as early as 1681 when he wrote:

If he painted, as sometimes happened, a nude woman
He chose no Greek Venus as his model
But rather a washerwoman or a treader of peat from a barn
And called this whim " imitation of nature "
Everything else to him was idle ornament. Flabby breasts
Ill shaped hands, nay, the traces of the lacings of the corsets on the stomach,
  of the garters on the legs,
Must be visible, if nature was to get her due.
This is *his* nature, which would stand no rules
No principles of proportion in the human body.

Sandrart also criticized Rembrandt for not using clean outlines. Thirty-five years earlier Huygens congratulated Rembrandt's generation for graduating from outlines; but the academic classicists insisted that line was more important than color or chiaroscuro. Sandrart takes Rembrandt to task for not having *the* proper style; his criticism is based upon the assumption that one mode of artistic expression is *per se* better than another. Although other modes of artistic expression have been substituted for the one Sandrart accepted, his assumption is still very much alive today.

Not all of Sandrart's criticism of Rembrandt is negative. As a painter Sandrart was sensitive to what he called the " universal harmony " of Rembrandt's light and shadow. He praised his color and the manner in which he rendered with vigor the simplicity of nature, his portraits and his little pieces. The latter is a reference to Rembrandt's early highly finished paintings which could be compared favorably with the then popular *Feinmalerei* of a Dou, Schalken or Mieris. Even Pels, who was so upset by Rembrandt's naked instead of nude women, agreed that Rembrandt had a tremendous talent; it was just too bad that he did not follow the rules.

One other point that Sandrart makes about Rembrandt must be mentioned. Sandrart complains that the miller's son did not know how to keep his station. This is severe criticism, for those who subscribed to the doctrines of the academy not only wanted to achieve beauty by rules, but also wanted to raise the social status of the artist. He was a blot on the profession: " er hat seinen Stand gar nicht wissen zu beachten und sich jederzeit nur zu niedrigen Leuten gesellet." Later critics will expand this theme; they will point out that Rembrandt did not wear velvet and a gold chain when he painted; and he even wiped his brushes on his clothes. The legend of Rembrandt the Slob has its origins in Sandrart.

The subjection of Rembrandt's work to academic criteria did not send Rembrandt into an artistic limbo. Hoogstraten, a former pupil of Rembrandt's who adopted much of the classicistic esthetic in his painting and writing, could still praise Rembrandt in 1678. He wrote that the *Night Watch* would outlive all its rivals because it is so original, artistic and forceful that it makes other Dutch group portraits look like playing cards. However, he adds—and one can almost detect a sigh—that it could have been less dark.

Late seventeenth-, eighteenth- and many nineteenth-century critics will find much to censure in Rembrandt's paintings, etchings and drawings; but even those who believed that his stylistic language made him *a priori* a bad artist found aspects of his work worthy of commendation. What these critics chose to laud or deplore throws light upon many facets of Rembrandt's work which we, as mid-twentieth-century observers, would tend to overlook. Each generation of critics constructed their own Rembrandt. The Rembrandt they saw tells us much about their critical frame of reference and their way of looking at the world. Some only saw the Rembrandt Pels saw: that which is seen so clearly in the artist's etchings of a nude woman made around 1631 (Bartsch, 198). Others overlooked that aspect of his work completely and only saw the Rembrandt who painted the *Self-portrait* in 1658 in the Frick collection. Writers will borrow, embellish or invent tales to prove Rembrandt was a realist interested only in low subjects, or will borrow, embellish or invent tales to prove he was never interested in the subject he represented and only used the subject to exercise his interest in light and shadow.

It is not difficult to understand why Eduard Kolloff, who in 1854 published in a book-length article in Friedrich von Raumer's *Historische Taschenbuch,* the first biography of Rembrandt based on the artist's works and seventeenth-century documents, complained that the list of errors made by previous Rembrandt biographers is longer than Don Juan's list of mistresses.

Bach: The Conflict Between the Sacred and the Secular

by Leo Schrade

Reprinted from the *Journal of the History of Ideas*—Vol. VII, No. 2, pp. 151-194

Understanding and esteem for Bach's music have developed in a way not altogether regular. The course of men's appreciation of Bach has moved back and forth, like the tides. The causes that have set these tides in motion have changed from time to time. Hence we always think we are "discovering" Bach anew. If signs are not wholly deceptive, a new wave seems to be rising here and now. A new historical interpretation may therefore be worth while.

Whenever in the past historical explanation has claimed to reveal the most ultimate and profound secrets of Bach's music, it has been only in the most general terms that the scholar, the historian, the philosophical interpreter have been able to fathom the depths of his work. Its sum and substance have been held to consist in the force of its religious quality, its spiritual power, its profundity of feeling, its abundance of humanity. We accept these terms as entirely appropriate. It seems that all who have a mind for his music draw upon such a terminology to express the ultimate and inexplicable. Such words are nebulous, and always exposed to danger; they are apt to be vague and empty. Their meaning as applied to Bach becomes clear only in the light of his own historical context. Was religious quality or intensity of feeling in fact the historical import of Bach and his work? And if so, was it the real force that gave his work its form? If Bach spoke the language of religion, of human depth and feeling, we must learn to understand its significance in terms of his own situation and problems, or else it merely calls forth our subjective and uncontrolled imagination. This is the true task of historical interpretation.

The domestic steadiness resulting from his social station as a burgher is probably the most striking, at any rate the most obvious, trait of Bach's life. It characterized all his kinfolk far and near. The Bachs lived for generations scattered over Thuringia and Saxony; they remained there. But despite the stout gravity of such an existence, Johann Sebastian Bach evinced throughout his life a peculiar restlessness, an anxiety hard to understand, and not in conformity with his usual firmness and composure. We are not referring to those sudden explosions of irascibility of which various stories are related. We mean the restlessness of the artist.

Wherever he resided, this perturbed state of mind in matters of art never left him. Continual search is a prominent characteristic of his musicianship. He had no apparent plan, but rushed uneasily from one artistic discovery to another. This may have been nothing more than an accidental and quite natural way of exploring local traditions wherever he happened to be staying. But these discoveries were more than chance encounters. They spring from the ideal he early conceived for his art; they derive from the goal he put definitely into words. To pursue this goal was his life-work, and it was this vocation that filled him with restlessness. It is at this point that we feel the historical tenseness of Bach's situation arising, it is in this sense that we must take his religious feeling as an historical phenomenon. Bach's artistic search grew out of the goal he set himself. In order to acquire the power to pursue it appropriately he moved about and absorbed all the music he could find.

The state of music he encountered was utterly confusing. Germany had no distinctive style of its own. It was Italy that set forth the dominating style of the baroque age. Because of this uncertainty about the prevailing musical style, a style which had its home outside his own country, and because of the necessity his goal laid upon him to search for all possible expressions and forms, the tension that runs through Bach's life seems to have arisen from the conditions of his times and not to be altogether personal. Musicians not in the most intimate contact with the center of style are exposed to the influence of all sorts of traditions; they will always search restlessly until they find that source. If such is the lot of truly great composers their fate becomes tragic. It is a situation with which it is of no avail to quarrel, but which again and again challenges the very great to revolt. Händel went to Italy after having fully experienced the perplexing musical state of Germany. Bach remained there.

This was likewise the result of necessity, and not of individual predilection. It was destiny that forced Bach into the position of a German organist and cantor, and consequently into all the narrow and limited forms of life that went with that position. In saying "destiny," we mean his goal, his vocation. Bach himself first described it in a document that is probably the most important of all the extant sources for understanding his aims. When in 1708 he submitted his resignation to the municipal council of Mühlhausen, at the age of twenty-three, he offered significant reasons. "Although it was my intention to advance the music in the divine service toward its very end and purpose (*Endzweck*), a regulated church music in honor of God; although it was also my intention here to improve the church music, which in nearly all villages is on the increase and is often better treated than here; although for the purpose of improvement I provided, not without expense, a good supply of the best selected church compositions, and also, in observation of my duty, submitted a project for the repair of the unsatisfactory and damaged organ, and, in short, would have fulfilled my obligations with enthusiasm: it so happened that none of this was possible without vexatious relations. . . . So God willed to bring about an opportunity that will not only put me in a better position so far as the subsistence of my livelihood is concerned, but will also make it possible for me, without annoyance to others, *to persevere in working for my very end which consists in organizing church music well.*"

Here for the first time Bach lays down the direction in which his work must grow. He characterizes the vocation in which he must serve all his life; his view of the goal is unusually clear and his will to pursue it unusually determined. His art is directed toward organizing church music, toward regulating it well to the honor of God. From this it has been concluded that Bach had a personal inclination toward and liking for sacred music—as though ends of this character have ever been the result of the individual's likes and dislikes! We may have forgotten that religion and the service it demands go far beyond the dispositions and inclinations of the individual; the obligations involved do not spring altogether from the "free" will of man. No "liberal" propensity called forth Bach's decision. The document of Mühlhausen becomes, indeed, one of the historic landmarks, its significance reaching out far beyond the personal development of Bach. Yet even from the individual point of view it is remarkable that a young man of twenty-three should set before himself, in full clarity and unrestrained determination, the goal of his life-work.

Bach's aim, then, is unusual in his time and of momentous consequence for him. His generation did not see church music as the one and exclusive form the art should or could have, to say nothing of the reform and reorganization which Bach held to be a necessity. It is true that Bach's inferiors if appointed church musicians—and most of them were—fulfilled their duties by placing traditional music in the service. There is no "end," no idea, not even a particular merit in disposing of duties such as fall to the musician's daily routine. Bach, however, brings in the idea of reform; he conceives of a new and inspiring aim; he intends to impart to church music a new structure. Such reforms are not invented because a person likes to invent them. On the contrary, an idea brings the reform to life; in this case it was the Lutheran idea of the Protestant church. Bach visualized a new regulation of religious life through music, a "birth of the Church out of the spirit of music," to give a famous expression a new turn.

The Mühlhausen document marks the last great moment of German baroque music. Almost at the same time Händel was definitely turning away from German musical conditions and toward the opera, as the ultimate opportunity for the artist to attain world fame and representative power. Bach dedicated himself to sacred music as the final opportunity to give expression to religion bound up with the church. Both Händel and Bach showed a mysterious assurance of decision; nearly all their further steps were but consequences once the decision had been made.

Bach accepted his work as of divine origin, as his vocation, not because of any individual inclination and not even because of personal piety, but in full recognition of the idea Luther had conceived of the church. So the whole musicianship of Bach obtains its meaning from his aim, which casts light upon all he did and worked for, against which any personal expression of life for its own sake fell back into insignificance. The determination of Bach, his assurance in approaching his work, his inner restlessness and continual search for artistic experience, all this derives from the grace of the vocation bestowed upon him as the medium through which to symbolize the idea of the church, faith, religion in his music. The process of development now to be unfolded, the advance Bach made in bringing the task into reality, reveals this destiny fully.

I

Bach spent his early years from 1685 to 1700, at Eisenach and Ohrdruf. The entire musical life was there organized around the municipality. Since the Reformation German music had drawn all its substance from the city. Musical compositions had to be furnished for all civic and religious events in the town. Training in music was carried on by the school as well as by the church, and the same persons often served in both places. In consequence of this unifying process, exemplified in the *"Kantorei,"* a musical institution most prominent during the age of the Reformation, the repertory of musical works in any one city was to an astonishing degree of one kind only—all alike. But this organization limited the effectiveness and activity of the musician to the single city in which he lived, regardless of the artistic greatness he might have achieved. There were elaborate rules which forbade any activity outside the town. Although a sort of illegal practice existed, such practice did not pay, as the delinquent musicians who lent their services to neighboring cities or villages had to expect severe punishment. The influence of this musical activity usually did not extend far beyond the range of view the church tower afforded. This extreme limitation is significant for the whole of German baroque music. We must keep this always in mind if we are to understand the calamities that befell the greatest of the German musicians during that period, not as personal misfortunes that call for sympathy, but as their inevitable historical destiny. Heinrich Schütz suffered severely from such limitations and narrow circumstances. Händel cast them off; he left all the institutions of the city and turned once and for all to the opera which granted wider scope.

Bach, however, grew up and remained in the small-town atmosphere and narrowness. Eisenach and Ohrdruf gave him his first experience of this type of music organization. But Ohrdruf had an additional significance. Although a very small place, it exposed Bach to influences the importance of which increased to proportions far beyond the size of the town. Strangely enough, problems significant for his artistic advancement also appear for the first time. Some decision with regard to his future course can be seen gradually taking form. Still more strangely, a great many essential traits begin to make their appearance at Ohrdruf; their significance will later increase. It is of extreme importance that at Ohrdruf Bach, though but a boy, came in contact with a religious movement that seemingly had no direct bearing on his music, but nonetheless was to accumulate considerable weight since it influenced his professional position. Ohrdruf brought home the first experience with Pietism. This religious movement had long had a firm hold on

Ohrdruf. The opposition between the orthodox and the Pietistic course seems to have been especially vehement there; any small town may give divergent opinions a greater violence of expression than the large city, where disunion is more readily covered up. Ohrdruf was such a stronghold of Pietism as to gain the dubious distinction of harboring even disreputable extremists who did great harm to the movement as a whole; and it is said that "zealots, seceders from other regions, found shelter" there.

The authorities of the school Bach attended were violently opposed to Pietism; in the most determined manner they uncompromisingly upheld the orthodox point of view. Every teacher of the school or officer of the town had, upon appointment, to take the oath on the so-called *formulae concordantiae* of the orthodox church; the signature established the procedure. Bach's brother, Johann Christoph, had also signed the orthodox formulae. Some letters by Christoph Kiesewetter, who had been since 1696 rector of the school Bach attended, give a very lively and instructive picture of Pietism at Ohrdruf; they portray the situation in the first decade of the eighteenth century.[1] We do not know in what way Bach, fifteen years old, may have taken part in the movement. That this schism which divided the whole community into two camps should have left him unimpressed it is impossible to think. On the contrary, we must assume that Pietism began to affect his religious thought fundamentally; later he possessed in his own library all the important literature of the Pietistic theologians. A religious experience appears side by side with his artistic beginnings. This much at least we must grant, that the period of Ohrdruf determined many of Bach's further steps.

It was then that the time of tension and restlessness began. An uncertainty with regard to the true character of musical style as well as to the whole state of music in Germany must have entered his mind. Not many years had passed since Heinrich Schütz had surveyed—at the end of his life—the state of German music; he had expressed many a word of despair and resignation, most frequently in his letters; he then no longer believed that his old ideal could be realized, of giving German music a unity of both style and

[1] Here we should mention a publication, important for the subject, but—so far as we can see—hitherto overlooked; Theodor Wotschke: "Der Pietismus in Thüringen," in *Thüringisch-Sächsische Zeitschrift für Geschichte und Kunst*, vol. 18 (Halle, 1929)

repertory. The condition Schütz had often described in tragic tones had not changed, either for the better or for the worse, until the time when Bach was on the verge of an important period. The musical traditions of the Bach family, his growing up in a small town, the type of training he obtained, all this allowed him little "free choice." Had he been given such a free choice, and had his view not been obstructed by the limitations of his early days, his preference might have turned to Italy, as Schütz in the past had gone south to search for the "true" musical style, as Händel was to go to Italy as the very source of the baroque opera. But Bach was heir to the traditions of a long line of ancestors who had all been musicians of the town's *Kantorei,* or organists. Training in their schools and his own excellent skill as organist were good enough reasons for continuing the work of his forefathers. To improve his skill in organ music Bach quite naturally turned his attention to the German North, where this branch of music was of high standing as regards both playing and composition. It possessed sufficient originality to differ distinctly from the organ music of the German South or from Italian music.

Bach came to Lüneburg in 1700, at the age of fifteen. Here, however, all that the German *Kantorei* stood for in traditional training as well as in the manner of composition made itself felt. Here any musician must have been exposed to the heavy impact of the most confusing influences. When a young composer came with the intention of getting a clear idea of what style in composition in his day should be, clarity was the last thing he could find. The repertory of the vocal music used at Lüneburg while Bach was a singer in the choir gives full evidence of the complete lack of any uniformity. And this, indeed, is very characteristic of the situation in which during the baroque period we find the *Kantorei,* an institution that had fulfilled its true function during the epoch of Dutch composition, from about 1450 to 1600, and in Germany especially during the age of the Reformation. Now the choral repertory of Lüneburg was in complete disorder. The names of the composers tell a confused story; they are: Aichinger, De Monte, Gabrieli, Gallus, Gastoldi, Grandi, Hammerschmidt, Ingegneri, Josquin, Adam Krieger, Lassus, Marenzio, Merulo, Monteverdi, Palestrina, Praetorius, Schop, Selle, Senfl, Vecchi, and Viadana In terms of musical style there were a good many Dutch compositions, but without any discrimination; all the shades of the Dutch style are represented, with the exception of its oldest type, that of Ockeghem; and also works of the same school that show distinctly the process of stylistic disintegration. In addition, the baroque style of the solo song as well as of the concerto was taken up. The Obsequies and Sacred Concerts of Heinrich Schütz were perhaps also part of the Lüneburg repertory. The accomplishments of not less than two centuries, from 1500 to 1700, were combined into the strangest mixture, entirely without order, without the slightest attempt to distinguish the different compositions by periods or countries. We must not assume, as has been done, that the old compositions were sung for any reason of "historical" interest, as we might be concerned with "the music of old." The obsolete works were *still* sung, and purely on the strength of the tradition in the *Kantorei;* when the more recent compositions began to be circulated, they were taken up as they became known and grafted upon the old stock. Consequently, the German baroque musician was confronted with an inheritance of spiritual power drawn from previous centuries. The musical service performed by the cantor afforded no clear view into the actual state of contemporary music. Bach met precisely this situation when he started at Lüneburg. From this, historians have concluded that such a vast repertory offered a rare opportunity to study musical composition on a really large scale, since it led the musician back to the technique of times past, even as early as 1500. The conclusion is unintelligent and unhistorical. In so far as the German baroque musicians were at all aware of the state of things, they suffered seriously from that grand scale, and it is we who have slighted the fateful consequences that arose from this situation.

Bach was on the quest, and his inquiries were answered by ancient and disorderly traditions, by a complex assortment of styles. Remote and recent epochs spoke to him at one and the same time with entirely different forms of expression. It was for this reason that the restlessness of the artist in dire uncertainty came over Bach and long remained with him. Lüneburg and the study of its choral music did not satisfy him. Bach explored at the same time the art of Loewe, whose work had no relation to the vocal tradition of the choir in which he was singing. He also studied the work of Böhm thoroughly. His early training in organ music called for further intensification of his knowledge in this field, and so he went to Hamburg to learn from Reinken. The musical repertory at the court of Celle, not far from Lüneburg, showed peculiar characteristics; hence it became an additional point of attraction. The ambitious miniature imitations of Versailles exposed the German baroque courts to the influences of French music. It was for this French character that Bach went to Celle. The stay at Lüneburg was also a constant turning about; with steadfast purpose Bach exploited all he could reach in the neighborhood. Characteristic of a development that proceeds without any certain guide, Bach took with greater seriousness the works he became successively acquainted with and attributed to them greater significance than most of them were entitled to, if viewed in the light of the whole musical achievement of the period. They turned out to be more than a momentary stimulus to his creative power. This, too, is significant. The models he encountered made their unmerited importance felt to the exclusion of anything else because there was nothing in sight that could adjust this relative experience to the "absolute" whole. Bach was in no real touch with the artistic vitality that always prevails in the center of style and carries everything before it, small and great alike. While during the period at Lüneburg he was steadily exploring the "true" state of music, whatever "truth" there was available, he perceived only what interested him as the future cantor and organist. Perhaps these are the most restless years in his life. It explains nothing, however, to attribute this to youth's insatiable thirst for knowledge. Bach stayed only two and a half years at Lüneburg; but despite its brevity the period brought him experience with the vocal music of the sixteenth and seventeenth centuries, with the works of Loewe, Böhm, Reinken, and the French baroque music. Indeed, they show an unusual diversity.

Bach was determined to begin his musical life as a cantor and organist. This his trips to Reinken in Hamburg make quite apparent. Not for a moment did he think of turning to Reinhard Keiser, the composer of operas. Hamburg was perhaps the only city in baroque Germany which through its opera afforded in a scope greater than usual and in splendid execution, a relatively adequate idea of baroque music. The plan to unite the prevailing Italian opera with the forms of the French court, the goal of Kusser, and to create out of such a unification a distinctive German opera on the grandiose scale of baroque man, the idea of Keiser, produced an achievement astonishingly close to the magnificent gesture with which the prominent men of the time showed themselves masters of their art. Through these works Hamburg became the only city where the narrowness of German musical conditions had been overcome. And on this point, all the differences of inner structure are brought out that separate Händel and Bach, their work as well as their characters. Händel went to Hamburg because of the significance he saw in Keiser's opera. His contact with the musical organization of the city and the branch of musical art that involved the cantor and organist was accidental, not sought after, and halfhearted. He became violinist at the opera, and his friendship with Johann Mattheson, a man who was to become well versed in the European aspects of music, probably opened his eyes. Here, Händel and Bach part with one another at this early stage, at the very beginning of their artistic careers. For their ideas about the "end and purpose" of musical art are fundamentally different. Bach went to Hamburg for Reinken, the organist. Again this decision reveals destiny, just as does Händel's resolution. The stay at Hamburg involved Bach still more deeply in the kind of life his musical goal forced him to choose.

Unfortunately, no document records the standard and skill of Bach's organ playing at this time. He was to be the master of his age in this field. But the beginning is obscure. We can take it for granted that he availed himself fully of the training in Böhm's school; he heard Reinken. But we do not know the degree of skill he had himself reached. It cannot have been inconsiderable. The events that followed the short period of Lüneburg make this assumption plausible. Though only eighteen years of age he must have been an organist of some renown.

From 1703 on Bach served as organist at Arnstadt. "Here he began most assiduously to make use of the works of the organists most famous at that time . . . to the advantage of his composition as well as of his playing," says the author of the necrology. Here began the process of elevating German musicianship within its well defined limits. Bach ennobled the office of cantor and organist from within, although the Germans around him were never aware of a process that would give an old office a new dignity. During the period at Arnstadt Bach in fulfilling his official duties came gradually closer to the clear idea about the end and purpose of his music he was shortly to formulate. The cantata "Denn du wirst meine Seele nicht in der Hölle lassen," composed at Arnstadt, is an indication of this aim. It took, however, the meeting with Buxtehude to reach absolute clarity. Bach was determined to visit him; and so he applied for a leave, which was granted for a month in 1705. At the time he arrived at Lübeck the Evening Music (*Abendmusiken*) in the church of St. Mary was at its height. Although these performances had a fairly respectable tradition, it was Buxtehude who gave them the form in which they became famous. The community of Lübeck took part in them, for religious rather than for merely musical reasons. Buxtehude gave the music the character of a liturgical service. The Protestant liturgy did not actually provide for a service of this kind, though it can be regarded as derived from the original Vespers. Tradition had treated it in an impersonal manner, using music regardless of the individual composer, as was the custom in other Protestant services; hymns, chorales, motets were sung. Buxtehude, however, succeeded in organizing the service into a religious whole, by making his music, to which he gave the forms of his time, set the tone throughout. He arranged the Evening Music as a musical liturgy with its own specific type and of his own making. Thus a unique category of church music came to birth in close relation to the liturgical act in whose service the music was intended to function. These evening services had a fairly wide reputation.

Hence Bach was attracted by Buxtehude, not only as the great master of the organ, but also as the inventor of a Protestant liturgy given significance through the music of the individual composer. Bach here experienced church music from an entirely new angle and discovered new possibilities for "organizing" church music as a whole. It even seems that he got a clear view of the "reorganization" he was soon to propose. At all events, never before had he approached the problems of Protestant church music as they were presented at Lübeck. The idea he found realized to a certain extent was this: Buxtehude, that is, an *individual* musician, arranged his own musical concertos for the Evening Music in such a way as to raise the new forms of Italian baroque into an *objective* church music through his appeal to the congregation. This work was complete in itself, based on liturgical tradition and creative in the sense that the music of a single composer produced a new religious service, even though limited in scope, for it comprised merely the five Sundays before Christmas. This form had as its goal the complete organization of the service through music.

The idea of the Protestant church had once more proved productive. The music of the individual composer was called upon to express an idea which must be regarded as the cradle of the Protestant liturgy, the idea of the part played by the congregation in offering the service of prayer and praise. It is not merely the solemnity of elevated language or the intensity of religious feeling that is the primary function of church music. These are only concomitant aspects; they are results perhaps, but certainly not the causes. The true aim is for the individual composer to use his music to organize the service. In the Evening Music of Buxtehude this ideal was realized on a small scale. It is a form of "regulated" church music in which the creative musician weds his work to the objective idea of church and liturgy. If Bach later on saw his particular problem to be the organization of a well-regulated church music, he may have thought of Buxtehude as one of his inspirers. We cannot assume, however, that Bach first learned the very ideal of church music as an entirely new thing from the organist of Lübeck. The "end" of his music was within him, regardless of how clearly he was aware of it. The goal if viewed on a large scale could raise the musician to such greatness as to make him the one and only creator of church music. His music will embody the idea of the whole service. His work must be the symbolic expression of the religious unity that the congregation realizes in the visible form of the service.

Not that Bach was looking for a new frame for his work, for a new organization of the service. The organization was there. But the "organizer," the spokesman of the congregation, should be new. The work will be only the medium; the whole responsibility for the unity of the music of the service is placed upon the individual composer. The only limits are the inner "law" of the artist and the vision he has of the idea of the church. If he should fail in obeying the inner law and in carrying out Luther's idea of the church, he would imperil the service and the musical liturgy as well. There has been no other musician who like Bach possessed the inner force to create church music in the spirit of Luther's church without breaking up the liturgy with an excess of the subjective, and by taking liberties with it as men are wont to do. Again, there has been no other musician whom the problem and the responsibility toward church and liturgy have stirred so deeply as they did Bach. Such a decision and such discoveries constitute the historical significance of Bach's stay at Lübeck and of his meeting with Buxtehude. Of course, the impressions he gained in his study of organ music were by no means of minor importance, since they seem to have rounded out his abilities as an organist and composer of organ music. But the intensive influences that guided his ideas as to an essentially new organization of church music were of far more consequence.

So fully did all this absorb him that he risked overstaying his leave of absence from Arnstadt. He had been granted a month. November passed by, and so did December. It was January 1706 when he once more visited Hamburg for the sake of seeing Reinken; he went to Lüneburg to call on Böhm, and at last arrived at Arnstadt at the end of January 1706. The authorities of the church were utterly indignant over his arbitrary absence. As soon as Bach started his work, he called forth violent protest by his new way of playing the organ; what was really involved, however, was his new style of composition for the organ rather than the mere technique of his performance. Displeasure with his innovations led to formal protests, in the course of which he was severely reminded of his neglect of duty in staying away from his job as he pleased. Finally it came to a break. Bach replied in very concise terms, sure of himself and of his doings: "I was at Lübeck in order to gain an understanding there of one problem and another connected with my art." The reprimand of the clerical authorities called his particular attention to what they took to be evil. Bach, they said, made many peculiar variations in the chorale; he smuggled many foreign tones into the melodies, and thus greatly confused the congregation. It is quite obvious that the new way of giving an individual interpretation to the objective chorale melody, the basis of the musical liturgy, met with apprehension on the part of the authorities. What was to Bach a new religious quality in church music they took to be nothing but a disturbance of the traditional forms. We need not go into the details of the dispute between him and the consistory. It appears that Bach was not at all inclined to compromise; he even seems to have welcomed the controversy as a good reason for resigning his post at Arnstadt. Then follows the exceedingly important phase of his life at Mühlhausen, in 1707.

The cantata begins to take on characteristics that grow more and more essential for his purpose, particularly when Bach develops it around the chorale melody. Like any other category of musical form in the baroque age, the chorale melody has values of its own, its objectivity, its traditional expression. Being an objective category it makes demands of its own which the composer must meet. It is a medium in which the subjective element of the musician must measure itself against the objective qualities of the category. This process underlies the treatment in which the composer recasts the traditional chorale: he breaks it up or expands it; he overlays it with a new surface; he creates a new chorale by ornamenting anew the melody of an old one. That the musician avails himself of the melody at all to build the cantata is purely a matter of structure and composition. The attempt to transform the melody is the result of the demands made by the objective category in the realm of musical form.

But for Bach this attempt springs at the same time from his resolve to interpret a religious reality anew. And here the significance of the text, of the Holy Word, plays its full part, and a distinctively Protestant one. The text stands, as it were, apart from the musical aspects of the melodic structure. Bach strove to create a new melody for the chorale; he exploited the meaning of the text and made it the basis for the melody. Thus he transformed the "traditional" chorale. The process was religiously justified in that he derived it from a relation between the religious meaning of the word and the melody as a new value. In order to be true to the religious sense of the word Bach had to reveal it in music by a closely realistic reproduction. The result was often a melody full of contortions, twists, expansions, brokenness, characteristics that are all significant of Bach's melody, but also indicative of the intensity with which he made his melody the true picture of the religious text. Its meaning was his main concern. Bach's melodies tend generally to realize these features, but they show them with particular clarity in the modified chorales. The power of artistic form emanates from the word which demands musical expression. For Bach attributed to the text the utmost significance; he endeavored to exhaust the religious value of each individual word in accordance with the fundamental Protestant attitude. The deepening of the musical forms by full admission of the individual word imposes upon the melody a rule of progression which cannot be explained by referring it to a melodic structure that has its own proper disposition as well as balance, independent and clear. Bach's characteristic individuality consists in something else. He submits the independent structure of the melody to the test of its adequacy to the necessities of the religious meaning inherent in the text. He interprets the word according to its inner qualities. He took the word as an object in the world of religion. As such, it finds its symbol in the melody. The broken melodic line, loaded with rhythmic complications, figurative material, ornaments, never as spontaneous and direct as the Southern baroque melodies, appears as the very expression of Bach's religious intensity.

It was typical of the baroque musician to recognize the categories of musical form. In this Bach hardly differed from other contemporary composers. But he also called upon these categories to symbolize the Holy Word, the object of the church. Without this any reorganization of church music in general was impossible. Bach clung to this idea. He renounced the way the categories were used and understood in Italy as well as in France. There they were taken to express man's bearing in life, his gesture in the world of appearance. Disregarding the categories as vehicles for expressing the grandiose entertainment of baroque life, Bach stripped them of the atmosphere in which they had been brought into existence. Making them responsible to the religious qualities of the sacred word, he combined two diverse elements: one was essentially and intentionally secular, the other made religious by Bach's aim.

While Bach's cantata "Gott ist mein König," composed at the beginning of his activities at Mühlhausen, does not yet reveal all the problems which are to play an essential part in the process of reorganizing church music through the symbolic interpretation of the religious word, the anxiety of his efforts to give the word its due increased because of new influences coming from the movement he had first experienced, although vaguely and immaturely, at Ohrdruf.

For the second time Bach encountered Pietism, and this time in such form as to wrest an inner decision from him. In matters of religious strife Mühlhausen had had abundant experience, which at times had been dearly paid for. The people of the town were able to trace it back to the Reformation when the Anabaptists, the adherents of Thomas Münzer, had started the revolution, political and religious. It was at Mühlhausen that Thomas Münzer was finally executed. Pietism fell here on a soil made fertile by religious conflicts. A violent contention broke out between Pietism and Orthodoxy. Passionate quarrels raged back and forth, from the church of St. Blasius, where Bach was appointed, to the church of St. Mary. On the side of Pietism was the new inwardness of the religious man, the introversion of the individual who makes his own inner self the very source of grace and religious intensity. But this subjective "inwardness" imperilled the forms of religious life as organized and guided by the church. On the other side stood the formalism of Lutheran orthodoxy. Since 1691 Pastor Frohne had advocated for the church of St. Blasius the new intensified religious attitude; from the very start, however, he made it clear that in recognizing the Pietistic movement he did not subscribe to certain disintegrating tendencies, a by-product caused by undisciplined fanatics and seditious hotheads.

When Pastor Georg Christian Eilmar took office at the church of St. Mary, the strife between the two factions broke out. Bach was caught in the very center. Frohne was the pastor of the church where he served as organist. A personal friendship bound him to Eilmar. But this position between the two factions reflected also an inner conflict, in which Bach felt himself drawn to both sides. While at Ohrdruf his youthful experience of Pietism had been prevented from growing, probably by the influences of education and advice in the family where he lived, now his situation at Mühlhausen could no longer save him from internal conflict. No longer could he fall back on the support that the advice of his relatives at Ohrdruf may have afforded. It is quite clear that Bach's nature would keep him aloof from the extremes of an unsteady fanatic. This side of Pietism never endangered him. But, of course, it was not the only side. Pietism as a new intensification of religious experience absorbed him. He was deeply agitated by the ideas to which Pietism gave expression, and the open strife may have increased rather than lessened his agitation. First of all: Pietism was always to him a matter of his own personal religion. He would not escape the decision as to the significance of Pietism for himself and his art. He could perhaps avoid an external decision with regard to his office. In any case, an open declaration of his stand could easily be forced from him. At all times he ran the risk of being brought face to face with such a demand by the authorities. This is, perhaps, another reason for his quick break with his consistory after the return from Lübeck.

At all events, such was the situation: many elements were in favor of the orthodox formalism, whereas his own inclination and his particular attitude toward the religious interpretation of the sacred word in worship and music drove him toward Pietism. The elements in favor of Orthodoxy were: his education and background; his own disposition, which led him to uphold the authority of tradition in general and to abhor all the immoderate exuberance and the revolutionary forces that were bound rashly to destroy the values of the past and the true sense of tradition; and finally, the close link that joined his vocation as an artist and his very position as well to the organization of the orthodox church. There was, furthermore, a factor that set him in definite opposition to Pietism. We know that Pietism favored an extremely puritanical attitude toward the arts and in particular toward music, whose artistic manifestations should have no place in the service of the true Pietist. It may be said that in view of such a principle any further question on this point becomes meaningless or purely theoretical. Actually such questions do not lose their meaning even if we disregard the fact that the authorities at the church of St. Blasius in no way hampered a liberal use of music in the service. But Pietism had now become for Bach an idea which involved his own religious and artistic feelings, quite apart from all its outward implications. We know what books were in Bach's own library, and that among them theological works had an outstanding place. We also know the scope of the Pietistic writings he possessed. All the great works with which the religious movement started off were in his hands, naturally the *Pia Desideria* of Spener first of all. And his Pietistic studies may very well have made him approach medieval mysticism; the Sermons of Tauler were also in his library.

Bach did not allow Pietism to make itself much felt in his external life. But he admitted that it exerted its influence upon his religious ideas of art. And here, indeed, Pietism was of far-reaching consequence. For the Pietist religious intensity came from his attitude toward the evangelical word of the Bible; he discarded the dogmatic meaning which tradition had honored. He devoted himself to the direct meaning of the word. He believed that intimate and spiritual conversation with God will reveal the true and pious sense of the word. He must endeavor to exhaust the inherent secrets of the word in order to find God through it. Whoever fails in humble piety and readiness to believe will not grasp the meaning of the word; to him it will remain closed. The Holy Word, therefore, is not symbolic of the dogma in its formal aspects. The act of interpreting the word depends on the pious intensity of the individual, not at all on the dogmatic sense that men of the past have established and sanctified.

It is Pietism that inspires Bach's attitude toward the religious text that is to be transformed into music. It is Pietism that accounts for his unswerving resolve to approach the concealed meaning of the word, for his devout contemplation of the religious value inherent in the word, and for his anxiety to do full justice to the word whose religious connotations the artistic form must not injure. Whenever he hears the sense God conveys to him through the word, he transmits it directly into music, as the religious element, "operated and operating." This interpretation of the word is equivalent to the creation of new religious realities, and it is the deepest expression of his piety in which he does homage to the meaning of the word as it is revealed to him. Only this Pietistic attitude can help to explain why Bach wanted the musical form, put so often into the most realistic appearance, to be understood as a religious symbol.

If Pietism produced Bach's characteristic approach to the Holy Word, it was also responsible for many a conflict he had to undergo. We can imagine how deeply this conflict affected him, if we take into full consideration that his artistic goal was once and for all church music; that church music called for a reorganization; that Bach was about to make the individual artist alone responsible for the creation of church music so organized that it would interpret the Holy Word in the spirit of Pietism; furthermore, that this goal was possible only within the forms of the orthodox church and could never be reached within Pietism; and finally, that Pietism must have repelled Bach because of its denial of artistic music while it still attracted him for personal religious reasons. And it is this contradictory situation that wrested from him the final decision. There was no escape for the man placed in the midst of antagonistic parties. As a matter of fact, he had no true choice; he did the only thing he could—he left the place. But before leaving Mühlhausen in 1708 he laid down—for all to read—a statement which made clear the very goal of his art.

II

After Mühlhausen the path toward fulfillment seemed free. Bach's goal was set and his work filled from within with a new religious intensity. Bach could do what he set out to do only in the position of an organist and cantor. At the time when he brought his work to its decisive phase, he probably did not foresee the consequences such a position would impose upon him. He could hardly have thought of the extreme narrowness from which his work would be doomed to suffer, since such a place had yielded to his forefathers and to his friends a solid foundation for honorable craftsmanship; tradition and experience prevented him from seeing limitation in it or finding fault with it. So he began the organization of church music. He started with organ compositions that should establish the world of new religious realities; they maintained, especially in the chorales and chorale preludes, a close relationship to the Holy Word and to religious emotion. He also began to compose cantatas on a systematic scale; he used texts by Salomo Franck and Erdmann Neumeister; the first perhaps the more intense and devout poet of the two, the latter the more original mind as regards the arrangement of new religious texts to set to music.

We know the ideas Neumeister set forth when he wrote his cantata texts for the purpose of religious intensification. "Having properly performed my official duties on Sundays in the church, I attempted to transform the most significant thoughts that were treated in the sermon into poetic language for my private devotional use.... Thus these cantatas came to birth." Considered as a musical liturgy, these new texts, essentially musical in their arrangement, offered three elements that contributed to Bach's own musical plans. First: the texts, written for all the Sundays of the church year, took on a liturgical function through their intimate connection with the sermon, which in its turn derived its special characteristics from the Gospel for the day and thus bore out the particular teaching of each Sunday or holy day in the year. Despite the "pious" form of subjective poetry which marked its origin, the cantata became part of the objective liturgy through being linked to the ecclesiastical calendar. There was nothing else in the cantata that made it liturgical. In full conformity with the topic of the sermon, the cantata was placed liturgically between the reading of the Gospel and the sermon.

Secondly, the new poem allowed the individual to penetrate completely the objective sphere of liturgy; this appears a prerequisite for the musician who would make the musical form interpret the religious element in the Pietistic sense. Neumeister regarded his texts as the expression of private piety. He spoke at some length of their poetic characteristics. He laid down the principle that the text of the cantata must express a specific emotion; at that time the various human emotions—"affections" in the baroque terminology—were classified and stereotyped in fixed patterns. Furthermore, being of religious character, it must include a thesis of ethical, or spiritual, import, a "moral." The music will, therefore, have a clear field to express the religious intensity of the affection. Thirdly, the text of the cantata provided for an intimate relation between the musical form and the style of the time. In fact, it is the musical composition of the period that dictated the arrangement of the poem. In Neumeister's own words, a cantata "does not look any different from a piece out of an opera which consists of recitatives and arias." He applied the baroque forms of music to organize the structure of the poem. The musical forms were accepted on the ground that the recitative, the aria, and, above all, the *da capo* aria were common to the Italian baroque cantata and to the opera.

To sum up: from its very origin, the poem placed strong emphasis on a certain religious feeling of intense but momentary character. The subjective situation, the starting-point for the poetry, shows the cantata to be an outgrowth of the individual's contemplative devotion and piety. It was the intention of the poet to lift man's mind to pious thoughts testifying to the intimate relation of man to God. This, too, implies a free subjective form of religious expression. Despite the many subjective elements in the poem, the cantata nevertheless found its way into the established liturgy. The process which led the poetical content through the moral to the sermon and finally to the Gospel was admitted into the ecclesiastical calendar. But here lies the sole relation between cantata and liturgy. The poetic content, however, is not always a safe ground on which to develop definite and organic forms within the liturgy. Such a relation between the liturgical order and the poetic content is essentially weak as well as flexible; and the poet has too much liberty to make the text a medium of arbitrary expression. As a matter of fact, the degree of safety depended entirely on the strength with which the composer realized this relation in each individual case.

Now the cantata as a species of poetry never claimed independent poetic value of its own. On the contrary, the poem was laid out with a view to the music from which it derived its structure in every detail. And this structure was admittedly of secular origin. Consequently, if the cantata was to be turned into a strictly ecclesiastical form, this had to be done through the music to which it was set, since the poem was without meaning in itself.

From the liturgical point of view the cantata should be more than an accidental contribution to the service. When Bach began to make the cantata the chief medium through which to reorganize church music, he conceived a twofold procedure. He put all the stress on the liturgical character, no matter how weakly and unreliably the poem might have expressed it, in order to attach the form as such indissolubly to the order of the divine service. He began to build up gradually a series of cantata compositions that would meet the requirements of the church calendar throughout the whole year. A great number of German baroque musicians had composed cantatas answering musical needs in the service; most of them took the cantatas merely as a welcome medium with which to bring church music closer to the prevailing secular style. Bach did much more. And here Pietism, or at least the Pietistic idea of the significance inherent in the religious word, makes its artistic influence felt. Bach carried the full meaning of the word into the music; he exploited its religious quality; he made all its secrets speak musically in piety. Through the music the meaning of the word became a new religious reality.

It is in this sense that we have called "the birth of the Church out of the spirit of music" the final achievement of Bach. If the text of the cantata retained its relation to the liturgy—and Bach held this to be indispensable—it would be intensified by the Pietistic interpretation he brought into it. Thus the very character appropriate to each season which the text attempted to keep would obtain its true qualification if the meaning of the text were transformed into a musical symbol. Again Orthodoxy and Pietism confront each other. For the composition of cantatas following the lessons of the calendar through the whole church year derives from orthodox formalism. The devout interpretation of the text, which we have tried to explain, comes from Pietism. This conflict will never leave Bach as long as he pursues his goal. We have anticipated many features in Bach's form of the cantata. In Weimar the scene was set for all he would achieve in this field. It took Leipzig for him to reach the final proportions of the cantata.

With the goal set there seemed to be nothing to hinder Bach

from straightforward advance. Everything appeared possible within the musical organization the German town provided. Bach did not doubt that accomplishment would come from his activities as an organist and composer of church music at Weimar. And he was right in not doubting. As yet the question of what place and recognition his music would attain in the rivalry of European countries, did not apparently trouble him. Either he did not realize the importance of such a question, or he avoided it in order to carry out his work faithfully. We have seen that it did not arise at Hamburg, where the musical conditions were very favorable for suggesting it to his mind. Much less did it occur to him at Lübeck. Arnstadt may perhaps have been too limited and too early a stage of his development to make him see the problem. And Mühlhausen brought full concentration on the religious aspects of this work. This is all the more amazing if we think of the contrast between Bach and Händel, who foresaw the question at a strikingly early age and acted accordingly. His inexplicable foresight was reason enough for him to sever his alliance with the musical organizations of the German baroque towns, once and for all. If Bach had not yet encountered the problem, it was his religious goal that kept him from doing so. In working at this task his field of activity was as small as the town where he did his work. And his renown as a composer, even though he declared his intention of reorganizing church music entirely, would hardly reach beyond the field within whose limits he was working. As long as his task controlled him, no doubt could arise, even if Bach were denied in advance the fruits of recognition as a composer and any influential effect upon the vast realms of truly European music. The compositions destined for the church in Germany failed to win acclaim in European circles.

But it is unthinkable that a composer of Bach's proportions would always be able to avoid measuring his own work against all other European music. Nowadays even very minor musicians think in international terms even before they begin really to compose. Sooner or later, Bach was bound to consider his European reputation. This must needs reveal to him the leading part Italy played in the concert of baroque music. As soon as Bach, in his restless search for possibilities of composition, came to strike out and make use of the musical categories of the Italian baroque, he would find what "style" meant among European forms and in the sense of Italian baroque. Then he would realize the true measure of greatness his own work had accomplished in the small town.

Apart from his work for the church he began during his Weimar period to study the Italian style in a more or less systematic way. These studies resulted in compositions which he himself expressly marked "*alla maniera Italiana.*" He wrote his concerti after the Italian model of Vivaldi. It has often been said that this new turn has a very simple explanation: Bach was proving anew how manifold were his artistic interests; he never overlooked any available form of musical expression, and hence he simply added one more experience. This is quite plausible and in a way true. Yet it does not hold true that all Bach's experience of "style" in music had the same historical meaning and bearing. The meeting with Buxtehude meant plainly something more than the acquisition of a certain technical skill. It would show a great lack of perception on our part were we to assume, for instance, that Bach's acquaintance with French music at Celle and his discoveries at Lübeck possessed the same significance. His new quest in the field of Italian music has likewise a different historical aspect. To be sure, it began with studies in style and form. The more systematically he explored the "*maniera,*" the more perturbed he must have grown. For the implications latent in all the forms of Italian music insinuated themselves and made Bach aware that formal studies involved at times more than mere manners of writing.

Bach learned gradually to view his works in the light of the whole of music. Here a danger would arise. A temporary leaning toward a certain manner of composing, or even the systematic imitation of Italian style, could not imperil his work. In the Italian forms, however, he encountered an expansive power and a predominance over the rest of European music. He recognized the actual conditions of music as they had been organized through the work of Italian baroque musicians. These conditions made him feel that his judgments had been practically perverted by his constant confinement within the German town. All the power with which Italians were directing European music pressed upon him. It made itself felt through the medium of compositions that were for all purposes and in all characteristics secular; Italian baroque music held the secular quality to be the essence of its being. With its style Italian music controlled all European music; Bach's music was limited to a single town. In its essential quality Italian baroque was secular; Bach's work was essentially sacred. In the light of such contrasts, the *maniera Italiana* presented itself, indeed, as far more than a style in the limited sense. Penetrating into a European range of music and musical activity, Bach must have come to doubt whether the work he had previously composed would ever attain the European rank to which, of course, he had a just title.

The recognition of all that Italian style implied had far-reaching consequences. Not only did it act as a corrective element: for the first time Bach availed himself of a European measure and learned to think in European terms. It also raised new hopes that he might himself reach out and seize upon an expansive power like that possessed by the Italian style, so that his own work might be heard throughout Europe. And finally, it caused dissatisfaction with the musical life in the German town. He must have seen clearly now that this type of musical activity would stifle his composition within the walls of the city, rob it of effect in the world at large. The organization of musical life through the *Kantorei*, though of venerable tradition, had grown entirely inadequate to absorb fully the *maniera Italiana* with which Bach was occupied. Did he now visualize the need for a reform of all musical life in Germany? We do not know. Heinrich Schütz, who found himself face to face with a situation not much different from the one Bach was now beginning to observe, at once drew his conclusions; he adapted the Italian baroque in the style of Monteverdi, but at the same time he recognized that mere transplanting of the new music into the traditional German organizations would not do. And Schütz laid down his ideas about the need of a reform. A man of sixty-three, he published his last work, the *Musicalia ad chorum sacrum, dass ist geistliche Chormusik*. In the preface, grandiose but depressing, he explained that he had failed in his reform, that the German musicians had not followed him, that they had accepted the new style only in part and on a petty scale; but in neglecting a simultaneous reform of the institutions that regulated musical training, they had merely lost the previous craftsmanship the old organization had the advantage of providing. He admonished German musicians to acquire the lost skill through the study of music in the style of the sixteenth century, obsolete but adequate for the *Kantorei* as the traditional school of training.

Bach found that the wide gap between Italian baroque as the

prevailing style and German musical life still existed. It is not probable that he desired to bring about a complete reform of German music as a whole. Moreover, with him the baroque epoch was entering upon its last phase. If the problems turned out to be precisely the same as they had been at the beginning of the period, a reform would come too late. Bach himself, toward the end of his life, came to see the dawn of a new age which he probably understood as little as his sons were to understand their own father.

Although a reform of German musical life was apparently far from his thought, the complete grasp of all that the *maniera Italiana* embodied would have brought home to him a revaluation of his work and of German musical art as well. That Bach went out of his way to seize upon the world-wide renown of Italian music for his own sake, cannot be doubted. Strange as it may seem, the more Bach's insight into the actual circumstances of German music grew, the more he, together with all that his work stood for, was imperilled. This might appear a contradiction, since it might seem strange to see danger in his very efforts to gain a far-reaching sphere of influence for his work. But there really was danger. Could Bach's music ever attain its due place in the music of Europe? Was it possible for him to gain a hearing for his work in the countries where Italians had settled the forms through which baroque Europe chiefly expressed itself?

The aim Bach had chosen for his work guided his decisions. There was the problem of reorganizing church music. This task could be carried out only if Bach remained in his position as organist and cantor. Such a position did not allow his works to have an echo in the European world of music. If Bach wanted to break through the narrowness in which his music had to live, he would have to give up his position. Were he to do so, he would betray the aim of his music. The vision of a vast province of action in the world of art was not in keeping with the idea of reforming church music. The two were incompatible. The new goal toward which Bach began to reach out was attractive enough. The prize might be a place in the European repertory, in which Bach's name was completely unknown; and perhaps a change from the depressingly minor situation of German baroque music might be a secondary reward. This glimpse into vast regions far beyond the walls of a town, even beyond the German-speaking countries, held out a new goal for his whole art. And the struggle between these two different goals, church music and the secular greatness of music in Europe, began slowly to take shape at Weimar while Bach was devoting himself to the study of the *maniera Italiana*.

But the choice had to be made. Indeed, Bach made one of the gravest decisions of his whole life. He discontinued his activity at Weimar. In 1717 he began his new work as Hofkapellmeister of Prince Leopold of Anhalt-Köthen, the court residing at Köthen. Bach had learned from the *maniera Italiana* that the culture of the courts was the medium through which musical composition would win acclaim in Europe. Perhaps his short visit to Dresden had its share in influencing his decision to leave Weimar. He was determined, unwilling to compromise. The authorities of Weimar did not want him to go; they made efforts to keep him. Bach insisted on leaving. So definitely had he made up his mind that he was ready to go to jail. This imperturbable determination is quite revealing. Behind it stands Bach's vision of a new goal for his music. To attain it was worth many a sacrifice.

In fact, Bach sacrificed things that must have been of the greatest value to him. If he had been known at all hitherto, outside the cities where he worked, it was as an organist that he enjoyed a good name. The only wider reputation he had gained was in the field of organ-playing. Bach gave all this up, at least so far as any official function was concerned. For Köthen took away from him just this activity. In order to understand this decision and his new aim fully we should not forget that from the day he left Weimar Bach never carried on any official activity as an organist, either at Köthen or later at Leipzig. He could have had no doubt that he must renounce his organ-playing before he made up his mind to go to Köthen. Moreover, Protestantism was of the reformed branch at the court of Köthen; it was Calvinistic. This also he must have known well in advance. No uncertainty could ever have entered his mind that the divine service at the court chapel would admit of any other sacred music than the Calvinistic melodies of the psalms. Such a severe curtailment could not possibly comply with the imposing structure of church music that Bach had originally visualized. There was not a single factor in the musical situation at Köthen favorable to Bach's art had he really wished to continue working toward his old aim, nothing that lent itself to realizing his plans for reforming church music.

If he nevertheless accepted the position at Köthen, he must have abandoned his first plan, and in doing this, he was swerving from the path that we might have expected him to follow to the very end. In accepting the offer of Duke Leopold, he was embarking upon a new program of musical art. He was rising to the position of "*Kapellmeister*," the only one that would cast in his way a different musical repertory that would conform to the spirit and style of the time. The *Kapellmeister*, representative of musical activity at the courts, and, as it were, spokesman of a form of life that had made an all-embracing "style" the guide for each and every human expression, was the one status in which the musician could reach out to the powerful manifestations that emanated from the style of nobility. An international reputation could come from such a position, in contrast to that of cantor, which at best led to local significance. Because the aristocratic form of life could be made the vehicle through which to give the work of the artist an international rank, musicians eagerly seized upon every opportunity to obtain a position as *Kapellmeister*. Such a position meant not only a new source of commissions for artistic works, or a pecuniary improvement for the individual artist (sometimes this was not even the case; some posts of *cantor* were actually more lucrative than those of *Kapellmeister*). It meant something intangible that money could not buy, the possibility of European rank as a musician. Händel had a genuine instinct for it, true to the nature of the baroque men, and he made it coincide with the aim of his work.

Bach heeded such an instinct once, and Köthen gave him the chance. He was fully aware of the opportunity the position of *Kapellmeister* afforded for a musician to mould his own destiny. When Leipzig later made an offer, Bach struggled against an inner warning not to return to the post of cantor; he even found it then—in his own words—beneath the dignity of a musician who held his honor in proper regard, to "step down" from the post of *Kapellmeister* to that of *cantor*. In still later years he turned his eyes now and again to the court of Dresden, from which he hoped to get at least the title of *Hofkapellmeister*. Even his return to the old goal that Leipzig brought into sight again, did not make him forget entirely what the position at Köthen had once held up to him as a promise.

The change of "end" in Bach's composition can be seen clearly if we compare the list of works he wrote at Weimar with those he composed at Köthen. The comparison is exceedingly instructive.

There are on the one hand the compositions of Weimar. The predominance of sacred works stands out and asserts itself as the contribution to his aim of reforming church music. In the first place there are the church cantatas which orginated in collaboration with Neumeister and Franck, about twenty in number. Next, there are the organ compositions, which by their great number as well as by their quality mark the whole Weimar period as a climactic point. (Even the *Orgelbüchlein* he arranged at Köthen draws upon chorale compositions written at Weimar.) The greater part of this organ music is made up of fugues, introduced by preludes or toccatas. There are about forty such compositions if we count the introductory piece and the fugue as one work. Lastly, there are the compositions for harpsichord and clavichord, similar in kind to the Weimar organ music, for the most part preludes, fugues, toccatas, fantasias. In addition to these works there are compositions—studies is perhaps the best term for them—that express the new relation to the ruling *maniera Italiana,* which Prince Johann Ernst, himself a lover of music and a composer as well, inspired and encouraged. It was because of the consequences Bach drew from this inspiration that he left Weimar for Köthen, where his exploration of the *maniera Italiana* went far beyond the scope of "studies."

It is clear from this list of works that it was church music that gave the compositions of the Weimar period their character. The peculiar conditions of Weimar favored the exclusiveness of the artistic standpoint Bach maintained in selecting musical categories each of which contributed its proper share to the ultimate range of a regulated church music. Whether Bach considered that the task he had set himself had been accomplished, in full or in part, must be doubted. The violence with which he severed himself from Weimar, the vision of a new goal which he now made the guide for his artistic work, render it obscure whether all he had done was in his own opinion a first step toward the reorganization of church music, or whether his departure was perhaps an admission of failure in the face of the insurmountable obstacles between his task and the general spirit of the times. At all events, the further Bach carried his religious work, the more bitter grew the conflicts with the authorities during each of the periods in which he devoted himself to this task.

On the other hand we have the list of works composed at Köthen. Its character is just as exclusive as that of Weimar. During the six years of his activity at the court, from 1717 to 1723, Bach neglected the church cantata entirely, and this neglect came abruptly. There are, in fact, only two that can, with certainty, be assigned to the Köthen period, and these are dedicatory works. Criticism of style may well succeed in relating one cantata or another to this period. But any new discovery would scarcely change the picture. With regard to organ compositions also, the situation is reversed from what it had been at Weimar. The composition of only one work is established, the great Prelude (Fantasia) and Fugue in G minor, written in 1720. Indeed, the whole list points to another origin and springs neither from the liturgical cantata, nor from the religious organ composition, nor from church music at all.

Again, we find quite a number of works for keyboard instruments. But here too Bach has changed plan and purpose, although the construction of preludes, fugues, fantasias, and toccatas still occupies his interest. First and foremost, however, the special meaning and technique of playing a keyboard instrument attracted him for purposes of instruction. With this end clearly in view he composed the *Clavier Büchlein* for his son Wilhelm Friedemann (1720), the *Noten Büchlein* for his second wife, Anna Magdalena (1721 and 1725), the first part of the *Wohltemperirte Clavier* (1722), the two-part inventions as well as the three-part symphonies which he combined into a special collection after the *Clavier Büchlein* for Wilhelm Friedemann. Next to these works, which became the imperishable documents of "house music" on the highest level of craftsmanship, he was attracted by the suite, that species of composition which so adequately reflected the gallant and cultivated taste of baroque life. In the field of keyboard music his efforts to cope with the structure and stylized expressiveness of the suite resulted in the collection of the English and French suites (1722/23). It has recently been found quite probable that the "English" suites derive their surprising name from a relation to Händel's suites of 1720, with which Bach's collection has, among other things, the opening in A major in common. The English suites may consequently have been written in 1721, owing the free and "unreflective" manifestation in which Händel's work abounds to a certain imitation of his style; at least this character seems to pertain more to the English than to the French suites.

A large part of the Köthen repertory is given to various forms of chamber music. Here, the *maniera Italiana* led Bach to adopt all the categories of composition used in performances in the "camera," at court. The repertory, then, shows the baroque sonata in a great variety of media. The solo sonata is represented by compositions for the violin, for the gamba, for violin and harpsichord, for flute and thoroughbass; there are sonatas for two violins, for two flutes with *basso continuo*, there is the sonata for violin, flute and thoroughbass in G major. Some of these sonatas, remarkably instructive, have Bach's own realization of the thoroughbass. And, finally, there come the compositions for the orchestra. The suite appears now as an overture with the orchestra as its medium of performance; the list of works shows also the three concerti for violin and orchestra and the D minor concerto for two violins and orchestra; and above all, the Brandenburg Concerti.

Instrumental works, for ensemble or keyboard, predominate in the repertory of Köthen, as did church music among the compositions written at Weimar. The change is sudden; it also is complete. Its significance cannot really be mistaken. Bach has moved out of the sphere of church music; he is building up a stock of compositions, new in the total range of his works; he is aiming at a sphere of art that Italian baroque had more and more successfully made the extreme opposite of church music, the realm of chamber music, indissolubly linked to the life of the court. Bach had foreseen all this. His foresight had led him to make his choice. It is utterly inappropriate to assume that it was merely the particular circumstances he encountered at Köthen that turned his work in a new direction. Actually, baroque music was always bound up with the objective situation in which it arose. For the local conditions to exert their influence upon the character of a musical work is, throughout the period and in every country, quite natural. This, however, was not at all open to question when Bach changed Weimar for Köthen. His foresight of all that was to come: the want of any opportunity to compose for the church, the loss of service as an organist; these stand against the materialistic explanation which would make the greatest work of musical art merely an outgrowth of circumstances without ever allowing for a decision made by the artist himself, and without taking into account the significance the work had for the composer which the historian must attempt to discover. How should the principal change in the repertory of Köthen be explained if we must discard the mere accident of circumstances as its sole reason? What else is there to be said if we cannot satisfy ourselves with the dry-as-dust statement of the factual change? What else but that Bach has set up a new goal for his art, that he has given up his former aim? We cannot escape the reasons that lie deep in the composer's attitude, which his repertory reflects in the nature of the compositions included, perhaps more clearly than in any other factor.

This shift in repertory was in conformity with an internal change in Bach's work. The struggle for repute in the ranks of European musicians, for a coincidence between his work and the spirit of the times, together with the desire to lift German music out of a narrowness that tradition had rendered unavoidable, bestows upon the period of Köthen momentous fascination. Bach begins to speak a European language in adopting the various species of instrumental music; and he makes the expressions of the life of the court his servants, hoping that their international quality will penetrate his work and abide to the end, so that the order of baroque nobility throughout the world may recognize that in them its own tones are resounding. Surely the new goal was no less worthy than the first. Indeed, the works of Köthen seem to abound lavishly with the life of the world and all its sweeping might. There is something common to all the compositions Bach wrote at Köthen, a particular tone almost unmistakable to recognize. They show Bach intent upon massive effects, fullness of sound, rhythms of an unimpeded vitality, upon characteristics by means of which many articles of the baroque age in all the arts expressed the harmony and order of the world, as well as the gesture of the law of baroque life.

Bach often appears to us as "introspective" or, better, as a discoverer of the constructive possibilities latent in objective and movable tones; he knows these "mathematical" secrets inherent in sound; he appears as a magician who understands how to take the soundings of the aptitude of tones to be combined one with another; this is a secret whose depth few of his contemporaries had penetrated. But here at Köthen there is still another Bach, less involved in the mysterious nature of tones as objects of the given world. Never again did Bach come out with so powerful a manifestation of vitality, never was he so certain of the sovereign gesture as an expression of life, never so full of self-assertion and of a natural demand for mastery, as in the grandiose scale of the Brandenburg concerti. Neither was he ever so free from the narrowness of the German burgher as in the Köthen period. Indeed, his work seems here to have absorbed the world tone which the baroque musicians strove to realize. While hitherto one element or another of his composition had always been bound to some tradition of the narrow German city, the European tone he strikes at Köthen is nowhere impaired by any such limitation. Is it then to be wondered at that Bach in years to come looked back upon Köthen as the happiest time of his life even from a personal point of view? The inner freedom he gained for his art, the contact with the whole of European music he thought he had found for his composition, the power the universal spirit of baroque life granted, the feeling of being in concord with the times, the strength that the communication with circumstances on a large scale and broader view afforded; all this eased his way of life and bestowed upon his work a convincing, spontaneous sweep, not always present in his composition. Oftener his music stirs men more through its deeply contemplative nature, through the "melancholia ingenii." The masterly directness, however, that emanates from the work of Köthen Bach never again attained. Händel commanded it as a bountiful gift of nature. Bach had to struggle for it; never did it come naturally to him; and only once did he fully succeed in casting off the inhibitions a cumbrous tradition made him bear.

Although the Köthen work did not make itself felt within European music as a whole—this was its true "end," foreseen or hoped for—its effect was not lost in a vacuum as was the case of Bach's other compositions. An astounding historical process springs from the work of Köthen. It is remarkable that Bach's sons should have taken up this work as the very starting-point for their own advance. They certainly neglected the later work, that of Leipzig, as much as all their other contemporaries did; they understood it as little as everyone else; they acted as though the work of Leipzig did not exist. But they seized upon the work of Köthen, whose spirit they followed and felt to be part of their own. They understood the direct address of this work to the European whole to be in keeping with the times. Bach's sons took it up and carried on from there, particularly Carl Philipp Emmanuel. It matters not what changes they were to bring into the message of Köthen; their primary understanding secured a direct line of development. Thus the Köthen Bach entrusted a heritage to the younger generation. Thus was the success, not an unconditional one and certainly not one that fulfilled all expectations. If the Köthen work did not really become part of Europe's music, at least it hammered out a link with which to hold old and young together. Thus Bach's efforts to give his composition a European message were not altogether in vain, even if the boundaries of Germany set the limit to the message.

Bach wrote in later years to one of his friends that he highly esteemed Prince Leopold of Köthen, both as lover of music and as connoisseur, and that he had hoped he could live and work at his court for the rest of his life. He was denied the satisfaction of doing so. Although he moved into an entirely new sphere of activities when he went to Köthen, he could not cut off his past as completely as he hoped to. That is to say, his reputation as an organist had grown so great that it now made certain demands upon him. Throughout the period of Köthen he was continually invited to test organs in nearby churches. During the early 'twenties certain occasions must have reminded him strongly of his previous task. At least the past frequently made itself felt through his close relations with organists. When the famous position of organist at St. Jacobi at Hamburg became vacant, the church where Neumeister was pastor, Bach was considered, Neumeister being the most ardent advocate of the call. But nothing came of it, and an organist far inferior to Bach was preferred. The decision disappointed Neumeister so deeply that he gave vent to his anger publicly in a sermon. These things may amount to no more than inconsequential interludes; but they must have sounded vivid enough to recall to Bach's mind the ideas he had entertained about the state of church music. His reputation as an organist did not allow sacred music to fall into complete oblivion. These interludes may have come like admonitions. They could in the long run accumulate enough weight to confuse the task Bach was accomplishing at Köthen. It also seems that a new turn of affairs at the court of Köthen may have lessened the readiness of the prince to patronize music. At any rate, Bach himself makes mention, though not altogether convincingly, of this change. Prince Leopold had married in 1722. And Bach wrote: "things seem to assume an appearance as though the musical inclination of the prince would grow somewhat lukewarm, since the new princess appears to be uninspired by the Muses"; an "amusa" she is said to have been. Be this as it may, Bach's activity at Köthen came to an end in 1723.

III

Then came Leipzig. It made the period of Köthen one of transition. The stage was set for the most tragic epoch of Bach's life, and the reason for the tragedy was that a fusion between German musical style and European music had never taken place. Bach returned to his first aim; it was to become his last. The possibility of reconciling through his own work the music of Germany with the musical spirit of the times seemed to have vanished forever. Bach revived the musical aim he had expressed in the document of Mühlhausen in 1708. If some works composed during the last year at Köthen show a new religious turn, they can perhaps be taken to indicate a reawakening of the old aim. It was in feeling his way back to the reorganization of a well-regulated church music that he first came in contact with Leipzig, especially through the St. John Passion, written for Leipzig and performed there. But any attempt to start the reorganization anew would of necessity lead him back into the narrowness of the cantor's function. For nothing had changed the fact that only in this position could he make a new and final effort toward his goal. The question became acute when the vacant post of cantor at St. Thomas's called for an appointment in 1722, the year of Kuhnau's death. At first, Bach did not apply for the position. It is well known that the council of the city did not consider Bach at all. Since the distinction of the post required the careful election "of a famous man," the council looked around for a musician thus qualified. Hence they negotiated first with the "world-renowned" Telemann, musical director at Hamburg. After failure to come to terms with him, Christoph Graupner, Hofkapellmeister at Darmstadt, was next in line. It is of great significance that neither of these men, regarded as really famous, held the position of cantor, although the council should, logically at least, have sought for a musician distinguished in this office; all the more as the formula of appointment expressly demanded that the musician to be installed should not compose church music that would sound like an opera. Despite the cantatas Graupner wrote, he can hardly be imagined as the right person to meet such a demand; and even the versatile and prolific Telemann does not appear to have been particularly fitted for the position, at least not as a result of his activity at Hamburg, since it was there that he had composed most of his operas.

The name of Bach, then, entered the discussion only after failure with both Telemann and Graupner. This fact has, historically speaking, a double significance; on the one hand for the extent of Bach's fame within Germany, and on the other for the way in which a musician's fame grew—surely, not in the position of cantor. The council of Leipzig significantly did not look among the cantors to find a man to occupy the post of cantor. Neither did Bach consider the post most desirable; he hesitated to accept the appointment when it came; he seems to have been fully aware of the limitations it would place again on the recognition of his work. We have already remarked that he thought "at first it could not at all comport with his dignity to become a cantor after being a Capellmeister." With the old goal probably in view, he finally resolved "to step down." And he said of Leipzig: "this post has been pictured to me so favorably that I finally took the risk in the name of God."

Gräfenhahn published a "*Rede der Musik*" in 1754. In an important passage he speaks of German musicians, mentioning only Händel and Telemann. Bach is not included, naturally because of his lack of recognition. The editor of Gräfenhahn's work, however, felt that he should complete the list of German musicians, "to the honor of the German nation," and he added first the name of Hasse, then that of Graun, and in the third place Bach, who immediately precedes musicians such as Weise, Pantalon, Heinichen, Quantz, Pisendel, Stölzel, Bümmler, all of them "great masters according to their kind." This reflects precisely what Germans thought of Bach's importance for German music.

After 1723, when the period of Leipzig began, Bach became more and more isolated. It is, however, not at all true that this growing isolation resulted from a certain quality of style in his music, in which it might be supposed that he was reaching out far beyond his own time in anticipation of the future. Bach's music had no bearing on the time to come. It fulfilled itself entirely within the baroque, in retrospect rather than in prophecy; this holds true even though finally the greatness of his composition has marked his work with that timelessness in which all great works of any period join each other.

Bach's isolation was his tragic destiny in history, bound up with his ideas for church music. When he took up this task again, it meant, as it were, a "home-coming": the mature Bach was returning to what he had once in his youth deemed final. This last vision of his goal came with stirring suddenness. Bach now held fast to it, with a determination from which an almost incredible productivity emerged. Within about eleven years, from 1723 to 1734, he composed approximately a hundred cantatas, the Magnificat, Sanctus, chorales, motets, the St. Matthew Passion, the Christmas Oratorio, and the B minor Mass, completed in 1738. As it were on the borderline between the period of Köthen and that of Leipzig stands the St. John Passion. By their elimination from the liturgy Bach's motets have merely maintained their old position as occasional works; the few motets he did write are nearly all compositions intended for funerals. Here again we have an extremely interesting fact indicative of the conflicting factors in German baroque music. For the cantor was now deprived of one of his oldest functions, the composition of motets. Instead of being discarded altogether, they were still kept in the Protestant service. Their liturgical place was at the beginning of the service. Since the cantor was no longer obliged to write new motets, the choir of St. Thomas selected the works for this liturgical purpose from the *Florilegium Portense* of Bodenschatz, a collection of motets whose sixteenth-century musical style was completely antiquated.

With his return to the religious task, Bach found his last form. If we now speak of a "style of Bach," we usually think of the work that originated at Leipzig, as though the last manifestations of his art summarized all he had been or could ever have been. While he was finding the final structure for his composition, the conflict with the tendencies of his time was growing gradually more intense. At length he succeeded in attaining the goal he had set himself. Yet success brought him complete loneliness as an artist; at the end, he was alone in fact. It was the great tragedy of his musicianship that at the close of his life he could say that he had accomplished what he set out to achieve. But his accomplishment echoed in a vacuum. This was a momentous catastrophe, not only for Bach but for the whole ideal of his work. His most mature compositions, significant of his later style, won no acclaim in their own time. This tragedy of his work could well be said to amount to a catastrophe for the whole musical situation in the middle of the eighteenth century, and, indeed, a far-sighted contemporary did say so. Any attempt to remedy the generally catastrophic situation of music drove Bach still further away from his own contemporaries. We have seen that his "successors," his sons, Carl Philipp Emmanuel in particular, and the so-called "early classics" turned to the works of Weimar and Köthen, when and if they maintained any link with Bach. Thus the cantor of St. Thomas's was left in increasing loneliness such as few have known. The language of the Leipzig Bach was never heard; and many a man who knew Bach's name thought he had grown silent altogther. Indeed, there are tragic undertones when, in conversation among friends and relatives, Bach was spoken of as the "old wig of Leipzig." Yet the old Bach was right when he considered his Leipzig works, the greatest he ever wrote, to have reached the state of fulfillment.

Quite naturally with the passing of the years he grew more and more irritable, peculiar, even stubborn and inaccessible. He would not compromise in any matter of principle even though in his relations with the authorities he bent the bow until it broke. He knew his task could not be tampered with; but he probably knew also that the gap between his work and the times was widening year by year. The Leipzig authorities spoke of the "incorrigible" Bach when they were confronted with this unwillingness to compromise. The struggle for the very goal of his music became more bitter every year. This can be seen in numerous documents. Of great importance in this respect is his *Brief, but utterly necessary outline of a well-regulated church music, with some additional unprejudiced consideration of its decline* of 1730. Four years later, with the appointment of Johann August Ernesti, who represented "enlightened rationalism," as the Rector of St. Thomas's, the old principle of the school, "to guide the students through the euphony of music to the contemplation of the divine," was discarded. The "Enlightenment" with which the new generation distintegrated religion confronted Bach from within as well as from without. His younger contemporaries began to shake their heads over what the "old wig" was doing at Leipzig. Attacks were even forthcoming on his music, on his "unnatural" style. The "pompous and confused character robs his compositions of the natural, and too great artificiality obscures their beauty." The attitude of the enlightened rationalist toward nature in art is clearly revealed in this criticism. The Leipzig Bach is still recognized as a great organist, but beyond that the younger men would not go. "This great man," they say, "has in no way explored the 'sciences' [humanities], the knowledge of which should be required from a learned composer." An odd thing to say of Bach of all men! But such was the injustice the enlightened younger generation inflicted upon the cantor of Leipzig if they happened to notice him at all. The angry disputes between Bach and the authorities of school and church, which are all set forth in lengthy documents, disputes the effects of which beclouded nearly the entire period of Leipzig, were not merely a controversy between individuals. They implied a collision between two times. It was this that sharpened the temper of everyone involved; and it was for this reason that reconciliation was impossible. The spirit of the Enlightenment admitted no understanding of Bach's task, and made the old style of his Leipzig work subject to criticism and neglect.

When later times brought an historical revival of Bach, the discovery—such it was in fact—that called the works into life for the first time began with the Leipzig compositions. Since the compositions of Weimar and Köthen had been to some extent transmitted to the younger generation, it was not necessary to make them accessible anew. They had already played their historical rôle through their influence on younger musicians. But with the Leipzig work the situation was different. There, everything had been forgotten. The Romantics, therefore, revived that part of Bach's work with which the historical connection no longer existed, if it ever had. Only then did we come to know what the particular style of Bach means in its essential character and climactic accomplishment. Ever since, when we speak of the "style of Bach," we mean that of Leipzig.

Although this later work accomplished at Leipzig has all the distinguishing marks of an unbroken unity, Bach himself, filled with boundless anger at the unsurpassable lack of understanding on the part of the authorities, often looked with envy as well as anguish toward the splendor of the court music at Dresden, where musical affairs were conducted in a way which Bach held up as an example to his superiors at Leipzig. His experience at Köthen had shown him the values of a "Hofkapellmeister." About the middle of his Leipzig period, in 1733, the year of the death of Augustus the Strong, he made contact with the court of Dresden. He strove to obtain an appointment there as Hofkapellmeister; and he lent his endeavor weight with a work he intended to dedicate to Augustus III; together with the St. Matthew Passion it now belongs to his greatest works. The cantata, which he had made the most substantial part of the Protestant liturgy, was entirely inappropriate for the Catholic court at Dresden. Hence the Protestant Bach wrote for a Catholic environment the B minor Mass for which he used, at least in part, some of his cantatas previously composed and now rearranged for the Latin text of the mass. It took him many an effort to extract a court "Predicate" from the Prince Elector. He set amazingly great store by this mark of distinction, which was nothing but a title. Later, the title was given him. He never forgot thereafter to lay the greatest stress upon the rank of Hofkapellmeister. His true position, however, was in no way affected; the title changed nothing. Because of the tension that existed between him and the authorities, he took some of his duties lightly in later years, as letters prove. He often went away without the request for permission he was required to submit whenever he planned a journey. He played the organ here and there with unmatched virtuosity. He made tests of organs, visited his sons and tried to keep up his relations with Dresden by fulfilling "obligations" he imagined himself under as Hofkapellmeister. The last church cantatas, among them "Du Friedefürst, Herr Jesu Christ," were completed in 1744 and 1745. Thereafter, organ composition came back into the foreground. This, too, was a return to the beginning. The last years closed the circle. His life ended, in 1750, with what had once started his artistic work, organ music.

IV

We shall not fully comprehend the whole greatness of Bach's work unless we have made clear its historical significance, which first finds far-reaching expression at Mühlhausen. The Leipzig years brought a complete break with his times. The sacred music of Leipzig was given a form beyond any of the tendencies the age produced. The style of the Leipzig Bach spoke neither to his times nor out of his times. His contemporaries were no longer stirred by it. After going to Leipzig, Bach preserved his work from any inner change. However flexible he may have been in his youth, in his later years he hardened himself against change, so far as the principal aim of his composition was concerned. Not that he had become incapable of development. He had reached the goal. His work grew to be so unapproachably compact and uniform that we perceive only its exceptional and complete independence, without being especially aware of any essential relation to the age of the Enlightenment. It appears as though Bach had shut out all intercourse with his times. This timelessness was the result not only of the greatness of his work; it emanated also from the religious goal of his art, which could only be realized in the inescapable narrowness of the sphere of his activity.

Bach spoke apart from the spirit of the age, although he was intent upon guiding it. Händel, on the other hand, was seized with the spirit of the times, of which he was at once servant and master. Händel created his work in accordance with this spirit, Bach ran counter to it. Händel was rooted in the effective and great associations of his time. Bach had once searched for them, but toward the end of his life he came to realize that in fact he had never found them. Händel reached his greatness within the times in which he lived, and through them, Bach against them. Hence Bach's "timelessness" made it possible—and this is true also from the historical point of view—to link the spirit of his work to other epochs which believed themselves closer to its essential aim than the age in which he lived. At times the steadiness of his character has been compared with that of the men of the Reformation; at times the form of his life has been found more akin to the men of the seventeenth century. Dilthey once said that the whole structure of his character belonged to the seventeenth century, when men were more staunch than Bach's own contemporaries; that, furthermore, "subjection to religion established his being," since his essential character rested upon "an unshakable religious feeling. . . . He seems to have known religious poetry only in connection with the chorale and related lyrics. Consequently, he did not move his own contemporaries to the measure of his genius."

We have attempted to set forth the general characteristics of Bach as well as the essentials of his work by searching for his historical significance. We cannot consider him anything but Protestant. The power and effect of his work lies, indeed, within Protestantism. But the form in which he expressed himself as a Protestant did not derive from his own times; it originated in sharp opposition to them, and he was powerless to force the Protestantism of his making upon the world around him. Just as the style of his later works developed apart from his own contemporaries, so the form of his Protestant religion had likewise no share in the prevailing ideas of the time. We should like to formulate this historical destiny through a parallel: Bach was driven into seclusion as an *artist,* and consequently also as a *Protestant;* or, he came to endure *religious* isolation, and consequently also that of his *art.*

The age, which Bach expected to accept his vision of a complete reform of church music, was wholly incapable of seeing its character and necessity. The rationalists attacked traditional religion from all sides, and they quickly found their way out of the church. One aspect of religion, individual religious feeling taken as the necessary intensive quality of religion, was preserved in part by Pietism. But this was not without grave peril; for it gave the individual an opportunity to seek religious expression outside the traditional church. Orthodoxy opposed this movement with the whole power of the canonical organization, which vindicated its claim to mold the religious life through dogma and tradition. Against this the Pietist maintained that the life of the church had declined to the mere administration of externals, completely subject to organization, which should never be allowed to assume more importance than the personal value of religion for which the individual must be held responsible. Bach was born into a time that did not seem equal to the task of eliminating the perilous elements in these movements. It now became possible to carry on religious life entirely outside the formal institution of the church.

It is for such reasons that church music as a whole necessarily declined, all the more since the leading musical style of the period took its rise quite apart from all sacred music. Bach was aware of the decline as no other musician of his day. In the existing state of the church he saw the urgent need for reform, which would effect a complete reorganization of the music in the Protestant service. His religious conscience as well as the weight of his religious responsibilities led Bach to this artistic task. He saw it always as directly bound up with the liturgy, since no musical reform could have any effect unless music and liturgy were taken as a unity. Pietism, however, had struck so hard a blow against the connections of music with liturgy as to preclude any reform of church music within its sphere. A genuine success might be expected only if the religious intensity of Pietism and the existing forms of the traditional liturgy could be brought together. Bach carried into his task the impetus that came from Pietism toward intensifying the religious life. This religious intensity, awakened in him by Spener and Tauler, set a new goal for the reform.

The question has often been raised as to the precise nature of this reorganization of musical liturgy. That a musician had arisen who succeeded in completing the music for the cult by furnishing cantatas for all the services of the year; one capable of creating music as an outgrowth of his own religious conscience; one religiously intense and able to stir the innermost spirit of man in religious expression; all this has the mark of highest distinction. But it does not suffice to answer the question fully. For other musicians in Bach's time also wrote cantatas, many of them even a series to cover the whole church year. But none of them was at one and the same time innovator and conserver in the spirit of the Protestant church.

"By leading the whole influence of the life of man's soul into a typical expression either of the poetic word or of music, a certain period comes to full awareness of its own religious feeling. Now, from the works of religious poets and musicians there are forthcoming intensities of the religious life which would otherwise slumber in the inscrutable depth of the human soul. The great epoch of the Protestant religion possessed such a knowledge of its own fullness and immeasurable profundity in the church chorale, in the sermon, above all, however, in religious music." Dilthey has thus expressed the way in which he understood the religious music of Johann Sebastian Bach. Music has raised "the Protestant religion, as it were, to eternity." Bach did this for the Lutheran religion. Is such an appraisal, then, the ultimate analysis of the ideal of his work, the ultimate interpretation of musical form in the realm of the church? Are there perhaps no other words to measure the immeasurable than those of religious feeling and intensity, whose vagueness is unbounded?

The baroque brought into music the motions of man's soul, the dynamics of the various states of the soul most profoundly and comprehensively expounded by Descartes and Mersenne. The musician had to understand this dynamics as the rhythm of the passions in human life. The passion of man, man himself became the powerful tenor upon which the composition of all baroque music had been built since the time when Claudio Monteverdi expressly refused to present inanimate matter unrelated to man, and proposed that man, his passion and his suffering, should be the subject-matter of art. Musicians thereafter embarked upon excited disputes about the matter; they did not cease to discuss the human affections to be expressed through musical composition.

When Bach began his work, he could draw on a fairly large range of forms and expressions established as tradition. He transformed human affection—in the baroque sense of the term—into a *religious reality of the church.* Pietism kindled in him, as well as in others, the states and passions of the soul as religious experiences. These must now be harmonized with the idea of the church, that is, within the congregation. Only thus could the idea of the church be expected to live. Church music, to spring from and flow back into the congregation, must be reorganized upon a sure foundation; for this only the most general all-embracing principle of art would suffice. This general principle should comprise all members of the congregation; and it should be comprehended by all of them as well. Furthermore, it should be one with the subject-matter of art in general and of musical composition in particular. For Bach never intended to depart from the musical language of the period in the manner of a revolutionary who would destroy tradition; he did not aim at breaking with his times; his work conformed entirely to the baroque style however far he expanded its possibilities.

Hence, the thought to be expressed in each particular composition, and the medium through which to renew church music in keeping with the idea of the church, must be brought into complete unity. This unity could be attained only through *affection,* the crucial element in the life of baroque man. For it is affection that has both a human and a musical basis; it can also be given religious significance. Affection, then, serves to organize the structure of the musical liturgy; it animates the individual musical work. Bach spiritualized the affections and made of them musical elements in the life of the church. That is to say, he imparted to them qualities that reflected the aspirations of the congregation and in which it could join with its own unbroken religious expression. Bach was not alone in looking upon affection as a phenomenon of art and composition; others had done so before him. It was his peculiar contribution that he gave it its place within the church. He understood it as something through which the religious intensity of the whole congregation might be expressed. He chose it as the sign and symbol for the benefit of the congregation. He took it as the Lutheran "confessio."

Bach also recognized the power of affection in the truly artistic sense. Affection was to the man of the baroque age perhaps the deepest secret of life. It was like an inexhaustible force always striving from within outward to find expression in human gestures; we are not able to say whence it comes, or what it is that continually renews it. This force retained its mysterious character in the music of the baroque. Men of the age were spontaneous in their understanding of the affections, because they felt in themselves their power. They thought of them as the various states through which man manifests his life in relation to the world. The succession of these states would form a dynamic rhythm rising and falling like a tide through his whole being, stirring body and soul alike. It is this rhythm that controlled the baroque conception of art.

Bach laid hold upon this property of the affections to move the whole being of man and brought it to bear upon the feeling of the congregation. Any affection should appeal to the congregation as a whole. The church, the symbol of the congregation, is the court of last resort to pass upon the religious value of the affections. Bach was, accordingly, in a position to remold the chorales along the same lines. The alterations he made in the traditional melodies are significant of this. He created a whole world of unchanging forms for certain ideas—mental and emotional images. We often speak of his "motives" or "symbols." Among these, his symbol for Jesus Christ, which he carries throughout his whole work, is the strongest in religious intensity and most prominent among the symbolic expressions of the congregation. Bach did not create such categories of types, motives and symbols to the exclusive end of a direct appeal through musical language; he created them in the service of the congregation. The affections obtained their lasting, symbolic forms in music, just as the sacred word retained its unalterable meaning. They were "confessions" of timeless values. Through them Bach accomplished the reorganization of Protestant church music. With them he proclaimed to a time devoid of understanding "the birth of the Church out of the spirit of music."

Goethe and the History of Ideas

by WALTER A. KAUFMANN

Goethe's 200th birthday seems a fit occasion for a reflection on his place in the history of ideas. Since his characteristic greatness was not primarily a function of his ideas, I shall begin by venturing a general suggestion about the human factor in the history of ideas and the way in which men make history. Then these considerations will be applied to Goethe as the setting for a few unorthodox perspectives which may be found fruitful: in particular, I shall seek to show briefly both how Goethe influenced the subsequent course of German history down to the Nazis, especially through his *Faust,* and how he revolutionized the form of the history of ideas. Throughout, the argument will be concerned with over-all structure rather than philological detail, and therefore left unencumbered by polemical references to the Goethe literature.

* * *

Students of the history of ideas are often preoccupied exclusively with the tracing of connections between ideas. This approach seems too narrow and does not allow for the proper appreciation of some of the most influential men. Among these is Goethe. He may remind us of what an age in awe of the achievements of the sciences, of a Copernicus, Darwin, or Einstein, is prone to forget: that men who make history without crowns and swords do not always do so by virtue of their theories.

Perhaps ideas as such are not the stuff of which history is made. They are hardly ever new and can usually be traced back to a previous thinker, often an obscure or minor figure—and if not, that generally proves only our ignorance. Goethe expressed this thought in the Mephistophelian epigram:

Wer kann was Dummes, wer was Kluges denken,
Das nicht die Vorwelt schon gedacht?[1]

Elsewhere, Goethe voiced the same insight in his own, characteristically more positive manner: "All that is clever has already been

---

[1] *Faust II,* Act II, Scene 1: "Who can think anything stupid, who can think anything clever, that the past has not thought before?"

thought; one must only try to think it once more."[2] There is novelty in selection and composition which need not be sterile, superficial, or eclectic: the new *Gestalt* may involve a radical revaluation of the several components. It may be, as it were, of one piece—not patchwork but the symbolic reflection of the vision and experience of a man.

The nature of novelty is, however, best revealed by the human being himself—most clearly by those men whose historical influence was greatest. Originality is the hallmark of character—and of the life in which character manifests itself. Ideas are universals which are revealed in time: not as propositions proclaimed by a godhead, but through experiences which, to be understood, require the formulation of ideas. In this sense, ideas are never primary: they are reflections of experience and grounded in it. And few experiences are as profound, fascinating, and disturbing as that of a great man.

Much of history, therefore, and especially of the history of ideas, consists in the untiring efforts of posterity to recapture by sheer force of thought some *"individuum ineffabile"*.[3] In this sense, history has its clue, at least in part, in the biographies of great men. And it is in this light that Goethe's place in the history of ideas must be considered. A brief reference to other men with whom he is at one in this respect will help to place him and accentuate the framework in which we should envisage his unique contributions.

Three eminent examples from antiquity will suffice to make the point. First, there is Socrates, the greatest of the Greeks—and we should certainly not agree with Montaigne that "to be the first man in Greece is to be an easy first in the world."[4] It may seem that Socrates was effective largely through his method which exerted so profound an influence on Plato. Yet this method was adapted from that of Zeno, the Eleatic, and later versions of the dialectic have gone back to Plato or even Zeno more often than to Socrates. In this respect Socrates is but a link in a long chain. It is even worse when we consider his ideas: we do not know what they were, and the *Apology* suggests strongly that he made a point

[2] *Maximen und Reflexionen I.*
[3] Goethe, letter to Lavater, September 9, 1780.
[4] *Essays,* transl. Trechmann, Book II, Chapter 36.

not of offering new ideas but of questioning old ones. What, then, of his influence? The *Apology*, together with the *Crito*, the conclusion of the *Phaedo*, and Alcibiades' speech in the *Symposion*, leaves no doubt that it was, more than anything, Socrates' personality which possessed the matchless mind of Plato and was reflected in his dialogues and, not a whit less, in all subsequent Greek and Hellenistic philosophy: Aristotelian and Cyrenaic no less than Epicurean and Stoic. The image of the proud and ironically disdainful sage who found in self-sufficient reflection a happiness and freedom far surpassing that of any plutocrat or despot —this truly original embodiment of human dignity captivated all the later thinkers of antiquity, became their ethical ideal, and led to a new conception of man. Socrates' fearlessly questioning iconoclasm and unhesitating decision to die rather than cease speaking out freely have had an equal impact on the modern mind. The character and bearing of this man have influenced the whole course of the history of philosophy more than has any idea or even any system.

Caesar, the greatest of the Romans, offers a strikingly similar picture. His name has entered the languages of the world, and his personality has revolutionized not only political theory but, far more, man's conception of himself and of his potentialities. Caesar did not develop a new form of government: there had been very similar administrations before, and those of the later Caesars, Kaiser, and Tsars were different from his in many ways. What the honorable Brutus could not kill was not an idea but, paradoxically, a life—and the personality which stood revealed in it.

Our last and most obvious example is Jesus.[4a] Recent apologists have sought to credit him with some new notion. Having lost their faith in the Trinity, they felt it incumbent on themselves to establish Jesus' greatness on the foundation of a novel insight; and whatever conception they fastened on, they have often defended with as much zeal and disregard for impartial scholarship as any dogmatist. While there is room for doubt whether Jesus had any new idea which could not be found in earlier Jewish or Hellenistic writers, not to speak of Taoists and Buddhists, it seems

[4a] The historic impact of the Incarnation falls outside the scope of the present essay.

plain that his character and life have made history even more than Socrates' or Caesar's. Subsequent thought and events, scarcely less than Western painting, can be viewed to a considerable extent as a ceaseless attempt to assimilate a character which has so far defied almost every effort.

There is no need for multiplying examples by proceeding, say, to Lincoln or Napoleon. The most influential men have made history neither by armed might nor by theories. If this view should seem to be prompted by some current vogue of anti-intellectualism, one may recall that Hegel, certainly neither an irrationalist nor one to deprecate philosophy, especially his own, arrived at much the same conclusion. Philosophy, he contended, is reflection and must necessarily look back rather than forward. Philosophic ideas, instead of making history, elicit its meaning only *ex post facto*, even as night descends and an era draws to a close:

When philosophy paints its grey on grey, a form of life has become old, and with grey on grey it cannot be rejuvenated, only comprehended. The owl of Minerva begins its flight only as the twilight sets in.[5]

Ironically, it was just Marx—renowned for his alleged deprecation of the ideational factor in history—who criticized Hegel for being too resigned about the efficacy of human thought. Perhaps human consciousness was actually assigned a more crucial rôle in Marx's interpretation of history, while Hegel emphasized the significance of individuality more than Marx did. But this is not the place to discuss the metaphysics of the world spirit, the "cunning of reason," the importance of the economic factor, or the problems of pluralistic causation. Suffice it to insist that one of the decisive elements in the historical process is to be found in the personalities and lives of its leading characters, and that Goethe was one of these.

* * *

Goethe's influence is clearly a function of his works as well as of his personality, and it might be supposed that his creations embody his ideas. After all, no other poet has developed such intricate scientific theories or been in such steady communion with the great intellects of his time. Goethe's novels manifest an increasing concern with intellectual issues, and so does his *Faust*. Moreover, he himself stressed his debt to Spinoza; the influence

[5] *Rechtsphilosophie*, preface.

of Leibniz may seem even more striking; and some of his finest poems appear to be philosophic. His aphorisms, letters, and conversations abound in keen insights. One cannot doubt that he had a most powerful intellect and surpassing wisdom. His characteristic greatness, however, is not a function of these qualities, and his great works are invariably *not* primarily vehicles for his ideas.

This goes without saying for such lyrical poems as *Über allen Gipfeln* or such outcries as *Prometheus* and the *Marienbader Elegie*. Yet it will be asked: what of *Faust,* so often hailed as Goethe's masterpiece? *Faust,* I should answer, is not a philosophic poem, and it neither reveals nor illustrates Goethe's *Weltanschauung,* let alone his "philosophy." The ideational *Leitmotif* of the drama—"*Wer immer strebend sich bemüht, Den können wir erlösen*"[6]—is, in this characteristically unqualified form, not even the core of Goethe's *magna confessio,* nor the theory for which one might find the experiment or demonstration in Goethe's life. We shall see later that Goethe and Faust are almost antithetical characters. First, however, let us inquire what the drama is, if it is not a poetic presentation of Goethe's ideas.

Neither Gretchen's death sentence at the end of *Faust I* nor the traditionally religious trappings of the closing scene of *Faust II* represent a theory of morals or religion. Shakespeare, not Dante, was our poet's model: instead of illustrating another man's philosophy, he let his poetic imagination reflect the cosmos, unimpeded by, and without the benefit of, any theoretical framework. "*Am farbigen Abglanz haben wir das Leben*"[7]—that is the poet's philosophy: not just Goethe's, but that of the poet in general. Goethe was a poets' poet and the embodiment of the aesthetic temperament no less than Socrates was the incarnation of the philosophic spirit.

Schiller's pertinent contrast of "naïve and sentimental (*sentimentalisch*)" poetry is well known, but one of Goethe's aphorisms is at least as relevant and incomparably more concise:

It makes a big difference whether the poet seeks the particular for the

[6] *Faust II,* last scene. "We can redeem him who exerts himself in constant striving."

[7] *Faust II,* Act. I, Scene 1. "In the colored reflection we have life."

universal or whether he beholds the universal in the particular. From the first procedure originates allegory, where the particular is considered only as an illustration, as an example of the universal. The latter, however, is properly the nature of poetry: it expresses something particular without thinking of the universal or pointing to it. Whoever grasps this particular in a living way will simultaneously receive the universal, too, without becoming aware of it—or only late.[8]

One should keep this in mind when one considers the usual disputes about Goethe's ideas. When the poet mitigated the original ending of *Faust I* by adding the line "She is saved," or when he concluded the *Wahlverwandtschaften* with a reference to the "friendly moment when they will once awaken again together," he was not avowing any faith in another life in which all wrongs are redressed. The essentially aesthetic bent of his mind and its sovereign Shakespearean playfulness—the word is not too extreme, if its literal denotation is allowed to soften it—are ignored all too often.

Some of the most celebrated quotations from *Faust* probably throw less light on their author than does this sarcastic retort, seeing that it came from the lips of one who so often referred to himself as a pagan:

I pagan? Well, after all I let Gretchen be executed and Ottilie starve to death. Don't people find that Christian enough? What do they want that would be more Christian?[9]

This rejoinder not only crystallizes—as perfectly as that can be done—the contrast between the original "glad tidings" (evangel) and the resentful bourgeois morality which purports to be Christian even while it insists on throwing the first stone; the remark also goes far to elucidate Gretchen's and Ottilie's fate. Primarily their deaths are an aesthetic reflection—*ein farbiger Ab-*

[8] *Maximen und Reflexionen* IV. Cf. Eckermann, July 5, 1827; Jan. 3, 1830; Feb. 1, 1831; and, above all, May 6, 1827: "They come and ask me which idea I sought to embody in my *Faust*. As if I knew . . . that myself! . . . Indeed, that would have been a fine thing, had I wanted to string such a rich, variegated . . . life . . . upon the meagre thread of a single . . . idea! It was altogether not my way to strive, as a poet, for the embodiment of anything abstract. . . . I did not have to do anything, but round out and form such visions and impressions artistically . . . so that others would receive the same impressions when hearing or reading what I presented."

[9] *Goethes Gespräche,* ed. Biedermann, II, 62.

glanz—of life. Beyond that, however, they represent an Olympic concession to society: the appeasing gesture of one whose paganism was anything but zealous, aggressive, or "Dionysian."

The last lines of *Faust I* and the *Wahlverwandtschaften* do not indicate the poet's adherence to any traditional dogma. They give aesthetic expression to his experience of human hearts ironically and hypocritically divided against themselves. Because there is no question here of any critique prompted by a rival theory of ethics, no new symbolism is required; and Goethe is naturally led to administer his rebuke—even this word is too intellectual—out of the very bosom of the tradition which he takes to task. In the same way, Christian symbolism is employed at the end of *Faust II* as a vehicle for the poet's negation of what he took to be conventional Christian morality: Faust is saved. What is revealed is not a new idea and certainly no philosophy, but the poetic vision of a world which preaches both the law and grace, conformity and individuality, convention and intention.

One may note that Goethe did not avail himself of Christian symbolism when he dealt with themes one would generally consider Christian, like the Incarnation or the redemptive power of love. Thus he transports us to Hindu India both in *Der Pariah* and in *Der Gott und die Bajadere.* He was not trying to allegorize traditional truths but seeking to express an original experience which called for new imagery. Perhaps the poems were first envisaged in the fresh encounter with some Indian lore. In any case, it was not a body of ideas but an unprecedented personal vision which had to be made manifest. To summarize: while Goethe's influence was a function of his works as well as of his character, the works themselves are not allegorical representations of ideas but the characteristic function of his personality.

* * *

These general reflections on the history of ideas and on the nature of Goethe's creations set the stage for our estimate of Goethe's influence. We shall not tarry over his well-known influence on Carlyle and Coleridge, on Matthew Arnold and Emerson, or over the equally familiar impact of his personality on Schiller's aesthetic theories—and hence on much subsequent work done in that field. Still better known and more important is the liberating effect of the young Goethe's character on the stuffy and sterile Germany of Klopstock and Gellert—the light he kindled in the hearts of a new generation, the age of genius he inaugurated. These matters need only be mentioned to be remembered.

There are other perspectives which lack this traditional sanction, and it is these I propose to deal with now. Let us proceed *in medias res*. Out of the Gothic chaos of the German past, Goethe distilled a national character which was accepted by his people as their ideal prototype: Faust. It is doubtful whether there is any real parallel to this feat—that a great nation should assign such a rôle to a largely fictitious character, presented to it so late in its history.

A nation's conception of itself determines in large measure its attitude toward its own past as well as—and this seems even more significant—toward its future behavior. Goethe's vision of Faust is therefore not only a major clue to the Romantics' anthologies and historiography but also a decisive factor in the shaping of German history during the past century and a half. This claim must seem extravagant to anyone unfamiliar with the idolatry of Faust in the German schools. Yet this *golem* has produced effects no less considerable than those of his maker, and our discussion will revolve around these two focal points and their interrelation—Goethe and Faust.

We behold Faust sacrificing Gretchen to his own self-realization—or, even more characteristically, Faust closing both eyes while Mephistopheles advances the fulfillment of his ultimate ambitions by ruthlessly destroying Philemon and Baucis. This egoistic disregard for the concrete human being, this utter ignorance of human rights and love, and this unbounded will to power over everything and everybody but one's self cause us to wonder why the interpreters of *Faust* have failed to find in it the frightful dangers of the German character and a prophetic vision of its later vices. The vast majority of German students, to be sure, have never heard of Philemon and Baucis (though they know of Gretchen)—but their teachers have; and the training, outlook, and ideals of generations of teachers and large portions of a nation's intelligentsia are of singular significance. Goethe's dramatization of Faust may thus be considered one of the many factors which helped to bring about historic outrages by giving the Germans so intoxicating a picture of themselves.

We may seem to have gone far in our speculation. Perhaps we find support in the consideration—hardly subject to any serious objection—that the vastly influential Romantic movement in Germany drew its inspiration from the work of the young Goethe.[9a] What was this movement if not a hopeless chase after his personality, the often ridiculous desire to equal his genius, his resurrection of Goetz, Faust, and the heroic past, and his cult of creativity? Here is the clue to much of Fichte's and Schelling's philosophies and to the literary activities of the Schlegels and Brentano.[10] And it was among these Romantics that modern German nationalism and Teutonism was bred. If theirs had a Christian tinge, so did Wagner's and Chamberlain's. If the Wartburg men were self-styled liberals, the Nazis called themselves socialists.[11]

Historical causation is extremely complex and cannot be dealt with adequately by the mere assertion of an influence. The question always remains why the later generation should have let itself be influenced by one factor rather than another. It would be rash to assume that priority entails responsibility. The present case offers a particularly striking illustration. For the Romantics' vision of neither Goethe nor Faust should be mistaken for the real Goethe who repudiated the Romantics unequivocally. He was the author of *Der West-Östliche Divan* no less than of *Faust*, a translator as well as a poet, and the coiner of the word, if not the concept of, *Weltliteratur*.[12] He ever insisted:

There is no patriotic art and no patriotic science! Both belong, like all that is high and good, to the whole world and can be promoted only by

[9a] What they saw in *Faust* and *Meister* were the conceptions of the young Goethe, rather than the later qualifications; and O. Harnack has shown how F. Schlegel read his own intentions into *Meister*, not Goethe's. Even these qualifications are unnecessary if "young Goethe" is understood as an inclusive contrast to "old Goethe."

[10] Schopenhauer's conception of the relentlessly striving Will may be considered a cosmic projection of Faust's ceaseless striving—pushing endlessly and purposelessly into infinity.

[11] The many striking similarities between the Wartburg "liberals"—Hegel has often been reviled for denouncing them—and the Nazis have been pointed out by Herbert Marcuse, *Reason and Revolution* (Oxford University Press 1941), 178 ff.

[12] Eckermann, January 31 and July 15, 1827, and *Werke, Ausgabe letzter Hand*, XLVI, 141, 260 and XLIX, 127, 137 ff.

universal and free interaction of all who live at the same time. . . .[13]

Is it Goethe's fault that he has never been popular with his people as the incarnate anti-Romantic and Good European? Yet it is a tragic fact that the Germans have, on the whole, worshipped Faust while having little use for the old Goethe.[13a]

Let us consider the vast difference between Faust and Goethe —the Faust of the second part no less than the first. Goethe, unlike Faust, did not sacrifice the present to the future or value the moment only as a foretaste of things to come. He knew that "a succession of consecutive moments is . . . always a kind of eternity," and he found "permanence in the transitory."[14] To Eckermann he said: "ever hold fast to the present . . . every moment is of infinite value, for it is the representative of a whole eternity."[15] When Goethe hurt others, whether the beloved Friederike or the young poet, Heinrich von Kleist, it was not—Faustlike—in the wanton quest of self-aggrandizement or an external projection of his power, but part of his daily dose of painful self-denial and his economy of creation: a matter of life and death today, not an unscrupulous calculated risk for the day after tomorrow. The cliché of Goethe's "great confession" should not deceive us into assuming any real parallel between the author and his heroes. The Gretchen tragedy is no more a portrayal of Goethe's treatment of Friederike than the infamous Weislingen or Tasso, so utterly lacking in self-control, are accurate representations of their maker. Goethe's own experience merely kindled his poetic imagination, and the creation of these splendid caricatures of his failings let him breathe more freely. Again, was it Goethe's fault if Germany could not assimilate his greatness, rejected him, and idolized—not indeed a golden calf but a scapegoat, Faust?

To be sure, we should not claim that Faust is nothing but the dross of Goethe's gradual refinement, although the Gothic past and the Romantic future were indeed what our poet sought to overcome. I should suspect that *Faust* reflects, to some extent,

[13] *Maximen und Reflexionen* V.

[13a] There is a striking difference in this respect between the popular attitude referred to here, and many excellent works about Goethe; e.g., Hehn's, Harnack's, Simmel's, Gundolf's, Beutler's.

[14] Goethe's last letter to Zelter.

[15] November 3, 1823.

Goethe's experience of the idol of his youth, Frederick the Great. It is often assumed, falsely, that the king's brilliant victories at the beginning of the Seven Years' War brought about his final triumph; but his early successes were wiped out by the disastrous defeat at Kunersdorf and the Russian occupation of Berlin. More memorable than any battle was Frederick's decision to hold out and to stay in the field, shifting small forces (no large ones were left) wherever they were most needed—never resting, although no reasonable chance of victory remained. Only the death of the Tsarina and her successor's stunning order to his troops to change sides saved the king:

Wer immer strebend sich bemüht,
Den können wir erlösen.[16]

And did not the aging king, in his last years, when peace had come, design a project to drain and colonize the Oder-Bruch? In some ways, the old Faust may reflect the personality of Frederick more than that of Goethe.

Unfortunately, the character of the enlightened anti-Gothic king has been less influential than its colorful reflection in *Faust*. Goethe himself, in the text of *Faust,* likened the Philemon and Baucis episode to the Biblical tale of Naboth's vineyard. Frederick, in an exactly parallel situation, let his miller keep his mill —not as a matter of capricious grace, but in explicit recognition of the rights of man. And Frederick's austere self-control, no less than the refinement of his personality, furnishes the most striking contrast to the Nazis. While one could trace the gradual and steady decline from Frederick and Faust through the Romantics and Wagner to the Hitler movement, one should keep in mind that the Nazis represent the ultimate fruition of all the failings of the German character—unmitigated by its undoubted genius.

To return to Goethe: he made history not only through his *Faust*. His *Divan,* for example, inspired Rückert's and Platen's artful translations of Persian poetry; and German scholarship has done much to give substance to Goethe's conception of world literature. Above all, however, the heritage of the mature Goethe was developed by Hegel, Heine, and Nietzsche. Perhaps this is more obvious in the case of the cosmopolitan poet than in that of

[16] See footnote 6.

the two philosophers, and a word of explanation may not be amiss.

The old Goethe has been made familiar in our time by Thomas Mann. Yet since Mann tends, rather more than Goethe, to draw self-portraits, he has exaggerated the bourgeois (*bürgerliche*) elements in his hero. I see Goethe more nearly as did Nietzsche, who was, incidentally, almost the first great German writer to realize and emphasize the surpassing greatness of the *old* Goethe and to find in the conversations with Eckermann, not in *Faust*, "the best German book."[17] Goethe as the living embodiment of *Selbstüberwindung* can be understood only against the background of his youth, of *Werther, Goetz, Prometheus,* and the *Urfaust*—but not as an old man embarrassed by the passions of his past, as one of millions whose maturity involves the loss of all their force and fire:

Nur der verdient sich Freiheit wie das Leben,
Der täglich sie erobern muss.[18]

Life he had to conquer ever again in his ceaseless combat with ill health and sickness unto death—and freedom, in his daily fight with passions which others, for the most part, do not know and which he harnessed into ever new creations.

Goethe so considered is the historic event which Nietzsche's whole philosophy attempts to recapture in aphorisms. Goethe, not Faust, served as the prototype of Nietzsche's superman. The "Bad Infinity"—to speak in Hegel's terms—of Faust's unbounded striving was explicitly repudiated by Nietzsche, who preached the glory of the moment. And the greatest power was, to Nietzsche's mind, not power over others but the perfect self-control and creativity of the old Goethe. To be sure, that did not keep his "Faustian" interpreters from following the established procedure of blandly putting Faust in Goethe's place.

Goethe's influence on Hegel was no less great and can be traced from Hegel's first book to his last—from his attempt in the *Phänomenologie* to emulate *Wilhelm Meister* by writing the *Bildungsroman* of God himself to the contention in the *Rechtsphilosophie* that freedom is to be found only in self-limitation and that, while absolute freedom can be found only in the realm

[17] *Der Wanderer und sein Schatten,* aphorism 109.
[18] *Faust II,* Act V, Faust's last speech: "He alone earns himself freedom and life who must conquer them daily."

of "Absolute Spirit," *i.e.*, in art, religion and philosophy, these pursuits must be grounded in a responsible civic existence—like Goethe's as a minister of state in Weimar.

Nietzsche, who also considered art and philosophy man's noblest enterprises, illustrated his diametrically opposite claim that they can prosper only apart from all civic existence and that culture thrives only at the expense of the State, by also citing Goethe —the Alpine recluse did not take the Weimar court as seriously as the Berlin professor. Moreover, Nietzsche was keenly aware of Goethe's Olympic contempt for civic conventions, and he insisted passionately and repeatedly on Goethe's anti-political opposition to the "Wars of Liberation."

Fichte, Schelling, Schopenhauer and Nietzsche could all have said to Goethe, with Hegel:

When I survey the course of my spiritual development, I see you everywhere woven into it and would like to call myself one of your sons; my inward nature has ... set its course by your creations as by signal fires.[19]

In other words, nineteenth-century German philosophy consisted, to a considerable extent, in a series of efforts to assimilate the phenomenon of Goethe. As in the case of Socrates, it was not a body of ideas that influenced the philosophers, but it was a personality which was variously reflected in their systems.

* * *

Having considered Goethe's surpassing significance for the contents of the history of ideas, let us conclude with a very few words about how he revolutionized its form. His highly personal poems and dramas should be considered together with the fact that his *Wilhelm Meister* established the genre of the *Bildungsroman*—a literary form taken up by the Romantics, by Gottfried Keller, and in our time by Thomas Mann and Hermann Hesse, to mention only a very few of the best known German writers. What is at stake is far more than a literary convention; it is a new way of approaching the human being, a new vision of man. Yet it is once again not a new theory or philosophic anthropology but a projection of Goethe's character and life. He experienced himself—if I may coin a phrase—*sub specie temporis,* and his character, life, and work cannot be understood except under the category of development.

[19] Letter to Goethe, April 24, 1825.

It is not a mere accident that we know so much more of Goethe's life and conversations than, say, of Shakespeare's. The bard's works, too, have been arranged in chronological order by the scholars, and Michelangelo's creations can also be studied in their development. That this is done, however, is due to Goethe. While the works of others did not require this approach, Goethe could not and did not wait for the professors of a future century to establish the probable sequence of his works. It was not a bare coincidence that he hired Eckermann and conversed with him, nor did he take a chance that some admiring genius after his death might write *Dichtung und Wahrheit*. It was Goethe who established the developmental approach to the human personality and the artist in particular. And here, too, it was his own character and life rather than any theory or proposition that made history.

Goethe was effective by his works no less than by his character; but though I should consider him incomparably the greatest German, this claim could not be founded on any single one of his works. No one of his creations is clearly superior to Beethoven's masterpieces. It is Goethe's personality which is unique, and we have tried to show why it would profit us to learn from him rather than from his dramas. In the end, we should apply to the poet himself his verse which reminds us that man is not a means to anything else, not even to the formulation or verification of ideas:

Höchstes Glück der Erdenkinder
Sei nur die Persönlichkeit.[20]

---

[20] *West-Östlicher Divan*, Buch Suleika: "Let personality alone be man's highest happiness." This interpretation of the verse as an imperative is debatable.

[Cf. my *From Shakespeare to Existentialism* (Boston, 1959); new revised edition with additions (Anchor Books, 1960) for some revisions of the above.]

The Social Background of Taine's Philosophy of Art*

by MARTHA WOLFENSTEIN

Reprinted from the *Journal of the History of Ideas*—Vol. V, No. 3, pp. 332-358

Taine's philosophy of art revolves around one central problem, the problem of the relation of history to values. The question is whether we can reconcile a universal standard of value with the historical variations of art and taste. Taine began by asserting that is was not possible. The theorist of art, he thought, should abandon the old project of judging art, and apply himself to the more useful work of correlating artistic phenomena with other facts of social life. This was his own intention as an historian of literature and the plastic arts. He wished to make his attitude as impartial as that of a botanist, observing that different kinds of vegetation appear under different climatic conditions. Taine could not, however, eliminate all considerations of value. Unacknowledged value-judgments forced their way into his historical studies. Eventually Taine recognized this fact, and confronted the task of formulating and justifying his implicit criteria. But the standard of value which he proceeded to elaborate remained uncoördinated with his earlier historical approach. His theory of value failed to overcome the difficulties which his historical observations had raised.

The intellectual struggle which appears in Taine's philosophy of art is part of a more intimate and at the same time a more widely social process. A thinker's ability to solve the problems that he undertakes is not a result exclusively of his wit and learning. It is also a function of his emotional attitudes and his relation to the society in which he lives. In the case of Taine, a basic ambivalence towards his society was responsible for the contradictions in his thinking about art. In order to integrate the historical and evaluational factors, a certain social adjustment is requisite. The thinker must be able to discover some institution or movement in his society which he can identify as the actual or potential agency for realizing what he considers valuable. Such an adjustment does not in itself constitute a solution of the problems of art criticism, but it provides a necessary condition for their

* This essay was completed on a fellowship from the American Association of University Women, 1940–41.

solution. In thinkers who succeeded better than Taine in solving the problem of history and values, some such adaptation was achieved.

I

Taine's writings on literature and lectures on art fall almost entirely between the dates of two revolutions, that of 1848 and that of 1870. The mention of these events in relation to Taine is not arbitrary. Let us begin with the year 1848. In that year, Taine, an ascetic young man of twenty, filled with an enthusiasm for philosophical ideas, entered l'École Normale in Paris. He came from a provincial family of very modest means, but of the professional class. His mother had decided that he should become a teacher, since in that profession it would not be necessary to buy him a practice. Absorbed in his studies, Taine remained aloof from the political events that were agitating Paris. His attitude at this time is revealed in his letters. He writes to a friend that both parties, the socialists and the reactionaries, revolt and disgust him. "It is a war between those who would leave others to die of starvation and keep everything for themselves, and those who strive to rob those who have anything."[1] In the same letter, he states that he has one or two firm opinions in politics. "The first is that the right of property is absolute." Committed in this way to regard the revolutionaries as robbers, Taine nevertheless takes a sufficiently unenthusiastic view of the bourgeois professional world in which his future course lies. Passing in review the professions of which his society affords a choice, he finds them all permeated by servility and mean interest. "Forced to sell myself, I have sold as little of myself as I could." In becoming a professor, he will be free except for eight hours a week.[2]

[1] *H. Taine, sa Vie et Correspondance*, I (Paris, 1902), 87, Letter to Prévost-Paradol, May 1849. Taine's political indecision expressed itself in abstention from voting.

[2] *Ibid.*, 90. Taine's dissatisfaction with his society is associated with dissatisfaction with himself. He wished to be a creative writer, but early abandoned hope of succeeding in that line. Cf. Hilda Norman, "The Personality of Hippolyte Taine," *PMLA*, XXXVI (1921), 543–4, on Taine's self-contempt because of his lack of artistic creativeness. In a youthful letter he wrote, "I feel that I am and will always be insignificant." Mme. Saint-René Taillandier, in "Mon Oncle Taine," *Revue Hebdomadaire*, VII (1931), 158, records a frequent saying of Taine's later years: "I have written twenty-two volumes. I would give them all to have written *La Chartreuse de Parme*." Taine did once try writing a novel, called *Étienne*

While Taine continued with his studies, the political reaction which the uprising of 1848 provoked was moving to reorganize the French school system. Up until this time the materialist and anti-clerical philosophy of the revolution of 1789 had prevailed; the bourgeoisie had used it in their struggle against feudal institutions. Following their successful revolution, they had made repeated attempts to exclude the influence of the Catholic Church from the educational system. Now, in their terror at the socialist threat, the bourgeoisie were driven to join forces with their old enemies.[3] It is related that after the revolution of February 24th the philosopher Victor Cousin, who held an influential position in the University, exclaimed to a friend, "Let us run and throw ourselves at the feet of the bishops; they alone are able to save us today."[4] The churchmen on their side were quick to point out that it was due to the dominance of the old revolutionary ideology in the University that so many unsound ideas had arisen. The leader of the Catholic party urged the reëstablishment of religious control of education as the antidote to socialism.[5] Consequently in 1850 there was enacted the Falloux law, which made possible the renewed ascendency of the Church in education, and implied the submission of the official philosophy to the requirements of Church dogma.[6]

The effect of this change was not immediately felt in l'École Normale, where the régime had been extremely liberal.[7] Taine was permitted to spend his formative years under the influence of an intellectual tradition which, little as he suspected it, stood under the threat of imminent suppression. Thus he was destined to graduate into an alien environment, and to find himself, half involuntarily, a rebel in the academic world. The first intimation

---

Mayran. Apparently discouraged, he left it unfinished. It was published posthumously in *Revue des deux Mondes* (1909).

[3] Charles Seignobos, *The Rise of European Civilization* (New York, 1938), 350–51; R. W. Collins, *Catholicism and the Second French Republic* (New York, 1923), 46.

[4] Collins, *op. cit.*, 270–71.

[5] *Ibid.*, 302–3.

[6] Seignobos, *A Political History of Europe since 1814* (New York, 1900), 167. There was continued curtailment of freedom of instruction under Napoleon III, particularly in the departments of philosophy and history.

[7] *Vie et Correspondance,* I, 113–15. The editor writes, "It seemed that l'École Normale was a privileged place, a sort of intellectual oasis which the reaction of 1850 was not able to touch."

which he had of his misfortune was when he came up for his final examination before a board of examiners from outside the school. Taine had in his adolescence abandoned the Catholic faith.[8] In his undergraduate years he had devoted himself to studying Spinoza, from whom he probably derived the belief in universal determinism which became one of his fixed principles. When in his examination he took Spinoza as the basis for discourses on morals and free will, it is not surprising that his clerically-minded inquisitors found his arguments "absurd."[9] Taine was regarded as a typical product of l'École Normale, for which the new educational authorities had already planned a thorough house-cleaning.[10]

Taine's failure on this examination marked the beginning of a series of academic reverses. Though his teachers and classmates had anticipated a brilliant career for him, he was sent away to an obscure provincial school, and there kept under strict and suspicious surveillance.[11] When the following year he was assigned a still more unsuitable post, he revolted against his uncongenial position, and resigned from the school system.[12] A further event acted to force Taine away from the field of philosophy and psychology, in which he had originally intended to specialize. His doctoral thesis on sensation was rejected. While this thesis was never published, we may infer its general tenor from Taine's later psychological treatise, *De l'Intelligence,* into which he incorporated all his earlier studies. Taine probably advanced the view that all the ideas of the mind are ultimately traceable to sensations. To the University authorities this must have seemed a reassertion of the proscribed eighteenth-century ideology.[13] It was as a result of this rejection that Taine turned to the less dangerous field of literature, and wrote a new thesis on La Fontaine. Meanwhile he assiduously attended scientific lectures to seek reënforcement for his heterodox philosophical views.

[8] C. C. Charaux, "Hippolyte Taine à l'École Normale," *Études Franciscaines* (XXXV, 1923), 567–8, recalls Taine's expressions of religious scepticism in his school-days.

[9] *Vie et Correspondance,* I, 126.

[10] *Ibid.,* 129.

[11] *Ibid.,* 142, 146.

[12] *Ibid.,* 307.

[13] Mary Duclaux, "The Youth of Taine," *Fortnightly Review,* LXXVIII (1902), 951. Taine's psychology "appeared the rankest materialism to the Idealists of 1850" (952), Taine's psychological analyses "brought him nearer year by year to the school of Condillac."

In 1857 Taine published *Les Philosophes Français du XIXe Siècle*. This book is a brilliant polemic against the spiritualistic or eclectic philosophy, most completely exemplified in Cousin, which had superseded the materialist philosophy of the eighteenth century. Taine contrasts the philosophical integrity of Condillac with the political opportunism and apologetic spirit of Cousin.[14] Cousin ends by offering his eclecticism as a support for the dogmas of the Church. His philosophy "does not depend on facts or analyses. Its first principle is to edify honest souls and to suit fathers of families."[15] It has succeeded because it fulfils certain requirements of the times. But it acts to repress all invention; it is impotent to lead any fresh intellectual movement. If its precepts were consistently carried out, all the new findings of science would have to be suppressed as subversive to public morality.[16] Taine discovers the corrupting motive of the official philosophy in its subordination to moral ends. To avoid such subversion of truth, Taine recommends that the philosopher should be, like the scientist, purely impartial. Taine himself follows this procedure. When he philosophizes, he steps out of his rôle as a member of society. What sort of practical consequences may follow from his inquiries does not concern him. One of his politically preoccupied opponents may object, "But you set up a revolution in the minds of Frenchmen." Taine in his philosophical rôle replies, "I know nothing about it. Are there such beings as Frenchmen?"[17]

II

The intention of maintaining scientific impartiality constituted the distinctive feature of Taine's approach to art. In *Les Philosophes Français* he had observed that Cousin judged every school of art according to whether it upheld the morality to which he was devoted. In contrast, Taine's scientific aesthetics "neither pardons nor proscribes; it verifies and explains."[18] In his thesis on

[14] *Les Philosophes Français du XIXe Siècle* (second ed., Paris, 1860), 135–40.
[15] *Ibid.*, 140.
[16] *Ibid.*, 36–9. The physiology of the brain, the correlation of different psychological abilities with different brain centers, undermines the doctrine of the immortality of the soul. The findings of embryology conflict with the orthodox doctrine of preformation, etc.
[17] *Ibid.*, 35–6.
[18] *Philosophie de l'Art* (12th ed., Paris, 1906), I, 12.

La Fontaine he had already announced this scientific approach.[19] He now proceeded to apply it in a long series of essays on literature, and later in his lectures on the plastic arts.[20]

The method of studying art which Taine chose as a basis and justification for his impartial attitude was the historical approach introduced by the Romantics. The Romantics had wished to combat the classical tradition in art and to rescue mediaeval art from the obloquy which it had suffered since the Renaissance. To this end they had formulated a set of historical arguments. Each epoch of history, they argued, had its distinctive institutions. Men were molded and remolded by these changing social forms. Thus men could not be regarded as the same throughout history. The peculiar institutions and the corresponding psychology of each period gave rise to different styles and standards of art. The merits of each artistic style were relative to the prevailing social institutions. The standards embodied in the art of one epoch could not be set up as authoritative for another. These general arguments were applied to the comparison of ancient and mediaeval art. The classicists were wrong to condemn mediaeval art on the score that it failed to conform to ancient canons. Mediaeval art had an excellence of its own, which derived from its appropriateness to feudalism and Christianity. However admirable ancient art might remain, it was necessary to recognize that the institutions to which it had been suited no longer existed. Thus modern artists could not hope successfully to emulate classical art. Their minds were formed by different institutions than the ancient ones. The institutions which were decisive in differentiating the modern from the ancient mind were those dating from the Middle Ages. The practical consequence then drawn was that the modern artist must regard the mediaeval tradition as the "indigenous" tradition, and seek to draw his inspiration from it and not from ancient models.[21]

This romantic doctrine was highly suited to Taine's purpose. It was necessary only to eliminate the programmatic conclusion,

[19] *La Fontaine et ses Fables* (6th ed., Paris, 1875), v. (First published in 1853.)

[20] In 1864, Taine was appointed professor of the history of art at l'École des Beaux-Arts. It was there that he delivered his lectures on the plastic arts.

[21] Cf. Mme. de Staël, *De l'Allemagne* (Paris, 1818), I, 264–6; Chateaubriand, *Le Génie du Christianisme* (Paris, 1852), I, 179; Ballanche, *Essai sur les Institutions Sociales, Oeuvres* (Paris, 1833), II, 398–9.

and the opposition of classical and romantic as two competing alternatives. Taine envisaged an indefinite number of historical epochs, each occasioning forms of art appropriate to it, each providing a subject for historical analysis. In the writings of the Romantics there had already been a tendency to transform the problem of the theorist of art from passing judgment on works of art to correlating them with developments in other provinces of social life.[22] The Romantics had also indicated the relativistic implication of their historical view,[23] which supported Taine's requirement of impartiality; artistic standards were not to be defended or combatted, but to be regarded as mere historical data.

The salient points of Taine's historical relativism may now be indicated. Taine observes that, since the beginning of the century, "it was perceived that a work of literature is not a mere play of imagination, a solitary caprice of a heated brain, but a transcript of contemporary manners, a type of a certain kind of mind."[24] The problem which he sets himself therefore is to discover what conditions of social life have given rise to a particular work or school of art.[25] It is necessary to recognize the diversities of art and taste which an historical survey reveals.[26] The basis for this variety is found in the appearance of different psychological types, corresponding to different historical situations. Taine criticizes the eighteenth-century philosophers who regarded men of the most diverse social conditions "as if they were turned out of a common mold."[27] He considers that there is in each period of history "a group of circumstances controlling man." Each historical situ-

[22] E.g., Mme. de Staël, *De la Littérature considérée dans ses rapports avec les Institutions Sociales;* Stendhal, *Histoire de la Peinture en Italie.*

[23] De Bonald, *Legislation Primitive*, II (Paris, 1829), 223. "Before comparing ancient and modern literature, it would be well perhaps to inquire whether a comparison between them is possible, whether our fable is the fable of the ancients, our tragedy the tragedy of the ancients, our epic the epic of the ancients, and finally whether our society is the society of the ancients; because literature is the expression of society, as the word is the expression of the man."

[24] *History of English Literature* (trans. by Van Laun, New York, Burt, 190–), I, 1. Chapters of this work were published as separate essays between 1856 and 1863. They were first gathered into a volume in 1863.

[25] *Ibid.*, 24.

[26] *Philosophie de l'Art*, I, 7. "If we pass in review the principal epochs of the history of art, we find the arts appear and disappear along with certain accompanying social and intellectual conditions."

[27] *History of English Literature*, I, 6.

ation "develops in man corresponding needs, distinct aptitudes, and special sentiments." The type that most fully exemplifies the qualities appropriate to the given conditions constitutes the ideal of the age. Taine sees passing in historical procession the Greek athlete, the mediaeval knight or monk, the Renaissance courtier, and the modern dissatisfied Faust-like man. In every age men award their admiration and sympathy to this current ideal, and the art of the period centers around it. The plastic arts represent it, as Greek sculpture embodied the athlete ideal; while the other arts appeal to the sentiments of the dominant type. Artistic excellence in any period is determined by conformity to the reigning ideal.[28]

It follows that it is impossible to ascribe exclusive authority to any single standard of artistic excellence. We look upon the works of the past with different eyes from those of the author's contemporaries. Often these works leave us quite unmoved, and it is only by means of historical study that we can reconstruct the type of mind that took pleasure in them.[29] The same discrepancy would appear if a survivor of a past epoch could be confronted with the art of more recent times. Taine imagines the horror which Balzac's style would inspire in an eighteenth-century French classicist. To a mind conditioned by the circumscribed regularity, the elegance and refinement of court life, Balzac would seem feverish, disordered, full of incongruous juxtapositions. It is just these qualities, however, which make him congenial to minds formed by the confusion and rapid tempo of nineteenth-century Parisian life.[30] "There is, then, an infinite number of good styles. There are as many as there are epochs, nations, and great minds. All differ.... The pretension to judge all styles by a single standard is as preposterous as the proposition to shape all minds in a single mold and to reconstruct all ages after a single plan."[31]

The scientific character which Taine imparted to the doctrines derived from the Romantics consisted largely in the superimposi-

[28] *Philosophie de l'Art*, I, 101–3. Cf. *Vie et Correspondance*, II, 265. "The beautiful is a fixed relation between variables, what mathematicians call a function."

[29] "Mme. de la Fayette," *Essais de Critique et d'Histoire* (Paris, 1858), 309, "The style and sentiments of Mme. de la Fayette are so remote from ours that we have difficulty in understanding them. They are like perfumes so fine that we can hardly smell them. So much delicacy seems to us like coldness or insipidity. A transformed society has transformed the mind." (First published 1857.)

[30] *Balzac: A Critical Study* (New York, 1906) 152. (First published 1858).

[31] *Ibid.*, 148–9.

tion of analogies borrowed from the natural sciences. For example, having read Darwin, Taine took the conformity of artistic styles to the prevailing social institutions as an instance of the law of natural selection.[32] Such analogies, which served to frighten the more timid of Taine's contemporaries, added little to his working basis of interpretation. Indeed, it must be admitted that the sociologist can find few usable hypotheses in Taine. In the introduction to his *History of English Literature* Taine presented his famous three factors of historical determination, the race, the milieu, and the moment. The race consists of the supposedly biological inheritance of a nation; the milieu includes physical environment and prevailing social institutions; and the moment, the acquired momentum which these institutions carry over from the past.[33] However, the difference between what is racially inherited and what is determined by temporary social conditions remains uncertain in Taine's own mind.[34] It is also impossible to differentiate in any concrete case between what he means to attribute to the milieu and what to the moment. Setting aside the geographical component of the milieu, the three factors reduce to one, an undifferentiated mass of social phenomena. Through much of the *History of English Literature* we find that Taine's historical method consists chiefly in interspersing facts of general social history with facts of literary history. His intention to adopt a social approach to art failed to mature into a set of concrete hypotheses.

III

Despite his constant professions of scientific impartiality, Taine could not help regarding the different artists and works of art that he analyzed as of unequal value. He attempted to disguise these value-judgments as judgments of what is typical of a particular age or nation. He calls some artists "greater" than others; but

[32] *Philosophie de l'Art*, I, 53–4.

[33] *History of English Literature*, I, 12–18.

[34] For example, in defining the character of the French race, Taine discovers its distinguishing mark in the capacity to develop consecutive ideas easily, clearly, and endlessly (*History of English Literature*, I, 82–3). Elsewhere he refers to the same intellectual peculiarity when he is defining the type of man produced by eighteenth-century French society (*The Ancient Régime* [trans. by John Durand, New York, 1896], 184 f.). For a detailed reduction of Taine's supposedly racial characteristics to socially acquired traits, cf. Paul Lacombe, *La Psychologie des Individus et des Sociétés chez Taine, Historien des Littératures* (Paris, 1906), 32–48.

he maintains that he means only to indicate their superior degree of conformity to their social environment. The *History of English Literature* abounds in such ambiguous judgments. For example, Taine calls Byron the "greatest" of modern English writers; but he explains this as meaning that Byron is the "most English."[35] Taine dislikes the Restoration dramatists; the reason he gives is that they attempted to borrow French forms which were unsuited to the English character.[36]

Here Taine borrows another doctrine of the Romantics. He repeats one of their most striking fallacies. The Romantics had argued that art is a product of the "indigenous" tradition; from this view they attempted to draw the consequence that art *ought* to be the product of this tradition. But the same relation cannot be asserted truly as an historical law and meaningfully as a normative one. If art is inevitably determined by the so-called indigenous tradition, it is meaningless to exhort artists to follow this precedent. They cannot do otherwise. On the other hand, if the imperative is meaningful, it must be that the so-called indigenous tradition is not the sole determinant of artistic production. In the case of the Romantics, the latter interpretation is applicable. The "indigenous" tradition to which the Romantics appealed was by no means the exclusive determinant of art in their society. Classical art, which they regarded as alien, had set the ruling standards for several centuries. The nineteenth-century classicist could cite precedent no less than the Romantic. The fallacy of appealing to history to decide disputes of value is thus apparent. Those who make this appeal always select one out of several historical precedents, while failing to make explicit the principle of value which has guided their selection.

Taine's use of the terms "most English" and "truly English" to discriminate among English writers is subject to the same criticism. Taine has selected, chiefly on the basis of implicit standards of value, certain English writers as superior. He then defines the English character in keeping with his favorites. Frequently it becomes necessary to alter the "typical" English character, as Taine admires writers of diverse affinities. For example, Byron is "most English" because he embodies the characteristically English spirit of rebellion. It is this which made it possible for Byron to sympa-

[35] *History of English Literature*, II, 344.
[36] *Ibid.*, I, 563–74.

thize with the heroes of the French Revolution at the very time his countrymen (all so much less English) were fighting to put down the Revolution.[37] However, Taine also admires Burke. Thus in discussing Burke's *Reflections on the Revolution in France,* Taine remarks, "Real England hates and detests the maxims of the French Revolution."[38]

If we examine Taine's procedure more closely we shall be able to uncover his suppressed criteria of value. In the *History of English Literature* he devotes much more space to some writers than to others. Shakespeare for example claims many more pages than any other Renaissance writer. Byron occupies a lengthy chapter, while Southey, the poet laureate of the day, is disposed of in a few pages. It would seem that Taine has selected for particular attention just those writers who are able to command admiration beyond the limits of their age and nation, those who are called "great" in retrospect. Taine, however, attempts to justify this emphasis from the point of view of his historical project. He had written earlier, "The more perfect a poet is, the more national he is."[39] Now he goes on to say, "When a work is rich, and one knows how to interpret it, we find there the psychology of a soul, frequently of an age, now and then of a race. In this light, a great poem, a fine novel ... are more instructive than a heap of historians with their histories. ... In this consists the importance of literary works: they are instructive because they are beautiful. ... It is by representing the mode of being of a whole nation and a whole age, that a writer rallies round him the sympathies of an entire age and an entire nation."[40]

Let us now ask what Taine means by the word "great" in this passage. Apparently there are four qualities of a work which Taine considers positively correlated: having "greatness," embodying the "psychology of the age," "representing the mode of being of a whole nation and a whole age," and "commanding the sympathies of the age and nation." Let us consider whether the latter three qualities invariably go together. If they do not, which of them is crucial in Taine's estimation of "greatness"?

I shall take Byron as a test case, since Taine considers him the

[37] *Ibid.,* II, 348–50.
[38] *Ibid.,* 108.
[39] *La Fontaine,* 344.
[40] *History of English Literature,* I, 25–6.

greatest of modern English writers. First, let us ask whether Taine makes out a case for Byron's rallying round him the sympathies of his age and nation. Such a case might be made out. But Taine on the contrary stresses the antipathy which Byron aroused in his compatriots.[41] Turning to the next possibility, did Byron express the prevailing attitudes of his age and nation? Here Taine assures us that Byron "fought all his life against the society from which he came." He attacked mercilessly the reigning hypocrisy and constraint of English society. It is not surprising "that Englishmen clamored and repudiated the monster," that Southey pontifically denounced him as a rebel "against the holiest ordinances of human society." So far from being at one with his contemporaries, Byron, according to Taine, stood "alone against all, against an armed society."[42]

There remains one characteristic which may still be correlated with what Taine considers great: "representation of the mode of being of a whole nation and a whole age." Here in fact is what Taine values most in an artist, veridical observation, seeing things "as they are." It was because of this capacity that Byron was able to penetrate the shams of English society, to perceive the misery underlying the surface decorum. His "poet's discernment" led him to see the truth.[43] This standard is the one which Taine applies throughout. He says of Shakespeare that he reproduces life entire without trying to ennoble it.[44] On the same basis he criticizes those writers who fail to be impartial observers.[45] He defines a novelist as "a psychologist, who naturally and involuntarily sets psychology at work. . . . He loves to picture feelings, to perceive their connections. . . . In his eyes they are forces, having various directions and magnitudes. About their justice and injustice he troubles himself little."[46] We may now recall that this artistic ideal had been explicitly adopted by certain novelists of Taine's day, notably

[41] Ibid., II, 345, "His ideas were banned during his life. . . . To this day, English critics are unjust to him. . . . He suffered the pain of the resentment he provoked, and the repugnance to which he gave rise."

[42] Ibid., 345, 351, 377–8.

[43] History of English Literature, II, 379. "True artists are perspicacious: it is in this that they outstrip us: we judge from hearsay and formulas. . . .; they . . . from accomplished facts and things."

[44] Ibid., I, 376, 424.

[45] Ibid., II, 220. Taine reproaches Fielding for his moralizing tendency.

[46] Ibid., 496.

Flaubert and Zola.[47] Thus Taine is unwittingly applying to the art of other times a standard peculiar to his own.

What I particularly wish to remark is Taine's inability to coordinate his implicit evaluational principle with his historical analysis. It is in respect to just that quality which Taine considers valuable in an artist that he fails to establish a social derivation. Taine's critics have argued that it is only the mediocre artist who "dates." The great artist does not succumb to the fashions of the moment, and so appears in retrospect undistorted by temporary peculiarities.[48] Contrary to what Taine had set out to prove, he agrees in practice with his critics. For him too, the great artist stands alone, his vision unobscured by the biases of his contemporaries. His strength resides in an individual quality, poetic perspicacity. In fact, of course, Taine himself cites plentiful evidence to show that Byron, for example, was far from being an isolated figure. At war with conservative English society, Byron was inspired by the ideals of the French Revolution. Taine is able to see Byron as a protagonist of these disappointed hopes.[49] Yet he is unable to establish any connection between these social relations and the quality in Byron which he admires.

Taine's conception of the great artist derives from his conception of his own method as a thinker. Regarding his opponents as determined by social motives, he was unable to see that his scientific aims also had an historical derivation. The historical line from which Taine drew his strength had fallen into official disrepute. And while he rejected the official philosophy he still could not identify himself with the opponents of the regime. Hence his conception of himself as holding aloof from all social influences, and his analogous conception of the great impartial artists.

[47] Flaubert, *Correspondance,* III (Paris, 1893), 117: "It is necessary that the moral sciences ... proceed like the physical sciences, impartially. The poet is now required to have sympathy with everyone and for everything, in order to understand and describe them." Cf. 331: "I believe that great art is scientific and impersonal." Zola, *Le Roman Expérimental* (Paris, 1887), 22: "The experimental novel is a consequence of the scientific evolution of the age; it continues and completes physiology. ... It substitutes for the study of the abstract man, the metaphysical man, the natural man subject to physico-chemical laws and determined by the influences of his environment; it is in a word the literature of our scientific age."

[48] Lacombe, *op. cit.,* 142–3. René Gibaudan, *Les Idées Sociales de Taine* (Paris, 1928), 107–8. Cf. A. O. Lovejoy, "Reflections on the History of Ideas," in the *Journal of the History of Ideas,* I, 1 (1940). See *supra,* 3–23.

[49] *History of English Literature,* II, 391.

IV

It may be argued that Taine's inconsistency in allowing his tastes to obtrude themselves in no way invalidates his basic doctrine of historical relativism. As opposed to this view, I should like to indicate that the breakdown of Taine's relativism may be traced to a doubtful psychological premise. Taine's underlying assumption is that human nature in general is an abstraction to which no content can be assigned. As we have seen, Taine holds that there is not one psychology but many, a different one for each age and nation. Taine does not, however, accept these many psychologies as mysteriously given and inexplicable (as Spengler does later). He attempts to indicate how these psychological differences come into being. There is in every historical period "a set of circumstances controlling man," an institutional organization which "develops in man corresponding needs, distinct aptitudes and special sentiments." This theory of the genesis of different psychologies involves at least one general psychological assumption, namely, that men's characters are conditioned by their social environment. Admission of this one general psychological law would not, however, seriously alter the relativist conclusion, that for each man those things are best which his upbringing impels him to pursue. A more decisive objection to relativism would be that it involves a dubious conception of the process of conditioning.

To put the argument in general terms, any theory of conditioning would seem to presuppose some unconditioned needs as a starting point. These needs can be directed to the pursuit of many different objects. However, not all the objects which a need has been persuaded to seek are equally capable of satisfying it. The pursuits instigated by modern advertising afford obvious examples. Men can learn to behave in a great variety of ways, but they cannot learn to be equally happy in all of them. It is this obstinacy of feeling, underlying the malleability of behavior, which the relativist overlooks. The relativist argues that no value-judgment can take precedence over any other. If I say that you value the wrong things, this is merely a rather impertinent way of expressing the fact that my upbringing has been different from yours. What the relativist fails to see is that the different upbringings themselves may be capable of comparison, on the basis of their relative fitness to promote the satisfaction of human needs. The doubtful conception of conditioning to which the relativist seems committed is that all instances of conditioning are equally adequate and successful; that the basic needs are equally amenable to every institutional pattern.[50]

Taine, while nominally committed to this view, was nevertheless unable to conceal his conviction that some institutions are better suited than others to satisfy human needs. Speaking of the consequences of ancient and mediaeval institutions, he wrote, "In Greece, we see physical perfection and a balance of faculties ... in the Middle Ages, the intemperance of over-excited imaginations."[51] The terms he uses betray clearly which set of social conditions Taine considered more conducive to human welfare. It was thus inevitable that Taine should sooner or later be forced to set up a universal standard of value.

However, Taine's historical relativism is not wholly invalidated by this necessity. The judgment that all social products satisfy human needs does not eliminate the applicability of historical qualifications. If we set up an ideal of human satisfaction, disregarding the actual and limited alternatives between which our social situation affords a choice, we are Utopian. Similarly, if we judge the works of the past without reference to the limiting conditions under which they were produced, we are guilty of what may be called "retrospective Utopianism." Within each social period, we may discriminate movements advancing and movements impeding the further satisfaction of human needs. In judging the activities and productions of each period, we must take as our standard the limit of satisfaction obtainable under the existing conditions. At the same time, it is necessary to observe the point at which altered conditions make possible the surpassing of a previous limit (or, in the case of retrogression, the unattainability of an earlier standard). Thus the ideal of any particular period is not to be mistaken for a universal norm.

[50] The view that there are universal human needs is confirmed by contemporary anthropologists, whose knowledge of the varieties of custom far exceeds that of nineteenth-century writers. Cf. Franz Boas, *The Mind of Primitive Man* (New York, 1924), 155–6: "Modern anthropologists proceed on the assumption of the generic unity of the mind of man." For a psychological analysis of how conformity to given social institutions may result in emotional conflicts and frustration, cf. Karen Horney, *The Neurotic Personality of Our Time* (New York, 1937), 286–9.

[51] *Philosophie de l'Art*, I, 101–2.

We may now specify the sense in which Taine's historical formula is acceptable. Taine wrote that "there is an infinite number of good styles. There are as many as there are epochs.... All differ.... The pretension to judge all styles by a single standard is as preposterous as the proposition to shape all minds in a single mold."[52] As it stands, this statement is ambiguous, since it is not clear what is meant by "a single standard." If the single standard is the very general one which requires the greatest possible satisfaction of human needs, the pretension to judge all styles by this standard is justified. But if the standard is the product of universal needs interacting with the limited possibilities of a particular historical situation, Taine is correct in saying that any single standard is of limited applicability.[53]

V

It was in the course of his lectures at l'École des Beaux-Arts that Taine became aware of the fact that he was really passing judgment on the works of which he had professed to give a purely impartial historical account. At the beginning of these lectures, Taine had announced, "My sole duty is to offer you facts, and to show you how these facts are produced."[54] However, at the end of a series of lectures on Italian art, in which the art of the high Renaissance had been set above that of every other period excepting ancient Greece, Taine was finally forced to admit, "We have always, and at every step pronounced judgment."[55]

It may be of interest to consider why Taine's evaluational bias, repressed and concealed in his literary studies, rose to the surface in his lectures on the plastic arts. During the period in which Taine wrote his most important essays on literature, from 1856 to 1864, he was unable to obtain any professorial post. He had no platform from which to speak, and was identified with no school or party.[56] His assumed attitude of historical detachment in his essays

[52] *Balzac,* 148–9.

[53] Considerable specification would, of course, be necessary to render these general propositions adequate to the requirements of art criticism. It is sufficient, however, for the present purpose if we define the minimal philosophic basis for a combined historical and evaluational analysis of art.

[54] *Philosophie de l'Art,* I, 12 (first published in 1865).

[55] "De l'Idéal dans l'Art," *Philosophie de l'Art,* II, 234 (first published in 1867).

[56] During those years, Taine gave private lessons, and held a post as examiner for a military academy.

corresponds to his actual social isolation. He felt it idle to adopt a pontifical rôle, and viewed with scepticism men's attempts to impose their values on others. In 1864, however, Taine was appointed professor at l'École des Beaux-Arts. As an officially approved lecturer he felt encouraged to express his already decided convictions. He was all the more disposed to yield to this impulse as he found his biases reënforced by the academic program. In this school young artists were still being consecrated in the classical tradition. In an essay on l'École des Beaux-Arts Taine relates how the pupils devoted "ten years of patience and good taste" to making a complete reproduction of Raphael's loggia from the Vatican. The atmosphere of the school was congenial to Taine. In the classical courtyard, decorated with a copy of Raphael's Galatea and casts from the Parthenon frieze, Taine found "a refuge for eyes wounded by the busy multitude . . . by the active and inexhaustible ugliness of Parisian life and work."[57]

In a series of lectures, "De l'Idéal dans l'Art" (1867), Taine made explicit the basis for his artistic judgments. He begins by maintaining that the judgments he has pronounced are not merely personal or arbitrary. The masterpieces of the high Renaissance "pass for the most beautiful in the judgment of all; all schools resort to them for models."[58] He has only repeated the "definitive judgments which posterity pronounces."[59] Here Taine falls prey to the illusion of universal agreement which absorption in an institution is apt to promote. Surrounded by the unanimity prevailing within the school, Taine loses sight of the variety of artistic tastes which his earlier historical studies emphasized. His appeal to the suffrage of posterity is also deceptive. Posterity is never unanimous.[60] The posterity which we invoke to give authority to our judgments is always a limited group, selected on the basis of their agreement with us.

[57] "L'École des Beaux-Arts et les Beaux-Arts en France," *Essais de Critique et d'Histoire* (6th ed., Paris, 1892), 373. This essay was written after Taine had been lecturing at the school for three or four years.

[58] "De l'Idéal dans l'Art," *Phil. de l'Art*, II, 275.

[59] *Ibid.*, 234.

[60] Cf. Charles Lalo, *L'Expression de la Vie dans l'Art* (Paris, 1933), 148. "Is the posterity which we call upon to judge equitably the Middle Ages our ancestors of the sixteenth, seventeenth and eighteenth centuries, in whom we recognize so much taste in other respects? Or is it the Romantics and ourselves? Are the Middle Ages, according to our taste, the posterity of the ancient world, the good judge of its monuments, which they used as a stone quarry?"

Taine's "De l'Idéal dans l'Art," however, signifies more than his assimilation to an academic institution. It provides the occasion for Taine to express his basic social attitudes. Like Ruskin and Morris, Taine takes art criticism as the basis for a general social critique. He glorifies the societies of the past which produced the art he most admires, and contrasts his own society with those golden ages. The Renaissance and Greek antiquity are the periods in which Taine considers men were happiest. In contrast there are two periods which Taine regards as characterized by human misery, the Middle Ages and the nineteenth century. Already in his *History of English Literature* Taine had written with enthusiasm of the "pagan Renaissance," in which the revival of invention and the increase of material goods raised men from the slough of mediaeval despond, emancipated them from theocracy, and concentrated their interests wholly on this world. After contrasting the Renaissance with the preceding age, he turns to compare it with later times. In Renaissance life there was "so open an appeal to the senses, so complete a return to nature, that our chilled and gloomy age is scarcely able to imagine it."[61] This two-directional comparison is significant. It is an antagonism engendered by his own society which imparts its animus to Taine's comparison of the Renaissance and the Middle Ages. Let us recall that Taine's polemical orientation had as its starting point his reaction against the Catholic revival which followed 1848. The moral and intellectual constraints which he condemns in mediaeval society are those which he sees revived in his "chilled and gloomy age."[62]

Taine's critique of social institutions is based on a contrast between the "natural" and the "civilized" man, which he borrows from the eighteenth-century philosophers (the same philosophers whom he had criticized earlier for thinking in such unhistorical terms). The ancient Greek and the Renaissance man are "natural," according to Taine, while the nineteenth-century man is typically "civilized." There are two sets of characteristics which distinguish these opposites. First, modern man is separated from

[61] *History of English Literature*, I, 169–72, 178.

[62] It may be fitting to recall here that even France was "Victorian" in the latter half of the nineteenth century. The French writers whom we think of as typically anti-Victorian were haled into Parisian law courts on charges of indecency: e.g., Baudelaire for *Les Fleurs de Mal*, Flaubert for *Madame Bovary*.

the man of ancient times by the institution of Christianity, which introduced psychological conflicts unknown to the pagan, and resulted in the development of the spirit at the expense of the body.[63] Taine here makes use of the comparisons which the Romantics had developed to differentiate the modern from the ancient; only Taine's sympathies are all on the side of the Greeks.[64] There is another circumstance that separates the "civilized" from the "natural," and that is a more advanced method of production and greater scientific knowledge. In ancient society there was relatively little division of labor. Men lived better-rounded lives, less confined by the narrowing influences of specialization.[65] Neither the ancients nor the men of the Renaissance lived in so much comfort and security as modern men. Consequently they were more rugged and robust. They were not overburdened with commodities like modern men who wear themselves out to obtain all the material things they regard as indispensable.[66] Finally, modern men know too much and think too much. Their minds are in an unhealthy condition, laden with too many facts and theories, troubled by too many problems. Thus they are estranged from the direct enjoyment of physical life familiar to their predecessors.[67]

It appears contradictory that Taine should associate the lack of physical enjoyment in modern life with the increased production of material goods, the more so as he had argued that it was just such an increase in production which had earlier rescued men from mediaeval other-worldliness. Moreover, it is puzzling that although modern men are separated from nature by Christianity it was possible for the men of the Renaissance, who followed the period of most complete church domination, to be pagans. Taine, however, is making a direct observation of fact. The continued advance of the productive activity initiated in the Renaissance had brought with it a renewal of inhibitions and spiritualism. With the material advance, there had been an ideological decline, as Taine had recognized earlier when he compared Cousin with

[63] "La Sculpture en Grèce," *Philosophie de l'Art,* II, 145 (first published in 1869).

[64] *Ibid.,* 158.

[65] *Ibid.,* 144.

[66] *Ibid.,* 137–40; "La Peinture de la Renaissance en Italie," *Philosophie de l'Art,* I, 149–50, 199–201 (first published in 1866).

[67] "La Sculpture en Grèce," 153–5; "La Peinture de la Renaissance en Italie," 165; "De l'Idéal dans l'Art," 301.

Condillac. But Taine does not understand the relationship between the two factors he correlates. He is unable to see the potentialities for still greater satisfaction of human needs latent in the accumulated material and intellectual equipment of his society. He fails to recognize the social agencies which prevent this equipment from being used to the greatest human advantage. Thus he attributes the frustrations which he observes to the equipment itself. He identifies the results of scientific advance with those of spiritualistic revival. Science, like Christianity, upsets the happy balance between mind and body; it produces men overly developed mentally, feeble physically.

Taine manifests a primitivist strain here which is extremely incongruous with his earlier enthusiasm for modern science.[68] In defending the achievements of the Renaissance, but rejecting those of any later age, Taine is forced into a reactionary position. It is interesting to note how much Taine differs from the eighteenth-century thinkers in the practical conclusions he draws from his theory of the "natural man." Where his predecessors demanded the liberation of the "natural man" from the fetters of "civilization," Taine is able only to dream of a golden age in the past before the fetters were imposed. It is to the Renaissance, the heroic opening phase of the bourgeois epoch, that Taine most frequently reverts.[69] Unable to free himself from the basic laws of bourgeois society, Taine recognizes its decline, but dares not think of its overthrow. The only way in which he can cling to the bourgeois order, and at the same time express his dissatisfaction with its later developments, is to revert to its more fruitful, earlier period.

[68] In saying that modern man knows too much and thinks too much, and that he is at the same time overburdened with too many problems, Taine is expressing his own unhappy predicament. Unable to resolve the conflict in his own mind, he asks, what good is all his learning? Taine's attitude towards science altered as he grew older. In 1866, he wrote that through understanding history we may learn to direct its course as we desire (*Essais de Critique et d'Histoire,* 12th ed., Paris, 1913, Preface to 2nd ed., xxiii). In later years he recommended science chiefly as a means of cultivating resignation of spirit (Cf. Norman, *op. cit.,* 548).

[69] Cf. Zola, "M. H. Taine, Artiste," *Mes Haines, Oeuvres Complètes,* XL, (Paris, 1929), 158-9. "M. Taine is not the man of his times nor of his body. If I did not know him, I would be inclined to picture him broad-shouldered, clad in large and splendid stuffs, dragging a sword, living in the full Renaissance." Zola discerns at the same time the compensatory character of Taine's enthusiasm for a more robust age. Taine "belongs indeed to our century of nerves. He is a sick and restless spirit having passionate aspirations towards strength and the free life."

It is for this reason that Taine makes such a contradictory impression, as a rebel hopelessly tied to the past.

The limitations of Taine's social outlook are manifest in the scale of values he sets up for the plastic arts. This scale ranges between two extremes, mediaeval art at the bottom and Renaissance and ancient art at the top. The two extremes are compared with reference to the "natural man," as the ideal of physical health. This ideal finds embodiment in Renaissance and ancient art, while the emaciated and sickly figures of mediaeval art represent the greatest deviation from it.[70] The Renaissance interest in the "natural man" is accompanied moreover by penetrating observation of anatomical structure, while mediaeval art is characterized by neglect of the empirical model.[71] In a certain sense, the points which Taine makes here may be conceded. Health is better than sickness; an attitude of valuing physical life is better than asceticism; and an interest in empirical observation is preferable to a lack of such interest. However, these judgments had become commonplaces by the time Taine wrote. They no longer indicated the direction of further social advance. It was only at a past moment of history that they had constituted crucial issues, in the period of transition from the Middle Ages to the Renaissance.[72] Taine transports himself in imagination back to this transitional period, and together with the heroes of the Renaissance fights the good fight against mediaeval tradition. Many of his judgments on art sound as if they came straight from Leonardo or Vasari. His mistake lies in that he takes the program of a particular historical school, and attempts to make of it a law for the arts of all times and places. According to Taine the plastic arts should never serve any function other than that which they served in the Renaissance. The representation of ideally healthy bodies constitutes the definitive purpose of the plastic arts.[73] It follows that when new social issues occasion new themes for art Taine can see nothing but decadence.[74]

[70] "De l'Idéal dans l'Art," *Phil. de l'Art*, II, 302–11.

[71] *Philosophie de l'Art*, I, 18–20.

[72] Insofar as the conquests of the Renaissance were called in question by the extreme reactionary movements of Taine's day, it was nevertheless impossible to defend them by a merely conservative, rear-guard action such as Taine's. This is demonstrated by the final outcome of Taine's thought, in *Les Origines de la France Contemporaine*, which landed him in the reactionary camp. See below.

[73] *Phil. de l'Art*, II, 279. "The genius of the masters consists in fashioning a race of bodies; thus regarded, they are physiologists, as writers are psychologists."

[74] *Phil. de l'Art*, I, 116–17.

His theory of artistic values denies the valid elements in his historical relativism.

VI

We may compare Taine with other writers who succeeded better than he in solving the problem of the relation of history to values. Both Hegel and Marx formulated conceptions of social development in which they combined historical and evaluational factors. While each of them assigned a different content to these factors, from a formal point of view the scheme was the same. Social products were evaluated by a universal standard. Yet their worthiness to be adopted or discarded at any particular time and place was decided by reference to the range of feasible alternatives.[75]

Taine differed from Hegel and Marx in his attitude towards the society in which he lived. Hegel was able, for official purposes at least, to accept the Prussian state of his day as the final and complete historical embodiment of the ideal. This constituted a somewhat anti-climactic conclusion to his grandiose vision of world history. Nevertheless it provided a basis for regarding history as the medium for the realization of values. Hegel's solution followed from his position as state philosopher, identifying itself with the dominant tendencies in his society. Marx's solution derived from an opposite social alignment. Marx was a critic of nineteenth-century society. However, he saw in this society accumulated resources which if properly reorganized would make possible an unprecedented satisfaction of human needs. And he proceeded to formulate a program by means of which society might be transformed in the desired direction. Thus Marx also was able to regard history as the medium for the realization of values, although he saw the desired fulfilment not in the present, but in the future.

In contrast to both Hegel and Marx, Taine was ambivalent towards the prevailing social order. He was dissatisfied with his society, but he was unable to break away from it. He could not be a thorough-going rebel, and abandon hope of ever becoming a mem-

[75] Cf. Hegel, *Logic* (trans. by Wallace, 2nd ed., London, 1892), 159-60; *Introduction to Hegel's Philosophy of Fine Arts* (trans. by Bosanquet, London, 1905), 196-99, 206-7. Engels, *Anti-Dühring* (New York, 1939), 206; Marx and Engels, *Sur la Littérature et l'Art* (selected by Jean Fréville, Paris, 1936), 27, 59-60. Proudhon also attempted to formulate a combined historical and evaluational approach to art; cf. his *Du Principe de l'Art et de sa Destination Sociale* (Paris, 1865), 102-3.

ber of the French Academy.[76] The way of Marx was closed to him. But the way of Hegel was also impossible. Taine was unable to become a state philosopher, an official apologist. His intellectual career had begun with a critique of such disingenuous thinkers, and he was never able quite to overcome this aversion. Moreover, since Hegel's day it had become increasingly difficult to cast an aura of idealization over the existing rulers. It had been possible to envisage Napoleon I as an embodiment of the *Zeitgeist*. It was more difficult to perform this imaginative feat in the case of Napoleon III.

VII

Despite the inhibited character of Taine's rebellious impulses, his earlier writings manifested a socially critical tendency which was sufficiently noticeable to alarm his more conservative contemporaries. His historical relativism contained a certain potency for dissolving social absolutes. The observation that different sets of values rise and fall with the appearance and disappearance of correlative social conditions, carried a disquieting implication if applied to currently honored precepts. Taine's historical relativism rested on a premise of psychological determinism. As we have noted, Taine held that men's actions and attitudes, even the most spiritual, are determined by their social environment. In this he was merely continuing the tradition of empirical psychology which, starting with Locke, had undermined the conception of the soul as containing innately certain timeless maxims of virtue. Locke had remarked that the so-called laws of God, when subjected to empirical analysis, were traceable to the teachings of one's nurse. In Taine's day a reaction had set in against such irreverent inquiries. Respectable thinkers were engaged in wrapping the soul once more in the old veils of mystery. Thus it was Taine's psychological determinism which drew the chief attack of his critics.[77]

[76] Taine's recurrent efforts to win official honors indicate that he was never wholly disillusioned with those who had them to bestow. Despite many rebuffs, Taine continued to submit his books for academic prizes. It was by gaining the favor of the Princesse Mathilde that he received his professorship at l'École des Beaux-Arts. In the end he became a member of the Academy.

[77] Sainte-Beuve, "Taine's History of English Literature," *Essays*, (trans. by Lee, London, 1892), 228. Sainte-Beuve records that the *History of English Literature* "terrified the timid and raised much opposition and resistance. . . . Rhetoricians in confusion took refuge behind real or pretended philosophers, themselves

The argument most persistently raised against Taine is that his determinism destroys the necessary basis for value-judgments. This necessary basis, according to Taine's critics, is the assumption that man is free, that regardless of his historical position he is able always to act according to the eternally Good, to paint after the model of the eternally Beautiful, and to frame his philosophy along the lines of the eternally True.[78] The aim of such thought is to place the particular values to which the thinker feels himself bound beyond the reach of historical necessity. Against the social tide which threatens to sweep away his limited ideals, a thinker of this type fortifies himself with the word-magic which speaks of eternal realms and the unchanging soul, and the typographical magic which prints "good," "true," and "beautiful" with capital letters.

The intention of Taine's critics is most clearly exemplified in Brunetière. Reviewing the development of Taine's thought, Brunetière observes the conflict between the impartial historical approach and the growing tendency to set up a standard of value. He notes with satisfaction that the values from which Taine had tried to detach himself are reaffirmed in his later writings. In "De l'Idéal dans l'Art," Taine reasserts aesthetic values. In his *Origines de la France Contemporaine,* he re-introduces moral criteria. When he portrays Marat, Danton, and Robespierre, it is not with "the curiosity of the amateur of moral zoology," but with "the indignation of the moralist."[79] Brunetière is satisfied with this outcome of Taine's thought. He believes that Taine has solved the problem of history and values.[80] Taine's aesthetic standard is, as we have seen, a defense of a limited historical tradition. But it satisfies Brunetière because it is so safely conservative. Similarly, Brunetière is satisfied to identify morality in general with that

---

drawn up for greater safety under the canon of orthodoxy; they saw in the author's method some sort of menace to morals, free will, human responsibility, and they loudly protested."

[78] Gibaudan, *op. cit.,* 118; Paul Bourget, "M. Taine," *Essais de Psychologie Contemporaine,* I (Paris, 1937), 221-3; Irving Babbitt, "Taine," *Masters of Modern French Criticism* (New York, 1912), 238; Giacomo Barzellotti, *La Philosophie de H. Taine* (Paris, 1900), 214; Edmond Schérer, "Taine's History of English Literature," *Essays on English Literature* (trans. by Saintsbury, New York, 1891), 80.

[79] Brunetière, "L'Oeuvre critique de Taine," *Discours de Combat* (2nd series, Paris, 1914), 248.

[80] *Ibid.,* 214, 222, 242.

particular moral outlook which brands the leaders of the French Revolution as criminals. Thus he is concerned not so much to see Taine solve his theoretical problem, as to see him reaffirm the conservative set of values which his relativism seemed to threaten.

While Taine's critics were alarmed by the destructive implications of his doctrines, Taine himself was unwilling to draw these consequences. Taine's essential conservatism is well illustrated in an episode of his later years. Paul Bourget wrote a novel, *Le Disciple*. In it, he relates how an elderly naturalistic philosopher is made to realize the morally destructive consequences of his ideas when a young disciple of his ends up in jail. Taine's reaction to this book is interesting. He writes to Bourget that the story has touched him very intimately and painfully. Its implications are such as to turn its readers either against morality or against science. The young hero attempts to justify his misdeeds by giving an empirical analysis of his emotional development. Young people of unstable moral character will rush to the conclusion that science condones immorality. People of strong moral principles, on the other hand, will be led to condemn science. Taine argues that the doctrine of psychological determinism in no way conflicts with the most rigid morality. He cites Calvin and Spinoza, the ancient Stoics and the Puritans, as men whose belief in determinism was combined with great moral severity.[81] It is evident that Taine has no intention of applying historical relativism to moral precepts. His invocation of moralists of such widely diverse historical backgrounds indicates his belief that morality is the same for all times. He has no quarrel with Bourget's moral presuppositions, according to which the disciple is a villain. For Taine, as for Bourget, this conservative, late nineteenth-century morality is the only morality.[82]

VIII

It was the events of the year 1870 which finally submerged the struggling remnants of liberalism in Taine's mind. The Franco-

[81] *Vie et Correspondance*, IV, 288–92.

[82] This "Victorian" prudery already manifested itself in Taine's *History of English Literature*. Despite his admiration for the Renaissance, Taine could not help being shocked by its lack of constraint. He finds the Elizabethans "foul-mouthed." They "delighted in conversation which would revolt us." On their stage, "decency is a thing unknown. . . . Shakespeare's words are too indecent to be translated." (I, 272, 378.)

Prussian war evoked in Taine an unsuspected strain of patriotism. The Commune shocked him as a crime against the Fatherland.[83] Amid the national disaster, Taine resolved to lend aid as best he could to a prostrate France. He began to project the work which was to occupy him for the next twenty years, to the end of his life, his study of *Les Origines de la France Contemporaine*. The purpose of this work was to discover what miscarriage in the national past had brought France to the unhappy position of 1870. Taine finds the starting-point of all France's subsequent misfortunes in the Revolution of 1789, and in the philosophy of the eighteenth century which he thinks inspired the Revolution. The first volume of *Les Origines* is an indictment of this revolutionary philosophy as the product of what Taine calls the "classical spirit." The essential trait of this spirit is its contempt for tradition, its proposal to found a new society on the grounds of reason alone.[84] In opposition to this doctrine, Taine summons up all the old arguments which the Romantics had forged as weapons against the French Revolution. Traditions are not fetters, but the inherited wealth which men receive from their ancestors. One cannot legislate for mankind in general, taken in abstraction from their concrete historical backgrounds.[85] Tradition is not opposed to reason; it represents the accumulated wisdom and experience of the ages. To break with it leads to anarchy and socialism.[86]

In thus taking up the defense of the tradition which the Revolution of 1789 had attacked, in repeating the arguments of royalists and Catholics, Taine renounced the liberal tendencies of his own youth.[87] The Commune of 1871 provoked in Taine the same reactionary impulse which the Revolution of 1848 had set up in so many of his contemporaries. Because in Taine this reaction was delayed, he found himself for twenty years in the position of an uneasy and half involuntary rebel. The historical argument which Taine uses against the French Revolution appears to be a political counterpart of his historical relativism in aesthetics.

[83] *Vie et Correspondance*, III, 60.
[84] *The Ancient Régime* (trans. by John Durand, New York, 1896), 204–5, 211.
[85] *Ibid.*, 214.
[86] *Ibid.*, 207–8, 231, 251.
[87] Alphonse Aulard, *Taine, Historien de la Révolution Française* (2nd ed., Paris, 1908), 330. Taine's "views on the Revolution add nothing to those which royalist pamphleteers had already expressed, either at the time of the Revolution, or under the Restoration."

However, we may observe here the ambiguity of historical relativism, its capacity for serving equally progressive and reactionary social purposes. Taine's earlier historical relativism, as exemplified in his studies of literature, had a certain tendency to unsettle established authority. The historical relativism of *Les Origines* manifests a directly opposite tendency. It is invoked to support the claims of antiquated institutions to indefinite perpetuation. Taine now came to be regarded as the man who, "in the face of advancing democracy, was able to restore to the governing classes of France their lost title-deeds."[88]

Having taken refuge in the camp of the reactionaries, from which he had struggled for so long to hold himself aloof, Taine was able to find small comfort there. He felt too strongly that the position of the class to which he was attached had become insecure. As he felt himself inescapably bound to the fortunes of this class, his sense of melancholy and of hopeless entanglement in a declining movement increased. He writes at the end of his life, à propos of *Les Origines*, "Probably I was wrong, twenty years ago, to undertake this series of researches; they have darkened my old age, and I feel more and more that from a practical point of view they will accomplish nothing; an enormous swift current is bearing us away; what good to record its depth and swiftness?"[89] This final despairing cry anticipates Spengler. At the same time, it indicates how far Taine is removed from the optimistic thinkers of the preceding century, whose philosophy provided his point of departure.

---

[88] R. A. Jones, "Taine and the Nationalists," *The Social and Political Ideas of Some Representative Thinkers of the Victorian Age* (edited by F. J. C. Hearnshaw, London, 1933), 249. Cf. Charaux, *op. cit.*, a Catholic retrospect on Taine. Charaux remarks how, with the publication of the first volume of *Les Origines*, the religious and spiritualistic contemporaries of Taine, who had formerly attacked him, became his enthusiastic admirers (563). In Taine's indictment of the Revolution, he speaks in the name of justice, even though "he does not call it, as we would, the justice of God" (580). Charaux ends with the thought that, if Taine had lived a little longer, he would probably have found his way back to the Church.

[89] *Vie et Correspondance*, IV, 338.

III

SOCIAL AND POLITICAL THOUGHT

History and the Humanities[1]

by HAJO HOLBORN

Reprinted from the *Journal of the History of Ideas*—Vol. IX, No. 1, pp. 65-69

The rôle of modern science in the destruction of the metaphysical outlook of western civilization and in the creation of modern rationalistic philosophies is universally acknowledged. The equally important part played in this process by the growth of modern historical thought is still far from being adequately appreciated. But Hume, Voltaire and their successors by pronouncing the belief in history as a manifestation of the will of Providence a superstitious myth did exactly what the scientists were doing with regard to nature. As all magic forces were excluded from the analysis of the universe history was henceforth understood as the knowledge of human actions and thoughts.

Since the eighteenth century this has constituted the fundamental assumption in the study of history. In its origins it was closely allied with a faith in progress and the infinite perfectibility of man. Thus even in the secular philosophies of history produced in the eighteenth and early nineteenth centuries the teleological character of the old religious interpretation continued, and it has remained a most formidable influence in modern historical thinking. The new Jerusalem was envisaged in various forms. Voltaire conceived it as progress toward general enlightenment and happiness, Hegel as the consciousness of freedom through the realization of a deified state, Marx as the achievement of real freedom in the paradise of a classless, and consequently stateless, society. Even when Comte, Spencer, and others replaced the speculative philosophy of history by a "positive," and that meant scientific, study of history the teleological structure survived.

Against these philosophical and sociological ideas the Historical School rebelled. It originated in Germany, but soon found its representatives in every country. It was by no means confined to the study of politics but embraced languages and literature, law and economics as well. Nobody questions today that these historical studies produced greater and more reliable results than those of any older school. After a century of tireless endeavor our

[1] This paper was read at the Princeton Bicentennial Conference "The Humanistic Tradition in the Century Ahead," which took place October 16–18, 1946.

knowledge of history now extends over vast reaches of human civilization. If, however, our generation inquires into the general assumptions underlying the work of the students of history in the nineteenth century as stated by these students themselves, we find them, with few exceptions, espousing philosophies which do not stand up under critical review. With few exceptions we see them under the spell of the expanding natural sciences. In their opinion the task of historical research was the reconstruction of the past from the sources which, if purged of certain falsehoods, would tell the story of the past by themselves. A steady accumulation of purified sources would in due course overcome whatever subjectivity existed in the individual historian. Philosophy was to be excluded from the field of history, since it imposed an arbitrary pattern, alien to historical reality.

Though such ideas are still widely held in the historical profession, they have often enough been exposed as a naïve rationalization of the practice of the historical student, explicable by the intellectual climate of the last century and particularly by the inevitable conflict between the modern empirical study of history and the old speculative philosophy of history. This philosophy of history, though it contributed greatly to the modern awareness of history, was at the same time an impediment to the critical reconstruction of the historical world. The emphasis on detailed factual evidence and the exclusion of a teleological construction of history was a logical necessity. But these circumstances did not justify a divorce of history and philosophy. How dangerous such a separation might become was amply demonstrated whenever the empiristic historians attempted to present a view of general history. In that case they could be seen borrowing heavily from the old philosophies of history which they themselves decried or, even worse, they were swayed by the naturalistic and materialistic ideologies of modern nationalism.

The study of history would inevitably lose any sense of direction and could not claim to yield objective and valid knowledge if its methods and aims were not lifted into clear consciousness and made the object of critical analysis. Philosophy and history are closely joined together, though their relationship is of an entirely different nature from that visualized in the eighteenth century. Philosophy cannot determine the contents of history by mere speculation.

Philosophy is as dependent on history as it is on science. When Kant wrote his *Critique of Pure Reason* he described the methods employed by the natural sciences. A critique of historical reason which Wilhelm Dilthey first postulated and to which a large number of scholars of the last and present generation have turned their attention would have to start in similar manner from the scrutiny of historical methodology.

But it is not only the epistemological concern which brings philosophy and history together. It is the fundamental problem of philosophy itself, the question "What is man?" which compels the philosopher to study history. For the subjective nature of man can be approached only through history. There is no new beginning in life. My every action and thought presupposes and contains an earlier background of thought and action. And what is true of individuals applies equally to civilizations or world history. In this sense Ortega y Gassett could recently say that "man has no nature, but only history."[2]

Such a statement is based on the recognition that historical time is something entirely different from time as it appears in nature. Any natural phenomenon takes place in time. But whether or not one uses words like history of nature, history of the universe, etc., it is evident, for example, that the chain reaction of an atomic bomb explosion, though it constitutes a sequence of events in time, is not *per se* a historical event. The historical significance of Los Alamos, Hiroshima and Nagasaki rests in the growth of the modern scientific mind, in the reasons which induced the American government to support the scientific and technological development of atomic energy and to employ it as a weapon in the final phase of the War. This is not the time to list all possible aspects of the invention of atomic energy that historians will have to treat. Suffice it to say that all of them will be subjects to be defined in terms of human motives, actions and reactions. For that reason they are unique events which will not repeat themselves, in contrast to the natural chain-reaction of an atomic explosion which will happen in the same form according to the same laws of nature whenever the same elements meet under the same circumstances.

The history of man, therefore, implies more than mere change

[2] José Ortega y Gassett, *Toward a Philosophy of History* (New York, 1941), 217, and *Concord and Liberty* (New York, 1946), 148.

in time. Historical time is meaningful time, made meaningful by singular human actions. The repetitious appetites and desires of man's physical being are not a subject of historical study. But, for example, the growth of specific forms of courtship and love in human civilization is a legitimate subject of historical inquiry. In addition to the principle of continuity history is determined by the principle of individuation. This process of individuation has most often been explained in a more or less Hegelian vein as the manifestation of reason. However, man always remains tied to his physical nature and human consciousness expresses not only reasoning thought, but will power and feeling as well. The historian will not expect history ever to reach a final goal beyond which human nature would be moved only by reason, or history would change into eternity.

The historian as a historian cannot even predict the outlines of the age immediately ahead with any claim to pronounce a valid judgment, since it would conflict with his basic premises and findings. History has neither a new beginning nor a final ending. It can only be conceived as the realization of the potentialities of man in historic time. But historical study, by retracing the struggle of man for the control of nature and by reviving the thoughts and conscious life of the past, offers the living generation the challenge to make its own vital decisions on the basis of a critical knowledge of the full scope of former human experiences and achievements. It thus enables the individual human being to expand his experience beyond his actual station in life or a historic society to absorb the fruits of events in which it had no part itself. The study of history opens the road to participation in the fullness of human civilization.

This participation has to be understood literally. Whereas the natural scientist perceives phenomena which have a reality independent from the observer history is only real in the consciousness of the historian. There is great significance in the fact, so annoying to many historians, that the word "history" means both history as actuality (*res gestae*) and written history. The past is present only as far as it is re-lived by the historian through sympathy and understanding. The central problems of a historical methodology or epistemology hinge upon the fact that an objective knowledge of the past can only be attained through the subjective experience of the scholar.

The study of history offers no escape from historicity and all the limitations of historic man apply to the individual student of history. As a matter of fact, without subjectivity we could not even hope to penetrate into history. Historians should keep their feet firmly planted in the life of their own age and participate bravely in its labors. They will not thereby gain answers to the problems of history, but they will be able to formulate questions with which to approach the past. And history gives answers only to those who know how to ask questions. Still, this is just the beginning of historical inquiry. The process of historical verification and understanding is a continuous struggle to move from a subjective towards a universal position, from a captivity in the floating and fortuitous moment of history, called the present, to a share in the objective human experiences as manifested in the historic civilizations.

The critical character of historical interpretation is ultimately determined by the underlying concept of man, which is not merely the result of a reading in the past but also of a simultaneous self-analysis of the observer. In this critical revival of the past the living generation achieves a higher consciousness of its own being. Therefore, historical study is a humanistic endeavor. Beginning with Cicero all the humanists desired to know the greatness and range of human nature and were animated by the faith that such knowledge would endow them with a greater capacity for the realization of the highest ideals in their own time. Modern historical study stands in this tradition, though it has changed almost all other ideas and methods of the humanism of former centuries. Today history is the approach to the knowledge of man and through history we acquire the wealth of former civilizations. The critical awareness of the potentialities of man enables us to act in our own time with higher insight and vigor.

The Theoretical Development of the Sociology of Religion
A Chapter in the History of Modern Social Science[1]

by TALCOTT PARSONS

Reprinted from the *Journal of the History of Ideas*—Vol. V, No. 2, pp. 176-190

The present paper will attempt to present in broad outline what seems to the writer one of the most significant chapters in the recent history of sociological theory, that dealing with the broader structure of the conceptual scheme for the analysis of religious phenomena as part of a social system. Its principal significance would seem to lie on two levels. In the first place, the development to be outlined represents a notable advance in the adequacy of our theoretical equipment to deal with a critically important range of scientific problems. Secondly, however, it is at the same time a particularly good illustration of the kind of process by which major theoretical developments in the field of social theory can be expected to take place.

Every important tradition of scientific thought involves a broad framework of theoretical propositions at any given stage of its development. Generally speaking, differences will be found only in the degree to which this framework is logically integrated and to which it is explicitly and self-consciously acknowledged and analyzed. About the middle of the last century or shortly thereafter, it is perhaps fair to say, generalized thinking about the significance of religion to human life tended to fall into one of two main categories. The first is the body of thought anchored in the doctrinal positions of one or another specific religious group, predominantly of course the various Christian denominations. For understandable reasons, the main tenor of such thought tended to be normative rather than empirical and analytical, to assert its own religious position and to expose the errors of opponents. It is difficult to see that in any direct sense important contributions to the sociology of religion as an empirical science could come from this source.[2] The other main category may be broadly referred to as that of positivistic thinking. In the phases which culminated in

---

[1] This paper was presented to the Conference on Methods in Philosophy and the Sciences at the New School for Social Research, New York, November 29, 1942.

[2] It was far less unfavorable to historical contributions than to those affecting the analytical framework of the subject.

the various branches of utilitarianism, this great stream of thought had, of course, long been much concerned with some of the problems of religion. In its concern with contemporary society, however, the strong tendency had been to minimize the importance of religion, to treat it as a matter of "superstition" which had no place in the enlightened thinking of modern civilized man. The result of this tendency was, in the search for the important forces activating human behavior, to direct attention to other fields, such as the economic and the political. In certain phases the same tendency may be observed in the trend of positivistic thought toward emphasis on biology and psychology, which gathered force in the latter part of the nineteenth century and has continued well into our own.

Perhaps the first important change in this definition of problems, which was highly unfavorable to a serious scientific interest in the phenomena of religion, came with the application of the idea of evolution to human society. Once evidence from non-literate societies, not to speak of many others, was at all carefully studied, the observation was inescapable that the life of these so-called "primitive" men was to an enormous degree dominated by beliefs and practices which would ordinarily be classified according to the common-sense thinking of our time as magical and religious. Contemporary non-literate peoples, however, were in that generation predominantly interpreted as the living prototypes of our own prehistorical ancestors, and hence it was only natural that these striking phenomena should have been treated as "primitive" in a strictly evolutionary sense, as belonging to the early stages of the process of social development. This is the broad situation of the first really serious treatment of comparative religion in a sociological context, especially in the work of the founder of modern social-anthropology, Tylor,[3] and of Spencer,[4] perhaps the most penetrating theorist of this movement of thought. Though there was here a basis for a serious scientific interest, the positivistic scheme of thought imposed severe limitations on the kind of significance which could be attributed to the observed phenomena. Within the positivistic schema, the most obvious directions of theoretical interpretation were two. On the one hand, religious phenomena could be treated as the manifestations of underlying biological or

[3] *Primitive Culture.*
[4] Esp. *Principles of Sociology,* Vol. I.

psychological factors beyond the reach of rational control, or interpretations in terms of subjective categories. Most generally this pattern led to some version of the instinct theory, which has suffered, however, some very serious scientific handicaps in that it has never proved possible to relate the detailed variations in the behavioral phenomena to any corresponding variations in the structure of instinctual drives. The whole scheme has on the level of social theory never successfully avoided the pitfalls of reasoning in a circle.

The other principal alternative was what may be called the "rationalistic" variation of positivism,[5] the tendency to treat the actor as if he were a rational, scientific investigator, acting "reasonably" in the light of the knowledge available to him. This was the path taken by Tylor and Spencer with the general thesis that primitive magical and religious ideas were ideas which in the situation of primitive men, considering the lack of accumulated knowledge and the limitations of the technique and opportunities of observation, it would reasonably be expected they would arrive at. With beliefs like that in a soul separable from the body, ritual practices in turn are held to be readily understandable. It is, however, a basic assumption of this pattern of thinking that the only critical standards to which religious ideas can be referred are those of empirical validity. It almost goes without saying that no enlightened modern could entertain such beliefs, that hence what we think of as distinctively religious and magical beliefs, and hence also the accompanying practices, will naturally disappear as an automatic consequence of the advance in scientific knowledge.

Inadequate as it is in the light of modern knowledge, this schema has proved to be the fruitful starting-point for the development of the field, for it makes possible the analysis of action in terms of the subjective point of view of the actor in his orientation to specific features of the situation in which he acts. Broadly speaking, to attempt to deal with the empirical inadequacies of this view by jumping directly, through the medium of anti-intellectualistic psychology, to the more fundamental forces activating human behavior, has not proved fruitful. The fruitful path has rather been the introduction of specific refinements and distinctions within the basic structural scheme with which "rationalistic positivism" started. The body of this paper will be concerned with a review

[5] See the author's *Structure of Social Action,* Chaps. II and III.

of several of the most important of these steps in analytical refinement, showing how, taken together, they have led up to a far more comprehensive analytical scheme. This can perhaps most conveniently be done in terms of the contributions of four important theorists, Pareto, Malinowski, Durkheim, and Max Weber, none of whom had any important direct influence on any of the others.

It is of primary significance that Pareto's[6] analytical scheme for the treatment of a social system started precisely with this fundamental frame of reference. Like the earlier positivists, he took as his starting-point the cognitive patterns in terms of which the actor is oriented to his situation of action. Again like them, he based his classification on the relation of these patterns to the standards of empirical scientific validity—in his terms, to "logico-experimental" standards. At this point, however, he broke decisively with the main positivistic tradition. He found it necessary, on grounds which in view of Pareto's general intellectual character most certainly were primarily empirical rather than philosophical, to distinguish two modes of deviance from conformity with logico-experimental standards. There were, on the one hand, the modes of deviance familiar to the older positivists, namely the failure to attain a logico-experimental solution of problems intrinsically capable of such solution. This may be attributable either to ignorance, the sheer absence of logically necessary knowledge of fact, or possibly of inference, or to error, to allegations of fact which observation can disprove or to logical fallacy in inference. In so far as cognitive patterns were deviant in this respect, Pareto summed them up as "pseudo-scientific" theories. Failure to conform with logico-experimental standards was not, however, confined to this mode of deviance, but included another, "the theories which surpass experience." These involved propositions, especially major premises, which are intrinsically incapable of being tested by scientific procedures. The attributes of God, for instance, are not entities capable of empirical observation; hence propositions involving them can by logico-experimental methods neither be proved nor disproved. In this connection, Pareto's primary service lay in the clarity with which the distinction was worked out and applied, and his demonstration of the essentially

[6] *The Mind and Society.* See also the author's *Structure of Social Action,* Chap. V–VII; and "Pareto's Central Analytical Scheme," *Journal of Social Philosophy,* I, 1935, 244–262.

prominent rôle in systems of human action of the latter class of cognitive elements. It is precisely in the field of religious ideas and of theological and metaphysical doctrines that its prominence has been greatest.

Pareto, however, did not stop there. From the very first, he treated the cognitive aspects of action in terms of their functional interdependence with the other elements of the social system, notably with what he called the "sentiments." He thereby broke through the "rationalistic bias" of earlier positivism and demonstrated by an immense weight of evidence that it was not possible to deal adequately with the significance of religious and magical ideas solely on the hypothesis that men entertaining them as beliefs drew the logical conclusions and acted accordingly. In this connection, Pareto's position has been widely interpreted as essentially a psychological one, as a reduction of non-logical ideas to the status of mere manifestations of instinct. Critical analysis of his work[7] shows, however, that this interpretation is not justified, but that he left the question of the more ultimate nature of non-cognitive factors open. It can be shown that the way in which he treated the sentiments is incompatible in certain critical respects with the hypothesis that they are biologically inherited instinctual drives alone. This would involve a determinacy irrespective of cultural variation which he explicitly repudiated.

It is perhaps best to state that, as Pareto left the subject, there were factors particularly prominent in the field of religious behavior which involved the expression of sentiments or attitudes other than those important to action in a rationally utilitarian context. He did not, however, go far in analyzing the nature of these factors. It should, however, be clear that with the introduction, as a functionally necessary category, of the non-empirical effective elements which cannot be fitted into the pattern of rational techniques, Pareto brought about a fundamental break in the neatly closed system of positivistic interpretation of the phenomena of religion. He enormously broadened the analytical perspective which needed to be taken into account before a new theoretical integration could be achieved.

The earlier positivistic theory started with the attempt to analyze the relation of the actor to particular types of situations common to all human social life, such as death and the experience of

[7] Cf. *Structure of Social Action*, 200 ff., 241 ff.

dreams. This starting-point was undoubtedly sound. The difficulty lay in interpreting such situations and the actor's relations to them too narrowly, essentially as a matter of the solution of empirical problems, of the actor's resorting to a "reasonable" course of action in the light of beliefs which he took for granted. Pareto provided much evidence that this exclusively cognitive approach was not adequate, but it remained for Malinowski[8] to return to detailed analysis of action in relation to particular situations in a broader perspective. Malinowski maintained continuity with the "classical" approach in that he took men's adaptation to practical situations by rational knowledge and technique as his initial point of reference. Instead of attempting to fit all the obvious facts positively into this framework, however, he showed a variety of reasons why in many circumstances rational knowledge and technique could not provide adequate mechanisms of adjustment to the total situation.

This approach threw into high relief a fundamental empirical observation, namely that instead of there being one single set of ideas and practices involved, for instance in gardening, canoe-building, or deep-sea fishing in the Trobriand Islands, there were in fact two distinct systems. On the one hand, the native was clearly possessed of an impressive amount of sound empirical knowledge of the proper uses of the soil and the processes of plant growth. He acted quite rationally in terms of his knowledge and above all was quite clear about the connection between intelligent and energetic work and a favorable outcome. There is no tendency to excuse failure on supernatural grounds when it could be clearly attributed to failure to attain adequate current standards of technical procedure. Side by side with this system of rational knowledge and technique, however, and specifically not confused with it, was a system of magical beliefs and practices. These beliefs concerned the possible intervention in the situation of forces and entities which are "supernatural" in the sense that they are not from our point of view objects of empirical observation and experience, but rather what Pareto would call "imaginary" entities, and on the other hand, entities with a specifically sacred character. Correspondingly, the practices were not rational techniques but rituals involving specific orientation to this world of supernatural forces and entities. It is true that the Trobriander believes

[8] See esp. "Magic, Science, and Religion," in *Science, Religion, and Reality*, J. Needham, ed., and *The Foundations of Faith and Morals*.

that a proper performance of magic is indispensable to a successful outcome of the enterprise; but it is one of Malinowski's most important insights that this attribution applies only to the range of uncertainty in the outcome of rational technique, to those factors in the situation which are beyond rational understanding and control on the part of the actor.

This approach to the analysis of primitive magic enabled Malinowski clearly to refute both the view of Lévy-Bruhl,[9] that primitive man confuses the realm of the supernatural and the sacred with the utilitarian and the rational, and also the view which had been classically put forward by Frazer[10] that magic was essentially primitive science, serving the same fundamental functions.

Malinowski, however, went beyond this in attempting to understand the functional necessity for such mechanisms as magic. In this connection, he laid stress on the importance of the emotional interests involved in the successful outcome of such enterprises. The combination of a strong emotional interest with important factors of uncertainty, which on the given technical level are inherent in the situation, produces a state of tension and exposes the actor to frustration. This, it should be noted, exists not only in cases where uncontrollable factors, such as bad weather or insect pests in gardening, result in "undeserved" failure, but also in cases where success is out of proportion to reasonable expectations of the results of intelligence and effort. Unless there were mechanisms which had the psychological function of mitigating the sense of frustration, the consequences would be unfavorable to maintaining a high level of confidence or effort, and it is in this connection that magic may be seen to perform important positive functions. It should be clear that this is a very different level of interpretation from that which attributes it only to the primitive level of knowledge. It would follow that wherever such uncertainty elements enter into the pursuit of emotionally important goals, if not magic at least functionally equivalent phenomena could be expected to appear.[11]

[9] *Primitive Mentality.*

[10] *The Golden Bough.*

[11] For example, the field of health is, in spite of the achievements of modern medicine, even in our own society a classical example of this type of situation. Careful examination of our own treatment of health even through medical practice reveals that though magic in a strict sense is not prominent, there is an unstable succession of beliefs which overemphasize the therapeutic possibilities of certain diagnostic ideas and therapeutic practices. The effect is to create an optimistic bias

In the case of magic, orientation to supernatural entities enters into action which is directed to the achievement of practical, empirical goals, such as a good crop or a large catch of fish. Malinowski, however, calls attention to the fact that there are situations which are analogous in other respects but in which no practical goal can be pursued. The type case of this is death. From the practical point of view, the Trobrianders, like any one else, are surely aware that "nothing can be done about it." No ritual observances will bring the deceased back to life. But precisely for this reason, the problem of emotional adjustment is all the greater in importance. The significance both practically and emotionally of a human individual is of such a magnitude that his death involves a major process of readjustment for the survivors. Malinowski shows that the death of another involves exposure to sharply conflicting emotional reactions, some of which, if given free range, would lead to action and attitudes detrimental to the social group. There is great need for patterns of action which provide occasion for the regulated expression of strong emotions, and which in such a situation of emotional conflict reinforce those reactions which are most favorable to the continued solidarity and functioning of the social group. One may suggest that in no society is action on the occasion of death confined to the utilitarian aspects of the disposal of the corpse and other practical adjustments. There is always specifically ritual observance of some kind which, as Malinowski shows, cannot adequately be interpreted as merely acting out the bizarre ideas which primitive man in his ignorance develops about the nature of death.

Malinowski shows quite clearly that neither ritual practices, magical or religious, nor the beliefs about supernatural forces and entities integrated with them can be treated simply as a primitive and inadequate form of rational techniques or scientific knowledge; they are qualitatively distinct and have quite different functional significance in the system of action. Durkheim,[12] however, went farther than Malinowski in working out the specific character of this difference, as well as in bringing out certain further aspects of the functional problem. Whereas Malinowski tended to focus attention on functions in relation to action in a situation, Durkheim

in favor of successful treatment of disease which apparently has considerable functional significance.

[12] *The Elementary Forms of the Religious Life.* See also *Structure of Social Action,* Chapter XI.

became particularly interested in the problem of the specific attitudes exhibited toward supernatural entities and ritual objects and actions. The results of this study he summed up in the fundamental distinction between the sacred and the profane. Directly contrasting the attitudes appropriate in a ritual context with those towards objects of utilitarian significance and their use in fields of rational technique, he found one fundamental feature of the sacred to be its radical dissociation from any utilitarian context. The sacred is to be treated with a certain specific attitude of respect, which Durkheim identified with the appropriate attitude toward moral obligations and authority. If the effect of the prominence which Durkheim gives to the conception of the sacred is strongly to reinforce the significance of Malinowski's observation that the two systems are not confused but are in fact treated as essentially separate, it also brings out even more sharply than did Malinowski the inadequacy of the older approach to this range of problems which treated them entirely as the outcome of intellectual processes in ways indistinguishable from the solution of empirical problems. Such treatment could not but obscure the fundamental distinction upon which Durkheim insisted.

The central significance of the sacred in religion, however, served to raise in a peculiarly acute form the question of the source of the attitude of respect. Spencer, for instance, had derived it from the fact that the souls of the dead reappeared to the living, and from ideas about the probable dangers of association with them. Max Müller, on the other hand, and the naturalist school had attempted to derive all sacred things in the last analysis from personification of certain phenomena of nature which were respected and feared because of their intrinsically imposing or terrifying character. Durkheim opened up an entirely new line of thought by suggesting that it was hopeless to look for a solution of the problem on this level at all. There was in fact no common intrinsic quality of things treated as sacred which could account for the attitude of respect. In fact, almost everything from the sublime to the ridiculous has in some society been treated as sacred. Hence the source of sacredness is not intrinsic; the problem is of a different character. Sacred objects and entities are symbols. The problem then becomes one of identifying the referents of such symbols. It is that which is symbolized and not the intrinsic quality of the symbol which becomes crucial.

At this point Durkheim became aware of the fundamental significance of his previous insight that the attitude of respect for sacred things was essentially identical with the attitude of respect for moral authority. If sacred things are symbols, the essential quality of that which they symbolize is that it is an entity which would command moral respect. It was by this path that Durkheim arrived at the famous proposition that society is always the real object of religious veneration. In this form the proposition is certainly unacceptable, but there is no doubt of the fundamental importance of Durkheim's insight into the exceedingly close integration of the system of religious symbols of a society and the patterns sanctioned by the common moral sentiments of the members of the community. In his earlier work,[13] Durkheim had progressed far in understanding the functional significance of an integrated system of morally sanctioned norms. Against this background the integration he demonstrated suggested a most important aspect of the functional significance of religion. For the problem arises, if moral norms and the sentiments supporting them are of such primary importance, what are the mechanisms by which they are maintained other than external processes of enforcement? It was Durkheim's view that religious ritual was of primary significance as a mechanism for expressing and reinforcing the sentiments most essential to the institutional integration of the society. It can readily be seen that this is closely linked to Malinowski's view of the significance of funeral ceremonies as a mechanism for reasserting the solidarity of the group on the occasion of severe emotional strain. Thus Durkheim worked out certain aspects of the specific relations between religion and social structure more sharply than did Malinowski, and in addition put the problem in a different functional perspective in that he applied it to the society as a whole in abstraction from particular situations of tension and strain for the individual.

One of the most notable features of the development under consideration lay in the fact that the cognitive patterns associated with religion were no longer, as in the older positivism, treated as essentially given points of reference, but were rather brought into functional relationship with a variety of other elements of social systems of action. Pareto in rather general terms showed their interdependence with the sentiments. Malinowski contributed the

[13] Especially *De la division du travail* and *Le suicide*. See also *Structure of Social Action*, Chap. VIII, X.

exceedingly important relation to particular types of human situation, such as those of uncertainty and death. He in no way contradicted the emphasis placed by Pareto on emotional factors or sentiments. These, however, acquire their significance for specifically structured patterns of action only through their relation to specific situations. Malinowski was well aware in turn of the relation of both these factors to the solidarity of the social group, but this aspect formed the center of Durkheim's analytical attention. Clearly, religious ideas could only be treated sociologically in terms of their interdependence with all four types of factor.

There were, however, still certain serious problems left unsolved. In particular, neither Malinowski nor Durkheim raised the problem of the relation of these factors to the variability of social structure from one society to another. Both were primarily concerned with analysis of the functioning of a given social system without either comparative or dynamic references. Furthermore, Durkheim's important insight into the rôle of symbolism in religious ideas might, without further analysis, suggest that the specific patterns, hence their variations, were of only secondary importance. Indeed, there is clearly discernible in Durkheim's thinking in this field a tendency to circular reasoning in that he tends to treat religious patterns as a symbolic manifestation of "society," but at the same time to define the most fundamental aspect of society as a set of patterns of moral and religious sentiment.

Max Weber approached the whole field in very different terms. In his study of the relation between Protestantism and capitalism,[14] his primary concern was with those features of the institutional system of modern western society which were most distinctive in differentiating it from the other great civilizations. Having established what he felt to be an adequate relation of congruence between the cognitive patterns of Calvinism and some of the principal institutionalized attitudes towards secular rôles of our own society, he set about systematically to place this material in the broadest possible comparative perspective through studying especially the religion and social structure of China, India, and ancient Judea.[15] As a generalized result of these studies, he found it was not possible to reduce the striking variations of pattern on the level of

[14] *The Protestant Ethic and the Spirit of Capitalism.*

[15] *Gesammelte Aufsätze zur Religionssoziologie.* See also *Structure of Social Action,* Chaps. XIV, XV, and XVII.

religious ideas in these cases to any features of an independently existent social structure or economic situation, though he continually insisted on the very great importance of situational factors in a number of different connections.[16] These factors, however, served only to pose the problems with which great movements of religious thought have been concerned. But the distinctive cognitive patterns were only understandable as a result of a cumulative tradition of intellectual effort in grappling with the problems thus presented and formulated.

For present purposes, even more important than Weber's views about the independent causal significance of religious ideas is his clarification of their functional relation to the system of action. Following up the same general line of analysis which provides one of the major themes of Pareto's and Malinowski's work, Weber made clear above all that there is a fundamental distinction between the significance for human action of problems of empirical causation and what, on the other hand, he called the "problem of meaning." In such cases as premature death through accident, the problem of *how* it happened in the sense of an adequate explanation of empirical causes can readily be solved to the satisfaction of most minds and yet leave a sense not merely of emotional but of cognitive frustration with respect to the problem of *why* such things must happen. Correlative with the functional need for emotional adjustment to such experiences as death is a cognitive need for understanding, for trying to have it "make sense." Weber attempted to show that problems of this nature, concerning the discrepancy between normal human interests and expectations in any situation or society and what actually happens, are inherent in the nature of human existence. They always pose problems of the order which on the most generalized line have come to be known as the problem of evil, of the meaning of suffering, and the like. In terms of his comparative material, however, Weber shows there are different directions of definition of human situations in which rationally integrated solutions of these problems may be sought. It is differentiation with respect to the treatment of precisely such problems which constitute the primary modes of variation between the great systems of religious thought.

[16] See especially his treatment of the rôle of the balance of social power in the establishment of the ascendancy of the Brahmans in India, and of the international position of the people of Israel in the definition of religious problems for the prophetic movement.

Such differences as, for instance, that between the Hindu philosophy of Karma and transmigration and the Christian doctrine of Grace with their philosophical backgrounds are not of merely speculative significance. Weber is able to show, in ways which correlate directly with the work of Malinowski and Durkheim, how intimately such differences in doctrine are bound up with practical attitudes towards the most various aspects of everyday life. For if we can speak of a need to understand ultimate frustrations in order for them to "make sense," it is equally urgent that the values and goals of everyday life should also "make sense." A tendency to integration of these two levels seems to be inherent in human action. Perhaps the most striking feature of Weber's analysis is the demonstration of the extent to which precisely the variations in socially sanctioned values and goals in secular life correspond to the variations in the dominant religious philosophy of the great civilizations.

It can be shown with little difficulty that these results of Weber's comparative and dynamic study integrate directly with the conceptual scheme developed as a result of the work of the other writers. Thus Weber's theory of the positive significance of religious ideas is in no way to be confused with the earlier naïvely rationalistic positivism. The influence of religious doctrine is not exerted through the actor's coming to a conviction and then acting upon it in a rational sense. It is rather, on the individual level, a matter of introducing a determinate structure at certain points in the system of action where, in relation to the situations men have to face, other elements, such as their emotional needs, do not suffice to determine specific orientations of behavior. In the theories of Malinowski and Durkheim, certain kinds of sentiments and emotional reactions were shown to be essential to a functioning social system. These cannot stand alone, however, but are necessarily integrated with cognitive patterns; for without them there could be no coordination of action in a coherently structured social system. This is because functional analysis of the structure of action shows that situations must be subjectively defined, and the goals and values to which action is oriented must be congruent with these definitions, must, that is, have "meaning."

It is of course never safe to say a scientific conceptual scheme has reached a definitive completion of its development. Continual change is in the nature of science. There are, however, relative degrees of conceptual integration, and it seems safe to say that the cumulative results of the work just reviewed constitute in broad outline a relatively well-integrated analytical scheme which covers most of the more important broader aspects of the rôle of religion in social systems. It is unlikely that in the near future this analytical scheme will give way to a radical structural change, though notable refinement and revision is to be expected. It is perhaps safe to say that it places the sociology of religion for the first time on a footing where it is possible to combine empirical study and theoretical analysis on a large scale on a level in conformity with the best current standards of social science and psychology.

When we look back, the schemes of Tylor and Spencer seem hopelessly naïve and inadequate to the modern sociologist, anthropologist, or psychologist. It is, however, notable that the development sketched did not take place by repudiating their work and attempting to appeal directly to the facts without benefit of theory. The process was quite different. It consisted in raising problems which were inherent in the earlier scheme and modifying the scheme as a result of the empirical observation suggested by these problems. Thus Malinowski did not abandon all attempt to relate magic to rational technique. Not being satisfied with its identification with primitive science and technology, he looked for specific modes of difference from and relation to them, retaining the established interpretation of the nature and functions of rational technique as his initial point of reference. It is notable again that in this process the newer developments of psychological theory in relation to the rôle of emotional factors have played an essential part. The most fruitful results have not, however, resulted from substituting a psychological "theory of religion" for another type, but rather from incorporating the results of psychological investigation into a wider scheme.

In order for this development to take place, it was essential that certain elements of philosophical dogmatism in the older positivism should be overcome. One reason for the limitations of Spencer's insight lay in the presumption that if a cognitive pattern was significant to human action, it must be assimilable to the pattern of science. Pareto, however, showed clearly that the "pseudo-scientific" did not exhaust significant patterns which deviated from scientific standards. Malinowski went further in showing the functional relation of certain non-scientific ideas to elements of uncertainty and frustration which were inherent in the situation of action. Durkheim called attention to the importance of the relation of symbolism as distinguished from that of intrinsic causality in cognitive patterns. Finally, Weber integrated the various aspects of the rôle of non-empirical cognitive patterns in social action in terms of his theory of the significance of the problems of meaning and the corresponding cognitive structures, in a way which precluded, for analytical purposes, their being assimilated to the patterns of science.[17] All of these distinctions by virtue of which the cognitive patterns of religion are treated separately from those of science have positive significance for empirical understanding of religious phenomena. Like any such scientific categories, they are to the scientist sanctioned by the fact that they can be shown to work. Failure to make these distinctions does not in the present state of knowledge and in terms of the relevant frame of reference[18] help us to understand certain critically important facts of human life. What the philosophical significance of this situation may be is not as such the task of the social scientist to determine. Only one safe prediction on this level can be made. Any new philosophical synthesis will need positively to take account of these distinctions rather than to attempt to reinstate for the scientific level the older positivistic conception of the homogeneity of all human thought and its problems. If these distinctions are to be transcended it cannot well be in the form of "reducing" religious ideas to those of science—both in the sense of Western intellectual history—or vice versa. The proved scientific utility of the distinctions is sufficient basis on which to eliminate this as a serious possibility.

[17] See the writer's paper, "The Rôle of Ideas in Social Action," *American Sociological Review*, III, 1938, for a general analytical discussion of the problem.

[18] Every treatment of questions of fact and every empirical investigation is "in terms of a conceptual scheme." Scientifically the sole sanction of such a conceptual scheme is its "utility," the degree to which it "works" in facilitating the attainment of the goals of scientific investigation. Hence the conceptual structure of any system of scientific theory is subject to the same kind of relativity as is all science. It is, however, essential not to confuse this element of relativity with "arbitrariness." It is subject to the disciplining constraint both of verification in all questions of particular empirical fact, and of logical precision and consistency among the many different parts of a highly complex conceptual structure. The "theory of social action" is by now a theoretical structure so highly developed and with so many ramifications in both these respects that elements structurally essential to it cannot be lightly dismissed as expressing only "one point of view."

Political Philosophy and History[1]

by LEO STRAUSS

Reprinted from the *Journal of the History of Ideas*—Vol. X, No. 1, pp. 30-50

Political philosophy is not a historical discipline. The philosophic questions of the nature of political things and of the best, or just, political order are fundamentally different from historical questions, which always concern individuals: individual groups, individual human beings, individual achievements, individual "civilizations," the one individual "process" of human civilization from its beginning to the present, and so on. In particular, political philosophy is fundamentally different from the history of political philosophy itself. The question of the nature of political things and the answer to it cannot possibly be mistaken for the question of how this or that philosopher or all philosophers have approached, discussed or answered the philosophic question mentioned. This does not mean that political philosophy is absolutely independent of history. Without the experience of the variety of political institutions and convictions in different countries and at different times, the questions of the nature of political things and of the best, or the just, political order could never have been raised. And after they have been raised, only historical knowledge can prevent one from mistaking the specific features of the political life of one's time and one's country for the nature of political things. Similar considerations apply to the history of political thought and the history of political philosophy. But however important historical knowledge may be for political philosophy, it is only preliminary and auxiliary to political philosophy; it does not form an integral part of it.

This view of the relation of political philosophy to history was unquestionably predominant at least up to the end of the eighteenth century. In our time it is frequently rejected in favor of "historicism," *i.e.*, of the assertion that the fundamental distinction between philosophic and historical questions cannot in the last analysis be maintained. Historicism may therefore be said to question the possibility of political philosophy. At any rate it challenges a premise that was common to the whole tradition of politi-

[1] A Hebrew translation of this paper appeared in *Eyoon—Hebrew Journal of Philosophy*, I (1946), 129 ff.

cal philosophy and apparently never doubted by it. It thus seems to go deeper to the roots, or to be more philosophic, than the political philosophy of the past. In any case, it casts a doubt on the very questions of the nature of political things and of the best, or the just, political order. Thus it creates an entirely new situation for political philosophy. The question that it raises is to-day the most urgent question for political philosophy.

It may well be doubted whether the fusion of philosophy and history, as advocated by historicism, has ever been achieved, or even whether it can be achieved. Nevertheless that fusion appears to be, as it were, the natural goal toward which the victorious trends of nineteenth- and early twentieth-century thought converge. At any rate, historicism is not just one philosophic school among many, but a most powerful agent that affects more or less all present-day thought. As far as we can speak at all of the spirit of a time, we can assert with confidence that the spirit of our time is historicism.

Never before has man devoted such an intensive and such a comprehensive interest to his whole past, and to all aspects of his past, as he does to-day. The number of historical disciplines, the range of each, and the interdependence of them all are increasing almost constantly. Nor are these historical studies carried on by thousands of ever more specialized students considered merely instrumental, and without value in themselves: we take it for granted that historical knowledge forms an integral part of the highest kind of learning. To see this fact in the proper perspective, we need only look back to the past. When Plato sketched in his *Republic* a plan of studies he mentioned arithmetic, geometry, astronomy, and so on: he did not even allude to history. We cannot recall too often the saying of Aristotle (who was responsible for much of the most outstanding historical research done in classical antiquity) that poetry is more philosophic than history. This attitude was characteristic of all the classical philosophers and of all the philosophers of the Middle Ages. History was praised most highly not by the philosophers but by the rhetoricians. The history of philosophy in particular was not considered a philosophic discipline: it was left to antiquarians rather than to philosophers.

A fundamental change began to make itself felt only in the

sixteenth century. The opposition then offered to all earlier philosophy, and especially to all earlier political philosophy, was marked from the outset by a novel emphasis on history. That early turn toward history was literally absorbed by the "unhistorical" teachings of the Age of Reason. The "rationalism" of the seventeenth and eighteenth centuries was fundamentally much more "historical" than the "rationalism" of pre-modern times. From the seventeenth century onward, the rapprochement of philosophy and history increased almost from generation to generation at an ever accelerated pace. Toward the end of the seventeenth century it became customary to speak of "the spirit of a time." In the middle of the eighteenth century the term "philosophy of history" was coined. In the nineteenth century, the history of philosophy came to be generally considered a philosophical discipline. The teaching of the outstanding philosopher of the nineteenth century, Hegel, was meant to be a "synthesis" of philosophy and history. The "historical school" of the nineteenth century brought about the substitution of historical jurisprudence, historical political science, historical economic science for a jurisprudence, a political science, an economic science that were evidently "unhistorical" or at least a-historical.

The specific historicism of the first half of the nineteenth century was violently attacked because it seemed to lose itself in the contemplation of the past. Its victorious opponents did not, however, replace it by a non-historical philosophy, but by a more "advanced," and in some cases a more "sophisticated" form of historicism. The typical historicism of the twentieth century demands that each generation reinterpret the past on the basis of its own experience and with a view to its own future. It is no longer contemplative, but activistic; and it attaches to that study of the past which is guided by the anticipated future, or which starts from and returns to the analysis of the present, a crucial philosophic significance: it expects from it the ultimate guidance for political life. The result is visible in practically every curriculum and textbook of our time. One has the impression that the question of the nature of political things has been superseded by the question of the characteristic "trends" of the social life of the present and of their historical origins, and that the question of the best, or the just, political order has been superseded by the question of the probable or desirable future. The questions of the modern state, of modern government, of the ideals of Western civilisation, and so forth, occupy a place that was formerly occupied by the questions of *the* state and of *the* right way of life. Philosophic questions have been transformed into historical questions— or more precisely into historical questions of a "futuristic" character.

This orientation characteristic of our time can be rendered legitimate only by historicism. Historicism appears in the most varied guises and on the most different levels. Tenets and arguments that are the boast of one type of historicism, provoke the smile of the adherents of others. The most common form of historicism expresses itself in the demand that the questions of the nature of political things, of *the* state, of the nature of man, and so forth, be replaced by the questions of the modern state, of modern government, of the present political situation, of modern man, of our society, our culture, our civilization, and so forth. Since it is hard to see, however, how one can speak adequately of the modern state, of our civilization, of modern man, etc., without knowing first what a state is, what a civilization is, what man's nature is, the more thoughtful forms of historicism admit that the universal questions of traditional philosophy cannot be abandoned. Yet they assert that any answer to these questions, any attempt at clarifying or discussing them, and indeed any precise formulation of them, is bound to be "historically conditioned," *i.e.*, to remain dependent on the specific situation in which they are suggested. No answer to, no treatment or precise formulation of, the universal questions can claim to be of universal validity, of validity for all times. Other historicists go to the end of the road by declaring that while the universal questions of traditional philosophy cannot be abandoned without abandoning philosophy itself, philosophy itself and its universal questions themselves are "historically conditioned," *i.e.*, essentially related to a specific "historic" type, *e.g.*, to Western man or to the Greeks and their intellectual heirs.

To indicate the range of historicism, we may refer to two assumptions characteristic of historicism and to-day generally accepted. "History" designated originally a particular kind of knowledge or inquiry. Historicism assumes that the object of historical knowledge, which it calls "History," is a "field," a "world" of its own fundamentally different from, although of course related to, that other "field," "Nature." This assumption distinguishes historicism most clearly from the pre-historicist view, for which "History" as an object of knowledge did not exist, and which therefore did not even dream of a "philosophy of history" as an analysis of, or a speculation about, a specific "dimension of reality." The gravity of the assumption in question appears only after one has started wondering what the Bible or Plato, *e.g.*, would have called that X which we are in the habit of calling "History." Equally characteristic of historicism is the assumption that restorations of earlier teachings are impossible, or that every intended restoration necessarily leads to an essential modification of the restored teaching. This assumption can most easily be understood as a necessary consequence of the view that every teaching is essentially related to an unrepeatable "historical" situation.

An adequate discussion of historicism would be identical with a critical analysis of modern philosophy in general. We cannot dare try more than indicate some considerations which should prevent one from taking historicism for granted.

To begin with, we must dispose of a popular misunderstanding which is apt to blur the issue. It goes back to the attacks of early historicism on the political philosophy which had paved the way for the French Revolution. The representatives of the "historical school" assumed that certain influential philosophers of the eighteenth century had conceived of the right political order, or of the rational political order, as an order which should or could be established at any time and in any place, without any regard to the particular conditions of time and place. Over against this opinion they asserted that the only legitimate approach to political matters is the "historical" approach, *i.e.*, the understanding of the institutions of a given country as a product of its past. Legitimate political action must be based on such historical understanding, as distinguished from, and opposed to, the "abstract principles" of 1789 or any other "abstract principles." Whatever the deficiencies of eighteenth-century political philosophy may be, they certainly do not justify the suggestion that the non-historical philosophic approach must be replaced by a historical approach. Most political philosophers of the past, in spite or rather because of the non-historical character of their thought, distinguished as a matter of course between the philosophic question of the best political order, and the practical question as to whether that order could or should be established in a given country at a given time. They naturally knew that all political action, as distinguished from political philosophy, is concerned with individual situations, and must therefore be based on a clear grasp of the situation concerned, and therefore normally on an understanding of the causes or antecedents of that situation. They took it for granted that political action guided by the belief that what is most desirable in itself must be put into practice in all circumstances, regardless of the circumstances, befits harmless doves, ignorant of the wisdom of the serpent, but not sensible and good men. In short, the truism that all political action is concerned with, and therefore presupposes appropriate knowledge of, individual situations, individual commonwealths, individual institutions, and so on, is wholly irrelevant to the question raised by historicism.

For a large number, that question is decided by the fact that historicism comes later in time than the non-historical political philosophy: "history" itself seems to have decided in favor of historicism. If, however, we do not worship "success" as such, we cannot maintain that the victorious cause is necessarily the cause of truth. For even if we grant that truth will prevail in the end, we cannot be certain that the end has already come. Those who prefer historicism to non-historical political philosophy because of the temporal relation of the two, interpret then that relation in a specific manner: they believe that the position which historically comes later can be presumed, other things being equal, to be more mature than the positions preceding it. Historicism, they would say, is based on an experience which required many centuries to mature—on the experience of many centuries which teaches us that non-historical political philosophy is a failure or a delusion. The political philosophers of the past attempted to answer the question of the best political order once and for all. But the result of all their efforts has been that there are almost as many answers, as many political philosophies as there have been political philosophers. The mere spectacle of "the anarchy of systems," of "the disgraceful variety" of philosophies seems to refute the claim of each philosophy. The history of political philosophy, it is asserted, refutes non-historical political philosophy as such, since the many irreconcilable political philosophies refute each other.

Actually, however, that history does not teach us that the political philosophies of the past refute each other. It teaches us merely that they contradict each other. It confronts us then with the philosophic question as to which of two given contradictory theses concerning political fundamentals is true. In studying the history of political philosophy, we observe, *e.g.*, that some political philosophers distinguish between State and Society, whereas others explicitly or implicitly reject that distinction. This observation compels us to raise the philosophic question whether and how far the distinction is adequate. Even if history could teach us that the political philosophy of the past has failed, it would not teach us more than that non-historical political philosophy has hitherto failed. But what else would this mean except that we do not truly know the nature of political things and the best, or just, political order? This is so far from being a new insight due to historicism that it is implied in the very name "philosophy." If the "anarchy of systems" exhibited by the history of philosophy proves anything, it proves our ignorance concerning the most important subjects (of which ignorance we can be aware without historicism), and therewith it proves the necessity of philosophy. It may be added that the "anarchy" of the historical political philosophies of our time, or of present-day interpretations of the past, is not conspicuously smaller than that of the non-historical political philosophies of the past.

Yet it is not the mere variety of political philosophies which allegedly shows the futility of non-historical political philosophy. Most historicists consider decisive the fact, which can be established by historical studies, that a close relation exists between each political philosophy and the historical situation in which it emerged. The variety of political philosophies, they hold, is above all a function of the variety of historical situations. The history of political philosophy does not teach merely that the political philosophy of Plato, *e.g.*, is irreconcilable with the political philosophy, say, of Locke. It also teaches that Plato's political philosophy is essentially related to the Greek city of the fourth century B.C., just as Locke's political philosophy is essentially related to the English revolution of 1688. It thus shows that no political philosophy can reasonably claim to be valid beyond the historical situation to which it is essentially related.

Yet, not to repeat what has been indicated in the paragraph before the last, the historical evidence invoked in favor of historicism has a much more limited bearing than seems to be assumed. In the first place, historicists do not make sufficient allowance for the deliberate adaptation, on the part of the political philosophers of the past, of their views to the prejudices of their contemporaries. Superficial readers are apt to think that a political philosopher was under the spell of the historical situation in which he thought, when he was merely adapting the expression of his thought to that situation in order to be listened to at all. Many political philosophers of the past presented their teachings, not in scientific treatises proper, but in what we may call treatise-pamphlets. They did not limit themselves to expounding what they considered *the* political truth. They combined with that exposition an exposition of what they considered desirable or feasible in the circumstances, or intelligible on the basis of the generally received opinions; they communicated their views in a manner which was not purely "philosophical," but at the same time "civil."[2] Accordingly, by proving that their political teaching as a whole is "historically conditioned," we do not at all prove that their political philosophy proper is "historically conditioned."

Above all, it is gratuitously assumed that the relation between doctrines and their "times" is wholly unambiguous. The obvious possibility is overlooked that the situation to which one particular doctrine is related, is particularly favorable to the discovery of *the* truth, whereas all other situations may be more or less unfavorable. More generally expressed, in understanding the genesis of a doctrine we are not necessarily driven to the conclusion that the doctrine in question cannot simply be true. By proving, *e.g.*, that certain propositions of modern natural law "go back" to positive Roman law, we have not yet proven that the propositions in question are not *de jure naturali* but merely *de jure positivo*. For it is perfectly possible that the Roman jurists mistook certain principles of natural law for those of positive law, or that they merely "divined," and did not truly know, important elements of natural

[2] Compare Locke, *Of Civil Government*, I, Sect. 109, and II, Sect. 52, with his *Essay Concerning Human Understanding*, III, ch. 9, Sects. 3 and 22.

law. We cannot then stop at ascertaining the relations between a doctrine and its historical origins. We have to interpret these relations; and such interpretation presupposes the philosophic study of the doctrine in itself with a view to its truth or falsehood. At any rate, the fact (if it is a fact) that each doctrine is "related" to a particular historical setting does not prove at all that no doctrine can simply be true.

The old fashioned, not familiar with the ravages wrought by historicism, may ridicule us for drawing a conclusion which amounts to the truism that we cannot reasonably reject a serious doctrine before we have examined it adequately. In the circumstances we are compelled to state explicitly that prior to careful investigation we cannot exclude the possibility that a political philosophy which emerged many centuries ago is *the* true political philosophy, as true to-day as it was when it was first expounded. In other words, a political philosophy does not become obsolete merely because the historical situation, and in particular the political situation to which it was related has ceased to exist. For every political situation contains elements which are essential to all political situations: how else could one intelligibly call all these different political situations "political situations"?

Let us consider very briefly, and in a most preliminary fashion, the most important example. Classical political philosophy is not refuted, as some seem to believe, by the mere fact that the city, apparently the central subject of classical political philosophy, has been superseded by the modern state. Most classical philosophers considered the city the most perfect form of political organization, not because they were ignorant of any other form, nor because they followed blindly the lead given by their ancestors or contemporaries, but because they realized, at least as clearly as we realize it today, that the city is essentially superior to the other forms of political association known to classical antiquity, the tribe and the Eastern monarchy. The tribe, we may say tentatively, is characterized by freedom (public spirit) and lack of civilization (high development of the arts and sciences), and the Eastern monarchy is characterized by civilization and lack of freedom. Classical political philosophers consciously and reasonably preferred the city to other forms of political association, in the light of the standards of freedom and civilization. And this preference was not a peculiarity bound up with their particular historical situation. Up to and including the eighteenth century, some of the most outstanding political philosophers quite justifiably preferred the city to the modern state which had emerged since the sixteenth century, precisely because they measured the modern state of their time by the standards of freedom and civilization. Only in the nineteenth century did classical political philosophy in a sense become obsolete. The reason was that the state of the nineteenth century, as distinguished from the Macedonian and Roman empires, the feudal monarchy, and the absolute monarchy of the modern period, could plausibly claim to be at least as much in accordance with the standards of freedom and civilization as the Greek city had been. Even then classical political philosophy did not become completely obsolete, since it was classical political philosophy which had expounded in a "classic" manner the standards of freedom and civilization. This is not to deny that the emergence of modern democracy in particular has elicited, if it has not been the outcome of, such a reinterpretation of both "freedom" and "civilization" as could not have been foreseen by classical political philosophy. Yet that reinterpretation is of fundamental significance, not because modern democracy has superseded earlier forms of political association, or because it has been victorious—it has not always been victorious, and not everywhere—but because there are definite reasons for considering that reinterpretation intrinsically superior to the original version. Naturally, there are some who doubt the standards mentioned. But that doubt is as little restricted to specific historical situations as the standards themselves. There were classical political philosophers who decided in favor of the Eastern monarchy.

Before we can make an intelligent use of the historically ascertained relations between philosophic teachings and their "times," we must have subjected the doctrines concerned to a philosophic critique concerned exclusively with their truth or falsehood. A philosophic critique in its turn presupposes an adequate understanding of the doctrine subjected to the critique. An adequate interpretation is such an interpretation as understands the thought of a philosopher exactly as he understood it himself. All historical evidence adduced in support of historicism presupposes as a matter of course that adequate understanding of the philosophy of the past is possible on the basis of historicism. This presupposition is open to grave doubts. To see this we must consider historicism in the light of the standards of historical exactness which, according to common belief, historicism was the first to perceive, to elaborate, or at least to divine.

Historicism discovered these standards while fighting the doctrine which preceded it and paved the way for it. That doctrine was the belief in progress: the conviction of the superiority, say, of the late eighteenth century to all earlier ages, and the expectation of still further progress in the future. The belief in progress stands midway between the non-historical view of the philosophic tradition and historicism. It agrees with the philosophic tradition in so far as both admit that there are universally valid standards which do not require, or which are not susceptible of, historical proof. It deviates from the philosophic tradition in so far as it is essentially a view concerning "the historical process"; it asserts that there is such a thing as "the historical process" and that that process is, generally speaking, a "progress": a progress of thought and institutions toward an order which fully agrees with certain presupposed universal standards of human excellence.

In consequence, the belief in progress, as distinguished from the views of the philosophic tradition, can be legitimately criticized on purely historical grounds. This was done by early historicism, which showed in a number of cases—the most famous example is the interpretation of the Middle Ages—that the "progressivist" view of the past was based on an utterly insufficient understanding of the past. It is evident that our understanding of the past will tend to be the more adequate, the more we are interested in the past. But we cannot be passionately interested, seriously interested in the past if we know beforehand that the present is in the most important respect superior to the past. Historians who started from this assumption felt no necessity to understand the past in itself; they understood it only as a preparation for the present. In studying a doctrine of the past, they did not ask primarily, what was the conscious and deliberate intention of its originator? They preferred to ask, what is the contribution of the doctrine to our beliefs? What is the meaning, unknown to the originator, of the doctrine from the point of view of the present? What is its meaning in the light of later discoveries or inventions?

They took it for granted then that it is possible and even necessary to understand the thinkers of the past better than those thinkers understood themselves.

Against this approach, the "historical consciousness" rightly protested in the interest of historical truth, of historical exactness. The task of the historian of thought is to understand the thinkers of the past exactly as they understood themselves, or to revitalize their thought according to their own interpretation. If we abandon this goal, we abandon the only practicable criterion of "objectivity" in the history of thought. For, as is well-known, the same historical phenomenon appears in different lights in different historical situations; new experience seems to shed new light on old texts. Observations of this kind seem to suggest that the claim of any one interpretation to be *the* true interpretation is untenable. Yet the observations in question do not justify this suggestion. For the seemingly infinite variety of ways in which a given teaching can be understood does not do away with the fact that the originator of the doctrine understood it in one way only, provided he was not confused. The indefinitely large variety of equally legitimate interpretations of a doctrine of the past is due to conscious or unconscious attempts to understand its author better than he understood himself. But there is only one way of understanding him as he understood himself.

Now, historicism is constitutionally unable to live up to the very standards of historical exactness which it might be said to have discovered. For historicism is the belief that the historicist approach is superior to the non-historical approach, but practically the whole thought of the past was radically "unhistorical." Historicism is therefore compelled, by its principle, to attempt to understand the philosophy of the past better than it understood itself. The philosophy of the past understood itself in a non-historical manner, but historicism must understand it "historically." The philosophers of the past claimed to have found *the* truth, and not merely the truth for their times. The historicist, on the other hand, believes that they were mistaken in making that claim, and he cannot help making that belief the basis of his interpretation. Historicism then merely repeats, if sometimes in a more subtle form, the sin for which it upbraided so severely the "progressivist" historiography. For, to repeat, our understanding of the thought of the past is liable to be the more adequate, the less the historian is convinced of the superiority of his own point of view, or the more he is prepared to admit the possibility that he may have to learn something, not merely about the thinkers of the past, but from them. To understand a serious teaching, we must be seriously interested in it, we must take it seriously, *i.e.*, we must be willing to consider the possibility that it is simply true. The historicist as such denies that possibility as regards any philosophy of the past. Historicism naturally attaches a much greater importance to the history of philosophy than any earlier philosophy has done. But unlike most earlier philosophies, it endangers by its principle, if contrary to its original intention, any adequate understanding of the philosophies of the past.

It would be a mistake to think that historicism could be the outcome of an unbiased study of the history of philosophy, and in particular of the history of political philosophy. The historian may have ascertained that all political philosophies are related to specific historical settings, or that only such men as live in a specific historical situation have a natural aptitude for accepting a given political philosophy. He cannot thus rule out the possibility that the historical setting of one particular political philosophy is the ideal condition for the discovery of *the* political truth. Historicism cannot then be established by historical evidence. Its basis is a philosophic analysis of thought, knowledge, truth, philosophy, political things, political ideals, and so on, a philosophic analysis allegedly leading to the result that thought, knowledge, truth, philosophy, political things, political ideals, and so on, are essentially and radically "historical." The philosophic analysis in question presents itself as the authentic interpretation of the experience of many centuries with political philosophy. The political philosophers of the past attempted to answer the question of the best political order once and for all. Each of them held explicitly or implicitly that all others had failed. It is only after a long period of trial and error that political philosophers started questioning the possibility of answering the fundamental questions once and for all. The ultimate result of that reflection is historicism.

Let us consider how far that result would affect political philosophy. Historicism cannot reasonably claim that the fundamental questions of political philosophy must be replaced by questions of a historical character. The question of the best political order, *e.g.*, cannot be replaced by a discussion "of the operative ideals which maintain a particular type of state," modern democracy, *e.g.*; for "any thorough discussion" of those ideals "is bound to give some consideration to the absolute worth of such ideals."[3] Nor can the question of the best political order be replaced by the question of the future order. For even if we could know with certainty that the future order is to be, say, a communist world society, we should not know more than that the communist world society is the only alternative to the destruction of modern civilization, and we should still have to wonder which alternative is preferable. Under no circumstances can we avoid the question as to whether the probable future order is desirable, indifferent or abominable. In fact, our answer to that question may influence the prospects of the probable future order becoming actually the order of the future. What we consider desirable in the circumstances depends ultimately on universal principles of preference, on principles whose political implications, if duly elaborated, would present our answer to the question of the best political order.

What historicism could reasonably say, if the philosophic analysis on which it is based is correct, is that all answers to the universal philosophic questions are necessarily "historically conditioned," or that no answer to the universal questions will in fact be universally valid. Now, every answer to a universal question necessarily intends to be universally valid. The historicist thesis amounts then to this, that there is an inevitable contradiction between the intention of philosophy and its fate, between the non-historical intention of the philosophic answers and their fate always to remain "historically conditioned." The contradiction is inevitable because, on the one hand, evident reasons compel us to raise the universal questions and to attempt to arrive at adequate answers, *i.e.*, universal answers; and, on the other hand, all human thought is enthralled by opinions and convictions which differ from historical situation to historical situation. The historical limitation of a given answer necessarily escapes him who gives the answer. The historical conditions which prevent any answer from being universally valid have the character of invisible walls. For

[3] A. D. Lindsay *The Modern Democratic State* (Oxford, 1943), I, 45.

if a man knew that his answer would be determined, not by his free insight into the truth, but by his historical situation, he could no longer identify himself with or wholeheartedly believe in, his answer. We should then know with certainty that no answer which suggests itself to us can be simply true, but we could not know the precise reason why this is the case. The precise reason would be the problematic validity of the deepest prejudice, necessarily hidden from us, of our time. If this view is correct, political philosophy would still have to raise the fundamental and universal questions which no thinking man can help raising once he has become aware of them, and to try to answer them. But the philosopher would have to accompany his philosophic effort by a coherent reflection on his historical situation in order to emancipate himself as far as possible from the prejudices of his age. That historical reflection would be in the service of the philosophic effort proper, but would by no means be identical with it.

On the basis of historicism, philosophic efforts would then be enlightened from the outset as to the fact that the answers to which they may lead will necessarily be "historically conditioned." They would be accompanied by coherent reflections on the historical situation in which they were undertaken. We might think that such philosophic efforts could justly claim to have risen to a higher level of reflection, or to be more philosophic, than the "naive" non-historical philosophy of the past. We might think for a moment that historical political philosophy is less apt to degenerate into dogmatism than was its predecessor. But a moment's reflection suffices to dispel that delusion. Whereas for the genuine philosopher of the past all the answers of which he could possibly think were, prior to his examination of them, open possibilities, the historicist philosopher excludes, prior to his examining them, all the answers suggested in former ages. He is no less dogmatic, he is much more dogmatic, than the average philosopher of the past. In particular, the coherent reflection of the philosopher on his historical situation is not necessarily a sign that, other things being equal, his philosophic reflection is on a higher level than that of philosophers who were not greatly concerned with their historical situation. For it is quite possible that the modern philosopher is in much greater need of reflection on his situation because, having abandoned the resolve to look at things *sub specie aeternitatis,* he is much more exposed to, and enthralled by, the convictions and "trends" dominating his age. Reflection on one's historical situation may very well be no more than a remedy for a deficiency which has been caused by historicism, or rather by the deeper motives which express themselves in historicism, and which did not hamper the philosophic efforts of former ages.

It seems as if historicism were animated by the certainty that the future will bring about the realization of possibilities of which no one has ever dreamt, or can ever dream, whereas non-historical political philosophy lived not in such an open horizon, but in a horizon closed by the possibilities known at the time. Yet the possibilities of the future are not unlimited as long as the differences between men and angels and between men and brutes have not been abolished, or as long as there are political things. The possibilities of the future are not wholly unknown, since their limits are known. It is true that no one can possibly foresee what sensible or mad possibilities, whose realization is within the limits of human nature, will be discovered in the future. But it is also true that it is hard to say anything at present about possibilities which are at present not even imagined. Therefore, we cannot help following the precedent set by the attitude of earlier political philosophy toward the possibilities which have been discovered, or even realized since. We must leave it to the political philosophers of the future to discuss the possibilities which will be known only in the future. Even the absolute certainty that the future will witness such fundamental and at the same time sensible changes of outlook as can not even be imagined now, could not possibly influence the questions and the procedure of political philosophy.

It would likewise be wrong to say that whereas non-historical political philosophy believed in the possibility of answering fundamental questions once and for all, historicism implies the insight that final answers to fundamental questions are impossible. Every philosophic position implies such answers to fundamental questions as claim to be final, to be true once and for all. Those who believe in "the primary significance of the unique and morally ultimate character of the concrete situation," and therefore reject the quest for "general answers supposed to have a universal meaning that covers and dominates all particulars," do not hesitate to offer what claim to be final and universal answers to the questions as to what "a moral situation" is and as to what "*the* distinctively moral traits," or "*the* virtues" are.[4] Those who believe in progress toward a goal which itself is essentially progressive, and therefore reject the question of the best political order as "too static," are convinced that their insight into the actuality of such a progress "has come to stay." Similarly, historicism merely replaced one kind of finality by another kind of finality, by the final conviction that all human answers are essentially and radically "historical." Only under one condition could historicism claim to have done away with all pretence to finality, if it presented the historicist thesis not as simply true, but as true for the time being only. In fact, if the historicist thesis is correct, we cannot escape the consequence that that thesis itself is "historical" or valid, because meaningful, for a specific historical situation only. Historicism is not a cab which one can stop at his convenience: historicism must be applied to itself. It will thus reveal itself as relative to modern man; and this will imply that it will be replaced, in due time, by a position which is no longer historicist. Some historicists would consider such a development a manifest decline. But in so doing they would ascribe to the historical situation favorable to historicism an absoluteness which, as a matter of principle, they refuse to ascribe to any historical situation.

Precisely the historicist approach would compel us then to raise the question of the essential relation of historicism to modern man, or, more exactly, the question as to what specific need, characteristic of modern man, as distinguished from pre-modern man, underlies his passionate turn to history. To elucidate this question, as far as possible in the present context, we shall consider the argument in favor of the fusion of philosophic and historical studies which appears to be most convincing.

Political philosophy is the attempt to replace our opinions about political fundamentals by knowledge about them. Its first task consists therefore in making fully explicit our political ideas, so that they can be subjected to critical analysis. "Our ideas" are only partly our ideas. Most of our ideas are abbreviations or residues of the thought of other people, of our teachers (in the broadest sense of the term) and of our teachers' teachers; they are abbreviations and residues of the thought of the past. These

[4] John Dewey, *Reconstruction in Philosophy* (New York, 1920), 189 and 163 f.

thoughts were once explicit and in the center of consideration and discussion. It may even be presumed that they were once perfectly lucid. By being transmitted to later generations they have possibly been transformed, and there is no certainty that the transformation was effected consciously and with full clarity. At any rate, what were once certainly explicit ideas passionately discussed, although not necessarily lucid ideas have now degenerated into mere implications and tacit presuppositions. Therefore, if we want to clarify the political ideas we have inherited, we must actualize their implications, which were explicit in the past, and this can be done only by means of the history of political ideas. This means that the clarification of our political ideas insensibly changes into and becomes indistinguishable from the history of political ideas. To this extent the philosophic effort and the historical effort have become completely fused.

Now, the more we are impressed by the necessity of engaging in historical studies in order to clarify our political ideas, the more we must be struck by the observation that the political philosophers of former ages did not feel such a necessity at all. A glance at Aristotle's *Politics, e.g.*, suffices to convince us that Aristotle succeeded perfectly in clarifying the political ideas obtaining in his age, although he never bothered about the history of those ideas. The most natural, and the most cautious, explanation of this paradoxical fact would be, that perhaps our political ideas have a character fundamentally different from that of the political ideas of former ages. Our political ideas have the particular character that they cannot be clarified fully except by means of historical studies, whereas the political ideas of the past could be clarified perfectly without any recourse to their history.

To express this suggestion somewhat differently, we shall make a somewhat free use of the convenient terminology of Hume. According to Hume, our ideas are derived from "impressions"—from what we may call first-hand experience. To clarify our ideas and to distinguish between their genuine and their spurious elements (or between those elements which are in accordance with first-hand experience and those which are not), we must trace each of our ideas to the impressions from which it is derived. Now it is doubtful whether all ideas are related to impressions in fundamentally the same way. The idea of the city, *e.g.*, can be said to be derived from the impressions of cities in fundamentally the same way as the idea of the dog is derived from the impressions of dogs. The idea of the state, on the other hand, is not derived simply from the impression of states. It emerged partly owing to the transformation, or reinterpretation, of more elementary ideas, of the idea of the city in particular. Ideas which are derived directly from impressions can be clarified without any recourse to history; but ideas which have emerged owing to a specific transformation of more elementary ideas cannot be clarified but by means of the history of ideas.

We have illustrated the difference between our political ideas and earlier political ideas by the examples of the ideas of the state and of the city. The choice of these examples was not accidental; for the difference with which we are concerned is the specific difference between the character of modern philosophy on the one hand, and that of pre-modern philosophy on the other. This fundamental difference was described by Hegel in the following terms: "The manner of study in ancient times is distinct from that of modern times, in that the former consisted in the veritable training and perfecting of the natural consciousness. Trying its powers at each part of its life severally, and philosophizing about everything it came across, the natural consciousness transformed itself into a universality of abstract understanding which was active in every matter and in every respect. In modern times, however, the individual finds the abstract form ready made."[5] Classical philosophy originally acquired the fundamental concepts of political philosophy by starting from political phenomena as they present themselves to "the natural consciousness," which is a pre-philosophic consciousness. These concepts can therefore be understood, and their validity can be checked, by direct reference to phenomena as they are accessible to "the natural consciousness." The fundamental concepts which were the final result of the philosophic efforts of classical antiquity, and which remained the basis of the philosophic efforts of the Middle Ages, were the starting-point of the philosophic efforts of the modern period. They were partly taken for granted and partly modified by the

[5] *The Phenomenology of the Mind,* tr. J. B. Baillie, 2nd edition (London, New York, 1931), 94. I have changed Baillie's translation a little in order to bring out somewhat more clearly the intention of Hegel's remark.—For a more precise analysis, see Jacob Klein, "Die griechische Logistik und die Entstehung der modernen Algebra," *Quellen und Studien zur Geschichte der Mathematik, Astronomie und Physik,* vol. 3, Heft 1 (Berlin, 1934), 64–66, and Heft 2 (Berlin, 1936), 122 ff.

founders of modern political philosophy. In a still more modified form they underlie the political philosophy or political science of our time. In so far as modern political philosophy emerges, not simply from "the natural consciousness," but by way of a modification of, and even in opposition to, an earlier political philosophy, a tradition of political philosophy, its fundamental concepts cannot be fully understood until we have understood the earlier political philosophy from which, and in opposition to which, they were acquired, and the specific modification by virtue of which they were acquired.

It is not the mere "dependence" of modern philosophy on classical philosophy, but the specific character of that "dependence," which accounts for the fact that the former needs to be supplemented by an intrinsically philosophic history of philosophy. For medieval philosophy too was "dependent" on classical philosophy, and yet it was not in need of the history of philosophy as an integral part of its philosophic efforts. When a medieval philosopher studied Aristotle's *Politics, e.g.*, he did not engage in a historical study. The *Politics* was for him an authoritative text. Aristotle was *the* philosopher, and hence the teaching of the *Politics* was, in principle, *the* true philosophic teaching. However he might deviate from Aristotle in details, or as regards the application of the true teaching to circumstances which Arisotle could not have foreseen, the basis of the medieval philosopher's thought remained the Aristotelian teaching. That basis was always present to him, it was contemporaneous with him. His philosophic study was identical with the adequate understanding of the Aristotelian teaching. It was for this reason that he did not need historical studies in order to understand the basis of his own thought. It is precisely that contemporaneous philosophic thought with its basis which no longer exists in modern philosophy, and whose absence explains the eventual transformation of modern philosophy into an intrinsically historical philosophy. Modern thought is in all its forms, directly or indirectly, determined by the idea of progress. This idea implies that the most elementary questions can be settled once and for all so that future generations can dispense with their further discussion, but can erect on the foundations once laid an ever-growing structure. In this way, the foundations are covered up. The only proof necessary to guarantee their solidity seems to be that the structure stands and grows. Since philosophy demands, however, not merely solidity so understood, but lucidity and truth, a special kind of inquiry becomes necessary whose purpose it is to keep alive the recollection, and the problem, of the foundations hidden by progress. This philosophic enquiry is the history of philosophy or of science.

We must distinguish between inherited knowledge and independently acquired knowledge. By inherited knowledge we understand the philosophic or scientific knowledge a man takes over from former generations, or, more generally expressed, from others; by independently acquired knowledge we understand the philosophic or scientific knowledge a mature scholar acquires in his unbiased intercourse, as fully enlightened as possible as to its horizon and its presuppositions, with his subject matter. On the basis of the belief in progress, this difference tends to lose its crucial significance. When speaking of a "body of knowledge" or of "the results of research," *e.g.*, we tacitly assign the same cognitive status to inherited knowledge and to independently acquired knowledge. To counteract this tendency a special effort is required to transform inherited knowledge into genuine knowledge by re-vitalizing its original discovery, and to discriminate between the genuine and the spurious elements of what claims to be inherited knowledge. This truly philosophic function is fulfilled by the history of philosophy or of science.

If, as we must, we apply historicism to itself, we must explain historicism in terms of the specific character of modern thought, or, more precisely, of modern philosophy. In doing so, we observe that modern political philosophy or science, as distinguished from pre-modern political philosophy or science, is in need of the history of political philosophy or science as an integral part of its own efforts, since, as modern political philosophy or science itself admits or even emphasizes, it consists to a considerable extent of inherited knowledge whose basis is no longer contemporaneous or immediately accessible. The recognition of this necessity cannot be mistaken for historicism. For historicism asserts that the fusion of philosophic and historical questions marks in itself a progress beyond "naïve" non-historical philosophy, whereas we limit ourselves to asserting that that fusion is, within the limits indicated, inevitable on the basis of modern philosophy, as distinguished from pre-modern philosophy or "the philosophy of the future."

The Study of Chinese Civilization*

by ARTHUR F. WRIGHT

Reprinted from the *Journal of the History of Ideas*—Vol. XXI, No. 2, pp. 233-255

When Westerners in the late XVIIIth and early XIXth centuries first turned to the serious study of Chinese civilization, they were influenced by a well-developed image of the object of their study. The Jesuits had, for their own reasons, given European man a peculiarly colored picture of that distant land, and the men of the Enlightenment had, in turn, put that picture to their own uses.[1] Objects from the hands of Chinese artists and artisans had been brought to Europe and proved to have an immediate appeal to the taste of the European upper classes.

Western scholars were persuaded that they were contemplating the oldest continuous socio-political order on earth with a record of that continuity so vast, detailed, and complex as to reduce any researcher to despair. They drew from the writings of the Jesuits and the Enlightenment the impression that Chinese civilization had an order, a stability, a symmetry, a "rationality" in strong contrast to the divided, uneasy, strife-ridden world of the West. This complex of impressions, together with the aesthetic appeal of Chinese objects of art, set the tone of the early European study of China. If it is true, as Max Scheler suggested, that the *aficionado* is the forerunner of the researcher, it would be correct to say that the sinophile is the forerunner, if not the father of the sinologue. As Europeans,[2] influenced by this sort of sinophilia, began their arduous progress toward some understanding of this remote cultural entity, they were guided in their choice of subject and in their methods and interpretations by the traditions of Chinese scholarship. After all, who could speak with more authority than those Chinese scholars who, as officials, had built and maintained that vast socio-political edifice and who, as writers, had celebrated its values, recorded its history, and organized its literary heritage? Thus the Europeans, in their early studies, were in a sense the captives of the tradition they studied and of the self-image of Chinese civilization which the perpetuators of that tradition had developed over the millenia.

From another vantage point, Japanese scholars continued, as they had for some thirteen centuries, to contemplate with awe the great

---

* This essay was first presented on the kind invitation of Professor Milton Singer and the late Robert Redfield to the Seminar on the Comparative Study of Civilizations held at the Center for Advanced Study in the Behavioral Sciences during the Spring months of 1958.

[1] Cf. Virgile Pinot, *La Chine et la formation de l'esprit philosophique en France* (Paris, 1932).

[2] Cf. Max Scheler, *Vom Ewigen im Menschen* (Leipzig, 1921), I, 94-5.

civilization of China to which Japan owed an inestimable cultural debt. Despite signs of restiveness in the XVIIIth and early XIXth centuries, the dominant tradition of Japanese scholarship was Confucian; Japanese scholars of China (*Kangakusha* ["Chinese Scholars"] or *Jusha* ["Confucianists"]) shared with Chinese literati a commitment to many of the ideas, the values, and the methods of study which had been evolved through the centuries in China. Japanese scholars tended to select the same problems for textual study, the same poetic models for appreciation and imitation, the same philosophic values by which they aspired to order the self and society. The intellectual and cultural context of their view of Chinese civilization was utterly different from that in which the early European sinologues worked, but both were subservient to the Chinese self-image; both were in thrall to the literary and cultural traditions of the Chinese elite.

If these scholars from China, Europe, and Japan had been able to meet and talk together in the years from 1800 to 1850, or even later, they would have been in general agreement about the history, the literature, the philosophy, and the society of China: they would have agreed with the Chinese scholar on what Chinese civilization was and what it meant; they would have been agreed on how that civilization should be studied. In what follows, we shall first attempt to describe as briefly as possible the Chinese self-image that imposed itself on Chinese and foreign scholars alike, forming and limiting what they thought and said about this civilization. Second, we shall sketch some of the complex ways in which this self-image broke up under the impact of catastrophic events and gradually lost its authority over Chinese and foreigners alike. Third, we shall suggest some of the new ways of looking at and evaluating this civilization which emerged in the wake of revolutionary change in China and in response to developments in the intellectual world of the West. Last, we shall attempt a brief appraisal of recent scholarship and of trends which suggest possibilities for future development.

The Self-image of Chinese Civilization in the Early XIXth Century

In speaking of the self-image of Chinese civilization at any given time, we must introduce a number of qualifications. First of all, there was no word in Chinese which carried quite the same freight of meaning and of ambiguity which our term "civilization" does. When the time came for the Chinese to translate our word 'culture' and 'civilization,' the common element in both the terms chosen was *wen* —a word with a galaxy of meanings: the ornamented as opposed to the plain, the written as opposed to the spoken, the suasive as opposed to the coercive, the refined as opposed to the crude, etc. But the root *civis*, citizen, or *civitas*, city, is nowhere expressed or implied. This is simply to caution that in none of the Chinese talk of their culture and its characteristics is " cityfication " implied or hinted at. Further, in the literature of imperial China there is little to suggest that concept of progressive, unilinear movement towards " civilization " which has been so prevalent in Western thought since the XVIIIth century. But one does find *wen* used in combination with other terms to mean something close to our ' civilize,' i.e., " to bring out of a state of barbarism, to instruct in the arts of life; to enlighten and refine." The reference of such phrases is generally to the aborigines and the peoples of the steppe frontiers whom the Chinese, through force and suasion plus the attractive power of their culture (*wen*), ' converted ' to the Chinese way of life.

The Chinese, in writing of their common culture, common traditions, and common social order, used the word *T'ien-hsia,* ' under-heaven.' And in naming the things which this concept included, Chinese of successive centuries, like other civilized peoples, simplified and sifted out of the plethora of known facts about their commonalty those things which they felt to be important and essential to it—a body of myth by which they thought, acted, and judged. The structure of these successive bodies of myth changed from age to age, and so did their constituent elements. But at all times certain elements persisted that would appear in the myths of any generation of imperial China, and about which they would say, " Without this, our Chinese order would cease to exist." If we look in upon the Chinese literati between 1750 and 1840, we may be able to sketch the outlines of the body of myth by which they lived, the self-image of their civilization which they accepted and imposed upon neighboring states and upon those in distant lands who attempted to study Chinese civilization.

Before turning to some components of this self-image, we must emphasize that it was the literati, the perpetrators and chief beneficiaries of the Chinese order, who formed it; it was they who made the selection from the literature and from the facts of experience; it was they who propagated it among the masses of the Chinese people; it was they who, through writing and the exercise of power, minimized or glossed over the cracks, the fissures, the tensions and deviations which were as characteristic of China as of any other society in the continuous process of development. In the same way, the literati as a whole tended to resist or ignore those occasional radical critics who challenged some but never all of the assumptions of their class about the nature of Chinese society.[3] The result is a self-image of

[3] As examples of such critics one might mention Huang Tsung-hsi (1610–1695), Ku Yen-wu (1613–1682), and Wang Fu-chih (1619–1692). For a summary of their

the civilization which has a deceptive symmetry, a self-consistency that belongs to myth and not to history.

In the interests of brevity, we shall attempt an outline of the self-image as it was about 1800, with the caution that on many of these items a voluminous literature exists and on the inter-relationships of these components far more could be said than the limits of the present paper permit.

1. China was a broad and populous and prosperous land located in the center of the flat earth and covered by the canopy of heaven. It was 'the central kingdom' (*chung-kuo*), the 'central land' (*chung-t'u*). (Jesuit maps of the world found acceptance only when they were revised to present China in the center of the page.)

2. China was 'central' in a cultural as well as a geographical sense (*Chung-hua:* 'The Central Cultural Florescence'). The Chinese had long conferred the blessings of civilization—writing, morals, rules of propriety, political institutions—upon those who had the misfortune to live beyond her borders and on those within who clung vainly to a more primitive way of life.

3. China was 'central' in politics as well. Through conquest and occupation, the Chinese imposed culture and political stability upon Central Asia, Tibet, Mongolia, and other lands far from the heart of the Empire. (These conquests were usually referred to by one or another euphemism suggesting that the subjugation of alien, often tribal, peoples was accomplished through 'the transforming virtue of the Son of Heaven,' i.e., through moral-cultural magnetism rather than military power.) Tributary states such as Korea adopted Chinese institutions, received the benefits of Chinese culture and protection, and showed their gratitude for the paternal concern of the Chinese emperor by sending regular tributary missions.

4. China had been and was self-sufficient, economically, ideologically, and in all other ways. "We have everything in abundance and require none of your manufactures," is the repeated reply to early Western requests for trading privileges. And to the Macartney mission's request (1793) that permission be granted to propagate Christianity, the Ch'ien-lung Emperor said, "Ever since the beginning of history, sage Emperors and wise rulers have bestowed on China a moral system and inculcated a code, which from time immemorial has been religiously observed by the myriads of my subjects. There has been no hankering after heterodox doctrines." [4]

---

views, cf. Ssu-yu Teng and John K. Fairbank, *China's Response to the West* (Cambridge, 1954), 6–10. On Huang, cf. William T. de Bary, " Chinese Despotism and the Confucian Ideal: a Seventeenth-Century View " in J. K. Fairbank, ed., *Chinese Thought and Institutions* (Chicago, 1957), 163–203.

[4] Cf. Bland and Backhouse, *Annals and Memoirs of the Court of Peking* (Boston, 1914), 330.

5. China's centrality, prosperity, and pre-eminence within the four seas were the legacy of the wise rulers of remote antiquity, of sages and their followers over innumerable generations who had formulated and developed the moral principles which were valid for all times and all peoples. Literate and responsible men of each generation were the guardians of the wisdom of the past; it was their duty to see that present reality was measured against immutable moral norms and that the history of China, seen as the record of men striving to realize the ideals of the sages, was scrupulously written and intensively studied.

6. Men discharging these responsibilities through study, contemplation, and writing perfected their character and became not only a learned but a moral elite. And, on the authority of the Classics, it was such men and only such men who should be entrusted with the management of the Chinese polity and society. Thus the scholar-official of 1800 saw himself as both guardian of the cultural heritage and the rightful wielder of power in state and society. Towards the masses he was to feel a paternal concern; the masses, on their part, were to feel gratitude and follow the directives and moral example of their betters.

7. The knowledge which, in its acquisition, perfected the character and gave the learned man his right to wealth, power, and status was varied, but the core was the Confucian Classics many of which he memorized in his youth. The Classics taught the cardinal virtues of filial submissiveness (*hsiao*), adherence to the rules of propriety (*li*), righteousness (*i*), loyalty (*chung*), etc. Historical works showed the working of these principles in past events. Poetry and painting, to be well regarded, should reflect the moral perfection of the poet or artist. Thus the cultural legacy of the past was the repository of wisdom, of guides to self-perfection and right action.

8. There were many ways to study this legacy. Since the phrases of the Classics contained all wisdom, commentaries on them contributed to self-development and guided posterity in understanding the words of the sages. Since the past was a repository of morally meaningful experience, the reconstruction of the past through the study of monuments, inscriptions, and historical texts was an estimable occupation for a man of learning. And, since it was a duty to express in a pleasing and proper style the truths one discovered, the study of literary exemplars was highly esteemed. Many more pedestrian studies were valued for the ways in which they rediscovered or reorganized segments of China's cultural past. Among these were bibliographical studies, collections of scattered works, local histories, collections of inscriptions, and encyclopedias. Such studies, bringing social prestige and often the rewards of public office, served to reinforce the accepted image of Chinese civilization in the minds of the

scholars and to perpetuate it from generation to generation.

This self-image was, as we have suggested, a simplification of the past and of the present. Like all such images, it had a symmetry and coherence which neither past nor present reality, in its fullness and variety, would confirm. It was the object of emotional commitment, and, in its composition, glossed over, ignored, or rationalized data and experience tending to impair its symmetry. Thus, for example, there had been centuries when the Chinese lost their cultural self-sufficiency and " hankered after heterodox doctrines " on a massive scale. And there had been many periods when the barbarians were ungratefully resistant to the meliorating influence of Chinese culture and instead imposed their harsh rule on the Central Kingdom itself; there were other periods when the tributary vassal states had failed to show grateful respect to their overlord. Under innumerable regimes, men of learning and character had been denied their proper status and public rôles or had been humiliated, driven from power, or killed. But these cases were rationalized into a martyrology meant to strengthen the moral fibre of the literati. In the world around him the scholar-official of 1800 saw much that was at odds with his image of Chinese civilization. In the earthy life of the villages, norms of propriety were often ignored, and the country gentry, however preoccupied with learning they might be, often failed to set the moral example which it was their duty to do. In hundreds of county seats the classically trained and presumably morally cultivated magistrates were less 'fathers and mothers of their people' than conscienceless exploiters. Evidence on every side testified to the power of the alien Manchu rulers—barbarians who, until recently, had resisted the supposedly irresistible magnetism of Chinese culture.

The literati's self-image of Chinese civilization survived—as all such images do—despite obvious conflicts with reality. It was sustained by the self-assurance of those who held it, by their cultural pride and relative isolation from external challenges. It was strengthened by the evident power of the Chinese state, the patent viability and prosperity of its socio-economic order. Even serious weakness and dislocation were rationalized in terms of a cyclical theory—a biological life-cycle analogy—which was itself a part of the body of myth we have just described. Such then are some of the aspects of the Chinese self-image of the years just before and after 1800, and some of the ways in which it sustained itself against the onslaughts of reality. It governed Chinese scholars' study and evaluation of their own civilization. Let us turn to its effects on sinologues in Japan and the West.

In the XVIIth and XVIIIth centuries, Japanese specialists on things Chinese (*Kangakusha*) were far more than academic 'sinologues.' As professional Confucianists (*Jusha*) many of them served the Tokugawa Shogunate and the feudal lords as ideologues, advisers on statecraft and ceremony, specialists on political economy, and teachers of Chinese morality and literature. The Kangakusha resembled the Chinese literati in having an interest both in scholarship and in the sphere of social and political action even though their field of action was limited by the warriors' monopoly of power.[5] Despite the fact that these Japanese scholars lived in a strikingly different society, much in their outlook shows the imprint of the image we have described; similarly much of their scholarship is motivated and directed in ways characteristic of the Chinese scholarly tradition.

For the Kangakusha, study of the Chinese Classics was the key to self-cultivation and to the welfare of state and society. Here are the fundamental principles of education as seen by Ito Jinsai (1627–1705), one of the greatest of the Kangakusha, whose school continued in operation until 1904: "First: education should perfect not only the mind but above all the will; in other words: it is more important to be a good man than to be a learned man. Second: education can only be achieved through the study and practice of the Way of the ancients, especially Confucius. This Way is their works, above all the *Analects*."[6] Ito regarded history, the Chinese histories, as *the* repositories of human experience, demonstrations, at their best, of the working of the moral dynamic in individual and collective life. The curriculum of Ito's school also included intensive study of the so-called "eight great prose writers of the T'ang and Sung Dynasties."[7] This was intended to develop a feeling for Chinese literary style and to perfect the student's ability to write in the only language proper for "civilized" men—Chinese.

There were various schools of Kangakusha, but disputes among them centered only on how and where to discover the true, correct, uncorrupted principles of the Chinese sages and on what interpretation of those principles to accept as authoritative.[8] We should say then that the Kangakusha tradition in Japan was unanalytical, save in moral-philosophic terms, of Chinese civilization. Its favorite medium was the commentary or interpretative essay on a Chinese work, a passage in the Classics, or an idea advanced by some Chinese thinker. It is thus in large part an exegetical tradition accompanied

[5] John W. Hall, "The Confucian Teacher in Tokugawa Japan" in David S. Nivison and Arthur F. Wright, eds., *Confucianism in Action* (Stanford, Calif., 1959), 268–301.

[6] Cf. Joseph Spae, *Ito Jinsai* (Peiping, 1948), 164.   [7] *Ibid.*, 173.

[8] Cf. William T. de Bary, "Some Common Tendencies in Neo-Confucianism" in *Confucianism in Action*, 25–49.

by the same concern for the discovery and preservation of every item about China's past that is characteristic of China's own scholars in the same period. The Kangakusha perpetuated in Japan the image of Chinese civilization we have described and the mode of studying that civilization which the literati tradition decreed. The emotional commitment to China which this involved and the disdain of the Japanese heritage which went with it did not go unchallenged, and the following attack suggests some of the points on which the nativists attacked the Kangakusha:

The perversity of the Confucians is that they know only China and are ignorant of our country. They grossly mock and sneer at things Japanese. While they are eating Japanese rice, wearing Japanese clothes, and living on Japanese soil, they praise China to the skies and have the deepest scorn for Japan. ... Such iniquitous Confucians are constantly praising China and prattling ' Chūka, Chūka ' (Chinese *Chung-hua*, central cultural florescence) whilst they scorn Japan and talk of ' Wazoku, Wazoku ' (customs of the dwarf barbarians—a classic Chinese way of referring to Japan). ... Though they are born in this country they know nothing of its morality, its practices, its ancient ways, its customs. They may be called ' men of wide learning and many talents ' (a Chinese cliché, *po-hsueh to-ts'ai*), but they are of no use to this country. Let them cease eating the rice produced in this land and starve to death, the sooner the better.[9]

In the very different society of Western Europe, the first serious study of China began, as we have suggested, in an intellectual climate where Romantic sinophilia lingered on as a legacy of the early Jesuit missionaries and of the Enlightenment. Yet, compared to the Japanese *Kangakusha,* living in a highly sinicized environment, the early European sinologues found the object of their study remote and perplexing. When Abel Rémusat (1788–1832) became the first holder of the Chair of Chinese at the Collège de France in 1814, he was wholly self-trained in Chinese and had developed his own vocabulary and grammar with only the dubious help of those earlier missionary writings that were available to him. The young Rémusat was by no means uncritical of the writings of missionaries, casual travelers, and the *philosophes,* but the literati self-image cast a part of its spell upon him: " Les Chinois sont une nation polie, paisible et laborieuse, et l'on peut dire qu'après les Européens il n'en est aucune qui ait fait d'aussi grands progrès dans la civilisation. Depuis la plus haute antiquité le savoir y a toujours été en recommandation, et l'ordre social fondé sur des institutions calculées d'après l'intérêt général. Libre de ce despotisme militaire que le musulmanisme a établi dans le

[9] From the *Ansai Zuihitsu* by Ise Sadatake (1717–1784), an authority on traditional Japanese military practices and a ritualist of the Shogun's court. Cf. *Kojiruien*, vol. 38 (Tokyo, 1933), 717–8.

reste de l'Asie, ignorant l'odieuse division des castes qui forme la base de la civilisation indienne, la Chine offre à l'extrémité de l'ancien continent un spectacle propre à consoler des scènes de violence et de dégradation qui frappent les yeux partout ailleurs. La piété filiale y est surtout en honneur. . . . La vénération même et l'obéissance qu'on doit au souverain et aux magistrats sont adoucies par une sorte de sentiment filial qui les inspire et les anoblit. . . . Il n'y a aucune caste privilégiée: tous les Chinois peuvent aspirer à tous les emplois auxquels on arrive par la voie des examens. . . ." [10]

The Chair of Chinese established in 1814 was regarded as complementary to the older posts in Arabic and Syriac, and thus Chinese studies were begun as a branch of 'Orientalism.' [11] This 'Orientalism' was the immediate intellectual context of Sinology in the early XIXth century and affected the growth and orientation of this new branch of learning. We might therefore inquire briefly into its origins.

One of the problems of late XVIIIth- and XIXth-century historical thought, influenced by the steadily increasing power and prosperity of Europe and by the idea of progress, was to categorize the histories of non-European peoples. This was done in several related ways. It was argued that Europe had the only 'history' worth consideration, that is, the only continuous series of stages in which the cumulative development of higher and higher forms of life could be discerned. In contrast, the civilizations of the Orient had a hierarchical and despotic organization which secured the changeless perpetuation of social and political institutions and of religion, mores, literature, and the arts; they were thus immune from change and exempt from history.[12] A corollary to this view was that these timeless structures were formed and perpetuated by certain basic ideas

[10] Abel Rémusat, *Nouveaux Mélanges Asiatiques* (Paris, 1829), I, 37.

[11] Cf. Henri Maspero, " La Chaire des Langues et Littératures chinoises et tartares-mandchoues." Extract from the jubilee volume on the occasion of the Fourth Centenary of the Collège de France (Paris, 1932), 355. In this section I shall concentrate on the development of Sinology in France because a) it is more self-consciously scientific than British Sinology which has continued to rely until recently on the occasional gifted amateur; b) it has greater unity and continuity than any other European tradition of Sinology; and c) it was long regarded as the center of methodological innovation.

[12] V. V. Barthold, *La Découverte de L'Asie,* translated from the Russian by B. Nikitine (Paris, 1947), 30. Barthold cites the statement of this position from the introduction to F. C. Schlosser, *Geschichte der Achtzehnten und Neunzehnten Jahrhunderts* . . . (Heidelberg, 1835). Herder as early as 1774 had argued that non-European civilizations were essentially static and thus irrelevant to any study of historical process. Cf. R. G. Collingwood, *The Idea of History* (Oxford, 1946), 90. J. S. Mill, writing in 1838, spoke of " Chinese stationariness." F. R. Leavis, ed., *Mill on Bentham and Coleridge* (London, 1950), 87.

and modes of thought. Some maintained that there was indeed a single 'altorientalische Weltanschauung.'

These views influenced the development of Sinology as a branch of Orientalism in the first half of the XIXth century and later. Negatively they tended to isolate 'Orientalists' from the rising tide of historical thought, and positively they tended to focus the attention of these scholars on the ancient books—the Zend Avesta, the Vedas, the Confucian Classics—assumed to contain the key ideas which would make the timeless cultures of the East intelligible. The concentration on the Classics was further justified by the authority of native scholarly opinions which Europeans reported; any Chinese literatus would have insisted, as our sketch of the self-image has intimated, that the Classics contained the fundamental principles on which the Chinese system had always rested and operated. Moreover, it was clear to any beginning student that the phrases and the metaphors of the Classics invariably recurred in every kind of Chinese writing.

For all these reasons, early European Sinology was concerned with Classical texts, their explication and translation. During Abel Rémusat's tenure at the Collège de France his three weekly lectures were divided between grammar and 'explication des textes.' Among these texts Rémusat, like the Chinese literati, preferred the Confucian to the Taoist which, however, he occasionally dealt with. In attempting to bring order into the Chinese collections of the Royal Library, he launched a massive bibliographical project which was planned to include a translation of the bibliographic chapters of the XIIIth-century encyclopedia *Wen-hsien t'ung-k'ao*.[13] The annotated translation favored by Rémusat and his successors may be regarded as the normal and accepted genre of writing among Orientalists, whether Assyriologists, Arabists, or what not. But in the case of Sinology, this type of work seems to me to be also in part a transplantation and an extension of the Chinese exegetical tradition and thus to suggest one of the ways in which the Western sinologue was subservient to the scholarly values of the Chinese literati. Rémusat's successor at the Collège de France, Stanislas Julien, began his teaching in the first semester of 1832 with an explication of one of the primers of a Confucian education, the *San-tzu ching*, and in the succeeding years translated in his classroom nearly all the Confucian Classics, often with reference to the orthodox commentaries of Chu Hsi.

Along with the dedicated study of the Chinese Classics and the acceptance of much of the literati self-image of Chinese civilization,

[13] Cf. Maspero, *op. cit.*, 357–59.

these pioneer sinologues had begun by looking at China from the outside and in doing so turned to the study of China's cultural relations with other countries. Rémusat's study of the record of a Vth-century Chinese Buddhist pilgrimage to India, followed later by Julien's studies of the Chinese pilgrim Hsüan-tsang, brought into doubt the myth of China's self-sufficiency and immunity to outside influence. As Rémusat's literary executor remarked in the introduction to Rémusat's greatest work, " A la Chine, *même, où tout est immuable,* de graves innovations s'introduisirent avec la secte nouvelle [i.e., Buddhism]; elles attaquèrent à la fois les moeurs, la philosophie, et jusqu'à la langue." [14]

As books and travelers' reports poured into Europe in an ever-increasing volume, descriptions of the Chinese Empire in operation, of its rebellions and repeated capitulations to the Western Powers, multiplied. Biased and imperfect as many of these were, they served on many points to contradict or undermine the bland self-image which the sinologue imbibed through his Classical texts. Though varieties of popular literature disdained by the Chinese literati were studied by Julien,[15] his successor's principal work was an exegetical work, the translation of a section of the *Wen-hsien t'ung-k'ao* devoted to China's barbarian neighbors to the east and south. And perhaps the most ambitious sinological enterprise by a European was James Legge's translation of the Chinese Classics which appeared between 1861 and 1872. In these, as Legge's necrologist said, the Classics were first given the meticulous attention usually reserved for Holy Writ, and in them the commentaries of Chu Hsi—orthodox in China from the XIVth through the XIXth century—were generally taken as authoritative.

The exegetical mode, the subservience to traditional Chinese scholarship continued to characterize European sinology until the 1890's. The change to another way of approaching Chinese civilization was prefigured by some of the developments noted above. It came in the late XIXth century when profound changes had occurred in the object of study and in the intellectual climates of China, Japan, and the West. This does not mean that the ancient self-image we have described or the modes of study it sanctioned and influenced were immediately destroyed. Rather it means that these things were slowly eroded by events and lingered on fragmented and dispersed, attracting the sympathies of individuals but never again dominating scholarly communities and traditions.

[14] Cf. C. Landresse, Introduction to *Foe Koue Ki ou Relation des Royaumes Bouddhiques* (Paris, 1836), xvi. Italics mine.

[15] Cf. Maspero, *op. cit.*, 361. Reference is to the popular dramas of the Mongol period.

The End of Imperial China and the Fragmentation of Its Self-image

The successive phases of China's retreat before a series of internal dislocations and external catastrophes (*nei-luan wai-huan*) are relatively well known and need not be detailed here. One of the striking features of this unplanned retreat to unprepared positions is that each withdrawal meant a relinquishment of more elements of that body of myth by which the Chinese literati had lived and rationalized their position in time, space, and culture. Chinese armies collapsed before the superior armament of the 'barbarians of the Western Ocean,' Chinese territory was relinquished to these same barbarians, trade was forced upon a country which cherished the illusion of self-sufficiency, and the propagation of a foreign and subversive religion was imposed in treaties exacted by force. As principles were conceded that had once seemed immutable, the Chinese literati divided their culture into its essence or basic structure (*t'i*) and its functions (*yung*) and maintained to themselves that compromise was possible on the functions but never on the basic structure. But as crisis followed crisis and the corrosive ideas of the West made dissidents of the younger literati, more and more was consigned to the realm of *yung* and what a few years before had been held to as essential was now seen as expendable.[16]

When, in 1897, the reformer K'ang Yu-wei published his volume *Confucius as a Reformer*, he painted the "peerless sage of ten thousand generations" as a reformer who sought authority for his program by extensive tampering with historical fact. K'ang's was perhaps a master-stroke for reform, but it further undermined the authority of the Classical tradition by which the Chinese literati had lived for centuries. When, a few years later and after a humiliating defeat at the hands of the Japanese, the 'dwarf barbarians of the Eastern sea,' the examination system was remodeled, the principle that classically educated and morally perfected men were the proper holders of power was finally abandoned. Western 'virtues'—military spirit, technical skill, patriotism—were to be fostered and rewarded. Shortly thereafter, the monarchy, which had successively shown that its charisma failed to sway the barbarians, that its moral influence could not sustain its subjects against the onslaught of alien ideas, that it was as ineffectual in civil government as in military organization, was abandoned and replaced by a republic. The great millennial edifice of institution and myth had at last collapsed. Its real and imagined

[16] On the process here summarized, cf. Mary C. Wright, *The Last Stand of Chinese Conservatism* (Stanford, Calif., 1957) and Joseph R. Levenson, "History and Value: The Tensions of Intellectual Choice in Modern China" in Arthur F. Wright, ed., *Studies in Chinese Thought* (Chicago, 1953), 146–194.

coherence was gone, but elements have survived until today, both in China and abroad, as objects of loyalty or nostalgia, as components of innumerable movements and ideologies which have sought to deal with the problems of modern China, and as conscious or unconscious elements in recent characterizations of Chinese civilization. This is why this debacle should be seen as the fragmentation and not the destruction of a self-image.

The Changing Image of China in XXth-Century Scholarship

For the reasons we have indicated—the authority of the literati self-image, the incubus of Orientalism, and the mass and complexity of documentation—the sinologue was slow to respond to the growth of historical and social sciences in XIXth-century Europe. Studies in the humanities and the social sciences evolved theories out of the common experience of Western man, theories for which the sinologue found, if he looked, scant confirmation in the isolated cultural entity with which he was concerned. Striking advances in philology and linguistics had been applied to many languages of the 'orient' but not to Chinese.[17] These experiences tended to perpetuate the illusion, common to the literati self-image and to much of Sinology, that China was unique. Historical science, perfecting its instruments of research and analysis, was at the high tide of its authority among the disciplines, but its Europocentrism was unabated; Hegel and Marx had reaffirmed the static a-historical character of Asian civilizations and Ranke had given his immeasurable authority to the same view: " At times the conditions inherited from ancient times of one or another oriental people have been regarded as the foundation of everything. But one cannot possibly use as a starting point the peoples of eternal standstill (*den Völkern des ewigen Stillstandes*) to comprehend the inner movement of world history." [18]

[17] Barthold, *op. cit.*, 153 remarks: " Toutefois même jusqu'à présent [1911], les sinologues n'ont adopté les méthodes de recherche élaborées par la science européenne que dans une proportion encore moindre que les représentants des autres branches de l'orientalisme." He goes on to suggest that the civilizations of the Near East have come within the scope of Western methods more readily because of the common roots shared by them and the West.

[18] *Weltgeschichte* (1881–88), part 1, quoted in Otto Franke, *Geschichte des Chinesischen Reiches*, vol. 1 (Leipzig, 1930), x. Franke, viii, quotes from Hegel's *Philosophie der Weltgeschichte* (1837): " The history of China itself does not develop anything and on that account one cannot engage in details of that history." And again: " We have before us the oldest state and yet no past, but a state which exists today as we know it to have been in ancient times. To that extent China has no history." Jules Michelet represents an exception to the prevailing view. Professor Meyer Schapiro has called my attention to a long rhapsody in which Michelet speaks of China as " une autre Europe au bout de L'Asie," and dreams of the possibility of a common culture of all mankind, Asian and Western. Cf. *Histoire de France au Seizième Siècle: Réforme* (Paris, 1855), 488–90.

The breaks in this impasse did not occur all at once nor at all the points along the frontier between Sinology and other disciplines; indeed the process is incomplete today. But when, in the academic year 1899-1900, Edouard Chavannes (1865-1918) first lectured on the *history* of China at the Collège de France this was the beginning of a major change.[19] And it was Chavannes who led the way towards a new critical method in dealing with the Chinese past. As the late Henri Maspero said of Chavannes' work, "... là où avant lui on avait vu ' la Tradition ' comme un bloc, il montra qu'il y avait à distinguer des époques et des auteurs chacun avec ses caractéristiques individuelles. Ce fut une des originalités de ses cours et de son oeuvre, les premiers où la sinologie européenne sut se dégager de l'emprise que la science indigène avait toujours exercée sur elle." [20]

Marcel Granet (1884-1940) broke through the barriers we have described at still another point and proved that the sociological study of Chinese antiquity was both possible and rewarding. With remarkable brilliance and virtuosity he read *through* the formalized Classical texts which on the surface mirrored the literati view of the culture and *into* the social reality behind them. Yet Granet was convinced that he could characterize Chinese society and thought with little reference to their development after the IIIrd century A.D. In this a-historical view he may possibly have been affected by the residual influence of the static conception of Asian civilizations and unquestionably was by the Durkheimian school of sociology to which he owed much of his method.

In the 1920's and '30's the use of the new methods for the study of China was broadened and deepened. The first history of China deriving its methods from European historiography and not from the literati tradition was that of Otto Franke which began to appear in 1930.[21] Yet the focus or theme of this work was the history of the

[19] W. A. P. Martin, the American friend of Chinese modernizers, seems to have been the first to recognize the great possibilities of the study of Chinese history through Western historical methods and a Western sense of problem. In his " Discourse on the Study of Chinese History," a presidential address presented to the Peking Oriental Society in 1886, he pointed to three key problems in Chinese history, to " three immense movements, each of which is as indispensable to the understanding of the present condition of China as are Kepler's three laws to the explanation of the solar system . . . ; they are: 1. The conquest of China by the Chinese; 2. The conquest of China by the Tartars; 3. The struggle between the centripetal and centrifugal forces of the empire." He remarks that ". . . no native writer appears to have grasped the significance or even formed a conception of any one of them." Extract from the *Journal of the Peking Oriental Society* (Peking, 1886), 10.

[20] Henri Maspero, " La chaire des Langues et Littératures chinoises et tartaresmandchoues " as cited in note 11, 364.

[21] Otto Franke, *Geschichte des Chinesischen Reiches, Eine Darstellung seiner Enstehung, seins Wesens und seiner Entwicklung bis zur Neuesten Zeit*, 5 vols. (Leipzig, 1930, 1936, 1937, 1948, 1952).

Confucian state and of the efforts of the literati to realize in institutional arrangements their ideal policy. Such a focus plus heavy reliance on the standard histories made the work far less destructive of the old literati-image than the cross-sectional sociological studies of Granet. Henri Maspero, whose critical study of Chinese antiquity used and developed the methods of Chavannes, also pioneered in other fields of research outside the orthodox limits of earlier Chinese scholarship. His were the first systematic studies in economic history and in the history of Taoism, the dissident tradition so long disdained by the Chinese literati.[22]

These must serve simply as examples of the ways in which Western Sinology began here and there to break out of the walls which had isolated it from the main currents of European intellectual life. The barriers were also attacked, as it were, from the outside. Max Weber boldly carried his sociological studies to India and China. In so doing he did not pretend to attempt total characterizations of those societies but to investigate " the relations of the most important religions to economic life and to the social stratification of their environment, to follow out both causal relationships, so far as it is necessary in order to find points of comparison with the Occidental development." [23] The analytical forays of Weber and other scholars with problem interests slowly demolished the old illusions that Chinese civilization was unique, without a history, understandable solely in terms of its immutable *Weltanschauung*. It became increasingly apparent to the world of Western learning that Chinese civilization had many characteristics which were analogous to those of other societies and that these characteristics—as the collapse of the old order so dramatically demonstrated—could change through time.

Analysis went forward with the use of one new discipline after another. But analysis implies " breakdown into components," and as this process proceeded, the holistic characterization of Chinese civilization once so easily made by reference to the literati's self-image—began to appear more formidable. We shall return to this problem at the close of this essay.

In Japan, the modernization which was pushed so rapidly after 1868 meant a turning away from China as sole cultural mentor. This

[22] Henri Maspero, *La Chine Antique* (Paris, 1927). Cf. also the volumes on Taoism and on history in his *Ouvrages Posthumes*, vols. 2 and 3 (Paris, 1950).

[23] Max Weber, *The Protestant Ethic and the Spirit of Capitalism*, translated by Talcott Parsons (London, 1930), 27. Weber's study of Confucianism and Taoism first appeared in 1922, and an English translation curiously entitled *The Religion of China* by Hans Gerth was published at Glencoe, Ill., in 1951. For a lucid account of Weber's analysis of Chinese society, cf. R. Bendix, *Max Weber, An Intellectual Portrait* (New York, 1960), 103–157.

process, together with the closely observed collapse of China's imperial order, shattered the image of China held by the Kangakusha and those whom they influenced. If the traditional learning of the Kangakusha was inadequate to explain a China where the old order was crumbling and where Japan, rapidly modernizing, saw herself as having 'vital interests,' then what should be the tools of interpretation? Clearly the historically oriented social sciences of the West, associated with the West's superior power and Western effort to understand its rapidly changing society, were the answer.

Significantly the Japanese did not call upon Western sinologues, isolated from the main currents of Western thought, to modernize Japanese studies of China. Rather they invited Dr. Ludwig Riess, a young German historian of the English Middle Ages and a devoted disciple of the school of Ranke, to introduce Western historical methods at Tokyo University.[24] Riess arrived in 1887. Within three or four years young Japanese scholars were applying this newly learned Western historiography to the study of China, thus perhaps disturbing the shade of Ranke for whom the Chinese were a people of "eternal standstill." Pioneer studies broke with many of the stereotypes which the Chinese literati and their Japanese representatives, the Kangakusha, had long maintained. Chinese history was no longer accepted as the literati had written it; other sources and the histories of Korea, Mongolia, and Central Asia were studied and used to criticize the official capital-centered accounts of the Chinese dynastic histories. Chinese history was no longer periodized according to dynasties but by developmental stages often grouped under that strange tripartite division of time which Westerners had stumbled into: ancient, medieval, and modern.[25]

The records of China's past were no longer seen as priceless repositories of relevant moral experience but as documents to be tested as to authenticity and credibility and then analyzed for the light they might shed on the development of some Chinese idea or institution.

[24] Cf. Aoki Tomitaro, *Tōyōgaku no seiritsu to sono hatten* ("The formation of East Asian studies and their development") (Tokyo, 1940), 146. Riess was born in 1861 and his doctoral dissertation presented at Leipzig in 1885; it was published in English translation by K. L. Wood Legh in 1940 as *The History of the English Electoral Law in the Middle Ages*. The work was dedicated to "the man who, of all my university teachers, has done most to lead me to understand the methods of research of the school of Ranke, and to think objectively, Dr. Hans Delbrück."

[25] A recent essay attacking this unfortunate invention of "a very indifferent German scholar, Keller or Cellarius ..." is to be found in Geoffrey Barraclough, *History in a Changing World* (Oxford, 1956), 54–63. The great Chinese historiographer Liu Chih-chi (661–721) had used an analogous scheme to segment China's long past, but these conventions were not adopted by Chinese historians generally. Cf. Edwin Pulleyblank, "Ancient, Medieval and Modern," paper read before the 9th Annual Conference of Junior Sinologues, Paris, 1956, mimeo., 2 pp.

And in the writings of many of these historians, China was not the sole object of attention but was placed in the context of Asian history.[26] Significantly the first professorship at Tokyo Imperial University to be occupied by one of the new historical scholars of China was called a chair of 'Eastern History' (tōyōshi), and scholarly nomenclature for referring to China abjured the old Sino-centric terms chūgoku (Central Kingdom) and chūka (Central cultural florescence) and used the simple transliteration 'Shina.' It should be noted, however, that with all this dramatic and rapid reorientation, Confucian moral texts were a required subject in the new national school curriculum, and kambun, the construing of classical Chinese texts in Japanese, was seriously studied in the new schools. The ideological needs of Japan's modern government made possible the perpetuation of fragments of the old Chinese learning within an entirely new context.

In the period from 1911 to 1925, stimulated by the Chinese Revolution, there was an increasing interest in the study of modern China, and an increasing number of new disciplines imported from the West were applied to the study of China: historical geography, archaeology, phonetics, social and economic history, and others. In the 1920's historical materialism began to have a pervasive influence on Japanese scholarship, and studies of China were at the vortex of controversy between Marxists and non-Marxists. Modern sociological and economic field-work was pressed forward as Japan's ambitions on the continent took shape, and interpretative links were forged between the living society of China and its past. The increasing volume of specialized studies tended to leave Chinese civilization atomized in discrete segments which were not readily assembled into a coherent characterization. Yet for the Japanese government, on the eve of continental expansion, characterization was needed as a basis for policy. Scholars became involved in the controversy over the nature and political evolution of modern Chinese society, and the view which won official acceptance—not without strong dissent—held that China was a culture, a way of life, that its peoples' loyalties were to these and not to the shaky nation-state of Republican China nor to its leaders. Hence China might once again be brought under alien (this time Japanese) rule providing the conquerors restored and respected the ancient culture. Another feature of this interpretation, traceable to Western origins, was that China was over-age, over-ripe, and incapable of any drastic change; all that was possible was a restoration

[26] According to Aoki, op. cit., 148, one of the most influential of the early histories which did this was the middle school text-book of East Asian history (Tōyōshi) published by Professor Kuwabara Jitsuzo in 1899. This text was used for the new subject of Tōyōshi introduced into the middle school curriculum in 1895.

of its old culture.[27] The lingering influence of the literati self-image can be detected in the first part of this interpretation, and it is less a synthesis of all that had been learned through scholarly analysis than a return, under the pressure of events, to old simplifications which study and field work had brought into doubt. This interpretation proved to be catastrophically mistaken as a guide to policy, and the post-war period has seen in Japan a rather feverish and searching reappraisal of scholarly views and analyses of Chinese history and society. Marxist theories of developmental stages, reinforced by a dynamic Communist regime in Peking, have exerted a powerful influence on Japanese studies of China. In some quarters one may discern the lineaments of a new 'Central Kingdom' image, but it is too early to predict how this will develop.

In China, unlike Japan and the West, the fragmentation of the old self-image was seen and felt in every aspect of life. Older men clung tenaciously to one or another fragment of the myth by which their ancestors had lived, while the young denounced it all as delusive and responsible for the sad plight in which China found itself. Politicians and reformers of every persuasion ceased to assess China's plight in terms of its ancient ideals. Rather, they held up Western institutions, Western history as norms from which China had deviated in disastrous ways. In the first quarter of this century the dominant mood of the younger intellectuals was critical and destructive of their native heritage, receptive to each of the successive waves of Western thought which broke over China. Their energies were absorbed first by the struggle for a viable polity, and later by the feverish effort to build a new popular culture on the ruins of the classical tradition. Controversies raged over the conflicting claims of science and humanism, over pragmatism and materialism, over democracy and authoritarianism. The underlying question in all these heated debates was: How can China survive in the modern world? Thus, every attempt to appraise Chinese civilization was made in the heat of controversy, and attacked or defended by those who saw this appraisal as part of a diagnosis leading logically to a prescription for China's ills. There was little time for research or reflection in a climate of opinion which favored the hasty polemic over the balanced analytical judgment.

Nevertheless, in the 1920's and '30's there were scholars who per-

[27] The writings of Naitō Torajirō, Yano Jin'ichi, and Inaba Iwakichi put forward, each with his own emphasis, this interpretation. Naitō's concept of the senescence of Chinese civilization was part of a life-cycle theory of civilization possibly influenced indirectly by Heinrich Rickert (1863–1936). Cf. Hisayuki Miyakawa, "An Outline of the Naitō Hypothesis and Its Effects on Japanese Studies of China," *Far Eastern Quarterly*, XIV (1955), 533–552.

sisted in the orderly and systematic study of Chinese history and society. In doing so they risked the scorn of the activists on one side and the surviving literati scholars on the other. When we consider some of these men and their work, it is clear that, as in the case of Japan, the new methods and concepts which they used seldom derived from Western sinology but usually from the historical and social sciences developed out of European society and European intellectual needs; much that was imported came to China via Japan. The progress which this handful of men made in the twelve or fifteen years before the Japanese invasion of 1937 is astonishing. Their first task was critical: the skeptical and disciplined reappraisal of every datum of China's past or present society and culture. The second was analytical: the search for patterns, frequencies, and continuities in the almost limitless body of data at their disposal. The third, for some, was an ultimate synthesis which would put Chinese civilization in a new and clearer perspective and thus enable reformers and activists to proceed on a sounder basis towards the building of a new culture and a new society.

In the field of history Ku Chieh-kang exemplifies the reorientation of the study of China in these years.[28] His critical spirit and his use of new methods for the study of China's past reflect an emancipation from the myths on which the culture of imperial China rested and from the methods of inquiry which the old order sanctioned.[29] The Confucian Canon was looked at afresh and each text was studied, not as a repository of wisdom but as a document with a history, with a greater or lesser degree of authenticity and credibility, with an analyzable relation to its time and authorship. As a corollary, much greater attention was given to the non-canonical works of the past which had been ignored or undervalued by the Confucian literati. In their critical approach to the past, Ku and his co-workers sought to free themselves from the tyranny of long-established schools of interpretation which, as Ku points out, presented the young scholar with approved 'hypotheses' and required of him only their further substantiation.

Studies of this critical sort mean the abandonment of any belief in immutable truths, or in the possibility of their final discovery. Ku says, " I can never experience the joy of being able to say ' Truth has

[28] Ku Chieh-kang, born in 1893, is still active as a historian in Peking. In what follows I draw heavily on Ku's *Symposium on Ancient Chinese History* (*Ku-shih pien*), 6 vols. (Peking and Shanghai, 1926-38), and on Arthur W. Hummel's translation of the preface to that work, *The Autobiography of a Chinese Historian* (Leyden, 1931).

[29] Ku also drew ideas and inspiration from noted skeptics and dissidents within Confucianism such as Ts'ui Shu (1740-1816), and K'ang Yu-wei (1858-1927).

at last revealed itself to me, hereafter there is nothing left to do'."[30] Guided by hypotheses, Ku and others sought to identify and eliminate forgeries, to rediscover and evaluate lost or neglected works. And, in response to the demand for 'national' scholarship accessible to a wider audience, Ku and men like him sought to make the records of the past and their own studies of the past intelligible. They published punctuated and annotated versions of ancient works, and translated some of them into the vernacular language, thus outraging the traditional scholars who would preserve the hallowed works of the past as the sole property of an erudite elite. The new scholars, under the influence of Western social sciences, saw that the traditional classifications of Chinese literature were useless as guides to the study of *problems* in Chinese history and society. The manifold uses of a single text were discerned, and articles and bibliographies began to sift from the traditional records materials for economic history, for historical geography, for sociology and all the many other fields of modern Western scholarship.[31]

The introduction of comparative methods in this period was as fruitful of new insights as it was destructive of the ancient myth of China's uniqueness and cultural homogeneity. Ku says of this innovation, "... our eyes have been opened to a new world of hitherto uninvestigated and unorganized materials; questions which once were believed to have no significance now take on an entirely new meaning."[32] As Chinese scholars began to find analogues in other cultures for what had been for ages regarded as uniquely Chinese, they found stimulation in the works of men like Granet and Maspero who had helped bring Sinology out of its isolation and into the realm of comparative studies. And they were inspired by Western experiences with field work to turn to the living sub-cultures of China for the study of linguistics, phonetics, folklore, sociology, and ethnology. In the 1930's field surveys of great importance were pushed through by newly trained Chinese social scientists.[33] The analysis of both the historical society and the living society of China proceeded apace.

[30] Hummel, *op. cit.*, 124.

[31] Among the many journals reflecting this development were: *Yu-Kung* ("The Chinese Historical Geography") which appeared from 1934 to 1937 [the first journal of historical geography appeared in Japan in 1900]; *Kuo-hsueh chi-k'an* ("Journal of Sinological Studies") which began to appear in 1923; *Shih-huo* ("Journal of Economic History") which began in 1934; *Chung-kuo jung-tsao hsueh-she hui-k'an* ("Bulletin of the Society for Research in Chinese Architecture"), I, 1 (July 1930).

[32] Hummel, *op. cit.*, 161.

[33] Some pioneer works of this type are: Hsiao-t'ung Fei, *Peasant Life in China* (London, 1938); L. K. Tao, *Livelihood in Peking* (Peking, 1928); S. Yang and L. K. Tao, *Standard of Living in Shanghai* (Peking, Institute of Social Research, 1931); Li Ch'ing-han, *Tsing Hsien; She-hui kai-kuan chiao-ch'e* ("A Sociological Survey of Ting Hsien") (Peking, 1933).

Yet the very progress of cultural analysis, bringing into play one after another technical discipline, seemed to make the day ever more distant when a new synthetic view of Chinese civilization could be soundly established. Such a synthesis, however preliminary, was a felt need not only for the continuous appraisal of special studies but for the practical purpose of planning China's transformation into a viable modern state and society. There thus appeared in Chinese scholarship a serious cleavage: the fact-finders, analysts, historical and textual critics pursued their specific lines of inquiry; those who felt the need of a new synthesis, undaunted by warnings that this was premature, embarked on system-building and attempted sweeping characterizations of China based on one or another theory imported from the West. By the end of World War II the gulf had widened between these two groups; a leading Chinese historian observed that the scholars committed to disciplined and limited research lacked any standard of relevance, while those committed to interpretation lacked that command of the data which alone could give their theories validity.[34]

The Chinese Communist state has imposed a resolution of this problem by decreeing a standard orthodox interpretation of Chinese history and society and ordering Chinese scholars to relate their work to it. A relatively integrated self-image of the civilization has been developed out of the Canons of Marxism-Leninism, and Chinese history is once again interpreted in the light of an official ideology. In a few fields of study such reinterpretations may prove fruitful, but in most fields the past record and present reality are warped and forced by reference to this new body of myth, and the foregone conclusion has replaced the hypothesis. The new self-image, like the old, is a simplification of the past and present; it has a symmetry and coherence which neither past nor present reality, in its complexity and variety, would confirm. Perhaps, a people long adrift from ancient moorings require such a myth for the conduct of their individual and collective lives. Whether China, with its new power in the world can impose this new myth on scholars and laymen outside the Communist world is a matter for speculation.

In the light of the history of the study of China, which I have sketched, it is not surprising that Chinese studies remain a retarded and underdeveloped field of Western scholarship. Let me point to some of the ways in which this history bears on recent Western sinology. The incubus of Orientalism is still with us. As late as 1937 American scholars interested in the development of Chinese studies urged that the first step should be the establishment of " depart-

[34] Ch'i Ssu-ho writing in the magazine *Ta Chung* (May 1946).

ments (which) would resemble in plan well-organized departments of Classical or Near Eastern languages. . . ."[35] And the commentarial tradition still dominates a great deal of serious scholarship.

Fragments of the ancient self-image linger as unacknowledged assumptions in scholarly work, are blandly accepted in semi-popular writings, or are reasserted in writings and pronouncements from Formosa.

In the West the intellectual need for some synthetic view, linked to the practical necessity of finding a basis for dealing with the Chinese, has stimulated theoretical constructions which often, ironically, serve as substitutes for substantive research. Northrop's 'undifferentiated aesthetic continuum' and related notions purport to explain 'the East' in terms of an *altorientalische Weltanschauung,* but ignore the vast body of accumulated knowledge about the *different* civilizations of Asia. Lily Abegg's 'envelopmental logic' offers another 'key,' but it opens a door into a dream world. On a more serious level Wittfogel's concept of hydraulic society is used to interpret the life and institutions of the Chinese and other historic civilizations. But the very title of his book, *Oriental Despotism,* is straight from Hegel, and enough data are now available to cast in grave doubt the picture of the Chinese as caught from the dawn of their history in an immutable complex of institutions explicable as the consequences of the need for water-control.

On the other hand, the West has made striking progress in many fields of Chinese studies. Linguistics, art history, the study of literature, social, economic and intellectual history are advancing slowly towards the standards which generally prevail in these disciplines. Modern Japanese scholarship on China is no longer ignored. Great enterprises such as the Sung Project centered in Paris,[36] the Modern

[35] " Memorandum on the Present Needs of Sinological Scholarship in America," May 17, 1937, signed by James R. Ware, George A. Kennedy, Ferdinand D. Lessing, and Peter A. Boodberg. The memorandum speaks with some condescension of providing " men whose primary interests are in other fields, such as history, political science, or philosophy, with a certain minimum training in the languages of the Far East," and of placing such men in the colleges. " We recognize the value of such activities, both for humanistic studies as a whole, and specifically for the development of Far Eastern studies. They enlarge academic and popular interest in the Far East, and prepare the ground for intensive cultivation of the field. From the point of view of Sinology, they may be classed as worthy and valuable propaganda."

[36] Professor Etienne Balazs who heads this project describes the reorientation of French Sinology: " The increasing interest in New China on the one hand, and the general tendencies developing in the humanistic sciences on the other, are not without repercussions in the domain of Chinese studies where the specialists will no longer be able to confine themselves to some eccentric corner of their private curiosities. The preceding generation's preoccupations with external forms, with the unique event and marginal contacts is giving way to the desire to seize structures, the content, and the significant facts and relations." A paper entitled " The Present

Chinese History Project at the University of Washington, and Modern Chinese Economic and Political Studies at Harvard complement the work of an increasing corps of scholars in many disciplines. These studies promise to lay the groundwork for more valid working hypotheses and general statements about Chinese civilization than were possible in the earlier stages of Sinology or are likely to develop in the shadow of the new Chinese self-image.

From this survey there arise some tentative conclusions relevant to general problems of the characterization and comparison of civilizations. One is that a great living civilization may impose its self-image on those who study it and affect the ways in which studies are conducted. Another conclusion is that characterization may be affected by a wide range of factors many of which are almost irrelevant to the object being studied: greater or lesser aesthetic appeal of the cultural products of the civilization; the vagaries of international politics and ideologies; the changes, intellectual and social, in the society in which the student of a civilization lives; the fortuitous organization of learning which may place the study of a particular civilization in an intellectual backwater.

All this suggests that characterizations of civilizations are conditioned by time, culture, and circumstances and that they have at best only a very provisional validity. Yet our survey indicates that men who are a part of a given civilization seek always to simplify it into a myth by which they can live and act. And those who study the same civilization from a distance are forever driven towards some simplified general view of the object they study. Sometimes this is a purely intellectual demand for some broad conception which will give importance and meaning to the study of some particular problem. At other times the demand for some holistic view may spring from considerations of international politics, from the need suddenly to 'understand' a whole people so that we can 'deal with them.' And the tendency in such cases is not to attempt the formidable task of the synthesis of available knowledge but to fall back on some earlier simplification or upon a passing intellectual fad.

In sum, the holistic characterization of such a civilization as the Chinese is a necessity for those within and those without its orbit. But our survey would suggest that simplification is always at war with analysis, that only rarely is a simplified image of this civilization held as a hypothesis; rather, it usually tends, for a variety of reasons, to devolve into an article of faith.

Situation of Chinese Studies in France" presented to the International Symposium on the History of Eastern and Western Cultural Contacts, Tokyo, Autumn 1957, mimeographed.

The Genesis and Character of English Nationalism*

by HANS KOHN

Reprinted from the *Journal of the History of Ideas*—Vol. I, No. 1, pp. 69-94

I

The awakening of a national consciousness in England came, in spite of the insular situation, later than on the continent. Only in the fourteenth century did the English language gradually replace the French in law courts and in official life. The Parliament began to hold its sessions in English in 1362, giving as the reason the fact that the French language was little understood by the people. But French literature retained its predominant influence among the educated classes, and of the greatest English poet of the fourteenth century, of Chaucer, it could be said that he was "remarkable for being one of the few masters in the very front rank of our literature whose work seems almost devoid of any definite patriotic impulse."[1]

Until the end of the fifteenth century England was a poor and backward country. England's population of somewhat more than three millions was then only half that of Spain, about a fourth of that of France, and about a fifth of that of Germany. The end of the Hundred Years War and the rise of the house of Tudor marked a milestone in the development of the English nation. The defeat in France and the withdrawal from the Continent in the long run strengthened England and laid the foundations for her greatness. Protected by the wall of the sea she felt herself safe against any attack from across the channel. Thus she could turn all her energies in an entirely new direction, towards the Atlantic Ocean. This turning-point in English history coincided with the turning-point of European economic and political life, when the center of the continent shifted from the Mediterranean, far away from the British Isles, to the Atlantic Ocean, beyond which new worlds of fabulous riches beckoned. Favored by these changes England could develop

---

* This essay is part of a study undertaken with the help of a grant-in-aid from the Social Research Council.

[1] Esmé Wingfield-Stratford, *The History of English Patriotism*, London, 1913, Vol. I, p. 78. A lonely forerunner of the new age to come in England in the sixteenth and seventeenth centuries was John Wycliffe, who translated the Bible into English and demanded the introduction of divine service in English.

earlier than any other European country certain fundamental conditions for the growth of modern nationhood and thus prepare the ground for the development of nationalism in the seventeenth century.

With the absence of foreign wars and with the growing expansion of economic life, the system of classes and castes, which elsewhere continued in its rigidity and checked the growth of nationalism, broke down in England. The common discussions in Parliament about the welfare of the land as a whole promoted the growth of a national feeling. The predominance of yeomen archers in the English army, in contrast to the continental armies with the knightly cavalry as their backbone, also played a part in shifting the emphasis from feudal loyalty to a more national sentiment. The aristocracy, greatly reduced in numbers by the internal Wars of the Roses, lost much of their warrior spirit. They were not separated by insurmountable barriers from the rising third estate.

In such an atmosphere of national security, expanding wealth and parliamentary influence, the conditions for the growth of individual liberty and of respect for the processes of law, and for the security and calculability of transactions guaranteed by law, could take root. Public opinion could become a factor carrying some weight in the decisions of those in authority; the emancipation of individuality and of private initiative from the bonds of medieval tradition and of feudal society coalesced with the slow growth of a feeling of self-confidence and self-reliance which became characteristic of the English in the sixteenth century.

The accession of the Tudors to power at the end of the fifteenth century laid the foundations for that national homogeneity which was the necessary condition for the later development of nationalism. Henry VIII played for English history and nationalism a role similar to that of the absolute kings on the continent; and the result of his reign was the growth of a conscious English stateism. He destroyed, finally, the bond which tied England to medieval universalism. He uprooted the last traces of feudal power in England, and did much to raise the strength of the middle class and of the gentry in whom the Tudors found their support. The new wealth which began to pour into England quickened the shift in the prestige and influence of the social classes.[2]

[2] Albert Frederick Pollard, *Henry VIII*, London, 1930. *Cf.* Lewis Einstein, *Tudor Ideals*, New York, 1921, p. 14. Henry's attitude to the Church corresponded

In the Elizabethan period the growth of power and of wealth, the beginning of colonial expansion, the increased literary activity, produced a feeling of intense patriotic pride, which had, however, nothing yet of the deeply-rooted, ever-present and all-pervading character of modern nationalism. The Renaissance still carried on the heritage of the Middle Ages in its emphasis upon the one great republic of letters which was the *una respublica Christiana,* in a secularized and intellectual form, a feeling well expressed by Samuel Daniel in his verses:[3]

> It be'ing the proportion of a happie Pen,
> Not to b'inuassal'd to one Monarchie,
> But dwell with all the better world of men,
> Whose spirits all are of one communitie;
> Whom neither Ocean, Desarts, Rockes nor Sands
> Can keepe from th' intertraffique of the minde,
> But that it vents her treasure in all lands,
> And doth a most secure commercement finde.

The Reformation itself preserved strong universalistic aspects. But the great cultural strides which, for the first time, England made in the last part of the sixteenth century, to catch up with the development in Italy and France, gave to the English a new feeling of importance, although for many years to come the civilization of

---

to the Renaissance tendency of the subordination of the Church to the State. As far as there was a national historiography in England at the time of Henry VIII, it limited itself to his praise, according to ancient models. He was made into a Roman hero and a Roman patriot. Some interest in the past of England was awakened, but it remained behind what the Renaissance did in other countries. There are a few expressions of typical Renaissance patriotism, such as that by John Poynet, the Bishop of Winchester (1514?–1556) who wrote: "Men ought to have more respect to their country than to their prince, to the commonwealth than to any one person. For the country and the commonwealth is a degree above the king." But this Renaissance spirit penetrated only very slowly into England. The first Renaissance historiographer in England, an Italian, Polydor Vergil, whom King Henry VII commissioned in 1507 to write a history of England, was struck as were other observers of the time by the fact that the English were little touched by the Renaissance spirit and were still deeply immersed in medieval piety. In the first book of his *Anglicae Historiae* he says, *nulla est hodie natio, quae ad divinum cultum pertineant, sanctius diligentiusque observet.*

[3] *The Complete Works in Verse and Prose of Samuel Daniel,* ed. by Alexander B. Grosart, London, 1885, printed for private circulation only, Vol. I, p. 287. The poem is dedicated to John Florio on the occasion of his translation of the Essays of Montaigne.

the two continental countries remained the example and the inspiration of English intellectual life. The new pride led to a closer observation of English life, its institutions and peculiarities, its traditions and history. Therein the English writers and antiquarians followed again the general trend of the Renaissance, with its newly awakened interest in research into the national past. Sir Thomas Smith's *De Republica Anglorum, The Manner of Government or Policie of the Realme of England* (1583), clearly points out the extent to which in the Tudor period the king was the center of the whole national life. "To be short the prince is the life, the head, and the authoritie of all thinges that be doone in the realme of England."[4]

Richard Carew, who had translated the first five cantos of Tasso's *Godfrey of Bvlloigne, or the recouerie of Hierusalem,* wrote *An Epistle concerning the excellencies of the English tongue* in which he claimed preeminence for the English language over all others, because it had borrowed from them all. William Camden, his contemporary, wrote after the example of the *Italia Illustrata* of Blondus a description of Great Britain, after having travelled throughout the land. His *Britannia, sive Florentissimorum Regnorum Angliae, Scotiae, Hiberniae, et Insularum adjacentium ex intima antiquitate Chorographica Descriptio,* published in 1586, became immediately a great success, and went within a short time through several editions of the Latin original and of the English translation. This patriotic pride found its most famous expression in the last years of the reign of Queen Elizabeth. It was then that Samuel Daniel wrote in his *Musophilus:*

> And who, in time, knowes whither we may vent
> The treasure of our tongue, to what strange shores
> This gaine of our best glory shall be sent,
> T'inrich vnknowing Nations with our stores?
> What worlds in th' yet vnformed Occident
> May come refin'd with th' accents that are ours?

[4] Sir Thomas Smith, *De Republica Anglorum,* ed. Alston, Cambridge, 1906, p. 62. On page 48 there is an evaluation of the importance of Parliament whose members "consult and shew what is good and necessarie for the common wealth, and to consult together, and upon mature deliberation everie bill or lawe being thrise reade and disputed upon in either house, the other two parties first each a part, and after the prince himself in presence of both parties doeth consent unto and alloweth." On English patriotism under Elizabeth see Elkin Calhoun Wilson, *England's Eliza,* Cambridge, Mass., 1939, especially Chapter III.

A few years previously John Lyly in his *Euphues and his England* had expressed a feeling which was to become common in the seventeenth century: "So tender a care hath HE alwaies had of that England, as of a new Israel, His chosen and peculiar people."[5]

In the sixteenth century the foreigners who had played a leading rôle in English economic and cultural life began to lose their prominence.[6] The growth of the English middle classes and of English learning rendered them gradually superfluous. The new feeling of English vitality, together with the new opportunities offered to a nation on the Atlantic shore, made itself felt in the beginning of English colonial enterprise. The English are not, as sometimes racial mysticism wishes to suggest, a race endowed by nature for adventures on the sea. No "Viking" blood has called them to discoveries and explorations. Down to the sixteenth century the English were a purely land-bred people. The great age of exploration belonged to the Spaniards and the Portuguese. Only slowly, under Queen Elizabeth and in the beginning of the seventeenth century, did the English become the great seafaring nation and begin to build an empire based upon navy and commerce. Even then, down to the time of Cromwell, there was no directed effort

[5] Samuel Daniel in his *Musophilus, op. cit.*, Vol. I, p. 255; see also Shakespeare, *Richard II*, Act II, Scene I, v. 40–53; *The Complete Works of John Lyly*, ed. by R. Warwick Bond, 1902, Vol. II, p. 205. See also p. 120: "The lyuing God is onely the Englysh God, wher he hath placed peace, which bryngeth all plentie, annoynted a Virgin Queene . . .", and on p. 211: "This peace hath the Lorde continued with great and vnspeakeable goodnesse amonge his chosen people of England." But for Lyly the center of England is not the people but the Queen. "A fortunate England that hath such a queene, ungratefull if thou praye not for hir, wicked if thou do not love hir, miserable if thou lose hir."—p. 208. There are very few instances in the Elizabethan literature where the English are compared to the chosen people. One of them we find in Richard Hooker's *Ecclesiastical Polity*, Book VIII, where he writes: "Our estate is according to the pattern of God's own ancient elect people, which people was not part of them the commonwealth, and part of them the Church of God, but the selfsame people whole and entire were both under one Governor, on whose supreme authority they did all depend." (ed. by Raymond Arron Houk, New York, 1931, p. 166.)

[6] *Cf.* H. A. L. Fisher, *The History of England from the Accession of Henry VII to the Death of Henry VIII*, (The Political History of England, ed. by W. Hunt and R. L. Poole, Vol. V.) London, 1906, pp. 215 *ff*. In 1517 a canon of St. Mary Spittal, Dr. Beale, incited his audience to violence by preaching that God had given the land to Englishmen as a perpetual inheritance and that the increase in poverty was due to aliens. But even in 1550 one third of the London population consisted of alien artisans.

comparable to that of the Iberian monarchies or of the Italian republics; at least for the beginnings it is true that the British Empire was founded in a haphazard way, though not entirely in a fit of absent-mindedness. For during the reign of Elizabeth the English people started to turn their attention more and more towards the sea; the exploits of Sir Walter Raleigh, the narrations of Richard Hakluyt, stirred their hearts. The victory of the Spanish Armada spurred imagination towards the domination of the seas. But it is characteristic that even at the end of the reign of Elizabeth, the greatest English poet in the infinite variety of his human types does not create for us a single English sailor.[7]

Thus the Tudor period laid the foundations for the growth of English nationhood. But the English people and the English culture had not yet come into their own. Even in the Elizabethan period the widespread fear that the English language had only a very limited future persisted. Literary criticism remained almost completely dominated by the classical standards of the past. There was as yet little feeling for English literature as English, and therefore great contemporary English poets, measured by the traditional and universal classical standards, could not be recognized in their own right.[8] Only with the beginning of the seventeenth century is a recognition of the English genius as peculiarly English expressed, and the point emphasized that rules of poetry and taste change with peoples and ages. Thus Samuel Daniel defended rhyme as suitable to the English language although unknown to classical poetry, and English architecture against the imitation of ancient styles. The moderns need not model themselves upon Greeks or Romans, for "we are the children of nature as well as they."

This emancipation from subjection to authority, biblical or ancient, this assertion of autonomy and of the possibility of progress was best mirrored in the new attitude towards science inaugurated by Francis Bacon. He represents the Tudor Renaissance in its utilitarian and experimental realism, in his faith in a universal,

[7] Gabriel Harvey challenged the English poets in 1592 to write an English national *epos* emulating Homer and glorifying the naval victory over the Spaniards.

[8] I am greatly indebted for some of the following material to the most valuable suggestions of my colleague, Dean Marjorie Hope Nicolson, whose special field of research is the intellectual history of seventeenth century England. I am also grateful to Dr. Grant McColley, research consultant at the Smith College Library, for his bibliographical information.

rational morality, in his desire for power over nature. A comparison of Bacon's *New Atlantis* with an earlier work like More's *Utopia* reveals a significant change in the attitude towards science and its power. Bacon lays much less stress on changes in economics or politics. He regards science as the vehicle for bringing in the millenium: "the enlarging of the bounds of human empire, to the effecting of all things possible." This belief led inevitably to optimism, as man did conquer more and more secrets of nature, learning how to command nature in such a way as to improve upon her. It was under this inspiration that the pessimism, or at least melancholy, predominant at the beginning of the seventeenth century—Robert Burton's *Anatomy of Melancholy* was published in 1621—was altered. In the *Novum Organum* Bacon first analyzes the reasons for despair, as generally advanced by those who were of the opinion that the ancients had done all the great things and that nothing was left for the moderns. Bacon then proceeds to analyze the reasons for hope, founded on his conviction that, by using the right method, man can and will command the world. Much quoted in the seventeenth century was the still famous passage in his *Advancement of Learning* in which he gave a new interpretation to the meaning and value of antiquity. "Surely the advise of the prophet is the true direction in this matter, '*State super vias antiquas, et videte quaenam sit via recta et bona et ambulate in ea.*' Antiquity deserveth that reverence, that men should make a stand thereupon and discover what is the best way; but when the discovery is well taken, then to make progression. And to speak truly, '*Antiquitas saeculi juventus mundi.*' These times are the ancient times, when the world is ancient, and not those which we account ancient, *ordine retrogrado*, by a computation backward from ourselves."[9]

This confidence in the future and in the growing powers of man through science singled Bacon out from most of his immediate contemporaries, but set the tone for the future. The belief was still common that the physical and intellectual forces of men were steadily declining and that the end of the world was approaching. On the strength of mystical calculations this event was anticipated

[9] Bacon's *Advancement of Learning* and the *New Atlantis*, 1905, p. 265 and p. 35 (*Advancement*, First Book, V, 1). The middle-class connection is well emphasized in *Advancement*, First Book, II, 5 (p. 16): "Only learned men love business as an action according to nature, as agreeable to health of mind as exercise is to health of body, taking pleasure in the action itself."

generally for the years 1600 or 1666. Godfrey Goodman published in London in 1616 *The Fall of Man, or the Corruption of Nature proved by the Light of our Naturall Reason,* in which he insisted that men were growing smaller, that no living generations could be compared to the giants of antiquity, that compared with the age of the patriarchs lives were getting shorter, animals were losing the strength and size of the ancient animals and the heavens and elements were wearing out. In a similar vein and at about the same time, John Donne wrote in his *An Anatomie of the World, wherein . . . the frailty and the decay of this whole World is represented:*[10]

> So thou sicke World, mistak'st thy selfe to bee
> Well, when alas, thou'rt in a Lethargie . . .
> If man were anything, he's nothing now.

But at the beginning of the seventeenth century new arguments began to be voiced, according to which the causes for the difference of historical periods and their attitudes were to be found, not in any essential difference between ancient and modern men, but in difference of climate, environment and national temperament. Therefore later generations had no less chances of greatness than the ancients. A growing historical way of thinking, an incipient understanding of literature against its historical and social background, coalesced

[10] The first edition of Godfrey Goodman's book was dedicated "To the QVEENES Most Excellent Maiestie, Ovr Most Graciovs Soueraigne Lady, and my most honoured Mistris Queene Anne." His pessimism about the world and nature is in contrast to his pride in the temporal achievements of England, expressed in the Introduction. "And thus as I haue endeuoured to shew the mercy and prouidence of God in generall to whole mankinde, especiallie for our soules health and saluation; so here making bolde to write vnto your Maiestie, I could doe no lesse, then take some notice of the temporall blessings, wherewith God hath blessed vs aboue other people. This blessing especially consists in gouernment, whereby we receiue the fruites of peace, of plentie, of happines, and liue securely vnder the protection of our Princes; this blessing seemes to bee proper to this nation, proper to this present age wherein wee liue; for I will not speake how in former times, this our Land was distracted with small principalities and gouernements; when it should seeme the greatest part lay waste in borders and confines when the strength was diuided within it selfe; I will onely beginne with the last age of our forefathers." (Sig. A5). The book of Goodman who became later Bishop of Gloucester, was republished in 1629 under the title *The Fall of Adam from Paradise proved by Natural Reason and the grounds of Philosophy.* The verses by Donne are from *Poems,* ed. by Herbert J. C. Grierson, Oxford, 1912, Vol. I, p. 232, 236, see also p. 238 f. Cf. also Raleigh's *History of the World* (1614), Pt. I, Bk. I, chap. V. Sec. 5.

with the growing pride in scientific progress into a slowly crystallizing national consciousness, into an optimistic belief in man's potentialities and in national achievement. Not only Bacon's but other widely read books[11] supported the new attitude of confidence. The controversy between the ancients and the moderns, which raged throughout the seventeenth century, was fought in England to a lesser degree on the battle fields of *belles lettres* and of aesthetic criticism (as it was in France) than in the field of experimental research and scientific progress. Thanks to this new spirit of scientific interest the English eventually achieved in the seventeenth century the leading position in this field, and men from all countries looked to the Royal Society of London for the Improving of Natural

[11] George Hakewill, *An apologie or declaration of the power and providence of God in the government of the world consisting in an examination and censure of the common errour touching natures perpetuall and universal decay* . . ." Oxford, 1630. The most important critical essays mirroring the attitude towards ancient and modern national standards in literature towards the end of the sixteenth century are Sir Philip Sidney, *An Apologie for Poetry* (*Elizabethan Critical Essays*, ed. G. Gregory Smith, Oxford, 1904, Vol. I, pp. 150–207), Sir John Harington, *A Preface, or rather a Briefe Apologie of Poetrie, and of the Author and Translator,* prefixed to his translation of *Orlando Furioso,* (*Ibid.*, Vol. II, pp. 194–211), Samuel Daniel, *A Defence of Rhyme,* (*Ibid.*, Vol. II, pp. 356–384). The new emphasis upon English national peculiarity and even superiority in comparison with French or classical standards was expressed in the second half of the seventeenth century in Sir Robert Howard, "Preface to Four New Plays," and "Preface to the Great Favourite, or the Duke of Lerma," (*Critical Essays of Seventeenth Century*, ed. by J. E. Spingarn, Oxford, 1908, Vol. II, pp. 97–111) and Sir William Temple, "An Essay upon the Ancient and Modern Learning," (*Ibid.*, Vol. III, pp. 32–72). Its strongest expression is found in John Dryden: "Indeed, there is a vast difference betwixt arguing like Perrault, in behalf of the French poets, against Homer and Virgil, and betwixt giving the English poets their undoubted due, of excelling Aeschylus, Euripides and Sophocles. For if we, or our greater fathers, have not yet brought the drama to an absolute perfection, yet at least we have carried it much further than those ancient Greeks; . . . Our authors as far surpass them in genius, as our soldiers excel theirs in courage." (*The Works of John Dryden,* ed. by Sir Walter Scott, revised by George Saintsbury, Edinburgh, Vol. XII, pp. 59 f.) In his *Of Dramatick Poesie* Neander strongly defends the superiority of English drama as compared with the French theatre. "We have borrow'd nothing from them; our Plots are weav'd in English Loomes," (ed. by T. S. Eliot, London, 1928, p. 53). A little later follows a defence of Shakespeare as "the man who of all Modern, and perhaps Ancient Poets, had the largest and most comprehensive soul." *Cf.* also George Morey Miller, *The Historical Point of View in English Literary Criticism from 1570–1770,* Heidelberg, 1913.

Knowledge as the center for experimental research in Europe. The first historian of the Society[12] insisted upon its cosmopolitan spirit. The members of the Society "openly profess, not to lay the Foundation of an English, Scotch, Irish, Popish, or Protestant Philosophy, but a Philosophy of Mankind. . . . If I could fetch my Materials whence I pleas'd, to fashion the Idea of a perfect Philosopher; he should not be all of one Clime, but have the different Excellencies of several Countries." But in this universal task the English have definitely assumed the undisputed leadership. Their attitude "has rous'd all our Neighbours to fix their Eyes upon England. From hence they expect the great Improvements of Knowledge will flow." Thus England "may justly lay Claim, to be the Head of a philosophical League, above all other countries in Europe. . . . If there can be a true Character given of the universal Temper of any Nation under Heaven; then certainly this must be ascrib'd to our Country-men; so that even the Position of our Climate, the Air, the Influence of the Heaven, the Composition of the English Blood; as well as the Embraces of the Ocean, seem to join with the Labours of the Royal Society, to render our Country a Land of experimental Knowledge. And it is a good Sign, that Nature will reveal more of its Secrets to the English, than to others; because it has already furnish'd them with a Genius so well proportion'd, for the receiving and retaining its Mysteries."

The idea of the superiority of the moderns thus soon became merged with the idea of the superiority of the English, as leaders in the new science of which even the ancients had been ignorant. Man's trust in reason,—as advanced by Descartes—in his senses and in observation,—as advanced by Bacon—for unveiling the secrets and laws of nature, found its most fertile soil in England, helped by the new feeling of liberty and tolerance germinating in the seventeenth-century Revolution. Even Bishop Sprat stressed the spirit of tolerance in 1667 when he wrote his *History of the Royal Society:* "It is dishonorable, to pass a hard Censure on the Religions of all other Countries: It concerns them, to look to the

[12] Thomas Sprat, *The History of the Royal Society of London for the Improving of Natural Knowledge*, 3rd ed., London, 1722. The book was first published in 1667. Sprat had helped to found the Royal Society. The quotations are from Part II, Section VI, pp. 63–65, and Section XX, pp. 113–115. Bishop Sprat also considered among the merits of the Royal Society its aversion to flowery language. "They have exacted from all their Members, a close, naked, natural way of speaking; . . . a native Easiness." (p. 113.)

Reasonableness of their Faith; and it is sufficient for us, to be establish'd in the Truth of our own." The new premonition of the immense possibilities which were opening up for the English and through the English for mankind found enthusiastic expression in John Dryden's *Annus Mirabilis*,[13] the year of wonders 1666, which by many people on the Continent was regarded as the date set for the end of the world.

> But what so long in vain, and yet unknown,
> By poor mankind's benighted wit is sought,
> Shall in this age to Britain first be shown,
> And hence be to admiring nations taught.

But in the seventeenth century the English were not only more engrossed in the new science than other contemporary peoples, they were also ahead of any other nation in political theory and political interest. Whereas Italy and Spain were declining, Germany was devastated economically and intellectually by the long-drawn horror of the Thirty Years War, and the French nation afforded the magnificent spectacle of a stable society on a classical basis, the English people were being deeply stirred by the convulsions of the Revolution. The tendencies of a nascent nationalism which had germinated under the Tudors now broke through in a volcanic eruption. It filled the English people with an entirely new consciousness, a sense that they, the common people of England, were the bearers of history and builders of destiny at a great turning point from which a new true Reformation was to start. For the first time the authoritarian and aristocratic tradition on which the Church and the State had rested was challenged in the name of the liberty of man. The English Revolution was a synthesis, far-reachingly important, of Calvinist ethics and a new optimistic humanism. Being a Calvinist revolution the new nationalism expressed itself in an identification of the English people with the Israel of the Old Testament.

II

The Puritan Revolution, in spite of its profound national and social implications, was fundamentally a religious movement for the assertion of those tendencies of the Reformation which had been suppressed by a ruthless authoritarianism in Germany. The theo-

[13] *The Works of John Dryden, op. cit.*, Vol. I, p. 63.

cratic radicalism of Calvinism joined with the primitive democracy of the Anabaptist and the spiritualist movements in the demand for the creation of a truly Christian Commonwealth, a Commonwealth in itself looking toward a universal Protestant polity. The primary inspiration of the Revolution was drawn from sources similar to those which had inspired the Hussite movement. But in the far-advanced stage of social and intellectual development of seventeenth-century England, the religious revolution turned into a liberating intellectual movement which definitely brought the Middle Ages to an end and initiated the social and political movements of the modern age.[14] The feeling of a great task to be achieved was not restricted to the upper classes. It lifted the people to a new dignity, of being no longer the common people, the object of history, but of being the nation, the subject of history, chosen to do great things in which every one, equally and individually, was called to participate. Here we find the first example of modern nationalism, religious, political and social at the same time, although it was not yet the secularized nationalism which arose at the end of the eighteenth century. But it was infinitely more than the stateism and patriotism of the Renaissance and of the age of absolute monarchies. Here we find for the first time a people aroused and stirred in its innermost depths, feeling upon its shoulders the mission of history, and finding a new meaning and a new luster in the word "liberty."

Some English writers of that time sought mooring for this new liberty in the past, in the traditions of English common law as against the rigidity of Roman law, in a reassertion of the Saxon common people against the Norman conquerors who had "destroyed all English liberties." Similar tendencies were again to emerge in the French Revolution. Politicians and scholars, monarchists as well as republicans, tried to justify their present position by an appeal to the past—not in the fashion of what was later to become romantic nationalism, but in an effort to strengthen their claims and demands as well as to protect their vested interests by the authority of the past. The awakening common people constructed a legendary past of freedom and equality as the background for the struggle of their ancestors against their "Norman masters," and regarded the liberty of all Englishmen as historically grounded. But far

[14] *Cf.* Ernst Troeltsch, *Die Bedeutung des Protestantismus für die Entstehung der modernen Welt*, 3rd. ed., München, 1924, p. 63. See also G. P. Gooch, *English Democratic Ideas in the Seventeenth Century*, 2nd ed., 1927.

more important than this ephemeral effort at a reinterpretation of the past was the immense surge towards the future, towards a new nationalism represented at that time by the English, destined, however, for the whole of humanity, and based ultimately on the ideas of natural law and reason. The new nationalism was fundamentally liberal and universal, carrying a message for all mankind and implying (if not always granting) the liberty and equality of every individual. On the road to this universalism based upon liberty and reason, the English people were to be the leader and teacher. They were to be an entirely new people, a reborn people, created by Cromwell out of Puritans and Sectarians, out of English, Scotch and Jews, out of all who were of the right mind, a godly people.[15]

This religious nationalism was experienced by the English people as a revival of Old Testament nationalism. As the writers of the Renaissance were inspired, in Italy, Germany, and France, by their familiarity with the classical authors into a new feeling of patriotism, so the English at the time of the Puritan Revolution were inspired by their *self-identification* with the Hebrews. But these attitudes were of fundamentally different consequence. It is sometimes difficult with Renaissance nationalism to determine whether the authors really meant or only quoted such sentiments, whether they only imitated the ancients, or transformed the inspiration into a new life of their own; and this Renaissance nationalism remained confined to the small educated class reading the ancient authors, and was therefore only a passing phenomenon quickly to be engulfed by the rising tide of the new theologizing. The English nationalism of the seventeenth century, however, became an indelible part of the mind and heart of all Englishmen: for its vehicle was the book open and known to every Protestant. "England became the people of a

[15] On this aspect of the Puritan Revolution, *cf.* Ernest Barker, *Oliver Cromwell and the English People*, 1937, pp. 82 *f.* An effort characteristic of present German historiography to find a racial consciousness in the English Revolution was made by Erwin Hölzle, "Volks- und Rassenbewusstsein in der englischen Revolution," in *Historische Zeitschrift*, Vol. 153, No. 1, but he can point out only very few indications of doubtful importance. *Cf.* also Georg Lenz, *Demokratie und Diktatur in der englischen Revolution 1640–1660*, München, 1933. One of the pamphlets against the Normans was John Hare's *Sanct Edward's Ghost or Antinormanism*, published in 1647, and soon followed by another pamphlet, *Plain English to our Wilful Bearers of Normanism*, which complained that the first pamphlet had not been noticed at all. Against the right of conquest of the Normans he pleaded for the law of nature and the necessities of the *salus populi*.

book, and that book was the Bible."[16] It was above all the Old Testament which inspired Cromwell and his generation. The whole thought and style of the period was deeply colored with Hebraism. The three main ideas of Hebrew nationalism dominated the consciousness of the period: the chosen people idea, the covenant, the messianic expectancy. They were professed with the old religious fervor, clothed in the very words of the Old Testament, but they radiated the new light of rationalism and liberty. In the struggle of the individual conscience against absolute authority, in the spiritual as well as in the political field, the fight for religious and for civic liberties coalesced into one enthusiastic effort which rooted the new liberty in the ethical ideal of prophetic religion. Like Israel in antiquity, the English now were called to glorify God's name on earth, to achieve the final Reformation and to teach nations how to live. Cromwell was compared to Joshua, and poets like Andrew Marvell and Edmund Waller glorified England as the center of a new *Weltpolitik* of universal liberty:[17]

> Whether this portion of the world were rent,
> By the rude ocean, from the continent;
> Or thus created; it was sure designed
> To be the sacred refuge of mankind.
>
> Hither the oppressed shall henceforth resort,
> Justice to crave, and succour, at your court;
> And then your Highness, not for ours alone,
> But for the world's protector shall be known.

This new liberty found its magistral expression in Milton's writings. When he returned from Italy in 1639 "wrapped in a vision of a regenerate England, he definitely conceived of himself as one

[16] J. R. Green, *A Short History of The English People*, New York, Harper, 1884, p. 455. William Tyndale, the most famous translator of the English Bible in the sixteenth century, stressed the similarity between the Hebrew and the English which he thought more related than English and Latin and even than English and Greek. "The manner of speaking (in Hebrew and English) is both one, so that in a thousand places thou needest not but to translate it into the English word for word." A. S. Cook, *The Bible and English Prose Style*, Boston, 1892, p. XI. See also Marjorie H. Nicolson, "Milton and the Bible" in Margaret B. Crook, *The Bible and Its Literary Associations*, New York, 1937, pp. 278–307.

[17] *The Poems of Edmund Waller*, ed. by G. Thorn Drury, new ed., New York, 1901. Vol. II, p. 11: "A Panegyric to my Lord Protector, of the Present Greatness and Joint Interest of His Highness and This Nation."

on whom also a burden was laid, and looked forward, as his share in the sacred task, to the composition of a great poem that should be 'doctrinal to a nation.' "[18] This poem was never written because Milton soon felt himself compelled into active political life, into the service of God and of his nation. "I saw that a way was opening for the establishment of real liberty; that the foundation was laying for the deliverance of man from the yoke of slavery and superstition; that the principles of religion, which were the first objects of our care, would exert a salutary influence on the manner and constitution of the republic."[19]

Milton was a man of the Reformation but he carried at the same time the spirit of the Renaissance forward into the eighteenth century. In all his deep religiosity lies a new jubilant this-worldliness. Man and society were in the center of his concern. He asked everyone "to place . . . his private welfare and happiness in the public peace, liberty and faith." "The great and almost only commandment of the Gospel is, to command nothing against the good of man, and much more no civil command against the civil good." "The general end of every ordinance, of every severest, divinest, even of Sabbath, is the good of man; yea, his temporal good not excluded."[20] His faith in human nature, his desire for the betterment of life was based on his pride in man's reason, in the right of the individual conscience. He saw the great arch-enemies of himself and of humanity in Custom and Authority. His plea for the liberty of unlicensed printing in the *Areopagitica* culminated in the outcry "Give me the liberty to know, to utter, and to argue freely according to conscience, above all liberties."[21] In his first *Defence of the People of England, concerning their right to call to account kings and magistrates and after due conviction to depose and put them to death,* he went beyond the declaration of the liberty of men to proclaim their fundamental equality:

[18] Sir Herbert J. C. Grierson, *Milton and Wordsworth, Poets and Prophets,* New York, 1937, p. VII.

[19] *Milton's Prose,* ed. by Malcolm W. Wallace, Oxford University Press, 1925, p. XI.

[20] *The Prose Works of John Milton,* London, George Bell & Sons, 1884–1889, Vol. II, p. 126; Vol. III, p. 353.

[21] *Milton's Prose, op. cit.,* p. 318. Milton points out that the censor uses the word *imprimatur* because "our English, the language of men ever famous, and foremost in the achievements of liberty, will not easily find servile letters enough to spell such a dictatory presumption in English." (p. 285.)

> No man who knows aught, can be so stupid to deny that all men naturally were born free, being the image and resemblance of God himself. . . . It being thus manifest that the power of Kings and Magistrates is nothing else, but what is only derivative, transferred and committed to them in trust from the People, to the Common good of them all, in whom the power yet remains fundamentally, and cannot be taken from them, without a violation of their natural birthright.

But his main concern remained the liberty of man, the autonomy of the rational being who is growing to full maturity and coming into his own. One may say that Milton was obsessed with the idea of liberty. It plays an important part even in his poetry; and its conception deepens as the troubled years brought the recognition of the problems attendant upon it. Liberty to him was religious, political and personal; he pleaded for liberty as the end of education, for liberty in marriage, for liberty in printing and publishing. He realized that liberty is not only an institutional but also a moral problem, that its concomitant is personal responsibility: the freedom and dignity of choice puts a tremendous burden of responsibility upon man and nation for their every decision. The real mark of freedom is Reason. Men can be free only so far as they control their lower faculties—appetites, desires and senses—by reason. "If men within themselves would be governed by reason, and not generally give up their understanding to a double tyranny, of Custom from without, and blind affection within, they would discern better, what it is to favor and uphold the Tyrant of a Nation."[22]

This new liberty Milton found represented in the English people of his time. An immense pride in their leadership of mankind rings through his words:[23]

> Lords and Commons of England, consider what Nation it is whereof ye are, and whereof ye are the governors: a Nation not slow and dull, but of a quick, ingenious, and piercing spirit, acute to invent, subtle and sinewy to discourse, not beneath the reach of any point the highest that human capacity can soar to. . . . Yet that which is above all this, the favour and the love of heaven we have great argument to think in a peculiar manner propitious and propending towards us. Why else was this Nation chosen before any other, that out of her as out of Sion should be proclaimed and sounded forth

---

[22] *Op. cit.*, pp. 331, 333, 326.

[23] *Op. cit.*, pp 312–315. The theme of liberty is taken up in *Paradise Lost* to be resumed with ever deepening implications in *Paradise Regained* and in *Samson Agonistes*.

the first tidings and trumpet of Reformation to all Europe. . . . Now once again by all concurrence of signs, and by the general instinct of holy and devout men, as they daily and solemnly express their thoughts, God is decreeing to begin some new and great period in his Church, even to the reforming of Reformation itself: what does he then but reveal Himself to his servants, and as his manner is, first to his Englishmen; I say as his manner is, first to us, though we mark not the method of his counsels, and are unworthy. Behold now this vast City; a City of refuge, the mansion-house of liberty, encompassed and surrounded with his protection; . . . What wants there to such a towardly and pregnant soil, but wise and faithful labourers, to make a knowing people, a Nation of Prophets, of Sages, and of Worthies. . . . For now the time seems come, wherein Moses the great Prophet may sit in heaven rejoicing to see that memorable and glorious wish of his fulfilled, when not only our seventy Elders, but all the Lord's people are become Prophets.

Thus the age-old shackles of authoritarianism have been removed: a nation has emerged of free men, without kings or aristocracy, free men politically as well as spiritually, without the aristocracy of priesthood, all of them prophets, a saintly people, a new Israel. The government of this new commonwealth will therefore correspond to the theocracy of ancient Israel:[24]

But God will incline them to hearken rather with erected minds to the voice of our Supreme Magistracy, calling us to liberty and the flourishing deeds of a reformed Commonwealth; with this hope that as God was heretofore angry with the Jews who rejected him and his form of Government to choose a King, so that he will bless us, and be propitious to us who reject a King to make him only our leader and supreme governor in the conformity as near as may be of his own ancient government; wherein we have the honour to precede other Nations who are now labouring to be our followers.

[24] *Op. cit.*, p. 356. Exalted passages in the Old Testament style are frequent with Milton. See *The Works of John Milton,* New York, 1931, Vol. III, Part I, p. 78 *f.*, 147 *f.* The following passage sounds entirely Cromwellian: "For he being equally near to his whole creation of Mankind, and of free power to turn his . . . fatherly regard to what Region of Kingdom he pleases, hath yet ever had this island under the special indulgent eye of his Providence." But a significant passage shows the Catholic temper of Milton's nationalism: "Nor is it distance of place that makes enmity, but enmity that makes distance. He therefore that keeps peace with me, near or remote, of whatsoever Nation, is to me as far as all civil and human offices an Englishman and a neighbour; but if an Englishman forgetting all Laws, human, civil and religious, offend against life and liberty, to him offended and to the Law in his behalf, though born in the same womb, he is no better than a Turk, a Saracen, a Heathen." (*Milton's Prose, op. cit.,* p. 341 *f.*)

And again: "Britain which was formerly styled the hot-bed of tyranny, will hereafter deserve to be celebrated for endless ages as a soil most genial to the growth of liberty." But this liberty is in no way destined for Great Britain alone. It is human liberty carrying a universal message to all the nations, even beyond the bounds of Christianity. In a famous passage Milton saw the whole of mankind watching and imitating the English Revolution: "I seem to survey, as from a towering height, the far extended tracts of sea and land, and innumerable crowds of spectators, betraying in their looks the liveliest interest, and sensations the most congenial with my own. . . . Surrounded by congregated multitudes, I now imagine that, from the columns of Hercules to the Indian Ocean, I behold the nations of the earth recovering that liberty which they so long had lost; and that the people of this island . . . are disseminating the blessings of civilization and freedom among cities, kingdoms, and nations."[25]

A new age had started, England was moving in gigantic strides at the head of mankind, under the leadership of great men, such as Cromwell and Milton himself. Milton knew Cromwell as the great leader to liberty; in spite of his enthusiastic admiration for him and his work he nevertheless did not hesitate to warn him, when it

[25] *Op. cit.*, pp. 376, 378. "For who is there, who does not identify the honor of his country with his own? What can conduce more to the beauty or glory of one's country, than the recovery, not only of its civil but of its religious liberty?" (p. 375). As a prophetic warning of the perversion of liberty which in recent times has been attempted in Europe we read today Milton's words: "For it is of no little consequence, by what principles you are governed, either in acquiring liberty, or in retaining it when acquired. And unless that liberty which is of such a kind as arms can neither procure nor take away, shall have taken deep root in your minds and hearts, there will not long be wanting one who will snatch from you by treachery what you have acquired by arms . . . If your peace and your liberty be a state of warfare, if war be the summit of your praise, you will, believe me, soon find peace the most adverse to your interests." (p. 403) In his *Defensio Secunda* Milton mentioned that "Greece herself, Attic Athens herself, as if coming to life again, expressed their applauses through their own Philaras, one of their noblest." Philaras was one of the earliest and isolated forerunners of Greek nationalism. Born in Athens at the end of the sixteenth century he lived in Italy and Paris. He appealed to Milton and to the Commonwealth to help Greece to regain her national liberty. (David Masson, *The Life of John Milton*, Vol. IV, London, 1887, p. 443.) Milton's reply to Leonard Philaras is preserved to us. (*The Works of John Milton*, New York, 1936, Vol. XII, pp. 54–59.)

appeared for a moment that Cromwell wished to make himself an autocrat, "for such is the nature of things that he who entrenches on the liberty of others is the first to lose his own and become a slave." The hero for him—and therein lies the immense liberating importance of the English Revolution—was not the man radiating power, the leader to conquest and expansion. "He alone is worthy of the appellation who either does great things, or teaches how they may be done, or describes them with a suitable majesty when they have been done; but those only are great things which tend to render life more happy, which increase the innocent enjoyments and comforts of existence, or which pave the way to a state of future bliss more permanent and more pure."

III

If Milton can be regarded as representative of the ideas of the Puritan Revolution,[26] Cromwell is much more than its incarnation. He has been called "the most typical Englishman of all time." "All the incongruities of human nature are to be traced somewhere or other in Cromwell's career. What is more remarkable is that this union of apparently contradictory forces is precisely that which is to be found in the English people, and which has made England what she is at the present day."[27] Cromwell's leadership marked the definite transition from religious medievalism to modern England, to the domination of middle class and trade interests. His mind was a curious mixture of religious, or more precisely Old

---

[26] *Cf.* Sir John Robert Seeley, *Lectures and Essays*, London, 1895, p. 112. Hilaire Belloc sees Milton as leading "the new religion of patriotism . . . , the transference to the English image of that feeling which hitherto had attached to Princes and before them to what had been the common religion of Christendom." (*Milton*, Philadelphia, 1935, p. 22.) See also Gertrude Hardeland, *Miltons Anschauungen von Staat, Kirche, Toleranz*, Halle, 1934; H. Poppers, *Der religiöse Ursprung des modernen englischen Freiheits-und Staatsideals. Die Geschichtsgestaltung des Independentismus*, Prague, 1936; Karl Völker, *Die religiöse Wurzel des englischen Imperialismus*, Tübingen, 1924.

[27] Samuel Rawson Gardiner, *Cromwell's Place in History*, London, 1902, pp. 116, 114. See Ernest Barker, *Oliver Cromwell and the English people*, 1937, p. 28; also Hermann Oncken, *Cromwell, Vier Essays über die Führung einer Nation*, Berlin, 1935; Helmuth Kittel, *Oliver Cromwell, seine Religion und seine Sendung*, Berlin, 1928.

Testament, enthusiasm and of a clear and rational discernment of the value of individual liberty. He more than any other awakened the consciousness of the English people as the chosen people, a consciousness in which every Englishman was called to participate. The religious enthusiasm was increased by the visible blessings conferred upon England at that time: the firm establishment of the union with Scotland, the consummation of the conquest of Ireland, the expansion of the colonial empire, the increase in the power of the navy, the growth of trade and commerce. Cromwell fought for "freedom of the individual conscience" in religious matters, for the "true freedom of the Christian man," but religious and civil liberties went hand in hand with him, the "free Church" demanded a "free State," his religious nationalism was full of modern political and social portent. His chosen people were no longer the Christians but the English, though they remained representative of the Christian and universal cause.

The cause for which he fought was indeed supra-national, the ideal of what he deemed true Protestantism and of the universal concern of humanity and liberty; but the interest of this cause coincided for him with the interest of the English people, who, in that hour of history, were fighting the Lord's battles. They were fighting them, however, only so long as they remained true to His ethical teachings, a saintly people, living in the service of God and blessed by Him for their righteous life. Again and again the words applied to the English people are words and images taken from the Old Testament. Cromwell's Ironsides went to battle inspired by hymns and songs from the Old Testament. A soldier's pocket-bible, printed in 1643 to show from the Holy Scriptures "the qualifications of His inner man, that is a fit Souldier to fight the Lord's battles," contained almost exclusively quotations from the Old Testament. Like the Old Testament prophets Cromwell felt the immense gravity of the burden laid upon him, and the desire to evade its heavy yoke. "I can say in the presence of God," he said a few days before his death, "in comparison with whom we are but like poor creaping ants upon the earth, I would have lived under my woodside, to have kept a flock of sheep, rather than undertook such a government as this is." The night before his death, however, he was heard to say: "I would be willing to live to be further serviceable to God and His people, but my work is done."[28]

[28] Charles Firth, *Oliver Cromwell and the Rule of the Puritans in England*,

With all his religious enthusiasm Cromwell foreshadowed clearly the coming secular nationalism. In 1656 he said that, while God's "most peculiar interest [is] His Church, that will not teach any of us to exclude His general interest, which is a Concernment of the Living People, not as Christians, but as human creatures, within these three Nations, and with all the dependencies thereupon." He was yet more outspoken the following year when he defined "the two greatest Concernments that God hath in the world. The one that of Religion . . . the other thing cared for is the Civil Liberty and Interest of the Nation. . . . If anyone whatsoever think the Interest of Christians and the Interest of the Nation inconsistent or two different things, I wish my soul may never enter into their secrets!" And three years before, in speaking of the wars and labors in Ireland and Scotland, he proclaimed as the aim, "to put the topstone to this work and make the nation happy."[29]

Throughout his activities and wars Cromwell was always filled with a conviction that the English were "a people that have had a stamp upon them from God; God having, as it were, summed up all our glory to nations, in an epitomy, within these ten or twelve years last past."[30] He completely identified the English people with ancient Israel; English nationalism was born in the great decisive hour of its history by repeating the experience of the chosen people,

---

London, 1925, pp. 440, 443. In the following Cromwell is quoted from *The Letters and Speeches of Oliver Cromwell*, with elucidations by Thomas Carlyle, ed. by S. C. Lomas, London, 1904. A new edition on the basis of the work of Mrs. Sofia C. Lomas is now in process of publication by Wilbur Cortez Abbott, *The Writings and Speeches of Oliver Cromwell*, with an introduction, notes and a sketch of his life, Cambridge, Mass., in 4 vols., Vol. I, 1937, Vol. II, 1939. Important source material on the rise of Puritanism is to be found in William Haller, *Tracts on Liberty in the Puritan Revolution 1638–47*, 3 vols., New York, 1935; and his *The Rise of Puritanism; Or, the Way to the New Jerusalem as Set Forth in Pulpit and Press from Thomas Cartwright to John Lilburne and John Milton, 1570–1643*, New York, Columbia University Press, 1938. See also W. K. Jordan, *The Development of Religious Toleration in England (1640–1660)*, Cambridge, Mass., 1938; A. S. P. Woodhouse (ed.), *Puritanism and Liberty, being the Army Debates (1617–49)* from the *Clarke Manuscripts*, London, 1938; and W. Fraser Mitchell, *English Pulpit oratory from Andrewes to Tillotson, a study of its literary aspects*, London, Society for Promoting Christian knowledge, 1932.

[29] Vol. II, p. 509; Vol. III, p. 30 *f.*; Vol. II, p. 358. See also Vol. I, p. 187 and Vol. III, p 172 *f.*

[30] Vol. II, p. 404 *f.* See also Vol. I, p. 217 *f.*

of the covenant, of the battles fought for the Lord. In his first speech to the Little Parliament in 1653 he addressed its members:[31]

> Truly God hath called you to this world by, I think, as wonderful providences as ever passed upon the sons of men in so short a time. . . . Truly you are called by God as Judah was, to rule with Him, and for Him. . . . Thus God hath owned you in the eyes of the world; and thus, by coming hither, you own Him: and, as it is in Isaiah 43, 21,—its an high expression; and look to your own hearts whether, now or hereafter, God shall apply it to you: "this people," saith God, "I have formed for Myself, that they may show forth my praise." I say, its a memorable passage; the Lord apply it to each of your hearts!

And four years later he summed up yet more strongly his conviction of God's guidance. The soil of Great Britain, he said,

> Is furnished,—with the best People in the world. . . . And in this People, in the midst of this People, you have, what is still more precious, a People that are to God 'as the apple of His eye,'—and He says so of them, be they many, or be they few! But they are many. A People of the blessing of God; a People under His safety and protection, a People calling upon the Name of the Lord; which the Heathen do not. A People knowing God; and a People fearing God. And you have of this no parallel; no, not in all the world! . . . You have a good Eye to watch over you. . . . A God that hath watched over you and us. A God that hath visited these Nations with a stretched-out arm; and bore His witness against the unrighteousness and ungodliness of man, against those that would have abused such Nations. . . .

Gesta Dei per Anglos: but for Cromwell England fought at the same time for civilization and for liberty, a liberty in which everybody, even Irishmen, should share. It was this spirit which pervaded his Declaration to the People of Ireland in 1650, which he intended "for the undeceiving of deluded and seduced people." Although his entire lack of knowledge of Irish history and of Irish social conditions caused him to misunderstand completely the situation in that unhappy land, he was sincerely convinced that the English army brought to Ireland a truly human life for all.[32]

---

[31] Vol. II, pp. 290 *ff.*; Vol. III, pp. 11–13. Among many other passages see his letter to Pembroke, Vol. I, p. 321, then Vol. I, p. 511 *f.*, Vol. II, p. 52 and also pp. 224 *ff.*

[32] Vol. II, p. 21. In this Declaration to the People of Ireland Cromwell first drew a wrong picture of the history of Ireland, painting it as an idyllic and peaceful community of Irishmen and Englishmen until wicked priests instigated and deluded the Irish. Cromwell was entirely sincere in his ignorance of history and this

We come to break the power of a company of lawless rebels, who having cast off the authority of England, live as enemies to human society . . . we come (by the assistance of God) to hold forth and maintain the lustre and glory of English liberty in a nation where we have an undoubted right to do it;—wherein the people of Ireland (if they listen not to such seducers as you are) may equally participate in all benefits, to use liberty and fortune equally with Englishmen, if they keep out of arms.

"Liberty" in the sense of individual liberty, and "fortune" in the sense of pursuit of happiness, both based upon the civilized security of due process of law: this the English Revolution of the seventeenth century began to establish for England and carried as its message to other nations. The seeds of modern secular civilization were planted and nurtured in a primarily religious revolution. The Puritans occupied in it a central position similar to that of the Jacobins in the French Revolution. As the Jacobins in France, so the Puritans left indelible traces on the character of nationalism in Great Britain and even more in New England. But the importance of the Puritan Revolution went infinitely beyond the circle of the Puritans. When the immense tension under which these crusaders for a new and more godly life labored, irretrievably broke down in the fatigue and disillusionment which preceded the Restoration, contemporary observers might well have thought the Puritan enthusiasm and strife in vain. But the birth of nationalism in the Puritan Revolution determined and still determines the character of English nationalism. England was the first country where a national consciousness embraced the whole people. It became so deeply ingrained in the English mind that nationalism lost its prob-

---

goes far to explain his cruelties. Mrs. Lomas remarks in her note on p. 9: "Not only was Cromwell not behind the other men of his day but he and they were all immeasurably in advance of their predecessors of a generation or two before; as may be seen by studying the letters of the rulers of Ireland at the end of Elizabeth's reign, with their triumphant relations of the 'good killings' not only of men, but of women and little children; their cold-blooded proposals for subduing the country by absolute starvation; their utter callousness in fact, as regards the sufferings or the lives of the Irish people." It is absurd to justify contemporary aggressor imperialism with its barbarisms and oppressions by past deeds of British imperialism: the changed circumstances, the progress in our reaction towards oppression and in our knowledge of history and social conditions have to be taken into account. Besides, Cromwell's imperialism had a liberal and liberating call, fascist imperialism denies liberalism and all liberating and humanizing efforts.

lematic character with the English. It is for this reason that English philosophical thought in the nineteenth century offers relatively little meditation upon nationalism, its theory and implications, compared with Italian, German or Russian thought, where the problem and the problematic character of nationalism occupied a central position.

From its origin English nationalism preserved its peculiar character; it has always been and still is closer than any other nationalism to the religious matrix from which it rose,[33] and is imbued with the spirit of liberty asserted in a struggle against ecclesiastical and civil authority. It never made the complete integration of the individual with the nation the aim of nationalism; it always put a great emphasis upon the individual and upon the human community beyond all national divisions. The Calvinist awareness of the infinite

[33] This "Hebraic nationalism" (Ernest Barker, *op. cit.*, p. 27) was not only characteristic of the origins of English nationalism in Cromwell's time. It colored all the sermons of the period. *Cf.* Ethyn Williams Kirby, "Sermons Before the Commons, 1640–42," in *American Historical Review*, Vol. XLIV, No. 3, p. 545. Many of the independent sects showed judaizing tendencies, practically all of them expected the establishment of Christ's kingdom on earth in connection with the re-admission of the Jews to England or with their return to Palestine or with their baptism. Henry Archer in his sermon of 1642, "The personal reign of Christ upon earth," set the date for the conversion of the Jews at about 1656 and for the coming of Christ at 1700. Another divine, John Owen, preached on October 13, 1652, a sermon before the House of Commons arguing that the Turk and the Pope had to be overthrown and the Jews brought back to their own before the kingdom could be established. "There were also differences of opinion as to the exact part the Jews were to play in setting up the kingdom, but it was to be an important one, and therefore they were to be favored, and admitted to England." (Louise Fargo Brown, *The Political Activities of the Baptists and Fifth Monarchy Men in England during the Interregnum*, Washington, American Historical Association, 1912, p. 24.) Cromwell himself favored the Jews and their resettlement in England, whence they had been expelled in 1290. His motives were characteristically twofold, his hope of the fulfillment of Messianic prophecy and his wish for their commercial support. The leading Jewish scholar, Manasseh ben Israel, published in 1650 first in Spanish, then in a Latin translation with a prefatory epistle to the Parliament of England, his "Esperança de Israel." (For text and history see *Manasseh ben Israel's Mission to Oliver Cromwell*, ed. by Lucien Wolf, London, Jewish Historical Society of England, 1901.) The question of the legal admission of Jews to England was not definitely settled in Cromwell's time, although in 1657 two leading Jews purchased land for a Jewish cemetery, and a nephew of Manasseh was admitted to the Royal Exchange as a duly licensed broker of the City of London, without taking the usual oaths involving faith in Christianity. (*The Jewish Encyclopedia*, Vol. V, p. 169.)

value of every individual continued to protect against uniformity in civil as much as in religious matters and against any tyranny. Religious life and sentiment in England were rarely of an other worldly character, withdrawing into the sanctuary of inner life and inner liberty. They were full of social activism, of a feeling of responsibility for the betterment of the conditions in this world, conscious of the common root of religious and political liberty as the foundation for a true commonwealth. The religious and liberal character of English nationalism determined also the peculiar development of English socialism in the nineteenth century, so different from the character of the socialist movements on the European continent. English socialism carried the deep impress of the Independentism of the seventeenth century, religious, liberal and humanitarian, but so also did English imperialism.

The birth of English nationalism likewise coincided with the definite rise of the new middle classes. Both developments had been prepared in the sixteenth century under the Tudor monarchs, both came simultaneously to their fruition in the seventeenth century. One of the factors involved in the birth of English nationalism was the rise of new social forces, the expansion of trade, the need for new social relations and their infusion with new emotions and loyalties. The new classes which came to power in the seventeenth century saw their own activities, their accumulation of wealth, their search for trade and outlets for their energy, in the light of this new nationalism. Their consciousness of the new power which accrued to them and through them to the nation, the pursuit of their own happiness and of the fortunes of the nation, went hand in hand with the consciousness of their mission, of their religious and moral duty, of their obligation to mankind. The new liberalism, the new faith in man and in reason, the new confidence in the blessings of God, infused into the new acquisitiveness, into the new capitalism, not only a feeling of progress and assurance, but also of a dedication to the service of something higher than individual gain or national interest. Continental observers often spoke sarcastically of the English people who seemed to serve both God and Mammon, and suspected cant whenever the English seemed to invoke moral principles. But as a result of the origin of English nationalism every manifestation of the English power, even if at many times brutal and bent upon exploitation, as is all imperialism, has been accompanied by a deep moral undercurrent, fundamentally Christian and liberal, which has been one of the most potent factors in shaping modern civilization. English imperial politics in the nineteenth century was power-politics, but in contrast to German or Russian power-politics of that day, never only power-politics. It seldom wholly lost the demand for and the promise of political and intellectual liberty and equal justice under law, and in its best representatives may always be discerned traces of the Puritan Revolution's enthusiastic hope and anticipation of the establishment of a universal kingdom of God on this earth.[34]

---

[34] The essential traits of the Puritan revolution—mitigated, relativized, humanized—returned in the revolution of 1688, and are plainly manifest in Locke's *Two Treatises of Government* and *Letters on Toleration* which largely shaped the character of both English and American nationalism. The humanitarian and universal character on the one hand, the national character on the other hand, are well put in the opening sentence of the first *Treatise of Government*: "Slavery is so vile and miserable an estate of man, and so directly opposite to the generous temper and courage of our nation, that it is hardly to be conceived that an 'Englishman,' much less a 'gentlemen,' should plead for it." With the fundamental similarities went certain important differences; but limitations of space prevent the writer from expanding this subject further here.

The Influence of Eighteenth Century Ideas on the French Revolution*

by HENRI PEYRE

Reprinted from the *Journal of the History of Ideas*—Vol. X, No. 1, pp. 63-87

No question is likely to divide students of the past more sharply than that of the action of philosophical ideas and literary works upon political and social events. Our age has been powerfully impressed by the economic interpretation of history proposed by Marxists; but it has also witnessed the important rôle played by men of letters and men of thought in the Spanish Civil War and in the Resistance movement of World War II. The conscience of many writers is more obsessed today than it has ever been by the temptation—some call it the duty—of "engaged literature." The affinities of many of the leading authors in France and other countries link them with the men of the eighteenth century. Sartre, Camus, Giono, Breton are not unworthy descendants or reincarnations of Voltaire, Diderot, Rousseau.

It may thus be useful to attempt a restatement of an old, and ever present, problem, without any presumptuous claim to renovate its data or its solutions, but with an honest attempt to observe a few conditions which are obvious but all too seldom met. A summation of such an immense and thorny question should be clear, while respecting the complex nature of reality. It should be provocative, in the sense that it should suggest that much remains to be said on these matters by young scholars determined to launch upon the study of ideas in relation to the Revolution. Above all, it should be impartial if that is humanly possible, concerning questions on which it is difficult not to take sides, and it should attempt to retain in these questions the life with which they are instinct, without on the other hand sacrificing objectivity or solidity.

I

The problem of the effect of the Philosophy of Enlightenment on the French Revolution is one of the most important problems that confront the pure historian as well as the historian of thought and of literature. It is without doubt the most complex of the thousand aspects involved in the study of the Revolution, that is to say the

* This article was translated into English by Arthur L. Kurth.

origins of the modern world. Together with investigation of the origins of Christianity and the end of the ancient world, this study concerns one of the two most important upheavals that the philosophically-minded historian can conceive: Taine and Renan, as well as Michelet and Tocqueville, the four most important French historians of the past century, had quite rightly realized its magnitude. This problem is inevitable for every teacher of literature who lectures on Voltaire and Rousseau to his students, for every historian of the years 1789–1799 in France, and likewise for every historian of these same years and of the beginning of the nineteenth century in Germany, England, the United States and Latin America. It presents itself to every voter who reflects even a little about the things in his country's past that he would like to maintain and those that he desires to reform.

But because it presents itself so insistently to everyone, this problem has often been met with solutions that are crude or at the very least lacking in necessary overtones; because it closely parallels our present-day preoccupations, it has aroused the partisan spirit; because it concerns not only facts but ideas it has favored excessively dogmatic generalizations on the one hand and on the other, the voluntary blind timidity of chroniclers who have chosen to see in the events of the Revolution nothing but a series of improvisations and haphazard movements.

There is for one thing a long and devious current of ideas which first springing forth as a swift and turgid torrent in the sixteenth century, becoming a more or less tenuous water-course in the great period of the reign of Louis XIV, and finally like a river encircling the most obdurate islets of resistance within its multiple arms, seems to have engulfed the eighteenth century in the years 1750–1765. More and more clearly, those who set forth and develop these ideas take it upon themselves to influence the existing facts, to change man by education, to free him from out-moded superstitions, to increase his political liberty and his well-being. In no way do they dream of a general cataclysm and several of them are not insensitive to the refined amenity of the life that surrounds them or to the exquisite blend of intellectual boldness and voluptuous refinement that characterizes their era.

Suddenly, this pleasant 18th-century security, ''Table d'un long festin qu'un échafaud termine,'' as Hugo's beautiful image calls it, crumbles. The Revolution breaks out, and within a few years, rushes through peaceful reforms, produces a profusion of constitutions, sweeps aside the old regime, devours men, and causes heads to fall. This great movement is certainly confused, turbulent and irrational like everything that men accomplish by collective action. However, lawyers, officers, priests, and journalists play a part in it that is often important. These men had grown up in an intellectual climate that had been established by Montesquieu, Voltaire, Rousseau, Raynal and Mably. May we accurately reach a conclusion of "Post hoc, ergo propter hoc"?

It would not have been so difficult to answer such a question if partisan quarrels had not needlessly clouded the issue. Frenchmen are incapable of viewing their nation's past dispassionately or accepting it as a whole. For a hundred and fifty years they have not ceased to be of different minds on their Revolution which is doubtless a proof that it is still a live question among them, while in other countries the revolution of 1688 or the revolution of 1776 is calmly invested with the veneration accorded to a buried past. It is a curious fact that the great majority of their political writers from Joseph de Maistre, Louis de Bonald, and Auguste Comte himself, to Le Play, Tocqueville, Taine, at times Renan, Barrès, Bourget, Maurras and many others, has pronounced itself hostile to the "great principles of '89" or at least to that which was drawn from these principles. Three fundamental assertions are the basis of most of the anti-revolutionary arguments. A) The Revolution was harmful and anti-French; it could only be attributed to foreign influences that perverted the French genius of moderation, restrained devotion, and obedience to the hereditary monarch. It was caused by foreign influences that contaminated eighteenth century thought: Locke, the English deists, the Protestants in general, the Swiss Rousseau, etc. . . . B) These corrupting ideas were introduced among the French people who had been sound and upright until then, by clubs called "Sociétés de Pensée" and by secret groups of conspiring intellectuals, the Freemasons for example and the "Philosophes" themselves, who formed an authentic subversive faction. (Augustin Cochin, *Les Sociétés de Pensée,* Plon, 1921.) C) The Revolutionary spirit is the logical outcome of the classical spirit strengthened by the scientific spirit. This spirit delights in abstraction, generalizes profusely, and considers man as a creature apart from his environment, isolated from his past; it lacks the subtle empiricism which characterizes the English reformists; it is ignorant of everything touching reality. Accordingly it sets out to make laws for universal man, without regard for France's age-old traditions or the local conditions of these provinces. This contention advanced with talent and a semblance of thorough documentation by Taine has beguiled a great number of excellent minds because of its specious clarity.[1]

These contentions have not stood the test of serious scrutiny by literary historians trained in more rigid methods since the dawn of the twentieth century. The penetration with which Gustave Lanson has laid bare many of our prejudices concerning the eighteenth century forms one of his best-established claims upon our gratitude. Numerous investigators, Frenchmen and Americans especially, have since followed upon the path that he had pointed out. Lanson's ideas in their turn have become accepted opinion and doubtless it will be necessary to modify and complete them in the future by adopting new points of view. It is none the less true that it is thanks to him and to Daniel Mornet after him that we can state today that the three assertions summed up earlier are contradicted by the facts. The French revolution is truly of French origin. If certain foreigners, in particular Locke, whose name may be found at almost all the century's crossroads of ideas, did exert a real influence in France, this influence was assimilated and naturalized there.[2] It had moreover implanted itself in a

[1] It is well-known that the documentation used by Taine has been checked by Aulard, with disastrous results for the philosopher, who is revealed as a mediocre analyst of documentary evidence and a hasty statistician (*Taine historien de la Révolution française,* Colin, 1907). Aug. Cochin in the work mentioned above has tried with little success to defend Taine against Aulard. Paul Lacombe, in *Taine historien et sociologue* (Giard, 1909), has shown that the sociologist in Taine often causes Taine the historian to advance ready-made or stock theses. A. Mathiez in the *Revue d'Histoire moderne et contemporaine* (VIII [1906–1907], 257–284) and H. Sée in *Science et Philosophie de l'Histoire* (Alcan, 1928), 383–398, have also exposed Taine's weaknesses as a historian.

[2] Tocqueville's work, *L'Ancien Régime et la Révolution* (M. Lévy, 1856), supports a thesis which is in some respects similar to Taine's on the spirit of abstraction of the Philosophes and the influence of their views as theorizing and dogmatic men of letters on their century; but Tocqueville's statements show more subtlety than those of Taine, even if their style is less colorful and sometimes stiffer in its dignified oratorical seriousness. The bulk of Tocqueville's work, which rests on sound documentary research, tends to prove that almost everything attributed to

group of ideas going back to Bayle, Saint-Evremond, Le Vayer, Naudé and Montaigne, which were quite as indigenous and "French" as the absolutism of Bossuet. The philosophical Clubs and similar groups that made themselves felt in France around 1750 and played an active part after 1789 are not all revolutionary—far from it! Furthermore, the part that they played in preparing the Revolution is nowhere clearly ascertained. The rôle of a gigantic conspiracy attributed by some to Freemasonry is a myth.

Finally and above all, nothing justifies the assertion made with assurance by Taine that the writers of the eighteenth century were men of reason alone with no experience of the realities of life. In their time there was some use of empty rhetoric, as there is in every time; the Revolutionaries for their part will cherish a type of eloquence reminiscent of the ancients, and be occasionally intoxicated with words; they will also have an ambition to proclaim universal truths and formulate principles for all men. It is not certain that this ambition is not one of the finest qualities of the French Revolution. But it would be a mistake to forget that the eighteenth century is a great century in science, as much or more so in experimental science as in deductive and abstract disciplines. The works of M. Mornet have proved that eighteenth-century thinkers were on the contrary suspicious of scholastic generalizations and of systems in general: they made observations and conducted experiments. They introduced into education the taste for very detailed empiricism and for actual practice in the arts and trades. They praised techniques and described them with care. They traveled like Montesquieu in order to see at close hand constitutions and the way people lived by them. They cultivated the soil, in the case of the physiocrats; lived on their lands, as did Helvetius; or administered provinces, like Turgot. The most thoroughgoing Revolutionaries had not, like Marx or Lenin, spent years in reading-rooms; they were petty lawyers in contact with the people, like Robespierre at Arras, veterinaries like Marat; in short, provincial men who knew the lives of the peasant,

---

the Revolution (often in order to condemn it) already existed in old France. He puts especially vigorous emphasis on the ownership of land, which came more and more into peasant hands well before '89, and on the general prosperity of the country, which along with discontent increased under Louis XVI.

the artisan and the humble country priest of France. Taine's abstraction existed chiefly in his mind, and perhaps in that of Descartes and in a few works of Rousseau. But the Revolution was hardly Cartesian and never put into practice as a complete doctrine the ideas of the *Contrat Social,* which are moreover as contradictory as they are logical.

II

So let us differ with those who claim a priori that the Revolution sprang from the teachings of the "Philosophes," only in order to justify their condemnation of both the Revolution and the teaching. But in opposition to this group, the admirers of the "Philosophes" and even more the admirers of Rousseau, who was not exactly one of the "Philosophes," have taken up the cudgels in an attempt to deny the responsibility or even the guilt of the eighteenth-century political writers in the upheaval that ensued. Particularly notable among these efforts is Edme Champion's abstruse but well-informed book: *Rousseau et la Révolution française* (Colin, 1909). Bringing the concept of retroactive responsibility into these matters is a questionable method. "My God!" Karl Marx is said to have exclaimed on one of the rare occasions when he seems to have called upon Heaven, "preserve me from the Marxists!" Rousseau has accused himself of enough sins without our taxing his memory with the errors of his followers. Without inquiring whether the Revolution was good or bad, which would be entirely too naïve in this day, may we not be able to show how and in what way it absorbed, reflected or brought to fruition the ideas of thinkers who had prepared it without wishing for it?

Professional historians generally tend to limit the part played by ideas in world events: the best of them devote, apparently for the sake of form, one or two chapters to the literature, painting and music of the periods studied by their manuals. But the history of civilization and culture is still very clumsily related to general history. Historians prefer to emphasize the purely historical causes of the Revolution: financial disorder, ministerial blunders, or the hostility of parlements that had been alienated by encroachments upon their prerogatives, etc. Perhaps in doing so they are choosing the easiest way. Their history does grasp the events, the things that change, that is, the things that would be presented in today's newspapers as facts or news: a tax-measure, a famine, the dismissal of a minister, a change in the price of bread, or a treaty. But it often fails to apprehend the slow subterranean movements which minds inclined to be too matter-of-fact find intangible, until they one day make their appearance as acts that make news or usher in a historical era. Now there are cases in which they never appear as acts; and orthodox history gives scant consideration to abortive movements or history's side-roads into which the past has ventured briefly only to turn back.

The history of ideas has the advantage of being able to give leisurely consideration to elements of history that changed only slowly and did not necessarily express themselves in events which demand attention by virtue of their suddenness. It would gladly declare that ideas rule the world. This would doubtless be an over-optimistic creed, if one did not add immediately that these ideas often turn into those truths wrapped in the gilt paper of falsehood that our contemporaries call in France "mystiques," or that they crystallize into a few fetish-words which imprison or falsify them. The history of the idea of progress has been sketched, although insufficiently in our opinion, by J. Delvaille and the English writer J. M. Bury. History itself would owe much to the man who would attempt to write the story of the idea of evolution, or the idea of revolution, the idea of comfort, or the idea of efficiency and the myth of success in the United States, among many others. On occasion he would have to go beyond the texts or interpret them, but this should not be forbidden provided that it is done with intellectual honesty. One must also remember the fact that the history of ideas is not simply the exposition of theoretical views expressed in philosophical writings, but at the same time the history of the deformations undergone by these ideas when other men adopt them, and also the history of the half-conscious beliefs into which ideas first clearly conceived by the few promptly transform themselves. In his lectures published in Buenos Aires in 1940 under the title *Ideas y creencias* the Spanish philosopher Ortega y Gasset has rightly claimed for these half-formulated "beliefs" a position in historical works on a par with that of ideas.

The difficulties presented by such a history of ideas when they become beliefs, articles of faith, or emotional drives and impel men to action are enormous: they should, by this very fact, challenge research-men. Up to now, sociology has failed to make over the study of literature to any considerable degree because histories of the prevailing taste and the environment in which a writer lived and of the social and economic conditions in which he was placed while conceiving his work have little bearing on the creation and even the content of the original work. But a knowledge of the public that greeted a literary work or of the work's subsequent career might on the contrary prove extremely fruitful. Such knowledge requires painstaking inquiry into the work's success, based on a great number of facts; it also demands a qualitative interpretation of history and statistics and the occasional intervention of that much-feared "queen of the world" called imagination. For the most read book is not the one that exerts the greatest influence. A hundred thousand passive or half-attentive readers who bought and even leafed through the *Encyclopédie,* for example, count for less than five hundred passionate admirers of the *Contrat Social* if among the latter may be counted Robespierre, Saint-Just or Babeuf. A school-master or a lecturer heard with interest may pass on Marx or Nietzsche to generations of barely literate people who will never guess the source of a thought that has modified their whole lives. It is not even necessary to have understood a book or even to have read it through in order to be profoundly influenced by it. An isolated phrase quoted in some article or a page reproduced at some time in an anthology, may have done more to spread some of the opinions of Montesquieu, Proudhon, or Gobineau than thirty re-editions of their writings bought by private libraries and commented upon by ten provincial academies.

In 1933 Daniel Mornet published on the subject sketched here his work entitled *Les Origines intellectuelles de la Révolution française* (Colin), which is a study of the spread of ideas justly termed a model of intellectual probity and discretion. Henceforth no one can consider this historical and philosophical problem without owing much to this solid book. The author has avoided the error of so many other writers who make the Revolution inexplicable by drawing a rough contrast between 1789 and 1670 or even 1715. He has followed the slow progress of the spread of new ideas from 1715 to 1747, then from 1748 to 1770, the date when the philosophic spirit had won the day. He has made very searching inquiries into the degree of penetration of the reformist spirit among the more or less learned societies and academies, in the letters of private individuals, in provincial libraries and even in educational curricula. His conclusions are new in many respects because of the exact information they offer and because they show those who are misled by the perspective of a later day into the error of limiting the group of "Philosophes" to five or six names, that writers half-unknown to us (Toussaint, Delisle de Sales, Morellet, Mably) were among those most widely read in the eighteenth century. With fitting reserve they tend to show that the thought of the century, by itself, would never have caused the Revolution if there had not been misery among the people as well; and that misery which was not a new thing at the time would not have brought about the Revolution if it had not had the support of opinion that had long been discontented and desirous of reform. It is clear that the Revolution had various causes including historical causes, meaning economic, political and financial causes as well as intellectual ones. However it would seem that Mornet has limited the rôle of the latter causes to an excessive degree and further work still needs to be done after his admirable effort.

The most obvious justification for further research lies in the fact that his investigation leaves off at 1787 because of the very purpose of his work. Now if a revolution was ready to break out at the time of the preparation of the "Cahiers de doléances" for the States-General it was not the Revolution that actually developed. Neither the days of June 20th and August 10th 1792, nor the death of Louis XVI nor the Terror, nor the constructive work of the Convention was contained in germ in the convocation of the States-General. In fact we know very little about the influence of Montesquieu, Voltaire and Rousseau himself on the different phases of the Revolution or the way in which they influenced certain actors in the great drama.

The special quality of the French Revolution, compared with other revolutionary movements in France or other countries, obviously lies in the titanic proportions of this upheaval but also in an ardent passion for thought, for embodying ideas in deeds, and for proposing universal laws. This accounts for the unparalleled world-wide influence of the work of destruction and construction which was accomplished between 1789 and 1795. An abstract passion for justice and liberty, the latter being sometimes conceived in strange fashion, inspired the men who made the Revolution and those who prepared it. The original tone that characterizes the Revolution and the verve that enlivens it, which are fundamental things although they elude the grasp of facts and figures, are due in part to the movement of thought and sensibility which goes from Montesquieu to Rousseau and from Bayle to the abbé Raynal.

III

If there is really one almost undisputed conclusion on the origins of the Revolution reached by historical studies coming from radically opposite factions, it is that pure historical materialism does not explain the Revolution. Certainly riots due to hunger were numerous in the eighteenth century and Mornet draws up the list of them; there was discontent and agitation among the masses. But such had also been the case under Louis XIV, such was the case under Louis-Philippe and deep discontent existed in France in 1920 and 1927 and 1934 without ending in revolution. No great event in history has been due to causes chiefly economic in nature and certainly not the French Revolution. France was not happy in 1788, but she was happier than the other countries of Europe and enjoyed veritable economic prosperity. Her population had increased from 19 to 27 millions since the beginning of the century and was the most numerous in Europe. French roads and bridges were a source of admiration to foreigners. Her industries such as ship-fitting at Bordeaux, the silk-industry at Lyons and the textile-industry at Rouen, Sedan and Amiens were active while Dietrich's blast-furnaces and the Creusot were beginning to develop modern techniques in metallurgy. The peasants were little by little coming to be owners of the land. Foreign trade reached the sum of 1,153 million francs in 1787, a figure not to be attained again until 1825. The traffic in colonial spices and San Domingo sugar was a source of wealth. Banks were being founded and France owned half the specie existing in Europe. So misery in France was no more than relative. But truly wretched peoples such as the Egyptian fellah, the pariah of India or even the Balkan or Polish peasant or Bolivian miners for example rarely bring about revolutions. In order to revolt against one's lot, one must be aware of his wretched condition, which presupposes a certain intellectual and cultural level; one must have a clear conception of certain reforms that one would like to adopt; in short, one must be convinced (and it was on this point that the books of the eighteenth century produced their effect) that things are not going well, that they might be better and that they will be better if the measures proposed by the reformist thinkers are put into practice.

Eighteenth-century philosophy taught the Frenchman to find his condition wretched, or in any case, unjust and illogical and made him disinclined to the patient resignation to his troubles that had long characterized his ancestors. It had never called for a revolution nor desired a change of regime; it had never been republican and Camille Desmouslins was not wrong in stating: "In all France there were not ten of us who were republicans before 1789." Furthermore he himself was not one of those ten. But only an over-simplified conception of influence would indulge in the notion that political upheaval completely embodies in reality the theoretical design drawn up by some thinker. Even the Russian revolution imbued as it was with Marxian dialectic did not make a coherent application of Marxism or quickly found it inapplicable when tried. The reforms of limited scope advocated by *L'Esprit des Lois, L'Homme aux quarante écus, L' Encyclopédie* and the more moderate writings of Rousseau struck none the less deeply at the foundations of the ancien régime, for they accustomed the Frenchman of the Third Estate to declaring privileges unjust, to finding the crying differences between the provinces illogical and finding famines outrageous. The propaganda of the "Philosophes" perhaps more than any other factor accounted for the fulfillment of the preliminary condition of the French revolution, namely, discontent with the existing state of things.

In short, without enlarging upon what is already rather well known we may say that eighteenth-century writers prepared the way for the Revolution, without wishing for it, because:

a) They weakened the traditional religion, winning over to their side a great number of clerics, and taught disrespect for an institution which had been the ally of the monarchy for hundreds of years. At the same time they had increased the impatience of the non-privileged groups by uprooting from many minds the faith in a future life which had formerly made bearable the sojourn in this vale of tears that constituted life for many people of low estate. They wished to enjoy real advantages here on earth and without delay. The concept of well-being and then that of comfort slowly penetrated among them.

b) They taught a secular code of ethics, divorced from religious belief and independent of dogma, and made the ideal of conduct consist of observation of this system of ethics, which was presented as varying in accordance with climate and environment. Furthermore they gave first importance in this ethical code to the love of humanity, altruism and service due society or our fellowmen. The ideas of humanity, already present in the teaching of Christ, in Seneca and Montaigne but often dormant, suddenly exert fresh influence over people's minds.

c) They developed the critical spirit and the spirit of analysis and taught many men not to believe, or to suspend judgment rather than accept routine traditions. In D'Argenson, Chamfort, Morelly, Diderot, Voltaire of course, D'Holbach, Condillac and many others, and even in Laclos and Sade, we will find the effort to think courageously without regard for convention or tradition, that will henceforth characterize the French intellectual attitude. From this time on, inequality with respect to taxation, the tithe paid to the Church, and banishment or persecution for subversive opinions will shock profoundly the sense of logic and critical spirit of the readers of the "Philosophes."

d) Lastly, these very thinkers who have often been depicted as builders of Utopias are the creators of history or the historical sense, or almost so. Montesquieu studiously examined the origins of law and constitutions and saw men "conditioned" by soil and climate in contrast with the absolute rationalists who were foreign jurists and not Frenchmen. Boulainvilliers and many others of lesser fame studied France's past. Voltaire's masterpiece is probably his work on general history. The result of this curiosity about history was two-fold: it encouraged faith in progress and convinced numbers of Frenchmen that it was their task to fulfill humanity's law, to endeavor to increase the sum of liberty, relative equality, "enlightenment" and happiness in the world; it also proved to many men of the law who examined old documents and the titles of nobility and property, that the privileges of nobility were based on a flimsy foundation. The respect that these bourgeois or sons of the people might have felt for the aristocrats was accordingly diminished, at the very moment when the bourgeois saw the nobles not only accept with admiration but take under their protection destructive writings produced by the pens of commoners: sons of tailors (Marmontel), vine-growers (Restif), cutlers (Diderot) and watch-makers (Rousseau). And the history of the origins of royal sovereignty itself seemed to them scarcely more edifying than that of the feudal privileges.

As for the means of dissemination of those ideas or new beliefs that the philosophes were spreading between the years 1715 and 1770 or 1789, it will suffice to enumerate them rapidly, for numerous studies have examined them: they were the salons, although very few of the future revolutionaries frequented society gatherings; the clubs, that more and more called for tolerance, preached deism, demanded the abolition of slavery (*Societé des Amis des Noirs*) and dreamed of imitating the American Revolution (*Club Américain*); books or tracts which made their appearance as works of small format, easily carried or hidden, lively and sharp in style and prone to surprise and arouse the reader; periodicals; the theatre especially after the coming of the "drame bourgeois" and the "comédie larmoyante," and then with Beaumarchais; and the education given in the secondary schools. Mornet's book sums up the essential material on the subject that can be found in documents. The other means of spreading new ideas, such as conversation, which is doubtless the most effective means man has always used to borrow and pass on new views, elude documentary research.

It is among the actors in the great revolutionary drama that investigations of broader scope might show us which of the ideas of the eighteenth century exerted influence and how and why they did so. Siéyès, among others, has been the subject of an exhaustive intellectual biography which has established with precision what the young abbé coming to Paris from Fréjus to devise constitutions owed to Descartes, Locke, and Voltaire in particular (for the negative side of his ideas), to Rousseau (for his impassioned logic) and to Mably. (Paul Bastid, *Siéyès et sa pensée*, Hachette, 1939). Another recent book, by Gérard Walter, is a study of Babeuf (Payot, 1937). It would be instructive to know how the minds of many of the revolutionaries were developed and by what books and meditations they were influenced; such men range from Mirabeau and Danton to Marat, from Rabaut de Saint-

Etienne to Hérault de Séchelles and from Desmoulins or Brissot to generals of the Convention who may have read Raynal and Rousseau with passionate interest, as Bonaparte did later. Only when many monographs have been written devoting at least as much if not more attention to the history of ideas and the psychology of the protagonists in the Revolution than to the facts of their lives of action, will we be able to make sure generalizations about the influence of Montesquieu or Rousseau on the France of '89 or '93.

IV

Montesquieu and Rousseau are certainly the two great names worthy of consideration in some detail. The presiding judge of the High Court of Bordeaux obviously did not want the Revolution; had he lived to see it, he would not have approved of its reorganization of the judiciary, nor its audacity in reform, nor the Declaration of the Rights of Man, nor even the interpretation of certain principles he himself had enunciated. Still he is one of the spiritual fathers of the first two revolutionary assemblies. Like so many other men who have made history, he influenced the fateful years of 1789–92 by what he did say almost involuntarily, by the thoughts other men read in his sentences and by the tone even more than by the content of his writings. His great work breathes a veritable hatred of despotism founded on fear; it shows no moral respect for monarchy, and so helped to alienate the most reasonable minds from it. The great principle of the separation of powers presumes the right to seize from the king the united powers that he believed he held as a whole by divine right. Finally, Montesquieu, however elevated his position as a citizen or as a magistrate may have been, uttered words which will assume a mystic authority in later times on the subject of the people's inherent good qualities and its ability to select its leaders: "The common people are admirable in choosing those to whom they must delegate some part of their authority," (II,ii) or "When the common people once have sound principles, they adhere to them longer than those we are wont to call respectable people. Rarely does corruption have its beginning among the people." (V,ii)

Finally, in his admirable XIth book, Montesquieu had defined liberty in terms that were to remain etched in people's memories: this liberty required stable laws, which alone could establish and protect it. These laws were also to correct economic inequality. Certainly its historical examples adduced in great profusion, highly technical juridical considerations, certain generalizations that had been too cleverly made symmetrical and its lack of order made this voluminous treatise hard to read. But Montesquieu's influence was not one of those that can be gauged by the number of readers: it expressed itself in action thanks to a few thoughtful minds who found in it a sufficiently coherent overall plan capable of replacing the old order which obviously was crumbling. Montesquieu's influence inspired a more important group of revolutionaries who were familar with only a few chapters of his work, but these chapters were filled with the love of freedom and the great feeling for humanity that condemned slavery and the iniquitous exploitation of some men by others.

Montesquieu's influence on the French Revolution began to decline at the time when Rousseau's was coming to the fore. Many studies have been devoted to the subject of Rousseau and the French Revolution; and the subject deserves still further study, for perhaps no more notable case of the effect of thought on life exists in the whole history of ideas and of dynamic ideas in particular. But this broad subject has too often been narrowed down by the most well-meaning historians. So many dogmatic and partisan statements had portrayed Rousseau as the great malefactor who was guilty of the excesses committed by the Terrorists and as the father of collectivism that, as a reaction, the best-disposed scholars set about proving by facts and texts that the author of the *Contrat Social* was guiltless of so many misdeeds. As a result they have belittled his influence. But there is some narrowness and naïveté in these scholarly arguments.

According to some, everything that Rousseau wrote already existed before his coming in the works of a number of writers and thinkers both at home and abroad and Jean-Jacques brought forth very little that was new. That is quite possible, and scholars have been able to make fruitful inquiries into the sources of the *Discours sur l'Inégalité* and the *Contrat*. But the fact remains that whatever Rousseau borrowed from others he made his own; he rethought it and above all felt it with a new intensity and set it off to advantage by his own passion and his own talent. What he owes to Plato or Locke suddenly "shook" the men of 1792 only because Rousseau had charged it with a new electric current.

Furthermore Rousseau is rife with contradictions and the most ingenious men of learning (Lanson, Höffding, Schinz and E. H. Wright) have not yet succeeded in convincing us of the unity of his thought. For Corsica and Poland he proposes finely adapted and moderate constitutions that do not seem to have sprung from the same brain as the *Contrat Social*. He writes a very conservative article on l'*Economie politique* for the fifth volume of the *Encyclopédie* while in his second *Discours* he had propounded anarchical theses burning with revolutionary ardor. "To expect one to be always consistent is beyond human possibility, I fear!" he himself had admitted in the second preface of the *Nouvelle Héloïse*. We will not go so far as to pay homage to Rousseau for his contradictions and may choose to reserve our unalloyed admiration for other systems of thought more dispassionate and logical than his. But an author's influence does not have much to do with the rigor and coherence of his philosophical system. In fact, it would not be hard to show that the thinkers who have contributed the most toward changing the face of the world exerted influence because of their contradictions, since very different periods and highly diverse individuals drew from them various messages of equal validity. Let us add with no ironic intention that because of this the ingenuity of the learned will never tire of seeking the impossible golden key to these disconcerting enigmas and that the hunger for systems, among those lacking the necessary imagination to construct new ones, will always exert itself to bring about a happy synthesis of the successive assertions of a Plato, a Montaigne, a Locke, Rousseau, Comte or Nietzsche.[3]

After all, as the historians tell us quite correctly, the *Contrat Social* is only a part of Rousseau's political thought and not the most important part in the eyes of his contemporaries; the author himself attributed only a rather limited importance to this logical Utopian book. Rousseau never seriously contemplated a revolution in France; he did not think that a republic was viable, or perhaps even desirable for France. One might even make the

[3] "Inconsistencies are the characteristic quality of men who have thought much, created abundantly and destroyed on a broad scale. They have necessarily said many things and among those things there are a great many that are at variance or even directly contrary to one another." This is the comment on Rousseau made in an article pertinent to the present subject by the solid founder of the School of Political Science: Emile Boutmy, in "La Déclaration des Droits de l'Homme et du citoyen et M. Jellineck," (*Annales des Sciences politiques,* 1902, pp. 415–443).

assertion supported by texts that Jean-Jacques, that *bête noire* of the anti-revolutionaries from Burke to Maurras, Lasserre and Seillière, was a timid conservative.[4] It is quite true (M. Mornet has proved this once again) that the influence of the *Contrat Social* was very weak between the years 1762 and 1789; the book caused so little disturbance that Rousseau was not even molested; and it is probable that Rousseau would have been frightened by certain inferences that were later drawn from his ideas. What he wrote in 1765 in no way justifies an assertion on our part that he would still have written the same thing in 1793 and so it is quite as conceivable that Rousseau might have violently changed his point of view and espoused the cause of the revolutionaries, had he lived long enough to receive their acclaim. And above all, without having consciously wanted the Revolution, Rousseau did a great deal, if not to cause it, at least to give it direction when it had broken out. The success of Rousseau's works and the reception accorded them in his life-time have been investigated in sufficient detail. From now on groups of research men might well give their attention to the enormous influence Rousseau exerted on the men of the Convention and on those of the Empire or the Restoration or on the Romantics. Granted that Rousseau was neither a republican nor a revolutionary, he was in revolt and that is no less important. A. Aulard who was not inclined to over-estimate the influence of the intellectuals on the French Revolution nevertheless accurately described the paradoxical result of any fairly broad study of this subject: "All these men in revolt want to keep the monarchy and all of them blindly deal it mortal blows. The French, monarchists to a man, take on republicanism without their knowledge."[5]

[4] Rousseau has depicted himself in the third of his *Dialogues* as "the man who is more averse to revolution than any one else in the world, . . . who has always insisted upon the maintenance of the existing institutions, contending that their destruction would only take away the palliative while leaving their faults and substitute brigandage for corruption." It is true that here he is making an effort to present himself in the most favorable light! In his *Jugement sur la Polysynodie de l'abbé de Saint-Pierre* (Vaughan, *The Political Writings of Rousseau* [Cambridge, 1915], I, 416), he gave the following warning in 1756: "Think of the danger of once displacing the enormous masses that make up the French monarchy! Who will be able to check the shock once it is given or foresee the effects it may produce?" In the eighth of his *Lettres de la Montagne*, he again exclaims: "Eh! How could I approve of any one's disturbing the peace of the State for any interest whatsoever. . . . ?"

[5] A. Aulard, "L'Idée républicaine et démocratique avant 1789," in the *Revolution française*, July-December 1898, tome 35, 5–45.

Not one of the men of the Revolution adopted Rousseau's philosophical system outright in order to put it into practice; that is only too plain. Not one of them understood Rousseau's thought in its subtleties, its contradictions and its alterations as the scholar of the present-day can understand it with the aid of much posthumous documentation: this is scarcely less obvious. Whatever chagrin it may cause minds devoted to strict methods, the unparalleled effect produced on the imagination of posterity by Montaigne, Rousseau or Nietzsche can be credited to quotations drawn from their contexts and probably perverted from their original sense. This influence is not so much an influence of ideas as it is an influence of *idées-forces,* to use Fouillée's expression, and exerts its power more by setting men's sensibilities aflame than by convincing their minds.

"Man is born free, and everywhere he is in chains." This peremptory formula from the first chapter of the *Contrat Social,* in conjunction with a few others which declared the sovereignty of the people inalienable and affirmed the right to revolt in the event of the usurpation of powers by the government, contributed immeasurably toward crystallizing in the general mind from 1789 on the resolve to make the king subject to the only true rights which were inherent in the people. On October 5th 1789 Robespierre and Barrère contended that the sovereign could not oppose the constituent power which was superior to him. The passion for equality which wildly inspires the Revolutionaries and the modern world after them owes no less to Rousseau's fundamental idea that law should rectify natural inequality (which he was not foolish enough to overlook) by means of civic equality. The XIth chapter of the 2nd book of the *Contrat Social* stated in striking terms: "For the very reason that the force of things always tends to destroy equality, the force of legislation must always tend to maintain it." The 3rd book of the same work castigated the vices to which kings are prone, for if they are not narrow or evil on attaining the throne—"the throne will make them so." That does not make Rousseau a partisan of republicanism or a democrat; but had it not been for such aphorisms, Saint-Just never would have proclaimed in his fine *Discours concernant le jugement de Louis XVI* of November 13th 1792: "Royalty is an eternal crime against which every man has the right to rise up and take arms... One can not reign in innocence."

The *Discours sur l'Inégalité* contained pages of impassioned rhetoric that were even more effective. The English writer C. E. Vaughan, who is a scrupulous commentator on the political writings of Rousseau, did not hesitate to state, after years of reflection of this subject: "Wherever, during the last century and a half, man has revolted against injustice and oppression, there we may be sure that the leaven of the second *Discours* has been working." (*Op. cit.*, i, 5) Doubtless Rousseau had never dreamed of the application of his declamations against property: but he had set forth the idea that inheritances ought to be whittled down by fiscal measures and that those who owned no lands ought to receive some, without necessarily advocating collectivism. He had also uttered against wealth words whose echoes will ring down the centuries: "It is the estate of the wealthy that steals from mine the bread of my children. . . . A bond-holder whom the State pays for doing nothing is scarcely different in my eyes from a highwayman who lives at the expense of the passers-by . . ., every idle citizen is a rogue."

The precautions with which Jean-Jacques had surrounded some of his bold affirmations quickly disappeared in the heat of action. The chapter called "Du Peuple," in the *Contrat Social* (ii, 8), was most cautious: but its author had nevertheless hinted in it that sometimes, in the life of peoples, "the State, set aflame by civil wars, is so to speak reborn from its ashes, and regains the vigor of youth in leaving the arms of death." People retained phrases from the *Emile* too,—the prophetic phrases in which the educator had proclaimed to the people of his time that they were approaching the era of revolutions when men would be able to destroy what men had built. These few phrases, gaining added violence in tone from the fact that they were detached from contexts that often contradicted them, seemed charged with new meaning when the great upheaval had broken out. Such was also the case of the mystic system of happiness taught by the Genevan "philosophe's" entire work. Man is born good; he is made to be happy; he may become so if he reforms himself and if his governments are reformed. We know how the echo of these doctrines will resound in the noble formulas of Saint-Just, who was perhaps the revolutionary most deeply steeped in Rousseau's thought.[6]

[6] On March 3rd 1794 (13 Ventose An II), "The Archangel of the Terror," as Michelet calls Saint-Just, declared before the Convention: "Let Europe learn that

The aspect of Rousseau that Albert Schinz called "the Roman Rousseau" exerted no less influence on that other myth which prevailed or raged among the men of the Revolution (and among the women, too, as in the case of Madame Rolland), the myth of the ancients and their passion for liberty and virtue. "The world has been empty since the day of the Romans," cried Saint-Just; and he stated to the Convention on February 24th 1793: "The Republic is not a Senate, it is virtue." The whole of Saint-Just's remarkable youthful work entitled: *Esprit de la Révolution et de la Constitution de la France* is imbued with Rousseauist themes and ends on this cry of regret: "France has only now conferred a statue upon J.-J. Rousseau. Ah! Why is that great man dead?"

Robespierre, whom Michelet maliciously called a "weak and pale bastard of Rousseau" because of his cult of the Supreme Being, was indebted to Rousseau to no lesser degree than Saint-Just, although he does not show the mark of the born writer that stamps the formulas of the terrorist guillotined at the age of twenty-seven. It was by assiduous reading of Rousseau that he formed his style: and his style served him as a powerful weapon. It seems that the young student from Arras met Rousseau in 1778, the year of his death, and never forgot it. "I saw thee in thy last days, and this memory is a source of proud joy for me," he declares later in his *Mémoires,* placed under the aegis of Rousseau, and promised to "remain constantly faithful to the inspiration that I have drawn from thy writings." Dozens of sentences which reiterate formulas from the *Contrat Social* might be extracted from his speeches. It was Rousseau who had helped to turn Robespierre away from Catholicism, and of course he was the man from whom Robespierre borrowed his cult of the Supreme Being; his *Observations sur le projet d'Instruction publique* pre-

---

you no longer want either a single unhappy victim of oppression or an oppressor in French territory; let this example bear fruit upon the earth; let it spread abroad the love of virtue and of happiness! Happiness is a new idea in Europe." In his *Fragments sur les institutions républicaines,* published after his death, the young disciple of Rousseau and the Romans wrote: "The day that I am convinced that it is impossible to instill in the French people ways that are mild, energetic and responsive but merciless against tyranny and injustice, I will stab myself." It is regrettable that there is in existence only an inadequate Swiss dissertation by S. B. Kritschewsky, *Rousseau and Saint-Just* (Bern, 1859) on the fine subject that the influence of Rousseau and other eighteenth century thinkers on Saint-Just's noble thought would make.

sented to the Convention in 1793 are based on the Rousseauist faith: "If nature created man good, it is back to nature that we must bring him." His speech made at the Jacobin Club on January 2nd 1792 against the war at that time desired by the Girondins rendered homage to Rousseau in impassioned terms: "No one has given us a more exact idea of the common people than Rousseau because no one loved them more."[7] The secret of the enormous influence exerted by Rousseau lay less in the substance of his thought than in the burning tone of a man who had lived his ideas and had suffered (or thought he had) because he had sprung from the people and had known poverty. "According to the principles of your committee," declared Robespierre to the Constituent Assembly on August 11th 1791, "we ought to blush at having erected a statue to J.-J. Rousseau, because he did not pay the property-tax." The history of ideas and their influence on persons and things is full of elements that defy all possibility of quantitative or statistical measurement. How can one estimate all that the men of the Revolution owed Rousseau in the way of fervor, mystic hope, logic that was impassioned and even fierce on occasion and —what is not less important, even for history, as Danton, Saint-Just and Robespierre were aware—the imperious and incisive style that made their formulas resound in twenty countries and across one hundred and fifty years? "One does not make revolutions by halves" or "the French people are voting for liberty for the world"—these aphorisms or decrees of Saint-Just, like certain phrases of Mirabeau, or a multitude of orators of lesser stature,[8]

[7] Here again this large subject deserves a lengthier and more recent monograph than the thesis of Richard Schass: *J. J. Rousseaus Einfluss auf Robespierre* (Leipzig, 1905).

[8] Among the speakers heard with interest at the time, one might mention D'Eymar, who had the honors of the Pantheon voted to Rousseau; Rabaut de Saint-Etienne, who often quoted Rousseau as one of the precursors of the revolution; the abbé Fauchet, who expounded the *Contrat* before a numerous audience, in 1790, at the "Universal confederation of the Friends of Truth." Mirabeau had long since (letter to Sophie of December 8th 1778) extolled "the sublime creative genius" of Rousseau, and had had homage paid to his widow on May 12th 1790. Marat had, so it is said, annotated the *Contrat* in 1788, and his sister Albertine testified how much he admired it. Let us hope that some historian with a knowledge of psychology will some day treat the great subject of "Napoleon the First and Rousseau." Even the remarks of the Emporer in old age show that he was attracted by Rousseau: the *Nouvelle Héloïse* was one of the first books he read on Sainte-Hélène. At the

and of Bonaparte himself, would not have been uttered, and would not have had the resonance that has kept them alive, if these men had not been imbued with the spirit and the style of the Citizen of Geneva.

The history of the cult of Rousseau during the French Revolution is easier to trace than that of his deep influence on the revolutionaries. The former has been studied in part, and the manifestations of this idolatry of Rousseau are often amusing. The setting-up of the bust of Jean-Jacques in the Constituent Assembly on June 23, 1790, the consecration of a street of Paris named after him in the same year, the repeated editions of the *Contrat Social* (4 editions in 1790, 3 in 1791, etc.), the constitutional articles put under his aegis, the decree ordering that Rousseau's ashes be brought to the Pantheon in 1794 and the pious emotion of the crowd, and lastly, the invocation to "his generous soul" by the Incorruptible One in his speech of May 7th 1794 on the religion of the Revolution and the pompous application of his declamations on the Supreme Being; all these things have been mentioned more than once and recently, too.[9] But the way in which Rousseau's influence profoundly modified the men and women of the revolutionary and imperial era, and then the romantics great and small, and the continuators of the Revolution, in and out of France, in the nineteenth and twentieth centuries: these are the questions that intellectual history seems to have been reluctant to investigate.

Its timidity is regrettable and our knowledge of the past suffers twice over because of it: first, because history that devotes itself

---

height of his glory, in 1806, he thought of organizing an official tribute to Rousseau, according to Stanislas Girardin. This same Girardin, in a curious passage in his *Memoires* (Michaud, 1834, vol. i, 190) reports this reflection (did he understand it correctly?) of the First Consul at Ermonville: "The future will tell whether it would not have been better for the peace of the earth if Rousseau and I had not existed."

[9] See Gordon McNeil: "The Cult of Rousseau in the French Revolution," *Journal of the History of Ideas*, April 1945, 196–212. Monglond's work *Le Préromantisme francais* (Grenoble, Arthaud, 1930) contains, especially in the second volume, chapters i and vi, the most thought-provoking evidence on the effect produced by Rousseau on sensitive souls of the revolutionary era. Monglond quotes (ii, 157) the curious sentence in which Bernardin de Saint-Pierre, in his *Etudes de la Nature*, had proclaimed some years before '89: "It seems to me that some favorable revolution is in store for us. If it comes, it will be letters that we will have to thank for it. . . . Oh men of letters! . . . . You alone recall the rights of man and of Divinity."

too exclusively to what we call material facts such as a military victory, the fall of a ministry or the opening-up of a railroad-track, seriously falsifies our perspective of what took place. The development of the Napoleonic legend, the quietly working influence of Rousseau or Voltaire, the growth of anti-clericalism and the elaboration of socialist myths are phenomena which are partly literary or sentimental in nature, but are second to no other order of phenomena in importance and in the effects they had on the course of human affairs. Our knowledge of the past suffers additionally because historians, by turning aside from the history of ideas and sentiments with their vigorous influence on the lives of men, abandon these research subjects to men less trained than themselves in exact methods of study; the latter are disposed to write with the sole intent of finding in the past arguments to support their political views or their partisan claims. Meanwhile youth is tempted to reject history as it is officially presented, as an endless series of wars, diplomatic ruses, crimes, examples of intense selfishness and the impotent efforts of men to bring more reason into the world. It refuses to lend credence to those who advise it that man has remained a religious and ideological animal even more than an "economic" creature. Youth's awakening, when it is suddenly placed face to face with the terrible power of ideas, myths and fanaticisms in the world, is sometimes a rude shock, as we have seen recently.

The Frenchmen in particular who have thought fit in the past few years to deny their eighteenth-century thinkers as traitors to the classic and monarchical tradition of France have only to open their eyes in order to ascertain that no French tradition is more alive than that of the Century of Enlightenment. Pascal and Descartes are doubtless greater; Montaigne has more charm and Saint Thomas more logical power: but it is Voltaire and Rousseau, and sometimes Montesquieu and Condorcet, that one finds almost always behind the living influence of France on the masses and the ideologies of South America, of the United States itself, of central and eastern Europe and that one will find tomorrow in Africa and Asia. The world of today expects from post-war France, and France herself expects from her political thinkers who had lost the habit of expressing themselves in universal terms during the last fifty years, a renewal and a modernization of her liberal ideas of the eighteenth century, boldly adapted to the social and economic problems of today, but still inspired by the same faith in man and his possibilities.

Students from other countries remind the French of this fact, lest they forget it too readily. Their studies on the influence of Voltaire and Rousseau on the French Revolution and the revolutions that ensued elsewhere in the world are becoming more numerous and sometimes more objective than the French ones. A Slavic scholar Milan Markovitch in a large and exhaustive book on *Rousseau et Tolstoi* (Champion, 1928) set forth in detail the Rousseauism of the Russian novelist, who in his adolescence carried the portrait of Jean-Jacques around his neck like a scapular and wrote the following message to the newly-founded Rousseau Club on March 7th 1905: "Rousseau has been my teacher since the age of fifteen. Rousseau and the Gospel have been the two great influences for good in my life." The German thinker Ernst Cassirer devoted a little book written in 1945 to commemoration of the admiration for Rousseau expressed by Goethe and Fichte as well as Kant who declared: "Rousseau set me right. . . . I learned to respect human nature."[10] Thoreau and D. H. Lawrence are indebted to the Genevan for a good half of their thinking. George Eliot, on meeting the philosopher Emerson in Coventry in 1848, found herself being asked by him what her favorite book was; Rousseau's *Confessions*, she answered; at which the American transcendentalist cried: "It is mine too." Shortly afterwards,

[10] Ernst Cassirer, *Rousseau, Kant and Goethe* (Princeton University Press, 1945).—Fichte openly proclaimed that he owed the revelation of his philosophical system to "the years when the French nation was fighting passionately for the triumph of political liberty. . . . To the French nation I owe my having been raised to those heights [of his *Doctrine of Science*]. . . . To her in some measure my system belongs." The influence of the French Revolution was equally strong on the philosopher who is often presented as the theorist of Prussian absolutism, Hegel. Two years before his death, in 1829, he wrote: "It was a glorious sunrise. All thinking beings then celebrated that dawn [of the French Revolution]. A sublime emotion then reigned, the enthusiasm for the spirit made the world quiver, as if, then only, a true reconciliation of the divine and the world had been achieved." In the *Phenomenology of the Mind*, a supreme function is also given to the French Revolution—it made a living synthesis between the two conflicting worlds of conscience: through that Revolution, "the two worlds are reconciled and heaven descends upon the earth." (See a posthumous article on "Hegel and Diderot's *Nephew of Rameau*," by the French philosopher Henri Mougin, in *Europe*, August 1926, 1–12.)

on February 9th 1849, she wrote Sara Hennel these extremely lucid sentences on the mechanism of intellectual influence:

> I wish you thoroughly to understand that the writers who have most profoundly influenced me are not in the least oracles to me. . . . For instance, it would signify nothing to me if a very wise person were to stun me with proofs that Rousseau's views of life, religion, and government were miserably erroneous,—that he was guilty of some of the worst *bassesses* that have degraded civilized man. I might admit all this: and it would be not the less true that Rousseau's genius has sent that electric thrill through my intellectual and moral frame which has awakened me to new perceptions; . . . and this not by teaching me any new belief. . . . The fire of his genius has so fused together old thoughts and prejudices, that I have been ready to make new combinations.[11]

In the face of such proofs of a fruitful and life-giving though possibly dangerous influence, an important English historian who was moreover an admirer of Burke and usually more moderate in his statements, but was conscious of the importance of ideas in the events of this world, Lord Acton, was impelled to exclaim: "Rousseau produced more effect with his pen than Aristotle, or Cicero, or St. Augustine, or St. Thomas Aquinas, or any other man who ever lived."[12]

---

[11] For this reference and the one preceding, we are indebted to Professor Gordon Haight, who is thoroughly familiar with all that touches on George Eliot.

[12] This quotation from Lord Acton is given by Herbert Paul as uttered in his presence. (Lord Acton, *Letters to Mary Gladstone* [New York, Macmillan, 1904], 10.)

Individualism in Jean Jaurès' Socialist Thought*

by Aaron Noland

Reprinted from the *Journal of the History of Ideas*—Vol. XXII, No. 1, pp. 63-80

When Pierre Leroux introduced the term 'socialism' more or less precisely defined into French political debate in 1833, he intended the term to serve as the antonym of the term 'individualism,' and he employed it to designate, in his words, "the doctrine or doctrines which, under one pretext or another, sacrifice the individual to society and in the name of fraternity or under the pretext of equality, destroy liberty."[1] Although Leroux later qualified the use of the term, applying it to what is now called 'authoritarian' or 'totalitarian' socialism, the fact remains that from Leroux's day to the present the view that socialism and individualism are fundamentally antithetical and that there is an irreconcilable opposition between socialism and liberty has retained considerable vitality and has received frequent reiteration in the literature on modern socialist thought. In our own time this view has been strengthened, and a new dimension of ambiguity added to the term socialism, by the rise of authoritarian and totalitarian regimes claiming the title of 'socialist' societies.

It is not surprising, therefore, that a good deal of serious writing on socialism in recent years should be characterized by a search for the roots and origins of contemporary authoritarianism and totalitarianism and by an emphasis on the anti-liberal, anti-individualist threads in the variegated, tangled skein of XIXth-century socialist thought. A few examples will illustrate the point. J. Salwyn Schapiro, the historian of liberalism, in his study (1949) of Pierre-Joseph Proudhon, calls attention to what he identifies as the latter's 'contempt' for the individual and his natural rights and for democratic institutions, including manhood suffrage and majority rule, and identifies Proudhon as a "harbinger of fascist ideas" and as a "herald

---

* This paper was presented before the First Meeting of the International Society for the History of Ideas, held at Peterhouse, Cambridge University, Sept. 2, 1960.

[1] Pierre Leroux, *Oeuvres* (Paris, 1850), I, 161 n., quoted in the Preface to "De l'Individualisme et du socialisme," *Le Contrat social*, IV (March 1960), 116. See also Elie Halévy, *Histoire du socialisme européen* (Paris, 1948), 17 n. In 1848, Alexis de Tocqueville characterized what he considered the irreconcilable conflict between socialism and democracy as an individualist institution in the following terms: "Democracy extends the sphere of individual freedom; socialism restricts it. Democracy attaches all possible value to each man; socialism makes each man a mere agent, a mere number. Democracy and socialism have nothing in common but one word: equality. But notice the difference: while democracy seeks equality in liberty, socialism seeks equality in restraint and servitude." *Oeuvres complètes d'Alexis de Tocqueville* (Paris, 1866), IX, 546, quoted in Friedrich A. Hayek, *The Road to Serfdom* (Chicago, 1944), 25.

of the great world evil of fascism." [2] In his study (1958) of the Saint-Simonians, Georg Iggers, while contending that Henri de Saint-Simon's social philosophy was not *étatiste* in character and could be considered authoritarian only by implication, insists that the philosophy of his followers, the Saint-Simonians, was hostile to individual liberties and that in its "conception of the state and of society constituted a thoroughgoing authoritarianism and totalitarianism." [3] Alexander Gray, in his history of socialist thought from 'Moses to Lenin' (1946), does not exempt Saint-Simon himself, arguing that "Saint-Simon and the Saint-Simonians alike, in their love of order, of hierarchy and of leadership, are at the roots of the tradition that blossoms in the full enunciation of the Führerprinzip." [4] Lastly, Ludwig von Mises, in his sweeping 'economic and sociological analysis' of the legacy of XIXth-century socialist thought (1951), finds that socialism (no qualification is made here) is destructive not only of individual liberties and freedoms but that it is "the spoiler of what thousands of years of civilization have created" and the promoter of "chaos and misery, the darkness of barbarism and annihilation." [5]

This re-examination of XIXth-century socialist thought in the light of the insights and perspectives derived from XXth-century political and social history, particularly the rise of 'socialist' totalitarian regimes, is, of course, proper; and as a result of many such efforts our understanding of this phase of XIXth-century intellectual history has been deepened and enriched. Yet, a note of caution should be sounded here. This emphasis on the roots or germs of totalitarianism contained in the work of some XIXth-century socialist theorists can easily lead to an unbalanced view of the legacy of socialist thought as a whole and, as a consequence, the liberal, democratic schools of socialist thought may be left in the shadows, neglected, and, indeed, as in the case of von Mises, lost sight of entirely. This is not the occasion to undertake a full scale examination of individualism in XIXth-century socialist thought, but it does seem worthwhile, if only in some small measure to redress the balance, to see how this matter was treated by a prominent socialist thinker of the late XIXth

[2] J. Salwyn Schapiro, *Liberalism and the Challenge of Fascism: Social Forces in England and France, 1815–1870* (New York, 1949), 365, 369, 349–351.

[3] Georg G. Iggers, *The Cult of Authority: The Political Philosophy of the Saint-Simonians* (The Hague, 1958), 103, 20. See also *ibid.*, 3, 7, 38, 185, and *The Doctrine of Saint-Simon: An Exposition*, trans. by G. G. Iggers (Boston, 1957), ix, xli, xliv–xlv.

[4] Alexander Gray, *The Socialist Tradition: Moses to Lenin* (London, 1946), 168.

[5] Ludwig von Mises, *Socialism: An Economic and Sociological Analysis* (New Haven, 1951), 23, 458, 467, 497, 592, and *passim*. See also Hayek, *The Road to Serfdom*, 24–31.

and early XXth centuries, Jean Jaurès, who was deeply committed to both socialism and individualism.

Born in 1859 at Castres in the south of France of a family identified with the provincial bourgeoisie, Jaurès was educated at the Collège de Castres and later at the Lycée Louis-le-Grand in Paris. In 1878 he entered the Ecole Normale Superiéure where his major subjects were philosophy, literature, and history. He was graduated in 1881 and shortly after began to teach philosophy at the Lycée d'Albi. In 1885 Jaurès actively entered the political arena, securing a seat in the Chamber of Deputies in the elections held that year. In the Chamber he voted as a liberal republican, although he did not identify himself with any group. In 1889 he returned to academic life and taught philosophy at the University of Toulouse. During the years 1889–1891 Jaurès prepared his two *thèses* for the *doctorat ès lettres,* one entitled *De la Réalité du Monde Sensible,* and a Latin *thèse* on the origins of German socialism (*De Primis Socialismi Germanici Lineamentis*). It was also during this period that Jaurès became a socialist and began to work out a philosophy that aimed at the reconciliation and unification of elements drawn from such diverse sources as ancient Greek thought, the writings of the *philosophes* and the Jacobins, the rich traditions of French socialist thought from Babeuf and Blanqui, through Fourier, Blanc, and Proudhon, to Malon and Fournière, the writings of German idealists, and of Marx and John Stuart Mill. Commenting on this unusual intellectual undertaking, one student of Jaurès' work declared: "his thought, temperament, and philosophy were dominated by a profound aspiration to achieve a synthesis—a synthesis which was quite a different thing from a superficial eclecticism. . . . He did not limit himself to simply juxtaposing contradictions. He grounded them in a rich and powerful harmony."[6] This "profound aspiration to achieve a synthesis," as will be indicated, lay at the heart of Jaurès' view of the relationship between socialism and individualism.

Jaurès returned to the Chamber in 1893 as a socialist, and with the exception of a single term (1898–1902) served as a deputy and provided the socialist group in the Chamber with vigorous leadership until his death in 1914. In 1904 Jaurès founded the newspaper *L'Humanité* and was its chief editor as long as he lived. In 1905 he took the lead in bringing about the creation of the unified French Socialist Party and until the outbreak of World War I played a prominent rôle in directing its course of action and in defining its

---

[6] Gaëtan Pirou, *Les Doctrines économiques en France depuis 1870* (Paris, 1946), 52. See also Charles Rappoport, *Jean Jaurès: l'homme, le penseur, le socialiste* (Paris, 1915), 104–114.

policies and programs. In addition to his work as deputy, editor, and party leader, Jaurès found time to write a number of books, including a massive 3,000 page work on the French Revolution, a work which found favor with a master of the subject, Alphonse Aulard. He also gave numerous lectures and public addresses in many European countries, in Great Britain, and in South America. When, on the night of July 31, 1914, he was shot dead by a deranged nationalist, Jaurès was at the height of his powers and enjoyed an international reputation as a spokesman for democratic socialism and as a defender of individual liberties.[7]

It is to an examination of this identification of socialism and individualism in the thought of Jaurès that we now turn. Attention will be directed to three aspects of this matter: (I) the rôle of the individual in history; (II) the rôle of the individual in the transition from the existing capitalist society to the future socialist society—this being a special case of the general question treated under (I); and (III) the status of individualism in the socialist society.

I

Jaurès accepted the Marxian notion that economic forces, "the modes of production and of property," were the "mainspring of human history." Just as in the case of the mass of individuals "l'essentiel de la vie" was one's occupation or *métier*, and just as this *métier* most frequently determined "the customs and habits, the thoughts, sorrows, joys, and even the dreams of men, in the same manner, at each period of history, the economic structure of society determines the political forms, the social mores, and even the general direction of thought." [8] Yet, at the same time, Jaurès insisted that these economic forces were not the only determinants in historical development. Moral, intellectual, and aesthetic ideas, operating in conjunction with economic, material forces were likewise of crucial importance: "In the great crises in the life of the world the economic forces are not the only ones in play—moral forces, concord, disinterestedness, and wisdom are sometimes decisive." [9] Economic forces act on individuals, but individuals are not 'machines' that respond automatically to stimuli. Individuals have sentiments and aspirations, visions and ideals—all of which react upon the impersonal, mechanical forces of

[7] For biographical details, see Marcelle Auclair, *La Vie de Jean Jaurès* (Paris, 1954) and J. Hampden Jackson, *Jean Jaurès* (London, 1943).

[8] Jaurès, *La Constituante, 1789-1791* (Paris, n.d.), 6. For Marx's views, see his *A Contribution to the Critique of Political Economy*, trans. by N. I. Stone (Chicago, 1904), 11-12; and *The Selected Correspondence of Karl Marx and Frederick Engels*, trans. by Dona Torr (New York, 1942), 475-477.

[9] Jaurès, *La Convention, 1792* (Paris, n.d.), 208.

the economy and on the social milieu as a whole; and in this manner some measure of conscious direction is imposed on the course of events.[10]

What was the origin of these non-material forces, these ideals? Jaurès maintained that they took shape in the mind and consciousness of the individual at the time the species *homo sapiens* first evolved from the lower stage of animality. Before the appearance of organized society, long before the formation of what could rightly be called an economic system, mankind had developed faint predispositions and tendencies of a spiritual character. First of all, mankind experienced what Jaures called "les sensations désintéressées." That is, as the human species evolved, the more or less purely animal responses to the environment, so necessary for survival in an ever-dangerous world of hunter and hunted, gradually became subordinated to responses of a far-less utilitarian character—to an awareness of the harmonies of sound and of the beauty of color and pattern in nature. A sense of the wonder and vastness of nature, of its "forces mystérieuses et profondes," impressed itself upon the emergent human consciousness, and in this way the universe, the world of nature, penetrated the animality of man "under a different form than that of the struggle for life." There was, then, in the evolving human being, "the need, the joy, the sheer enchantment of melody and of harmony," and little by little over a vast expanse of time there blossomed in the human consciousness an aesthetic sense and a capacity to experience disinterestedness.[11]

Gradually, as man developed the ability to view the world about him with detachment, to put a sort of 'aesthetic distance' between himself and his natural environment, he learned, Jaurès believed, to grasp the general in the particular—to discern the generic resemblance amidst individual diversities and variations. With this there came the first feelings of empathy, of that "sympathie imaginative" which enabled one member of the human species to understand and feel vicariously the joys and sorrows of another. A communion of spirits and sensibilities was now possible. Finally, at this point in the evolution of human consciousness and self-awareness, there came into being in the mind of man what Jaurès called "a sense of unity," a vague awareness of the relatedness of all things and of all the forms and forces of life. For this reason it could be said that man was, almost from the beginning of his existence "a metaphysical animal," since the essence of metaphysics, Jaurès held, was "the search for a

[10] Jaurès, *La Constituante*, 7–8; *Pages choisies de Jean Jaurès*, eds. Paul Desanges and Luc Mériga (Paris, 1922), 381–384.

[11] Jaurès, *Idéalisme et matérialisme dans la conception de l'histoire* (Paris, 1946), 14.

total unity in which all phenemona and laws are included." [12]

As men grew increasingly aware of their essential identity and unity as a species and as their capacity to share common experiences deepened, a cluster of vaguely defined notions—"the consciousness of human dignity, a faith in the grandeur of man and in his potentiality for infinite development, respect for the individual, and the obligation to assure reciprocal respect for all individuals and to draw them closer to one another in an ever more comprehensive association that would be regulated in accordance with the laws of harmonious liberty"—inter-related notions that Jaurès subsumed under the idea of justice, took root in the conscience of man and henceforth profoundly influenced his conduct.[13]

All these aesthetic and moral sentiments and ideas had evolved in the mind of man long before any sort of economic system, as the term is customarily used, had come into existence. When, in time, a structured economy did become a characteristic feature of society, these ideas and sentiments came under the strong influence of the economy, and reciprocally, the former exercised a powerful influence on the latter. The movement of history, according to Jaurès, was thus determined in part by the operation of the impersonal, mechanical forces of the economy, of the mode of production, as described by Marx, and in part by the desire and will of individual human beings to embody in their social and economic institutions the ideas and sentiments that humanity had borne "within its soul" since time immemorial.[14]

Throughout history humanity has struggled against oppression and exploitation to achieve an ever-fuller realization of the idea of justice—"one of the decisive springs of human action"—in the words of Jaurès; and it was the moral and spiritual force of this aspiration for justice in human relations which gave "intelligible direction" to the evolution of history. In all the economic systems that have ever existed, man has been regarded, Jaurès contended, as a machine, as a commodity, and as a means. This had done violence to man's self-image as a sensate, volitional being and has perpetually outraged his sense of justice. The progressive transformation of economic forms, of

[12] *Ibid.*, 15. See also Rappoport, *Jean Jaurès*, 403–407, and I. Benrubi, *Les Sources et les courants de la philosophie contemporaine en France* (Paris, 1933), II, 734–735.

[13] *Pages choisies de Jean Jaurès*, 228–229. See also Jaurès, *La Constituante*, 7–8. Cf. Proudhon's conception of justice in his *De la Justice dans la révolution et dans l'église* (4 vols., Paris, 1930–35), especially I, 263, 271, 280, 291, 305–306, 324–326, 423, 426.

[14] *Pages choisies de Jean Jaurès*, 228, 232, 234, 236, 381. See also *Oeuvres de Jean Jaurès*, ed. Max Bonnafous (9 vols., Paris, 1931–39), VI, 69. Cited hereafter as *Oeuvres*.

economic systems, from primitive cannibalism to slavery, from slavery to serfdom, and from serfdom to the wage system of modern capitalism had been determined, in Jaurès' view, by the unending pressure exerted by individuals throughout history to realize "the whole idea of human justice" and the rich potentialities of man's nature. "Since the whole process of history springs from the essential contradiction between the nature of man and the use that is made of man, this process must tend towards an economic order in which the use that is made of man will be in conformity with his nature." Thus, it was through a series of economic forms or systems, each of which embodied to a greater extent than the last the human ideal, that humanity was "realizing itself." [15]

The upshot of Jaurès' analysis of the rôle of the individual in history—of the significance of the energies, aspirations, and ideals of individual human beings in determining the course of events—was his discovery that the individual was as important a factor in historical causation as the economic forces described by Marx, and that the two were complementary rather than opposing factors: "They merge in a unique and indissoluble development, because, though one cannot consider man apart from his economic relationships, neither can one consider economic relationships apart from man; and while history is from one aspect a phenomenon evolving in accordance with mechanical laws, it is at the same time an aspiration working itself out within the framework of an ideal." [16]

II

Since the Renaissance and the Reformation, the significance of the individual in history, which, to Jaurès, was discernible in whatever age or epoch one examined, had taken on added dimension. The rise of science and rational thought, the economic growth of the industrial and commercial middle-class in the XVIIth and XVIIIth centuries, and "the great humane philosophic movement of the XVIIIth century" all served to enhance the rôle of the individual as a force in history and to give "an audacity and élan" to the public mind which had been unknown before. In the modern period, every human being, in Jaurès' view, had become "a center of energy, consciousness, and action." More aware than ever before of his own interests and values, the individual was now capable of "a prodigious animation." [17]

To Jaurès, all this was apparent in the French Revolution, which, of the paramount historical events of modern history, was the most

[15] Jaurès, *Idéalisme et matérialisme*, 17. See also Rappoport, *Jean Jaurès*, 153–155, 395–398, 402–403, 407.

[16] Jaurès, *Idéalisme et matérialisme*, 18. See also *Pages choisies de Jean Jaurès*, 234.

momentous in promoting the fuller realization of the individual's aspiration for justice and for the development of socialism. If the ideas of the *philosophes* had not penetrated the consciousness of countless individuals where they were caught up and merged with the age-old, immanent ideal of justice, the ideas would not have been able to stir these individuals to action, and the Revolution itself, however well prepared by the economic and social conditions of the time, might not have taken place. In 1789, however, the minds of "an overwhelming, self-conscious majority" of individuals did meet "in the clearest, most precise affirmations," and the Revolution was accomplished.[18]

Jaurès contended that the leadership of the revolutionary forces, drawn largely from various sections of the middle-class, was prepared by its education and by its awareness of its economic interests to turn the Revolution to the profit of its own class. Consequently, the Revolution "too often did not comprehend justice and right except under the form of bourgeois society," believing that it had done enough in eliminating the absolute monarchy and feudal privileges and in preparing the ground for laissez-faire capitalism with its legitimation of private property.[19] Nevertheless, in proclaiming the Declaration of the Rights of Man and Citizen (September 3, 1791) and subsequently in establishing the Republic, the Revolution had set in motion forces that were destined, in Jaurès' view, to carry it far beyond the confines staked out for it by its bourgeois leadership. It was to the everlasting credit of the Revolution to have proclaimed that "man and the citizen have rights, that these rights were imprescriptible, and that age-old and time-honored privileges had no real claim against these rights; it is to the honor of the Revolution to have proclaimed that in each individual human being there is the same native excellence, dignity, and rights. When the Revolution proclaimed this symbol of justice, when it declared that governments and societies should be subject to the positive laws derived from this idea of human rights, the Revolution not only fashioned a new world, it created a new philosophy of history: it made of right, of justice, the driving force, the supreme goal of history and of the forward movement of all mankind." [20] In addition, the Revolution had recognized that *all* the individuals comprising the nation—rather than a single ruling family—possessed the title to "la propriété politique" of France, and that political sovereignty resided in the people as a whole.[21]

[17] *Oeuvres*, VI, 301, 304, 325. [18] *Ibid.*, 305.
[19] *La Petite République*, August 26, 1901; *Pages choisies de Jean Jaurès*, 229.
[20] *Ibid.*, 229–230. [21] *Oeuvres*, III, 46.

It was on the basis of these impressive achievements and all that they implied that Jaurès maintained that "le socialisme tout entier" was contained in embryo in the French Revolution, and that the extension of its principles of justice and sovereignty from the political sphere to the economic would lead inevitably to the creation of a socialist society.[22] How, Jaurès asked, could freedom and justice be guaranteed to all in a society where the great mass of individuals possessed no property or wealth but their labor power and were obliged, in order to live, to sell this power to a small group of individuals who possessed the means of production, distribution, and exchange? Writing more than a century after the French Revolution, Jaurès contended that the Declaration of the Rights of Man would remain an "illusion" for the great mass of individuals unless property relations were altered to make society the responsible repository for the wealth of the nation. Indeed, to Jaurès, there existed since the Revolution a "contradiction" between the political and economic orders in society. To be sure, an elaboration and development of the idea of political sovereignty born in the Revolution had led subsequently to the introduction of universal manhood suffrage and democratic political institutions and to the acknowledgment of the fitness of all individuals, including workers (proletarians), to have a say, as citizens, in the political affairs of the nation. Yet, in the economic order, these same proletarians still had no share in the direction and management of industrial and commercial enterprises.[23]

Furthermore, in present-day society, Jaurès asserted, the proletarians were obliged to pay the property owners, the bourgeoisie, a "tax" for the "privilege of working." To find work, the proletarians had to deliver themselves into the hands of those who owned the machines and other means of production as well as the sources and supplies of raw materials, i.e., the bourgeoisie. "Naturally this capitalist class," Jaurès wrote, "taking advantage of its power, makes the working class pay a large fee." This fee comes out of the labor of the proletarians—from their labor power—and, hence, the work energies of each proletarian were not really his own property. "And since, in our society founded on intensive production, economic activity is an essential function of every human being—since work forms an integral part of personality—the proletarian does not even own his own body outright." Thus, the proletarian "alienates a part of his activity, a

---

[22] *Ibid.*, 45–47. See also André Hauriou, "Jaurès et la démocratie," *Revue d'histoire économique et sociale*, XXXVIII (1960), 9–18.

[23] "Declaration of Principles" of the French Socialist Party, formulated by Jaurès in 1902, in *Quatrième Congrès général du Parti socialiste français, tenu à Tours du 2 au 4 mars 1902* (Paris, 1902), 406–407.

part of his being" for the benefit of another class.[24] To end this alienation and injustice, it was necessary, Jaurès affirmed, to transfer into the economic order the democracy and the sovereignty of all individuals already realized in large measure in the political order; and "just as all citizens exercise political power in a democratic manner, in common, so they must exercise economic power in common as well."[25] Since social injustice has its origin in the existence of opposing classes—one which oppresses and one which is its victim—the latter "must be enfranchised, and with it society as a whole. All differences of class must be abolished. . . . The cooperation of all citizens must be substituted for the unjust and offensive rule of the minority. This is the only way all individuals can be emancipated. And that is why the essential aim of socialism, collectivist as well as communist, is to transform capitalist property into social property."[26]

How was this transformation of society to be brought about? Jaurès agreed with Marx that the contradictions within the capitalist system rendered it vulnerable and created economic and social problems of such magnitude that only the institution of a new social order could resolve them.[27] But if the evolution of the capitalist system itself set the stage for a social revolution, the "direct, immediate, continuous, and decisive intervention" of the great mass of individuals rendered it inevitable.[28] It would be wrong, Jaurès thought, to count "on a sort of mechanical development, on the irresistible march of events" to bring about this revolution: "No, it is on individual human beings, on their initiative, emancipated reason, and fortified will" that one must count "pour la grande transformation économique."[29] More than ever before, the rôle of the individual was of central importance: "For the first time since the beginning of history, man claims his rights as a man—all his rights." He was now seeking the full affirmation of his individuality and the complete embodiment of his sense of justice in human relations and social institutions.[30]

[24] *Oeuvres*, VI, 347, 348; Jaurès, *Studies in Socialism*, trans. by M. Minturn (New York, 1906), 4.

[25] *Quatrième Congrès*, 406. See also *Oeuvres*, III, 234–235.

[26] *Ibid.*, VI, 349.

[27] Karl Marx and Friedrich Engels, *Le Manifeste communiste*, trans. by Charles Andler (Paris, 1906), I, 30–41; K. Marx, *Capital: A Critique of Political Economy*, trans. by Samuel Moore and Edward Aveling (Chicago, 1906), I, Ch. XXXII. See also *Pages choisies de Jean Jaurès*, 386.

[28] *Ibid.*, 388–389. See also Jaurès, "Socialisme et liberté," *La Revue de Paris*, XXIII (December 1898), 488–489.

[29] *Oeuvres*, III, 257. See also Jaurès, "Le Socialisme français," *Cosmopolis*, IX (January 1898), 113.

[30] *Oeuvres*, VI, 366–367.

"Let no one object," Jaurès wrote, "that it is useless and even foolish to invoke justice, that justice is a metaphysical conception that can be twisted in any direction." Indeed, in modern society the word 'justice' was taking on in the minds of individuals "an ever larger and more precise meaning." It now meant that "in every man, in every individual, humanity ought to be fully respected and exalted." This "true humanity" could only exist where there was independence, where the individual could actively exercise his energies and will and enjoy the right to develop fully all his faculties, adapting himself to society in a free and spontaneous manner. In the present society, Jaurès asserted, where so many individuals "are dependent on the favor of others and are at their mercy, where individual wills do not cooperate freely in the work of society, and where the individual submits to the law of the community under duress or force of habit and not from reason alone—there human nature is degraded and multilated." And it was because an ever-increasing number of individuals were coming to the realization that "only by the abolition of capitalism and the establishment of socialism could humanity come into the fulness of its heritage" that their intervention could be counted upon as the decisive factor "in the immense social transformation that is coming." [31]

Although Jaurès did not entirely rule out the possibility of a violent revolution, he personally favored peaceful methods and believed that the existence of political democracy would enable this transformation to be carried out without recourse to force. Force had largely been rendered obsolete by the introduction into modern society of universal suffrage, which was, in Jaurès' words, "the revolutionary instrument of the modern period." [32] The conquest of the state's political power—the act which Jaurès considered prerequisite for the formation of a socialist order—would be carried out in all probability in a legal manner, by individuals casting ballots at the polls. "The socialist revolution shall be accomplished not by the action—the sudden surprise stroke—of a bold minority, but by the clear and concordant will of the immense majority of the citizens." [33]

III

As we have seen, the transformation of society, in Jaurès' view, was to be brought about not only by the impersonal forces of history, "par la force des choses," but also by the active intervention of individuals, "par la force des hommes, par l'énergie des consciences et

---

[31] *Oeuvres*, VI, 353.   [32] *La Dépêche de Toulouse*, April 8, 1893.
[33] *Oeuvres*, VI, 305. See also *ibid.*, 301–302, 306, 325, 327, 329–330, 331–343, and Jaurès, *Le Manifeste communiste de Marx et Engels* (Paris, 1948), 17–18, 25–26.

des volontés." [34] But on the morrow of the revolution that would usher in the socialist society, what would the status of individualism be? Jaurès was aware of the fears expressed by many of his contemporaries that the creation of a socialist society might well mean the diminution of liberty, with the individual subjected to arbitrary constraints, his initiative curbed, his formal education and his intellectual life as a whole prescribed within narrow limits by a new dogmatism, his function and status in the economy determined for him by a centralized bureaucracy, and with life in general reduced to a drab, monotonous affair, devoid of all joy and spontaneity—in brief, the fear that socialism meant a new tyranny, a universal servitude.[35] To Jaurès, however, these fears were largely without foundation; and he endeavored as best he could to set them at rest.

In the socialist order that Jaurès envisioned, liberty—in the fullest meaning of the term—would be "sovereign" and the individual would be "the supreme end." Socialism itself, to Jaurès, was nothing more or less than the complete affirmation of all the rights of the individual. Indeed, as Jaurès put it: "There is nothing superior to the individual." No "celestial authority" existed in the universe which could mold the individual to its own conceit or subordinate humanity to its own "ends, glory, or mysterious designs." And just as man was not "an instrument in the eyes of God," he certainly was not, in Jaurès' view, an instrument of mortal men. Paraphrasing the slogan of the insurrectionist Auguste Blanqui (1805–81)—"Ni Dieu, Ni Maître"—Jaurès declared: "There is no master above humanity, and there is no master within humanity itself." [36]

From this exalted conception of the individual and the notion that "le socialisme est l'individualisme logique et complet," [37] it followed that man was certainly 'the measure of all things,' and that in a socialist society the value of all institutions would be relative to the individual: "It is the individual human being, affirming his will to liberate himself completely, to live and grow, which will henceforth give virtue and life to both institutions and ideas." [38] And it was this

[34] Jaurès, *La Constituante*, 9.

[35] Yves Guyot, *La Tyrannie socialiste* (Paris, 1893), 29, 243–246, and *passim;* Emile Faguet, *Le Libéralisme* (Paris, 1903), 220–224; Anatole Leroy-Beaulieu, "Collectiviste et anarchiste: dialogue sur le socialisme et l'individualisme," *Revue des deux mondes*, CIL (1898), 721–762; Arthur Desjardins, "Le Socialisme et la liberté," *Revue des deux mondes*, CXXI (1894), 29–62; Jaurès, "Socialisme et liberté," *loc. cit.*, 481, 487, 515.   [36] *Ibid.*, 497–498, 500, 506. See also *Oeuvres*, III, 247.

[37] Jaurès, "Socialisme et liberté," *loc. cit.*, 499.

[38] Jaurès, "Socialisme et liberté," *loc. cit.*, 505–506.

yardstick that Jaurès applied to the institutions of the future socialist society.

To those who feared that the socialist state, because it would be the repository for the property of the nation as a whole, would prove to be a repressive instrument, Jaurès declared that while the national state (*la patrie*) had a central rôle to play in the future order, it would not be an absolute value in and of itself. It was true that to socialists their movement was rooted in the state and that for a long time after the establishment of a socialist order the state would "furnish the historical setting" for the existence of that order and it would be "the mould in which the new justice" would be cast.[39] At the same time, however, it was important to note that the state, in Jaurès' thought, "is not the end; it is not the supreme goal. It is a means for attaining liberty and justice. The goal is the emancipation of every individual: the end is the individual." The state was not above human rights: "No, it is not superior to the conscience of man. It is not superior to the human being." Jaurès avowed that the day the socialist state moved against the rights of the individual—"against the liberty and dignity of the human being"—it would lose its justification for being, for the state "only retains its legitimacy to the extent that it secures individual rights."[40]

As for the danger that in the socialist order the individual would lose his initiative and economic freedom of action to the 'fonctionnaires' of an authoritarian bureaucracy in command of the economy, Jaurès believed that this would be avoided by decentralizing control of the national economy and by introducing a "régime électif" into its administration. In structuring the socialist economy, several forms of organization would be brought into play, and this would serve to curb any tendency towards authoritarianism on the part of the nation's central economic organ. In each branch of industry, commerce, and agriculture, labor unions (*syndicats*), agricultural cooperatives, and professional and artisan groups would be formed. Communal and regional federations of such groups would also come into being. All these economic groups would share in the administration of the economy, playing an active, creative rôle in the formation and execution of economic policy. Thus the central economic organ (responsible for fixing prices, determining the value of labor, maintaining full employment, and guarding the nation as a whole against monopoly practices by any economic group) would be counter-balanced by a

[39] *Oeuvres*, VI, 349-350.
[40] Jaurès, "Socialisme et liberté," *loc. cit.*, 505. See also Jaurès, *L'Eglise et la laïcité* (Paris, n.d.), 14.

multiplicity of other economic organizations.[41] "It can be said with assurance," Jaurès wrote, "that the substitution for the privileges of capital is not going to be the depressing monotony of a centralized bureaucracy. No, the nation, in which is vested the sovereign social right of property, will have numerous agents—local government units, cooperative societies, and trade unions—which will give the freest and most flexible movement to socialized property." [42]

Concerning the liberty of the individual in this projected socialist economy, every precaution would be taken to safeguard, "avec une énergie particulière," the rights and initiative of the individual and to reconcile them with the general interests of "la communauté organisée." [43] Jaurès did not believe that the individual had to remain detached and isolated in order to retain his liberty: "What is essential to liberty is that where the individual participates in social action, he is able to act with all the forces of his nature, and, in addition, where there is a vast coordination of social forces and social enterprises, he is able to choose, in accordance with the free choice of occupations and the exercise of preferences, that place to act which is most suitable to him—finally, that he is able to influence, by all the power of thought, will, and conviction that is in him, the general direction of the common effort." [44] In capitalist society, for the great mass of individuals, Jaurès asserted, these essential conditions did not obtain, and they were only "cogs" in the vast industrial machine, possessing neither initiative nor responsibility, for they did not "determine the purposes for which they worked nor did they regulate the *mécanisme d'autorité* under which the work was performed." As workers they made the economy function; but in no way did they determine its course.[45]

In the socialist economy, on the other hand, the individual, in Jaurès' view, would no longer be an "inert cog," and his initiative, far from being curbed, would be greatly enhanced and developed. In each of the organs of the economy, from the local group to the central authority, the *régime électif* would function: as in the political sphere, all citizens, in their rôles as producers, would have the right to vote for their officers and would select those who would represent them in other economic organs. Moreover, by their votes they would deter-

[41] *Oeuvres*, III, 132, 195–200, 203, 288–291, 295–399 *passim*. See also Maurice Boitel, *Les Idées libérales dans le socialisme de Jean Jaurès* (Paris, 1921), 85, 103, 150–153, 169–171.

[42] *Oeuvres*, VI, 359.

[43] *Ibid.*, III, 161, 185; VI, 349. See also Jaurès, "Socialisme et liberté," *loc. cit.*, 516, and Boitel, *Les Idées libérales*, 86–91.

[44] *Oeuvres*, III, 283.

[45] *Oeuvres*, VI, 348.

mine what is to be produced as well as the method of production.[46] Hence, by extending the *régime électif* from the political sphere into the economic, Jaurès endeavored to translate into reality Proudhon's vision: "Chaque individu est également et synonymiquement producteur et consommateur, citoyen et prince, administrateur et administré." [47]

Just as in the organization of the socialist economy the freedom of the individual would be the touchstone, so, to Jaurès, freedom of the mind would be the guiding principle in education and in intellectual life generally in the socialist society. A basic assumption of Jaurès' was that in this world there were no 'sacred truths,' no spheres or subjects of intellectual concern that were closed to free and public investigation, and that the governing idea in all matters of the mind was "the sovereign liberty of the human spirit." To Jaurès, this meant that "no authority of any sort, no power or dogma ought to limit in any way the perpetual effort, the perpetual quest of human reason," and that "in this world humanity itself is *une grande commission d'enquête* whose functioning no governmental intervention, no intrigue in heaven or on earth should be allowed to restrain or distort." [48] Education in the socialist society would thus be *laïque* in character, and human reason and the search for truth would be sovereign. No indoctrination of any sort, even of socialism, would be permitted, for to Jaurès such indoctrination could only produce in students "un esprit serf." Indeed, Jaurès insisted that when the day came that socialists would be empowered to establish schools "the duty of the teacher would be never even to pronounce before the students the word 'socialism.'" [49]

Finally, in the socialist society envisioned by Jaurès, existence would by no means be 'weary, stale, flat, and unprofitable,' and social justice would not be attained at the cost of the joy and spontaneity of life. Quite the contrary: the equitable and rational organization and control of the forces at the disposition of mankind would enhance life in all its aspects. The life of man would not only be "more harmonious and balanced, but fuller, more vibrant, and richer"; the "power and drive of man's instincts" would not be attenuated, but rather "disciplined and harmonized by a high, noble culture." [50] As we have

[46] *Ibid.*, III, 196–198, 257–258, 329–356.

[47] Proudhon, *Idée générale de la révolution au XIXe siècle*, quoted in Boitel, *Les Idées libérales*, 172.

[48] *Pages choisies de Jean Jaurès*, 104. See also *ibid.*, 90, 92, 109, 112, 113; Jaurès, *L'Eglise et la laïcité*, 27, 28, 32; Jaurès, *Action socialiste* (Paris, 1899), 152, 154–155.

[49] Speech in the Chamber of Deputies, January 1909, quoted in Boitel, *Les Idées libérales*, 116. See also *ibid.*, 115, 117.

[50] *Oeuvres*, III, 374; IV, 352–353.

seen, Jaurès did not conceive of socialism merely, or even primarily, in economic terms. To him the question of the 'emancipation' of the oppressed was indissolubly bound up with the status of human culture in general. In the last analysis, socialism was a moral ideal, the "greatest and most efficacious that has yet appeared in the world of man," concerned as it was with "l'ennoblissement de l'humanité tout entière." [51]

What disturbed Jaurès most in the social order of his day was not the economic deprivation of the lower classes but the "moral suffering" inflicted on the great mass of men by the incessant struggle for the necessities of life and economic status as well as by the "monstrous inequality" that was, to him, characteristic of capitalism. Jaurès was appalled by the "endless waste of human intelligence," the blunting of sensibilities induced by "an inert and mechanical existence" and by "stupefying, excessive labor," and by the distortion of the very meaning and purpose of life itself.[52] Work, Jaurès believed, should be "a natural function and a joy; often it is nothing more than servitude and suffering." Work should be a struggle of all mankind against "inanimate things, the fatalities of nature and the problems of life; instead, it is the war of man against man." In this state of affairs, some individuals become the slaves of their wealth just as others become the slaves of their poverty—slaves all, in Jaurès' view, because "those men are not free who have neither the time nor the strength to follow the noblest instincts of their minds and their souls." [53] More than this: in the "narrow and bleak existence" which is the lot of almost all men the deeper meaning and the mystery of life itself is lost sight of and forgotten. The business man is absorbed in managing his enterprise and making money, the workers are submerged in the "deep abyss of their misery," while the politicians are caught up in battles and intrigues that give them no respite. "All of us tend to forget that before everything else we are *men,* perceptive beings, at once autonomous and ephemeral, lost in an immense universe full of mystery. We tend to forget the significance of life and to neglect the search for its full meaning; we overlook the real values, *le calme du coeur, la sérénité de l'esprit.*" [54]

When, under socialism, "brutal competition" between individuals is replaced by cooperation and "fraternal emulation," when men have

[51] *Ibid.,* III, 261, 272. See also *Pages choisies de Jean Jaurès,* 114.

[52] Jaurès, *Action socialiste,* 106–107; *Pages choisies de Jean Jaurès,* 332–333; Boitel, *Les Idées libérales,* 46.

[53] Jaurès, *Action socialiste,* 107; Jaurès, *Studies in Socialism,* 184–185. See also *Oeuvres,* III, 269–270; IV, 305–306.

[54] *Pages choisies de Jean Jaurès,* 257.

learned "to govern social phenomena as they are learning to govern natural phenomena"[55] and, consequently, men themselves will, in the words of Friedrich Engels, "with full consciousness fashion their own history" and humanity will ascend from "the realm of necessity into the realm of freedom,"[56] for the first time, Jaurès declared, a truly 'human' society will come into being: "Every human being shall have more leisure time, more freedom of spirit to develop his physical and moral being. For the first time in human history, there will be a civilization of truly free men; and it will be like the brilliant and charming civilization of ancient Greece, except that it will grow out of universal humanity instead of expanding on a foundation of slavery."[57] Jaurès did not believe that socialism would bring to mankind "un bonheur tout fait," automatically produced by the new society. *Le bonheur* would always remain an individual achievement, the conquest of those who "shall know how to cultivate in themselves the profound meaning of life and to exhalt and discipline their faculties so as to bring within their ken the supreme joys of human existence."[58]

Fyodor Dostoevsky once expressed the fervor of his religious commitment by saying that "If anyone could prove that Christ is outside the truth, and if the truth really did exclude Christ, I should prefer to stay with Christ, and not with the truth."[59] Jaurès was committed to both socialism and liberty. But what if events were to prove that liberty was outside of socialism and that socialism *did* exclude liberty? What would Jaurès' choice be? Fortunately, we have an unequivocal answer. In an article entitled "Organisation socialiste," which appeared in the *Revue socialiste* (Paris) in April 1895, Jaurès declared: "If, in the social order that we are dreaming of, we would not at the very outset encounter liberty—*la vrai, la pleine, la vivante*

[55] Jaurès, *Studies in Socialism*, 178; *Oeuvres*, III, 359; Boitel, *Les Idées libérales*, 46, 156.

[56] F. Engels, *Anti-Dühring: Herr Eugen Dühring's Revolution in Science*, trans. by Emile Burns (New York, 1939), 310. See also Rappoport, *Jean Jaurès*, 402.

[57] *Oeuvres*, IV, 352. "La vie de l'homme, dans l'ordre socialiste sera infiniment complète, délicate et subtile, toute pleine de contrastes et de variétés .... L'homme nouveau sera le plus compliqué et le plus riche de vie qu'ait connu encore l'histoire" (*ibid.*, III, 283). Cf. Marx's assertion that in the future socialist society "the full and free development of every individual forms the ruling principle" (*Capital*, 649), and the statement in the *Communist Manifesto* that "Dans la société communiste, le travail accumulé ne sera qu'un moyen d'élargir, d'enrichir, de stimuler la vie des travailleurs" (*Le Manifeste communiste*, I, 45).

[58] *L'Humanité*, August 13, 1905, quoted in Boitel, *Les Idées libérales*, 45.

[59] Quoted in Avrahm Yarmolinsky, *Dostoevsky: A Life* (New York, 1934), 300. See also F. Dostoyevsky, *The Possessed* (New York, 1936), 253.

liberté—we would draw back towards the present society. We would do so in spite of the disorders, iniquities, and oppressions of this society; because even if in it liberty is only a lie, nevertheless it is a lie that men still find themselves able to call a truth, a truth capable at times of touching the heart. Or, if it were to prove necessary because of the shock of disappointment to recoil even further, we would follow Jean-Jacques Rousseau to some hidden corner of a forest where one could hope that no human being had ever visited before. . . . Rather solitude with all its shortcomings than social constraint: rather anarchy than despotism in any shape or form. . . . Justice, for us, is inseparable from liberty."

The Double Standard*

by KEITH THOMAS

Reprinted, with revisions, from the *Journal of the History of Ideas*—Vol. XX, No. 2, pp. 195-216

" Anything wrong about a man was but of little moment . . . but anything wrong about a woman, . . . O dear! "—Mrs. Wortle, in *Dr. Wortle's School* by Anthony Trollope (1881).

This paper is an attempt to explore the history of an idea which has been deeply rooted in England for many centuries and which by its effect upon law and institutions as well as upon opinion has done much to govern the relations of men and women with each other. Stated simply, it is the view that unchastity, in the sense of sexual relations before marriage or outside marriage, is for a man, if an offense, none the less a mild and pardonable one, but for a woman a matter of the utmost gravity. This view is popularly known as the double standard.

It is an idea which has made itself felt in most aspects of English life. In the field of opinion it gives rise to such maxims as " young men may sow their wild oats," " a reformed rake makes the best husband," " two maidenheads meeting together in wedlock, the first child must be a fool " or, in modern language, " it is best if the man is ' experienced '." Correspondingly, it teaches that a woman who has lost her honor has lost all and it leads to a great exaltation of female virginity for its own sake. " Chastity in women," said a politician in 1923, " is a star that has guided human nature since the world began, and that points far higher and teaches us of the other sex things which we could not otherwise know. We bow in humble reverence to that high star of chastity, and we celebrate it in song and poetry. But I do not think that any mere man would thank us for enshrining him in such a halo." [1] Both before and after marriage men were permitted liberties of which no woman could ever avail herself and keep her reputation. From Henry I to George IV most of the Kings of England kept mistresses and their examples were followed by many of their subjects. At the court of Charles II, where debauchery was almost a proof of loyalty, Francis North, Lord Guildford, was seriously advised to " keep a whore " because, we are told, " he was ill looked upon for want of doing so." [2] But on the other hand if a woman once fell from virtue her recovery might be impossible.

From this state of affairs sprang the extreme wenching attitude associated with periods like that of the Restoration. Society trained up its daughters to trap men into matrimony without yielding any of its benefits in advance, so the men hit back in the only way they

---

* I am much indebted to discussions with Mr. Alan Tyson, although I fear that he is unlikely to accept many of my conclusions.

[1] *Parliamentary Debates (Commons)*, 5th Ser., Vol. 160, col. 2374.

[2] R. North, *The Lives of . . . Francis North, Baron Guildford, . . . Sir Dudley North . . . and Dr. John North* (London, 1826), II, 164.

could.[3] The illicit nature of their attempts on female chastity constituted a large part of their attraction. "I'd no more play with a man that slighted his ill fortune," says Fainall in Congreve's *The Way of the World*, "than I'd make love to a woman who undervalued the loss of her reputation."[4] Or, as Jeremy Collier put it, "difficulty and danger heighten the success, and make the conquest more entertaining."[5] The role of seducer and rake was more attractive than that of husband. As Mr. Badman remarked, "Who would keep a cow of their own that can have a quart of milk for a penny?"[6] It has been argued that in eighteenth-century England there was a decline in marriage, or at least a rise in the proportion of bachelors.[7] It is perhaps significant that it was also in the eighteenth century that the demand for virginity in the brothels of England culminated in a mania of defloration which contemporary observers agreed was without parallel in Europe.[8]

When men took liberties, women had to be educated to tolerate them, and in the great mass of didactic literature for young ladies one of the main themes was that women should recognize that the double standard was in the nature of things, and that model wives should turn a blind eye to their husband's liaisons. Here is the first Marquis of Halifax writing to his daughter at the end of the seventeenth century:

You are to consider you live in a time which hath rendered some kind of frailties so habitual, that they lay claim to large grains of allowance. The world in this is somewhat unequal, and our sex seemeth to play the tyrant in distinguishing partially for ourselves, by making that in the utmost degree criminal in the woman, which in a man passeth under a much gentler censure. The root and excuse of this injustice is the preservation of families from any mixture which may bring a blemish to them: and whilst the point of honour continues to be so plac'd, it seems unavoidable to give your sex the greater share of the penalty .... Remember, that next to the danger of committing the fault yourself, the greatest is that of seeing it in your husband. Do not seem to look or hear that way: If he is a man of sense, he will reclaim himself ... if he is not so, he will be provok'd, but not reformed .... Such an undecent complaint makes a wife much more ridiculous than the injury that provoketh her to it.[9]

[3] On this see Mr. Christopher Hill's brilliant article, "Clarissa Harlowe and her Times," *Essays in Criticism*, IV (1955), esp. 324.   [4] Act I, scene 1.

[5] "Of Whoredom," in *Essays upon Several Moral Subjects*, III (3rd ed.) (London, 1720), 114–115.

[6] J. Bunyan, *Life and Death of Mr. Badman*, ed. J. Brown (Cambridge, 1905), 154.

[7] H. J. Habakkuk, "Marriage Settlements in the Eighteenth Century," *Trans. Roy. Hist. Soc.*, 4th Ser., Vol. 32 (1950), 24.

[8] I. Bloch, *Sexual Life in England Past and Present*, trans. W. H. Forstern (London, 1938), 176.

[9] *Miscellanies by the Right Noble Lord, The Late Marquess of Halifax* (London, 1700), 17-18.

But if society was to allow men comparative sexual freedom and at the same time keep single women virgin and married women chaste then a solution had to be found which would gratify the former without sacrificing the latter. The answer lay in prostitution and the widespread view that a class of fallen women was needed to keep the rest of the world pure.

The classic statement of this belief is to be found in W. E. H. Lecky's *History of European Morals*, where he describes the prostitute:

a figure which is certainly the most mournful, and in some respects the most awful, upon which the eye of the moralist can dwell. That unhappy being whose very name is a shame to speak; who counterfeits with a cold heart the transports of affection, and submits herself as the passive instrument of lust, who is scorned and insulted as the vilest of her sex, and doomed, for the most part, to disease and abject wretchedness and an early death, appears in every age as the perpetual symbol of the degradation and the sinfulness of man. Herself the supreme type of vice, she is ultimately the most efficient guardian of virtue. But for her, the unchallenged purity of countless happy homes would be polluted, and not a few who, in the pride of their untempted chastity, think of her with an indignant shudder, would have known the agony of remorse and despair. On that one degraded and ignoble form are concentrated the passions that might have filled the world with shame. She remains, while creeds and civilisations rise and fall, the eternal priestess of humanity, blasted for the sins of the people.[10]

But the view of the prostitute as a necessary evil and a buttress for the morals of the rest of society goes back to a time long before Lecky. "Remove prostitutes from human affairs," wrote St. Augustine, "and you would pollute the world with lust." [11] Aquinas compared her to a cesspool in a palace, unpleasant but necessary.[12] And in the eighteenth century that engaging writer Bernard Mandeville, who argued that private vices were public benefits, produced *A Modest Defence of Publick Stews* (1724) in which he made a strong case for state-regulated brothels. The existence of male lust had to be recognized; even Socrates had confessed in his old age that when a girl touched his shoulder "he felt a strange tickling all over him for five days." [13] This lust had to be channelled off by way of the stews if female chastity (which he shrewdly analyzed as an artificial combination of honor and interest [14]) was to be preserved. "If courte-

---

[10] W. E. H. Lecky, *History of European Morals* (London, 1913), II, 282-283.

[11] *De Ordine*, ii, 4, quoted in E. Westermarck, *Christianity and Morals* (London, 1939), 363.

[12] Cited in G. R. Taylor, *Sex in History* (London, 1953), 21.

[13] Mandeville, *A Modest Defence*, iv.   [14] *Ibid.*, 42.

zans and strumpets were to be prosecuted with as much rigor as some silly people would have it, what locks or bars would be sufficient to preserve the honor of our wives and daughters? " [15]

Whether or not it existed for the sake of wives and daughters there can be no doubt that prostitution was widespread in England throughout the whole of medieval and modern times. It was regarded as universal and inevitable and it received a good deal of official sanction from the state. Regulations for the management of the stews at Southwark were issued by Henry II and these licensed brothels survived until the reign of Henry VIII. They came under the jurisdiction of the Bishop of Winchester and their inhabitants were popularly known as " Winchester geese." It is impossible to quote reliable figures, but it is clear that by Victorian times prostitution in London and the industrial cities was carried out on an enormous scale. In 1841 the Chief Commissioner of Police estimated that there were 3,325 brothels in the Metropolitan district of London alone [16] and this calculation takes no account of part-time prostitution produced by inadequate female wages. " I am afraid," said Gladstone in 1857, " as respects the gross evils of prostitution, that there is hardly any country in the world where they prevail to a greater extent than in our own." [17]

The most horrible aspect of this state of affairs lay in the different standards applied to the prostitutes themselves on the one hand and to the men who availed themselves of their services on the other. As late as 1871 a Royal Commission declared, " we may at once dispose of (any recommendation) founded on the principle of putting both parties to the sin of fornication on the same footing by the obvious but not less conclusive reply that there is no comparison to be made between prostitutes and the men who consort with them. With the one sex the offence is committed as a matter of gain; with the other it is an irregular indulgence of a natural impulse." [18] Such indulgence was made possible by the law. In 1881 a Select Committee reported: " In other countries female chastity is more or less protected by law up to the age of twenty-one. No such protection is given in England to girls above the age of thirteen." [19] Until 1875 the age of consent had been only twelve and when in 1885 it was finally raised to sixteen the vehement opposition which had previously greeted this proposal was only overcome by the publicity afforded to the sensational prosecution of the journalist W. T. Stead who had delib-

[15] *The Fable of the Bees,* ed. F. B. Kaye (Oxford, 1924), I, 95-96.
[16] G. R. Scott, *A History of Prostitution from Antiquity to the Present Day* (London, 1954), 98.   [17] *Parliamentary Debates,* 3rd Ser., Vol. 147, col. 853.
[18] *Report of the Royal Commission upon the Administration and Operation of the Contagious Diseases Acts* (London, 1871), I, 17.

erately purchased a young girl from her mother for five pounds, had her virginity certified by a midwife, took her to a brothel for a night and finally shipped her abroad—all to show just what could be done under the then existing state of the law. His subsequent articles in the *Pall Mall Gazette,* entitled *The Maiden Tribute of Modern Babylon,* caused an outcry and made reform inevitable. Yet Stead himself was sent to prison and, as he remarked of the House of Lords, "Stringent legislation against the fraud and force by which brothels are recruited could hardly be expected from legislators who were said to be familiar visitors at Berthe's in Milton Street, or Mrs. Jeffries's in Chelsea."[20]

In no way did these legislators demonstrate the direction of their sympathies in this matter more clearly than in the passing of the Contagious Diseases Acts. These were a series of measures issued in the 1860's. They were modeled on a scheme devised by Napoleon and they provided for a system of state regulated prostitution in the garrison towns of England. Under their provisions any woman could be arrested merely on the suspicion of a plain-clothes government spy and be compelled to sign a voluntary submission to be medically examined once a fortnight or else vindicate her character in the police court. After a notable campaign led by Mrs. Josephine Butler the Acts were repealed in 1886. They had led to much incidental hardship and cruelty, but their main relevance to our purpose here is that they represent the high-water mark of the tendency we have been describing. By their bland assumption that prostitution was a permanent and necessary evil and by their direct application of the double standard in that all regulation and medical examination applied to the women alone they yield an interesting commentary on a too often forgotten aspect of Victorian England.

The branch of English law, however, which best illustrates the effects of the double standard and the tenacity with which it survived is that relating to divorce. Here we see how, during those periods when divorce and remarriage have been allowed, adultery on the part of the married woman has almost invariably been recognized as valid grounds for such a divorce, but the wife, on the other hand, has very seldom been entitled to seek the dissolution of the marriage solely on the grounds of a similar offense on the part of her husband. A brief survey of the facts should serve to demonstrate this point.

In Anglo-Saxon times the conventions governing marriage and divorce are shrouded in a certain amount of obscurity, but it appears that under ancient Germanic law adultery was, strictly speaking, not a crime that a man was capable of committing against his wife at all.

[19] *The Truth about the Armstrong Case and the Salvation Army* (London, n.d.), 6. [20] *Ibid.,* 7.

If he were punished, it would be not for unfaithfulness to his wife, but for violating the rights of another husband. For similar misconduct on her part, however, the wife was sometimes put to death—which would have obviated the need for any divorce proceedings.[21] The code of King Ethelbert suggests that divorce was possible at the will of either spouse,[22] but in the penitentials of Theodore we see the clear operation of the double standard. In cases of adultery discretion was exercised in favor of the husband. Should the wife be unfaithful he had the right to repudiate her, but if he committed adultery she was unable to free herself from him save by his departure for a monastery.[23]

After the Norman Conquest all matrimonial cases were dealt with in the spiritual courts and came under the jurisdiction of the canon law. This did not recognize the existence of divorce at all, at least not in the sense of divorce with the right of remarriage (*divortium a vinculo matrimonii*); although, if the parties were sufficiently rich or influential, it was usually possible to find an impediment on the grounds of which the marriage might be annulled, so that it was deemed never to have taken place. The ecclesiastical courts, however, could grant a separation (*divortium a mensa et thoro*) by which the marriage was effectively brought to an end, although neither party would be allowed to remarry. Adultery by either partner was good grounds for a separation and here it might seem as if the double standard went into abeyance. But such an impression would be misleading, for in practice it usually only the husband who was in a position to take advantage of this. The wife was seldom able to claim a separation from her husband. The reasons for this were economic; she would probably be unable to support herself during such a separation, because, although separated, she was still subject to all the legal disabilities of a married woman. In other words, she was now in a state of virtual outlawry, for her husband retained all his rights over her property, including even the wages she might earn after her separation; she was incapable of conducting a legal action by herself, and she could not even claim access to her children. All she had was a small allowance in the shape of alimony and the payment of this was often difficult to enforce. As a result it was only those wives of higher social status with independent property rights secured to them by

[21] G. E. Howard, *A History of Matrimonial Institutions* (Chicago & London, 1904), II, 35–36. Cf. J. R. Reinhard, " Burning at the Stake in Medieval Law and Literature," *Speculum*, XVI (1941).

[22] F. L. Attenborough, ed., *The Laws of the Earliest English Kings* (Cambridge, 1922), 15.

[23] A. W. Haddan and W. Stubbs, *Councils and Ecclesiastical Documents* (Oxford, 1871), III, 199.

equity who were in a position to take advantage of their theoretical right to gain a separation from a husband on the ground of his adultery.

The jurisdiction of the spiritual courts survived the Reformation and the law remained unchanged until 1857. But from the end of the seventeenth century a new factor emerged: divorce by Act of Parliament. A marriage might be dissolved and the partners allowed to marry again as a result of a petition and bill presented to the House of Lords. This procedure made divorce with the right to remarriage legal in England for the first time since the Norman Conquest, but its effects were limited. The process was enormously expensive and few people were in a position to take advantage of it—to be precise, there were only 317 such divorces granted in the whole period up to 1857.[24] Of these only about half a dozen were granted at the suit of a woman. Whereas adultery by the wife was regarded as good grounds for granting the husband a divorce, she on the other hand had no hope of getting her bill through if she had no stronger claim than that of infidelity on the part of the husband. The doctrine was that the marriage should be dissolved only if circumstances had arisen which were deemed such as to make the continuance of the union impossible. Adultery by the wife *was* such a circumstance, but adultery by the husband was not. In *Mrs. Moffat's Case* (1832) it was stated that the husband had "committed an act of infidelity on the very night of his marriage, and occupied himself afterwards in constant experiments on the chastity of his female domestics, by one of whom a child was born to him." Her petition for divorce was rejected. The opinion of parliament was that the wife should forgive the guilty husband but that the husband *could not* forgive the guilty wife. Another rejected petition was that of Mrs. Teush in 1805, whose husband had treated her with great brutality and was living openly with a mistress by whom he had had several children. Lord Eldon said that "he never recollected a more favorable representation given of any woman; but yet, on general grounds of public morality, he felt it his painful duty to give a negative to the original motion;" and the Bishop of St. Asaph was of the opinion "that however hard the rule might press upon a few individuals, it would, on the whole, be better if no bill of this kind were passed."[25] Only if her husband's adultery was incestuous adultery or was greatly aggravated by other circumstances was the wife entitled to expect a divorce.

Although England was the only Protestant country in Europe to maintain this distinction, it was not discarded in 1857, when matri-

---

[24] J. Roberts, *Divorce Bills in the Imperial Parliament* (Dublin, 1906), 7.

[25] J. Macqueen, *A Practical Treatise on the Appellate Jurisdiction of the House of Lords and Privy Council* (London, 1842), 658, 603–4.

monial jurisdiction was transferred from the realm of canon law to a new civil divorce court. In permitting dissolutions of marriage the new court was to follow the rules which had governed the earlier divorces by Act of Parliament. The husband merely had to prove one act of adultery committed by his wife, but his wife had to show her husband guilty of adultery *plus* some other injury—bigamy, cruelty, desertion, incest, rape, or unnatural offenses. " It had ever been the feeling of that House," said that Lord Chancellor, introducing the bill in the Lords, " indeed, it was a feeling common to mankind in general that, although the sin in both cases was the same, the effect of adultery on the part of the husband was very different from that of adultery on the part of the wife. It was possible for a wife to pardon a husband who had committed adultery; but it was hardly possible for a husband ever really to pardon the adultery of a wife." [26] Despite a good deal of opposition, notably from Gladstone, the double standard was preserved in the act of 1857 and it was only in 1923 that the grounds for divorce were made the same for both sexes.

Prostitution and divorce have provided us with two examples of the way in which the law enforced the double standard, but there are many others, for instance, the laws relating to the property of married persons. Should either spouse die intestate, the surviving partner was allowed to retain a proportion of the property of the deceased. The wife had a third of the estate as her dower, the husband was permitted by what was called *courtesy* to remain in possession until his death of all the land which the couple had held during the wife's lifetime in her right, provided a child had been born to them. The double standard appears in the conditions under which dower or courtesy might be forfeited. The wife lost her dower if she was proved to be unfaithful, but a similar act of adultery did *not* deprive the husband of his courtesy.[27] The same distinction applied also to unmarried women, for under feudal law an heiress who was demonstrated to have been unchaste was deprived of her inheritance—a penalty which was not demanded of a man who had behaved in a similar manner.

As a final instance of the double standard at work in English law, let us recall that until half-way through the nineteenth century the

[26] *Parliamentary Debates*, 3rd Ser., Vol. 145, col. 490. A stronger view was expressed by Sir John Nicholl in 1825: " Forgiveness on the part of wife, especially with a large family, in the hopes of reclaiming her husband, is meritorious; while a similar forgiveness on the part of the husband would be degrading and dishonourable." J. Haggard, *Reports of Cases argued and determined in the Ecclesiastical Courts at Doctors' Commons, and in the High Court of Delegates* (London, 1829–1832), I, 752.

[27] T. E., *The Lawes Resolutions of Womens Rights* (London, 1632), 146 has some spirited remarks on this topic.

husband was entitled to use violence and physical restraint to secure the person and services of his wife (her *consortium*) whereas she was able to regain her renegade husband only by means of a court order for restitution of conjugal rights.

There is therefore abundant evidence for the extensive operation of the double standard in both English law and opinion in medieval and modern times.[28] But it is hardly necessary to add that this double standard did not meet with uncritical acceptance by all elements in the community. In particular, two main currents of opinion ran counter to it. The first was that of Christianity.

The idea of reciprocal fidelity was not unknown in pre-Christian times, but it is undeniable that it received a new emphasis from Christian teaching. Christ's own treatment of the woman taken in adultery was frequently cited as justification for not discriminating against the woman alone. The attitude of the medieval church was mixed and it is easy to detect a wide discrepancy between theory and practice; nevertheless, the idea that unchastity was as much a sin for the one sex as for the other steadily gained ground,[29] and with the Reformation the attack on the double standard grew stronger. The English Reformers of the sixteenth century were generally in favor of divorce and most of them would have allowed it to the wife for the husband's adultery. The *Reformatio Legum Ecclesiasticarum* drawn up under Edward VI would have permitted the innocent party of either sex to remarry.[30] Similarly, most of the later Puritan writers urged equality of the sexes in divorce and enjoined chastity as a duty for men and women alike. "Keep chaste till the coming of the Lord Jesus," wrote Daniel Rogers; "Know that this is an equal duty of both, . . . think not thy husband tied to this rule, O woman; nor thou thy wife tied, O husband, and the other free: the tie is equal."[31] Perkins declared that the husband's superiority gave him no immunity from the prohibition against adultery,[32] and William Gouge wrote, "I see not how that difference in the sin can stand with the tenour of God's Word." It might be that greater consequences followed from a lapse on the part of the wife, but at least "God's Word

[28] For a discussion of some of the consequences of the double standard as it operates in modern American society see I. L. Reiss, "The Double Standard in Premarital Sexual Intercourse. A Neglected Concept," *Social Forces*, Vol. 34, No. 3 (March 1956).

[29] *Dives and Pauper* (1493), 6th Commandment, cap. 5, actually says that the husband's adultery is the more serious offense, on the grounds that he is the woman's superior and the greater the sinner, the greater the sin.

[30] E. Cardwell, ed., *The Reformation of the Ecclesiastical Laws* (Oxford, 1850), 51.

[31] *Matrimonial Honour* (London, 1642), 181-2.

[32] *Workes* (Cambridge, 1609-1613), III, 53.

maketh no disparity between them." [33] By the time of the Restoration the attitude of most divines was that adultery was as great a sin in the husband as in the wife, but that account had to be taken of the more enduring consequences when it was committed by the latter.[34] Up to the nineteenth century this position was the standard one, and in the debate on the Divorce Bill in 1857 most members agreed that the sin was the same but that the effects were different. By itself, therefore, the Christian insistence upon the equality of the two sexes before God was not sufficient to bring about a radical change in social attitudes, since by their own admission its exponents did not claim to provide a yardstick by which the full consequences of unchastity might be measured.

The other main source of opposition to the double standard was the ever-growing current of what can only be described as middle-class respectability. From the seventeenth century, if not earlier, there becomes apparent a strong tendency to place a new and heightened emphasis upon the values of family life and to deplore any aristocratic or libertine conduct which would be likely to jeopardize domestic security. This attitude is intimately connected with Puritanism, though it stems from certain strong material values as well. It is associated with propriety and prudery and is exemplified in the attack on the Restoration stage. It is also essentially a middle-class morality, which the rich despise and the poor cannot afford. Sexual promiscuity was condemned because it was incompatible with the high emotional values expected from marriage, because it was wasteful, and because it took time and money which would have been better spent in the pursuit of a gainful occupation.

The representative exponents of this outlook were totally opposed to the double standard. " It is certain," wrote Richard Steele, " that chastity is . . . as much to be valued in men as in women." [35] He deplored the state of affairs by which the world "instead of avenging the cause of an abused woman, will proclaim her dishonour; while the person injured is shunned like a pestilence, he who did the wrong sees no difference in the reception he meets with, nor is he the less welcome to the rest of the sex who are still within the pale of honour and innocence . . . I know not how it is, but our sex has usurped a certain authority to exclude chastity out of the catalogue of masculine virtues, by which means females adventure all against those who have nothing to lose." [36] Jeremy Collier attacked the aristocratic seducer.

[33] *Of Domesticall Duties, Eight Treatises*, 3rd. ed. (London, 1634), 221.

[34] R. B. Schlatter, *The Social Ideas of Religious Leaders, 1660–1688* (London, 1940), 28–9.

[35] *Tatler*, No. 58, also quoted by R. Blanchard, " Richard Steele and the Status of Women," *Studies in Philology*, XXVI, 3 (1929), 349.

[36] *The Guardian*, No. 45 (2 May, 1713).

"Why," he asked, "is not he that steals a woman's honour as uncreditable as a common surpriser of property [37] .... What think you of sending a wench to Bridewell, and doing nothing to the fellow that debauch'd her, tho' sometimes the first is single, and the other married?" [38]

Since the late seventeenth century there has always existed a large body of middle-class opinion which has regarded illicit sexual activity outside marriage as equally unrespectable in men and women alike. Yet its influence has been limited, in that its main attention has always been directed towards safeguarding the chastity of married women and of the daughters of respectable families. Towards the large body of lower class and of "fallen" women it has been less indulgent. Moreover, the emphasis on outward respectability has resulted in the absence of any serious deterrent against successfully conducted clandestine activity. Concealment has always been more difficult for women than for men; as for the Victorian father the volume of nineteenth-century prostitution tells its own tale.

Before we embark upon the question of why this double standard existed, there are two observations which should be made.

The first is that the double standard is in no way peculiar to England. The moral and legal codes of most advanced peoples reflect the same distinction. The Hindus, the Mohammedans, the Zoroastrians, the ancient Hebrews, all to a greater or lesser extent regarded chastity as primarily a female virtue, an essential quality for all women, but for men, if perhaps an ideal, yet scarcely an attainable one.[39] But it is not true that a high value has been set on female chastity by the whole human race at every stage in its development. As Locke remarks, "He that will carefully peruse the history of mankind, and look abroad into the several tribes of men, and with indifferency survey their actions, will be able to satisfy himself, that there is scarce that principle of morality to be named, or rule of virtue to be thought on ... which is not, somewhere or other, slighted and condemned by the general fashion of whole societies of men, governed by practical opinions, and rules of living quite opposite to others." [40] Some societies have set great value on female chastity; some have not. And if it is admitted that it is comparatively rare for infidelity by married women to be condoned, then it has also to be recognized that active contempt for unmarried females who are still virgin is by no means infrequent. There is, therefore, no reason to believe that the origin of the double standard lies in the nature of things. It is

---

[37] "Of Whoredom," op. cit., 123.   [38] Ibid., 129.

[39] E. Westermarck, *The Origin and Development of the Moral Ideas* (London, 1906–1908), II, 427–8.

[40] *An Essay Concerning Humane Understanding* (London, 1690), 19.

not to be found in every society and we may reasonably conclude that when it does appear, as in England, we may discuss it as a genuine product of historical circumstance.

The second observation is that the double standard is not to be found in all levels of English society with the same intensity. In particular, it has been much less marked in the lower classes. This is made clear by a volume of nineteenth-century comment the force of which cannot be gainsaid, even when all allowances for the deficiencies of the observers have been made. "There is no chastity among the absolute poor," wrote Place in 1822.[41] A country vicar reported to a Royal Commission, in 1843, "I remark also a particular deficiency of the women as to chastity; in many instances they seem hardly to comprehend or value it as a virtue."[42] The Poor Law Commissioners of 1834 were told that "it is scarcely possible in a civilised country, and where Christianity is professed, for there to be less delicacy on the point of chastity than among the class of females in farm service and the labouring community generally[43] . . . . The moral sanction is wholly ineffective amongst the labouring classes."[44] "Sexual intercourse was almost universal prior to marriage in the agricultural district," wrote Gaskell; "marriage was generally deferred till pregnancy fully declared itself." He went on to explain that this kind of intercourse "must not be confounded with that promiscuous and indecent concourse of the sexes which is so prevalent in towns, and which is ruinous alike to health and to morals. It existed only between parties where a tacit understanding had all the weight of an obligation—and this was, that marriage should be the result. This, in nineteen cases out of twenty, took place sooner or later.[45] But there is little doubt that what indignant observers like Gaskell mistook for the effects of the Industrial Revolution upon the morality of the cotton mills represented merely the standards which the laboring classes had always known and which overcrowded housing conditions now did everything to encourage.[46] Among the lowest classes of society the tradition of promiscuity was too strong to allow the emergence of so sophisticated a concept as that of the double standard.

[41] Quoted in M. C. Stopes, *Contraception*, 6th ed. (London, 1946), 280.

[42] *Reports of Special Assistant Poor Law Commissioners on the Employment of Women and Children in Agriculture* (London, 1843), 201.

[43] Parliamentary Papers, 1834, XXXVII (Appendix C to Report of Poor Law Commissioners), 407.

[44] *Ibid.*, 394.

[45] P. Gaskell, *The Manufacturing Population of England* (London, 1833), 28, 31.

[46] M. Hewitt, "The Effect of Married Women's Employment in the Cotton Textile Districts on the Organization and Structure of the Home in Lancashire, 1840–1880" (London, Ph.D. thesis, unpub'd) 1953, 73.

With these reservations in mind we may now turn to consider some possible explanations as to the origin and cause of this double standard.

Of these explanations the first is the one which the present writer is least competent to discuss, for it is matter of psychology, but it is an important one which has to be considered at the very outset. In one of his essays Freud describes what he regards as a common characteristic of civilized men: their inability to fuse the two currents of love and sensuality into love for one person and the resulting tendency to find with women of a lower social order, whom they despise, that sexual satisfaction which they are unable to obtain from their relationship with their wives, for whom they feel only tenderness, affection, and esteem. Of such men he says that " where they love they do not desire and where they desire they cannot love." [47] This dissociation of sexual attraction from the other elements of love and the inability to focus both on a single object Freud attributes to the frustration of intense incestuous fixations in childhood. He admits that women to some extent are also subject to this dissociation, which in their case takes the form of frigidity and occasionally produces Lady Chatterley-like situations. But, on the whole, it seems fair to say that the conclusion which follows from Freudian psycho-analysis is, in the words of one of its best-known exponents, that " with women the directly sexual elements of love are more frequently aroused together with the elements of tenderness and esteem, than is the case with men." [48]

Now if this were true it would suggest that when people have regarded an act of marital infidelity on the part of the woman as having far greater significance than a similar act committed by the man they were doing no more than stating a psychological fact. Such an explanation would go a long way towards accounting for the existence of a double standard of morality. It lends much support to Mr. Gladstone's analysis in the debate on the 1857 divorce bill of the " mode in which temptation operates on parties guilty of adultery according as they are men or women. I believe that a very limited portion of the offences committed by women are due to the mere influence of sensual passion. On the other side, I believe that a very large proportion of the offences committed by men are due to that influence." [49] The findings of the Freudian school of psycho-analysis have to be considered by the historian of morals who endeavors to disentangle the permanent factors from the variable. Thus Dr. Ernest

---

[47] " On the Universal Tendency to Debasement in the Sphere of Love," (trans. A. Tyson), in *Works* (Standard Ed.), ed. J. Strachey *et al.*, XI (1957), 183.

[48] J. C. Flügel, *The Psycho-Analytic Study of the Family*, 3rd ed. (London, 1929), 112.

[49] *Parliamentary Debates*, 3rd Ser., Vol. 147, cols. 1273–1274.

Jones once declared that "prostitution is not altogether a mere *faute de mieux* replaceable, for instance, simply by making early marriage possible." [50] He added that "in a large number of typical cases potency is incompatible with marital fidelity, and can be attained only at the cost of adultery," [51] and that " there is reason to think that the state of affairs would not be so very dissimilar if the social restrictions on sexuality were greatly diminished." [52]

If all this is accepted, then our search for the origins of the double standard would be at an end, for it would have to be recognized that it was no more than an inevitable by-product of a permanent feature of human pyschology, namely the inability of the male to find complete satisfaction within marriage. But it is scarcely as simple as all that. There are good reasons to believe that the conclusions of Freudian psycho-analysis, represented as valid for the whole human race and reinforced by numerous indisputed case-histories as they are, do not necessarily hold outside the nineteenth-century, Western European middle-classes from whom they were derived. It is not just that Freud held many of what we would now regard as characteristically Victorian prejudices and in his attitude to women embodied many of the patriarchal assumptions of his time.[53] What is more serious is that he rarely seems to have considered the possibility that what he regarded as permanent attributes of human nature might have been more temporary affairs influenced or determined by economic and social factors which his investigations did not take into account.

It is true that the incestuous motif which he identified as the fundamental cause of dissociation and therefore of the double standard is less easy to explain away as merely the product of one society than are the various subordinate causes such as the view of the sexual act as something degrading. On the other hand the universal existence of this incestuous fixation would seem to be equally hard to establish. It is not clear exactly how propositions relating to the unconscious are to be proved or disproved, but it can at least be seen that Freud's account of dissociation can hardly be a complete statement of the facts, since there obviously do exist men who succeed in uniting the two streams of love, and since he leaves curiously uncertain the plight of the large majority of men—those of the lower strata of society for whom there exists no class of socially inferior women at whose expense they may gratify their sexual appetites.

[50] E. Jones, *Papers on Psycho-Analysis*, 3rd ed. (London, 1923), 569.
[51] *Ibid.*, 575.
[52] *Ibid.*, 576.
[53] Cf. C. Thompson, " Cultural Pressures in the Psychology of Women," *Psychiatry* (Aug. 1942) V, 3.

Those features of sexual morality which Freud explains by reference to incestuous fixations can, I think, be equally well accounted for in terms of the *mores* of a society that held that sexual desire unadorned was something no respectable lady could ever confess to having known, that produced prostitution by paying single women inadequate wages, and, by assuming that men should conduct the political and professional affairs of the world while women confined themselves to domestic affairs, created a situation in which the casual onlooker would have agreed with Byron that

> Man's love is of man's life a thing apart,
> 'Tis woman's whole existence.

In short, it may be argued that Freud was analyzing not the cause of the double standard, but the result.

A better-known solution to our inquiry was provided by a highly successful interpreter of English life, Dr. Johnson. He regarded female chastity as of the utmost importance because " upon that all the property in the world depends." [54] As for adultery, " confusion of progeny constitutes the essence of the crime; and therefore a woman who breaks her marriage vows is much more criminal than a man who does it. A man, to be sure, is criminal in the sight of God; but he does not do his wife a very material injury, if he does not insult her; if, for instance, from mere wantonness of appetite, he steals privately to her chambermaid. Sir, a wife ought not greatly to resent this. I would not receive home a daughter who had run away from her husband on that account.[55] ... Wise married women don't trouble themselves about infidelity in their husbands.... The man imposes no bastards upon his wife." [56]

There is obviously a good deal of truth in this. A valid reason for discriminating against the adultery of a married woman is that it might well produce bastard children who then intrude into the husband's inheritance. But as an explanation for the double standard it is far from complete. If " confusion of the progeny constitutes the essence of the crime," then the woman should be blameless if there is no confusion or if there is no progeny. When Boswell quoted the example of the lady who " argues that she may indulge herself in gallantries with equal freedom as her husband does, provided she take care not to introduce a spurious issue into his family," Johnson retorted, " this lady of yours, Sir, I think is very fit for a brothel," [57] yet there was logically no reason why he should have disapproved of her argument. Even on Johnson's premises it is clear that the double standard derives from something more than fear of bastard children.

Yet, fundamentally, female chastity has been seen as a matter of

---

[54] G. B. Hill and L. F. Powell, eds. *Boswell's Life of Johnson* (Oxford, 1934–1950), V, 209. Cf. *Ibid.*, II, 457.   [55] *Ibid.*, II, 55–6.   [56] *Ibid.*, III, 406.

property; not, however, the property of legitimate heirs, but the property of men in women. The language in which virginity is most often described should tell us this, for it is that of the commercial market. "The corrupting of a man's wife, enticing her to a strange bed," says *The Whole Duty of Man,* "is by all acknowledged to be the worst sort of theft, infinitely beyond that of goods." [58] A maid who loses her virginity is described by a sixteenth-century writer as "unthrifty" [59] and a hundred years later a poet tells us that "Wives lose their value, if once known before." [60] In other words, girls who have lost their "honor" have also lost their saleability in the marriage market.

The double standard, therefore, is the reflection of the view that men have property in women and that the value of this property is immeasurably diminished if the woman at any time has sexual relations with anyone other than her husband. It may be that this only pushes our investigation back one stage further, for the reasons for the high value set on pre-marital virginity, on retrospective fidelity, as it were, are hard to find and they certainly spring from something more than mere certainty of the legitimacy of the children. Nor do they derive entirely from the fear that a woman who has been unchaste before marriage is likely to be unchaste again, for there have always been men like Angel Clare in *Tess of the d'Urbervilles* who are totally unable to entertain the idea of marriage with a woman who has experienced sexual relationships with another man, no matter how extenuating the circumstances, or who in casual or venal intercourse would insist on a virgin for a partner.[61]

At all events this attitude is to be found in many different kinds of patriarchal society, even if it has varied in intensity according to the social level of the persons concerned and has been weakened by some economic circumstances and strengthened by others. Although reinforced by the growth of capitalism and the influence of the middle-classes it was not entirely derived from those phenomena in the way that some Marxist writers, for example, have suggested. "The heaven-blest merit of chastity," which is so exquisitely celebrated in *Comus,* one of them asserts, "is not unconnected with the Puritan-capitalist reaction against irresponsible consumption." [62] Despite its

[57] *Ibid.*, III, 25.   [58] London (1804), 152.
[59] L. Vives, *The Instruction of a Christen Woman,* trans. R. Hyrde (1541), f. 16ᵛ.
[60] G. Goodwin, ed., *The Poems of William Browne of Tavistock* (1894), II, 160.
[61] Flügel, *op. cit.*, 115–6. By way of example, we may cite the customers of the eighteenth-century brothels mentioned above.
[62] E. Rickword, "Milton: The Revolutionary Intellectual," in C. Hill, ed., *The English Revolution, 1640* (London, 1949), 108, note 1. Cf. C. Hill, "Clarissa Har-

comic overtones, there is an element of truth in this statement in that the middle-class outlook which emerged in the seventeenth and eighteenth centuries, although superficially opposed to the double standard, did much to intensify existing ideas on the subject of female chastity. But it is not a complete answer and the thinly-veiled implication—banish capitalism and banish the double standard—is, it has to be recognized, just not true. What, for example, could provide a better instance of this allegedly peculiarly *bourgeois* view than this law dating from the pre-capitalist times of King Ethelbert? " If one freeman lies with the wife of another freeman, he shall pay the husband his or her wergeld and procure a second wife with his own money, and bring her to the other man's home." [63] The adulterer was expected to buy the aggrieved husband a new wife because the first had been paid for in money. Modern anthropologists, however, agree that the insistence on pre-nuptial chastity is not a result of the system of wife-purchase, but goes back before it, and that the most that can be said is that such a form of marriage provided an additional reason for an existing prohibition.[64]

Yet much of English feudal law was based on the need to protect the property rights of the woman's father or husband. A female heir who was unchaste during the period of her custody was excluded from her inheritance because the advantage to the lord of her marriage might now be lost through her having lost her honor.[65] At a lower social level the same principle applied. The lord of the manor assumed the right to take a fine from girls who bore illegitimate children in exactly the same way as he took fines from those of his tenants who sought permission to give their daughters in marriage.[66] In each case he was losing the value of the woman's marriage, because that depended upon her chastity.

The laws relating to seduction illustrated the same principle. The abduction of heiresses only became a public crime as opposed to a private injury in the reign of Henry VII, and under Elizabeth I it was made a felony without benefit of clergy.[67] But everything depended upon the woman being an heiress.[68] If she owned no land

---

lowe and her Times," *loc. cit.*, 331. " Insistence on absolute pre-marital chastity goes hand-in-hand with the bourgeois conception of absolute property, immune alike from the king's right to arbitrary taxation and the church's divine right to tithes."

[63] Attenborough, *op. cit.*, 9.

[64] M. Ginsberg, *Essays in Sociology and Social Philosophy*, II, *Reason and Unreason in Society* (London, 1956), 81.

[65] G. May, *Social Control of Sex Expression* (London, 1930), 6, note 1.

[66] D. M. Stenton, *The English Woman in History* (London, 1957), 83.

[67] 3 Hen. VII, c. 2. 39 Eliz., c. 9.

[68] W. S. Holdsworth, *A History of English Law* (London, 1925), VIII, 427–9.

or goods then her forcible abduction was a much less serious offense. In the late seventeenth century men were hanged for stealing heiresses, but the women had to be heiresses. In feudal society there was always somebody with a financial interest in every woman's marriage whether she was an heiress or not, but when this situation disappeared it was only the chastity of women with property which continued to be legally protected, because the loss in the case of landless women was nobody's but their own. On the other hand, the father was always at liberty to bring an action against his daughter's seducer on the grounds of the loss of her services which he had thus incurred.[69] Similarly the injured husband could bring against his wife's seducer an action for criminal conversation to recover damages for the loss of his wife's *consortium*. This action was based on the legal fiction that as the husband and wife were one person at law the wife was consequently incapable of consenting to adultery and the husband might therefore claim damages for trespass and assault. This action for criminal conversation was abolished in 1857 but survived in the form of the damages the husband might claim from the co-respondent, the adulterer being liable because he had infringed the husband's right of property in his wife.

Needless to say, none of this worked in reverse. The wife had no claim for damages against her husband's mistress; and on the only occasion in modern English history when adultery was made a criminal offense, and a capital one at that, in 1650, it was the adultery of the married woman and not of the married man which was made punishable.[70] The Puritans took such strong action against adultery, partly because of their respect for the Mosaic law and partly because of the great value they set on family life, but they still adhered to the double standard, based as it was on nothing more than men's property in women.

This deeply entrenched idea that woman's chastity was not her own to dispose of persisted for a long time and was reinforced by the system of arranged marriages which prevailed in the higher reaches of society for most of English history. As long as these unions were a means of social and economic advancement and as long as the bridegroom expected his partner to be a virgin, so long have the arrangements of society been specially designed to preserve female chastity. A woman could no more be unchaste than she could resist her

---

[69] As Sjt. Manning remarked, " the quasi-fiction of *servitium amisit* affords protection to the rich man whose daughter occasionally makes his tea, and leaves without redress the poor man whose child is sent unprotected to earn her bread amongst strangers." Holdsworth, *op. cit.*, 429.

[70] C. H. Firth and R. S. Rait, *Acts and Ordinances of the Interregnum, 1642-1660* (London, 1911), II, 388.

parents' commands concerning her marriage. Rogers tells us how a Puritan preacher " once said to a coy virgin, ' thy virginity is not all thine to dispose of: in part it's thy parents ', father hath a stroke in it, mother another, and kindred a third: fight not against all, but be his whom they would have thee.' " [71] Once married, her chastity was transferred to another owner. "A woman hath no power of her own body, but her husband," wrote Vives; " thou dost the more wrong to give away that thing which is another body's without the owner's licence." [72]

The absolute property of the woman's chastity was vested not in the woman herself, but in her parents or her husband. And it might be sold by them. "For very need," writes one of the Pastons, " I was fain to sell a little daughter I have for much less than I should have done by possibility." [73] Even the husband might do a little marketing himself. In 1696 Thomas Heath was presented by the churchwardens of Thame for cohabiting unlawfully with the wife of George Fuller, "having bought her of her husband at 2¼d the pound." [74] In the eighteenth and nineteenth centuries foreigners were firmly of the opinion that Englishmen could sell their wives, provided they put a halter around their necks and led them into the open market; and in fact many actual transactions of this kind seem to have taken place.[75] One does not have to prove the widespread existence of wife-selling in order to be able to assert that until the mid-nineteenth century the ownership of most women was vested in men, but it provides an interesting if somewhat exaggerated illustration.

The double standard, therefore, was but an aspect of a whole code of social conduct for women which was in turn based entirely upon their place in society in relation to men. The value set on female chastity varied directly according to the extent to which it was considered that women's function was a purely sexual one. Until modern times women were, broadly speaking, thought of as incomplete in themselves and as existing primarily for the sake of men. Hence the contempt for unmarried women—" old maids " who had failed to achieve the main purpose of their existence. The virtue of women was relative to their function and their function was to cater to the needs of men. For this task the first qualification was chastity;

[71] D. Rogers, *op. cit.*, 303.   [72] L. Vives, *op. cit.*, f. 66r.

[73] J. Gairdner, ed. *The Paston Letters, 1422–1509* (London, 1900–1901), *Introduction*, clxxvi.

[74] S. A. Peyton, ed., *The Churchwardens' Presentments in the Oxfordshire Peculiars of Dorchester, Thame and Banbury* (Oxford Records Society, 1928), 184.

[75] *Notes and Queries*, 1st Ser., VII (1853), 602–3; 4th Ser., X (1872), 271, 311, 468–9; H. W. V. Temperley, " The Sale of Wives in England in 1823," *The History Teachers' Miscellany* (May 1925), III, 5.

hence, chastity was the essence of female virtue. In the sixteenth century Vives had written that "no man will look for any other thing of a woman, but her honesty: the which only, if it be lacked, is like as in a man, if he lack all that he should have. For in a woman the honesty is instead of all." [76] Three hundred years later the sentiment was repeated when Josephine Butler in the course of her travels was told that "A woman who has once lost chastity has lost every good quality. She has from that moment '*all the vices.*' " [77]

It is not for us to comment here on the ironies of a code of morality which made virtue and honor a mere physical fact to which intention and circumstance were not relevant. As finally developed in the eighteenth century, this view of honor held out no hope to an injured girl save the unlikely *deus ex machina* of marriage, what Fordyce called "a sponge to wipe out in a single stroke the stain of guilt." [78]

From this prime insistence on woman's chastity emerged most of the other social restrictions upon her conduct. As Mrs. Knowles said to Dr. Johnson, "the mason's wife, if she is ever seen in liquor, is ruined; the mason may get himself drunk as often as he pleases, with little loss of character."[79] And not only sobriety was expected, but modesty, delicacy, bashfulness, silence and all the other "feminine" virtues. For centuries the ideal woman was a Griselda, passive and long-suffering, or a Lucrece who put death before dishonor.[80] And in courtship women existed to be pursued, not to do the pursuing. Ultimately such conduct was regarded as springing not merely from the usages of society, but from the fundamental attributes of female nature itself. The claim of men to the exclusive sexual possession of women resulted not only in two separate codes of conduct, but in a highly exaggerated view of the innate differences between the two sexes themselves.

[76] Vives, *op. cit.*, f. 17ᵛ.
[77] J. Butler, *Personal Reminiscences of a Great Crusade* (London, 1896), 149.
[78] Quoted on 171 of I. Watt, *The Rise of the Novel: Studies in Defoe, Richardson, and Fielding* (London, 1957).
In this connection it is noteworthy to see how Richardson advances from the repulsive marriage-covers-all morality of *Pamela* (the story of a maid-servant who holds off the advances of her lecherous employer until he has agreed to marry her) to the superior theme of *Clarissa*, who is raped after being drugged and can find escape only in death, yet whose chastity of intention remains unchallenged. See C. Hill, "Clarissa Harlowe," *loc. cit.*
[79] G. B. Hill and L. F. Powell, *op. cit.*, III, 287.
[80] For example, Isabella in *Measure for Measure* (III, i, 104–106). She cannot yield her chastity to save her brother but
    Isabella: O, were it but my life,
                       I'd throw it down for your deliverance
                       As frankly as a pin!
    Claudio: Thanks, dear Isabel.

The final step in the campaign to protect female chastity was the most remarkable of all, for it amounted to nothing less than the total desexualization of women. It is now well-known how the eighteenth century witnessed the triumph of the new feminine ideal afforded by Richardson's Pamela—delicate, insipid, fainting at the first sexual advance, and utterly devoid of feelings towards her admirer until the marriage knot was tied.[81] Slowly there emerged two quite different standards of what constitutes propriety for either sex. And the origin of these standards can be seen quite clearly in the male desire to build a protective fence round male property—female chastity.

The association of sexuality primarily with men and the male organ was not new and may well have some basis in fact, particularly in the case of younger people. Dr. Kinsey tells us that " the average adolescent girl gets along well enough with a fifth as much sexual activity as the adolescent boy." [82] Be this as it may, this distinction was fostered out of all proportion by the tendencies we have been describing. An article in *The Westminster Review* for 1850 remarked that, save in the case of fallen women, sexual desire in women was dormant " always till excited by undue familiarities; almost always till excited by actual intercourse. . . . Women whose position and education have protected them from exciting causes, constantly pass through life without ever being cognizant of the promptings of the senses. . . . Were it not for this kind decision of nature, which in England has been assisted by that correctness of feeling which pervades our education, the consequences would, we believe, be frightful." [83] Less stress on the effects of education was laid by the leading authority on sexual matters in later Victorian England, who declared that " happily for society " the supposition that women possess sexual feelings could be put aside as " a vile aspersion." [84]

Respectable Victorian wives therefore were educated to regard the act of procreation as a necessary and rather repulsive duty; and of course the process was circular. The sense of shame in the woman and the lack of consideration on the part of the man, who was, after all, encouraged to regard this particular part of matrimony as existing primarily for his benefit, led women to take an unduly fastidious attitude and helped to create the enduring legacy of frigidity in women, all traces of which have not yet departed.

[81] See R. P. Utter and G. B. Needham, *Pamela's Daughters* (London, 1937) and I. Watt, *The Rise of the Novel*.

[82] A. C. Kinsey, W. B. Pomeroy, C. E. Martin, *Sexual Behaviour in the Human Male* (Philadelphia and London, 1948), 223. A. C. Kinsey offers his own explanation of the double standard in *Sexual Behavior in the Human Female* (Philadelphia and London, 1953), 322, 411–12.

[83] *The Westminster and Foreign Quarterly Review* (April–July 1850), 457.

[84] Acton, quoted by H. Ellis, "The Erotic Rights of Woman," *The British Society for the Study of Sex Psychology, Publication No. 5* (London, 1918), 9.

As a final proof that the double standard was based on something more than fear of the risk of illegitimate children, some of the arguments deployed by the opponents of birth-control may be cited. Although a modern feminist work speaks in passing of "the comparative unimportance of physical fidelity now that birth-control is possible," [85] it does not seem that contraception by eliminating some of the consequences has eliminated everything which went into making the double standard. At the famous trial of Mrs. Besant and Charles Bradlaugh for publishing Knowlton's *Fruits of Philosophy*, a manual on birth control, the prosecuting counsel described the work concerned as a "dirty, filthy book" which would enable the "unmarried female" to "gratify her passions." [86] In doing so he was clearly revealing that his demand for female chastity was not based upon the dread of illegitimate children at all. And yet it may be that all the details of the double standard are mere elaborations of the central fact that when a man and a woman have sexual relations the woman may conceive whereas the man will not. The whole social and ethical structure may well follow from this in practice without following logically. "When a general rule of this kind is once established," says Hume, "men are apt to extend it beyond those principles from which it first arose ... and though all these maxims have a plain reference to generation, yet women past child-bearing have no more privilege in this respect than those who are in the flower of their youth and beauty ... the general rule carries us beyond the original principle, and makes us extend the notions of modesty over the whole sex, from their earliest infancy to their extremest old age and infirmity." [87]

Hume's remarks notwithstanding, it seems that the English insistence on female chastity cannot be explained by reference to the fact of child birth and elaborations thereon, but that the solution is more likely to be found in the desire of men for absolute property in women, a desire which cannot be satisfied if the man has reason to believe that the woman has once been possessed by another man, no matter how momentarily and involuntarily and no matter how slight the consequences.

I am well aware that this conclusion leaves many questions unanswered, notably why this desire for property in women should vary in degree according to the social level of the men concerned. This problem, together with allied questions, must be left to future investigators. My main concern here is to pose the question, not to provide all the answers.

[85] I. Clephane, *Towards Sex Freedom* (London, 1935), 230.   [86] *Ibid.*, 108
[87] *Theory of Politics*, ed. F. Watkins (London, 1951), 124–5.

Jane Addams on Human Nature[1]

by MERLE CURTI

Reprinted from the *Journal of the History of Ideas*—Vol. XXII, No. 2, pp. 240-253

It is somewhat curious that in tributes to Jane Addams (1860–1935) occasioned by her centennial year, no serious consideration has been given to her place in American intellectual history. One finds merited praise of her personality and of her contributions to the woman's movement, to social welfare, and to international peace. Her understanding and appreciation of the immigrants in our midst and what she did to help them become Americans without losing a feeling for their Old World heritage have been rightly recalled. But the ideas she held, their relation to her time and her life, have not apparently seemed worthy of analysis and evaluation.

Three main considerations go a long way toward explaining this. Jane Addams did not in any of her writings systematically set forth her social ideas in a way to please the scholars nowadays who set great store on what is called intellectual sophistication. Her ideas, in her books and essays, are subordinated to the larger social and human purposes and activities to which her life was dedicated. The pages abound with straightforward, unpretentious but often moving and penetrating reports of interviews with well known public figures and of participation in meetings of social workers and advocates of peace. Her writings are chiefly concerned with her everyday experiences over forty odd years at Hull House.

A second reason for the neglect of Jane Addams' thought may be that in her own day a public image was developed in some quarters which did her scant justice. She was widely appreciated, but certain critics, influenced by the stereotype of the sentimental do-gooder which was common among intellectuals, were close to condescension in their judgments of her. Agnes Repplier, for example, wrote of her "ruthless sentimentality." Theodore Roosevelt once dubbed her "poor bleeding Jane" and "a progressive mouse." Such judgments no doubt have lingered and confirmed many in accepting a stereotype—a Jane Addams whose easy optimism blinded her to the depth of the "tragic view of life" so popular now in many intellectual circles.

The neglect of her ideas may also be related to a present discouragement over the uses women have made of the vote, to which she attached so much importance, and, even more likely, to the contemporary strength of nationalism and of the forces in the world that make the abolition of war seem at best remote.

It is not my purpose to try to elevate Jane Addams into a major

[1] This essay was presented as the first William I. Hull Lecture at Swarthmore College, October 16, 1960, under the joint sponsorship of the William J. Cooper Foundation and the Swarthmore College Peace Collection.

figure in our intellectual life. But on re-reading her ten books [2] it seems clear that if justice has been done her heart and her social vision, it has not been done her mind. Her ideas illuminate in sensitive and often keen ways major movements of thought in her time. Nor can the significance of her life be understood unless thoughtful attention is given to the rôle that ideas played in that life. Further, at its best, the writing in which her ideas are expressed rises to a level of literary distinction.

The thought of Jane Addams might be considered in any of a number of ways. I have chosen to use a central theme as a key to her ideas and feelings—her conception of human nature. The term itself occurs frequently in her writings. It was not common in her time to give the term an explicit, formal definition, and she herself did not do so. But it is clear that she did not limit it to the native equipment of men. For her, human nature encompassed the experiences and potentialities of the growing organism, in infancy, childhood, adolescence, and old age. She appreciated the dynamic factors in motivation and saw in the universal desire of individuals to be recognized and appreciated as unique persons, and the consequence of society's failure to make such recognition, the key to much behavior. She recognized the nature and rôle of sex in the life of the individual, but she also saw its relation to civilization. In her view of human nature, play and recreation are basic needs which brook denial only at heavy cost. Fighting is of course a part of human nature, but so is cooperation. Above all, her image of man emphasized the idea that the differences separating social classes and distinguishing immigrants and Negroes from old stock Americans, are far less important than the capacities, impulses, and motives they share in common.

In *Twenty Years at Hull House* the author noted that in 1889, when she went to live on Halstead Street, she was without any preconceived social theories and economic views. These, she added, were developed out of her experiences in Chicago. True, but the foundations for these theories and views rested on already formulated conceptions of human nature which, as she herself recognized, began to take shape in early childhood. Such recognition was natural enough, for by 1910, when the book was published, social workers as well as parents and educators were familiar with the great importance G.

[2] All of Jane Addams' books were published by the Macmillan Company: *Democracy and Social Ethics* (1902), *Newer Ideals of Peace* (1907), *The Spirit of Youth and the City Streets* (1909), *Twenty Years at Hull House* (1910), *A New Conscience and an Ancient Evil* (1912), *The Long Road of Woman's Memory* (1916), *Peace and Bread in Time of War* (1922), *The Second Twenty Years at Hull House* (1930), *The Excellent Becomes the Permanent* (1932), *and My Friend Julia Lathrop* (1935); *Jane Addams, A Centennial Reader*, edited by Emily Cooper Johnson, 1960. The Jane Addams papers are in the Swarthmore College Peace Collection.

Stanley Hall had long been attaching to childhood experiences. And so it was natural for Miss Addams to begin her autobiography by referring to the theory that "our genuine impulses may be connected with our childish experiences, that one's bent may be traced back to that 'No man's land' where character is formless but nevertheless settling into definite lines of future development."

These reminiscences reveal some of the basic conceptions of human nature later to be more or less explicitly formulated in writing and richly implemented in living. One finds repeated reference, for example, to the presumably innate tendency of children to seek in ceremonial expression a sense of identification with man's primitive life and kinship with the past, perhaps a compensation for the child's slowness to understand the real world about him, and certainly an instrument toward that end. This conviction, made intellectually respectable by early XIXth-century German philosophers and in Jane Addams' young womanhood by G. Stanley Hall (the recapitulation theory), was to figure in the importance she attached to the esthetic impulse and to children's play. The theory that in play children satisfy an innate need to live over the experience of the race seemed to her both reasonable and realistic. Adolescent behavior, which some thought stemmed from original sin, she looked upon as a natural expression of an instinct too old and too powerful to be easily recognized and wisely controlled. She noted also that children love to carry on, either actually or in play, activities proper to older people. This trait she thought of as also grounded in the need to repeat racial experience, and as expressing itself regardless of precept or inculcation. "The old man," as she put it, "clogs our earliest years."

Another early formed foundation stone for her image of man was the conviction that the basis of childhood's timidity, never altogether outworn, stems from "a sense of being unsheltered in a wide world of relentless and elemental forces." It is at least in part because of this fear and loneliness, she thought, that the child, and the adult which he becomes, needs affection and companionship. Jane Addams realized, of course, long before she wrote the autobiography, that in her own case this feeling of being unsheltered was accentuated by the fact that she had been deprived of her mother by death in her third year and by the further fact that a physical deformity both isolated her and gave her a sense of inadequacy and inferiority. But she was sure that all children share in greater or less degree this sense of fear and loneliness and that its major antidote is understanding and love. Also in her case the sense of timidity and loneliness was compensated for by the close and affectionate father-daughter relationship. The father's way of assuring her of his acceptance of her cemented the bond more tightly. It is hard, she reflected, to account fully for a child's adoring affection for a parent, "so emotional, so irrational, so tangled with the affairs of the imagination."

It came to be clear to Jane Addams, as it is so patently clear to us, that her father greatly influenced her ideas about the nature of mankind. A substantial miller imbued with the democracy of the Illinois frontier and of his hero Mazzini, John Addams' views of human nature reflected his abolitionism, his great admiration of Lincoln, and his commitment to Hicksite Quakerism. His complete lack of racial prejudice and his firm conviction that the similarities of men far outweigh the differences, were an indelible influence in the forming of the daughter's view of human nature. So too was his belief in the essential equality of men and women. These beliefs were reinforced by his Quaker heritage and the essentially classless society of this Illinois farm community. When his young daughter was troubled about the doctrine of foreordination, and asked her father to explain it to her, he replied that probably neither she nor he had the kind of minds capable of understanding the doctrine. In other words, as Jane Addams later recalled the conversation, some minds are capable and fond of dealing with abstractions while others are at home with concrete facts and immediate problems: this simple typology explained much that she later observed at Hull House in heated discussions over socialism and anarchism. Her father continued by adding that it made little difference whether one was the sort to understand such doctrines as predestination as long as he did not pretend to understand what he didn't. "You must always be honest with yourself inside, no matter what happens." This idea, so basic in Quaker tradition, stuck with the girl. The discussion ended with the suggestion that there may be areas of unfathomed complexity, incapable at least at the present stage of man's rational development, of being fully comprehended. In Jane Addams' view of human nature there was a large place for the contemplation of life's mysteries.

The instruction and associations of Rockford Seminary did not greatly alter these foundations for a conception of human nature. Jane Addams, like her fellow-students, read textbooks on mental philosophy, but the static and sterile approach in most treatises of this kind at best stimulated discussions outside class on such questions as the freedom of the will. The reading of Emerson strengthened her sense that human nature includes both rational and intuitive capacities. But as she was introduced to new ranges of feminism, she felt dissatisfied with the old belief in the ascendancy of intuition in the feminine mind. Under the influence of the positivism which she discovered, she concluded that women ought to study intensively at least one branch of natural science to make the faculties clear and more acute. Following graduation from Rockford, she tried studying medicine in Philadelphia but found she had little taste or aptitude for the sciences and dropped the course.

During the Rockford years and the brief Philadelphia experiment, Miss Addams' awareness of death and sorrow took on, especially through her study of Plato, a universal dimension: human existence had always been an unceasing flow and ebb of justice and oppression, of life and death. She heard about Darwinism and accepted it. The acceptance and interpretations she gave to evolution became a fresh and vastly important component in her image of man.

Like so many young women college graduates of the time, Jane Addams went to Europe in search of further culture. The four years she spent abroad were shadowed by long and painful illnesses and a depressing sense of failure. Thus her years of further education were not altogether roseate. But she continued to learn. Experiences in the great art galleries and study of man's early artistic expressions in the pyramids and in the catacombs sharpened her vague feeling that the esthetic component is basic in man's nature. But this was not all, for she interested herself further in the positivism which she had discovered in her reading at Rockford.

When she saw that for all their enthusiasm about human brotherhood, the positivists did little or nothing to implement the idea, she sought light elsewhere. This she found in her growing awareness of the human wretchedness in the great urban slums and in the programs of the British social settlement pioneers. Increasingly she felt that many college women in their zest for learning and in their search for individual culture departed too suddenly from the active, emotional life led by their grandmothers and great grandmothers. The rewards of the search for individual knowledge and culture paled as she became more deeply convinced of the far greater importance of learning from life itself. Education and artistic effort, she decided, were futile when considered apart from the ultimate test of the conduct it inspired, when there was no relationship between these and the human need of the poor and the suffering. Thus without benefit of William James and John Dewey, who only later reenforced her views of human nature, she became, as her friend Dr. Alice Hamilton said, something of a pragmatist, determined to test ideas and values about life in the actual laboratory of life. But the pragmatism that later provided support for an enlarged view of human nature did not lead to a rejection of presuppositions more or less unconsciously acquired and interwoven with Christian humanism and Christian mystery.

Closely related to pragmatism and more important in her own intellectual growth had been the doctrine of evolution. No one of the other late XIXth- and early XXth-century movements of thought— the so-called new psychology of the experimental laboratory, or

Freudianism, or Marxism—to all of which she responded, exerted so far-reaching an influence on Jane Addams' view of the nature of man as did the teachings of Darwin and his disciple Kropotkin, who spent some time at Hull House in 1901.

For Jane Addams, the evolutionary view of human nature postulated certain primordial types of behavior and potential types of behavior. On many occasions she referred to these, in the fashion of those days, as instincts. Man shared some of these with other animals. But in the process of evolution, of survival through adaptation, he came to have impulses that set him apart from other animals in somewhat the way that the human hand enabled him to claw his way to a civilization denied his less well equipped fellow creatures.

Her view of the inherited basic equipment of man emphasized the special importance of the extremely early appearance in man's long struggle upwards, of the tribal feeding of the young. This human instinct sprang out of or was at least closely related to man's innate gregariousness and to the ability first of mothers and then of males to see in the hunger of any young symbolical relationship to the hunger of their own offspring. Our very organism, Jane Addams wrote, holds memories and glimpses of "that long life of our ancestors which still goes on among so many of our contemporaries. Nothing," she continued, "so deadens the sympathies and shrivels the power of enjoyment, as the persistent keeping away from the great opportunities for helpfulness, as a continual ignoring of the starvation struggle which makes up the life of at least half the race. To shut oneself away from the race life is to shut one's self away from the most vital part of it; it is to live out but half the humanity to which we have been born and to use but half our faculties." This desire for action to fulfil social obligation was so deep-seated a heritage that to deny its expression, she thought, was more fatal to well-being than anything save disease, indigence, and a sense of guilt.

Here we have the corner stone of all that Jane Addams did in sharing her life with less fortunate neighbors, in encouraging measures designed to prevent the young and the old from being exploited, and in mobilizing in war-time food for helpless hungry mouths wherever they might be. For marvelous though human nature was in its adaptability, it had never "quite fitted its back to the moral strain involved in the knowledge that fellow creatures are starving."

The reading of Kropotkin and others led to the belief that this human instinct or trait appeared perhaps a million years or more before man developed a proclivity to kill masses of his own kind. This method of settling differences, many anthropologists held, had become common among human beings a mere twenty thousand years ago. It was used by only one other species, ants, which like human beings, were property holders. Thus Jane Addams might respectably hold, and she did, that the earlier instinct, with its implications of human solidarity, could under proper conditions exert an even stronger pull over behavior than competing forces, less deeply seated. In other words, man's primordial concern for group feeding of the young and the sense of responsibility for helping those in need which was related to it, might check and control the more recently acquired habit of mass killing of one's own kind. In the growth of international institutions and the evidences that love of man was crossing provincial and national boundaries, she saw hope for an emerging pacifism that in time would make war as obsolete as slavery had become. In sum, her reading convinced her that war, like slavery, was a relatively recent man-made institution. The argument that pacifism could never triumph because of man's inborn and unchangeable pugnacity, was no more valid, she thought, than the pre-Civil War argument of Southerners that slavery could never be abolished because it is ingrained in human nature itself.

In an address at the Boston Peace Congress of 1904, Miss Addams began to spell out the implications of this position, a position more positive in character than the non-resistance ideas of her hero, Tolstoy. In that address she anticipated William James' "Moral Equivalents of War" in suggesting that the subhuman and dark forces which so easily destroy the life of mankind might be diverted into organized attacks on social maladjustments, on poverty, disease, and misfortune, on one hand, and into the closely related "nurture of human life" on the other. It might in particular be diverted from destructive outburst into war by taking heed from the successful example of the immigrants of diverse and even hostile traditions who had learned to live as friends in America's cities. This view was developed in her book *Newer Ideals of Peace,* published in 1907. In the poorer quarters of our cosmopolitan cities she found multitudes of immigrants surrendering habits of hate and of aggression cherished for centuries, and customs that could be traced to habits of primitive man. She not only saw that they surrendered these habits, she also witnessed innumerable and sustained examples of the pity and kindness based on an equally ancient, or even more ancient, instinct: the instinct of pity and kindness toward those in the group whose need was even greater than that of the others. "In seeking companionship in the new world the immigrants are reduced to the fundamental equalities and universal necessities of life itself. They develop power of association which comes from daily contact with those who are unlike each other in all save the universal characteristics of man." To put it in other words, the pressures of a cosmopolitan neighborhood seemed to be the simple and inevitable foundations for an international order in somewhat the same way that the foundations of tribal and national morality had already been laid.

This hope suffered a blow during the first world war when an emotional crisis showed that many immigrants had not in living together actually shed the heritage of Old World hatreds. But the outbreak of the war brought to the fore another belief also rooted in her conception of human nature. Jane Addams found a great many soldiers in hospitals in the several belligerent countries who expressed the wish that women everywhere would use their influence to end the struggle. She knew, of course, that women as well as men in all the fighting countries were supporting the war. Yet she reflected that, just as an artist in an artillery corps commanded to fire on a beautiful cathedral would be "deterred by a compunction unknown to the man who had never given himself to creating beauty and did not know the intimate cost of it, so women, who have brought men into the world and nurtured them until they reach the age of fighting, must experience a peculiar revulsion when they see them destroyed, irrespective of the country in which these may have been born."

Such intimations received confirmation at the meeting of women from several countries at The Hague in 1915. Here it was said again and again that appeals against war and for a peaceful organization of the world had been made too largely a matter of reason and a sense of justice. If reason is only part of the human endowment, then emotion and the deepest racial impulses must be recognized, modified, utilized. These deep racial impulses admittedly include the hatred of the man who differs from the crowd: but this would be softened by understanding and education. Also involved are those primitive human urgings to foster life and to protect the helpless of which women were the earliest custodians. Involved too are the gregarious instincts shared with the animals themselves—instincts which women as noncombatants might now best keep alive. Such were some of the supports in her concept of human nature on which Jane Addams now leaned.

When her own country entered the war in 1917 she kept faith with the instrumentalist conviction that the processes or methods by which goals are approached or achieved, are more important than acceptance of so-called practical means that are in fact incompatible with the ends. She had always felt that temperament and habit—also important ingredients in human nature—kept her in the middle of the road. Now circumstances drove her to the extreme left of what had been the peace movement. She faced the opprobrium of society and the loneliness of standing out against mass judgment, wondering at times if such deviation as hers might not be only arrogance. But she fell back on the lesson her Quaker father had taught her: that what was most important was always to be honest with oneself inside, no matter what happened, that the ability to hold out against friends and society in a time of crisis depends "upon the categorical belief that a man's primary allegiance is to his own vision of the truth and that he is under an obligation to affirm it."

She also found comfort in reminding herself of the universality of sorrow and death and in pondering—she knew it was at the risk of rationalization—on what seemed to be one of the lessons of the evolutionary view of human nature. If the deviant pacifist invited the deeply rooted biological hatred meted out to one who by nonconforming threatened the security of the group, there was after all another side of the evolutionary coin. All forms of growth begin with a variation from the mass. Might not the individual or group that differed from the mass be initiating moral changes and growth in human behavior and affairs? Might not he who was damned as a crank or pitied as a freak in times of stern crisis actually be leading in the growth of a new moral sense for his society? In view of the complexity and mystery of life's purposes, who could say? And finally, the difficulties of being a pacifist in war time were made a bit more bearable by keeping in mind what seemed another lesson from evolution: that the virtues of patriotism and the martial traits remained only as vestiges after they had actually become a deterrent to future social progress.

In other ways, too, the evolutionary view deeply influenced without moulding Jane Addams' ideas about human nature. This view also influenced, in an unknown measure, her own conduct. During the first years on Halstead Street nothing was more pitifully clear to her than "the fact that pliable human nature is relentlessly pressed upon by its physical environment." The Socialists, more than any other group, seemed to realize this, and seemed also to be making an earnest effort to relieve that heavy pressure. She would have been glad to have the comradeship of that "gallant company" had the Socialists not so firmly insisted that fellowship depended on identity of creed. In making this comment she was for the moment probably overlooking a Socialist emphasis on class conflict: for though she recognized the existence of such a conflict, she was not convinced that it was inevitable.

And so, unable to find comfort in a definite ideology which "explained" social chaos and pointed to logical bettering of physical conditions, Jane Addams went at the matter differently. Without bitterness or self-righteousness she tried to help labor and management learn the lesson of cooperation. She tried to educate public opinion and legislators to an appreciation of the fact that there is a definite relation between physical conditions and human behavior: that long and exhausting hours of labor at deadening tasks are likely to be followed by a quest for lurid and exciting pleasures. Moreover, the power to overcome such temptation reaches its limit almost automatically with that of physical resistance. "The struggle for existence," she wrote in *Democracy and Social Ethics* (1902), "which is so much harsher among people near the edge of pauperism, sometimes leaves ugly marks on character." Society had begun to apply this evolutionary principle to the bringing up of children. It had finally come to expect certain traits and behavior under certain conditions, to adapt methods and matter to the child's growing and changing needs. But society was slow to apply this principle to human affairs in general. In our attitudes toward the poor, the alcoholic, the prostitute, the outcast, she wrote, we think much more of what a man or woman ought to be than of what he is or what he might become under different and better conditions.

Here is an important factor in Jane Addams' approach to social work. She sensed the limitations in what the scientific charity groups and case workers had come to look on as the only true kind of helpfulness but what all too often seemed to those to be aided, ruthless imposition of conventions and standards that were incomprehensible. Pity might seem capricious and harmful to the new type of social case worker, but she should not forget that a theory of social conduct is a poor substitute for tenderness of heart which need not be blind to the complexity of the situation.

The deeply human interest in and appreciation of all sorts of people, including those in trouble, led Jane Addams to an early appreciation of the rôle of sex in deviant behavior and tragedy. It is noteworthy that a girl reared in the Victorian period was able to speak as frankly as she did and to recognize sex as "the most basic and primordial instinct of human beings." It is remarkable that she so early saw in the sex instinct a source of creativity in the arts and that she recognized its close association with play, which she also thought to be an inherent need in humankind. Basic and all important as the sex instinct was, it had always, from the beginnings of the race itself, been in some way controlled in the expression it took. But, in her view, our modern industrial city as it was in the 1890's not only failed to provide sensible, humane, and necessary forms of regulation of the instinct but invited its commercial degradation and exploitation and encouraged its expression in delinquent behavior and in enduring human tragedy.

More specifically, the American city with its anonymity, its uprooted families, its ill-adjusted immigrants, its commercial exploitation of the labor of girls and boys and young men and women in grim shops and factories in an almost never-ending workday, provided no opportunities for the development of comradeship and recreation save in gaudy and sensation-evoking saloons, dance halls and similar money-making establishments. Loneliness was the fate of innumerable girls who struggled against poverty and who had no decent opportunities for making friendships. "It is strange," wrote Miss Addams in 1911, "that we are so slow to learn that no one can safely live without companionship and affection, that the individual who tries the hazardous experiment of going without at least one of them is prone to be swamped by a black mood from within. It is as if we had to build little islands of affection in the vast sea of impersonal forces lest we be overwhelmed by them." Boys, to be sure, found companionship in gangs. But deprived of opportunities for natural expression of adolescent revolt in healthy recreation, the gang was at best an antisocial institution leading naturally to delinquency and a life of defeat, alcoholism, violence, and crime.

One might suppose in view of the innumerable examples of the rôle of sex in leading to ruthless exploitation one the one hand and to grim tragedy on the other, that Jane Addams would have accepted the Calvinist theory, with which she was familiar, of the innate depravity of mankind. On the contrary, with her faith in the pliability of human nature she held that just as our society brings out unfortunate behavior, so it is also capable of evoking wholesome relationships, social idealism, and artistic creativity if society assumes responsibility in a great area of human drive and experience, sex, which it had ignored, or condemned, or permitted to be degraded. She quoted General Bingham, Police Commissioner of New York, to the effect that there is "not enough depravity in human nature" to keep alive the very large business of commercial prostitution. "The immorality of women and the brutishness of men have to be persuaded, coaxed, and constantly stimulated in order to keep the social evil in its present state of business prosperity."

Jane Addams, like other Americans imbued with the teachings of pragmatism, did not draw any separating line between theory and practice. If, as she insisted, the regulation of this great primitive instinct had a long history and if that regulation had evolved with civilization, indeed, with the race itself, it was important to recognize the fact that its regulation now needed to be better adapted to the conditions of urban and industrial life.

Understanding the nature of sex was the first step in developing a better regulation of it. The cooperation of parents and schools might do much to bring about a more healthy understanding of and attitude toward sex. Sane education could be furthered not only through classes in biology and hygiene. It could also be encouraged through the study of literature and history which provide rich examples of the ill-effects of mere suppression or mere indulgence, and which also give abundant illustration of the ennobling expression of sex in altruism. Also important in her view was the expression of the creative aspects of the sex instinct in music and art—which the ancient Greeks had so well understood. "In failing to diffuse and utilize this fundamental instinct of sex through the imagination," she wrote, "we not only inadvertently foster vice and enervation, but we throw away one of the most precious implements for ministering to life's highest need." It is, to be sure, no easy thing to substitute the love of beauty for mere desire, to place the mind above the senses. But "the whole history of civilization," as she kept reminding her generation, "has been one long effort to substitute psychic impulsion for the driving force of blind appetite." Jane Addams took pains again and again to make clear that this was quite different from the mere parental and social imposition of repression.

Understanding the nature and potential relationships between sex, altruism, and esthetic creativity was, however, not enough. What was also needed was community provision for the expression of the sex impulse in wholesome companionship, in social idealism put into practice, and in the provision by society of adequate means for the expression and development of the play instinct. For this too was so basic and inherent a constituent of human nature that it could neither be safely repressed nor, in modern urban life, left to chance. The thwarting of all these basic instincts, the failure of contemporary society to provide proper channels for their expression, explained, Jane Addams insisted, much of the tragedy that stemmed from leaving the sex instinct isolated from intelligent direction and manifestation. It is worth noting in passing that she came to these views without benefit of Freud, at least as far as we know. When, in the 1920's, she first spoke of him in her writings, it was less to find support for her thesis than to regret the popular interpretation which focused attention on the driving need for direct and overt sex expression.

But understanding and sublimation of the sex instinct are not in her view enough. Society, she insisted, must put an end to certain conditions that tempted boys and girls into degrading expressions of the sex impulse. It can not do this merely by sanctioning benevolent welfare capitalism, such as that exemplified in the paternalism at Pullman. For like a modern King Lear, George Pullman could not understand that his regimentation of the workers presumably in their own interest led to "a revolt of human nature" against the denial of their own participation in what affected every detail of their lives. State intervention against long hours, poor pay, and the grueling monotony of tending machines in factory and sweatshop was a more positive need. The trade unions were working in this direction and early found in Jane Addams a strong supporter. But the community, she said, must also provide an environment in which, after an exhausting workday, youth and older workers might find the right sort of companionship and release from nervous tensions. Only by this means and through adequate pay would the toilers be freed from the temptation and necessity of finding pleasure in saloons and dubious dance halls.

Society can, in short, Miss Addams believed, reestablish under modern conditions the ancient tie between the sex impulse and artistic creativity and wholesome relaxation from the nervous tension of modern industrial labor. And it can also provide the means by which the social idealism of adolescence can find constructive outlet in helping others. Hull House pioneered in all this; but Jane Addams was sufficiently realistic to appreciate the need of a broader institutionally and socially supported program, and to work toward that end. In brief, people need not be allowed to fall into esthetic and social insensibility and into an indulgence of basic instincts that is unsatisfying, wasteful, and often tragic.

How much of the analysis of human nature which Jane Addams so unpretentiously made seems valid in the light of experience and present-day knowledge? One must report that some of her concepts are no longer entertained by competent psychologists. The theory that children in their growth recapitulate racial experiences, for example, now has few adherents. Nor would psychologists describe as instincts some of the motives and behavior she regarded as inborn and unlearned. But in her day psychologists did accept the instinct theory, and in following them she was *au courant*. She was on more solid ground in early emphasizing the importance of childhood experiences and of sex well before even psychologists had generally recognized it. It is true that she was too optimistic in thinking that degrading forms of expression of the sex impulse would disappear if bitter poverty were eliminated and adequate recreation made available. Our society has gone far toward achieving these ends, yet the degrading forms of expression seem to be as much of a problem as ever. But it is hard to measure the effects of changing conditions, and a great deal can of course be said for her conviction that the sex impulse can be modified and channeled into varied and often elevating expressions.

Miss Addams was also a pioneer in America in appreciating and using constructively the now well established fact that the great modes of adjustment in life, whether considered individually or socially, develop through influences of which each participant is often unconscious as he struggles to adapt himself to continuing and changing conditions. And though motivation research, unknown in her day, has made substantial progress, her discussion of motivation was unusually perceptive and is still largely acceptable. Her explanation of the deviant behavior of youth as a blundering effort to find adventure and self-expression in a society which provides few opportunities for either, is still central in the most informed approaches to the problems of delinquency. A case can also be made for her thesis that the talents and experiences of women in bearing children, in nurturing life, and in housekeeping and homemaking have been important factors in what they have done with the vote and through organization in helping to raise standards of community welfare.

It is perhaps in Miss Addams' discussion of the relation of war to human nature that the limitations of her analysis and her program are most apparent. One need not minimize the contributions of women in the continuing struggle against war. But her ideas about the potential rôle of women in this struggle, which she associated with a strongly ingrained compassion and reverence for life, would probably seem to her, were she alive today, to have been overstressed. The fact that immigrants in the United States seem quickly to forget ancient hatreds and learn to live together in peace, has been cited by various writers here and abroad. But Miss Addams' expectation that this demonstration would have an effect on international cooperation does not appear to have been realized. It also seems clear that she overstressed as a factor for peace what she regarded as the primordial appearance in the race of group responsibility for feeding infants and children regardless of parentage. The fact that loyalty to the nation and mass killing appeared historically late has not thus far rendered these patterns of behavior subordinate to the compassionate traits in human nature which she thought to be much older and therefore stronger in pull.

On the other hand, social scientists generally endorse Miss Addams's early arrived at insistence that the things that make men alike are more important than the things that differentiate them. If this is the case, then it may be that in our trials and errors and in our efforts to adjust our behavior to the world community we now recognize as a fact, we have not yet found adequate means for institutionalizing the implications of the fact that men share common characteristics regardless of culture. Also relevant to the discussion is the general agreement of psychologists and other social scientists that man's action or behavior is largely explained in terms of his social relationships.

Perhaps we have not yet sufficiently tested Jane Addams' conviction that there will be no peace until the world community is no longer divided into the repressed, dimly conscious that they have no adequate outlet for normal life, and the repressing, the self-righteous and the cautious who hold fast to their own. Perhaps we have not yet tested sufficiently her overarching conviction that if life is often mean, unprofitable and tragic, if it is at other times feeble and broken, it is because we have not yet learned the lesson, and acted on it, that these evidences of what some call the tragic flaw in human nature, result not from man's essential and unchangeable limitations, but rather follow from our failure to understand ourselves and others.

IV

PHILOSOPHICAL AND RELIGIOUS THOUGHT

Extradeical and Intradeical Interpretations of Platonic Ideas

by HARRY A. WOLFSON

Reprinted from the *Journal of the History of Ideas*—Vol. XXII, No. 1, pp. 3–32

The history of philosophy, especially that philosophy which hired itself out as a handmaiden to theology, is a succession of conflicting views and of attempts to reconcile them. Philosophy, which affects a language of its own, would describe it as a dialectical process of thesis, antithesis, and synthesis. Theology, which occasionally stoops to speak the language of ordinary men, would describe it as a process of peacemaking between mutually misunderstood friendly opinions. But, while in theology peacemakers are pronounced blessed and are they who inherit the kingdom of dogma, in philosophy synthesizers are often blasted and castigated as infringers upon the Law of Contradiction.

In my talk tonight * I shall deal with two opposite interpretations of Platonic ideas and the attempts to reconcile them, tracing their history through successive generations of descendants of these Platonic ideas down to the philosophies of Descartes and Spinoza. I shall try to tell the story briefly, simply, sketchily, confining myself to highlights and to the main plot of the story, without going into the intricacies of the topics that come into play. My purpose in selecting this topic for a lecture dedicated to the memory of Whitehead is to illustrate to some extent the truth of his saying that "the safest general characterization of the European philosophical tradition is that it consists of a series of footnotes to Plato." [1]

I. LOGOS

Among the things which Plato somehow left unexplained about his theory of ideas is the question of how these ideas are related to God. His statements on this point produce conflicting impressions. Sometimes he uses language which lends itself to the interpretation that the ideas have an existence external to God, either ungenerated and coeternal with God [2] or produced and made by God.[3] They are thus extradeical. Sometimes, however, he uses language which lends itself to the interpretation that the ideas are the thoughts of God.[4] They are

---

* Delivered as the Alfred North Whitehead Lecture at Harvard University, 1960. Parts of Sections I and II, in expanded form, were delivered as the Grace A. and Theodore de Laguna Lecture at Bryn Mawr College, 1957, and as one of the three Walter Turner Candler Lectures at Emory University, 1959.

[1] *Process and Reality* (New York, 1929), 53.

[2] *Timaeus* 28 A, 29 A, 52 B; *Philebus* 15 B.   [3] *Republic* X, 597 B–D.

[4] Early modern students of Plato who found such a view in Plato are listed by Zeller, *Philosophie der Griechen* II, 1⁴ (Leipzig, 1921), 664, n. 5 (*Plato and the Older Academy* [London, 1876], 243, n. 53).

thus intradeical. Modern students of Plato, from Karl Friedrich Hermann to our own Raphael Demos, try to solve these as well as all other real or seeming contradictions by a method which may be called the method of periodization. They assume that these different views about ideas in their relation to God were held by Plato at different periods of his life, and so they classify his dialogues according to certain chronological schemes and speak of early dialogues, middle dialogues, and later dialogues.

In antiquity, however, students of Plato did not know of this convenient method of exegesis. They followed another method, equally convenient. It may be described as the method of selection and rejection. What the followers of this method did was simply to select one set of statements in Plato and accept them as representative of his true philosophy and to reject all the other statements as of no account. And so among the early students of Plato, there were two opposing interpretations of his ideas in their relation to God. According to one interpretation, the ideas have a real existence outside of God: they are extradeical. According to another interpretation, which identifies Plato's God with mind, they are thoughts of God: they are intradeical.[5] These two interpretations of Platonic Ideas in their relation to God are brought out most poignantly in a statement which comes from the third century, but may reflect earlier traditions. "Plato," it says, "asserted that there are three first principles of the universe, God and matter and idea," and then, reflecting the two opposite interpretations of Plato, it goes on to say that, with respect to the idea, Plato at one time says that "it subsists by itself" and at another time says that "it is in thoughts [of God]."[6]

It is to be noted, however, that in the various passages restating the intradeical interpretation, two modes of expression are used. In the passage quoted, the expression used is that the idea is in thoughts (ἐν νοήμασι). Similarly in two other passages, the expression used is that "the idea is an incorporeal substance in the thoughts (ἐν τοῖς νοήμασι) and fancies of God"[7] or that "the ideas are substances separate from matter, subsisting in the thoughts and fancies of God, that is, of mind."[8] But in a fourth passage, the expression used is that "the idea, in relation to God, is His act of thinking (νόησις)" and that "whether God be mind (νοῦς) or something mental, He has thoughts (νοήματα), and these thoughts are eternal and immutable, and, if this be so, there are ideas," and the author then goes on to explain that by saying that

[5] On this interpretation, see M. Jones, "The Ideas as Thoughts of God," *Classical Philology*, 21 (1926), 317–326.

[6] Pseudo-Justin Martyr, *Cohortatio ad Graecos* 7 (PG 6, 256 A).

[7] Aëtius, *De Placitis Philosophorum* I, 3, 21 (H. Diels, *Doxographi Graeci*, 288).

[8] *Ibid.* I, 10, 3 (309).

there are ideas he means that God acts by certain rules and plans and that the order observed in nature is not the result of mere chance.[9] Similarly in a fifth passage, the expression used is that the idea is "the thought (διάνοια) of God." [10] The difference between these two modes of expression on the face of them would seem to be quite striking. But still, taken in their textual and historical setting, the two mean the same, the difference between them being only verbal. When in the third passage, for instance, ideas are spoken of as substances separated from matter and as subsisting in the thoughts of God, it means the same as when in the fourth passage ideas are spoken of as the well regulated and planned process of God's thinking and thoughts. The different form of expression used in the third passage, as well as in the first and second passages, is only to show pointedly how, on the one hand, Plato differed from Aristotle who "admitted the existence of forms or ideas, but not as separated from matter or as patterns of what God has made" [11] and how, on the other hand, he differed from Zenonian Stoics, who "profess that the ideas are nothing but the conception of our mind." [12] In fact, all those who interpreted the Platonic ideas intradeically were already under the influence of the Aristotelian teaching that in God, because He is immaterial and a mind (νοῦς) which is always actual, the process of thinking (νόησις) and the object of thinking (νοούμενον) are identical with His own self.[13] Even Plotinus, who in his interpretation of Plato, as we shall see later, does not identify God with mind, but still believes that according to Plato the ideas are intramental, argues, quite evidently on the basis of that Aristotelian teaching, that though in our thought we distinguish between Nous, which is that which thinks, and the ideas, which are the object of its thinking, still they are both one and even identical, seeing that Nous is always in a state of "repose and unity and calm," [14] that is, in a state of actuality, for in Nous, as he says elsewhere, there is no transition "from the potentiality of thinking to the actuality of thinking." [15]

While these two contrasting methods of interpreting the Platonic ideas were followed by pagan philosophers, a new method was introduced by the Jewish philosopher Philo of Alexandria. His method may be described as that of harmonization. According to this method, all the statements in Plato, however contradictory they may appear to be, are assumed to be true, and out of all of them a harmonious com-

[9] Albinus, *Didaskalos* IX, 1 and 3 (ed. P. Louis).
[10] Hippolytus, *Refutatio Omnium Haeresium* I, 19, 2 (ed. P. Wendland).
[11] Aëtius, *op. cit.* I, 10, 4.   [12] *Ibid.* I, 10, 5.
[13] *Metaph.* XII, 9, 1074b, 34; 1075a, 3–5.
[14] *Enneades* III, 9, 1.   [15] *Ibid.* II, 5, 3.

posite view is molded, in which all the apparently contradictory statements are made to live in peace with each other. Such a method of interpretation had been used, from earliest times, by Jewish rabbis in their effort to harmonize contradictory statements in the Hebrew Scripture and it was later also used by Augustine, in his *De Consensu Evangelistarum,* as a way of harmonizing the contradictory statements in the Gospels.

Philo's interpretation of Platonic ideas occurs in his various comments on the story of creation in the Book of Genesis. A composite summary of these comments may be stated as follows: When God by His own good will decided to create this world of ours, He first, out of the ideas which had been in His thought from eternity, constructed an "intelligible world," and this intelligible world He placed in the Logos, which had likewise existed previously from eternity in His thought. Then in the likeness of this intelligible world of ideas, He created this "visible world" of ours.[16]

Students of Plato cannot fail seeing a resemblance between this version of the story of creation of the Book of Genesis with the story of creation in Plato's *Timaeus.* As told by Plato in the *Timaeus,* there is a God, who is called the Demiurge, the Creator. Then, besides the Demiurge, there is a model ($\pi\alpha\rho\dot\alpha\delta\epsilon\iota\gamma\mu\alpha$),[17] which is coeternal with the Demiurge. This model is called the "intelligible animal"[18] and contains in itself "intelligible animals."[19] The Demiurge is said to have looked at the intelligible animal and in its likeness he created this world of ours, which is called "the visible animal."[20]

Comparing these two accounts of the creation of the world, one can readily see that what Philo was trying to do was to interpret the story of creation of the Book of Genesis in terms of the story of creation in the *Timaeus.* In fact, we know that this was his purpose.

But, though there is a resemblance between these two accounts of creation, there are also some differences. I shall mention here three such differences.

First, in the *Timaeus,* the contrast between the preexistent ideas and the created world is described as a contrast between the "intelligible animal" ($\zeta\hat\omega o\nu$ $\nu o\eta\tau\acute o\nu$) and the "visible animal" ($\zeta\hat\omega o\nu$ $\dot o\rho\alpha\tau\acute o\nu$). In Philo the contrast is described as one between the "intelligible world" ($\kappa\acute o\sigma\mu o\varsigma$ $\nu o\eta\tau\acute o\varsigma$) and the "visible world" ($\kappa\acute o\sigma\mu o\varsigma$ $\dot o\rho\alpha\tau\acute o\varsigma$). At first sight the change would seem to be only verbal and of no significance. But upon further study of Plato's and Philo's philosophies we may discover that it involves two problems upon which Philo differed from Plato. To begin with, it involves the problem of the existence of a world-soul.

---

[16] *De Opificio Mundi* 5, 20ff. Cf. chapter on "God, the World of Ideas, and the Logos," in my *Philo* (Cambridge, Mass., 1947), I, 200–294.
[17] *Timaeus* 29 B. [18] *Ibid.* 39 E. [19] *Ibid.* 30 C. [20] *Ibid.* 29 D.

To Plato, there is a world-soul, a soul which exists in the body of the world, just as there is a soul which exists in the body of any living being. The world is therefore to him a visible animal, and the ideas are therefore described by him as an intelligible animal. To Philo, however, there is no world-soul. Though occasionally he uses the expression "soul of the world," he never uses it in the sense of a soul immanent in the world. The function of the Platonic, as well as the Stoic, world-soul, which is a soul immanent in the world, is performed in Philo's philosophy partly by the Logos, which with the creation of the world becomes immanent in it, and partly by what he calls the Divine Spirit, which is an incorporeal being not immanent in the world. Without a soul, the world to Philo was not an animal being. Then, it involves the problem of the existence of ideas as segregate beings. To Plato in the *Timaeus,* the intelligible animal contains only the ideas of the four kinds of living creatures in the universe, namely, the celestial bodies, birds, fishes, and land-animals.[21] There is no evidence that it contains even the ideas of the four elements, though such ideas are mentioned or alluded to in the *Timaeus*.[22] All the ideas, therefore, with the exception of those of living creatures, exist in segregation from each other. To Philo, however, all the ideas are integrated into a whole, namely, the intelligible world; and their relation to the intelligible world is conceived by him as that of parts of an indivisible whole, which as such have no real existence of their own apart from that of the whole.

Second, in the *Timaeus* there is no mention of a place where the ideas exist; in Philo the ideas are said to have their place in the Logos. Now, while the term Logos occurs in Greek philosophy, having been used ever since Heraclitus in various senses, it was never used in the sense of the place of the Platonic ideas. We must therefore try to find out how Philo happened to come to this concept of a Logos as the place of the Platonic ideas.

In trying to find an answer to this question, let us start by examining carefully the passage in which Philo introduces the Logos as the place of ideas. In that passage, he begins by saying that, just as the plan conceived by the mind of an architect, prior to its execution, exists in no other place but the soul of the architect, so the intelligible world of ideas, prior to creation of the visible world, existed in no other place but "the divine Logos." He then adds the following rhetorical question: "For what other place could there be ... sufficiently able to receive and contain, I say not all, but any one" of the ideas of this intelligible world?[23] This rhetorical question quite evidently con-

---

[21] *Timaeus* 39 E. [22] *Ibid.* 51 B f. Cf. R. D. Archer-Hind in his Introduction to his edition of the *Timaeus* (London, 1888), 34–35; F. M. Cornford, *Plato's Cosmology* (London, 1937), 188–191. [23] *De Opificio Mundi* 5, 20.

tains a challenge. It implies that somebody did suggest some other place for the ideas and Philo, convinced that that other place, or any other place that might be suggested, could not properly be the place of the ideas, challenges that somebody as well as anybody else to show whether any other place could properly be the place of the ideas. Fortunately we are able to identify that somebody who suggested another place for the ideas. It is Plato. In several passages Plato touches upon the question of the place of the ideas. In one of these passages, he states that the idea of beauty, and quite evidently any of the other ideas, is "never anywhere in anything else,"[24] a statement on the basis of which Aristotle generalizes that Plato's ideas are "nowhere"[25] or "not in place."[26] In other passages he speaks of the ideas as existing in a "supercelestial place"[27] or in an "intelligible place."[28] Combining these passages, we may conclude that what Plato means to say is this: the ideas do not exist in any place in the visible world, but they exist in the "supercelestial place" or "intelligible place," which is outside the visible world. But what is that supercelestial or intelligible place outside the world? It can be shown, I believe, that Philo took this supercelestial or intelligible place of Plato to mean an infinite void outside the world, for, though Plato explicitly denied the existence of a void within the world,[29] there are statements in his writings which could have been interpreted by Philo to refer to the existence of a void outside the world. It happens, however, that Philo, under the influence of Aristotle, denied the existence of a void even outside the world.[30] And so, with the elimination of what Plato designated as the place of the ideas, he locates the ideas in "the divine Logos" and, challenging one and all, he asks rhetorically, "for what other place could there be" for the ideas?

But how did Philo come to substitute the Logos as the place of ideas for Plato's vacuum outside the world? The answer is that he came to it by a process of reasoning arising from a passage in Plato's own works. He started, we may imagine, with a passage in *Parmenides* (132 BC), in which Socrates, who poses as one not altogether convinced of the existence of ideas as real beings, raises the question whether an idea may not be only a "thought (νόημα), which cannot properly exist anywhere except in souls (ἐν ψυχαῖς)." Souls here means human souls, for it is in this sense that the term was understood by Aristotle in a passage where, with evident reference to this passage in the *Parmenides*, Aristotle says that "it has been well said that the soul is a place of forms or ideas," adding, however, "that this does not

---

[24] *Symposium* 211 A. [25] *Phys.* III, 4, 203a, 9. [26] *Ibid.* IV, 2, 209b, 34.
[27] *Phaedrus* 247 C. [28] *Republic* VI, 509 D; VII, 517 B.
[29] *Timaeus* 80 C. [30] Cf. *Philo*, I, 241–242.

apply to the soul as a whole but only to thinking soul (ψυχὴ νοητική)."³¹

Now it can be shown that Philo made use of this statement of Aristotle,³² and we may be justified in assuming that he also knew the original statement in *Parmenides*. Let us then imagine that, on reading these two statements, Philo asked himself: if ideas, according to those who question or deny their real existence, exist in a human thinking soul, which exists in a body, why should not those who believe in the existence of real ideas say that they exist in a thinking soul which does not exist in a body? Does not Plato himself believe in a bodiless preexistent soul as well as in a bodiless immortal soul? And so Philo has arrived at the conclusion that the ideas exist in an unbodied thinking soul. It is perhaps on the basis of these passages, too, and by the same kind of reasoning that those who interpreted the Platonic ideas intradeically came to identify the God of Plato's philosophy with its Nous.

Then, let us further imagine that, on having arrived at this conclusion, Philo began to look for a single Greek word for the expression "thinking soul" used by Aristotle. It happens that the Greeks, by the time of Philo, had two words for it, *nous*, "mind," and *logos*, "reason," so that Philo had to decide between these two words, and he decided in favor of Logos. What made him decide in favor of Logos may be assumed to be a threefold consideration. First, that which was to contain the intelligible world of ideas as the model for the visible world that was to be created was, according to Philo, to serve as a sort of instrument by which the visible world was to be created by God.³³ Second, the Greek term "Logos," which besides "reason" means also "word," is used in the Greek version of Scripture as a translation of the Hebrew term *dabar*, "word," so that in the verse "by the word of the Lord the heavens were established" (Ps. 33/32: 6) the Logos is represented as a sort of instrument by which the world was created. Third, a parallel to this use of the term Logos in the scriptural verse quoted may have been seen by Philo in Plato's statement that all animals and plants and inanimate substances "are created by *logos* [that is, reason] and by divine knowledge that comes from God."³⁴

It is this threefold consideration, we may assume, that has led Philo to decide in favor of the use of the term Logos to that of Nous. An indication that the term Logos is used by him as the equivalent of Nous, as well as a substitute for it, in the sense of an unbodied Nous, in contrast to the embodied Nous implied in Aristotle's statement that the "thinking soul" is the place of ideas, is his statement that the Logos is "the Nous above us" in contrast to the human thinking soul

---

[31] *De Anima* III, 4, 429a, 27–28.
[32] Cf. *Philo*, I, 233, 247.
[33] Cf. *Philo*, I, 261–282.
[34] *Sophist* 265 C.

which is "the Nous within us." [35] And as an indication that it is the scriptural verse that caused him to decide in favor of the Logos is his use of the term Wisdom (σοφία) as the equivalent of Logos and his description of Wisdom also as that "through which the world came into existence," [36] for in Scripture, corresponding to the verse "by the word (*logos*) of the Lord the heavens were established" (Ps. 33/32: 6) there is the verse "by wisdom (*sophia*) God founded the earth" (Prov. 3: 19).

Since by Logos is meant Nous, when Philo speaks of the Logos as the place of the intelligible world, he means thereby that the relation of the Logos to the intelligible world, and hence also to the ideas which constitute the intelligible world, is after the analogy of the relation of the thinking mind to its object of thought. Now, according to Aristotle, in the case of immaterial things, the thinking mind is identical with its object of thought.[37] The Logos is, therefore, conceived by Philo as being identical with the intelligible world and hence also with the ideas which constitute the intelligible world.[38]

The third departure from Plato's *Timaeus* is his rejection of its view that the ideas were ungenerated[39] and outside the Demiurge, who is said to have looked at them and used them as a model in the creation of the visible world.[40] Philo undoubtedly knew of the other kind of statements about the ideas in the other dialogues of Plato and presumably he would also know of the two contrasting interpretations current in his time. Neither of these interpretations, however, was acceptable to him. The extradeical interpretation was unacceptable, because it implied the existence of eternal beings besides God, but to Philo, besides God, there could be no other eternal being.[41] Nor could the intradeical interpretation be acceptable to him. For, if it meant that the ideas were in thoughts of God as real beings really distinct from Him, then it implied that in God there existed something other than himself. But this was contrary to Philo's interpretation of the scriptural doctrine of the unity of God as meaning absolute simplicity.[42] And if it meant that the ideas were thoughts of God and hence identical with Him, then it meant a denial of the existence of ideas as such, but, according to Philo, those who denied the existence of incorporeal ideas are condemned in Scripture as "impious" and "unholy," [43] for, on the basis of certain scriptural verses and a Jewish tradition, he held that the belief in the existence of ideas as real beings was one of the fundamental teachings of Moses.[44] And so, what did he do? He

---

[35] *Quis Rerum Divinarum Heres* 48, 236.
[36] *De Fuga et Inventione* 20, 109; cf. *Quod Deterius Potiori Insidari Soleat* 16, 54.
[37] *Metaph.* XII, 9, 1075a, 3–4. [38] Cf. *Philo*, I, 248–252.
[39] *Timaeus* 52 A. [40] *Ibid.* 28 A.
[41] Cf. *Philo*, I, 322. [42] *Ibid.*, 172–173; II, 94ff. [43] *Ibid.*, 164. [44] *Ibid.*, 181–186.

introduced a new interpretation of the Platonic ideas in their relation to God. According to this new interpretation, the Logos, together with the intelligible world of ideas within it, at first, from eternity, existed as a thought of God; then, prior to the creation of the world, it was created as a real incorporeal being distinct from God.

In Philo, then, Platonic ideas were integrated into an intelligible world of ideas contained in a Nous called Logos, so that the original problem of the relation of Platonic ideas to God became with him a problem of the relation of the Nous or the Logos to God, and the problem was solved by him by the assumption of two successive stages of existence in the Logos, an intradeical one followed by an extradeical.

From now on, in the history of philosophy, ideas will be treated either, after the manner of Plato himself, as segregated beings, or, after the manner of his interpreter Philo, as integrated into an intelligible world placed in a Logos or a Nous, and the original problem of extradeical and intradeical, or the solutions thereof, will be applied either to the ideas themselves or to the Logos or Nous.

II. TRINITY [45]

Philo preached his philosophical sermons in the synagogues of Alexandria at the time when Jesus, known as Christ, preached his hortatory and admonitory sermons in the synagogues of Galilee. About half a century later there appeared one of the four standard biographies of Christ, the Fourth Gospel, the Gospel according to St. John. This biography of Christ is based upon the theory, introduced by Paul, that before Christ was born there was a preexistent Christ, an ideal Christ, an idea of Christ. This preexistent idea of Christ, which in the epistles of Paul is called Wisdom or perhaps also Spirit is described in this biography of Jesus by the term Logos. which is conventionally rendered into English by the term Word. And we are all acquainted with the opening verse in the Gospel according to St. John: "In the beginning was the Word, and the Word was with God, and the Word was God" (1: 1). Then, like the Logos of Philo, which became immanent in the created world, the Logos of John, which is the preexistent Christ, became immanent, or, as it is commonly said, incarnate, in the born Christ. And we are all, again, acquainted with the verse toward the close of the Prologue of the Gospel according to St. John: "And the Word was made flesh" (1: 14).

In this Prologue of the Fourth Gospel, there are some striking similarities between the Logos of Philo and the Logos of John. But two main characteristics of the Philonic Logos are missing in the Johannine Logos, or, with regard to one of them, it is not clearly stated.

[45] This section is based upon the chapters dealing with the Trinity in my *Philosophy of the Church Fathers* (Cambridge, Mass., 1956), I, 141–364 (henceforth *Church Fathers*).

There is no hint at all that the Logos of John, which is the idea of Christ, contains in itself the intelligible world of ideas and there is no clear statement that before its incarnation it had two stages of existence, one from eternity as the thought of God, and then, with the creation of the world, as a real being distinct from God.

These two missing characteristics were supplied in the second century by those Church Fathers known as Apologists, who, having been born pagans, were before their conversion to Christianity students of philosophy. As they themselves tell us, what has led them to their conversion was the reading of Scripture, the Hebrew Scripture, naturally in the Greek translation. From internal evidence of their writings, we may gather that they used the works of Philo as a sort of commentary upon Scripture. From these works of Philo they became acquainted with Philo's interpretation of Platonic ideas, at the centre of which was the term Logos. When, therefore, in the Fourth Gospel they read the opening sentence, "In the beginning was the Logos," they identified this Logos with the Philonic Logos and thus, without the Johannine Logos ceasing to mean the preexistent Christ, it acquired the two main characteristics of the Philonic Logos.

To begin with, like the Philonic Logos, the Johannine Logos began to contain the intelligible world of ideas, so that it was no longer a single idea, the idea of Christ, but it became the place of the intelligible world consisting of all ideas. Then, again, like the Philonic Logos, it was made to have two stages of existence prior to its incarnation: first, from eternity it was within God and identical with Him; second, from about the time of the creation of the world it was a generated real being distinct from God. Once these two innovations were introduced, Fathers of the Church began to look in the New Testament for proof-texts in support of them. For the first of these two innovations, two Fathers of the Church, Origen and Augustine, at one time thought that they had found a supporting proof-text in Jesus's saying, "I am not of this world" (John 8: 23), from which they tried to infer that there was another world, and that that other world was the intelligible world of ideas.[46] Ultimately, however, this inference was rejected, for different reasons, by both of them.[47] A satisfactory proof-text for this first innovation was, however, discovered by them in the verse stating that through the Logos were all things made by God (John 1: 3). Following Philo in his description of the Logos, they interpreted this verse to imply that the Logos was used by God as a sort of architect's blueprint, which contained the plan for the structure of the world and thus it contained the intelligible world of ideas.[48] As for the second

---

[46] Origen, *De Principiis* II, 3, 6; Augustine, *De Ordine* I, 11, 32 (PL 32, 993).

[47] Origen, *loc. cit.*; Augustine, *Retractiones* I, 3, 2.

[48] Origen, *In Joannem* XIX, 5 (PG 14, 568 BC); Augustine, *In Joannem* I, 9. Cf. *Church Fathers*, I, 277-8, 283-4.

innovation, again, two of the Fathers of the Church, Tertullian and Clement of Alexandria,[49] took the verse "In the beginning was the Logos" to mean that "in the beginning of the creation of the world the Logos came into being." Now the Greek ἦν which is used in this verse for the English "was," in classical Greek means "was" and not "came into being," for the latter of which the Greek would be ἐγένετο. But their interpretation of ἦν as meaning "came to be" may be justified on the ground that in the Greek translation of the Hebrew Scripture, the Septuagint, the Greek ἦν, through its use as a translation of the Hebrew *hayah*, which means both "was" and "came to be," acquired the additional meaning of "came to be."[50]

Following Philo, too, these early Fathers of the Church added to the Logos another preexistent incorporeal being, the Holy Spirit, thus together with God and the Logos making three preexistent real beings, subsequently to become known as hypostases or persons. Now the Holy Spirit is mentioned in the New Testament, but it is not clear whether it is meant to be the same as the preexistent Christ, and hence the same as the Wisdom of Paul and the Logos of John, or whether it is meant to be a preexistent being different from the preexistent Christ. The Apostolic Fathers, who flourished before and up to the middle of the second century, were still uncertain about it. But the Apologists, under the influence of Philo, definitely declared the Holy Spirit to be distinct from the Logos. Like the Logos, the Holy Spirit was held by them to have been at first intradeical and then became extradeical.

But on one point did the Apologists differ radically from Philo.[51] To Philo, who followed the traditional Jewish conception of God as the maker of things after the analogy of an artisan, the Logos entered its second stage of existence by an act of making or creating, except that the making was out of nothing, since God is an omnipotent artisan and is in no need of material for any of his acts of making. Consequently, like any product of an artisan's making, which is not the same as its maker, the Logos is not the same as God. Though Philo applies to the Logos several terms meaning divine, he never applies to it the term God in the real sense of the term. The Apologists, however, who followed the Christianized mythological conception of God as the begetter of things, after the analogy of natural procreation, conceived of the entrance of the Logos into its second stage of existence as having been effected by an act of begetting or generating and

[49] Cf. *Church Fathers*, I, 198 and 213–214.

[50] Cf. my article "Philosophical Implications of Arianism and Apollinarianism," *Dumbarton Oaks Papers*, XII (1958), 14.

[51] On what follows, see the chapter on "The Mystery of Generation," in *Church Fathers*, I, 287–304.

consequently, as in any act of natural generation, where that which is generated is like that which generated it, the Logos to them is God like the God who generated it. Later Christian theologians, Augustine, followed by Thomas Aquinas, tried to explain the Godship of the Logos by referring to the philosophic principle that all living beings reproduce their kind. They illustrated it by quoting the Aristotelian statement that "man begets man," [52] to which St. Augustine added "and dog dog" [53] and which St. Thomas paraphrased by saying "as a man proceeds from a man and a horse from a horse." [54] Subsequently the term God was extended to the Holy Spirit, so that each of the persons, the Father, the Son or Logos, and the Holy Spirit, was God.

These three persons of the Trinity, however, though each of them a real being and each of them God and each of them really distinct from the others, constituted one God, who was most simple and indivisible. Consequently, the Logos, in so far as it was really distinct from God the Father and God the Holy Spirit, was extradeical: but, in so far as it was an indivisible part of an indivisible triune God, it was intradeical. This was a new kind of harmonization of extradeical and intradeical, which may be described as harmonization by unification. How three distinct real beings, each of them God, could be harmonized and unified into one God, without infringing upon the Law of Contradiction, the Fathers of the Church tried to explain by various analogies up to a certain point, but beyond that point they admitted that the Trinity was a mystery.

As part of the mystery of the Trinity is the conception of the relation of the ideas within the Logos to the triune God. According to Philo, so also according to the Church Fathers, the ideas within the Logos were identical with the Logos. But, whereas to Philo, by reason of their being identical with the Logos, they were, like the Logos during its second stage of existence, extradeical, to the Apologists, despite their being identical with the Logos, they were not like the Logos during its second stage of existence both extradeical and intradeical by unification: they were only intradeical. The reason for this is as follows: It happens that among the Church Fathers from the earliest times there existed the view that the distinction between the persons of the Trinity is only with respect to some causal relationship existing between them, which later came to be described by the terms paternity, filiation, and procession. In every other respect they are one, their unity consisting in the indivisible unity of the one God which they all constitute. Since they all constitute one God, whatever is said of any of the persons of the Trinity, with the exception of the terms which describe the one single distinction between them, applies to the

[52] *Metaph.* VII, 7, 1032a, 23–24; cf. IX, 8, 1049b, 27–29.
[53] *Contra Maximinum Arianum* II, 6. [54] *Sum. Theol.* I, 27, 2c.

one indivisible God which they all constitute. Accordingly, when the intelligible world of ideas is said to exist in the Logos and to be identical with the Logos, it really means that it exists in the one indivisible God, which the three persons constitute, and it is with that one indivisible God that it is identical.

This, then, was the philosophic situation during the second century after the Christian era. Three interpretations of Platonic ideas existed side by side. Among pagan philosophers, the Platonic ideas were treated as segregated beings, and were interpreted either (1) extradeically or (2) intradeically. In Philo and the Church Fathers they were treated as integrated into an intelligible world placed in a Logos, but, whereas to Philo the Logos together with the ideas within it (3) was both intradeical and extradeical by succession, to the Apologists (4) the Logos was extradeical and intradeical both by succession and by unification, but the ideas were only intradeical.

Then, in the third century, something new happened both in Christian philosophy and in pagan philosophy. Christian philosophy had its centre in Alexandria under Origen and pagan philosophy had its centre in Rome under Plotinus.

Both Origen and Plotinus start their philosophy with three principles, which are coeternal. Both of them call these principles hypostases.[55] Both of them describe the first hypostasis, who is God, as Father.[56] Both of them describe the second hypostasis as being eternally generated from the first[57] and call him son[58] and image.[59] Both of them make their second hypostasis contain the intelligible world of ideas.[60] So far forth they are in agreement. But then they begin to differ. Origen, as in Christianity, calls his second hypostasis Logos. Plotinus calls it Nous and, in direct opposition to those who called it Logos, he explicitly denies that the second hypostasis is the Logos of the first.[61] Again, the third hypostasis is called by Origen, as in Christianity, Holy Spirit;[62] Plotinus calls it Soul[63] and, again, in direct opposition to those who called it Spirit, he uses the term spirit in a material sense and therefore argues that it cannot be soul.[64] Then,

---

[55] Origen, *De Principiis* I, 2, 2; *In Joannem* X, 21 (PG 14, 376 B); *Contra Celsum* VIII, 12 (PG 11, 1533 C); Plotinus, *Enneades* II, 9, 2; V, 1, 7; V, 8, 12; VI, 7, 29.

[56] Origen, *De Princ.* I, 2, 6; Plotinus, *Enn.* III, 8, 11.   [57] Origen, *De Princ.* I, 2, 4; *In Jeremiam,* Hom. IX, 4 (PG 13, 357 A); Plotinus, *Enn.* V, 1, 6; VI, 8, 20.

[58] Origen, *De Princ.* I, 2, 4; Plotinus, *Enn.* III, 8, 11.   [59] Origen, *De Princ.* I, 2, 6; Plotinus, *Enn.* V, 1, 7; V, 4, 2; V, 6, 4; V, 9, 2; VI, 2, 9.

[60] Origen, cf. above at n. 44; Plotinus, *Enn.* V, 9, 9.

[61] *Enn.* VI, 7, 17. So also, in opposition to the Christian use of Logos as a designation of the second hypostasis only, he says: "The soul is the *logos* and a certain *energeia* of the Nous, just as the Nous is of the One" (*Enn.* V, 1, 6).   [62] *De Princ.* I, Praef. 4.   [63] *Enn.* V, 1, 10.   [64] *Ibid.* IV, 7, 3–4.

also, following Christian tradition, Origen calls his Logos God; and, while a real being distinct from his first hypostasis, it constitutes with it one God. Plotinus, however, is reminiscent of Philo. Like Philo, who calls his Logos simply "God," without the definite article "the," in contrast to the true God, who is called "the God," with the definite article "the," [65] and also describes it as "the second God" [66] in contrast to the true God who is "the first God," [67] Plotinus calls his Nous God in the sense of πᾶς, "all," that is, in an indefinite sense, in contrast to God in the sense of τίς, "who?", that is, in a definite sense,[68] and he also describes it as "the second God" [69] in contrast to the God, whom he usually refers to as "the First" [70] or whom he may have even described as "the first God." [71] Accordingly, to Origen, the Logos is eternally both extradeical and intradeical by unification, but the ideas within it are intradeical, whereas, according to Plotinus, the Nous, together with the intelligible world of ideas within it, are extradeical.

How did these two systems at once alike and different originate?

Here I am going to suggest an answer for which there is no direct documentary evidence. There is only circumstantial evidence, the kind of evidence on which a defendant standing trial for murder may be acquitted by a jury of his peers, and on which, I believe, a historian of philosophy may venture to build a theory even at the risk of being condemned by fellow historians as indulging in flights of fancy.

My explanation is this: Both Plotinus and Origen were students at one time, though not at the same time, of Ammonius Saccas in Alexandria. "Ammonius," according to Porphyry as quoted by Eusebius, "was a Christian, brought up in Christian doctrines by his parents, yet, when he began to think and study philosophy, he immediately changed his way of life to conform to that required by the laws." [72] We may assume, I believe, that during his Christian period, like Clement of Alexandria,[73] he interpreted Plato in terms of the Philonic twofold stage theory and applied the same interpretation to

---

[65] *De Somniis* I, 39, 239–240. [66] *Quaestiones in Genesin* II, 62, and cf. *Legum Allegoria* II, 21, 86. [67] *De Migratione Abrahami* 32, 181; 35, 194; *De Vita Mosis* II, 26, 205.

[68] *Enn.* V, 5, 3. [69] *Ibid.* [70] *Ibid.* V, 5, 11.

[71] *Ibid.* III, 9, 9, according to some reading of the text. See ed. Bréhier (1925) and ed. Henry & Schwyzer (1951) *ad loc.*

[72] Eusebius, *Historia Ecclesiastica* VI, 19, 7. It must be noted that Eusebius denies the apostasy of Ammonius (VI, 1, 10). Among modern scholars, some say that Eusebius was mistaken in denying the apostasy of Ammonius Saccas (cf. Lawlor and Oulton's note on VI, 19, 10 of their English translation of Eusebius), while others say that Porphyry was mistaken in making Ammonius Saccas born a Christian (cf. Bardy's note on VI, 19, 7 of his French translation of Eusebius).

[73] *Church Fathers*, I, 266–270.

the Johannine Logos and, by reason of the mystery of the Trinity, while the Logos during its second stage of existence was both extradeical and intradeical by unification, the ideas within it were only intradeical. Then, when Ammonius gave up Christianity, we may further assume, he gave up the interpretation of Plato in terms of the Philonic twofold stage theory and substituted for it the theory of eternal generation; he also gave up the primarily Biblical term Logos and the strictly Biblical term Holy Spirit and substituted for them the purely philosophical terms Nous and Soul; finally, discarding the Christian mystery of the Trinity, his Nous, the substitute for the Christian Logos as the place of the intelligible world of ideas, was no longer equal with God, no longer the same as God, and no longer forming together with God and the Soul one God, and hence no longer both intradeical and extradeical by unification. Plotinus, a pagan, adopted this new philosophy of Ammonius in its entirety. Origen, a Christian, adopted from it only the concept of eternal generation, which he applied to the Christian Logos, but this he did only on purely Christian religious grounds, considering the principle of eternal generation less open to misunderstanding and misinterpretation than the twofold stage theory.

Truly speaking, then, the philosophy of Plotinus, known as Neoplatonism, in so far as its theory of ideas is concerned, is a paganized version of the Christian version, which in turn is a Christianized version of the Philonic Jewish version of Plato's theory of ideas. Thus the theory of ideas of both Origen and Plotinus are a third generation of the descendants of Plato's ideas.

In Christianity, the Origenian harmonization of extradeical and intradeical by the method of unification prevailed and it became the orthodox creed of the Church. But it met with opposition. It was felt by many Christians, described by Origen as those "who sincerely profess to be lovers of God," [74] that the conception of a God, in whom there was a distinction of three real beings each of whom was God, was incompatible with the conception of the unity of God, which was the common profession of all Christians. The various attempts at explaining the unity of God ultimately meant the reduction of the conception of unity to a relative kind of unity,[75] which to them was unacceptable. They had before them, therefore, two choices, either to deny that the Logos was God or to deny the reality of its existence.[76] Some followed the first alternative. They are the Arians. Others followed the second alternative. This had many exponents. But we shall refer to them, after one of its exponents, as Sabellians. Denying the

[74] *In Joannem* II, 2 (PG 14, 108 C); cf. *Church Fathers*, I, 580ff.
[75] *Church Fathers*, I, 312ff.   [76] Cf. *ibid.*, chapter on "Heresies," 575ff.

reality of the Logos, in a passage in which they refer to the Logos as the Son, they declared that "the Father is Son and again the Son Father, in hypostasis one, in name two." [77] And when the Holy Spirit was proclaimed by orthodoxy to be also God, they declared that "the term Father and Son and Holy Spirit are but actions and names." [78] In other words, they rejected the orthodox conceptions of the Logos as being simultaneously both extradeical and intradeical by unification and made it only intradeical, in the sense of identical, and, of course, with it also the ideas within it were intradeical.

In pagan philosophy, similarly, the Plotinian conception of a Nous, in which the ideas integrated into an intelligible world was located, prevailed until the pagan schools of philosophy were closed by the order of Emperor Justinian in 529. But one notable exception is to be mentioned, and that is the theory of Ammonius Hermiae, who was at the head of the pagan school of philosophy in Alexandria at about the middle of the fifth century. In his commentary on the *Isagoge,* a work by Porphyry, who was a student of Plotinus, this Ammonius tries to answer questions raised by Porphyry with regard to the ideas of Plato— questions not with regard to the relation of the ideas to God but rather with regard to their relation to individual things in the world. After solving in his own way the phase of the problem with regard to ideas which was raised by Porphyry, Ammonius, of his own accord, tries to solve the problem of the relation of the ideas to God. His answer is contained in the following statements. First, he says, "He who fabricates all things contains in himself the paradigms of all things" [79] and "if He knows that which He makes, it is at once evident that the forms exist in the Fabricator." [80] Then, trying to prove that this is also the view of Plato, he says [81] that Plato, who, in contradistinction to Aristotle, describes the ideas as being "intelligible, subsisting in themselves" (νοηταί, αὐταὶ καθ' ἑαυτὰς ὑφεστῶσαι),[82] as being "really substances" (ὄντως οὐσίας),[83] and as "first substances" (πρώτας οὐσίας),[84] means thereby that "God contains in himself the models of the genera and species." Here then we have in pagan philosophy a continuation or revival of the old pre-Plotinian, or rather pre-Philonic, treatment of ideas as beings segregated from each other and as the thoughts of God.

[77] Athanasius, *Oratio contra Arianos* IV, 25 (PG 26, 505 C).
[78] Epiphanius, *Adversus Haereses Panarium* LXII, 1 (PG 41, 1052 B).
[79] *Ammnius in Porphyrii Isagoge sive V Voces* (ed. A. Busse), 41, lines 20–21.
[80] *Ibid.,* 42, lines 5–6.   [81] *Ibid.,* 44, lines 1–4.
[82] Reflecting Plato's description of ideas as νοητά (*Tim.* 30 C) and as things which are αὐτὰ καθ' αὑτὰ ὄντα (*Tim.* 51 B).   [83] Reflecting Plato's description of ideas as οὐσία ὄντως οὖσα (*Phaedrus* 247 C).   [84] Not found in Plato as a description of ideas, but it probably reflects Plato's description of ideas as ἀΐδιος οὐσία (*Tim.* 37 E).

Thus beginning with the third century both in pagan philosophy, as represented by the Neoplatonism of Plotinus, and in Christian philosophy, as represented by orthodoxy and Sabellianism, the Platonic ideas were integrated into an intelligible world. In pagan philosophy it existed in a Nous which was extradeical; in Christian philosophy it existed in a Logos which was either, as in orthodoxy, both extradeical and intradeical by unification or, as in Sabellianism, only intradeical. As for the ideas within the Logos or Nous, in Christianity they were purely intradeical; in Neoplatonism they were extradeical along with the Nous with which they were identical.

III. ATTRIBUTES

Six hundred and twenty-two years roll by since the rise of Christianity and a new religion appears—Islam. In the Scripture of this new religion, the Koran, God is described by what the followers of this religion like to refer to as "the ninety-nine most beautiful names of God," such, for instance, as "the living," "the powerful," "the wise," and so forth up to ninety-nine. Early in the history of this religion there arose a view, first with regard to only two of that list of ninety-nine names and then also with regard to other names of that list, that each name by which God is designated reflects some real being existing in God as something distinct from His essence, but inseparable from it and coeternal with it. Thus, for instance, when God is described as living or wise or powerful, it means that life or wisdom or power exist in Him as real, eternal beings, distinct from His essence. These real beings in God corresponding to the names by which God is designated are known in Arabic by two terms, one of which, as we shall see, came to be known to philosophers of the West as "attributes."

This view, it can be shown, could not have originated in Islam spontaneously but it could have originated under Christian influence in the course of debates between Muslims and Christians shortly after the Muslim conquest of Syria in the VIIth century.[85] In these debates, we may assume, Christians tried to convince the Muslims that the second and third persons of the Trinity are nothing but the terms "wisdom" and "life" or "wisdom" and "power," which in the Koran are predicated of God, and that there is nothing in the Koran against the Christian belief that the predication of God of either pair of these terms reflects the existence in God of real beings, or persons or hypostases, as they called them. The Muslims could find no flaw in the reasoning and no objection to the conclusion. They therefore

[85] See my papers "The Muslim Attributes and the Christian Trinity," *Harvard Theological Review*, 49 (1956), 1–18, and "The Philosophical Implications of the Problem of Divine Attributes in the Kalam," *Journal of the American Oriental Society*, 79 (1959), 73–80.

accepted the view that in God there were real beings to correspond to certain terms predicated of Him in the Koran. But then, when the Christian debaters continued to argue that these two persons of the Trinity, the second and the third, are Gods like the first persons, the Muslims balked and quoted against them the Koranic verses, "say not three ... God is only one God" (4: 169) and "they surely are infidels who say, God is the third of three, for there is no God but one God" (5: 77). Thus there had arisen in Islam the belief, which became the orthodox belief, that certain terms predicated of God have, corresponding to them, real existent beings in God, called attributes, which are coeternal with God, but eternally inseparable from Him, and because they were eternally inseparable from God and because also they were not called God, the unity of God, so vehemently insisted upon in the Koran, is preserved.

That this is how the problem of attributes had originated in Islam can be shown by arguments evidential, terminological, and contextual. To begin with, among Muslims themselves there were those who in this doctrine of attributes saw an analogy to the Christian doctrine of the Trinity. Then, the two Arabic terms for what we call "attributes," namely ṣifāt and ma'āniyy, are translations of two Greek terms, χαρακτηριστικα and πράγματα, which were part of the technical vocabulary of the Trinity. Finally, the two "most beautiful names of God," which originally were taken by Muslims to reflect real attributes in God, correspond exactly to the names by which the second and third persons of the Trinity came to be known to Muslims through Christians writing in Arabic.

This, we imagine, is how the theory of attributes was introduced in Islam.

No sooner, however, had the belief in real attributes been introduced than there arose opposition to it. This opposition was like the Sabellian opposition in Christianity to the reality of the second and third persons of the Trinity. It saw in the assumption of real attributes, even though not called Gods, a violation of the true unity of God. Like Sabellianism in Christianity, therefore, which declared the second and third persons of the Trinity to be mere names of God designating His actions, this opposition declared the terms predicated of God in the Koran to be only names of God, designating His actions, and hence the so-called attributes are not real beings and other than the essence of God: they are identical with His essence.

And so the controversy in Christianity over the persons of the Logos and the Holy Spirit in their relation to God became in Islam a controversy over the relation of the attributes to God. The orthodox Muslim position was like, though not exactly the same as, orthodox Christian position. The attributes, like the second and third persons of the Trinity, were both extradeical and intradeical, except that, unlike the second and third persons of the Trinity, which were intradeical and extradeical by unification, that is, they were at once the same as God and other than He, these orthodox Muslim attributes were intradeical and extradeical by location, that is, they were in God but other than He. The unorthodox position of the Antiattributists in Islam corresponds to Sabellianism in Christianity.

The Muslim attributes are not ideas. They lack the essential characteristic of the Platonic ideas, that of being preexistent patterns of things that come into existence. But they may be considered as the third generation of Platonic ideas through two generations of Logos, being as they were direct descendants of Logos and the Holy Spirit of the Christian Trinity. It can be further shown that with the gradual introduction of Greek philosophy into Islam, the problem of attributes became identified with the problem of Platonic ideas, or rather with the problem of universals, as the problem of Platonic ideas was known by that time, and with that the controversy between Attributists and Antiattributists in Islam became a controversy over universals as to whether they were extradeical or intradeical.[86] It was during this new phase of the problem that a new conception of the relation of attributes to God, or perhaps only a new way of expressing their relation to God, made its appearance. It is known as the theory of modes (*aḥwāl*). Dissatisfied with the orthodox view that attributes are really "existent" in God and with the unorthodox view that attributes, being mere names, are "nonexistent," the exponents of this new theory declared that attributes, now surnamed modes, are "neither existent nor nonexistent." [87] Of course, they were charged with infringing upon the Law of Excluded Middle, but theologians and philosophers that they were they were not fazed by this difficulty: they found a way of getting around it.

While in Islam the problem of attributes was raging, there was no such a problem in Christianity, that is to say, there was no controversy over the question as to what was the meaning of terms, outside the terms Father, Logos or Son, and Holy Spirit, in their relation to God, when predicated of Him. The old distinction between the Logos, which was both extradeical and intradeical by unification, and the ideas within the Logos, which were only intradeical, was formally given expression by the last of the Church Fathers, John of Damascus, in the distinction drawn by him between "persons" and "names." [88] The Logos, as one of the three persons of the

[86] To be fully discussed in my work *The Philosophy of the Kalam*, in press.

[87] Baghdādī, *Al-Farq bayn al-Firaq* (ed. M. Badr, 1910), 182, line 5; Shahrastānī, *Nihāyat al-Iqdām* (ed. A. Guillaume, 1934), 133, line 4.

[88] Cf. *De Fide Orthodoxa*, I, 6–8 and 9.

Trinity is a real being, but the ideas within the Logos, such as the ideas of goodness, greatness, powerfulness, and the like, are not real beings; they are only "names," so that their distinction from the Logos as well as from one another is only nominal, derived from the various ways in which the Logos appears to the mind of man through its various operations in the world. Since they are only various names of the Logos, by the principle that whatever is predicated of one of the persons of the Trinity is predicated of the triune God as a whole, they are various names of the triune God as a whole. Accordingly, when you say God is Father and Logos the Holy Spirit, the relation between the three predicates and the subject as well as the relation between the three predicates themselves is a real relation and they are all one by the mystery of the Trinity. But when you say that God is good or great or powerful you merely predicate of God different "names." Thus, without using the term "attribute" and without raising a problem of attributes, the Fathers of the Church arrived at a position like that of the Antiattributists in Islam. In fact, it can be shown, that the Antiattributists in Islam were influenced by this view of the Church Fathers.

This distinction between "persons" and "names," or between the Logos as the place of ideas and the ideas within it, in their relation to God, was generally accepted in Christianity. The ideas within the Logos continued to be called "names" and there was no problem of "attributes" corresponding to such a problem in Islam. But then four events happened which resulted in the introduction of the problem of divine attributes into mediaeval Christian philosophy. Let us study these four events.

The first event was the publication and subsequently the condemnation of the *De Divisione Naturae* by John Scotus Erigena. In that work, published in 867, Erigena deals with what he calls "the primordial causes of things," which he says the Greeks call "ideas" and "prototypes." [89] Following the Church Fathers, these ideas are placed by him in the Logos, but, departing from the Church Fathers, who considered the ideas within the Logos as identical with the Logos, Erigena distinguished them from the Logos. This may be gathered from his statements that "before the ages, God the Father begot (*genuit*) His Word, in whom and through whom He created (*creavit*) the most perfect primordial causes of all natures" [90] and also that while "we believe that the Son is wholly coeternal with the Father, with regard to the things which the Father makes (*facit*) in the Son, I say they are coeternal with the Son, but not wholly coeternal." [91]

---

[89] *De Divisione Naturae* II, 2 (PL 122, 529 B); II, 36 (615 D–616 A). Cf. E. Gilson, *History of Christian Philosophy in the Middle Ages* (London & N. Y., 1955), 117–119.

Note the two distinctions drawn between the Logos and the ideas it contains: the former is begotten, the latter are created or made; the former is wholly coeternal with God, the latter are not wholly coeternal with the Logos. Being thus not identical with the Logos, they are not identical with God, and therefore they are not mere "names" of God. Accordingly, while God is described by him as "that which creates and is not created," the ideas are described as "that which is created and creates." [92] Here then we have, in deviation from the traditional Christian view, a view approaching the orthodox Muslim view on attributes.

Erigena's deviation from the traditional Christian view on the relation of the ideas to God passed unnoticed by his contemporaries. While his *De Praedestinatione* was condemned twice during his lifetime, his *De Divisione Naturae* was not molested during his lifetime, nor was it molested for a long time after that. The Schoolmen during the four centuries following Erigena were engaged in the problem of universals, which is concerned primarily with the problem of the relation of ideas to sensible objects, and paid little attention to the problem of the relation of the ideas to God. It was not until the beginning of the XIIIth century, at the Council of Paris (1209) that his *De Divisione Naturae* was condemned; and one of the reasons for its condemnation was its theory of ideas. The writ of condemnation on this point reads as follows: "The second error is his view that the primordial causes, which are called ideas, that is forms or exemplars, create and are created, whereas, according to the Saints, since they are in God, they are the same as God, and therefore they cannot be created." [93] This is event number one.

Then, prior to the condemnation in 1209 of Erigena's work, Gilbert of la Porrée was accused at the Council of Rheims, in 1148, of believing that, when such terms as goodness, wisdom, greatness and the like are predicated of God, they are not designations of perfections which are identical with God, but rather a "form" which is placed in God and by which He is God, analogous to the universal term "humanity," which, when predicated of the subject "man" does not designate that which is identical with the subject but rather a "form" in the subject by which the subject is man.[94] This prompted the Council to draw up a profession of faith, which, directly in opposition to the alleged view of Gilbert, maintained that "God is wise only by a wisdom which is God himself; eternal by an eternity which is God himself; one only

---

[90] *Ibid.* II, 21 (560 B).   [91] *Ibid.* (561 C).   [92] *Ibid.* I, 1 (441 B).

[93] "secundus est, quod primordiales causae, quae vocantur ideae i. e. forma seu exemplar [sic], creant et creantur: cum tamen secundum sanctos idem sint quod Deus: in quantum sunt in Deo: et ideo creari non possunt" (quoted in Johannes Huber, *Johannes Scotus Erigena* [Munich, 1861], 436).

by a unity which is God himself; [God] only by a divinity which is He himself; in short, He is by His own self wise, great, eternal, one, God."[95] The difference between Gilbert and the Council is strikingly like the difference between the Muslim Attributists and Antiattributists. The formula used by the Council is exactly the same as that reported in the name of the Antiattributist Abū al-Hudhayl, which reads as follows: "God is knowing by a knowledge which is himself, and He is powerful by a power which is himself, and He is living by a life which is himself."[96] This is event number two.

Then something else happened. Early in the XIIIth century, certainly before 1235, there appeared a Latin translation of Maimonides' work *The Guide of the Perplexed,* which contained an account of the Muslim controversies over the problem of divine attributes and a presentation of his own elaborate theory in opposition to the reality of attributes. This Latin translation was made not from the original Arabic, in which the book was written, but from one of its two Hebrew versions. In that Hebrew version, the Arabic term *ṣifah,* which, as said above, reflects the Greek term χαρακτηριστικόν used in connection with the Trinity, was translated by two Hebrew terms, *middah* and *to'ar.* These two terms, in turn, are translated by three Latin terms: *dispositio, attributio,* and *nominatio.*[97] Of these three terms, each of which reflects one of the senses of the two Hebrew terms as well as of their underlying Arabic term, the term *attributio,* used in this translation in the sense of a divine predicate, is of special interest. By the time this translation was made, the Latin term *attributio* or *attributum* in the technical sense of "predicate" was not altogether unknown. According to the *Thesaurus Linguae Latinae* it was used in that technical sense by Cicero. But it was never used, as far as I know, as a designation of terms predicated of God, either in a work originally written in Latin or in a work translated from the Arabic into Latin. In the Latin translation of Ghazālī's *Maqāṣid al-Falāsifah,* which was made in the XIIth century by John Hispalensis, the Arabic *ṣifah* is translated, not by *attributio* or *attributum,* but by *assignatio.*[98] The verb *attribuere*[99] and the noun *attributio*[100] do indeed occur in the Latin translation of Avicebrol's *Fons Vitae,* also made in the XIIth century by John Hispalensis, but from the context it may be gathered that in both its

---

[94] Cf. Geoffrey d'Auxerre, *Libellus contra Capitula Gilbert Pictavensis Episcopi* (PL 185, 597 CD; 617 A). [95] *Ibid.* (618 A).

[96] Al-Ash'arī, *Maqālāt al-Islāmīyīn,* ed. Ritter (1929–30), 165, lines 5–7.

[97] Rabi Mossei Aegyptii, *Dux seu Director dubitantium aut perplexorum.* Lib. I, Cap. XLIX, Fol. XVIIIa, line 28; Cap. LI, Fol. XVIIIb, line 41 (Paris, 1520).

[98] *Algazel's Metaphysics,* ed. J. T. Muckle (1933), 62, line 2; cf. Arabic text: *Maqāṣid al-Falāsifah* (Cairo, no date), 149, line 12.   [99] Avencebrolis (Ibn Gabirol), *Fons Vitae,* ed. Clemens Baeumker (1895), 92, line 27.   [100] *Ibid.,* 182, line 9.

forms the term is used not in the sense of "predicate" and still less in the sense of "divine predicate" but rather in the sense of "gift," "addition," "cause." This is event number three.

The fourth event is a double header.

Between the years 1245–1250 and between the years 1254–1256 Albertus Magnus and Thomas Aquinas respectively published their commentaries on the *Sentences* of Peter Lombard. In these commentaries, both of them for the first time use the term "attributes" instead of the traditional term "names" as a description of the ideas within the Logos predicated of God. Moreover, both of them, as soon as they introduced the term "attributes," raised the question, which, as phrased by Albert, reads: "Whether attributes in God are one or many?" [101] and, as phrased by Thomas, reads: "Whether in God are many attributes?" [102] The meaning of the question is whether the attributes are really distinct from God and from each other or not. Once this question was raised with regard to attributes, Thomas raised it also with regard to "names," phrasing his question to read: "Whether names predicated of God are synonymous?" [103] meaning, again, whether the ideas contained in the Logos and traditionally designated by the term name are really distinct from God and from each other or not. Moreover, once St. Thomas raised the question of the relation of the ideas to God under the guise of the question with regard to attributes and names, he raised the question directly with regard to ideas. Thus in the very same work, the commentary on the *Sentences,* in which he for the first time introduced the term attribute and the problem of attributes, he raised the question "Whether the ideas are many?" [104] and the same question appears also in some of his later works.[105] Here again the question is whether the ideas are really distinct from God and from each other or not. In other words, he raised the question whether the Fathers of the Church were right in assuming that the ideas within the Logos were only names and intradeical or whether they were wrong.

This is the succession of events in the history of post-Patristic Christian philosophy relating to the problem as to whether the ideas within the Logos are intradeical or not: (1) the condemnation of the alleged Gilbert's view on the reality of the distinction between the perfections of God; (2) the condemnation of Erigena's theory of ideas; (3) the introduction into Christian philosophy of the term "attributes" in the sense of divine predicates and withal a knowledge of the

---

[101] Albert, *In I Sent.* III, 4.   [102] Thomas, *In I Sent.* II, 1, 2.
[103] *Sum. Theol.* I, 13, 4; cf. *Cont. Gent.* I, 35; *De Potentia* 7, 6; *Compend. Theol.* 25.
[104] *In I Sent.* XXXVI, 2, 2.   [105] *Sum. Theol.* I, 15, 2; *De Veritate* 3, 2; *Cont. Gent.* I, 54; *Quodl.* IV, 1.

Muslim controversies about it; (4) the use of the term "attribute" and the raising of the problem of attributes by Albertus Magnus and Thomas Aquinas. The question naturally arises in our mind whether there is any causal connection between the first three events and the fourth event. In answer to this question, it may be said that with regard to the first two events there is an argument from silence showing that there is no connection between these two events and the fourth event. Neither Albert nor Thomas, throughout their discussions of the problem of attributes, makes any reference or allusion to Erigena or to Gilbert. Besides, while Gilbert was accused of believing in a real distinction between the perfection predicated of God and God, he was not accused of believing in a real distinction between the perfections themselves; quite the contrary, he is said to have believed that all the perfections predicated of God constitute one form in God.[106] There is, however, evidence of a connection between the new problem raised about attributes and the Latin translation of the work of Maimonides. First, there is St. Thomas himself, who in his commentary on the *Sentences,* after introducing the term attribute and raising the problem of attributes, quotes Maimonides and takes issue with him.[107] Second, there is Occam, who, arguing for a nominalistic conception of attributes, says: "The holy men of old did not use that word attributes (*attributa*) but in its stead they used the word names (*nomina*), whence, in contrast to certain moderns who say that divine attributes are distinct and diverse, the ancients said . . . that divine names are distinct and diverse, wherefrom it follows that they laid down a distinction only with reference to names and a diversity only with reference to signs, but with reference to the thing signified they laid down unity"; [108] and in support of this Occam goes on to quote Augustine and Peter Lombard. The term "attributes" was thus regarded by Occam as a new-fangled term, of recent origin, which had come to replace the old traditional term "names," and he makes it unmistakably clear that there was no problem of the relation of attributes to God as long as "names" was used instead of "attributes," and that the problem arose only with the introduction of the term "attributes." With all this, are we not justified in assuming that the use of the term attribute and the rise of the problem of attributes in mediaeval Christian philosophy had its origin in the Latin translation of Maimonides' *Guide of the Perplexed?*

[106] *Op. cit.* (597 CD).   [107] *In I Sent.* II, 1, 3 c.

[108] *Quodlibet* III, 2: "Sancti antiqui non utebantur isto vocabulo attributa, sed pro isto utebantur hoc vocabulo nomina. Unde sicut quidam moderni dicunt quod attributa divina sunt distincta et diversa, ita dicebant antiqui . . . quod nomina divina sunt distincta et diversa, ita quod non posuerunt distinctionem nisi in nominibus et unitatem in re significata et diversitatem in signis" (quoted by P. Vignaux in *Dictionnaire de Théologie Catholique,* Vol. 11, col. 757).

In their attempt to solve the problem, the Schoolmen were all unanimous in rejecting the reality of attributes predicated of God. So far forth, they were all aligned against the Muslim Attributists. But there were differences of opinion among them as to how to express this opposition to the reality of attributes. Three different ways of expressing it developed in the course of the discussion.

First, Thomas Aquinas, having introduced the term attribute and having raised the problem of attributes, laid down certain fundamental views which were shared by all other Schoolmen.

The starting point in St. Thomas's discussion of the problem raised by him is that ideas and attributes are in God. With regard to ideas, having in mind his own statement elsewhere that "the Word of God is rightly called conceived or begotten Wisdom, as being the wise conception of the divine mind," [109] he says that the "ideas" are "in the divine Wisdom" or "in the divine mind," and this divine wisdom or "divine mind" is subsequently spoken of by him as the "divine essence" and "God himself." [110] With regard to attributes, in answer to the question "Whether in God are many attributes," he starts by saying that "in God there is wisdom, goodness, and the like." [111]

Then, as a qualification of the statement which was his starting point, St. Thomas tries to show that, while ideas and attributes are in God, they are not in God as real beings. With regard to the ideas which are in God, he argues against their reality on the ground that there is no "real plurality in God other than the plurality of persons," [112] maintaining, therefore, that the relations between the ideas in God "are not real relations, such as those whereby the persons are distinguished, but relations understood (*intellecti*) by God," [113] so that ideas are many, only in the sense that "God understands many models proper to many things" [114] or "that many ideas are in His intellect as understood by Him," [115] or that "although these ideas are multiplied in their relations to things, they are not really distinct from the divine essence." [116] Combining these statements, we gather that in reality all the ideas in God are one and, of course, identical with God, but God in His wisdom causes them to be multiplied in things. Similarly with regard to attributes, he says that, unlike the persons of the Trinity, each of which signifies "a real thing" (*res*) [117] and which are "really (*realiter*) distinct from each other," [118] so that "there are many real things (*res*) subsistent in the divine nature," [119] the plurality of attributes which are affirmed of God are "in God wholly one in reality (*re*) but they differ in reason (*ratione*)"; [120] or, as he also phrases it, "the

[109] *Cont. Gent.* IV, 12.   [110] *Sum. Theol.* I, 44, 3 c.   [111] *In I Sent.* II, 1, 2 c.
[112] *Ibid.* I, 15, 2, obj. 4.   [113] *Ibid.*, ad 4.   [114] *Ibid.*, c.   [115] *Ibid.*, ad. 2.
[116] *Sum. Theol.* I, 44, 3 c.   [117] *Ibid.* I, 29, 2 c; I, 30, 4 c.   [118] *Ibid.* I, 30, 2 c.
[119] *Ibid.* I, 30, 1 c.

names attributed to God signify one thing" but "they signify that thing under many and diverse distinctions of reason (*sub rationibus multis et diversis*)," [121] so that God "is one in reality (*re*), and yet multiple according to reason (*secundum rationem*), because our intellect apprehends Him in a manifold manner, just as things represent Him in a manifold manner." [122]

That the attributes of God are "multiple only according to reason" is thus St. Thomas's way of expressing his denial of any real distinction between the attributes and the essence of God and between the attributes themselves.

Another expression, however, for the same purpose of denying any real distinction between the attributes and God and between the attributes themselves, is used by Duns Scotus. The expression used by him is "formal distinction" (*distinctio formalis*).[123] Whether this "formal distinction" is something different from St. Thomas's "distinction of reason" is a moot point.[124] But if it is assumed to be different, the difference has been stated as follows: "The attributes are distinguished from the essence not indeed actually in reality (*realiter*) or by reason only (*ratione tantum*) but formally (*formaliter*) or by a distinction which is midway between real and of reason." [125] If this is what the expression "formal distinction" means, then it reminds one of the expression "neither existent nor nonexistent" used by the Muslim Modalists; [126] and, like the Modalists' expression it could be objected to on the ground of its being an infringement on the Law of Excluded Middle; but, if such an objection is raised, it could be answered in the same way as the Modalists answered the objection raised against their expression.

Opposed to the description of the anti-realistic conception of attributes by either the expression "distinction of reason" or the expression "formal distinction" is Occam. As we have seen, he prefers the good old term "names" to the new-fangled term "attributes." He therefore maintains that the terms predicated of God are distinguished from God and from each other only "with reference to names" (*in nominibus*) or "with reference to signs" (*in signis*).[127] As the equivalent of "names" and "signs," he uses also the term "concepts" (*conceptus*),[128]

[120] *In I Sent.* II, 1, 3 c. [121] *Sum. Theol.* I, 13, 4 c. [122] *Ibid.*, ad. 3.
[123] *Opera Oxoniensis, I Sent.* II, 7 (Op. VIII, 602–605). See E. Gilson, *History of Christian Philosophy in the Middle Ages*, 461–462 and n. 63 on page 765.
[124] Cf. Bernard Jansen, "Beiträge zur geschichtlichen Entwicklung der Distinctio formalis," *Zeitschrift für Katholische Theologie*, 53 (1929), 318.
[125] Francis Noel, *Theologiae R. P. Fr. Suarez, Summa, seu Compendium*, I: *De Deo Uno et Trino*, I, i, 10, 2 (Vol. I, 24). [126] Cf. above at n. 87.
[127] Cf. above n. 108. [128] *In I Sent.* Dist. II, Qu. II F, where with reference to divine attributes, he says: "non sunt nisi conceptus vel signa quae possunt praedicari

though in St. Thomas *conceptio,* which he uses as the equivalent of *conceptus,* means the same as *ratio,* and hence *distinctio conceptus* would mean the same as *distinctio rationis.*

These three expressions are all meant to be a denial of the reality of attributes. The difference in phrasing, to my mind, does not mean a difference in the degree of reality which they each deny. St. Thomas in his detailed explanation of what he means by his "distinction of reason" makes it clear that, even with the qualification that the "reason" is not "from the side of the reasoner only" (*tantum ex parte ipsius ratiocinantis*) but also "from the peculiarity of the very thing" (*ex proprietate ipsius rei*),[129] he does not mean by it any diminution in the degree of his denial of the reality of attributes; he only means by it to emphasize that the attributes, which are in no sense real, are not definable, that is to say, they are not univocal terms, and also that they are not generic or fictitious or equivocal or synonymous terms.[130] And to my mind, again, just as the phrases used by St. Thomas as qualifications of his "distinction of reason" do not mean a diminution in the degree of his denial of the reality of divine attributes, so does not also the expression "formal distinction" used by Duns Scotus. If there is at all any difference in meaning between the different expressions used by them, it is to be found with reference to something in which they openly and outspokenly disagree with each other. Now they happen to be openly and outspokenly in disagreement as to whether attributes are predicated of God univocally or not. St. Thomas takes the negative;[131] Duns Scotus takes the affirmative.[132] But, as we have seen, St. Thomas explains his "distinction of reason" plus its qualification to mean the negation, among others, also of the univocal interpretation of divine attributes. We may therefore conclude that, if Duns Scotus had chosen the expression "formal distinction" with a view to emphasizing some difference between himself and St. Thomas on the question of divine attributes, the difference which he wanted to emphasize was that of his approval of the univocal interpretation of divine attributes. Similarly the different formula used by Occam, to my mind, once more, does not mean an increase in the degree of his denial of the reality of attributes; it only means that he felt that the denial of the reality of attributes should be expressed more strongly and more clearly and in a form, such as suggested by him, which would be less likely to be misunderstood by the unwary and to mislead them

---

vere de Deo" (quoted by P. Vignaux in *Dictionnaire de Théologie Catholique,* Vol. 11, col. 756).

[129] *In I Sent.* I, 2, 3 c.   [130] *Ibid.;* cf. *Sum. Theol.* I, 13, 4–5; *Cont. Gent.* I, 32–35.
[131] *Ibid.*   [132] Hieronymus de Montefortino, *Ven. Johannis Duns Scoti Summa Theologica,* XIII, 5 (Vol. I, 318–322).

into endowing attributes with some measure of reality. In the history of religions, many a hotly debated problem was not so much over actual beliefs as over the manner in which to formulate actual beliefs, behind which there was always the fear that a wrong formulation might lead the unwary astray.

Thus toward the end of the XIVth century there were in mediaeval Christian philosophy two types of descendants of Platonic ideas, the Logos and Attributes. The Logos was the place of the ideas and, through the Logos of Philo, was the third generation of the descendants of Platonic ideas; attributes were the terms by which the ideas within the Logos were designated and, through the Muslim attributes, were the fifth generation of the descendants of the Platonic ideas. It is to these two types of Platonic ideas that the original question as to whether the Platonic ideas were extradeical or intradeical was transferred. The answer given to this question differed in each of these two types of descendants. The Logos was both extradeical and intradeical by unification; attributes were only intradeical.

Centuries roll by and the scene is shifted from the Schoolmen, who were professional teachers of philosophy, to Descartes and Spinoza, who were free-lance philosophers, Descartes a free-lance roving philosopher, Spinoza a free-lance non-roving philosopher.

Descartes, heir to mediaeval Christian philosophy, followed faithfully the traditions of that philosophy. God to him was still immaterial and hence he insists upon the simplicity and indivisibility of God.[133] Following Christian tradition, he declares that the Logos, as one of the persons of the Trinity is both extradeical and intradeical by unification and that hence the Trinity is a mystery. He thus says with regard to the persons of the Trinity that he denies that "there can be discerned between them a real distinction in respect of the divine essence, whatever be admitted to prevail in respect to their relation to one another"; [134] and, with regard to the Trinity itself, he says that it is a doctrine "which can be perceived only by a mind illumined by faith." [135] Following the vocabulary of the Schoolmen, he refers to such terms predicated of God as "eternal, infinite, omniscient, and the creator of all things which are outside of himself" [136] as "attributes." [137] From his classification of attributes into those which are in "things themselves" (*in rebus ipsis*) and those which are "only in our thought" (*in nostra tantum cogitatione*) [138] it may be inferred that divine attributes belong to the latter and that the distinction between these attri-

[133] *Meditatio* III (*Oeuvres*, ed. Adam et Tannery, VII, 50, lines 16–19).
[134] *Sextae Responsiones* 10 (*Oeuvres*, VII, 433, line 27 to 444, line 2).
[135] *Ibid.* (443, lines 23–27). [136] *Medit.* III (*Oeuvres*, VII, 40, lines 16–18).
[137] *Correspondance* 299 (*Oeuvres*, III, 297, lines 15–17).

butes and God and between these attributes themselves is what he describes, by the phrase used by St. Thomas, as being a "distinction of reason (*distinctio rationis*),"[139] and, like St. Thomas, he explains that by that "distinction of reason" he does not mean a "reason" which is only of the "reasoner" (*ratiocinantis*) but one which has a "foundation in things" (*fundamentum in rebus*).[140] In fact, Descartes himself confesses that in his conception of God and His attributes he follows tradition, for in his letter to Mersenne (July 1641) he writes: "by the idea of God I understand no other thing than that which all other people are accustomed to understand when they speak of Him."[141]

Spinoza, heir to mediaeval Jewish philosophy supplemented and panoplied by mediaeval Christian philosophy, parted from the fundamental conception of God as an immaterial being common to both these philosophic traditions. He boldly asserts that God is not pure thought; He is both thought and extension. How he came to this view he explains in geometrical language in Propositions II–VI of *Ethics* I and in plain language in Chapter II of *Short Treatise* I.[142] But, while his God is extension as well as thought, He is simple and indivisible. How extension can be simple and indivisible is explained by him in a Scholium to Proposition XV of *Ethics* I and in Epistola XII addressed to Ludovicus Meyer.[143] But still, while thought and extension are each simple and indivisible, they are different from each other. How then could he say of God that He is both thought and extension, without making Him composite and divisible? His answer is that thought and extension are related to God after the analogy of goodness and greatness and the like in their relation to God as conceived by philosophers before him, including Descartes. They are attributes of God, which are distinguished from God only in thought or by a distinction of reason. And so he formally defines attribute as "that which the intellect perceives of substance, as if constituting its essence,"[144] or, as he informally describes it, as that which is the same as substance but is called attribute with respect to the intellect (*respectu intellectus*).[145] Knowing also that, in the history of the problem of attributes, those who denied their reality, spoke of them as names, Spinoza refers to the attributes of extension and thought as two names of God and explains the unity of God, despite His having two attributes, by the example

[138] *Principia Philosophiae* I, 57.   [139] *Ibid.* I, 62.
[140] *Correspondance* 418 (*Oeuvres*, IV, 349, lines 26–30); cf. above at n. 129.
[141] *Ibid.* 245 (*Oeuvres*, III, 393, lines 25–27).
[142] Cf. chapter on "The Unity of Substance" in my *Philosophy of Spinoza* (Cambridge, Mass., 1934), I, 79–111.   [143] Cf. chapter on "Infinity of Extension," *ibid.*, 262–295.
[144] *Eth.* I, Def. 4.   [145] *Epist.* 9 (*Opera*, ed. Gebhardt, IV, 46, line 4).

of the third patriarch, who is one, despite his having two names, Jacob and Israel.[146]

And yet, with all this background, reaching far and wide into history, students of Spinoza treat the attributes in his philosophy as if they were inventions of his own mind. With their bare wit they try to extract some rootless meaning out of his mnemonic phrases and, if sometimes they happen to summon external aid, they make him split hairs with Descartes or share honors with Berkeley.

At the beginning of my talk I said that I would trace the history of the two interpretations of Platonic ideas through the successive generations of descendants of these ideas. Let me now, by way of summary, list the generations through which I have tried to trace the continuity of these two interpretations. As there is no better method of showing the continuity of a historical process than that used by the Biblical historiographers in those genealogies which begin with the words "Now these are the generations," I shall adopt this literary device and begin:

Now these are the generations of Platonic ideas.

And Plato lived forty years and begat the ideas.

And the ideas of Plato lived three hundred years and begat the Logos of Philo.

And the Logos of Philo lived seventy years and begat the Logos of John.

And the Logos of John lived six hundred years and begat the attributes of Islam.

And the attributes of Islam lived five hundred and fifty years and begat the attributes of the Schoolmen.

And the attributes of the Schoolmen lived four hundred years and begat the attributes of Descartes and Spinoza.

And the attributes of Spinoza lived two hundred years and begat among their interpreters sons and daughters who knew not their father.

---

[146] *Ibid.* (lines 9–11).

St. Augustine and the Christian Idea of Progress: The Background of the City of God*

by THEODOR E. MOMMSEN

Reprinted from the *Journal of the History of Ideas*—Vol. XII, No. 3, pp. 346–374.

In the summer of the year 410 Rome fell to a Visigothic army under King Alaric. Since the city suffered relatively little external damage, modern historians have sometimes been inclined to regard that conquest or sack of Rome as a rather insignificant incident. We should be wary, however, of any tendency to belittle the event, remembering that it impelled Augustine to write *The City of God*. In view of the impact this work has had upon the development of Christian thought, it can certainly be said that the fall of Rome in the year 410, which motivated its composition, marks a momentous date in the intellectual history of the western world.

Moreover, Augustine was not the only contemporary to be profoundly impressed by that event, as several other writings show. It may suffice here to quote a few sentences from St. Jerome, who was at that time living in Bethlehem. When he received the news of "the havoc wrought in the West and, above all, in the city of Rome" (*Epist.* 126, 2), he expressed his feelings in the preface to the first book of the *Commentaries on Ezekiel*, which he was then writing: "When the brightest light on the whole earth was extinguished, when the Roman empire was deprived of its head and when, to speak more correctly, the whole world perished in one city, then 'I was dumb

---

* This article was already in the hands of the printer when I got a copy of the essay by J. Straub, "Christliche Geschichtsapologetik in der Krisis des römischen Reiches," *Historia* (1950), 52–81. Prof. Straub's article does not discuss the idea of progress and the other Christian and pagan conceptions of history which were current before and throughout the fourth century. His main objective is rather, for the period from 378 to the aftermath of the fall of Rome in 410, to deal "mit der Rolle, welche die christlichen Apologeten in jenem epochalen Umwandlungsprozess gespielt haben, in dem der römische Staat zugrundeging, aber die mit dem Staat aufs engste verbundene Kirche ihre eigene Existenz zu behaupten und sich für die Teilnahme an der neu zu bildenden Völkergemeinschaft der Welt des Mittelalters freizumachen suchte" (p. 54). Of particular value is Prof. Straub's clarification of the views which Augustine and Orosius had concerning the Christian attitude toward the Roman empire.—Unfortunately I was unable to consult the articles by H. v. Campenhausen, O. Herding, and W. Loewenich, all of which, according to Straub, *l.c.*, p. 52, n. 1, deal with Augustine's historical conceptions.

with silence, I held my peace, even from good, and my sorrow was stirred' (*Psalm* 39, 2).'' And in the preface to the third book of the same work Jerome asked: "Who would believe that Rome, built up by the conquest of the whole world, has collapsed, that the mother of nations has also become their tomb?"[1]

To understand the profound consternation of Jerome and his contemporaries we must realize that the fate of Rome meant infinitely more to the people of late antiquity than the fate of any city, even the most renowned, would mean to the western world today. For many deeply rooted ideas and beliefs, and numerous superstitions, were connected with the very name and existence of that city. One need recall only the famous lines of Vergil's *Aeneid* (1, 278f.), in which Jupiter says: "To the Romans I assign limits neither to the extent nor to the duration of their empire; dominion have I given them without end." This notion of "the eternal city," the capital of a universal empire, "the golden Rome," we find reflected in the works of almost all the pagan writers and poets of the first centuries of our era, whether they were of Latin, Greek or Oriental origin.[2] Thus, at the end of the fourth century, the pagan general and historian Ammianus Marcellinus declared (*Histor.*, 14, 6, 3) that "as long as there are men, Rome will be victorious so that it will increase with lofty growth." And around the year 400 the Christian poet Claudianus wrote (*On the consulate of Stilicho*, 3, 159f.): "There will never be an end to the power of Rome, for luxury and pride resulting in vices and enmities have destroyed all other kingdoms."

During the same period the attitude of the Christians toward the Roman empire was divided. On the one hand there ran within early Christianity an undercurrent of strong hatred of the Roman state and of everything that state stood for. This hostility, nourished by Jewish traditions and strengthened by the persecutions, manifested itself in the apparently widespread expectation that some day the prediction of the angel in the *Book of Revelation* (14, 8) would be fulfilled: "Babylon [*i.e.*, Rome] is fallen, is fallen, that great city, because she made all nations drink of the wine of the wrath of her fornication."

---

[1] Throughout this article I have based the text of my quotations from the Church Fathers on the translations in the three series of *The Select Library of the Ante-Nicene Fathers*, and of the *Nicene and Post-Nicene Fathers* (1885–1900); very frequently, however, I have found it necessary to make changes in the translations, for which I have to take the responsibility.

[2] See E. K. Rand, *The Building of Eternal Rome* (1943).

On the other hand, the official spokesmen of the early Church always remembered that Jesus himself had ordered his disciples to "render unto Caesar the things which are Caesar's" (*Matthew,* 23, 21), and that St. Paul had demanded obedience to the Empire when he wrote in his *Epistle to the Romans* (13, 1): "Let every soul be subject unto the higher powers; for there is no power but of God: the powers that be, are ordained of God." In accordance, then, with these explicit orders of Christ and St. Paul, every adherent of the faith had to pay his outward respect, at least, to the established authorities of the state.

But many Christians showed themselves willing to go even farther and actually hoped and prayed for the continuance of the Roman empire. This affirmative attitude grew out of certain historical and eschatological ideas which went back to both pagan and Jewish traditions.[3] In the Hellenistic era there had developed in the East a theory which saw history take its course in a sequence of great or, rather, universal monarchies. Four of these empires were to follow one another, and the series was to conclude with a fifth monarchy which, it was believed, would last to the end of the world. This idea of the four or five monarchies was adopted by some of the Roman and Greek historians, and it appeared likewise in Jewish literature. For the great image seen in a dream by Nebuchadnezzar (*Daniel,* 2, 31ff.) and the four beasts seen by Daniel himself (7, 1ff.), were explained by the pre-Christian tradition in terms of an interpretation of world history: these visions were believed to signify symbolically that history takes its course through the succession of four universal monarchies; the disintegration of the last of the four empires was assumed to usher in the end of the world.

In the latter part of the second century and in the first part of the third century Christian theologians like Irenaeus of Lyons, Tertullian and Hippolytus adopted these pagan and Jewish traditions and expressed their opinion that the Roman empire "which now rules" (Irenaeus, *Against Heresies,* 5, 26, 1), should be considered to be the fourth monarchy.[4] All these Christian authors shared the belief that

[3] The most recent treatments of this question have been given by J. W. Swain, "The theory of the four monarchies: opposition history under the Roman empire," *Classical Philology* (1940), 1–21; H. L. Ginsberg, *Studies in Daniel* (1948), 5–23.

[4] See the list of authors who identified the fourth monarchy with the Roman empire, which has been compiled by H. H. Rowley, *Darius the Mede and the Four World Empires in the Book of Daniel* (1935), 73ff.

the fall of the last empire would be a most ominous event. Thus, Tertullian said in his treatise *On the Resurrection of the Flesh* (ch. 24), in which he interpreted a passage in St. Paul's *Second Epistle to the Thessalonians* (2, 7), that the Antichrist will appear after the Roman state has been scattered into ten kingdoms. On the basis of this eschatological belief Tertullian declared very emphatically in his *Apology* (ch. 32, 1): " There is also another and greater necessity for our praying in behalf of the emperors and the whole status of the empire and Roman affairs. For we know that only the continued existence of the Roman Empire retards the mighty power which threatens the whole earth, and postpones the very end of this world with its menace of horrible afflictions." In the early fourth century Lactantius stated even more explicitly in his *Divine Institutions* (7, 25, 6–8): " The fall and the ruin of the world will shortly take place, although it seems that nothing of that kind is to be feared as long as the city of Rome stands intact. But when the capital of the world has fallen . . . who can doubt that the end will have arrived for the affairs of men and the whole world? It is that city which still sustains all things. And the God of heaven is to be entreated by us and implored—if indeed His laws and decrees can be delayed—lest sooner than we think that detestable tyrant should come who will undertake so great a deed and tear out that eye by the destruction of which the world itself is about to fall."

During the fourth century a number of commentators on the *Book of Daniel,* including Eusebius and John Chrysostom in the East, Jerome and Sulpicius Severus (*Sacred Histories,* 2, 3) in the West, continued to identify the fourth monarchy with the Roman empire. Cyril of Jerusalem (*Catechetical Lectures,* 15, 12) followed even more closely the line of Irenaeus, Tertullian and Lactantius, by declaring: " The Antichrist is to come when the time of the Roman empire has been fulfilled and the end of the world is drawing near."

In view of the persistence of this concern for the continuance of Rome it seems safe to assume that in the year 410 many contemporaries regarded Alaric's conquest of Rome as the realization of the long-dreaded " fall of Rome " and considered the end of the world to be imminent. A reflection of this superstitious fear we find, I think, even in the words of Jerome, that " the whole world has perished in one city."

Augustine was, of course, well aware of both the pagan belief in "eternal Rome" and the eschatological speculations of his fellow-Christians. He rejected emphatically the one idea as well as the other. As to the pagan notion, he pointed out (*Sermon* 105, 9) that "the earthly kingdoms have their changes" and that only of the Kingdom of Christ it can be said: "There shall be no end" (*Luke*, 1, 33). He continued (*ibid.*, § 10): "They who have promised this to earthly kingdoms have not been guided by truth but have lied by flattery." He quoted the famous line from Vergil—whom he calls rather slightingly "a certain poet of theirs"—and remarked: "This kingdom which you [Jupiter] have given 'without limits to its duration,' is it on earth or in heaven? Certainly it is on earth. And even if it were in heaven, yet 'heaven and earth shall pass away' (*Matthew*, 24, 35). Those things shall pass away, which God Himself has made. How much more rapidly shall that pass away which Romulus founded?" As to the meaning of the passage in St. Paul's *Second Epistle to the Thessalonians* (2, 7): "Only he who now holdeth, let him hold until he be taken out of the way,"[5] Augustine was much less certain than Tertullian, who had concluded from these words that the duration of this world is bound up with the duration of the Roman empire. Augustine knew (*City of God*, 20, 19 E–F)[6] that "some think that this refers to the Roman empire," and he granted that such an interpretation, in contrast to some others, "is not absurd." But at the same time he felt obliged to state: "I frankly confess that I do not know what St. Paul meant."

In reply to those Christian thinkers who attempted to figure out the exact date of the end of the world and connected the coming of that event with concrete developments and with definite historical incidents like "the fall of Rome," Augustine declared (*City of God*, 18, 53 A–B)[6] that such a question "is entirely improper." For he pointed out that Christ himself told his disciples: "It is not for you to know the times and the seasons which the Father hath put in His own power" (*Acts*, 1, 7). "In vain, then," Augustine stated, "do we attempt to compute and determine the years which remain to this world." Whoever undertakes that kind of calculation, Augustine con-

---

[5] The above translation is based on the text of the *Itala* quoted by Augustine; the version in the *King James Bible* reads: "Only he who now letteth will let, until he be taken out of the way."

[6] My quotations from *De civitate Dei* are based on the Latin text edited by J. E. Welldon, 2 vols. (1924), and on the translation by M. Dods, *The City of God*, 2 vols. (1872); frequently, however, I have replaced Dods' translation with my own.

cluded, "uses human conjecture and brings forward nothing certain from the authority of the canonical Scriptures."

Another argument which in several of his sermons Augustine employed, though in a more incidental fashion, is the observation that, after all, Rome was still standing, in spite of the disaster of the year 410. For instance, in the *Sermon on the Ruin of the City* he said that Rome, unlike Sodom, was not completely destroyed, and in another discourse (*Sermon* 105, 9) he declared: " The city which has given us birth, according to the flesh, still abides, God be thanked." He added (§ 11): "An end there will be to all earthly kingdoms. If that end be now, God alone knows. Perhaps the end is not yet, and we, because of a certain weakness or mercifulness or anguish, wish that it may not yet be." Augustine confessed (§ 12) that he himself was "entreating the Lord for Rome," not because he believed the duration of that one city would guarantee the duration of the whole world, but simply because there were many fellow-Christians in Rome, dear to him as all other Christians were.[7]

Since Rome did, in fact, survive, the old belief in its eternity also survived for many centuries to come, and with it persisted the popular superstition, in spite of its rejection by Augustine, that the final "fall" of the city would signify the coming end of the world. Only one of many testimonials to that belief may be quoted. In a British text of the early eighth century, which was wrongly ascribed to the Venerable Bede, we find the following lines:

> As long as the Colosseum stands, Rome also stands.
> When the Colosseum falls, Rome also will fall.
> When Rome falls, the world also will fall.[8]

The denial of the pagan belief in the eternity of Rome and the rejection of any connection between Christian eschatology and specific historical events occupy, however, only a rather minor place in the whole context of *The City of God*. Augustine felt justified in making short shrift of these ideas because he regarded them as either mere superstitions or futile conjectures.

[7] Cf. also *Sermon* 81, 9; all three sermons mentioned were preached in the years 410 and 411: see A. Kunzelmann in *Miscellanea Agostiniana* (1931), II, 449f., 500. On these sermons see also M. Pontet, *L'exégèse de S. Augustin prédicateur* (1944), 454, 471–76.

[8] Pseudo-Bede, *Flores ex diversis, quaestiones et parabola*, ed. Migne, *Patrologia Latina*, 94, col. 543; cf. F. Schneider, *Rom und Romgedanke im Mittelalter* (1926), 66f., 251.

The real purpose of his great book he stated in a number of places but nowhere more concisely than in the work entitled *Retractations* (2, 68, 1), which he wrote after the completion of *The City of God* in the year 426. He defined his primary objective as follows: " In the meantime Rome had been overthrown by the invasion of the Goths under king Alaric and by the vehemence of a great defeat. The worshippers of the many and false gods, whom we commonly call pagans, attempted to attribute that overthrow to the Christian religion, and they began to blaspheme the true God with even more than their customary acrimony and bitterness. It was for that reason that I, kindled by zeal for the house of God, undertook to write the books on *The City of God* against their blasphemies and errors."

The accusation was very old that Christianity was responsible for the miseries of the world. The pagans claimed that the Christians, through their refusal to honor the traditional deities, were provoking the wrath of the very gods whose favor had raised Rome to her universal power. The Christian apologists found it easy to refute the charge. One of the most precise expressions of their customary reply is contained in Tertullian's *Apology* (40, 3, 5). Tertullian addressed the pagans as follows: " Pray, tell me, how many calamities befell the world as a whole, as well as individual cities, before Tiberius reigned, before the coming, that is, of Christ? " He asked: " Where were your gods in those days when a deluge effaced the whole earth or, as Plato believed, merely its plains? " And he concluded: " The truth is that the human race has always deserved ill at God's hand .... Therefore one ought to know that the very same God is angry now, as he always was, long before Christians were so much as spoken of."

Augustine used exactly the same kind of argument throughout the first five books of *The City of God,* only in a much more elaborate and detailed fashion than Tertullian, Arnobius, Lactantius and other apologists of the third century had done before him. He went still further and commissioned his younger friend Orosius to write an entire history of the world from a point of view which is best described by Orosius himself in the dedication to Augustine of his *Seven books of Histories against the Pagans:* " You bade me to discover from all the available data of histories and annals, whatever instances past ages have afforded of the burdens of war, the ravages of diseases, the horrors of famine, terrible earthquakes, extraordinary floods, dreadful eruptions of fire, thunderbolts and hailstorms, and also instances of the cruel miseries caused by murders and crimes against man's better self." [9] Orosius proved himself indeed "the true compiler of the evils of the world," as Petrarch (*Familiares*, 15, 9, 10) was to characterize him scornfully many centuries later. But in spite, or perhaps because, of their admitted prejudices and their preconceived ideas, Augustine's and Orosius's systematic expositions of the old apologist conceptions of world history in general and of Roman history in particular were to determine the historical outlook of most western writers to the time of the Italian Renaissance.

However, that traditional apology fills only one section in the first part of *The City of God*.[10] In the second half of the work (books XI to XXII) Augustine wanted to offer much more than a mere defense, as he stated himself in his *Retractations* (2, 68, 2): "In order that no one might raise the charge against me that I have merely refuted the opinions of other men but not stated my own, I devoted to this objective the second part of the work."

Of the vast number of ideas which Augustine set forth as his "own opinions," only one problem will be discussed here, that of "History": how does history take its course and is there any meaning to be found in the sequence of events from the beginning of this world to the present age and to the day of the Last Judgment?[11]

How deeply Augustine was concerned with the question of the

[9] Quoted from J. W. Woodworth's translation of Orosius's *Seven Books* (1936), 1.

[10] The second section of the first part of the work, which consists of books VI to X, can be passed over in this article because Augustine did not deal in it with historical problems but set out to disprove the assertions of those philosophers who "maintain that polytheistic worship is advantageous for the life to come" (*Retractations*, 2, 68, 1).

[11] See the comprehensive analysis of the main body of ideas of Augustine's main work, which has been recently presented by W. J. Oates in his introduction to *Basic Writings of St. Augustine* (1948), I, ix–xl; and by E. Gilson in his introduction to D. B. Zema's and G. G. Walsh's translation of *The City of God* (1950), I, pp. XI–XCVIII.—Of the vast literature dealing with Augustine's historical ideas, I can list only some of the most recent treatments: R. J. Defferari and M. Keeler, "St. Augustine's City of God: its plan and development," *American Journal of Philology* (1929), L, 109–37; U. A. Padovano, "La Città di Dio: teologia e non filosofia della storia," *Rivista di Filosofia Neo-scolastica* (1931), supplem. vol. to vol. XXIII, 220–63; H. I. Marrou, *S. Augustin et la fin de la culture antique* (1938; see esp. 131–35, 417–19, 461–67); H. Fuchs, *Der geistige Widerstand gegen Rom in der antiken Welt* (1938); C. N. Cochrane, *Christianity and classical culture; a study of thought and action from Augustus to Augustine* (1944; esp. 397–516); W. M. Green, "Augustine on the teaching of history," *University of California Publications in Classical Philology* (1944), XII, 315–32; K. Löwith, *Meaning in History* (1949), 160–73.

philosophical or rather, from his point of view, the theological interpretation of the meaning and course of history, is shown by those chapters of *The City of God* in which he discussed the problems of the origin of the world and the uniqueness of its creation. He rejected the view that this world is eternal and without beginnings, and he stated that it was definitely created in time and will come to an end in another definite moment in time, a moment known to God alone. In connection with his discussion of " this controversy about the beginnings of things temporal" (12, 13 E) Augustine wrote (12, 14 A): " The philosophers of this world believed that they could or should not solve that controversy in any other way than by introducing cycles of time, in which they asserted that the revolving of coming and passing ages would always be renewed and repeated in the nature of things and would thus go on without cessation." In this sentence Augustine was obviously referring to the cyclical theory of history held by Platonists, Stoics and other Greek schools of philosophy.[12] But although he mentioned no name, it becomes evident from the context of the passage just quoted that he knew that this cyclical view was also maintained by Origen, who attempted to support it in a somewhat qualified fashion through quotations from the Scriptures, for instance the famous sentence in *Ecclesiastes* (1, 9): " There is no new thing under the sun." In his Latin translation of Origen's text Rufinus considerably modified these views, but this did not prevent Jerome from attacking them sharply. Augustine was even more emphatic in his refutation when he exclaimed in *The City of God* (12, 14 E): " Far be it from the right faith to believe that by these words of Solomon [*i.e., Ecclesiastes*] those cycles are meant in which [according to these philosophers] the revolving of the same periods and things is repeated." He found it logical that those thinkers " erroneously wandering around in cycles, find neither entrance nor exit," for he was convinced that " they do not know how the human race and this mortal condition of ours took its origin nor how it will be brought to an end " (12, 15 A). Those " false cycles which were discovered by false and deceitful sages," he believed, " can be avoided in the sound doctrine, through the path of the straight road (*tramite recti itineris*)."[13]

[12] Cf. K. Löwith, *l.c.*, 162–65, 248 n. 15; J. Baillie, *The Belief in Progress* (1951), 42–57.

[13] *City of God*, 12, 14 B.—C. N. Cochrane, *l.c.*, 245, stated that " we find Origen, for instance, protesting vigorously against the Platonic theory of cycles " But

To Augustine, then, history takes its course, not in cycles, but along a line. That line has a most definite beginning, the Creation, and a most definite end, the Last Judgment. Within this definite period of time the greatest single event was, of course, the appearance of Christ. "For," Augustine said (12, 14 F), "Once Christ died for our sins and 'raised from the dead dieth no more' (*Romans*, 6, 9); . . . and we ourselves, after the resurrection, 'shall ever be with the Lord' (*I Thessalon.*, 4, 17)." It seems that here Augustine was arguing again indirectly against Origen who, according to Jerome, "allowed himself to assert that Christ has often suffered and will often suffer, on the ground that what was beneficial once, will always be beneficial," and who also, "in his desire to confirm the most impious dogma of the Stoics through the authority of the Divine Scriptures, dared to write that man dies over and over again.[14]

From Augustine's conception of the course of history it follows that every particular event that takes place in time, every human life and human action, is a unique phenomenon which happens under the auspices of Divine Providence and must therefore have a definite meaning. The roots of this linear conception of history, as distinguished from the cyclical theories of the Greeks, went back to Hebrew ideas which had been further developed by the early Christian theologians.[15] But it was Augustine who elaborated those ideas most fully

---

Cochrane and, following him, R. Niebuhr, *Faith and History* (1949), 65, based their assertion exclusively on one passage in Origen's writings (*Against Celsus*, 4, 68) and neglected the much more detailed treatment of this problem in Origen's book *On first principles*, 2, 3, 1-5; 3, 5, 3; 4, 13. P. Koetschau, in his edition of Rufinus's translation and of the Greek fragments of *On first principles* (*Origenes Werke* [1913], V, 113f., 120), commented on Rufinus's modifications of the original text and printed the relevant remarks made by Jerome on Origen's belief in a series of many worlds: see the English translation of Koetschau's edition by G. W. Butterworth, *Origen, On first principles* (1935), 83-89, 238f.; J. Baillie, *l.c.*, 74ff., seems to overlook, too, the fact that Origen shared the cyclical theory, although in a modified form.

[14] See Butterworth, *l.c.*, 88 n. 4 (Jerome, *Apology*, 1, 20) and 83 n. 1 (Jerome, *Epist.*, 96, 9).

[15] On the Hebrew conceptions, see H. Butterfield, *Christianity and History* (1950), esp. 1-4, 57-62, 68-88; on the Christian views, see O. Cullmann, *Christus und die Zeit; die urchristliche Zeit- und Geschichtsauffassung* (1946); R. G. Collingwood, *The Idea of History* (1946), 46-52; J. Baillie, *l.c.*, 57-87; Th. Preiss, "The vision of history in the New Testament," *Papers of the Ecumenical Institute* (1950), V, 48-66; J. Daniélou, "The conception of history in the Christian tradition," *ibid.*, 67-79.

and consistently and thus determined the theology of history which prevailed throughout the Middle Ages and was to influence the philosophies of history of modern times.

When Augustine decided to combat the cyclical theories, he was probably motivated, as we have seen, by his knowledge that this pagan view was shared, to a certain extent at least, by a prominent, though suspect and even heretical, Christian thinker, Origen. But it appears that there existed still another philosophy of history at that time, which from Augustine's point of view was even more dangerous than the cyclical theory because it was very widespread among the Christians of his own as well as previous generations. To Augustine the truly problematic and the most objectionable theory of history must have been a conception which may be called " the Christian idea of progress."

When in 1920 J. B. Bury published his book on *The Idea of Progress,* he wrote (20f.) that " the idea of the universe which prevailed throughout the Middle Ages and the general orientation of men's thoughts were incompatible with some of the fundamental assumptions which are required by the idea of progress." But more recently, a number of scholars have pointed out that, to a certain degree, such an idea can actually be found among some of the early Christian thinkers.[16] A systematic treatment of this complex topic does not yet exist and it cannot be given in a brief essay. But in the following an attempt will be made at least to set forth some examples from early Christian writings, which may serve to illustrate the nature of that idea.

One might be inclined to find the first instance of the conception of progress in that part of Christian literature which dealt with the question of the Millennium. For some of the early theologians, including Justin, Irenaeus and Lactantius, interpreted the apocalyptic prediction of Christ's future reign of one thousand years in terms of a very material bliss. But this peculiar notion cannot be truly said to express a belief in " progress," because the Messianic kingdom of the future was not to come into existence through a gradual or evolutionary process but rather through the dramatically sudden second coming of Christ. Moreover, even before Augustine's time thinkers like Origen and Tychonius had successfully discredited that very

[16] See, *e.g.,* E. K. Rand, *Founders of the Middle Ages* (1929), 13–22, 291; Rand, *The Building of Eternal Rome* (1943), 72, 189ff.; C. N. Cochrane, *l.c.,* 242–47, 483f.; K. Löwith, *l.c.,* 60f., 84, 112f., 182ff.; J. Baillie, *l.c.,* 19–22, 94–96.

materialistic notion of the Millennium and had interpreted the conception in a primarily spiritual sense.[17] This became Augustine's own opinion also, because in the writings of the later period of his life, which dealt with eschatological speculations, he made it very clear that the question of the Millennium has nothing to do with any kind of earthly prosperity but has reference only to the necessarily imperfect realization of the divine in this world.

But apart from these speculations concerning the Millennium we find that some of the most prominent Christian apologists voiced views which implied the belief that under the auspices of Christianity the world had made concrete progress in historical time and that further progress could be expected. Those writers asserted that the new creed was bringing blessings to the whole of mankind, not merely to its own adherents. They pointed to the historically undeniable fact that the birth of Christ had taken place at the time of the foundation of the Roman empire by Augustus and the establishment of the *Pax Romana* on earth. As the appearance of Christ coincided with a marked improvement of all things secular, so, the early apologists argued, the growth of the new faith will be accompanied by further progress.[18]

The first testimony to this conception is to be found in the *Apology* which Bishop Melito of Sardis addressed to Emperor Antoninus Pius in the middle of the second century. According to Eusebius' *Ecclesiastical History* (4, 26, 7-8), Melito wrote: " Our philosophy [*i.e.*, Christianity] flourished first among the barbarians; then, during the great reign of your ancestor Augustus, it spread among your people and, above all, it has become to your own reign an auspicious blessing. For from that time the power of Rome has grown in greatness and splendor. To this power you have succeeded as the desired heir and you will continue it with your sons if you safeguard that philosophy which grew up with the empire and took its start under Augustus.... The best evidence that our doctrine has been flourishing for the good

[17] On the ideas concerning the Millennium, see, *e.g.*, E. Bernheim, *Mittelalterliche Zeitanschauungen in ihrem Einfluss auf Politik und Geschichtschreibung* (1918), esp. 63-109; A. Wikenhauser, " Das Problem des tausendjährigen Reiches in der Johannes-Apokalypse," *Römische Quartalschrift* (1932), XL, 13-36; Wikenhauser, " Die Herkunft der Idee des tausendjährigen Reiches in der Johannes-Apokalypse," *ibid.* (1937), XLV, 1-24; J. Baillie, *l.c.*, 60-64, 79-83.

[18] On the discussion of these arguments, see also E. Peterson, *Der Monotheismus als politisches Problem* (1935), 66-88; J. Geffcken, *Zwei griechische Apologeten* (1907), esp. 63, 92.

of an empire happily started in this: since the reign of Augustus no misfortune has befallen it; on the contrary, all things have been splendid and glorious, in accordance with the wishes of all."

Around the year 200, Tertullian expressed the same idea, though somewhat more cautiously. He wrote in his *Apology* (ch. 40, 13): "And for all that is said, if we compare the calamities of former times [with those of our own era], we find that they fall on us more lightly now, since the earth has received from God the believers of the Christian faith. For since that time innocence has put restraint on the wickedness of this world and men have begun to plead with God for the averting of His wrath."

These two apologists, then, did not merely content themselves with rejecting the pagan accusation that Christianity was responsible for the misfortunes of the era; on the contrary, they dared to take the offensive and claimed that their faith was making a positive contribution to the well-being of the Roman empire.

From this assertion there was but a single step to the expression of the belief that the universal acceptance of the Christian religion by the Roman world would lead to a still greater degree of security and prosperity. The pagan Celsus, in the middle of the third century, raised the question as to the consequences of such an event. Origen replied to Celsus' question with utmost confidence (*Against Celsus*, 4, 69): "If all the Romans were to pray together in full harmony, then they would be able to put to flight many more enemies than those who were discomfitted by the prayers of Moses when he cried to the Lord." Fifty years after Origen, around the year 300, Arnobius expressed the same belief in his treatise *Against the Pagans* (1, 6): "If all without exception, who consider themselves men, not in form of body, but in power of reason, were willing to lend, for a little while, an ear to [Christ's] salutary and peaceful prescriptions and were not, swollen with pride and arrogance, to trust to their own senses rather than to His admonitions, then the whole world, having turned the use of iron into more peaceful occupations, would live in the most placid tranquillity and would unite in blessed harmony, maintaining inviolate the sanctity of treaties."

This conviction that the appearance of Christ has led to a general improvement of the material conditions of the world and that its universal acceptance will lead to a still greater progress, was set forth by Melito and Tertullian, by Origen and Arnobius, during a period when their faith was suppressed by the official authorities of the Roman state. When, in the reign of Constantine, the great turning-point arrived and Christianity was not only tolerated but became the religion most favored by the emperor, it was natural that hope for progress rose still higher. Thus even Lactantius, once the champion of eschatological ideas in their most extreme and pessimistic form, dared to express rather optimistic expectations at the very end of his book *On the Death of the Persecutors* (ch. 52): "The Lord has destroyed and erased from the earth those proud names [of the anti-Christian rulers]. Let us therefore celebrate the triumph of God with joy. Let us frequently praise the victory of the Lord. Day and night let us offer our prayers to the Lord that He may establish for all time the peace which has been given to His people after [a warfare of] ten years."

Constantine showed himself most eager to adopt the idea that the worship of the true and omnipotent God was bound to benefit his empire in a material sense. In a letter written shortly after his decisive victory at the Milvian Bridge in the year 312, he declared (Eusebius, *Eccles. Hist.*, 10, 7, 1): "From many facts it appears . . . that the lawful recognition and observance [of the Christian faith] has bestowed the greatest success on the Roman name and singular prosperity on all affairs of mankind, blessings which were provided by the divine beneficence." Constantine's highly materialistic conception of his relationship with the Christian God was very much in accordance with the religious notions of the ancient Romans.[19] It was the old principle of *do ut des:* "I give that you may give." The emperor argued: I, Constantine, do something for you, God, so that you may do something for me; likewise, of course, God himself was assumed to expect gifts in return from those to whom he had extended favors. This idea of a commutative contract between God and man found reflection in the politico-ecclesiastical writings of quite a few of the Christian authors of the fourth century, beginning with Constantine's court-bishop, Eusebius of Caesarea. It was a complete ideological reversal: once the pagans had charged that the worship of the Christian God was the source of all the calamities of the empire; now, Constantine had the symbol of the cross displayed in the principal room of his new imperial palace in Constantinople; according to Eusebius' *Life of Constantine* (3, 49), "this symbol seemed to the

---

[19] On this point, see H. Berkhof, *Kirche und Kaiser; eine Untersuchung der Entstehung der byzantinischen und theokratischen Staatsauffassung im 4. Jahrhundert* (1947), esp. 14–18, 31–34, 55–59, 66, 70.

beloved of God [Constantine] to have been made as a safeguard of the empire itself."

The principle of *do ut des* was most emphatically rejected by Augustine, for it was wholly contrary to his conception of the relationship between God and man, even the great of this world.[20] Thus he stated in *The City of God* (4, 33) that in God's eyes earthly power and all similar things temporal are not important gifts and that therefore God "bestows them on both the good and the bad." In discussing the question of the *imperator felix*, Augustine admitted (*City of God*, 5, 25 A) that God "gave to the emperor Constantine, who was not a worshipper of demons but of the true God Himself, such fulness of earthly gifts as no one would even dare to wish for." But Augustine continued: "Lest, however, any emperor shall become a Christian in order to merit the blessed felicity of Constantine—when everyone ought to be a Christian for the sake of the eternal life—God took away [the Christian prince] Jovian far sooner than [his pagan brother, the emperor] Julian, and He allowed [the Christian emperor] Gratian to be slain by the sword of a tyrant."

These sentences in *The City of God* sound as if they were written expressly against Eusebius, who had declared in his *Life of Constantine* (1, 3, 3), with specific reference to the emperor: "God, that God who is the common Saviour of all, has treasured up with Himself, for those who love religion, far greater blessings than man can conceive, and He gives even here and now the first-fruits as a pledge of future rewards, thus assuring in some sort immortal hopes to mortal eyes."

Eusebius based his belief in the effectiveness of the principle of *do ut des* on a very definite interpretation and philosophy of history.[21] He emphasized (*Demonstratio Evangelica*, 3, 7, 139) even more strongly than Melito and other Christian thinkers during the previous centuries, that "it was not through human merit that at no other time but only since the time of Christ most of the nations were under the single rule of the Romans; for the period of His wonderful sojourn among men coincided with the period when the Romans reached their summit under Augustus, who was then the first monarch to rule over most of the nations."[22] This concurrence of the appearance of

[20] Cf. Berkhof, *l.c.*, 205–209.
[21] Cf. H. Berkhof, *Die Theologie des Eusebius von Caesarea* (1939), 45–50, 55f., 58f.; E. Peterson, *l.c.*, 66ff.
[22] See the similar passages in Eusebius' *Theophania*, 3, 2; *Praeparatio Evangelica*, 5, 1.

Christ on earth and the founding of the universal empire by Augustus "was not by mere human accident" but it was "of God's arrangement." Whereas the earlier interpreters of that concurrence had stated it simply as a historical fact, Eusebius believed himself capable of adducing proof from the Scriptures that those events were long before predicted by God. Thus he quoted in all the works in which he discussed the "synchronising" of the birth of Christ with the reign of Augustus, the following passages from the Old Testament: "In His days the righteous shall flourish and abundance of peace" (*Psalm* 72, 7); "He shall have dominion also from sea to sea, and from the river unto the ends of the earth" (*Psalm* 72, 8); "And they shall beat their swords into plowshares, and their spears into pruninghooks: nation shall not lift up sword against nation, neither shall they learn war any more" (*Isaiah*, 2, 4).

These quotations are highly remarkable. For according to tradition these prophecies were to be understood as predictions of the future Messianic Kingdom, as we can learn from their interpretation by men like Irenaeus (*Against Heresies*, 4, 56, 3), Tertullian (*Against Marcion*, 3, 21) and Lactantius (*Divine Institutions*, 4, 16, 14). It seems that previous to Eusebius only Origen (*Against Celsus*, 2, 30) had ventured to refer the passage in *Psalm* 72, 7 to the *Pax Romana*.[23] But the full elaboration of Origen's suggestion was left to Eusebius, who gave the most bluntly secular interpretations to these scriptural texts. Witness the passage in Eusebius' *Praeparatio Evangelica* (1, 4): "In accordance with these predictions [*i.e.*, of *Psalm* 72 and of *Isaiah*, 2, 4], the actual events followed. Immediately after Augustus had established his sole rule, at the time of our Saviour's appearance, the rule by the many became abolished among the Romans. And from that time to the present you cannot see, as before, cities at war with cities, nor nation fighting with nation, nor life being worn away in the confusion of everything." Eusebius saw a close parallel between the victory of Christian monotheism and the growth of the Roman monarchy. Thus he stated in his *Theophania* (3, 2):[24] "Two great powers sprang up fully as out of one stream and they gave peace to all and brought all together to a state of friendship: the Roman

---

[23] It may be noted that Origen interpreted the passage in *Isaiah*, 2, 4 in an entirely spiritual sense; see *Against Celsus*, 5, 33; *Against Heresies*, 6, 16.

[24] Translated from the Syriac by S. Lee, *Eusebius on the Theophania* (1853), 156f.; cf. the very similar passage in Eusebius' *Praise of Constantine*, 16, 4–5.

empire, which from that time appeared as one kingdom, and the power of the Saviour of all, whose aid was at once extended to and established with everyone. For the divine superiority of our Saviour swept away the authority of the many demons and gods, so that the one Kingdom of God was preached to all men, Greeks and barbarians, and to those who resided in the extremities of the earth. The Roman empire, too—since those had been previously uprooted who had been the cause of the rule by many—soon subjugated all others and quickly brought together the whole race of man into one state of accordance and agreement."

To Eusebius the greatest gains made by mankind since the days of Christ and Augustus were the abolition of wars, foreign and civil, and the establishment of peace and security, the time-hallowed ideals of the *Pax Romana*. But he saw also other improvements. For instance, he declared in his *Praeparatio Evangelica* (1, 4): " Of the benefits resulting from God's doctrines which have become manifest on earth, you may see a clear proof if you consider that at no other time from the beginning until now, and not through the merits of any of the illustrious men of old but only through Christ's utterances and teachings, diffused throughout the whole world, the customs of all nations have been set aright, even those customs which before were savage and barbarous." Because of the strict discipline of the new faith men have learned to lead a moral life, to refrain from hostility toward others and to master their own emotions and passions. Eusebius concluded his enumeration of all the improvements made in the political, legal and moral spheres by asking: " How, then, can anyone . . . refuse to admit that our doctrine has brought to all men good tidings of very great and true blessings, and has supplied to human life that which is of immediate advantage toward happiness? "

There was no doubt in Eusebius' mind that mankind, under divine guidance, had made progress from the pre-Christian era through the three centuries of the gradual ascent of the new Church to the reign of Constantine in which he himself lived. He declared in his *Praise of Constantine* (16, 8): " As those predictions concerning our Saviour [*i.e., Psalm* 72, 7–8, and *Isaiah*, 2, 4] were foretold and delivered in the Hebrew tongue many ages before, so in our own times they have become really fulfilled and the ancient testimonies of the prophets clearly confirmed." Great as the advances made by mankind were, still further progress was expected by Eusebius. For he asserted (*ibid.*, 6): " Although the object of the Roman empire to unite all nations in one harmonious whole has already been secured to a large degree, it is destined to be still more perfectly attained, even to the final conquest of the ends of the habitable world, by means of the salutary doctrine and through the aid of that Divine Providence which facilitates and smooths the way [of the Empire]."

In his recent essay on *The Idea of Progress,* G. H. Hildebrand stated [25] that this idea includes three principles: "First, the belief that history follows a continuous, necessary, and orderly course; second, the belief that this course is the effect of a regularly operating causal law; and third, the belief that the course of change has brought and will continue to bring improvement in the condition of mankind." The first two of these principles were always implied in the Christian belief that every single event and consequently also the course of historical events as a whole take place under God's will and in accordance with the plan of Divine Providence. But it remained for Eusebius to add the third principle, the optimistic belief in continuous improvement, and thus to develop a full-fledged Christian idea of progress.

Eusebius' idea was taken up by some of the most prominent theologians of the fourth and early fifth centuries, both in the eastern and the western parts of the Church.[26] This is shown by the interpretations which John Chrysostom, Ambrose, Jerome, Cyril of Alexandria and Theodoret of Cyprus gave in their various commentaries on *Psalm 72* and *Isaiah* (2, 4), and we may add, on the passage in *Psalm 46* (v. 9), which reads: "He maketh wars to cease unto the end of the earth." Like Eusebius all the writers just mentioned explained these passages in terms of the *Pax Romana* and its earthly achievements, and it seems that of the great theologians of the fourth century only Athanasius and Basil expounded them in a strictly spiritual sense.

When Augustine wrote his *Enarrations on the Psalms,* he replaced the explanations of the above passages with interpretations wholly different and entirely his own. For instance, Origen, Eusebius, John Chrysostom and Ambrose had declared that the words of *Psalm 46:* "He maketh wars to end," had been realized in the reign of Augustus; Basil alone had explained that passage in exclusively religious terms. But whereas Basil had contented himself with simply setting forth his personal exposition, Augustine accompanied the commentary which

[25] *The Idea of Progress; a Collection of Readings;* selected by F. J. Teggart; revised edition with an introduction by G. H. Hildebrand, 4.

[26] Cf. E. Peterson, *l.c.*, 71–88.

he wrote in 412, two years after the fall of Rome, with a polemic directed against the interpretation given by so many of his famous predecessors.[27] For although he did not mention any name, there seems to be no doubt that he was taking issue with the current view when he denied categorically that the prediction of a reign of peace had been fulfilled in any material or historical sense: " There are still wars, wars among nations for supremacy, wars among sects, wars among Jews, pagans, Christians, heretics, and these wars are becoming more frequent" (*Enarration on Psalm 45, 13* = 46, 9). In Augustine's opinion, external peace was not yet achieved and, in fact, it would not even matter if it actually had. Only that peace matters which, through divine grace, man finds in himself, by his complete submission to the will of God. " When man learns that in himself he is nothing and that he has no help from himself," Augustine said, " then arms in himself are broken in pieces, then wars in himself are ended. Such wars, then, destroyed that voice of the Most High out of His holy clouds whereby the earth was shaken and the kingdoms were bowed; these wars He has taken away unto the ends of the earth."

In his *Enarration on Psalm 71, 10* (= 72, 7), Augustine commented on the passage: " In His days righteousness (*iustitia*) shall arise and abundance of peace until the moon be exalted."[28] These words, Augustine declared, " ought to be understood as if it were said: there shall arise in His days righteousness to conquer the contradiction and the rebellion of the flesh, and there shall be made a peace so abundant and increasing ' until the moon be exalted,' that is until the Church be lifted up, through the glory of the resurrection to reign with Him." Righteousness and peace in the words of the psalmist ought not to be confused, then, with the notions of *iustitia* and *pax* of the earthly state. Those highest Christian ideals have not yet been nor will they ever be embodied in the secular organization of the Roman empire, but they will be realized in the spiritual community of the eternal Church. The theologically untenable identification of the Messianic ideal with the historical reality of the *Imperium Romanum* could not have been rejected more radically than was done by Augustine in his commentary.

[27] Cf. E. Peterson, *l.c.*, 97f.; as to the date of *Enarration on Psalm 45*, cf. S. M. Zarb, " Chronologia enarrationum S. Augustini in Psalmos," in *Angelicum* (1947), XXIV, 275–83.

[28] The above translation of *Psalm* 72 is based on the text of the *Itala* used by Augustine.—This *Enarration* was written between 415 and 416; see S. M. Zarb, *op. cit.*, *Angelicum* (1935), XII, 77–81.

Augustine was fully aware of the fact that in his exegetical works he was frequently deviating from his predecessors on essential points. No less a man than Jerome had told him so very bluntly in two letters written in the year 404 (*Epist.* 105 and 112), that is, long before Augustine wrote his *Enarrations on Psalms 45 and 71*. It is interesting to note that Jerome specifically referred to Augustine's " little commentaries on some of the Psalms, which, if I were disposed to criticise them," Jerome said (*Epist.* 105, 2), " I could prove to be at variance, I shall not say with my own opinion, for ' I am nothing ' (*I Corinth.*, 13, 2), but with the interpretations of the older Greek commentators." [29] In his reply Augustine stated in unmistakable terms (*Epist.* 82, 3) that he felt justified in deviating from views held by previous commentators in any instance in which he considered himself to be in full accordance with the Scriptures; for he declared that " of only those books of the Scriptures, which are now called canonical, do I most firmly believe that their authors have made no error in their writing." He continued: " But the others I read in such a way that, however outstanding the authors are in sanctity and learning, I do not accept their teaching as true on the mere ground of the opinion held by them, but only because they have succeeded in convincing my judgment of its truth either by means of those canonical writings themselves or by arguments addressed to my reason." The definite nature of this statement entitles us to ascribe great significance to the fact that Augustine interpreted the Messianic predicions of the Old Testament in a fashion so fundamentally different from that of some of the most renowned earlier theologians, both Greek and Latin, who had found in those passages the promise of material well-being and progress to be achieved by man on earth and in the course of history.

Augustine's rejection of these conceptions appears even more noteworthy when we remember that it was during his own lifetime that the Christian idea of progress as developed by Eusebius became the crucial issue in a basic controversy. This was the famous affair of the Altar of Victory in Rome, the great conflict, the last one in history, between pagan traditionalism and Christian progressivism.[30] That

[29] We do not know to which of Augustine's "little commentaries" Jerome referred; Augustine started writing his *Enarrations* in the last decade of the fourth century; cf. Zarb, *op. cit.*

[30] On this affair, see esp. J. R. Palanque, *S. Ambroise et l'empire Romain* (1933), 131-36, 221f., 278f., 307, 358-64, 510, 536; J. Wytzes, *Der Streit um den*

incident, with its later repercussions, forms the immediate background of the composition of *The City of God.*

Ever since the days of the Republic the statue of Victory had stood in the building of the Roman Senate, and the meetings of the Senate used to be opened with the burning of incense at the altar of the goddess. In the mid-fourth century emperor Constantius ordered the removal of the statue, but Julian the Apostate had it restored to its old place. It was taken away once again in the year 382. The pagan members of the Roman Senate were naturally very much disturbed, and in the year 384 the most highly respected member of that group, Symmachus, submitted an impressive plea to the reigning emperors for the restoration of the Altar of Victory. Symmachus argued on the basis of the principle of *do ut des,* but he used the principle, of course, according to the pagan mode of thought. The ancient deities, he declared, have raised Rome to her great position, and for that reason Rome owes them gratitude (Symmachus' *Relatio,* §§ 3 and 8). Symmachus let the personification of Rome address herself to the emperors (§ 9): "Excellent princes, fathers of the country, respect my years to which pious rites have brought me. Let me use the ancestral ceremonies, for I do not repent of them. Let me live after my fashion, for I am free. This worship has subdued the world to my laws, these sacred rites repelled Hannibal from my walls and the Gauls from the Capitol." In the same spirit Symmachus sounded an emphatic warning (§ 4): "We are cautious as to what may happen in the future, and we shun portentous actions."

The leading Christian figure of that time, Bishop Ambrose of Milan took it upon himself to reply to the plea made by the great pagan statesman. In his refutation of Symmachus' assertion that Rome rose to power through the favor of the pagan gods, Ambrose employed, of course, the old arguments of the Christian apologists. But he went farther. He, too, let Rome speak for herself (*Epist.* 18, 7). But whereas Symmachus' *Roma* had pleaded for the preservation of the time-honored traditions of the past, Ambrose's *Roma* appealed to the idea of progress. "It is no disgrace," she declared, "to pass on to better things." And in answer to Symmachus' traditionalist argument that "the rites of our ancestors ought to be retained," Ambrose asked (§ 23): "Why should we do so? Has not everything

---

Altar der Viktoria (1936); L. Malunowicz, *De ara victoriae in curia Romana quomodo certatum sit* (1937); M. Lavarenne in his edition of the works of *Prudence* (1948), III, 85–90.

made advances in the course of time toward what is better?" In both the memoranda which he addressed to the then reigning emperors, Ambrose made it clear that he shared the current belief that Christianity was a progressive factor in history. It may be remarked in passing that Ambrose, like Eusebius and Symmachus, believed that the relationship between God and man is largely determined by the principle of merit and reward. For instance, in his treatise *On Faith* (2, 16), Ambrose did not hesitate to find the explanation for the defeat of the emperor Valens in the battle of Adrianople in 378 in the fact that Valens was an Arian heretic: on the other hand he predicted with full confidence the victory of the emperor Gratian over the Visigoths because the new ruler confessed the orthodox faith.[31]

In the year 384, the question of the Altar of Victory was settled in accordance with Ambrose's wishes, but during the next two decades the pagan faction of the Roman Senate continued to work, with varying success, for the restoration of the statue. Thus around the year 403, the poet Prudentius decided to present once more the Christian point of view in regard to that problem.[32] His poem entitled *Against Symmachus* was the greatest poetical expression the Christian idea of progress ever found in early western Christendom. According to Prudentius, God had assigned to the Romans the task of conquering the world and establishing a universal empire so as to pave the way for the spread of the universal religion. The mission of the Roman empire was to become finally the Christian empire. That great turn took place under Constantine who, in Prudentius' words (1, 539f.), "accustomed Romulus' state to be powerful for ever in a dominion derived from above." In his description of the universal and eternal Christian empire as it was established by Constantine, Prudentius used phrases (1, 541–43) which are almost identical with those which Vergil once had made Jupiter say: "[Constantine] did not set any boundaries nor did he fix limits of time; he taught an imperial power without end so that the Roman valor should no longer be senile nor the glory which Rome had won should ever know old age." This Christian Rome, Prudentius said (1, 587–90), which "has dedicated herself to Thee, O Christ, and has passed under Thy laws, and is willing now, with all her people and her greatest citizens, to extend her earthly rule beyond the lofty stars of the great heavens." Pru-

[31] Cf. H. Berkhof, *Kirche und Kaiser*, 90–94, 173–82.

[32] On the Date of Prudentius' *Contra Symmachum*, cf. L. Malunowicz, *l.c.*, 99f.; M. Lavarenne, *l.c.*, III, 89f.

dentius recalled Symmachus' assertion that it was only because of the help of the ancient gods that neither the Gauls nor Hannibal had succeeded in completely overwhelming Rome. He let his personification of the Christian *Roma* reply as follows (2, 690–95): " Whosoever tries to impress me again with the memories of past defeats and ancient calamities, he ought to see that in this age of yours [*i.e.,* that of the Christian emperors] I no longer suffer anything of that sort. No barbaric enemy shatters my walls with a javelin and no man with strange weapons, attire and hairdress wanders around the city he has conquered and carries off my young men into transalpine prisons."

These lines were written around the year 403. In 410 Rome fell to Alaric and Visigothic " strangers wandered around the city they had conquered." Under these circumstances many contemporaries, pagan as well as Christian, must have remembered the sombre warnings of Symmachus, which had been so recently discussed again and so optimistically rejected by Prudentius. In the year 410 Alaric had achieved that complete conquest of Rome which hundreds of years before Hannibal had failed to accomplish, and the long-dreaded " fall of Rome " had taken place almost immediately after a Christian poet had assured his listeners that it could not happen now and never would.

The reactions of the pagan and Christian contemporaries were profound and radical, as we learn from the *Sermon on the Fall of the City*, which Augustine preached shortly after the event.[33] The pagans said to the Christians (§ 9): " As long as we brought sacrifices to our Gods, Rome stood; now when the sacrifice to your God is triumphant and abounds and the sacrifices to our gods are prevented and forbidden, see what Rome is suffering." And the Christians, according to Augustine's sermon (§ 6), were shocked and bewildered by the fact that in spite of the many holy places in the city, in spite of the tombs of St. Peter and St. Paul and many other martyrs, " Rome is miserable and devastated, Rome is afflicted, laid waste and burnt." Augustine was naturally much more concerned about the reactions of the Christians than about those of the pagans. For in the aftermath of the year 410 it had become evident that Christianity included within its ranks many people who had been won over to the new faith simply because of its external triumph. To them Christianity meant primarily the belief in the effectiveness of the principle of *do ut des,*

[33] The Latin text of Sermon 296 has recently been re-edited by G. Morin, in *Miscellanea Agostiniana* (1930), I, 401–19.

which had been taught by Eusebius and his followers. Such a faith, based as it was on essentially materialistic foundations, and such a shallow optimism was of necessity badly shaken by the turn of events. How deeply conscious Augustine was of the problem presented by those worldly-minded Christians is revealed by another sermon which he preached after the fall of Rome. In bitter words he condemned (*Sermon* 105, 13) " those blasphemers who chase and long after things earthly and place their hopes in things earthly. When they have lost them, whether they will or not, what shall they hold and where shall they abide? Nothing within, nothing without; an empty coffer, an emptier conscience."

This was the situation, from the ideological point of view a very critical situation, which motivated Augustine to write *The City of God*. He realized that one single event, the " fall of Rome," had an impact upon the thinking and the feeling of his contemporaries which went far beyond its material importance. The significance attributed to the event resulted from the central position which the destiny and fate of " eternal " Rome occupied in the existing conceptions of history, whether they were pagan or Christian. If Augustine, then, wanted to combat in a truly fundamental fashion the interpretations of that " fall of Rome," he could do so only by setting forth his own ideas concerning the course and the meaning of history. Therefore he was willing to devote thirteen years of his life to the most comprehensive study of the problem of history, a problem which up to the year 410 had been of merely incidental interest to him.

In attempting to solve that problem, Augustine found, as we have seen, that he had to reject practically all the current conceptions of history. He did not share the sentiments of those among the early Christian writers to whom any concern about history was superfluous in view of the presumably imminent end of this world, and he had no interest in eschatological speculations and calculations regarding the future millennium. Neither could he, of course, accept the cyclical theory as it was held by some of the pagan schools of philosophy and, in a modified form, by Origen. And he saw most clearly how perilous it was for the Christian faith to proclaim, as Eusebius and others had done during the fourth century, a belief in " progress," if that notion was understood in any kind of materialistic sense. For under the existing circumstances it was inevitable that " most of the pagans," as Augustine said in his *Enarration on Psalm 136, 9*, asked the question: " Is it not true that since the coming of Christ the state of human affairs has been worse than it was before and that human affairs were once much more fortunate than they are now?"[34] Every emphasis on the idea of secular progress was bound to lay the Christian cause wide open to attacks by the pagans and to the disillusionment of the half-hearted Christians. Both groups could rightly find that all promises of worldly success were totally disproved by the catastrophe of the year 410—and there might be more and worse disasters to come.

In contradistinction to all these conceptions Augustine's own views concerning history represent a basic reiteration and systematic elaboration of Hebrew and early Christian ideas.[35] To him history was the *operatio Dei* in time, it was "a one-directional, teleological process, directed towards one goal—salvation," the salvation of individual men, not of any collective groups or organizations.[36] Ever since the creation of the world there have existed two cities, the city of God or the community of those who "wish to live after the spirit," and the earthly city or the community of those who "wish to live after the flesh" (*City of God*, 14, 1 C). Of the twelve books of the second part of *The City of God*, eight books deal with the origin (*exortus*) and the end (*finis*) of those two cities, that is with the Creation and the Last Judgment. Only the middle section (books XV to XVIII) deals with that period of time which is commonly considered to be the historical era, and even within that section Augustine gave his main attention to those men and events which belonged to "the heavenly city which is a pilgrim on earth" (18, 54 K). The fact that only one book of *The City of God* (b. XVIII) treats historical developments proper, shows clearly that Augustine regarded the purely secular aspects of the drama of mankind as relatively insignificant.

The content of that middle section of *The City of God* comprising books XV to XVIII has been defined by Augustine as follows (15, 1 C): "It now seems right to me to approach the account of the course [of the two cities] from the time when those two [*i.e.*, Adam and Eve] began to propagate the race to the time when men shall cease to

[34] This *Enarration* was written between 410 and 413; see Zarb, *l.c.* (1939), XVI, 289f.

[35] See above, note 15.

[36] See K. Löwith, *l.c.*, 170f.; E. Frank, "The role of history in Christian thought," *The Duke Divinity School Bulletin* (1949), XIV, 74.

propagate. For this whole time or world-age, in which the dying give place and those who are born succeed, is the course of the two cities which are under discussion." Twice in the passage just quoted, and in two other passages (11, 1 C and 18, 54 K), Augustine used the word *excursus* to define the historical process which is taking place between the Creation and the Last Judgment.[37] In other passages of *The City of God,* and more frequently, he employed the words *procursus* and *procurrere* for the development within the same span of time.[38] What is the meaning of these words? When we look in the translations of *The City of God* by John Healey and by Marcus Dods, we find that they translated the noun *procursus* most frequently with " progress," but also with " history," " proceedings " and " advance," the verb *procurrere* with " run its course," " run on," " proceed " and " progress," and the word *excursus* with " progress," " progression," " career " or " course." In their recent translation of *The City of God,* Fathers Demetrius B. Zema and Gerald G. Walsh translated the word *procursus* with " progress " and *excursus* with " development." Do we have to assume, then, that Augustine believed that the course of the two cities on earth takes place in some form of evolutionary progress? Such an assumption appears highly improbable. For not only were the two words *procursus* and *excursus* used interchangeably throughout *The City of God* and in the description of this work in Augustine's *Retractations* (2, 69, 2),[39] but in a letter which was written shortly after the completion of *The City of God,* Augustine said explicitly that the section under discussion " sets forth the *procursus* or, as we have preferred to say, the *excursus* [of the heavenly city]."[40] In retrospect, then, Augustine himself considered the term *excursus* more adequate. To equate that word with " progress " seems very questionable, both from the linguistic point of view and in consideration of the modern connotation of this term.

The best key to the right understanding of this particular ter-

[37] Cf. *City of God,* 15, 9 D: *praeterit saeculi excursus.*

[38] *E.g., City of God,* 1, 35 B; 10, 32 U; 15, 1 D; 16, 12 A, 35 A and 43 I; 17, 1 A, 4 A and 14 A; 18, 1 A, B, C and 2 G.

[39] M. Dods, *The City of God* (1872), I, p. VIII, and, following him, G. H. Hildebrand, *The Idea of Progress* (1949), 110, translated the words *excursum earum siue procursum* in *Retractat.* 69, 2, with " their history or progress."

[40] The text of this newly found letter to Firmus has been published by C. Lambot in *Revue Bénédictine* (1939), LI, 212; the passage reads: *procursum siue dicere maluimus excursum;* it has been translated by Zema and Walsh, *l.c.,* I, 400, with " its progress or, as we might choose to say, its development."

minology seems to be provided by a passage in *The City of God* (15, 21 E), in which Augustine said: " The reckoning of the times [in the Scripture] begins after the two cities have been set forth, the one founded in the business of this world, the other in the hope for God, but both coming out from the common gate of mortality, which is opened in Adam, so that they might run on and run out (*procurrant et excurrant*) to their separate proper and merited ends." The history of the two cities, according to this passage, has the same starting-point, the fall of Adam; from that point they follow each its own course to the terminal point in time, the Last Judgment. Thus Augustine conceived of the historical process in the form of two tracks the courses of which have been laid out by God and are to be followed by the successive generations of the citizens of the two communities. In the terms of that figure of speech it was possible for Augustine to use the words " run on " and " run out " as synonyms and to say that the city of God on earth " proceeded in running out its course." [41]

With regard to the course of the heavenly city it may be said that there is a " progress," not of any materialistic nature, but in the sense that there is a gradual revelation of the divine truth communicated by God to man, especially through the prophecies predicting the future Messiah (see, *e.g.*, 18, 27).[42] Augustine declared (10, 14 A): " Like the correct knowledge of an individual man, the correct knowledge of that part of mankind which belongs to the people of God, has advanced by approaches through certain epochs of time or, as it were, ages, so that it might be lifted from the temporal to the perception of the eternal and from the visible to that of the invisible." In the spiritual realm, therefore, according to Augustine, mankind has grown up from the time of its infancy through the phases of childhood, adolescence, young manhood and mature manhood to its old age (*senectus*) which has begun with the birth of Christ. That growth of the spiritual enlightenment of the human race found its clearest expression in the scheme of " the six ages," to which Augustine alluded in the passage just quoted and into which he divided the

[41] *City of God*, XIX, 5 A: . . . *ista Dei civitas* . . . *progrederetur excursu*. . . .
[42] Cf. K. Löwith, *l.c.*, p. 172: " . . . there is only one progress: the advance toward an ever sharper distinction between faith and unbelief, Christ and Antichrist . . ."; according to J. Daniélou, *l.c.*, 70, it was Irenæus of Lyons who first saw that " the reason for this progression is of a pedagogical nature."

course of the heavenly city on earth.[43] The summit has been reached with the appearance and the gospel of Christ, and no further fundamental change will take place in the spiritual realm to the end of time.

In regard to the developments in the sphere of the earthly city, Augustine emphasized repeatedly in his historical survey the mutability and the instability of human affairs. Cities, kingdoms and empires have risen and fallen throughout the course of history, and this will always be the case. For, Augustine declared (17, 13 C) " because of the mutability of things human no security will ever be given to any nation to such a degree that it should not have to fear invasions inimical to its very existence." Augustine admitted that the Roman empire had achieved more than any other state, and he granted that the pagan Romans had possessed certain qualities which might be called virtues, though not in the full and true sense of the word. At the same time Augustine, like his pupil Orosius, maintained that for many centuries the Roman empire was involved in a process of moral disintegration, in a decline which had started long before the times of Christ and Augustus.[44]

Eusebius and the other Christian progressivists of the fourth century had strongly stressed the coincidence of the birth of Christ and the reign of Augustus, for they saw the counter-part of the religious summit in the erection of the " eternal " Roman empire and in the establishment of the " universal " *Pax Romana*. Whereas that observation occupied a central position in their conceptions of history, Augustine passed over it in a single sentence, by simply stating (18, 46 A): " While Herod reigned in Judaea and, after the change of the republican government, Caesar Augustus was emperor in Rome and pacified the world, Christ, man manifest out of a human virgin, God hidden out of God the Father, was born of Judah in Bethlehem." Whereas according to Eusebius and his followers the history of man had taken a fresh start at that time and had " progressed " toward a new culminating-point under Constantine, when the Roman empire reached the fulfillment of its mission by becoming Christian, Augustine stopped his historical account precisely with the appearance of

[43] See *City of God*, 15 C A; 16, 24 F and 43 G; 22, 30 O–P; the most detailed exposition of that scheme is to be found in Augustine's treatise *De Genesi contra Manichaeos*, I, 23–24, in Migne, *Patrologia Latina*, XXXIV, 190–94; cf. W. M. Green, *l.c.*, 320–27.

[44] Besides many passages in *The City of God*, see a letter written by Augustine in the year 412 (*Epist.* 138).

Christ. To him the period following that event and extending to his own days and to the end to come, was not a modern era but it was "the *senectus* of the old man, the last age in which the new man is born who now lives according to the spirit."[45] God has revealed all the truth that is to be communicated to man in this world, and henceforth the history of both the heavenly and the earthly cities has no fundamentally new lessons to teach. Augustine did not share the optimism of Eusebius and others; on the contrary, he spoke of his own era as "this malignant world, these evil days" (18, 49 A), and he reckoned even with the possibility of future persecutions of the Church and the faith (18, 52). He reminded his readers (16, 24 H) that, according to Christ's own words, the terminal period of history will not be an era of secular peace and earthly prosperity but just the opposite: "About the end of this world the faithful shall be in great perturbation and tribulation, of which the Lord has said in the Gospel: 'For then shall be great tribulation, such as was not since the beginning of the world to this time, no, nor ever shall be' (*Matthew*, 24, 21)."

In Augustine's opinion, then, there is no true "progress" to be found in the course of human history. He was, of course, well aware of the fact that "the human genius has invented and put to practical use many and great arts . . . and that human industry has made wonderful and stupefying advances" (22, 24 K-L). But at the same time he pointed out a fact which has been overlooked all too often by believers in the blessings of material progress, the fact that the ingenuity and the inventiveness of man have also their destructive aspects: "And for the injury of men, how many kinds of poison, how many weapons and machines of destruction have been invented." This dual aspect of the development of human history results from the very nature of the forces determining its course. "In this river or torrent of the human race," Augustine said toward the end of *The City of God* (22, 24 A), "two things run the course together, the evil which is derived from the parent [Adam], and the good which is bestowed by the Creator."

---

[45] Augustine, *De Genesi contra Manichaeos*, I, 23, 40, in Migne, *l.c.*, XXXIV, 192.

Christian Myth and Christian History

by LYNN WHITE, JR.

Reprinted from the *Journal of the History of Ideas*—Vol. III, No. 2, pp. 145-158

As the study of intellectual history is intensified, it becomes increasingly clear that from the IVth century until the middle of the XVIIth, and even, although with decreasing vigor, until the middle of the XIXth, the Christian religion was the principal force molding the European and American mind. Whether by its direct action or by reaction against it, whether through its doctrinal formulations or through the secularized vestiges of dogma which became the liberal creed of the Enlightenment, the Church proved herself, when not the *mater,* at least the *matrix* of Western thought. For the historian of our ideas, whatever his personal beliefs, *extra ecclesiam non est salus*.

Yet during the past three centuries, and especially the past three generations, Christianity has been shaken not so much by external attack as by internal crisis. The Church and its cargo weathered not only the tempest of the barbarian invasions and the collapse of antiquity, but likewise survived without irreparable damage the much less difficult squalls marking what is generally considered to be the passage from the Middle Ages to modern times. Now, however, a greater peril has appeared: what the storms have spared the worms may be destroying. The timbers of the Ark may no longer be sound.

This religious crisis lies at the very vortex of the maelstrom of our time: to maintain the contrary is to misunderstand the place which Christianity occupied among us for fifteen centuries, and which, in some part, it still holds. Yet while contending floods of polemic literature have swirled about the discoveries of Copernicus, Darwin, and the Biblical critics, not enough attention has been given to the exact and sympathetic analysis of the difficulties besetting traditional theology. Perhaps the issues have been too palpitating to encourage objective examination: agnostics, inflamed with an almost evangelical zeal, have been bent on smashing ecclesiastical "infamy" with every available bludgeon; while theologians have fought a rear-guard action, chiefly, it would seem, with intellectual smoke-screens designed to cover retreat. But surely we cannot understand the fevers of our age until we arrive at the true historical diagnosis of the malady afflicting contemporary religion; and for this a preliminary dissection of the anatomy of orthodoxy is indispensable.

The Christian claims to be unlike other men: he dwells amphibiously in two worlds. Born into the realm of time, he is likewise sacramentally *renatus in aeternum*. As a result, for the Christian every event has a double but unified significance appropriate to the duality of his experience. He enjoys two modes of perception, two distinct but simultaneous ways of viewing each phenomenon; he has two types of information, not *drawn* from time and eternity respectively, but *seen* from them just as we see a thing through two eyes. He likewise uses two methods of expressing these parallel perceptions: one is history; the other is myth.

History is a coherent account of events which occurred in time. Speculation about the general nature of the time-sequence is therefore an inevitable by-product of the writing of history, and, more remotely, of the effort to make ethical decisions for action. Greco-Roman antiquity held to various notions of cyclical recurrence, usually involving degeneration within each cycle, or, less frequently, to a theory of endless and meaningless undulation. Faith that the historical process is unique and that it has a moral purpose first appeared in Europe as a Christian dogma, the elements of which were mainly taken over from popular Judaism. The Hebrews seem to have started with the usual Mediterranean legend of the Golden Age of innocence, the Garden of Eden, and to have thought of history as a progressive decay, through Adam's fault, possibly in cycles. The Jewish people, however, were intense patriots, and under Assyrian, Babylonian, Persian and Macedonian conquest they never lost hope that some day Jehovah would make Israel, his chosen race, supreme over the whole earth. They came to feel, under the religious leadership of the Prophets, that they were a nation with a moral mission in history: to set up God's kingdom on earth and to teach the gentiles his will. But successive uprisings and defeats convinced many Jews that only supernatural aid could accomplish this end, aid in the form of a Messiah. Mingled with these Messianic hopes there flowed a turbid stream of apocalyptic thought, springing (it would seem) chiefly from Persian sources, and teaching a Last Judgment over which the Messiah should preside at the end of historical time.

Inevitably, it was in terms of some such view of the nature of history that the preaching of Jesus was understood by his first followers. And when his life and words were, in their eyes, completely validated by what they believed to be his resurrection and ascension, they naturally felt that what had been in a sense hypothesis was now proved fact: "Since by man came death, by man came also the resurrection of the dead." Adam's fall explained the coming of the Messiah, and Jesus' death and resurrection pointed clearly towards his return and judgment. Consequently, the Christian view of history carried a power of immediate and overwhelming conviction: it was no longer mere speculation, but rather it was based on the empirical fact of an historic personality. The significance of that fact, however, was understood in terms of Adam's fall and the expectation of the judgment: to Christians this symmetrical interpretation of history came to be as important as the fact of Jesus, because it made the Incarnation intelligible.

Naturally, to the early Christians, the pagan belief in purposeless temporal undulation was entirely unacceptable, and the idea of cosmic repetitive cycles was the worst of blasphemies. From such a theory it follows, writes Origen, "that Adam and Eve will do once more exactly what they have already done; the same deluge will be repeated; the same Moses will bring the same six-hundred thousand people out of Egypt; Judas will again betray his Lord; and Paul a second time will hold the coats of those who stone Shephen." Obviously no such notion could be held by a Christian: "God forbid," cries St. Augustine, "that we should believe this. For Christ died once for our sins, and, rising again, dies no more." The axiom of the uniqueness of the Incarnation required a belief that history is a straight-line sequence guided by God. And as the Church became the exclusive cult of the Roman Empire, the doctrines of undulation and recurrent cycles vanished from the Mediterranean world. No more radical revolution has ever taken place in the world-outlook of a large area. In the early Vth century St. Augustine elaborated on Judeo-Christian foundations the first developmental philosophy embracing all human history. During the Middle Ages and Renaissance, step by step, this Augustinian providential interpretation was very gradually secularized into the modern idea of progress, which until recently dominated Western historical thinking.

But today an increasing group of historians, disenchanted with historical optimism, confesses that the idea of human progress is intelligible only in terms of the theological assumptions on which it originally rested: without the dogma of the Incarnation, the dynamic and rectilinear view of time traditional in our Western culture (a concept which has done much to invigorate that culture) tends to die out. Having lost faith that God revealed himself uniquely at one single point in history, we are relapsing, they say, into the essentially static or repetitive view of the time-process typical of antiquity and of the East. It is increasingly evident that history as Westerners generally have conceived it is an expression of Christian ideas about the nature of time.

The second means of expressing Christian experience is myth, defined as the dramatization in temporal terms of things seen from the non-temporal standpoint of eternity. The Church salvaged from pagan mysticism a mode of thinking which permitted the abstraction from temporal happenings of universals which seem to manifest themselves repetitively in time; and myths were developed as the best means of sharing the perception of these universals. Despite its fictional form, myth is not mere fiction. A myth is not about something that once happened, but rather about something that is always happening: the narration of an eternal event. Myths are firmly anchored to the world of everyday happenings because they dramatize the universals which have been thought to be discoverable behind temporal events. However, unlike the historian, the myth-maker starts not with the particular, but, by illumination of the spirit, with the abstraction of something timeless. The experiential basis of myth-making can perhaps be grasped, at least by analogy, from Mozart's supposed letter to a friend:

The whole composition, though it be long, arrives in my head almost complete, so that I can survey it, like a lovely picture or a beautiful person, at a glance. In my imagination I do not hear the parts successively, but I hear them, as it were, all at once. . . . And to hear them thus, all together, is much the best way!

Similarly some fourteen centuries earlier the Neoplatonist Sallustius remarked of myth that it "did not happen at any one time, but always is so: the mind sees the whole process at once; words tell part first, part second."

Myth-making is therefore an analytical process, with an element of arbitrary art in it. Myth is successful to the extent that its dramatic sequence enables any one meditating on the myth to reverse the analysis, to synthetize and to share the eternal perception from which the myth-maker started. It is a legitimate and necessary form of symbolic expression, closely akin to allegory, to dramatic poetry, and to fable. But although one may discuss a myth, one can never completely convey or explain its content in any other medium, because in the best myths dramatic presentation still leaves many meanings compounded in a counterpoint of significance which is destroyed by further analysis. Even when myth is believed to be identical with history, it is always enveloped in an atmosphere of *double entendre,* and, as though to insist that it never really happened in time, it incorporates elements of wonder and fantasy.

For example, consider the very simple myth, told in the valleys of California, of how the orange got its golden color. A long time ago the fruit of the orange tree was a dingy brown, like a potato. But when Herod commanded the slaughter of the children of Bethlehem, St. Joseph and St. Mary fled with the baby Jesus to Egypt. After days of journeying across barren mountains and hot desert they at last reached the great valley, green against the desolation, and sank down exhausted in an orchard of oranges. And the trees in compassion bent their branches low, offering their fruit to the Holy Family. Seeing which, the Christ child smiled and blest the trees; and ever since then the fruit of the orange has been like gold of the Mother Lode.

Clearly the eternal event dramatized in this myth could not be expressed so compactly in any other way. Merely to assert that a Christ-like personality glorifies all nature, to say that the creature is redeemed by love of its Creator, that man is saved by sacrifice, is only to scratch the surface of the verities which through mythical form are perceived "all together," fused in simultaneous harmony.

Myth-making is found not simply among primitive people but among civilized as well: no sharp line can be drawn between Homer and Aesop. However, it is true that while the myths of primitive cultures deal frankly with the gods and achieve their anti-historical emphasis by means of miracle, the myths of advanced societies, in which a more vivid sense of the transcendence of the divine has been achieved, generally try to express eternal events by other means, replacing miracle by deliberate and sometimes comic unreality. But whether it be simple or sophisticated, myth attempts for eternity what a prism does for light: it breaks up various elements which are found unified and entire, and presents them in sequence to the human eye.

Since ideologically the Christian moves in two planes at once (time and eternity, nature and grace) he sees everything as both history and myth. To be sure, the historical content of Christian myth-history has at times been tenuous in the extreme. The Virgin

Birth, for example, quite apart from difficulties arising from its admittedly miraculous character, would appear to be denied by the very documents upon which it purports to rest, inasmuch as the genealogies preserved in the Gospels of St. Matthew and St. Luke both trace the descent of Jesus from King David through St. Joseph and thus flatly contradict the nativity stories contained in those same records. But the Virgin Mother, undefiled yet productive, bearing Christ into the world by the action of the Spirit of God, is so perfect an analogue of the most intimate experience of the soul, that powerful myth has sustained dubious history; for, to the believer, myth and history have been one.

The traditional Christian world-view is bifocal. Inevitably, therefore, paradox is the most natural style of Christian formulation. Beliefs which to the logical secular mind (limited as it is to the temporal perspective) seem mutually exclusive, are to the Christian mutually sustaining. To adopt another, and perhaps more exact, metaphor from physics: the Christian life is conducted in the magnetic field between the poles of time and eternity. To destroy either pole would destroy the magnetic field, the vital tension which keeps the Christian life healthy: and that is what the Church has commonly meant by heresy.

This bipolarity between myth and history, eternity and time, permeates all Christian institutions and doctrines, although the relative importance of the two elements has varied greatly in different periods. The chronic tension in Christendom between the priestly and the prophetic traditions is generally represented as a conflict between conservative and radical, but it goes much deeper: it reflects the clash of two types of religion, the active and the contemplative. The one, primarily Jewish in origin, emphasizes conduct and the bringing in of the Kingdom of God on earth; the other, Greco-Oriental, is chiefly concerned with the salvation of the individual, conceived as a member of a timeless *civitas Dei*. No sooner had the Edict of Milan in 312 made Christianity a tolerated religion, than this struggle came into the open and rocked the Church. In 314, at the Council of Arles, it was decided that the validity of a sacrament does not depend upon the morality of the priest officiating. Since that day Christianity has tended to fluctuate between puritanical moralism and amoral sacramentalism. Fortunately, despite wide variations of emphasis between different centuries and different groups, the great body of Christians has kept the middle ground of orthodoxy, has balanced its perceptions of time against those of eternity and, in disregerd of all logic, has successfully combined in its doctrine of the Church the mutually exclusive conceptions, on one hand, of the dynamic, visible *ecclesia militans,* a "saving institution" trying to draw men to God, and, on the other hand, of the contemplative, invisible *ecclesia triumphans,* "the body of the elect," enjoying, whether in this life or the next, the beatific vision.

In specific matters of dogma the bipolarity of time and eternity, history and myth, is so evident that illustrations may be chosen almost at random. The Roman Catholic Church has long discouraged discussion of the logically insoluble problem of free-will versus predestination; and in 1937, assembled at Edinburgh, the leading theologians of the Protestant and Eastern Churches similarly affirmed both contradictory doctrines, declaring that no attempt to reconcile them philosophically can be considered part of the Christian faith. Seen through the bifocal glasses of Christian experience there is, indeed, no conflict: God in eternity has predestined every action, but we experience our temporal destiny as freedom. To a philosopher this does not make sense. But that does not disturb a Christian, who claims to know things of which philosophers are ignorant. The same may be said of the dogma of the human and divine natures of Christ, declared at Chalcedon to be perfect, each in its own way, not identical and not separate. Temporally and historically Jesus is, according to the creeds, completely human. Eternally and mythically, Christ is God. No one has ever pretended to tell what this means, but millions have claimed it to be the central fact of their experience. Similarly the Kingdom of God is eternally "within you" and temporally "to come." And nowhere is the paradox made necessary by Christian bifocalism more evident than in the contradictory doctrines of the Judgment. Immediately at death there is a preliminary judgment, since through death the soul passes out of the category of time. But at the end of historical time all the dead will rise for a final judgment, which logically is superfluous. Clearly, however, these two judgments are the same supposed phenomenon viewed first eternally and then temporally.

To summarize: the Church has never doubted that God exists outside the categories of space and time. God made time as a function of his creation; but in God there is neither before nor after: in the words of the Johannine Christ, "Before Abraham was, I am." Time is a human mode of perception: it does not limit God. Everything that has ever taken place in time, or will take place, existed (and exists) in God's mind, or (to speak in temporal terms) in God's foreknowledge and intention, before the Spirit brooded over the waters. And this includes the Fall of Adam, the Incarnation of Christ, the Last Judgment, and the detailed history of every individual soul.

As a result, the Christian lives in a peculiar state of consciousness, mixing inextricably the temporal and the eternal. The keenest intellect among theologians, St. Thomas Aquinas, coined a word to express it: *aevum*, as distinct from *tempus* and *aeternitas*. He defines *aevum* as "the mean between eternity and time," *medium inter aeternitatem et tempus*, partaking of both.

The Christian, then, aspires to dwell in both time and eternity. He insists with all his might that God works in history, but he knows likewise that in the pilgrimage of his own soul the whole historical drama of salvation is recapitulated, and, as in the Negro spiritual, he trembles at the mystery of it: "Were you there when they crucified my Lord?" Transcendent reality reveals itself historically to the race and in parallel myth to the individual. Adam fell, and falls in us; God became man but once, yet the Christ-child nestles next to every heart touched by the Holy Spirit; a young man once hung on a cross in perfect and complete atonement for the sins of all generations, yet he bleeds on every altar; Christ rose, and we rise in Christ; he will come again, and he comes perpetually; he will judge, and we are daily judged.

This belief in a double manifestation of the divine mind through identical history and myth has been the very core of Christianity, enabling men to conceive in time, and thereby to become, what eternity is.

But by the end of the last century this bifocal Christian worldview had been rendered untenable in the thinking of countless millions. The "Copernican" revolution was slow to undermine it, probably because the new cosmology, which in no way challenged the concept of a creation, seemed at first to have little relevance to time and history. However, as men came to believe that every star was a sun, and that surely, in the depths of space, there must be other inhabited worlds, each with its own history and therefore with sin and the need of redemption, doubts arose: in the newly discovered universe one Bethlehem seemed scarcely sufficient. The Church saw the peril from afar, and sent to the stake Giordano Bruno, the first great evangelist of "the infinity of worlds." For, as the Fathers had so vigorously asserted, to a Christian time must be unique: there cannot have been two historic Incarnations. Yet even to many of the devout, the notion of the plurality of inhabited spheres seemed to challenge the Christian axiom that the drama of sin and salvation is played but once.

Attempts were made to assimilate the new astronomy to the Catholic tradition, but too often these degenerated into fantasy. For example, in the *Traité de l'Infini Créé*, widely circulated in the later XVIIIth century, the anonymous author, probably a cleric, posits in the infinite universe an infinity of Saviors supervising an infinity of Last Judgments, and ingeniously suggests that when each planetary system is dissolved at its Judgment, the saved are mustered to form a legion of angels, led by their particular Man-God, to battle for redemption of souls in less complete worlds, whereas the damned become demons with contrary intent. Such extravagances helped to discredit the notion of a plurality of *Heilsgeschichten*, but could not altogether obscure the objections which modern astronomers had raised to the inherited Christian view of the time-process. The effort to encompass the new cosmos within the great tradition culminated in the last year of Victoria's reign in Alice Meynell's *Christ in the Universe*:

> With this ambiguous earth
> His dealings have been told us. These abide:
> The signal to a maid, the human birth,
> The lesson, and the young Man crucified.
>
> But not a star of all
> The innumerable host of stars has heard
> How he administered this terrestrial ball.
> Our race have kept their Lord's entrusted word.
>
> Of his earth-visiting feet
> None knows the secret, cherished, perilous,
> The terrible, shamefast, frightened, whispered, sweet,
> Heart-shattering secret of his way with us.
>
> No planet knows that this
> Our wayside planet, carrying land and wave,
> Love and life multiplied, and pain and bliss,
> Bears, as chief treasure, one forsaken grave.
>
> Nor, in our little day,
> May his devices with the heavens be guessed,

    His pilgrimage to thread the Milky Way
Or his bestowals there be manifest.

    But in the eternities,
Doubtless we shall compare together, hear
A million alien Gospels, in what guise
He trod the Pleiades, the Lyre, the Bear.

    O, be prepared, my soul!
To read the inconceivable, to scan
The million forms of God those stars unroll
When, in our turn, we show to them a Man.

Yet with all its sincerity and insight, this poem marks a fateful break from orthodoxy: the uniqueness of time and history is gone: Christ is become Krishna of the myriad Incarnations.

And already the revolution in biology had given the *coup de grâce* to the traditional Christian interpretation of history. Hitherto Christian myth and Christian history had been the same; Adam falls when we sin (that is the myth), but in fact Adam did fall (that was history); by sacramental grace we rise from the dead in Christ (that is the myth), but all of Christian history pivots on the dated resurrection of an historical man, Jesus of Nazareth; Christ judges us in our every act (that is the myth), but Christ may come on clouds of glory tomorrow morning (that has been the historical expectation of the Christian community). Christianity above all other religions had rashly insisted that its myth really happened in time. It was not merely a dramatization of the common denominator of all religious experience: it was likewise a sequence of historic events. But the traditional Christian history has depended for its validity upon its symmetry: it must stand or fall as a unit. If historically one man, Adam, did not fall, then the unique historical Incarnation of God in one man, Christ, loses its point, and the expectation of the historical Last Judgment crumbles. But by the later XIXth century most educated men had concluded that as a temporal fact Adam did not fall. Doubtless theories of evolution would continue to be modified, but no conceivable mutation of biological science could rehabilitate Adam as an historical individual.

The new astronomy had undermined confidence in the uniqueness of the Incarnation; the new biology destroyed the symmetry of Christian history which had been designed by the devout to explain that Incarnation. Consequently, in the opinion of many men, the entire structure collapsed, and faith in the singleness and purpose of the time-process waned. Under the aging Victoria there occurred a shift in the world-outlook of Europe and America more important than any since the days of Constantine. If the latter marked the beginning of the Middle Ages, historians of the future, gifted with a perspective denied us today, may well conclude that the former marks their true end.

For multitudes reared in the traditional faith, the bipolarity which had been basic in Christianity seemed now lost: the pole of eternity remained, but the pole of time had been destroyed, and with it vanished the magnetic field in which, for nearly two millennia, the Christian life had flourished. To many intelligent men and women whose hearts yearned to be Christian, this crisis marked the end of Christianity: if the nexus of myth with historical fact was broken, then, they maintained, the myth loses its conviction. Or, as others have suggested, the American and European mind is so steeped in respect for concrete fact that it instinctively rejects the myth or symbol which strays too far from history. If this diagnosis be correct, then we seem doomed to succumb to one of the new and dynamic myth-making religions which now for decades have been waging their *jihads:* to some successor of National Socialism with its consciously formulated myth of the chosen race making history under a Messianic Leader; to Communism with its new Israel, the proletariat; or more probably to some fanaticism not yet envisaged. Our political maladies are integrally related to our religious uncertainties. Myth-history Western men must have; and if Christian myth-history fails them they will find it elsewhere.

But to sing a Requiem for Christianity may be premature. Now for decades some of the keenest theologians have been hailing the smashing of the traditional myth-history as pure gain. Merely as a conspicuous example: Reinhold Niebuhr, the most seminal religious thinker of contemporary America, stoutly maintains that myth is the necessary language of religion, but that no myth is capable of conveying its full freight of truth until it is a "broken" myth, *i.e.*, one which is severed from history and clearly recognized to be a sign pointing from the temporal order to a reality beyond. "What is true in the Christian religion," he writes, "can be expressed only in symbols which contain a certain degree of provisional and superficial deception." Even about Jesus we must tell little lies in the interest of a greater truth: "The message of the Son of God who dies upon the cross, of a God who transcends history and is yet in history, who condemns and judges sin and yet suffers with and for the sinner, this message is the truth about life. It cannot be stated without deceptions but the truths which seek to avoid the deceptions are immeasurably less profound. Compared to this Christ who died for men's sins upon the cross, Jesus, the good man who tells all men to be good, is more solidly historical. But he is the bearer of no more than a pale truism."

Here indeed is something new in Christian theology! Rejecting the old identification of myth and history, it is an effort to validate the significance of history by transcending the temporal facts of history. To compare the Jesus of history unfavorably with the Christ of myth, to go on to speak disparagingly of "the chronological illusion" in regard to the Last Judgment: this is to make a virtue of the catastrophe which has destroyed the traditional Christian bifocalism.

But many who are drawn toward such views accept them reluctantly, fearing lest indifference to history bring some diminution of ethical fervor: the Christian myth, they agree, remains "true," but the stripping of the historical husk from traditional dogma would seem to deprive the time-process of moral meaning. When faith in the righteous culmination of history is lost, men look for the vindication of their ideals outside history. When time is conceived to be vagrant, morality is cultivated as an ascetic means of reaching spiritual perfection and of transcending the senseless flux. In such a religious atmosphere the belief emerges that while the individual man may be moral, society is immoral by its very nature, since it is hopelessly enmeshed in a temporal tangle having no reference to eternal reality. Personal ethics may survive, but the activist, the prophet and the champion of social justice go unheeded because men of religion have lost interest in history: temporal events are an illusion, a veil through which sage and saint try by meditation and worship to penetrate towards the timeless Absolute. To many Christians, social ethics has significance, prophetic religion has a dynamic, only in the framework of that purposive view of history which Christianity inherited from the Jews and which now would appear to have been destroyed.

We may, indeed, be turning in the direction of the Orient. In the East, especially in India, men have never taken history and time very seriously or felt them vividly to be real. Buddhism and Hinduism, in particular, have consciously elaborated and used myths as symbols of eternal truths quite without concern for historical accuracy. By losing its focus on time and history, by concentration on eternity and myth, Christianity might, in fact, be able to absorb the Orient into Christendom more easily than has proved possible with its traditional historical-activist emphasis. But would we Westerners, trained so long by Christianity itself to think in historical terms, have any truck with an eternity-oriented cult?

Clearly, of all types of Western Christianity, Roman Catholicism, which concentrates its devotion upon the timeless Bethlehem and Calvary of the Mass, can most easily adjust itself to the new religious tendencies. Indeed the papal promulgations in 1854 of the dogma of the Immaculate Conception of St. Mary by St. Anne, and in 1950 of the dogma of the bodily Assumption of the Virgin into heaven, show that the average Roman Catholic, unlike the average Protestant, is already able to find complete religious satisfaction in myth which has no relation to documented history. But for two centuries the various Protestant Churches, led by the Methodists and Anglicans, have almost instinctively been adapting themselves in a Roman Catholic direction. The Orientals, who have long claimed that our Occidental activism is a symptom of religious immaturity, may therefore be complacent at the prospect that out of the present religious crisis, the greatest since that of antiquity from which Christianity itself emerged, there may well come a more quietistic and contemplative form of Western religion.

Our later-XXth century is, in fact, more hospitable to the idea of a religion expressing itself in terms of arbitrarily constructed symbols than would have been conceivable even fifty years ago. Contemporary psychology, philosophy, semantics, linguistics, mathematics and aesthetics are permeated by the recognition of the necessity of symbolic systems not merely for communication but for thought, and to some extent even for sensory perception itself. Today not merely all myths but all other symbols as well are "broken": that is, they are seen to be not descriptions of things symbolized but signposts pointing in the direction of things. Yet without such arbitrary symbols we cannot cope with experience: we can know fact only in terms of fancy. Even in dealing with the beliefs of "primitive" peoples, scholars no longer use the word *superstition* with its old self-assured ring. Indeed it is a word which has gone out of style, not through indifference to error but because we see that error is inherent in all observation of fact.

In such a context does the breaking of Christian myth-history have the shattering consequences which once it seemed to have? Adam indeed is gone, but sin remains; the apple is withered, but the moral perils of new knowledge have never been more evident; the serpent crawls away, but not temptation. The eternal event, the thing which "always is so" is unaffected by changes in cosmology or biology. Christian myth remains the most compelling expression of man's timeless spiritual experience evolved by any religion.

As the dust of old scientific-theological controversies settles, one thing grows clearer: like the first disciples, we still stand facing a cross, a love and an agony which demand explanation. Drawing on its Jewish traditions, the early Church flanked the cross with an apple at one end of time and a trumpet at the other. That symmetry is destroyed, but its crux remains. In every age men have cast a net of symbols to catch truth, and it is the nature of symbols that as their mesh is fine they obscure what they capture. Yet in each generation this man who was crucified reaches through the enveloping web and touches us with bleeding hands; and we may touch his side.

The Historical Background of Maritain's Humanism[1]

by G. G. COULTON

Reprinted from the *Journal of the History of Ideas*—Vol. V, No. 4, pp. 415-433

I

M. Jacques Maritain is perhaps the most distinguished and influential of the neo-Thomists who would fain take us back to the medieval Schoolmen. The title he chooses seems, at the very outset, an abuse of terms. The word "humanism" in its original and ordinary acceptation stands for a striving towards the widest and deepest comprehension of man and the universe: in short, for what the ancients knew as "philosophy," the love of wisdom. Yet M. Maritain asks us to apply the time-honored name to what is, in effect, a comparatively narrow specialization in medieval metaphysics. Where we are promised "true humanism," we find ourselves put off with little more than an old theology refurbished.

Controversy, taken in its plain dictionary sense, apart from invidious associations which have given it a bad name, lies at the very foundation of human progress. Socrates, Pascal, Lessing, to name only three of the thinkers whom the world could least have spared, were among the most active of controversialists. Christianity itself was born and nurtured in controversy. This it is which compels us to examine M. Maritain's historical claims with the same unsparing strictness with which he examines modern life —or, it might perhaps be more truly said, modern Parisian life, sophisticated, feverish in its manifold activities and its extreme contrasts.

History without controversy would carry the world little farther than alchemy did. There is no safer guarantee against mere wishful thinking, with its concomitant of slavish copying from author to author, than the knowledge that we must publish explicit references, and be prepared to defend them under cross-examination. So long as the breach of this common-sense rule is condoned by ordinary readers, and even by academic teachers, history will

[1] In its references to Jacques Maritain's interpretation of the Middle Ages, this study is based chiefly upon his volume, *True Humanism* (English translation, Geoffrey Bles, 1938).

earn, and will deserve, its present low estimate among the public in comparison with the exact sciences. The propagandist has the temporary advantage of a Dr. Goebbels: his bad coin drives out the good.

The present world is torn between rival and mutually exclusive cultural values, in a struggle which ordinarily shapes itself in the form taken in M. Maritain's book: Past *versus* Present. Here we are on ground where the accuracy of our historical calculations is as necessary as in a trigonometrical survey. Professor Whitehead utters a much-needed warning. "Nothing," he writes, "does us more harm in unnerving men for their duties in the present, than the attention devoted to the points of excellence in the past as compared with the average failure of the present day."[2] And the harm is all the greater in proportion as these "excellences" are purely imaginary. There is a terrible temptation to depreciate this poor workaday world to which, after all, we are wedded, in comparison with the meretricious charms of an imaginary past.[3]

History is an integral part of philosophy in the original sense; yet history was practically non-existent in medieval scholasticism. There was no university chair for it. One of the latest of the Schoolmen (extolled sometimes as an "Aquinas redivivus") looked back upon what the Ages of Faith had done for history "with shame and disgust."[4] Even to the present day, history is the weakest point of Roman apologetics. Renan has told us how that which drove him out of the Church was not her philosophy but her history. Leo XIII is often praised as a specially learned and broad-minded Pope; in a famous Encyclical he extolled St. Thomas with almost divine honors. Yet in another Encyclical (September 8, 1899), he explicitly prohibited the French clergy, in their historical studies, from looking critically into any question upon which the Church has given her verdict. Such intellectual regimentation is necessarily inimical to free history.

M. Maritain's history of philosophy is falsified by an almost fundamental (although of course unconscious) *suppressio veri*. St. Thomas, and all the idolized Schoolmen, drew some of their most important conclusions by rigid logic from unverified assump-

[2] *Science and the Modern World* (ed. Pelican), 237.
[3] Cf. R. H. Tawney, *Religion and the Rise of Capitalism* (ed. Pelican), 67.
[4] Melchior Cano, *Loci Theologici* (1550), lib. XI, c. 6. He specially deplores the glaring contrast between pagan historiography and the Lives of the Saints.

tions. For instance, their Bibliolatry and their lurid eschatology lie at the root of their terrible conclusion that pertinacious nonconformists must be burned. No modern bishop in any church would dare to rehearse to an educated congregation in so many words the description of Hell and its torments which Aquinas gives at the end of his great *Summa Theologica*. Yet if he had sifted and rejected such assumptions and refused to recant, he would have been burned himself. It does not materially alter the case that no base fear of personal consequences restrained him here, but simply a thousand-year-old mental atmosphere which precluded the very notion of verifying with philosophic care some of his most fundamental premises.[5]

In this connection we may say, without disrespect, that M. Maritain copies his chosen master only too well. We may submit him to the same psychological analysis which he applies to that Soviet creed which is his Public Enemy No. 1, yet which has on that very account a peculiar fascination for him. The young Marxist, he points out, is "moved by the same mystical vertigo" as an ardent Christian; he lives "under the domination of a violence drunk with logic."[6] Here he illustrates not only his own attitude, but also that of the Schoolmen to whom he would recall us, who are so well summed up by his brilliant colleague Étienne Gilson.[7] M. Maritain, while admitting the genuine enthusiasm of "a certain number of young Communists," continues: "But when they interrogate themselves, do not these men find that at the same time, as if not to embarrass this enthusiasm, certain fundamental things are left in shadow, by a sort of involuntary censorship which retards or inhibits awareness?"[8] Is he not here describing, with curiously unconscious felicity of expression, precisely his own position?[9]

[5] I have emphasized this in detail elsewhere, e.g., in *Romanism and Truth* (1930; out of print), I, ch. 27; and in *Studies in Medieval Thought* (1940), 139 ff.

[6] *True Humanism*, 59, 263.

[7] *Philosophie au Moyen Âge*, 312, 313. "De là enfin notre goût inné de l'abstraction, due raisonnement *a priori*, de la clarté logique, et notre habitude, si surprenante pour des esprits anglo-saxons, de régler notre conduite sur des principes abstraits, au lieu de la soumettre aux exigences des faits."

[8] P. 30.

[9] It is noticeable how often, with the same unconsciousness, M. Maritain states objections against the totalitarian Soviet State which seem equally applicable to any totalitarian Church. E.g., pp. 28, 32, 77, 89, 128 n, 141, 153, 263, 278. Cf. also his *Crépuscule*, 89, 91.

Every man's mind has its blind spots: strive as we may, we run much of our life in blinkers of birth or of environment. But let us cleave to a sort of Occam's razor in history: *Non sunt multiplicandae caecitates praeter necessitatem.* In the Roman Church, as in present-day Germany and Russia, an authoritative *Trespassers Forbidden* adds to the temptations of ordinary human weakness in the historian.

These are serious criticisms to pass upon an author who has attracted so much attention by his disinterested zeal and his remarkable literary qualities; therefore I must supply such documentary corroboration as my space will permit.

II

Let us follow M. Maritain through two matters to which he recurs over and over again. He contends that modern civilization has robbed the ordinary man of two great human attributes, Freedom and Dignity. These are so closely inter-related that they may be treated together.

It was a legal and religious commonplace, throughout the Middle Ages, that society was providentially divided into three classes, typified in the Priest, the Knight and the Laborer. This was not a strict caste-system; movement was not prohibited between class and class; but the laborer was taught that, apart from exceptional cases, he must be content with his humble lot.[10] Since some ninety per cent of the population were agricultural laborers, it seems paradoxical to claim for such a distribution of society that it added notably to human dignity. We seldom find the medieval ecclesiastic writing of the laborer with the sympathy which is fashionable in modern literature, and which reposes upon a solid substratum of honest brotherly feeling.

In the Middle Ages proper—*le Haut Moyen Âge*—a very large proportion of the population of Europe—probably more than half—were unfree men, serfs. There were different degrees of servage: yet in 1280 the Abbot of Burton had the strict letter of the law on his side when he reminded his discontented bondmen that they "possessed nothing but their bellies."[11] St. Thomas, commenting on Aristotle's politics, finds many points to alter; but he passes

[10] Marc Bloch gives a typical quotation from the Blessed Raimon Lull (*Camb. Econ. Hist.*, I, 277).

[11] W. Ashley, *Introd. to Eng. Econ. Hist. & Theory,* part. II (1893), 277.

uncontradicted the Aristotelian conclusions that, in an ideal state, the peasant has no full rights of citizenship, that the division between fighting and working castes is natural and profitable, that agriculture is a necessary but illiberal occupation, and that "in the best state, if matters can be exactly as we wish, there should be slaves,[12] robust of body, that they may well labor the earth, but deficient in understanding, lest they be inventors of wiles against their masters." They should be "poor-spirited, and not all of the same tribe," lest they "plot against their lords." To this St. Thomas adds two biblical arguments: (a) Adam's fall made the majority of mankind into hereditary slaves, and (b) Christ's blood is on the head of the Jews, who are therefore born slaves of the Christian Church, which may dispose of their goods as it pleases her.[13] This last maxim had been enshrined in Canon Law at a far earlier date. Thus the institution of bondage, ever since Adam's fall, is justified as economically sound and morally defensible not only by that pre-eminent Schoolman whom Leo XIII recommends as an almost infallible guide, but also (I believe) by every other Schoolman who discusses the subject, except the heretic Wyclif; and even he did not envisage general enfranchisement as practicable. In fact, serfdom lasted longest on Church estates, while even slavery proper far outlasted the Reformation in Italy and the city of Rome. Alexander VII dealt in slaves as late as the mid-seventeenth century. The first Pope to brand slavery as unchristian was Gregory XVI in 1839.

Such, in the matter of the common man's liberty and dignity, was the medieval theory. Let us pass to the even more important question of medieval practice.

While the serf worked in the harvest field, his lord's overseer held the rod over him,[14] for the master was legally entitled to

[12] Or "serfs," *servos*. Both theologians and lawyers in the Middle Ages sometimes left the most important points undefined: thus we can seldom be sure whether the writer, in his most formal arguments, is speaking of *slave* in the ancient sense or *serf* in the medieval.

[13] See Aquinas, *Sum. Theol.* 1ª 2ᵃᵉ q. 94. art. 5. iii., and especially the commentary on Aristotle's *Politics,* completed by his pupil, Peter of Auvergne (Parma Edition), XXI, 368–9, 377, 658–62, 680. For the Jews, see *Sum. Theol.* 2ª 2ᵃᵉ q. 10. art. 10. e. Aquinas's follower Egidio Colonna approved of *servitus* as a Christian institution (Th. Brecht, *Sklaverei,* 63). Gury, one of the most authoritative writers on morals, "cannot quote any existing Church law against it" (*ibid.,* 65).

[14] See my *Medieval Village,* facing p. 51, phototype from Brit. Mus. MS. Roy. 2B. vii. f. 78. b.

chastise the man with all severity, short of death or maiming. The serf had no protector in Magna Carta: that foundation-stone of English liberty deals only with freemen. M. Maritain reproaches modern society with the commonplace reminder, unfortunately true so far as it goes, that the working man is often called a "hand." But, after all, that is only in vulgar parlance; the word is never consecrated in formal legal speech. Yet the medieval serf was so far de-humanized that, in legal phrase, he possessed not a *familia*, but only a *sequela*—"brood," or "litter." If he sent his son to school he was fined, since the scholar's tonsure would bring the boy into the praying class, and thus the lord would lose a prospective laborer. So, also, if he married his daughter outside the manor: for there again the lord was defrauded of his legal moiety of a *sequela*. On the Continent, that job was sometimes arranged by dividing the children between the girl's lord and the man's. For instance, three of the greatest Benedictine houses in Europe, Marmoutier, Fleury, and Blois, had a standing tripartite treaty for such division of servile litters.[15]

All these trespasses upon natural parental rights are consecrated in legal terminology: the serf "buys his own flesh and blood"; he is a bondman by the mark *de sanguine suo emendo*.[16] It is quite false to claim, as apologists echo from mouth to mouth, that family life was more sacred in those days than in ours. When the serf died, his little possessions often paid a death-due to the lord, and perhaps to the parson also, on a more extravagent ratio than is demanded in peacetime from any modern estate short of the wealthiest class.[17] Every year the priest took his tithe and, from his pulpit, solemnly committed to hell all who might wilfully refuse it. This was an income-tax of ten per cent on gross earnings, without allowance made for working expenses; moreover, it was often exacted even from menial servants. Normally, such bondage was an ineffaceable lifelong birth-blot, so that on some manors it was

[15] *Miracles de St. Benoit* (Ed. Certain), 57.

[16] See *Camb. Econ. Hist.*, I, 447; and cf. R. H. Tawney, *Religion and the Rise of Capitalism* (Pelican ed.), 67.

[17] In 1352, the House of Commons petitioned the King against "the extreme exactions which the spiritual men used in taking of corpse-presents or mortuaries; for the children of the dead should all die for hunger, and go a-begging rather than they would of charity give to them the silly cow which the dead man ought, if he had but only one; such was the charity of them" (Wilkins, *Concilia*, III, 739). We must make allowance, of course, for the highly-colored language of such petitions.

a punishable offence to reproach a man with the nickname of *nativus*.[18] It is to the credit of humanity that the out-and-out slavery of antiquity was gradually softened down into the half-way status of servage. But this partial denial of human rights became practically extinct only towards the end of what M. Maritain repeatedly calls "the decline" of the Middle Ages.[19]

Let us pass on to the wider relations of rich and poor. Throughout the medieval centuries, writers of all classes deafen us with their outcry against "the Almighty Dollar," to put it into modern terms. One of the tritest medieval slogans is from Ecclesiastes: *Pecuniae obediunt omnia;* and the fountain-head of this corrupt greed is almost universally ascribed to the Roman Court. There is no book so instructive for ordinary medieval mentality as *Piers Plowman;* and in that book the main theme is the omnipotence of Lady Meed (Unlawful Gain), whether in the royal or the papal courts of justice. It was among St. Bernard's and St. Thomas More's main claims to sanctity that, though their exalted position gave them abundant opportunities, neither was known ever to have taken a bribe. The ordinary economic helplessness of the poor was everywhere a commonplace theme. The Franciscan Berthold of Regensburg says: "because the fishes are poor and naked, therefore they devour each other in the water; so also are the poor folk; because they are helpless, therefore they have divers wiles and deceits. . . . None are so false as the country-folk among each other." Another moralist[20] draws a comparison most unflattering to his own age. In Gospel times, he says, the dogs of Dives licked the sores of Lazarus under his table; but nowadays they bite him and chase him away.

[18] The "freedom" and "dignity" of the French peasant under the Ancien Régime inspired one of the most vitriolic passages of La Bruyère's *Caractères,* "Les Paysans et les Laboureurs."

[19] It is difficult to follow M. Maritain's logic when, compelled to recognize some flaw in the Middle Ages, he excuses it by pleading that this was during the "decline." Even though this plea were true in fact (which is by no means always the case) what is its cogency? An institution is no less responsible during its decline than during its heyday of power. If medieval society was so admirably organized, upon such a foundation of eternal realities, why did it decline after the Great Pestilence (the favorite date for apologists) into a decay which finally bred violent revolt, potent still after these four hundred years?

[20] I think, Cardinal Hugues de St. Cher in the late thirteenth century, but my reference is among my papers in England.

Another most pressing question is that of anti-Semitism. What of freedom and dignity did the Jew enjoy? M. Maritain relies upon Léon Bloy's exculpation of the Church here, in flagrant contradiction with notorious historical facts. M. Bloy writes: "Ce candide Moyen Âge détestait les Juifs pour l'amour de Dieu. . . . La guerre aux Juifs ne fut jamais dans l'Église que l'effort mal dirigé d'un grand zèle charitable. La Papauté les abrita contre la fureur de tout un monde."[21] I have printed elsewhere[22] three sources from the eighth to the twelfth century, in which clerical writers complacently describe such solemn ecclesiastical buffetings of Jewish hostages, in "expiation" for Christ's death, as Hitler himself has hardly surpassed in cold-blooded cruelty.[23] Popes did indeed sometimes protect Jews from the mob, but their contemporaries attributed this to the same cupidity which prompted lay princes also to foster the Hebrew usurers as milch-cows. No Pope ever attempted to remove from Canon Law that decree which condemned the Jew as a slave and his goods as legally seizable by the Church. St. Thomas More tells us of a lady who, convinced with much difficulty that Mary was a Jewess, exclaimed: "So help me God and halidom, I shall love her the worse while I live."[24]

M. Maritain holds up Puritanism and Jansenism as the two main disfigurations of Christianity bred by the Reformation.[25] Here he voices a popular delusion for which academic historians are partly responsible through their neglect of thorny or controversial points in social and religious history. The medieval Church was strongly puritanical in theory, though in practice it so often took the line of least resistance. Extremists of the Reformation earned their unenviable reputation through the psychological error of trying to enforce practical reality upon the theories to which their forefathers had done lip-service for a thousand years."[26] If we study the Lives of the Saints in the original records, we con-

[21] Mme. Maritain, *Les Grandes Amitiés*, 177.

[22] *Life in the Middle Ages*, II, 23 ff.

[23] Duchesne, *Scriptores*, III, 430; Adhémar de Chabannes, *Chronicon* (ed. Chavanon), 175; Bouquet, *Historiens*, XII, 436. Cf. Aquinas, *Summa Theol.* 2ª 2ᵃᵉ, X, 10. c; XII. ad. 3; *ibid.*, LXVIII. 10 ad. 2.

[24] *English Works* (1557), 136.

[25] P. xv.

[26] (1) I have worked this out at some length in *Medieval Studies*, No. IV, reprinted from *Contemp. Review* (Aug. 1905); and again in *The Medieval Village*, 240 ff. and Appendix 31. Fuller evidence still in *Review of the Churches* for July, 1925.

stantly find characteristics ordinarily associated with the term *puritan,* a sour repudiation of mere earthly attractions, a kill-joy piety, an unhealthy egocentric brooding over the chances of personal salvation, and, at the opposite extreme, the complacent assurance of personal election. Throughout the Middle Ages, pious folk set great store upon the gift of tears in prayer. We have one instance where the Blessed Umiliana assisted nature with quicklime,[27] and the lately-discovered autobiography of Margery Kempe supplies evidence for such feelings on an extravagant scale.[28] The Blessed Angela of Foligno, spiritual instructress to Dante's Ubertino da Casale, found so great a hindrance to religious life in family ties that she prayed God for their removal, "and so it befel that, within a brief space, her mother first, and then her husband, and presently all her children, passed away from this world."[29]

With all St. Francis's cheerful serenity, an admiring disciple warns us that he disliked downright laughter;[30] so also was it with St. Bernard, and monastic disciplinarians harp constantly upon this theme. The *joculator, jongleur,* professional minstrel and play-actor, was granted by clerical moralists only the slenderest chances of salvation; thus the denial of holy ground to Molière's body was a normal medieval survival. The village dance on Sundays and holy-days, so dear to the peasant, was reprobated by Schoolmen and preachers with striking emphasis and unanimity; for the Church traced it back to Aaron's idolatrous gambols before the Golden Calf. The friction here was all the greater, because the medieval laborer, like *Uncle Tom's* Negro, reacted often against his hard lot in riotous mirth. For working on Sundays or the great holy-days, a peasant or artisan might be heavily fined. St. Bernard and St. Francis, with other saints, were contemptuous of elaborate art in architecture or imagery. Though St. Francis loved music and song, a party developed in his Order which disliked organs and complicated chant.[31]

[27] Wadding, *Annales Minorum, an.* 1246. Cf. my *Five Centuries of Religion,* I, 356.

[28] E. E. T. S., Vol. 212 (1940).

[29] Wadding, *an.* 1309, § XI. It will be seen how relevant this spirit is to the theory that the Middle Ages were penetrated with peculiar respect for family life.

[30] *Speculum Perfectionis,* c. 96.

[31] See my *Five Centuries of Religion,* I, 80 and 470, where two pages are filled with references.

Closely connected with this is the medieval attitude towards God's earth. M. Maritain advances the mere mention of St. Francis's name as sufficient proof that the Middle Ages had a love of God so intimate that it spread from Him to his whole creation: "in the purest hearts a mighty love, exalting nature above itself, extended even to things the same fraternal piety."[32] He has evidently no conception of the extent to which St. Francis was not typical here, but highly exceptional. Far more normal was St. Dominic, who is recorded by one admiring disciple to have plucked a sparrow alive because it fluttered into his lamp and was therefore an emissary of Satan to hinder his sacred studies.[33] Or, again, that monkish chronicler of Fleury, who, having related how a pet peacock was healed by St. Benedict's intercession, warns us formally against regarding this as a precedent; since "we know that God careth not for these irrational beasts, save in so far as they contribute to the use and necessities of rational beings."[34] The Society for the Protection of Animals is practically unknown in Catholic countries. The wilder aspects of nature, it is notorious, appealed little to the medieval poets.[35] Despite the claim of healthy fundamental optimism which M. Maritain makes for the Middle Ages, it is almost impossible to find a writer who seriously claims general advance for his own age. Almost everywhere the tone is that of Horace's classic lament,

> Aetas parentum, pejor avis, tulit
> Nos nequiores.

M. Maritain is very severe upon present-day marriages, applying to them that most damning epithet in the modern political vocabulary: they are "bourgeois."[36] We may indeed admit that modern society lends itself here to criticism, but he goes sadly astray in looking upon the materialistic *mariage de convenance* as a product of the Reformation. It is in fact one of the oldest of institutions, and it flourished in feudal Europe when as yet the citizen class scarcely existed. Léon Gautier, a loyal panegyrist of the Middle Ages, is shocked to find this trait everywhere in the

---

[32] P. xv.

[33] Gérard de Frachet, *Lives of the Brethren* (ed. J. P. Conway), 290.

[34] *Miracles de St. Benoît* (ed. Certain), 253. It is strange that the good monk was not reminded here of Christ's words about the sparrows.

[35] Further evidence in my *Five Centuries of Religion*, I, 368–9.

[36] Pp. 190–192.

romances of chivalry: he writes: "Whatever may be said, these are not conditions for truly free marriage; or to speak plainly, for a truly Christian one." The dominant business element was open and undisguised. Squire Stephen Scrope writes to Sir John Paston, "I was fain to sell a little daughter I have for much less than I should have done by possibility."[37] The classical and imperishable manual on this subject is the *Ménagier de Paris*, written in Chaucer's life-time and introduced to modern readers by Eileen Power, who truly characterizes the Middle Ages as "a time of *mariages de convenance*."[38]

Even Church law, while it claimed to control marriage as a sacrament, was of a laxity incredible to the modern educated Roman Catholic. A boy and a girl might bind themselves for life by a mere verbal undertaking on both sides, without church or priest or witness, followed by physical conjunction.[39] Though divorce was nominally forbidden, yet it was so easily procurable by bribery and perjury that, as Gautier confesses again, "here was a revival, under canonical and pious forms, of the ancient [Roman] practice of divorce."[40] St. Peter Damian, bosom friend of Gregory VII, wrote "money sets the marriage laws in motion": a rich man can persuade judges who would be pitiless to the poor.[41] "The Sacrament of Matrimony," wrote one of the greatest Churchmen about 1200, "is turned to derision among the layfolk."[42] Erasmus asked Katharine of Aragon why the Church could not secure marriage by some such clear legal forms as the State had long used for far less important civil contracts: then "the world would not see so many unhappy and perplexed marriages, and so many divorces."[43] This was in 1526: four years later, that plea was painfully relevant to the Queen's own case.

The growth of the Mary-cult did little to raise women's status; for, after all, the preacher had logic on his side when he argued

[37] *Paston Letters* (1901), introd. p. clxxvi; see also *Piers Plowman*, C. XI. 256, and J. Gower, *Mirour*, 17245 ff.

[38] *Medieval People*, ch. IV (Pelican, 93).

[39] Pollock and Maitland, *Hist. Eng. Law*, II, 391. This was unknown even to Cardinal Gasquet, who enjoyed a considerable reputation in his Church for medieval scholarship. (*Parish Life in Medieval England*, 207.)

[40] *La Chevalerie*, 352.

[41] Migne, *P.L.*, CXLIV, 283–5.

[42] Petrus Cantor, in Migne *P.L.*, CCIII, 235.

[43] *Opera* (1705), V, 627, 641, 666, 670.

that the victory over Satan was all the more glorious for having been gained by one of the weaker sex. In itself that frailty was unquestioned; Chaucer's wife of Bath scarcely exaggerated when she complained that it was impossible to find praise from any clerical pen for any female outside the list of canonized saints. Troubadour poetry is notorious for its frequent insincerity. And, even in poetry, wives and daughters frequently felt the weight of the Knight's fist. In Canon Law wife-beating was explicitly permitted.[44] The standard medieval book on the education of children is that of the Knight of La Tour-Landry, who treats such marital violence as a matter of course even in the highest circles.[45]

Even in Utopia, the implication is that the good man may chastise his wife as he does his children.

One final note on this question of "freedom" and "dignity." The medieval censorship of high academic thought, far stricter than is commonly represented, was perhaps less mischievous on the whole than the leaden tyranny over smaller persons. England accepted the Inquisition, with its legalized torture-chamber, only for a few months, under the strongest papal pressure, in the affair of the Templars. But when the Lollards had compromised the justice of their cause by dabbling in politics, State came into equal partnership with Church in the repression of men's struggles for what they believed to be a Bible-religion. Archbishop Arundel, in his conciliar decrees of 1407-8, condemned to the stake all persons who should translate or read any unauthorized English Bible—at a time when no authorized version existed—or should misinterpret or contradict any papal decree or decretal, or refuse to take oath in the law courts, in reliance upon Christ's and St. James's prohibition of swearing.[46]

But, it is often argued, modern "freedom" is merely illusory: the common man has been robbed of that which his ancestors recognized as the Pearl of Price, for which the merchant sold all that he had; we have lost or are losing the True Faith. Such a plea brings us into the region of imponderables; and those who are insensible to this temperamental appeal can retort in good scholastic terms, *Quod gratis asseritur, gratis negatur.* Yet to some extent this

[44] Gratian *Decretum*, glosses to pars I, dist. XXV, c. 3; pars II, causa VII, q. 1. c. 29; causa XXXIII, q. 2. 10; cf. *ibid.*, q. 5. cc. 15–7.
[45] E.E.T.S., vol. 33, pp. 23, 25, 27, 81, 95.
[46] Wilkins, *Concilia*, III, 314 ff.

plea comes among the ponderables of history; for Descartes, with his insistence on the greater significance of deeds than words, is in effect repeating Christ's *By their fruits ye shall know them.* It is not only that the long perspective of time shows us excessive anti-clerical and anti-religious violence in countries such as Spain and Mexico, where Protestant preaching and education have been almost or quite unknown.[47] More significant still are the recorded confessions of our medieval ancestors themselves, monotonously pessimistic, as to the substantial atheism or paratheism of the multitude. Achille Luchaire, one of the most learned of medievalists, recognized what was great in the twelfth century, but sums up in one scathing sentence: "La vraie religion du moyen âge, il ne faut pas s'y tromper, c'est le culte des reliques."[48] Like all epigrammatic generalizations, this must be taken with a liberal grain of salt; yet it is scarcely more damning than the judgment passed upon the mass of common folk by St. Bernardino of Siena and St. Antonino of Florence, men who had preached more sermons and heard more confessions than any other churchman of their century.

But (pleads M. Maritain on p. 8) we must make allowance for this period as one of "decline": this is "the end of the Middle Ages, in the long agony of the 15th century, when the dance of death caracoled through men's minds and St. Vincent Ferrer announced the coming end of the world." Yet in fact all this was characteristic not of that century only, but of the whole medieval period. The Dance of Death was not a more grisly artistic subject than the realistic Dooms of earlier centuries; and the immediate coming of AntiChrist was a still older theme. Ordericus Vitalis, about 1120, is as painfully haunted by Apocalyptic terrors as St. Vincent; so were the early Cistercians and Franciscans and Dominicans. From *Piers Plowman* comes the complaint: "God is def now a dayes and deyneth nouht us to huyre."[49] St. John Fisher caps this, in a book written about 1500 for his devotee, the King's mother: "An we take heed and call to mind how many vices reign nowadays in Christ's Church, as well in the clergy as in the common people, how many also be unlike in their living unto such in times

[47] Mr. Eyre's *European Civilization* frankly recognizes this; the bare facts are fully stated on pp. 1502–3 of vol. VI, but without any serious attempt to discuss their significance.

[48] 2me Ed., 30.

[49] C. xii. 61; cf. B. i. 7.

past, perchance we shall think that Almighty God slumbereth not only, but also that He hath slept soundly a great season."[50]

For it was not in material conditions only that the common man of the Middle Ages would have been surprised to find himself held up as a model for posterity. The neglect of religious education was scandalous, as described in conciliar decrees and corroborated in every direction by crosslights from formal documents.[51] "The ignorance of the priests," proclaimed Archbishop Pecham at his Lambeth Council of 1287, "casteth the people into the ditch of error"; and this was repeated, *totidem verbis,* by Wolsey in 1518 at his Council of York. By a singular irony of history, no standard English translation of the *Pater Noster* existed until Henry VIII published one in his *Primer.* Of all the Seven Sacraments, Confirmation alone brought no fees to the officiant; and we have supporting evidence for Archbishop Pecham's complaint at the end of the 13th century, that there were "numberless people, grown old in evil days, who had not yet received the grace of Confirmation."[52] Even among the priests, from the early thirteenth century onwards, official visitations record, and many undesigned coincidences of time and place go to corroborate, the most startling frequency of ignorance. Bishop Hooper found many who could not name the Author of the *Pater Noster,* or specify whereabouts it was to be found.[53] Yet these things will not be found incredible if we reflect that, in religion as elsewhere, a totalitarian régime spells monopoly, with the consequences, sooner or later, of inelasticity and inefficiency. Those religious thinkers who are most averse from Caesaropapism should reflect most seriously upon the similar evils of Papocaesarism. There must always be dangerous possibilities in intellectual regimentation.

III

In reaction against past Protestant unfairness, scholars are now tempted to indulgence the other way; and some of the best,

[50] *Fisher's English Works* (E.E.T.S., 1876), 170.

[51] For detailed evidence on this and the following points, see my *Medieval Village* (Camb. Univ. Press), and No. VII of my *Medieval Studies, Religious Education before the Reformation,* reprinted from *The Contemporary Review* of Oct. 1906.

[52] Wilkins, *Concilia,* II, 53.

[53] See my *Europe's Apprenticeship* for eighty pages of evidence as to the frequency of Latin ignorance among the clergy.

enjoying general and well-earned respect, are often found to dread the suspicion of partiality more than the undoubted error of omitting important but invidious truths in pure good nature. It has thus become academic "good form" to ignore some of the most important surviving sources for the study of medieval civilization. This is a grave accusation, but let us see whether it cannot be justified by the mere recital of fifteen titles, which alone my space will here permit. It will be noted that they begin in the hey-day of the Middle Ages, and continue from century to century until the end.

Let us begin with (I) St. Bernard's *De Consideratione*, addressed to his former pupil Eugenius III.[54] Next, (II) Grosseteste's speech before the Cardinals at the First Ecumenical Council of Lyon.[55] (III) The Introduction to the Statutes of the Papal Legate Othobon in 1268.[56] (IV) Roger Bacon's pleas to Clement IV.[57] (V) The Memorial drawn up for the Second Ecumenical Council of Lyon, at the Pope's request, by the Bishop of Olmütz.[58] (VI) The similar Memorial by Humbert de Romans, General of the Dominicans.[59] (VII) and (VIII) The Memorials drawn up for the Ecumenical Council of Vienne, at the request of Clement V, by the Bishops of Angers[60] and Mende.[61] (IX) Alvarus Pelagius, *De Planctu Ecclesiae*, written at papal command.[62] (X) The Petition of 1414 from Oxford University to Henry V.[63] Omitting the speeches by great churchmen at Constance and Basel (though these themselves are often very superficially treated), we come to (XI), the *Liber Veritatum* of the celebrated Chancellor of Oxford University, Thomas Gascoigne.[64] Next comes (XII), Trithemius, in his official orations to the Abbots and monks of the Reformed Congre-

[54] Migne, *P.L.*, vol. 185.
[55] E. Brown, *Fasciculus etc.*, II, 255.
[56] Wilkins, *Concilia*, II, 15.
[57] *Opera Inedita*, R. S., 399 et passim.
[58] Raynaldus, *Annales*, an. 1273, § vi.
[59] Mansi, *Concilia*, XXIV (1780), 120, 130.
[60] Guillelmus Major in *Mélanges Historiques – Choix de Documents* (Imprimerie Nationale, 1877), 479.
[61] Durandus, *De Modo Generalis Concilii Habendi* (Paris, 1671) pars II, tit. 53.
[62] *De Planctu Ecclesiae* (Ed. of 1517), lib. ii.
[63] Wilkins, *Concilia*, III, 363.
[64] *Loci e Libro Veritatum* (Ed. J. E. T. Rogers). The whole bulky manuscript from which these excerpts are made is in the Bodleian Library: it looks as though the passages omitted would repay careful study.

gation of Bursfelde.[65] For (XIII) and (XIV) we have Memorials to the King of France in 1493 from the Abbots-General of Marmoutier and Cîteaux at the Assembly of Tours;[66] and finally (XV), the Memorial of Pico della Mirandola to Leo X in 1513 for the Ecumenical Lateran Council.[67]

Here, then, we have a continuous series of state documents—for such they are in effect, addressed explicitly or implicitly to the highest civil or ecclesiastical authorities by Churchmen of conspicuous rank, piety, and orthodoxy. These men rehearse in detail their views upon the most desperate sores of the Church, and cry directly or indirectly for reform *in capite et membris* as the only alternative to moral bankruptcy and revolution. St. Bernard's words, for instance, are at least as significant as are the first distant mutterings in Fénelon or Vauban of the French revolutionary storm. Guillaume Durand's *De Modo Generalis Concilii Habendi*, again, is as detailed in its complaints against the Hierarchy as the *Cahiers* are against the Ancien Régime. If to ignore those French instances would be an unthinkable treason against common-sense in history, what excuse can be pleaded for the academic ignorance or neglect with which these medieval parallels are steadily treated?

It is now half a century since Rashdall's *Universities of Europe* opened my eyes to many obscure corners of ecclesiastical and social history. Yet even now, after all those years, I cannot recall ever to have met, in print or in person, any medievalist who shows intimate and critical acquaintance with even a quarter of that list; indeed, the large majority seem not even to suspect the existence of documents which open to us not by-paths alone, but the very high-roads of thought and life in that far-off age. Pierre Dubois and Marsilius do receive the attention they deserve; but those two witnesses must be discounted to this serious extent, that they were political enemies of the Papacy. Where is it that we can find anything like the same minute care, by students of equal ability, expended upon writers even more eminent in rank, inspired not by animosity but by profound devotion and respect for the papal office? Who chooses such subjects for Ph.D. theses?

Not, of course, that we can uncritically take the very best of this

[65] *Opera Pia et Spiritualia* (Mainz, 1604), especially *Dehortationes ad Monachos*.
[66] Both are printed in *Analecta Gallicana*, II, 333 ff.
[67] *Opera* (Basel, 1601), 886.

evidence at its bare face value. But we have ample sources elsewhere for checking it. St. Bernard, for instance, is most emphatic on the obscuration of justice through clouds of dispensations from Rome, annulling any existing law. For such dispensations we have a mass of independent documentary proof; we can trace them not as diminishing, but as growing almost in geometrical ratio from generation to generation. Grosseteste, again, insists that the monasteries are doing untold harm by the appropriation of parish churches; and here the episcopal registers give us detailed statistics, not only for the multitude of such appropriations, but even, in many cases, for the sums thereby taken from the parish and the poor. Bacon inveighs against University morals; but so, also, in even stronger terms, do Cardinal Jacques de Vitry in St. Francis's time and the Italian Professor Benvenuto da Imola in Chaucer's. Bacon's condemnation of the Vulgate Bible text current in his day is emphatically supported by the most learned, perhaps, of all modern medievalists, Fr. Denifle of the Vatican Archives. Bacon's complaint that Bible study was being throttled by that of the Sentences can be checked by a great deal of circumstantial evidence which has never yet been scientifically exploited. When he points to the neglect of Greek study and translations, he is supported by notorious facts. But on the other hand, when he insists on scholastic miscomprehensions of Aristotle, the facts seem to show that he is doing great injustice to the best of his contemporaries.

IV

Many of us who are not Americans believe that this Century of the Common Man will necessarily be also, in many things, an American Century. The United States will possess more money for libraries, more students with greater leisure for study, than any other part of the world. The developments of this last quarter of a century, mainly through the efforts of the Medieval Academy of America, have already been remarkable. Masses of ancient documents have been released in the auction-room from the cold storage of centuries, and are being submitted to scientific examination in their new transatlantic homes. Here, then, is the chance for any University which may be sternly resolved to plan ahead for fifty years, for removing the stigma, all the darker in proportion as it is unconscious, that History is neglecting obvious and essential sources of knowledge with an obscurantism which cannot be charged against any of the physical or exact sciences.

Just seventy-five years ago, in June, 1868, at the Lycée Impérial de St-Omer, I saw one of my schoolfellows hauled off to the school prison, a noisome hole, for the crime of playing the Marseillaise on the music-room piano. From that Second Empire in France, the Third Republic was born in blood, to sink again in blood after an existence of seventy years. Who will guarantee that the coming régime will not be born in blood, spilt again between those who think with M. Maritain and those who are passionately convinced of the contrary? Reconstruction after this present war will need the sternest regard both to principles and to facts. The whole world will be faced by the eternal struggle in its acutest form—eternal at bottom under different names and from different angles—of Tradition *versus* Adventure in politics, sociology and religion. We cannot afford to neglect any means of getting nearer, if only by almost imperceptible degrees, to the truths of past human experience.

But how are we to do this, so long as one side is debarred by official proclamation from probing to the very roots, and the other side refrains for appeasement's sake? How, under these conditions, can we ever form that "Third Party" so earnestly desiderated by M. Maritain? He envisages an organization like the Society of Friends, which shall enlist all men of good will, whatever their creed or their no-creed, and absorb them so wholly in their high basic ideal as to avoid disputes about points of detail. For the growth of such a super-Quaker organization, what soil could be more fertile than the English-speaking Americas, with their ingrained habits of experiment and compromise, and their many undenominational social affiliations which already exist? There are grave dangers, of course, in the stolid "Anglo-Saxon"[68] belief that, so long as we take care of the facts, the principles will take care of themselves. But is it not even more dangerous to shape our facts by our principles, and build our Temple of Thought upon wishful thinking? Let each follow his own natural bent, but not at the expense of the other. The clear classification and symmetrical shaping of thought may be the peculiar mission of the "Latin"

---

[68] Following here, for convenience, Professor Gilson's brief label. But, of course, the American continent owes even more than Europe to its multiple mixture of different races.

mind, but it is up to the scholars of newer countries to display the energetic pioneer virtues of their ancestors.

No artist has ever given greater impression of imagination and facility than J. M. W. Turner. But when his aristocratic lady-pupil begged for the "secret" of one particular effect in the water-color he had lent her to copy, his answer was: "Make my kind regards to Major Fawkes, and tell him I have no secret but damned hard work." Under much vague academic talk about "historical method," the securest foundation will always be found in Virgil's *labor improbus,* joined to solid common-sense. In 1888, at Heidelberg, a scientist and ex-diplomat, Baron C. R. v. d. Osten-Sacken, made to me, à propos of the Boss Tweed scandal, a remark which practically anticipated Lord Tweedsmuir's recent eulogy: America has a remarkable power of improvisation to meet emergencies. Here, then, is an emergency calling for courage and resolution. Let a capable research student—or, preferably, two from different angles—be put on to earn their Ph.D. by releasing some of the highlights of the Middle Ages from under their age-long bushel. Let us have less History according to the Scribes, and far more History for the Common Man.

The Idea of God in Elizabethan Medicine

by PAUL H. KOCHER

Reprinted from the *Journal of the History of Ideas*—Vol. XI, No. 1, pp. 3-29

When Christianity conquered the ancient world, it faced the problem of absorbing, along with the other pagan learning, a system of Graeco-Roman medicine which had become fairly well divorced from any type of religious thought. Positivism was the keynote of this system. Its practitioners, whatever their personal beliefs about the meaning of the universe, inclined to treat health and disease strictly as matters of natural cause and effect. This conscious pulling in of horizons occurred as early as the writings of the Hippocratic school. The tenor of even such a work as *The Sacred Disease* was that no disease was peculiarly holy or more immediately derived from the gods than any other. All were equally susceptible of natural explanation in terms of causation by climate and bodily constitution. Aristotle and Galen admitted God as the supreme architect of anatomy and physiology but not as the adjudicator of sickness and health. The comprehensive survey *De Medicina* by the Roman writer Cornelius Celsus traversed the whole field without once accepting a supernatural agent in medical events. In the Christian theocracy, where everything had to be subordinated to theology, what was needed was a way of incorporating the obviously useful findings of pagan medicine into a strictly Christian context. That context was provided mainly by the Bible itself, which emphatically established disease as a function of the wrath of God, healing medicines as a function of his mercy, and the physician as his instrument.

On this general basis a firm integration of all pagan medical learning (including the accretions of Arabic science) with the Christian world-view was achieved during the great period of synthesis in the Middle Ages. One can see the results in such medieval works as Lanfranc's *Chirurgia,* John of Arderne's *Treatise of Fistula in Ano,* and Guido de Cauliaco's *Cyrurgia.* The religious rationalization of medicine there founded was passed on without change to Elizabethan writers, both clerical and scientific. We shall observe presently that these two groups differed somewhat in the emphasis they assigned to different parts of the theory. But mainly it was satisfactory to both. The clergy were of course committed to keeping medicine, as one important field of human knowledge and practice, closely tied to theology. And the doctors, too, despite some contemporary charges of atheism, were most of them pious men who took encouragement from the belief that their work was ordained of God and divinely directed to the relief of man's suffering.

Precisely what, then, were the details of this theology of medicine? The first proposition was that man's body, having been created by God in his own image, is a beautiful and perfect work, a microcosm. It is, in fact, the most exquisite of all physical fabrications, revealing the divine genius of its architect. As God's goodness

is most manifestly and chiefly declared unto us by holye scripture . . . Euen so secundarily as in a sensible glasse, maye we beholde the same his goodnesse, wysdome, and prouidence, in the framinge of the bodie of man with the use of the partes therof as it were in a secreate shoppe and forge of his maruelous woorkmanshippe.[1]

Indeed, one of the chief reasons for studying human anatomy is that it leads to appreciation of God's greatness as a builder.[2] Every part of the body is perfectly designed for its appropriate end:

Thus if we wel perpend the construction, and composition of the partes, and bones of the hand, our senses shall soone conceiue the maner of the action, with no lesse admiration, in beholdyng the handy worke of the incomprehensible Creator: who not one mite, or portion of a part hath sited any where, that serueth for no end, or utilitie to the body: for how fit to apprehend are the handes, and how prompt to moue are the fingers . . .[3]

In the same way, the head admirably protects the brain and gives a commanding location to the eyes, and so on. Thus the argument from design exhibited in man's body is an unanswerable refu-

---

[1] Thomas Gemini, *Compendiosa totius Anatomiae delineatio*, 1559, sig. A2ʳ of the Dedication. Similarly, Andreas Laurentius, *A Discourse Of The Preservation Of The Sight*, 1599, pp. 15–16. Unless the contrary is specified, all books mentioned in this paper were published in London, most of them between 1550 and 1610, although a few earlier and a few later publications will be included. Some contemporary foreign medical works translated by Englishmen and published in England will be drawn upon.

[2] John Vigo, *The most excellent worckes of Chirurgery*, 1550, fol. 1ʳ.

[3] John Banister, *The Historie of Man* (1578), fol. 31ʳ; Thomas Vicary, *The Englishemans Treasure* (1586), 15–17. Such teleological interpretations of anatomy had been frequent in Galen.

tation of atheism.[4] Of course this masterpiece of the celestial craftsman is corrupted by disease and death, but these are results of man's own sin through Adam. Corruptions of this sort, though they may spoil the workings of the soul in the body, never affect the soul itself, which remains untouched through all physical vicissitudes and departs when the body dies.

Secondly, God has foreseen man's need of medicines and has mercifully endowed all living creatures, all animals, trees, herbs, grasses, all metals and minerals, with medicinal properties for his healing:

. . . the arte of Medecine, was geuen to mankinde, by the almightie Lord God, that it might helpe our weke and frayle nature, in the time of most greuous sicknesse, sent unto us for our sinnes, for if we should always remaine in health, & in good and perfect state, neither should we know our selues, neither yet the great might, and power, of the Lord God, which doth geue health, and sicknesse, neither should we seeke out the vertue of his creatures, as herbes, trees, stones, mettals, mineralls, beastes, foules, fishes, and all other things, that crepeth on the face of the earth, which hath receued of the high and mightie Lorde, both qualities, and properties to helpe, and cure, most greuous diseases, being rightly aplied and used, according to reason & experience . . .[5]

By a divine instinct sick or wounded animals seek out those herbs which will do them good, but man, with God's aid, must carry on the search for medicine by observation and reason.

Thirdly, God sends the physician to discover and administer these remedies implanted in nature. Adam was originally gifted with a complete knowledge of materia medica, but when this was lost through the Fall[6] the Lord raised up a long series of histor-

[4] Thomas Tymme, *A dialogue philosophicall* (1612), "To the Reader." In books against atheism the argument from the design of the human body was often used as proof of the existence of God. See Philip de Mornay, *The Trewnesse of the Christian Religion* (1587), 7; Robert Parsons, *The Seconde parte of the Booke of Christian exercise* (1590), p. 36; John Dove, *A Confutation of Atheisme* (1605), 22–27. From the foregoing citations and those in the preceding three footnotes it is clear that medical research was not generally labeled as the sin of curiosity or made widely subject to theological censure in England.

[5] Thomas Gale's *A briefe declaration of the worthy Arte of Medicine*, sig. A1^r, prefacing his translation of *Certaine Workes of Galens* (1586). Also William Bullein, *Bulwarke of defence againste all Sicknes* (1562), sig. ii^r; Timothy Bright, *The sufficiencie of English Medicines* (1580), 9, 23.

[6] Tymme, *loc. cit.*

ical physicians, beginning with some of the Biblical patriarchs and continuing on through supposed heathen gods like Apollo and Aesculapius who were really actual men, down to Hippocrates and Galen and beyond, to resuscitate this lost knowledge:

. . . God the great Creator & fashioner of the world, when first he inspired Adam by the breath of his mouth into a living and breathing man, he taught him the nature, the proper operations, faculties and vertues of all things contained in the circuit of this Universe. So that if there be any who would ascribe the glory of this invention to man, he is condemned of ingratitude even by the judgment of Pliny. But this knowledge was not buryed in oblivion with Adam: but by the same gift of God was given to those whom he had chosen and ordained for Phisicke, to put their helping hands to others that stood in need thereof . . . Which thing Iesus the sonne of Sirach the wisest among the Iewes, hath confirmed saying: Honor the Physition with the honnor due unto him, for the most High hath created him because of necessity: and of the Lord commeth the gift of healing. The Lord hath created Medicines of the Earth and he that is wise will not abhorre them.[7]

Physicians, therefore, are emissaries of the Almighty in the exploration of the natural causes of disease and the treatment of the sick.[8]

But, a fourth proposition, God provides not only the human body, the physician, and the medicine; he provides also the disease to punish man's wickedness. Human life

. . . is subiecte to diseases . . . which for the most part do encrease dayly, euer the iust vengeance of God falling upon us for greate abhominations, and without doubt will euermore endure, unless we do repent and liue in his commaundementes. And to passe ouer al the whole swarmes of so many, both old and new diseases, wherewith the body of man (alas for our sinnes) is continually tormented and vexed . . . as Lepries, Agues, Cankers, Poxes,

[7] Ambroise Paré, *Workes* (1634), Preface, sig. A2r. Other good accounts of the religious history of medicine were given by Iaques Guillemeau, *The Frenche Chirurgerye* (Dort, 1597), fol. 1r&v; Christopher Wirtzung, *The General Practise of Physicke* (1605), 1–5; Peter Lowe, *The Whole Course of Chirurgerie* (1597), sig. B1r&v; John Banister, *A Needefull treatise of Chyrurgerie* (1575), fol. 2r ff. of the Epistle Dedicatorie.

[8] John Cotta, *A Short Discoverie of Ignorant Practisers of Phisicke* (1619), 120: "And thus must the true physition euer behold God as his guide, and be gouerned and directed by his hand. For God is nature aboue nature, and nature is his hand and subordinate power: God being therefore the cause of causes in nature, he is the giuer of health and life in nature, and the Physition is his seruant and minister therein."

Goutes, Palsies, Dropsies, reums, Pthisikes, other out of number . . . what paine or punishment can there be immagined to put us in remembraunce of our own wickednes, cause us to detest our abhominable liuings, and to call for mercy with lamentable hearts more then this onely plage & scourge of God commonlie called the pestilence?[9]

All infirmities come equally from God, but the great epidemics most clearly signify his wrath. And all come usually through the ordinary channels of nature, though the possibility of direct infliction by God without ordinary means must always be reserved.

Hence a final proposition that God likewise determines the outcome of each sickness in the individual patient. The doctor must humbly recognize that he is a servant of the divine will. Since the primary cause of disease is supernatural, the first remedy must be prayer and moral reform, but, since the supernatural works usually through the natural, physical remedies also must be applied:

. . . in the time of Pestilence, Penitencie and Confession are to be preferred before all other Medicaments, and withall to change the place for a more pure ayre.[10]

God has set in advance a death hour for each man. If this has arrived, no prayers or medicaments can save the patient:

. . . thynke not that no man can be holpen by no maner of medecynes, yf so be God do sende the sicknes, for he hath put a tyme to euery man, ouer the which tyme no man by no art nor science can not prolonge the time: for the nomber of monthes and dayes of mans lyfe God knoweth.[11]

Inasmuch, however, as no man can guess in advance whether the destined death hour is at hand, the doctor is always bound to do his best to preserve life.

By these various ligatures medicine was thus bound very closely to theology. Indeed the connections could not well have been much tighter. Completely dominating medicine, God was re-

[9] Thomas Phayre's preface to *A Treatise of the Pestilence* appended to Jehan Goeurot's *The Regiment of Life* (1596), sig. Ll^r. Also William Bullein, *Regiment againste Pleurisi* (1562), sigs. A4^v ff.; Simon Kellwaye, *A Defensative against the Plague* (1593), fol. 1^v.

[10] Thomas Vicary, *The English Mans Treasure* (1633), 250. Similarly, Thomas Moulton, *Myrrour of Helth* [1550 (?)], sigs. A8^v, B5^r ff.

[11] Andrew Boorde, *The Breuiary of Healthe* (1552), fol. vi^r. Warde's epistles to Alessio's *Secretes* (1568), fol. 2^v; William Bullein, *Dialogue against the feuer Pestilence* (1564), fol. 77^r.

garded as the source of the human body, of all medical materials, of the physician's knowledge, of the disease itself, and of its final event. So ran the generally accepted theory. Yet the most important thing about a theory is not that it exists but how it exists, how it is interpreted, contorted, utilized, or avoided by actual classes of people under particular circumstances.

Briefly, the whole doctrine was regarded as false and dangerous by two small groups of extremists on opposite sides of the issue. On what might be called the far right wing were the Elizabethan mystics and ascetics, the ultra religionists who despised worldly life as a clog upon the union of the soul with God. For them, man's body was vile.[12] Prolonged study for its health could lead only away from the single essential care of salvation, if not into perilous curiosity about God's secrets. Men of this otherworldly temper tended strongly to reject or minimize the natural causation and treatment of disease in favor of the supernatural. Later on we shall see how this attitude issued in the sect of so-called "Stoical Christians," who denied that plague was infectious. It did not suffice, however, to overcome the more practical and worldly strain featuring most Elizabethan religion, and so remained a minor element.

On the extreme left wing can be distinguished a small fringe of medical men who had become either outright atheists or at least disbelievers in the Christian concept of Providence. Their direction was towards a complete materialism which ruled out altogether any supernatural explanation of what happened to the body. In their eyes, disease was a purely natural phenomenon capable of being dealt with by a positivistic method only. William Bullein's *Dialogue against the feuer Pestilence* (1564) satirizes this view in the person of a Medicus who worshipped Aristotle instead of God and denied the dualism of body and soul.[13]

[12] See, typically, T. R.'s *The Anatomie of the minde* (1576), Preface to the Reader; and contrast Nicholas Gyer's *The English Phlebotomy* (1592), A3^r. Gemini, *op. cit.*, sig. A1^r of the Dedication, inveighed against those who "when they heare or reade certein wordes of holy scripture speakynge against the fleshe and the worlde, do greatly mistake those woordes and folyshly dyspise and contemne the maruelous creatours of God wherin shyneth the poure and wysdome of his inuisible deitie . . ."

[13] Fols. 6^v to 8^v, 24$^{r\&v}$, 38^r, etc. For other references see Kocher, "The Physician as Atheist in Elizabethan England," *Huntington Library Quarterly*, X, 3 (May, 1947).

And *The difference betwene the auncient Phisicke and the latter Phisicke* (1585) by R. B., a Paracelsan, accuses orthodox Galenism of fostering belief in a mechanistic, materialistic universe in the running of which God has no part:

And because (O mercifull God) the heathnish Phisicke and the heathnish Philosophie doth not acknowledge, that it is thy power and vertue that bringeth forth all thinges that growe, and that thy working power doth preserue and maintaine all thinges: and that it is thy curing vertue that helpeth and cureth all deseases, greefes and infirmities, by such meanes as it pleaseth thee, or without meanes: therefore they cleaue fast to their false imagined naturall causes and meanes of helpe, forgetting thee: whereby many of them become Atheists.[14]

Despite this latter partisan slur, it seems quite unlikely that many Elizabethan doctors really put out of their minds the belief in God as working behind all the physical appearances of illness. The medical writings of the period bear convincing witness to the fidelity of the great majority of doctors to this belief, though with many fine gradations of stress.

Let us look at some concrete instances. The most devout among contemporary medical works were likely to lean upon religion not merely in their prefaces but pervasively throughout their texts, sometimes culminating in a closing prayer for divine aid. So ardent is the tone as to leave no doubt of its genuineness of feeling. Books of William Clowes, the prominent surgeon, may serve as good examples. His *Treatise of the disease called Morbus Gallicus* (1585) devotes most of its three-page opening Epistle to an admonition, both long and strong, that sexual disease is God's punishment for the sin of lust. Likewise the first three pages of the text are suffused with the idea that man must amend his moral life to escape syphilis. Clowes even protests (page 5) that no reader should expect help from the medicines he is about to describe "but such as fully purpose to liue honestly: for the God otherwise will bring a cursse upon the verie medicines, and take away the benefit of healing, by that meanes." The next 33 pages give a discussion of various preparatives and purgations, bloodletting and diet, during the course of which a digressive complaint against the hordes of quacks then scandalizing the medical profession leads Clowes into a defense of

[14] Sig. A6ᵛ.

the honor of medicine, with full citation of the text from Ecclesiasticus 38 requiring honor for the physician (page 8). Pages 38 to 46 comprise case histories of actual cures wrought by Clowes through fumigation and rubbing with a mercury ointment. In several of these cases, after detailing his therapeutic methods, he adds that the cure was effected "through the helpe of almightie God, to whome be all glory for euer. Amen." He then ends the book with a fervent prayer to God to bless the physician's labors "that thy power giuing force to these medicines, they may bee effectuall to the remouing the griefes of thy people." Likewise from Clowes' other books, *A prooued practise for all young Chirurgians* (1588), *A Profitable and Necessarie Booke of Obseruations* (1596), and *Treatise for the Artificiall Cure of Struma* (1602), it is clear that he was a devout man who bore his religion constantly in mind while practising surgery. The works of William Bullein, John Woodall, and Thomas Gale are other examples of the intense penetration of medical writing by religious feeling. A number of additional books might be classified as warmly pious throughout, but, on the whole, they remained a minority group. Lest there be any attempt to correlate piety with lack of ability, we should remark that the men just named were among the ablest of the Elizabethan physicians and surgeons.

The average Elizabethan work on medicine or surgery is much less intent on religion. It normally makes a pious reference or two in the preface and dedicatory epistle, but when it buckles down to the business of medical analysis it is likely to forget the supernatural, except for a possible passing allusion now and then. Thus John Banister's *Needefull treatise of Chyrurgerie* (1575) in its two Epistles Dedicatorie cites Ecclesiasticus against the maligners of the medical profession and allots two pages to God's sending of medicines to men, but in its actual text gives over a hundred pages to discussing types, causes, and treatment of ulcers without once mentioning supernatural cause or supernatural cure. *The birth of mankynde* (1585) by Eucharius Roesslin is a practical work of several hundred pages on obstetrics. Measures to promote conception of a child are said to operate only "by the grace of God" (fol. 126ʳ), and symptoms of approaching death in a pregnant mother are listed which would cause the physician to "commit the cure of her to the handes of almyghtie God." Otherwise, religion is limited to several of the usual statements in the Prologue. The 484 closely printed pages of Philip Barrough's *The Method of Phisick* (1596) describe the causes and treatment of hundreds of ailments as if no God existed, with but two exceptions: the supernatural as well as the natural origins of pestilence are admitted in the section on the disease (pp. 246–54), and the religious justification for the physician's right to search the secrets of nature is stated in the preface. In books of this kind religion becomes largely a prolegomenon and an appendix to medicine. The majority of Elizabethan medical publications fall loosely within this general class.[15]

Then there is also a smaller class of treatises in which religion does not appear at all, or so infinitesimally as to be negligible. Several books of prescriptions for miscellaneous infirmities, like Johannes de Vigo's *Lytell Practyce in Medycyne* (early blackletter, no date) and John Banister's *An Antidotarie Chyrurgicall* (1589), are quite devoid of religious reference. Robert Recorde's sensible book on urinalysis, *The Urinall of Physick* (1567), has only this one brief phrase at the end of its preface addressed to the Surgeons' Company of London: "I . . . with earnest affection, commit you unto God, whiche is the right instructor of al true knowledge, Fare you wel." John Caius gave his entire *Boke against the disease commonly called the sweate* (1552) to a scientific commentary on the sickness as a thing of this world, not alluding to God until the very last sentence, couched in the conditional: "If other causes ther be supernatural, theim I leue to the diuines to serche, and the diseases thereof to cure, as a matter with out the compasse of my facultie." So conscious and explicit an exclusion of religion from medicine, however, is not usually to be found even in books of this general type, where the omission is usually silent, and no doubt often unpremeditated.[16]

[15] Other samples: Thomas Newton, *The Olde-mans Dietarie*, 1586; Leonardo Fioravanti, *A Short Discours uppon Chirurgerie*, 1580; Peter Levens, *The Path-way to Health*, 1632 (first printed in 1587); Thomas Rainold, *Compendious Declaration of a certain lateli inuented oile*, 1551; Andrew Boorde, *A Regimente of health*, 1562.

[16] Other books of this type: Walter Cary, *The Hammer for the Stone*, 1581; A. T., *A Rich Store-house for the Diseased*, 1596; *The Englishmans Doctor*, 1607. The able work of Christopher Langton, *A Treatise declaring the principal partes of phisick*, 1547, Bk. 3, chap. 1, even discusses the causes of disease without including the supernatural. George Baker's works on medical chemistry are in this category, as is also William Harvey's revolutionary *De Motu Cordis*.

Recognizing always that the foregoing triple grouping of medical works cannot be rigid and that each book has its own peculiar quality of religious tone depending on the relative length, ardor, frequency, context, and subject-matter of its embodiments of accepted religious theory, we can still conclude that Elizabethan medical literature in the mass was heavily weighted toward religion. There was no discernible trend away from it during the period. Books at the end of the era seem just as pious as those at the beginning. No increase can be noticed in the relative numbers of works excluding the whole supernatural element, as a possible prelude to the separation of religion from the theory of medicine. What can be said, however, is that the average Elizabethan writer on the subject preferred to reserve his recognition of the larger religious significations of his work for his prefaces and to keep his feet on the common earth when giving the actual medical information itself. Noteworthy also is the fact that books on plague and other devastating epidemics have on the whole a much deeper religious tone than do books on non-epidemic infirmities. Devout feelings of the Elizabethan people clustered more passionately around these great universal diseases which seemed like overwhelmingly fearful revelations of the wrath of God. They were a natural focus of piety to which the sentiments of the doctors themselves appear to have gravitated quite genuinely. Without these large numbers of pestilence books, and sections on pestilence in general compendiums, the medical literature of the epoch would undoubtedly have been considerably more secular than it is.

There remains the question whether this literature favors some portions of the theology of medicine more than others, and, if so, in what ways and for what reasons. The conclusion will be clear that medical writers sometimes had motives other than spotless piety in using religious theory and that there were certain tensions between them and the religionists, even the moderate religionists who made up the bulk of the theological school.

Of the five main propositions which, on an earlier page, were described as constituting the theology of medicine, the first three justified medicine whereas the last two tended to make claims upon it. The divine craftsmanship of the human body, the divine intention that all nature should be explored for its medicinal properties, and the divine commission to doctors to apply and extend the healing art were all clear encouragements to medical science.

On the other hand, God's control over the coming of disease and over its healing were, under some interpretations, limiting factors upon medicine. Obviously the writers of medical works felt a good deal more ease and zest in using what was encouraging than what was constricting, and governed their selections accordingly.

The religious justification of medicine was, indeed, their chief rock of defense against the perpetual and widespread attacks leveled against the profession during this era. If preachers accused medical science of atheism, they might be answered with a quotation, from Guy de Chauliac or almost any subsequent work on anatomy, that among the reasons for studying the human body "The first and the greatest is for the meruayle of the great power of God to the creator of men, that so hath made them to his lykenesse and forme."[17] If other preachers spoke of the danger to the soul in knowing too much about the world, they could be confronted with the text from Ecclesiasticus 38 that God created medicines of the earth, and the inference, as in John Banister's *Historie of Man* (1578):

In fine, there is nothing so highe in the heauens aboue, nothing so low in the earth beneath, nothing so profound in the bowels of Arte, nor any thing so hid in the secretes of nature, as that good will dare not enterprise, search, unclose, or discover.[18]

If the derisive word went round among the people that doctors killed more than they cured and that they were the only murderers privileged to bury their dead without penalty of law, it was comforting to be able to point to the long religious history of medicine since the days of Adam and to remark that Christ and his apostles were healers.[19] The doctors themselves were very sensitive about the abominable state of medical practice in England at

[17] *Guydos Questions* (1579), fol. 5^v; Vigo, *Chirurgery,* chap. 1, fol. 1^r.

[18] Sig. A2^v. Also Bullein's *Bulwarke* (1562), sig. ii^r: "There is nothyng so secrete hidden, within the minerals of the yearth, or lurkyng so lowe under the floodes of the sea: but by meanes and policie, thei are brought to use. Their names, qualities, and natures, are knowen, unto the wittie hedde of mankinde, to this ende, to helpe mankinde, in the tyme of his bodily infirmitie. These God hath ordained by his diuine prouidence, that euery creature sencible and insencible, should serue his beste creature, mankinde." Similarly, John Dove, *Confutation of Atheisme,* 26; Gyer, *Phlebotomy,* sig. A3^v; Burrough, *Method of Phisick,* sig. A4^r.

[19] See the defences of medicine in Thomas Gale's preface to *Certaine Workes of Galens,* 1586; Pedro Mexia, *A Pleasaunt Dialogue concerning Phisicke and Phisitians* 1580; Erasmus, *Prayse of Phisyke,* n.d.

the time because of its infestation by droves of quacks and sorcerers unchecked by a licensing system. Ecclesiasticus 38 is undoubtedly the Scriptural text most zealously cited in contemporary medical books.[20]

We may emphasize also that these same religious ideas could be, and were, used by the Paracelsans and others in support of their new discoveries. If anything, the Paracelsans invoked God oftener than did the rival Galenists. In his *Compendious Declaration of the Excellent vertues of a certain lateli inuented oile* (1561) Thomas Rainold argued that:

. . . it can not be trueli denied, but that in this oure time god hath stearid up excellent vertuous witts whiche so straitli call to examination al the doctrine and documents lefft from the auncients, waieng, & so aduisidlie trieng, the sincere from the contrarie, that if thei procead as thei haue begun, it is like within feu yeares, that science will be so renuid, refreshid, and purgid, that thei whiche hitherto haue boren al the bruit, & haue obtainid all autorite, wil leese a greate portion of there creadit . . .[21]

John Hester was the center of early Paracelsan activity in England. Not only in his independent works, like *The Key of Philosophie* (1596) and *Pearle of Practise* (1594), but also in his translations of Paracelsus, Du Chesne, and Fioravanti he relied constantly on the idea that God intended the Paracelsans to advance medical science. It could never have been the divine will that all progress should cease with Galen and Avicenna. Especially in new diseases like syphilis, which was unknown to the ancients, God was revealing new remedies to mankind through the Paracelsans. No matter now unpopular these remedies might be at first with the orthodox Galenists it was the Christian duty of each Paracelsan to publish them lest he be guilty of hiding his talent. In this way, comparable to the way in which the explorers of the New World found a religious incentive for their hardships, the new chemists were encouraged to go on with their work. It is certainly wrong to think of Elizabethan religion as inhibiting new ideas in medicine.

[20] See John Hall's epistle to his translation of Lanfranc's *Excellent Woorke of Chirurgerie* (1565), fol. ii^r; John Securis, *A Detection of the daily abuses committed in physick* (1566), sig. D3^r; Bullein, *Gouernment of Health* (1595), fol. 3^r.

[21] Sig. B3^v–B4^r. A like defence of Paracelsan medicine is made by William Vaughan's *Naturall And Artificiall Directions for Health* (1600), 67; Francis Anthony, *The Apologie of Aurum Potabile* (1616), 19. See also Thomas Tymme's forespeech to Du Chesne's *The Practise Of Chymicall Physicke* (1605), fol. 1^v.

The case was different when it came to those parts of the theology of medicine which announced God as the ultimate source of all bodily weal and woe. Here the problem was to reconcile this doctrine with a science of medicine which, if it was to be a science at all, had to be able to depend on an order of nature at least relatively predictable. General recourse was therefore had in medical thinking to the view that when God acted upon man's body he did so by natural means. But let us see how this view was actually applied in concrete cases.

As regards the divine origin of all physical ailments, most medical writers did not bother to mention it except in discussions of plague and venereal disease. Wounds, fractures, agues, dropsies, and the like were analyzed solely according to natural origins. For example, William Clowes made much of the supernatural cause of syphilis in his book on *Morbus Gallicus* but said nothing about God's sending the wounds, ulcers, and tumors he described in his books on surgery. Walter Cary in his *Farewell to Physicke* (1583) wrote of headache, sore eyes, heartburn, rheum in the lungs, and so on, but only in his chapter on plague listed a supernatural as well as a natural reason for the sickness.[22] Apparently, the lesser and more obvious infirmities did not carry the mysterious horror which, in the case of pestilence, led men's thoughts to God, or the moral obloquy which, in the case of syphilis, produced the same result.

Where plague was concerned, medical writers were fairly unanimous in recognizing the supramundane element. But their general disposition was to give it far less space than they gave to mundane explanation, and a far inferior emphasis. Sir Thomas Elyot's *The Castell of Helth* (1572), although a fairly pious document, sets aside four pages for the solely naturalistic explanation of plague and only this final sentence for the other: "But here I alwaye except the power of God, which is wonderful, and also mercifull, aboue mans reason or counsell, preseruing or stryking whome, whan, and where it shall like his maiestie, to whome bee glory and prayse euerlasting. Amen" (fol. 95ᵛ). Elyot evidently

[22] Cary's discussion of plague covered pp. 45–50, but he gave only half of page 46 to the supernatural. In the same class was Petrus Valentinus' *Enchiridion Medicum* (1612), a 72-page general survey of medicine which brought in the supernatural only in one sentence of its 2-page essay on plague (p. 60); John Jones, *A Diall for all Agues* (1566), sig. F7ᵛ ff.

regarded the supernatural as something unaccountable, apart from and superimposed upon the natural, with which it was not his function to deal in a book on medicine. In the same way, Philip Barrough's *The Method of Phisick* (1596) offers only a grudging welcome to the idea in this one sentence of his eight-page discussion of plague:

> Also we doe not deny, but that sometime great plagues & pestilence be sent of God for the grieuous sinnes and horrible offences of men, wherewith he punisheth the great offences of us: whereof there be many euident testimonies in the Prophets, and specially in Ezechiel cap. 5.[23]

In many another such treatise, God's intervention was similarly reduced to an "also" which doctors "doe not deny" but do not exert themselves to affirm either.[24] It was something to be admitted at the outset and thereafter, in effect, ignored. It belonged mainly to the province of the theologian, who was a specialist in such matters and might be expected to know what to do about them. In truth there was nothing much that doctors, as doctors, could contribute in that field. They were specialists in the natural. Thus a distinct practical separation of medicine from religion inevitably obtained in the Elizabethan age, however close their assimilation in theory. Let us emphasize, however, that this was a separation rather than an opposition.

The point which medical writings were chiefly concerned to bring out was that when God sent pestilence he did so by natural means, like the influence of planets, weather, corrupted air or unwholesome humors in the body. To these man might add by dissipation and bad diet ruinous to his constitution. But God did not often bypass or pervert the normal order of nature through direct, unintermediated, miraculous inflictions of disease. This struggle of the medical writer to assert both the ordinary inviolability of natural law and the possibility of its violation on extraordinary occasions by God stands out vividly in Paré. God, he said, is

> ... the beginning and cause of the second causes, which cannot well without

[23] P. 247. His full analysis of plague occupies pp. 246–54. Similarly, Peter Turner's *Concerning Amulets or Plague Cakes* (1603), especially p. 10.

[24] This is true, though in somewhat lesser degree, even of the more pious medical works on plague, e.g., Thomas Lodge, *A Treatise of the Plague* (1603); Simon Kellwaye, *A Defensative against the Plague* (1593); and Christopher Wirtzung, *The General Practise of Physicke* (1605), 653 ff.

the first cause goe about nor attempt, much lesse performe any thing. For from hence they borrow their force, order, and constancy of order; so that they serve as Instruments for God, who rules and governes us, and the whole World, to performe all his workes, by that constant course of order, which hee hath appointed unchangeable from the beginning. Wherefore all the cause of a plague is not to bee attributed to these neere and inferiour causes or beginnings. . . On the contrary, wee ought to thinke . . . That even as God by his omnipotent Power hath created all things of nothing, so he by his eternall Wisedome preserves and governes the same, leads and enclines them as he pleaseth, yea verily at his pleasure changeth their order, and the whole course of Nature.

This cause of an extraordinary Plague, as wee confesse and acknowledge, so here we will not prosecute it any further, but thinke fit to leave it to Divines, because it exceeds the bounds of Nature, in which I will now containe my selfe. Wherefore let us come to the naturall causes of the plague.[25]

Here in a single paragraph Paré stated in naked juxtaposition both that nature was "unchangeable from the beginning" and that God "verily at his pleasure changeth" it, and then hurried on to his real business, which was with its unchangeableness, its functioning as a system.

Most clergymen agreed in the main with this position. However anxious they were to preserve the theoretical possibility that God might occasionally choose to act by miracle, they had to concede that usually he did not. Their complaint, however, was that doctors tended to stress these natural second causes at the expense of the supernatural first cause, and thus substitute nature for God. So Roger Fenton, a preacher, enumerated in *A Perfume against the noysome Pestilence* (1603) five possible natural sources of plague, and cautioned:

But the iudgement of Moses reacheth further, in that he maketh it an effect of Gods wrath: for whatsoeuer secondarie causes doe concurre hereunto, certaine it is, that the wrath of God is the principall: which being kindled and sent forth, doth fire the rest and set them all a working. He is purblind, as the Apostle speaketh, and cannot see a farre off, who looketh onely upon inferiour causes.[26]

Evidently the difference between the clergy and the medical profession was one of emphasis. The clergy began from God and

[25] *Workes*, Bk. 22, chap. 2, p. 818.
[26] Sig. A7r.

treated his use of natural causes as an incidental consequence, whereas doctors began from nature and saw God as a distant activator who was somewhat out of their sphere. Henoch Clapham's sermon, *An Epistle upon the present Pestilence* (1603), displays typical clerical impatience with this tendency:

> Beloued, God hauing smitten our Citie with the Pestilence, behold, booke upon booke, prescribing naturall meanes as for naturall maladies, but little said of spirituall meanes, for spirituall maladies, which should giue life to the former. To speake and act in such cases, as sole Naturians, is of Christians to become Galenists, and of spirituall to become carnall.[27]

It is easy to see how this difference of stress sometimes led to charges of atheism against the physician.

Despite these disagreements, however, doctors and most preachers made common cause against the still more radical Christian view, entertained by the so-called Stoical or fatalistic Christians,[28] that God smote plague victims directly, without employing any natural process. This view was held, apparently, by sizeable segments of the Elizabethan population and by a few clerics of an especially otherworldly turn of mind. It was the fruit of panic and hysteria during the great epidemics, when, for no visible reason, thousands of healthy people seemed to drop dead, while other thousands, no more healthy, survived. What could be the cause except that God in his unsearchable will was striking down his selected victims? The foul sores and buboes of the disease were "God's tokens" or the literal marks of his hand. According to Thomas Nashe's *Christs Teares Over Ierusalem* (1593):

> Hye hande I may well terme it, for on many that are arrested with the Plague is the print of a hand seene, and in the very moment it first takes them, they feele a sencible blow gyuen them, as it were with the hande of some stander by.[29]

---

[27] Sig. A3ʳ. This also is the point of view expressed by such other preachers as James Godskall, *The Kings Medicine For This Present yeere 1604* (1604), sig. E4ʳ, and Henry Holland, *Spirituall Preservatives against the pestilence* (1593), fols. 15ᵛ–16ʳ; Miles Coverdale, *How a Chrysten man ought to flye the Plague* [1537 (?)], sig. A3ᵛ.

[28] This title was conferred by Thomas Cogan, *The Haven of Health* (1584), 269.

[29] Ed. McKerrow, II, 171–72. Holland, *op. cit.*, 15ʳ: "Because the Lordes power and might more appeares & is more manifested in this great euill, than in anie other, I thinke it not fabulous what I haue heard some reporte, that they haue seene as it were the print of a hand upon the armes and other partes of the bodie, of sundrie smitten with the Pestilence."

If this was the dramatic method by which God killed, it followed that plague was not contagious at all. Each patient had his own private case of the disease, not contracted from other sufferers. Therefore all preventive and therapeutic measures were quite futile. Quarantines imposed by the health authorities need not be observed, sanitation was waste effort. The only thing necessary was to trust in the Lord as required by Psalm 91:

> I will say of the Lord, He is my refuge and my fortress: my God, in him will I trust.
> Surely he shall deliver thee from the snare of the fowler, and from the noisome pestilence . . .
> A thousand shall fall at thy side, and ten thousand at thy right hand; but it shall not come nigh thee.

So, by a twist of rationalization, the popular terror of death gave rise to the complete disregard of death. If you looked hard enough at the 91st Psalm you could see that the Lord would not let you die, no matter how many others died—others, presumably, who trusted him less than you did.

But neither the medical profession nor the great majority of churchmen could allow such a doctrine to flourish. It thrust aside the whole science of medicine. Even clergymen who insisted on the primacy of God in the causation of plague realized that age-long experience showed the disease to be catching. Also, it was obvious that a scrapping of all physical precautions by these sectarians jeopardized the life of everybody else. Hence numerous sermons were preached and books written against them during the Elizabethan period, especially in the 1590's and early 1600's when the plague was at its worst. The whole of preacher James Balmford's book, *A Short Dialogue Concerning The Plagues Infection* (1603) is a refutation of "that bloudy errour, which denieth the Pestilence to be contagious: maintained, not onely by the rude multitude, but by too many of the better sort" (sig. A2^v). Much of John Ewich's *Of the dutie of a faithfull Magistrate* (1583) likewise inveighs against them.[30] Theodore Beza's *A shorte Treatize of the Plague* was translated into English in 1580 for the same purpose.

Inasmuch as most of the debate was waged on a theological level around the interpretation of Psalm 91, most medical books

[30] Fol. 4^r of John Stockwood's Epistle Dedicatorie.

do not take part in it. The issue, however, is mentioned frequently enough in the contemporary medical literature to show that doctors were aware of its dangers. For example, Cogan's *Haven of Health* (1584) and Jones' *A Dial for all Agues* (1566) both denounced the attitude on theological as well as medical grounds, arguing that plague was certainly infectious and that God intended man to use all possible natural means to preserve his life.[31] To fail to do so was really to commit the sin of suicide. And the question was serious enough to rouse the apprehensions of the Government itself. The official *Orders thought meete by her Maiestie to be executed throughout the Counties of this Realme* (1588) for the combating of plague contains this order:

Item, if there be any person Ecclesiastical or laye, that shall holde and publishe any opinions (as in some places report is made) that it is a vayne thing to forbeare to resort to the infected, or that it is not charitable to forbid the same, pretending that no person shall dye but at their tyme prefixed, such persons shalbe not onely reprehended, but by order of the Bishop, if they be ecclesiasticall, shalbe forbidden to preache, and being laye, shalbe also enioyned to forbeare to utter such dangerous opinions upon payne of imprisonment . . .[32]

Besides plague, one other form of possible direct supernatural action upon the human body concerned physicians. This was demonic possession, whereby a devil was supposed to enter the body, taking control of all its faculties, or the analogous affliction of witchcraft whereby a witch sent a devil to twist and torture her victim's limbs, procure sexual impotence, and the like. But the extent to which Elizabethan medicine actually bothered about these possibilities has been vastly overestimated. One can read dozens of treatises on all aspects of medicine without encountering a single reference to the subject. When it appeared at all, it was stringently limited to cases of epilepsy or mental illness. And even in those cases the physician seldom gave it more than passing mention, often only in order to say that many putative instances of demonism were nothing more than misunderstood physical and mental ailments. Konrad Gesner's *The Treasure of Euonymus*

[31] Cogan, 268–71; Jones, sig. G3^r; I. W., *A Briefe Treatise of the Plague* (1603), sig. A3^r; William Warde's epistle to his translation of Alessio's *Secretes* (1568), fol. 2^v.

[32] Sig. B2^v. This order was reissued without change upon James I's accession in 1603.

(1559) prescribed a powder as a cure for them: "Manye also that bee Limphatici, that is, mad or Melancholicke, whome they beleued commonly to be resorted unto of Deuils, we haue cured them with ye same" (p. 331). Sponsored by such writers as Wier and Reginald Scot, the explanation of witches as being often merely psychopaths had taken firm hold during the closing decades of the sixteenth century. *A Discourse of the Preservation of the Sight* (1599) by Andreas Laurentius exclaims:

Auicen noteth that melancholike persons sometimes doe such strange things, that the common people imagine them to bee possessed. How many famous men be there in this our age, which make scruple to condemne these olde witches, thinking it to bee nothing but a melancholike humour which corrupteth their imagination, and filleth them with these vaine toyes (p. 98).

The enlightened physician, Edward Jorden wrote his *Discourse of the Suffocation of the Mother* (1603) to point out that this ailment, apparently a form of hysteria, should be distinguished from demonic possession:

I doe not deny but that God doth in these dayes worke extraordinarily, for the deliuerance of his children, and for other endes best knowne unto himselfe; and that among other, there may be both possessions by the Diuell, and obsessions and witchcraft, etc. and dispossession also through the Prayers and supplications of his seruants, which is the onely meanes left unto us for our reliefe in that case. But such examples being verie rare nowadayes, I would in the feare of God aduise men to be very circumspect in pronouncing of a possession: both because the impostures be many, and the effects of naturall diseases be strange to such as haue not looked throughly into them.[33]

In other words, the devil was a last resort in Elizabethan medical diagnosis. Most doctors never got around to using him at all. His appearance, though still possible was "very rare nowadayes" and should not be admitted until every other kind of natural explanation had first been tried. Moreover, like God whose agent

---

[33] Sig. A3ʳ et passim. Gyer, *English Phlebotomy*, sig. A4ᵛ, shared this view. John Cotta in *A Short Discoverie of Ignorant Practisers in England* (1619), 56, tried to hold open the possibility of witchcraft, but used most of his space in arguing that various trances, sleeps, and convulsions were really natural symptoms of disease (59–72). Cf. Paré, *Workes*, Bk. 25, chaps. 13–17. It is interesting to notice that writers on psychology seem to have made more of the devil than did writers on medicine. See Timothy Bright, *A Treatise of Melancholie* (1586), 205–29; Levinus Lemnius, *The Touchstone of Complexions* (1581), 20ff.; Juan Huarte, *Examen de Ingenios*, 92ff. He was, of course, indispensable in books on witchcraft, whether popular or learned.

he was, Satan was no affair of the doctor's anyway. The only method of routing him was by prayer. So, much more than was the case with God, the doctor simply passed the devil by.

As God was primarily responsible for sending disease, so he cured it or made it fatal, again usually through natural means. The same types of medical books which ignore or play down the former idea do the same thing to the latter, and in the same ways. Treatises on plague are likely to make brief mention of prayer and moral reformation as the first of all remedies before proceeding to extended discussion of physical therapy. This kind of conjunction is exemplified in William Bullein's *The Government of Health* (1595):

Against the said influences al christian men must pray to God to be their defence, for they be Gods instruments to punish the earth. . . . Then one must make a fire in euerie chimney within the house, and burne sweete perfumes to purge this foule aire.[34]

In other types of diseases, it is interesting to notice that the idea of divine healing was usually not invoked except in extraordinarily difficult and dangerous cases. Thus the books of the pious William Clowes, *Observations* and *Struma*, favor the idea chiefly when the patient seems in danger of death. In the easier cases the surgeon might be inclined to feel that he had effected the cure himself.

Miraculous cures worked by God without natural means are either not alluded to at all in medical books or, if mentioned, are carefully restricted. In Bullein's *Dialogue betwene Sorenes and Chyrurgi* (1562) a character named Sorenes expresses the wish that nowadays God would perform such miracles of healing as in Biblical times. He is rebuked by another character called Chirurgeon:

Sorenes, Sorenes! Thou saiest not well, for it is rather a tempting of God, then a beleuing in God, to looke or wishe for miracles, for faithfull men nedes none. And I trust thou are faithfull, therfore thou nedest no miracle, but rather consider this, Christ healed the bodies of Sicke menne, twoo maner of waies, the one by vertue of his heauenlie worde, whereby we be taught that he is God. The seconde he healed somtime with claie, with

[34] Fol. 30^v. Also Leonardo Fioravanti's *Chirurgerie*, p. 21^r, and *A Ioyfull Iewel* (1579), 3 ff.; Benedict Canutus, *Treatyse ageynst pestilence* [1510 (?)], sig. A3^r; Cary, *Farewell to Physicke*, 45–6.

spitte etc. wherein we be learned, and he also haue learned us, in the tyme of our sorenes, prudentlie to use Goddes instrumentes and meanes, yea, not with claie or spitte, yet with presious herbes, fruites, gummes etc. For God hath ordeined theim onelie to helpe his people. . .[35]

We are familiar with this unremitting pressure by doctors to eject the supernatural from Elizabethan medicine. Nevertheless, an exception with respect to scrofula, the king's evil, was universally acknowledged. Clowes in his *Struma* agreed that when the English or French king touched a scrofulous patient, intoning the words "The King toucheth thee, the Lord make thee whole," a divine power flowed through his fingers capable of healing cases incurable by human art. In his text, however, Clowes said that he could not presume to discuss this supernatural gift, and confined himself instead to "the true path-way of Artificial gifts (which God of his great goodnes giueth to men of Arte)."[36] Whether from motives of humility, indifference, or disdain, medical men of letters certainly inclined strongly to do the same.

Exorcisms, charms, amulets, incantations, and the like were also condemned as futile and superstitious. Any physician using them was ridiculed by his colleagues as a quack.[37] Indeed as one of the chief devices favored by renegade doctors and "empirickes" in cheating the ignorant public they were a principal target for the scorn and indignation of the reputable practitioner. Both the College of Physicians and the Barber-Surgeons Company made constant, if unavailing efforts to stamp out this practice, efforts which are fully reported in their records.[38]

[35] Fol. 9ʳ, bound in with Bullein's *Bulwarke*, 1562. Juan Huarte, *Examen de Ingenios*, 15–19 made the same point very emphatically. Cf. Bullein, *Regiment against Pleurisi*, sig. B1ᵛ.

[36] P. 68 and A2ᵛ. See also Securis, *A Detection*, sig. B5ʳ.

[37] See especially John Hall's *An historiall Expostulation Against the beastlye abusers, both of Chyrurgerie and Physyke,* appended to his translation of Lanfranc; and the vigorous contempt of Clowes in *A prooued practise for all young Chirurgians*, sig. A3ʳ. John Oberndoerffer in *The Anatomyes of the True Physition*, 1602, p. 16, attacked the impostors who ". . . that they may colourably and cunningly hide their grosse Ignorance, when they know not the Cause of Disease, referre it unto Charmes, Witchcrafts, Magnificall Incantations, and Sorcerie, vainely, and with a brazen forehead, affirming that there is no way to help them, but by Characters, Circles, Figure-castings, Exorcisme, Coniurations, and other Impious, and Godlesse Meanes." Cotta, *Short Discoverie*, p. 49 ff.

[38] Charles Goodall, *The Royal College of Physicians of London* (1684), and Sidney Young, *The Annals of the Barber-Surgeons of London* (London, 1890).

Upon review of the whole situation we can now distinguish four main types of attitude toward the rôle of God in disease. A small group of medical atheists held that disease came by natural processes only. Most doctors, however, accepted the addition that these processes were set in motion by God. Most clergymen, shifting the emphasis, spoke of God as the originator of disease though normally using natural means. At the other extreme, a minority group of Stoical Christians preached that God struck the individual victim directly without using natural means. Between the first and the last groups there was obviously no common ground. The atheists were materialists, the Stoical Christians spiritualists. But the two moderate parties shared a common acceptance of both sides of the Elizabethan dualism, body and spirit. And since these parties represented the great majority of Elizabethans there was no sharp split between the dominant views of the relations between medicine and religion during this period.

Both parties wished to preserve the idea that God was an active power in man's affairs, as well as the idea that a normally inviolable order of nature existed. The former may be regarded as primarily a religious need of the human heart, the latter as a necessary basis of all science. But it would be misleading to think of the clergy as interested only in the one, and the medical profession only in the other. Doctors were human beings who felt their own religious needs and inclined to accept the solutions current in the society in which they had been educated. And the priesthood were too pragmatic to blink the fact that the world seemed to run a natural course or to ignore the very considerable corpus of systematic information which had been gathered about it. Indeed many clergymen, especially in the country districts, practised medicine on the side;[39] many doctors had studied theology at one time or another.

If Elizabethan religion had consistently taught that, since its

[39] Cotta in his *Short Discoverie*, 86–9, loudly complained that too many clergymen were dabbling in medicine, "making themselues roome in others affaires, under pretence of loue and mercie." In the preface to his *Phlebotomy* (1601), sigs. A6ᵛ–7ʳ, Simon Harward, a minister, defended his writing a book on medicine: ". . . the coniunction betwixt the body and soule being so neere, and the sympathy so great, I see no cause but that he which studieth Diuinity, may lawfully now and then so bestow a spare houre in viewing of the remedyes ordeyned of God for mans infirmities, that he may be able in corporall extremities to yeeld reliefe as well particularly to himselfe, as in common to his good friends." Also, Gyer, *Phlebotomy*, sig. A7ʳ.

creation, the universe operated solely according to a system of natural law never broken by God, most of its ground of conflict with science would have disappeared. But the Elizabethan concept of God was much too personal to permit any such concession. Their homocentric religion visualized God as wielding the world's natural forces to punish or reward the behavior of mankind on a moral basis. If men became wicked, God set in motion certain stellar influences, meteorological phenomena, pollutions of the air, and so on, which ended by producing plague as a punishment. Similarly, if the human community then repented sufficiently with prayer and moral reformation, God would initiate another sequence of natural events which would remove the plague. One therefore gets the impression from reading both sermons and medical books that the natural order was considered quite flexible and responsive to man's fluctuations of good and evil conduct. Doctors and preachers had in mind a picture of God beginning numerous short-term chains of causation designed to achieve particular afflictions and cures, instead of persisting in a single long-term chain of causation capable of producing them all.

This, as I say, was implicit in statements of the general popular view of the matter. They did not trouble themselves to explain how God fitted all his different responses to human vice and virtue into a physical pattern of nature, nor what happened to the pattern when God chose to act directly by miracle. Theologians in the library might labor to show that God's scheme at the beginning of creation was ample enough to foresee and contain all these separate chains of natural causation, miracles, and choices of human free will in one tremendous order. But as soon as they passed out of the library and became teachers of men they were bound to talk as if God's anger, mercy, or reward were spontaneous reactions to the behavior of their parishioners. To have described all the world's happenings as a single gigantic scheme operating since the first moment of time, whether that scheme was strictly predestined or merely foreseen by God, would have taken the heart out of the people sitting on the church benches. What was the use of prayer, for instance, unless it might alter the issue of events, might induce God to change his mind? Why lead the good life in order to escape the plague, if it had been settled, or even foreknown, ages ago that through the design of nature you were going to catch it anyway? So popular religion had to hold fast to the idea of the flexibility of God's manipulation of natural law according to the variations in human morality.

But this same flexibility so necessary to religion was a principle of uncertainty most unwelcome to medical science. The doctor had a difficult enough task in trying to understand the normal workings of disease without having to consider abnormal appearances and sudden mutations arising from moral factors outside his ken. The result seems to have been that in practice he simply did not consider them. He might admit that disease was a punishment for sin or a trial of virtue, but he nevertheless went ahead telling people how to avoid disease and how to get rid of it after it had been contracted. In this program he was protected by another theological doctrine, that God requires man to take all available natural measures of self-preservation. But on the theoretical plane it certainly demanded a nice nimbleness of thought to explain why God should exhort men to try all means to avoid the very illness which God himself was sending on purpose as a divine infliction.

In order to solve this dilemma some theologians, followed by some medical men, made an ingenious distinction between plagues sent by wholly supernatural means as exhibitions of heavenly wrath and plagues which, though initially motivated from God, arrived through exclusively natural phenomena and were not instruments of moral instruction.[40] The former could not be treated by medicines, the latter could. Obviously, doctors in general could make nothing of these supersubtle refinements. All plagues looked alike to them, killed victims in the same ways, and called for the same effort of prevention and therapy. A doctor could not stop to ask his patient whether he was dying of a supernatural plague, or a natural one. Of course, after the man was dead it might be useful to conclude that the plague had been supernatural.

Physicians got into similar difficulties with the belief, validated by a text from Job (14:5) and affirmed by theologians, that each man's death hour had been set by God before the man had ever been born. Here was a fixed event. So in every case of serious illness for the individual or epidemic for the community

[40] Ewich's *The Dutie of a Magistrate*, fol. 3r&v of the Author's Preface; Cary, *Farewell to Physicke*, 46; Vicary, *English Mans Treasure* (1633), 246; Paré, *Workes*, Bk. 22, chap. 2, p. 818; Valentinus, *Enchiridion Medicum*, 60.

the argument quite logically arose that it was useless to apply medicines because if the destined death hour had arrived the patient would die anyway, and if it had not, he would not. This was in fact the argument accepted by the Stoical Christians which gave rise to so fatalistic an attitude in large portions of the population during severe epidemics and seriously hindered the work of quarantine. In strict logic there was no good answer to this surrender of action once the premise was accepted that the hour of death had been predetermined.

It would have been much easier to let the premise go, but the clergy set out to save it and at the same time to champion the health regulations, by various interesting evasions. One was to harp on the familiar idea the God had put medicines on the earth for man's use and had enjoined him to use every possible natural measure to prolong his life. In support of this view, numerous Biblical figures like Abraham, David, Jacob, and Elias could be cited[41] who had certainly made every effort to save their own lives without worrying about metaphysical considerations as to whether God had predetermined that they should live or die. Most ingenious, however, was the device of some preachers who declared that although a man could never postpone the date set for his natural death, he might definitely hasten it by neglecting at any time to use natural means, including medicines, for his own preservation.[42] The effect of this was really to unfix the fixed event of death and to restore the incentive to use remedies, since these might at least change the present outcome. No one could tell in advance whether a given sickness was or was not destined to lead to the natural death hour.

Doctrinal gymnastics of this kind were fascinating devices to save side by side both the sense that human life was under the hand of the Almighty and the sense that it was in man's own keeping. But the doctor could not pay them much heed. He might believe that the life span of every individual was foreordained, but as a practical man he had to assume when he approached the bedside that he could perhaps save the sick man's life. Clearly the doctrine was sharply hostile to medical science. It was given some

[41] E.g. Jones, *Dial for all Agues*, sig. G4^v; Bullein, *Dialogue against Pestilence*, fol. 41^r.

[42] Boorde, *Breuiary of Healthe*, fol. vi^r. Cf. Coverdale, *How a Chrysten Man . . .*, sig. C4^v.

verbal notice in medical treatises, but their whole dynamic was to push towards a cure in even the apparently most hopeless cases.

Because we have spoken of some instances in which the theology of medicine did not affect actual practice, the question may be asked whether it ever had practical consequences in any degree. In some of the more obvious ways, it did not. Doctors do not seem to have relied habitually on prayer and moral counsel in treating the sick. Their books occasionally gave a form of prayer to be said before or after a perilous operation, but when narrating case histories they did not describe the physician as praying or probing into his patient's moral soundness.[43] The average sick man, I think, would have been dismayed to see the doctor go down on his knees. It would have given him a poor opinion of his chances of recovery. Nor would the average doctor have been quick to discover supernatural manifestations in any case he was treating, certainly not witchcraft or demonic possession. With regard to God's intervention, he would probably hide behind the doctrine that the Lord acts almost always by natural means, leaving the burden of proof as to possible rare exceptions upon the theologian.

On the other hand, his inherent piety had, no doubt, less definable effects on his professional conduct. His sense of the presence of a watchful God was good for his standard of ethics. The idea of the religious derivations of medicine gave him a satisfaction in the honorableness of his calling and a feeling of unison with God's purposes in the work of healing. The same idea encouraged new medical discovery and research, on the theory that the Creator intended man to know all the wonder of the human body and all the hidden virtues of drugs. It is hard to say to what extent the physician's belief in God's ultimate control over disease may have discouraged him from putting forth his most strenuous efforts to prevent or to cure it. Probably in some tem-

---

[43] This was true, for example, of the numerous case histories told by William Clowes and Peter Lowe. The charter of St. Bartholomew's hospital in London as set forth in *The Ordre of S. Bartholomewes* (1553), E4^r, directed surgeons: "Also at all such tymes as ye shall go to the dressyng of any diseased persone in this house, asmuche as in you is, ye shall geue unto hym or her, faithfull and good coũsaill, willing them to mynde to sinne no more, and to be thankefull unto almighty GOD, for whose sake they are here comforted of men." But the charters of public charitable institutions are notoriously more pietistic than the surrounding society.

peraments it did promote a disposition to give up a little sooner. In others, since God was thought to work through the physician, it might have had the opposite effect. But in critical cases, when the doctor had done all he could and the issue was still in doubt, the tendency must have been to feel that the outcome was now in the hands of God. And among the sometimes uncontrollable decimations of the plague, the idea that God was punishing a wicked people must often have passed from a textbook platitude into a dreadful conviction. Thus the Elizabethan doctor's religion lay close under the surface of his science, ready to break out whenever the circumstances were so extraordinary or so terrible as to fall beyond the bounds of his knowledge and summon thoughts of a divine agency.

It is therefore false to sum up the relations of medicine to the idea of God in this period in facile terms of a conflict between science and religion. Religion had taken medicine into its house, and if one or two of the rooms were somewhat stuffy, the others were spacious and hospitable enough. Tensions did persist. They were tensions between the doctor's need for an idea of regularity in nature as a basis for science, and the religious need for an idea of irregularity as expressive of transcendent manipulation by God. But since almost everybody conceded that God very seldom injected any such irregularity by direct, miraculous action, the medical man had both a congenial intellectual climate and virtual freedom of action in which to carry forward his work. He could always ignore in his practice the theoretically possible exceptions. And that other, more normal and regular type of irregularity which came from God's acting through nature to impose moral sanctions on mankind did not greatly bother him either, because it could not change his diagnosis and treatment of actual cases of disease. So religion and medicine reached during the Renaissance a *modus vivendi* reasonably suitable to both. Under it medicine flourished and produced its Vesalius, its Paré, its Harvey, and many others. Those of us today who are interested in seeing on what terms science and religion can be compatible may study with respect this instance of their fairly harmonious accommodation.[*]

[*] The opportunity to do this and other work in the field of Renaissance science and religion I owe to a fellowship from the John Simon Guggenheim Memorial Foundation.

"Preparation for Salvation" in Seventeenth Century New England

by PERRY MILLER

Reprinted from the *Journal of the History of Ideas*—Vol. IV, No. 3, pp. 253-286

In the second half of the seventeenth century the clerical and political leaders of the Puritan colonies in New England became convinced that their societies were steadily degenerating. From about 1650 on, as the founders were laid to rest and the second generation attempted to take up the work, it seemed to every pious observer that the spirit of the fathers was dying with them. In sermon after sermon, especially those delivered on formal and public occasions, to the General Courts on annual election days or to particular congregations on the days appointed for public fasts, the ministers traced the accelerating "declension," and repeatedly called upon the people to repent their sins and reform their ways lest the God who had blessed their fathers should now wreak a terrible vengeance upon them. Afflictions and disasters, such as plagues, crop-failures or Indian wars, were exhibited as the preliminary manifestations of His wrath, to be followed by still more terrible judgments if the reform were not forthcoming. In 1679 the ministers met at Boston in a formal Synod, drew up a systematic survey of the evils, and launched an even more vigorous campaign to incite the people to recovery.[1]

Whether the colonies had in fact so woefully fallen off need not concern us. The point is that the ministers, and in all probability most of the people, believed that the case was desperate, and the staggering tabulation of sins, crimes, and offenses published by the Synod in 1679 furnished sufficient documentation. What does concern us is that the leaders of these Calvinist communities, believing that they were faced with destruction, called upon their people to reform, although not a man among them yet entertained any serious doubts about the doctrine of divine determinism. They maintained the absolute sovereignty of God and the utter depravity of man; they held that whatever came to pass in this world was ordained by providence, and they attributed the success of the founders not to human abilities or to physical opportunities, but

[1] Cf. Williston Walker, *The Creeds and Platforms of Congregationalism* (New York, 1893), 427 ff.

solely to God, who had furnished the abilities and brought about the opportunities by His providential care. Therefore the question was bound to present itself to divines and statesmen of the second generation, could any merely human effort arrest the moral decline? Was not it a fact in the irresistible plan of God, just as the triumph of the first generation had been decreed in Heaven? If God was withholding His grace, could the people be expected to become saints, and if He was depriving them even of "restraining grace" could they possibly avoid yielding to every temptation? And if God, even while rendering them powerless to resist, was at the same time augmenting the temptations, what point could there be in summoning the society to repent?

Any other nation, having such absolute control over all the agencies for molding public opinion, might have gone directly to work. But a Puritan state, anxious though it was to excite the populace, could not merely preach repentance and expect the mass of men to obey. Before it could call upon them to reform, it had first to prove that there were legitimate provisions in the accepted theory of the community for assuming that they could if they would. Was there any authorization in the Word of God—as it had been definitively expounded by the founders—for summoning the populace to this work? For the Puritan, this was the all-important question. If he could not prove that the founders had bequeathed him a principle to serve in the emergency, he could not invent one of himself, for that would be to commit the horrid crime of "innovation."

Unfortunately the leaders in the second half of the century were aware that in one fundamental respect their situation differed from anything the founders had foreseen. John Winthrop had declared that the societies of New England were in a direct covenant relationship with Jehovah, exactly as the chosen people of the Old Testament had been; they had agreed with Him to abide by the rules of righteousness, to practice the true polity, to dedicate themselves to doing His will on earth. If they lived up to their promise, He would reward them with material prosperity; if they faltered, He would chastise them with physical affliction until they reformed. When he proclaimed this national covenant, Winthrop had not been troubled by the fact that a majority of the settlers were presumably not regenerated. Only one-fifth of the adult population could give such evidence of their sanctification as would admit them to the covenant of a particular church, but Calvinist theory did not prevent the remaining four-fifths, even though unnumbered among the visible saints, from sharing in the covenant of the nation or from acting their part in its fulfillment. According to the doctrine of all Reformed communities, there existed a realm of conduct which was within the competence of a merely "natural" ability, wherein unregenerate men could be expected to behave one way rather than another because of ordinary pressures, the law, the police, moral persuasion or the promptings of their conscience. Whether they were saints or not, all men could be required to furnish the state a purely "external" obedience, to abstain from murder or theft, to take no usury and to pay their debts. A holy state, received into a covenant with God, differed from an uncovenanted one not because all its citizens were saints but because therein saints could determine and administer the laws and the natural inhabitants be either incited or compelled to obey. In Massachusetts and Connecticut these conditions were fulfilled. The mass of the planters were earnest beings who, by voluntarily migrating, demonstrated that they were eager to do whatever was within the command of their "natural ability." Furthermore, the leadership was a monopoly of certified saints, who were enabled through grace not only to practice good laws but to enforce obedience upon the body politic. Thus the terms of the national covenant could be complied with, though but a small minority were capable of entering the personal Covenant of Grace. The national covenant bound men only to "external" righteousness, without presuming the essential sanctity of every individual. In his great oration of 1645 Winthrop explained that all those who enter a civil society—he obviously meant both the godly and the ungodly—no longer have the right to exercise their impulses to evil, but are now committed, by their own assent, to obeying the authority which is set over them for their own good, and to doing only that which is inherently good, just, and honest. Hence he could summon all inhabitants, church members or not, to a public repentance. The national covenant obliged the community only to an outward rectitude, and required that God punish all violations with a physical affliction, but it also promised that an outward reformation would procure an immediate deliverance. No doubt God would never consent to take a society into such a national covenant which did not contain some men sanctified by the Spirit, inwardly as well as externally, but a core of them was adequate as long as they were in control.

For the founders there did exist a real distinction between the realms of nature and of the Spirit, and such actions as required no supernatural assistance were altogether sufficient to ensure the public welfare. The original saints could earn their liberation from all social distresses by carrying their unconverted neighbors to at least a constrained compliance with the good, just, and honest—which would fully satisfy the public justice of God. But thirty or forty years later the ministers had built up the picture of a universal depravity, and it seemed clear that the society was no longer responding to providential corrections, let alone to the laws against usury and excessive apparel. They put the blame upon all alike, and called for action from all. One of their principal complaints was the infrequency of sound conversions, and the purely numerical consideration, which had been of no consequence to John Winthrop, thus became tremendously important. It was now absolutely imperative that the vast number of non-members, who had supposedly committed themselves to the extent of their natural ability (or been committed by their fathers), who were regularly convened on the days of humiliation and urged to repent, be assured that they could do something. The children of the saints were troubled about their own calling and election, which to many was not so "sure" as that of their fathers had been; a large number were members by only a "Half-Way" covenant which left their inward condition in some perplexity, and they also had to be convinced, whether they were truly regenerate or not, that they could achieve at least the external obedience. Certainly the mass could no longer be carried or driven by the saints, for the saints were not equal to the task. Had it been merely a matter of recalling approved Christians from temporary lapses, the clergy would have had clear sailing, but in 1679 they had to face the fact, by their own admissions, that the whole body politic was in a bad way, and that a reform which touched only a segment would not be enough. In order to effect a national recovery, the whole nation had to be recovered; the declension was a social phenomenon, and it seemed to bring social consequences, plagues, wars, and famines. Hence these determinists were the more obliged to find some method for appealing to natural men, for persuading the unregenerate that they could achieve enough sanctity to preserve the society, though they might never be able to save their souls. The whole people, citizens and inhabitants, church members and non-members, recorded their vow to repent and reform on the many days of humiliation, but their promise would remain an empty gesture unless they could be convinced that they did have the power to keep it without first having to be numbered among the spiritually elect.

It might seem, when the leaders returned to first principles and studied the works of their fathers, that they were caught in the inexorable logic of Calvin. All things in their world were ordained by God, and if He decreed that a people were to decline, no human hand could fend off the appointed outcome. So the founders had conceived the world. They had, it is true, carved out a small island of liberty in the sea of determinism, which was the Covenant of Grace, but even that Covenant was a very slight curtailment of God's awful despotism. The great English theologians from whom New England learned the "federal" doctrine had delivered themselves without equivocation. William Perkins, for instance, condemned all "Pelagians" who would seek the cause of predestination in men, as if God ordained them only after He foresaw which would receive or reject the offer of salvation. The decrees have no cause beyond God's arbitrary pleasure, and Perkins dismissed as "subtile deuices" all attempts to mitigate this "hard sentence."[2] William Ames worked out more carefully the rationality of the Covenant, but he always insisted upon the irrationality of a transcendent might behind it, and agreed that no foreknowledge of God should ever be presupposed to His determinations.[3] John Preston would argue that according to the logic of the Covenant men were justly condemned for not doing what they could do, but he would also declare, "God hath kept it in his power to draw whom he will, to sanctifie whome he will," and would expound the natural freedom of men with this qualification, "yet it is not in any mans power to beleeve, to repent effectually."[4] Hence John Ball's *A Treatise of the Covenant of Grace,* published in 1645, in some respects the most daring excursion in the whole literature, could not avoid the embarrassing question: "To what end doe the promises and threatenings [of the Covenant] tend . . . if God doe worke all things by his effectual power in them that believe?" Ball could not answer his own question, and took refuge in the conventional

[2] Wlliam Perkins, *Works* (London, 1612–13), I, 107–11.

[3] Ames, *The Marrow of Sacred Divinity* (London, 1643), 105.

[4] John Preston, *The Saints Qvalification* (London, 1633), 236, 237.

distinction between God's revealed and hidden will. Openly He demands obedience of all men, but secretly He gives the ability only to the few already elected: "That is, he invites many in the Ministry of his Word, and externall administration of the Covenant, whom he doth not inwardly instruct and draw." If you concluded, therefore, that the offer of the Covenant was a "giftelesse gift," Ball could reply only that you were an unthankful servant and perverse being.[5] But the ministers of New England by 1679 had to deal with a race of the unthankful and perverse.

The founders faithfully echoed such teachers. Cotton pointed out that God could pour His grace upon the most abominable sinners, so that "If he take pleasure to breathe in a man, there is nothing can hinder him, it will blow upon the most noysome dunghill in any place, and be never a whit the more defiled." Logic compelled him to suggest that the best way to become a saint might be "to have run a lewd course of life," since a Calvinist God would then be the more challenged to show His power,[6] but such reflections were sadly out of order in 1679. Thomas Hooker seemed to be no more helpful: man is darkness and God is light, he said, and darkness is unalterably opposed to light; "Thou canst resist a Saviour, but not entertaine him, doe what thou canst."[7] In fact, the ministers, who in the *Report* of the Synod bade all men reform, also renewed their allegiance to the *Westminster Confession,* which explicitly stated that "God from all eternity did by the most wise and holy Counsel of his own Will, freely and unchangeably ordaine whatsoever comes to pass," and further declared that until grace comes the natural spirit must be "passive" and utterly incapable of moral action. "A natural man being altogether averse from that good, and dead in sin, is not able by his own strength to convert himself, or to prepare himself thereunto."[8] With what right, therefore, could the divines rally depraved generations to repent in the name of the fathers, who had taught that a people to whom God chooses not to give His grace are impotent? If men may sit all their lives under the most clear dispensations of the Gospel and yet remain impenitent—Samuel Willard testified at the end of the century, "woful experience tell[s] us that there are a great many

[5] Ball, *A Treatise of the Covenant of Grace* (London, 1645), 343.
[6] Cotton, *The way of Life, or Gods VVay and Course* (London, 1641), 113, 117.
[7] Hooker, *The Soules Vocation* (London, 1638), 230-1.
[8] Walker, *Creeds and Platforms,* 370-1, 377-8.

that do so"[9]—with what face could the ministers preach reformation? What inducement could they offer the average man or what hope of success could they hold out?

It was at this point that the second and third generations began to perceive the advantages in an idea which the founders themselves had devised, which they had heroically vindicated against all opposition and bequeathed to their children as an indispensable part of New England orthodoxy. Though Calvinism pictured man as lifeless clay in the potter's hand, and the *Westminster Confession* asserted that the natural man could not convert himself or even "prepare himself thereunto," the New Englanders had been able to maintain that there did exist a state of "preparation for salvation." We should note at once that the seeds of this difficult and dangerous idea are to be found in the writers whom the New Englanders studied even before the migration. Perkins, Preston, and Ames were Calvinists, and undoubtedly had no intention of propounding any belief at variance with the accepted creed, but they were also the formulators of the Covenant or "federal" version of Calvinism, in which they managed to present Jehovah as consenting to deal with sinners according to the terms of a covenant.[10] As soon as the relationship of God to man was conceived in this fashion, the corollary became obvious that the terms of a covenant may be known in advance. Men must still receive grace, which is dispensed arbitrarily according to sovereign decrees, but the very fact that God does propose terms means that there may be a moment in time between absolute depravity and the beginning of conversion in which the transaction is proposed. Men may not be able to do anything until they are regenerated, but until then they can listen and meditate. Grace is a covenant, and the essence of a covenant, these theologians never wearied of explaining, is an agreement between two agents, both of whom must know the conditions. If election be a flash of lightning that may strike at any moment, men cannot place themselves in its path, nor cultivate any anticipatory attitudes, but when it comes as a chance to enter a contract, they must first of all learn what is to be contracted. Though God gives His son freely, Preston said, "yet except we take him, that gift is no gift; therefore there must be a taking on our part."[11] A man must have his quill sharpened for the signa-

[9] Willard, *A Compleat Body of Divinity* (Boston, 1726), 427.
[10] Cf. Perry Miller, *The New England Mind* (New York, 1939), Ch. 13.
[11] Preston, *The Nevv Convenant, or The Saints Portion* (London, 1629), 172.

ture and the wax warmed for his seal. God has graciously put aside His overwhelming might in order to treat with men in a rational negotiation, "that we might know what to expect from God, and upon what termes."[12] If we may know the terms, we may be encouraged, in advance of our conversions, even while we possess nothing more than our "natural gifts," to commence a course of obedience. Once regeneration was conceived not as a sudden prostration but as a gradual process commencing with an initial stage of negotiation, it became possible, even probable, that men should undergo a preliminary state of "preparation" before they actually were called.

The English formulators were concerned chiefly to establish the fact that regeneration is a process in time, capable of being analyzed into temporal units. They concentrated attention not so much on the crisis of conversion but on the moment just preceding it, when the Covenant of Grace was being tendered to a sinner but was not yet taken up. In Perkins the idea of preparation first appeared as little more than a conventional instruction to preachers that they should spare no pains with their people: "This preparation is to bee made partly by disputing or reasoning with them, that thou mayest thorowly discerne their manners and disposition, and partly by reproving in them some notorious sinne, that being pricked in heart and terrified, they may become teachable."[13] Among his successors the idea took on increased dimensions. We can trace through their works an expanding realization that previous to the signing of a covenant there must be a period in which man is instructed and solicited, that before a simple regeneration he may be careless but before a covenant he must learn to stipulate. The federalists denounced Arminianism because they said that no amount of good works merited any consideration from God, but at the same time they taught sinners provisions for their possible conversion. Preston, for example, said that the worst of sinners may be called without any antecedent humbling of the heart, just as a sick man does not need a sense of sickness in order to be cured, but nevertheless "if he be not sicke, and have a sense of it, he will not come to the Physitian."[14] Coming to the physician will not in itself work a cure, but it may be "a preparative sorrow." Though a reprobate may have the sense and yet never be saved, the elect

[12] Obadiah Sedgwick, *The Bowels of Tender Mercy* (London, 1661), 6.
[13] Perkins, "The Art of Prophecying," *Works* (London, 1631), fol. 670.
[14] Preston, *The Breast-Plate of Faith and Love* (London, 1630), 13.

are seldom taken into the Covenant of Grace until after they too have had it. In general the evidence indicates that these theologians had succeeded, even before 1630, in investing the word "preparation" with a distinct connotation, making it mean a period in time during which men could acquire a "sense" which was not yet an actual conversion but which might be a forerunner of it, an experience that all men might have, since it was not limited merely to the elect,[15] which could be construed as a hopeful augury of ultimate success and could be demanded of all men, whereas an authentic work of the Spirit would have to wait upon the disposition of God.

To establish this thesis the covenant theologians undertook a labor which won them fame throughout Protestant Europe and which was assiduously carried on by their New England disciples, a subtle analysis of the temporal process of regeneration, so that they were able to give elaborate descriptions of every step, beginning with the most minute diagnosis of the dawning of a premonition. Yet all this while, their loyalty to the basic Protestant doctrine of salvation by faith required them to insist that, no matter how slight this first movement might be, it should be attributed to no effort of man but solely to the grace of God. Hence their conception of a state of preparation, as something that came before even the most infinitesimal rumble of faith, was exceedingly welcome. Preparation did not need to be called a saving act of the human will; it could be set forth as no meritorious work in any Arminian sense, not even as part of faith at all, but as a mere inclination to accept faith, should faith ever come. This much a corrupt man might do, for it was really no motion of his soul; it was no lifting of himself by his own bootstraps, but simply an attitude of expectancy. Had the mechanism of regeneration still been phrased exclusively in the language of Calvin, as a forcible seizure, a holy rape of the surprised will, there would have been no place for any period of preparation, which would have been conceivable only as the first moment of an effectual calling. But when regeneration was understood to be the offer and acceptance of a covenant, even though the power to accept it must come from God, men could

[15] Cf. Preston, *Remaines* (London, 1637), 193: "The preparative sorrow is nothing else but a sorrowing for sinne, as it causeth punishment, or a sorrowing for some Iudgement likely to ensue, and pronounced against him, but this is not the true sorrow: a reprobate may have this sorrow, which shall never be saved ... it hath his originall from nature."

make themselves ready to entertain it, since they could know in advance what form it would assume and what response it would entail. Though God might do as He pleased, it was noted that normally those who most strove to prepare themselves turned out to be those whom He shortly took into the Covenant of Grace.

So far as the somewhat obscure passages from the early writers can now be made out, they do not exhibit any interest in the social implications of the idea. These writers still assumed the distinction between the realms of nature and of grace; at this point they were concerned with salvation, not with politics. The conduct of society, the observance of the moral law in domestic and business affairs, was to them a matter of regulation and compulsion. Good laws were to be enforced, and even the most drastic forms of Calvinism always assumed that men had the physical power to obey whatever laws the state imposed. Such actions had nothing to do with salvation, and were not a part of preparation. Of course a saint would endeavor to be a good citizen, but the performance of his civic duties did not earn his redemption. The idea of preparation, as formulated by Perkins, Preston, and Ames, met a spiritual need; it encouraged men to seek holiness in the midst of a determined universe. But almost as soon as the idea was propounded, it began to reveal that it did in fact have social as well as spiritual consequences, for while a man was undergoing a work of preparation in the hope that it might be followed by a conversion, he would be making every effort, out of his own volition, to perfect his external behavior. He would have a positive incentive to righteous conduct, although he could not yet be said to be a true saint or even to have a hope of salvation. But though he might finally go to Hell, if while he lived in this world he prepared himself, he would *ipso facto* fulfill the terms of the national covenant. Thus the rapid development of the idea, first among the theologians of English Puritanism and then among the leaders of New England, is a symptom of the change that came over the Puritan movement as it became concerned more with the conquest of power than with the pursuit of holiness. Sixteenth-century Puritans were driven by one consideration above all others, the salvation of their souls, and they set out to cleanse the Church as a proof of their sainthood, but in the seventeenth century Puritans became organized into a political party and thereupon had to take more thought for the strategy of winning a political victory. The problem of determinism never bothered men who were already convinced of their election, for they were free to do God's will; but when saints banded together to capture the English state, or after they had captured the new states in New England, they had to find more effective means of getting all the people, the mass of the unregenerate whom they were now to govern, started on the road they had travelled in the sheer exuberance of zeal. In the practical terms of social regulation, their problem now was to excite the people to moral action. Almost from the beginning the leaders perceived that to depend merely upon the sanctions of the law, upon the coercion of natural abilities, was not enough. Yet according to Calvinist doctrine, if men were ever to perform anything beyond the limits of nature, they had to be supplied with grace. Hence for the sake of the social welfare, as much as for the welfare of particular souls, it became necessary that men be made gracious. Yet grace was dispensed only by God, according to the secret pleasure of His will, and men could not be converted by any amount of external compulsion. But preparation was not a supernatural work. All men could achieve it, and all men therefore could be called upon to prepare for grace, and thereby to exert themselves in precisely such a course of moral conduct as was required of all the society by the national covenant.

We should not be surprised that Thomas Hooker, the virtual dictator of Connecticut and one of the most socially minded among the early ministers, should be also the greatest analyst of souls, the most exquisite diagnostician of the phases of regeneration, and above all the most explicit exponent of the doctrine of preparation. Thomas Shepard and Peter Bulkeley followed his lead. All three agreed that preparation was not a meritorious work; they took infinite precautions lest their doctrine be construed in any Catholic or Arminian sense. Hooker would explain that no natural action can prepare for supernatural grace, and that the effectual operation of the Word must never be thought to depend upon anything that a man may do by himself, "not upon any preparation which was done, nor any performances . . . but meerly upon the power and good pleasure of the Lord."[16] After justification the will has acquired a new power, "whereby it is able to set forth it selfe into any holy action," but in the first stage it is merely wrought upon, "and I am a patient and doe onely endure it: but I have not any spirituall power to doe any thing of myself."[17] Bulkeley put it in

[16] Hooker, *The Application of Redemption* (London, 2nd ed., 1659), 297–8.
[17] Hooker, *The Sovles Preparation for Christ* (London, 1632), 156.

the language of the federal theology: after God has taken us into a covenant with Him, He requires a positive performance of its terms, but "first the Lord doth dispose us and fit us to a walking in Covenant with him," and in these hours we must remain passive.[18] In fact Hooker and his friends were so eager to prove their orthodoxy that they would indulge in statements as extreme as any to be found in the history of New England, and consequently their real position had been generally misrepresented.[19] Since the sinner must be at first "meerly patient," said Hooker, God is at liberty to give or to deny grace to whom He pleases, and may justly refuse it to the most prayerful and conscientious, *"for it is not in him that wils and runs, but in God that shews mercy."*[20] By the same token God may bestow it "upon such who neither prize nor profit at al they have." The Puritan God was a capricious Jehovah whose favor did not follow upon any good work of man—it "hangs not upon that hinge."[21]

We may very well ask what Hooker and his group could conceivably accomplish when they prefaced the doctrine of preparation by such qualifications. To appreciate the significance of their work we must remember that had they definitely broken with the Calvinist system, had they openly advocated the natural freedom of men to perform deeds that would secure salvation, they would have been branded as Arminians. So Hooker was extremely careful to insist upon the natural impotence of the unregenerate. He was not endeavoring to preach even the possibility that holy actions might be performed by natural men, but he was endeavoring to mark off a number of chronological phases in the sequence of regeneration and then to argue that the first might be undergone by some who ultimately did not continue through the others, who finally proved to be reprobates. The important point was to establish the factual existence of this probationary period, to demonstrate that regeneration was not a precipitate or instantaneous transformation and that the first degree did not always or necessarily lead to the second. There is an "order" in God's proceedings, Hooker said: first He takes away the resistance of the soul by an irresistible operation, whereupon the soul "comes to be in

[18] Peter Bulkeley, *The Gospel-Covenant* (London, 1651), 319.
[19] Cf. Frank H. Foster, *A Genetic History of the New England Theology* (Chicago, 1907), 26, 31–5.
[20] Hooker, *The Application of Redemption*, 309.
[21] *Ibid.*, 299.

the next passive power" and is disposed to a spiritual work—"*vult moveri.*"[22] In his preface to Rogers' *Doctrine of Faith,* a handbook much prized among the people, Hooker called attention to a passage wherein Rogers wrote that we cannot tell exactly when faith is born, whether after a man has fully apprehended Christ or when he first hungers for Him; this, Hooker remarked, ought to settle all disputes about preparation, for all should agree that in the first stage "there is as it were the spawne of Faith, not yet brought to full perfection."[23] But this first conviction need not be regarded as a "fruit" of faith, only as a preliminary negotiation. Of course such beginnings must be initiated by the Lord—"I have no power of my selfe, but onely receive it from the Lord";[24] when the will is first turned toward God, it is "not onely the bare power and faculty of the naturall will" at work, but that will turned by God's efficiency, yet at this point God is still acting from the outside, as when He moves any object in nature, not from within as He does after He has filled the heart with His Spirit.[25] Hence there is a space between depravity and sanctity, a hiatus during which the human will is being influenced but is not yet transformed, a state which Hooker characteristically illustrated in a metaphor, comparing it to the moment when a clock that was running out of order is stopped but not yet repaired. At that moment, "the clocke is a patient, and the workman doth all," yet whenever the workman is the Holy Ghost and "where ever it is soundly wrought," the operation "will in the end be faith and grace."[26] Hooker's reputation among Puritans was great because he was the expert chronometer of regeneration, offering the most acute discriminations of preparation, vocation, justification, adoption, and sanctification, but his most impressive thought was devoted to the first action in the series. Through this doctrine he did more than any other to mold the New England mind.

However, his teachings were not universally accepted by all Puritans. They were opposed even by some of the federalists, who saw in them, despite Hooker's elaborate safeguards, a sophistical form of Arminianism. Pemble, for example, without men-

[22] *Ibid.,* 395–6.
[23] John Rogers, *The Doctrine of Faith* (London, 1629), A10.
[24] Hooker, *The Soules Vocation* (London, 1638), 204–5.
[25] Hooker, *The Unbeleevers Preparing for Christ* (London, 1638), 32.
[26] Hooker, *The Sovles Preparation for Christ,* 157–8.

tioning Hooker by name, attacked his doctrines in the *Vindiciae Gratiae*, declaring that such actions as Hooker identified with preparation could not be encompassed by the unconverted. "They are not antecedents, but consequents and parts of true conversion," whereas any preparative actions produced merely by human efforts could be "no efficient causes to produce grace of conversion."[27] Giles Firmin attacked both Hooker and Shepard specifically, on the ground that their doctrine caused seekers after God much unnecessary discouragement since it made them distrust the first acting of the Spirit for fear it might prove no more than an abortive preparation. They demanded more of men than God required and called upon them not merely to repent but to go beyond repentance, whereas according to Firmin the battle was won just as soon as men were able to lament their sins.[28]

The majority of New England divines followed Hooker, but there was one ominous exception. John Cotton generally figures as the chief "theocrat" of Massachusetts and is popularly remembered as the dictator of its intellect, yet in fact he differed widely from his colleagues, and his dissent came near to causing his ruin. On this fundamental point Hooker's influence eclipsed Cotton's, and his share in the formation of American Puritanism is correspondingly the larger. The full story of the opposition is difficult to reconstruct, because the authorities made every effort to play it down; nevertheless, the noise of their disagreement resounded through the Calvinist world. Enemies of the New England Way were quick to make the most of it, the Presbyterian Baillie, for instance, scoring a blow when he sneered that Winthrop and Welde, in their narrative of the Antinomian episode, did all they could "to save Mr. *Cottons* credit," yet they could not so falsify the story but what "they let the truth of Mr. *Cottons* Seduction fall from their Pens."[29] The halting sentences in which Cotton endeavored to reply do more to confirm our suspicions of a difference than to persuade us of the asserted agreement, nor do we need to search very far into his writings to find the theological basis for his divergence.

Cotton's position was simplicity itself. Though he was a "fed-

[27] William Pemble, "Vindiciae Gratiae," *Workes* (Oxford, 1659), 78, 81–4.

[28] Giles Firmin, *The Real Christian* (London, 1670), "To the Reader."

[29] Charles Francis Adams, *Antinomianism in the Colony of Massachusetts Bay, 1636–1638* (Prince Society, Boston, 1894), 364.

eralist," he was first of all the man who sweetened his mouth every night with a morsel of *The Institutes*. He was persuaded that between the natural and the regenerate man lay a gulf so immense that only divine grace could bridge it. If a man performs a single action appropriate to the elect, he has then and there become one of them. There can be no half-way conversion; a man is either one or the other, and those who once receive grace will infallibly persevere through all short-comings to an ultimate glorification. Therefore what Hooker and Shepard called preparation was for Cotton simply the impact of grace, and the prepared were already saints. "A man is as passive in his Regeneration, as in his first generation."[30] If we are "fitted" for good deeds, the first motion must be a work solely of God, who alone can fit us, and once He gives the smallest competence, He has thereby signified His irrevocable favor. Hence, as Cotton saw it, the first motion no less than the last is "true spirituall Union between the Lord & our souls;" define it as closely as possible, it is still from God.[31] The natural heart is totally "drowsie," and "for our first union, there are no steps unto the Altar."[32] Can a blind man prepare himself to see?[33] Hooker's doctrine creates a false sense of security, for it tells men that preparation consists in a disposition to wait upon Christ, and those who have brought themselves by their own efforts to such a seeming surrender thereupon give over striving. The supreme refinement of deceptive faith has always been a self-induced determination to wait upon Christ: "there is no promise of life made to those that wait & seek in their own strength, who being driven to it, have taken it up by their own *resolutions.*" Should we try to reassure ourselves by reflecting that if we cannot work we can believe, or that if we cannot believe we can wait until we come to believe, "here is still the old roote of *Adam* left alive in us, whereby men seeke to establish their owne righteousnesse."[34] There can be no safe building upon such resolves, for they are produced by mechanical causes, even when induced by the persuasive eloquence of the pastor at Hartford.

Cotton was the better Calvinist, and he knew it: not only would he plead the authority of federalists like Pemble in rejecting prepa-

[30] Cotton, *The New Covenant* (London, 1654), 55.
[31] *Ibid.*, 28–9.
[32] *Ibid.*, 54.
[33] Cotton, *The way of Life* (London, 1641), 182.
[34] *The New Covenant,* 196–7, 182; cf. 19–25, 54–5, 58–80.

ration, he would also cry out, "Let *Calvin* answer for me."[35] Nevertheless Hooker triumphed in New England, for the good and sufficient reason that Cotton's doctrine fathered the awful heresy of Antinomianism. Modern historians often find the technicalities of this dispute so abstruse as to lead them comfortably to conclude that it was meaningless, but its social consequences became immediately apparent when Mrs. Hutchinson declared that she had come to New England "but for Mr. Cotton's sake" and added, "As for Mr. Hooker . . . she said she liked not his spirit."[36] Mr. Hooker, it will be remembered, aided by Shepard and Bulkeley, was the principal prosecutor in her trial before the Synod, and did not check the expression of his satisfaction upon her expulsion.

Anne Hutchinson took her stand upon Cotton's doctrine of a radical distinction between regeneration and unregenerateness, asserting that in no sense whatsoever could works have anything to do with justification, that they could not even be offered as "evidence," and that a true saint might consistently live in any amount of sin. She wiped out all Hooker's fine-spun discriminations between a state of preparation and a state of adoption; she presented the clear-cut alternatives of an absolute union with Christ or an utter disseverance. Her followers regarded preparation as the most offensive among the tenets of the New England clergy, and cited Hooker and Shepard as proof positive that the ministers were preaching a "covenant of works." If Hooker would allow that a man could do something, anything, before he was redeemed, which could also be done by those who eventually went to perdition, what was this but Popery? The Antinomians emphatically declared that the sinner "for his part, must see nothing in himselfe, have nothing, doe nothing; onely he is to stand still and waite for Christ to doe all for him."[37] They disapproved any preaching of the "law," any pressing of duties upon the unconverted, any calling them to faith and prayer; to exhort even the elect to fulfill their obligations was superfluous, not because saints would be perfect but because those who are concerned about their conduct are still under the obsolete covenant of the law. To them it seemed that Hooker, though he professed the impotence of nature, set men to work of themselves and promised the unconverted that somehow they might take the first step toward grace if only they would try;

[35] *Gospel Conversion* (London, 1646), 22; cf. 18–19, 30, 46.
[36] Adams, *Antinomianism,* 272.
[37] *Ibid.,* 74.

therefore, as Anne Hutchinson saw it, the people were misled into thinking themselves justified no further than they could perceive themselves enabled to perform good works, although the essence of Protestantism was the assurance of justification through the free promise of forgiveness. Election did not admit of degrees proportioned to the extent of the endeavor, nor could any amount of sin reverse the divine decree; justification was absolute and final, in and by itself.

Anne Hutchinson announced that she had learned her doctrine from Cotton, and throughout her ordeal wrapped herself in the mantle of his authority, to the consternation of the authorities. Even after the Antinomians were exiled, and Cotton had utterly renounced them, they would not give him up. In the heat of the conflict the elders brought Cotton to a conference, "drew out sixteen points, and gave them to him, entreating him to deliver his judgment directly in them." Winthrop remarks that many copies of his reply "were dispersed about"; seven years later, one Francis Cornwell published in England what purported to be an authentic version, with a dedication to Sir Harry Vane—for that erstwhile friend of Mrs. Hutchinson was now a power in the land. The book was so popular that two more editions appeared in 1646 and a fourth in 1647,[38] and when copies were brought to Boston there must have been anguish in the parsonage of the First Church. Winthrop says that at the conference Cotton cleared some doubts, "but in some things he gave not satisfaction";[39] in Cornwell's version he appears to have given none at all. The issue in 1637, says the editor, came down to this: the renegade clergy "would not believe themselves justified, no further then they could see themselves work; making their Markes, Signes, and Quallifications, the causes of their Justification," whereas the Antinomians upheld the true Protestant position that the evidence of justification is to be discerned "onely by Faith in the Free Promise."[40] Cornwell exhibited Cotton adhering to the Antinomian sense. Being asked whether there are any conditions in the soul before faith "of dependance unto which, such promises are made," he replied

---

[38] *Sixteene Questions of Seriovs and Necessary Consequence, Propounded unto Mr. John Cotton* (London, 1644); *A Conference Mr. John Cotton held at Boston* (London, 1646); *Gospel Conversion* (London, 1646); *Severall Questions* (London, 1647).

[39] John Winthrop, *Journal* (ed. J. K. Hosmer, New York, 1908), I, 203, 207.

[40] *Gospel Conversion*, A5.

roundly, no: "To works of creation there needeth no preparation; the almighty power of God calleth them to be his people, that were not his people."[41] In other answers, still according to Cornwell, Cotton asserted that to evidence one's justification by his sanctification is Popery, that "Such a Faith as a practicall Sillogisme can make, is not a Faith wrought by the Lords Almighty power," that no conviction wrought by natural means, even by evangelical preaching, should be confounded with a true work of faith, for "the Word without the Almighty power of the Spirit is but a dead Letter," that God does not give His grace upon condition of our becoming prepared, because "it is not his good pleasure to give us our first comfort . . . from our owne righteousnesse."[42] In these words the Antinomians were content that their cause be stated; they then appealed to the judgment of Protestantism whether the divines in New England, following the way of Hooker and of preparation, had not betrayed the Bible Commonwealth.

Anne Hutchinson said that but one minister besides Cotton remained faithful, her brother-in-law, John Wheelwright, who came to grief when, on the fast-day appointed for a public lamentation over the controversy, he delivered a sermon which the authorities found "incendiary." The text of that discourse does not immediately suggest, to an age insensitive to the fine shading of theological dispute, exactly wherein it was subversive, but if it be read in the light of the times, in view of the then agitated state of the question of preparation, its inflammable substance becomes all too evident. Wheelwright later repudiated Mrs. Hutchinson, or at least the errors charged upon her; yet like Cotton he opposed the doctrine of preparation and therefore by implication accused his colleagues of apostasy. "To preach the Gospell," he declared, "is to preach Christ . . . & nothing but Christ . . . so that neither before our conversion nor after, we are able to put forth one act of true saving spirituall wisdome, but we must haue it put forth from the Lord Jesus Christ, wth whom we are made one."[43] Hooker, Shepard, and Bulkeley were bending all their ingenuity to tabulating the successive periods of conversion, but Wheelright flatly announced that when the Lord converts a soul, He "revealeth not to him worke, & from that worke, carieth him to Christ, but there is nothing revealed but Christ, when Christ is lifted vp,

[41] *Ibid.*, 1, 5.
[42] *Ibid.*, 6, 16–17, 18, 28.
[43] Charles H. Bell, *John Wheelwright* (Prince Society, Boston, 1876), 163.

he draweth all to him, that belongeth to the election of grace.'' If men think they are on the highway to salvation after they have traversed the first mile but are not yet united to Christ, "they are saued w^{th}out the Gospell." "No, no," he exclaimed, "this is a covenant of works."[44] If so, then the ministers of New England were not Protestants, and the friends of Wheelwright might warrantably conclude that Christians should refuse them a hearing, that they might take even more violent measures against them.

Therefore Wheelwright was banished, but John Cotton was not. There were many reasons why the authorities were unwilling to send away their most renowned scholar, but one is forced to suspect that he owed his preservation to the fact that he was still more reluctant to go. Wheelwright would disown the extravagances of the Antinomians,[45] but he would not compromise on preparation; Cotton bent before the storm and saved his standing in the holy commonwealth at the expense of his consistency. Perhaps this statement is too severe, for in works presumably written after 1638 Cotton still stressed the strictly Protestant version of the Covenant of Grace, which, he said in a book published five years after his death, "is not of our will, but of the Lords, that takes away our strong heart, and gives us a soft heart before any preparation."[46] Nevertheless, it is clear that Cotton learned at least a degree of caution from his unhappy experience, and his subsequent references inevitably suggest that he so moderated his opinions as to make himself no longer able to speak frankly. The account which he gave in his reply to Roger Williams is so patently evasive, so utterly fails to correspond to the narrative of Winthrop, and is so denuded of feeling that every line rings with a hollow sound. He had never, according to his own account, given any countenance to the "sundry corrupt, and dangerous errors" of the "Familists," but instead had publicly preached against them. The orthodox brethren had then said to the erring party, "See, your Teacher declares himselfe clearely to differ from you," and they had replied, "No matter . . . what he saith in publick, we understand him otherwise, and we know what he saith to us in private." On no other grounds than these was bred a "jealousie" in the country "that I was in secret a Fomenter of the

[44] *Ibid.*, 164.
[45] *Ibid.*, 199.
[46] Cotton, *An Exposition upon The Thirteenth Chapter of the Revelation* (London, 1656), 211.

Spirit of Familisme, if not leavened my selfe that way."[47] In this account and in others he confessed that he had meditated fleeing from Massachusetts, since in the opinion of many, "such a Doctrin of Union, and evidencing of Union, as was held forth by mee, was the *Trojan* Horse, out of which all the erroneous Opinions and differences of the Country did issue forth,"[48] yet, he protested, he did not have to go, not because he changed his mind, but because "private conference with some chiefe Magistrates, and Elders" revealed the welcome fact that he was in essential agreement with them after all! At the Synod he at last discovered the "corruption of the Judgement of the erring Brethren" and saw the fraudulence of their pretense of holding forth nothing but what they had received from him, "when as indeed they pleaded for grosse errors, contrary to my judgement," and therefore he "bare witnesse against them."[49] This happy resolution was not a matter of his being recovered, but "the fruit of our clearer apprehension, both of the cause and of the state of our differences, and of our joynt consent and concurrence in bearing witnesse against the common heresies, and errors of Antinomianisme, and Familisme, which disturbed us all."[50] Therefore he could reply to Baillie that there had never been any question of his "Seduction"—"all of us hold Union with Christ, and evidencing of Union by the same Spirit, and same Faith and same holinesse."[51]

But what of Cornwell's embarrassing pamphlet? Cotton could do nothing but denounce it as a forgery and publish what he swore were the replies he had given in the cross-examination of 1637. The student finds himself wondering how, if Cornwell's version is accurate, Winthrop could have said at the time that Cotton cleared some doubts, or how, if Cotton's own version is true, Winthrop should have added that in other things he gave no satistion. At any rate, what Cotton now presented sounds strangely different from his previous statements. He described himself replying to the question of whether our union with Christ be complete before and without faith, that though from one point of view we are united to Christ as soon as He elects us, "yet in order of

[47] Cotton, *A Reply to Mr. Williams* [1647] (*Publications of the Narragansett Club*, Vol. II, Providence, 1867), 80–4.
[48] Adams, *Antinomianism*, 360.
[49] *A Reply to Mr. Williams*, 83.
[50] *Ibid.*, 376.
[51] *Ibid.*, 362.

nature, before our faith doth put forth it self to lay hold on him," we may be among the elect without a final union—an admission that gave Hooker every right to introduce a period of preparation. When asked if justification could be evidenced by a "conditionall" promise—a word he formerly had denounced—he hedged: "The Spirit doth Evidence our Justification both wayes, sometimes in an absolute Promise, sometimes in a conditionall," and though he would still hestitate to take "saving qualifications" as a "first evidence" of justification, he would generously grant that "A man may haue an argument from thence (yea, I doubt not a firm and strong argument)."[52] Since Hooker had carefully defended his thesis against Arminian constructions, Cotton could seek refuge in the same disavowals; the promises of the Covenant, he could say, have no efficacy in themselves to bring men to faith unless the Spirit accompanies them, "yet this is the end to which God giveth them, to stir up the Sons of men."[53] Consequently, men are not to rest but are to be exhorted "to provoke themselves and one another, to look after the Lord." He would still insist that in the first work of conversion a man must be passive; nevertheless, urged on by his colleagues, he would say, "There are many sins which a man lives in, which he might avoid by very common gifts, which would he renounce, God would not be wanting to lead him on to further grace."[54] This was exactly what Hooker meant by "preparation."

Cotton was much too valuable to be sacrificed unnecessarily, and in the 1640's he vindicated the wisdom of the authorities by rendering the New England Way yeoman service in its dispute with the Presbyterians, but on this point he never dared again to speak with authority. If he touched upon it, he would preface his remarks, "Reserving due honour to such gracious and precious Saints, as may be otherwise minded."[55] Eager as he was to prove

[52] Cotton, *The Way of Congregational Churches Cleared* (London, 1648), Pt. I, 41–7.

[53] Cotton, *The New Covenant*, 89.

[54] Cotton, *Christ the Fountaine of Life* (London, 1651), 174.

[55] This phrase occurs in *A Treatise of the Covenant of Grace* (London, 1671), 35; this volume is the third edition of *The New Covenant* (London, 1654). In the first version the courteous gesture is lacking; an objection is propounded, "whether doth not the Lord give us some saving Preparations before Jesus Christ?" and to this question itself is appended an explanation for its existence, "for there be those that are gratious Saints, that have conceived that there are some gratious Qualifica-

the basic unanimity of New England, he could not altogether conceal his well-known opinions, and he had to admit a degree of difference: "though some may conceive the Union wrought in giving the habit, and others rather refer it to the act: and some may give the second place to that, whereto others give the first."[56] Yet his strategy was always to minimize the importance of these differences; he went conspicuously out of his way to approve the treatises of Shepard and Hooker, particularly Hooker's *The Sovles Preparation,* and smoothed over his former objections with the mild qualification, "wherein . . . they sometime declare such works of Grace to be preparations to conversion, which others do take to be fruits of conversion."[57] In every case, he protested that he and they were entirely at one upon all essentials, holding alike that whosoever did come under a saving work of the Spirit had to experience a preparation of some sort. His effort to drape the conflict in the robes of harmony was assiduously seconded by the other spokesmen for New England, their deliberate obscurantism indicating not only how wide but how dangerous the breach had been. The issue made a deep impression upon the seventeenth century, and as late as 1690 George Keith, then speaking as a Quaker and hailing in Anne Hutchinson a forerunner of George Fox, embarrassed his New England opponents by reminding them that Cotton had been closer to his doctrine and to hers than to theirs.[58] Even at the end of the century the leaders were main-

---

tions, which the Lord giveth to prepare for Jesus Christ." Cotton is here represented as replying in a short and positive dictum, that such a notion "would be prejudiciall unto the grace and truth of Christ" (53). In the revised text of 1671 the question stands alone, without the explanation, and Cotton begins his reply by first expressing due honor to the precious saints who disagree with him; he humbly professes that he cannot "discern" any preparation and modestly suggests that the idea "seemeth to be" prejudicial to the Gospel. Both editions were printed after Cotton's death; Allen says in his preface to *The New Covenant* that the text was "taken from the Authors mouth in Preaching, was afterward presented unto him with desire of his perusal and emendation of it; which being done (and indeed the interlinings of his owne hand doe plainly testifie his correcting of it)," he then delivered the manuscript to a gentleman of Boston who brought it to London (p. A7 verso). Whether the revision of the later edition represents an "interlining" of Cotton's own hand or of his editor's may be questioned, but in either case it testifies to a weakening or blurring of his originally clear-cut opposition.

[56] Adams, *Antinomianism,* 362.
[57] *The Way of Congregational Churches Cleared,* Pt. I, 75–6.
[58] Keith, *A Refutation of Three Opposers of Truth* (Philadelphia, 1690), 68.

taining the defensive tactics of the founders; in a preface to Cotton Mather's *The Everlasting Gospel* in 1700, Higginson granted that Cotton had "differed from some of his Brethren in *The Souls Preparation for Christ*" and had contended that "some" took certain works to be *"preparations to Conversion, which others take to be fruits of Conversion";* however, Higginson insisted, the disagreement never became a serious issue, because all agreed that such works must be achieved by every person who undergoes the effectual influence of the Spirit. *"And so the Difference is but Logical, and not Theological."*[59]

The fact of the matter is, however, that in 1637 the difference had been not only theological but social and political, and had Cotton stood his ground either he would have had to flee or the society been torn asunder. He did not stand his ground, and his uneasy references to the affair in subsequent years are oblique admissions that he and not Hooker made the concession. Hooker seemed to be tightening his victory when, in sermons delivered at Hartford in the 1640's, he began an exposition of preparation with the remark, "I shall not only speak mine own Judgment, but the Judgment of all my fellow Brethren, as I have just cause, and good ground to beleeve,"[60] and then proceeded to expound preparation in direct contradiction to the views of Cotton. After guaranteeing their orthodoxy by a blanket assertion that they were not Arminians, Hooker and his brethren serenely defined preparation as a work that should be demanded of all men as a "condition" of their salvation. The Antinomians had succeeded only in convincing them of the supreme need for a more vigorous pressing of moral responsibility upon all the people; the horror of Anne Hutchinson's heresy was simply that "most of her new tenents tended to slothfulnesse, and to quench all indevour in the creature."[61] She had declared before the Synod, "The Spirit acts most in the Saints, when they indevour least," and the Synod had answered, "Reserving the special seasons of Gods preventing grace to his owne pleasure, In the ordinary constant course of his dispensation, the more wee indevour, the more assistance and helpe wee find from him."[62] The last embers of Antinomianism had to be

[59] B 6 verso.
[60] *The Application of Redemption,* 309.
[61] Adams, *Antinomianism,* 163.
[62] *Ibid.,* 109.

beaten out, and Hooker showed the clergy how to wield the one flail that would serve, the doctrine of preparation. With Cotton subdued, Hooker preached repeatedly upon it. "The soule of a poore sinner must bee prepared for the Lord Jesus Christ, before it can receive him."[63] The people must do something to receive God or else never expect Him: "only he watcheth the time till your hearts be ready to receive and entertaine him."[64] When the soul perceives—if it listened to Hooker it could not help but perceive— that it cannot save itself, it "falls downe at the foot of the Lord, and is content to be at Gods dispose," and though at that moment it has no dominion over its sin, "yet it is willingly content that Jesus Christ should come into it."[65] Hooker never preached long without a metaphor: a sharp sauce, he explained, will not "breed a stomacke, yet it stirres up the stomacke,"[66] and so a godly preparation, though it may not breed faith, may yet stir up the stomach of faith—and conduct.

The connection of the Antinomian outburst with the further development of the idea of preparation can be traced explicitly in the works of Thomas Shepard. When he described a sort of heretics who hold that there is no sorrow for sin but what is common to both the reprobate and the elect and who insist that genuine grief can come only after the soul is in Christ by faith, his listeners had no trouble knowing whom he meant, or in following his assertion that such heretics are in error because a man who gives no previous thought to his sins is in no position to receive grace, even the irresistible grace of God. No doubt it would be Pelagian to say that a man can dispose himself of his own power, but some antecedent disposition is necessary; a form cannot be joined to matter until the matter is prepared, until it is made "such a vessel which is immediately capable" of the union.[67] Shepard acknowledged that this is a difficult doctrine; even angels may be "posed" by the problem of explaining how men may yield themselves to Christ so that all their fruit comes from Him and not from themselves, but Shepard was certain that before any soul experiences a supernatural change it must learn to "lie

[63] *The Unbeleevers Preparing for Christ*, 2.
[64] *The Sovles Implantation* (London, 1637), 47–8.
[65] *Ibid.*, 85, 34.
[66] *Ibid.*, 234.
[67] Thomas Shepard, *Works* (ed. John A. Albro, Boston, 1853), I, 160–63.

like wax" beneath the seal.[68] This learning was what he and Hooker understood by preparation.

The real import of a Puritan doctrine is seldom found in the formal statement. To protect their orthodoxy, theologians would hedge every proposition with innumerable qualifications; but once they had proved and vindicated a doctrine, they were free to reveal its true meaning in their "applications." In their exhortations Hooker and Shepard disclosed the great utility of the doctrine of preparation, namely that they could demand of every man, no matter how sinful, that he make the requisite and feasible preparations, and they could blame him for his own damnation if he refused. Of course, Hooker would explain, if a man's relief depended upon his own endeavors, he would certainly fail: the soul cannot choose Christ "out of the power of nature;" nevertheless, an inn must be prepared to receive the guest, else He will pass by to another lodging.[69] In another characteristic simile, he declared that it is with the soul as with a woman in child-birth: "when her throwes come often and strong, there is some hope of deliverance; but when her throwes goe away, commonly the child dies, and her life too."[70] If a man should argue, "I can do nothing for my self, therefore I will take a course that no man shall do any thing for me," humanity would call him mad; instead, he can and must conclude, since he is able to do nothing of himself, "therefore I must attend upon God in those means which he useth to do for all those he useth to do good unto."[71] Assuredly, unregenerate though he be, a man can avoid the grosser temptations; it is not in your power to make the Gospel "effectual," but it is in your power to doe more than you doe, your legs may as well carry you to the word, as to an Ale-house." You can read pious books as well as "Play-books"; "you may sing as well Psalmes as idle songs." By the doctrine of preparation, in short, the people of New England, nominally professing a rigid Calvinism, could still be told, "doe what you are able to doe, put all your strength, and diligence unto it."[72] At the very least, if they could not resist the ale-house and the play-book, they could "wait" upon God:

[68] *Ibid.*, III, 307-08.
[69] *The Unbeleevers Preparing for Christ*, 40.
[70] *The Sovles Preparation for Christ*, 189.
[71] *The Application of Redemption*, 320.
[72] *The Saints Guide* (London, 1645), 117.

It is true indeed, we cannot doe it, but by Christ, it is the grace of Christ, the power of Christ, the spirit of Christ that doth help us to get our selves from under iniquitie; yet notwithstanding we must labour to get our selves from under it, and Christ will help us. . . . It is the Lords Almighty power that hath possesst us with this libertie and freedome from iniquitie, but yet notwithstanding before we can come to inioy a full libertie from all iniquitie, we must fight for it, and wage the battels of the Lord.[73]

The people could not excuse themselves by pleading that they were disabled, for with the very argument they showed that they were *"not yet* WILLING *to be made* ABLE.*"*[74] Hooker never hesitated to exhort the unregenerate: "It is possible for any Soule present (for ought I know or that he knows) to get an humble heart."[75] The customary ending of a Hooker sermon was an encouragement to all men "that you would indeavour, and be perswaded to get an interest in Christ."[76] Likewise, Thomas Shepard held it a "slothful opinion" to believe that since no activity of grace can be received except from God, men should attempt nothing.[77] Peter Bulkeley indicated the connection of the doctrine with the federal theology by reasoning that, since grace is an offer of a contract, a man can humble himself before God, confess his depravity and intreat God for a chance to enter the covenant. Generally, Bulkeley promised, God will receive those who come to Him, and "Thus you see the way to enter into Covenant with God."[78]

Here at last was a fulcrum for the lever of human responsibility, even in a determined world. Here was something a man could do, here was an obligation that could be urged upon him, no matter how impotent his will. He could at least prepare, he could wait upon the Lord. Of course, his preparation would be worthless if it did not lead to faith, but it was not, like faith itself, so far above the reach of a mortal being that he could do nothing toward attaining it. Whatever was lost or gained in this restatement, one thing was sure: it ruled out all forms of Antinomianism. In 1657 Hooker's fellow Congregationalists in England, Goodwin and Nye, published his *Application of Redemption* with their

[73] *The Saints Dignitie, and Dutie* (London, 1651), 38.
[74] *The Application of Redemption,* 143.
[75] *The Sovles Hvmiliation* (London, 1638), 207.
[76] *The Saints Dignitie, and Dutie,* 118.
[77] *Works,* II, 401.
[78] *The Gospel-Covenant,* 51.

hearty endorsement, admitting that Hooker had been accused of "urging too far, and insisting too much upon that as *Preparatory,* which includes indeed the beginnings of true Faith," but they were now ready to agree with him, because they in England were suffering what New England had endured in 1637, a wave of Antinomian fanaticism, and they hoped that Hooker's volume would set to rights "those that have slipt into *Profession,* and Leapt over all both *true* and *deep Humiliation* for sin, and *sence of their natural Condition."*[79] With this to recommend the doctrine, that it provided both an antidote to Antinomianism and a working basis for stirring up the sinful will without running to the opposite extreme of Arminianism, no wonder it become a prized possession of the New England mind! And no wonder that as the decades passed and the leaders became more and more worried over the declension, as they were obliged to find means for stimulating the zeal of the flagging generations, they enlarged and magnified the scope of preparation.

The next stage in the development of the doctrine is marked by John Norton's *The Orthodox Evangelist,* published in 1657, which was a treatise upon the particular "evangelical truths" that were then being widely opposed "in this perillous hour of the Passion of the Gospel." There were many Antinomians, mystics, seekers, and Quakers abroad, and therefore Norton devoted three long chapters to preparation; he did not so much extend Hooker's idea as give it systematic formulation, but by that very act, by stripping off Hooker's rhetoric, he caused further implications to emerge. He was compelled, for instance, to distinguish between works which are preparatory in the sight of God—which are achieved only by the elect—and those judged by man, which are to be measured by the rule of charity and to be considered in many cases merely as grounds for hope, not as the signs of a completed redemption. Leaving secret things to God, Norton was able to insist that preparatory works in the second sense might legitimately be required of everybody. His definitions emphasized the temporal element, making preparation a period in which a man is neither a sinner nor a saint, but in some tentative half-way condition: "By preparatory Work, we understand certain inherent qualifications, coming between the carnal rest of the soul in the state of sin, and conversion wrought in the Ministry." It is a "common work of the Spirit," whereby "the soul is put into a

[79] *The Application of Redemption,* C 2 verso.

Ministerial capacity of believing immediately," whereas the unprepared soul is incapable of directly receiving faith."[80] He stressed constantly that God works conversion not by a violent invasion of the psyche but by degrees: " 'Tis in the works of Grace, as we ordinarily see in the works of Nature; God proceeds not immediately from one extream unto another, but by degrees."[81] Norton again recited all the safeguards against Arminianism; he denied that preparatory works have any causal influence upon vocation, and repeated that even the preparing soul is passive. Yet he carried the analysis so far beyond Hooker that not only was he able to describe preparation as a part of the process of conversion, but to dissect preparation itself into a process, with an array of component stages: believing in the holiness of the law, realizing the nature of sin, learning the message of Christ, comprehending the need for repentance, and finally waiting upon Christ in the use of means under the Gospel Covenant. All this, let us remember, was presented as pertaining only to preparation, during which the soul remains passive! Preparation, as Norton said, "worketh not any change of the heart, yet there are in it, and accompanying of it, certain inward workings, that do dispose to a change."[82] He did not demand that every individual run through all the stages he marked out; in fact, he declared, the least measure is enough to put a soul into a "preparatory capacity," and since certainty of election is not always possible in this life, a work of preparation among the as yet unconverted, even if it be not followed by a visible operation of the Spirit, must still be taken as a hopeful sign. In any event, it was clear that preparation could be accomplished by the unregenerate. Arminians and Pelagians allowed too much to preparation—one wonders what more they could allow!—but Norton's chief concern was to counter those "Enthusiasts" who were denying the usefulness or indeed the very existence of any preparation. Hence the conclusion for him, even more explicitly than for Hooker, was the moral duty of all men to seek for preparation, even though it would not guarantee their salvation: "That it is the duty of every one that hears the Gospel to believe, and that whosoever believeth shall be saved; but also it ministers equal hope unto all (answerable to their preparatory proceeding) of believing,

[80] John Norton, *The Orthodox Evangelist* (London, 1657), 130.
[81] *Ibid.*, 135.
[82] *Ibid.*, 154.

and being saved."[83] That the soul should first be prepared and then called to faith, instead of being called without warning, "is the method of the Gospel, ought to be the direction of the Ministry, and course of the Soul; Christs own way, and therefore the most hopefull and most speedy way for attaining of faith and salvation thereby."

Increase Mather came back to Boston in 1661, believing it the last stronghold of Protestantism and resolved to maintain all doctrines in their most rigorous form; just as he at first opposed the Half-Way Covenant, even though his father was a principal advocate, so also he held to Cotton's views on preparation. In 1669 he declared conversion a miracle, far beyond the power of nature to produce or even approach,[84] and in 1674 was preaching "men are altogether *passive* in their *Conversion*."[85] But meanwhile New England sank into the mire of apostasy, and he above all others thundered the need for reform. Very shortly he found himself obliged to remodel his thinking, starting not from abstract doctrines but from the facts with which he was contending. He changed sides on the Half-Way Covenant, and before long he also altered his views of preparation, declaring that while the gate is indeed strait, yet God requires men to strive for entrance, and consequently "they should do such things as have a tendency to cause them to Believe."[86] Others in his generation, under the same circumstances, likewise found charms in the same thought. Samuel Willard was too skilled in the traditional theology ever to lose sight of natural inability; he would explain that when a man repents, "it is God by his Spirit that enforms him with this power and grace," and he held it an error to "put a Divine honour upon Moral swasion, as if it could of it self attract and draw the heart after it,"[87] yet whenever he exhorted the congregations, he pointed out that in preparation, as apart from regeneration, they have a power of working upon themselves. "It is one of Satans cheats, to tell us we must wait before we resolve."[88] In his *Compleat Body of Divinity* he defined preparation as that time in which the soul

[83] *Ibid.*, 171.

[84] Increase Mather, *The Mystery of Israel's Salvation* (London, 1669), 90.

[85] *Some Important Truths about Conversion* (London, 1674. 2nd ed., Boston, 1684), 5.

[86] *Sovl-Saving Gospel Truths* (Boston, 1703. 2nd ed., Boston, 1712), 22-7.

[87] Willard, *Mercy Magnified on a penitent Prodigal* (Boston, 1684), 212.

[88] *Ibid.*, 215-16.

is not yet redeemed but is merely in "*a posture and readiness for the exerting of the act of Faith, which follows thereupon.*"[89] Even at this date there were debates among the orthodox, and many whom Willard respected still denied the existence of any preparatory works; but he repeated the arguments of Hooker and Norton, and added a few of his own, to prove once more that men may be called upon to prepare themselves if not to convert themselves.[90] In 1690 a committee of ministers attempted to moderate the confusion that followed the revolution against Andros by issuing a manifesto of the ancient creed of New England; admitting that men are saved or rejected entirely by the will of God, they hastened to insist, nevertheless, that there are "some previous and preparatory common works" which may be accomplished by all, though in those who afterwards fall away "we deny them to be the beginnings of true justifying or saving faith."[91] Most sermons in the last decades of the century exhibit the same alternation between an assertion of human impotence and an incitation to preparation, and in one breath denounce the "insignificant and unsavoury" belief that men's efforts have any value while in the next they exhort men to greater efforts. The inconsistency no longer bothered the preachers, and once having stated the conventional inability, they were at liberty to press upon their congregations an obligation to act, as though John Calvin had never lived. If accused of Pelagianism they answered that preparation was not salvation and therefore not a matter of grace. How may I know that I have Christ? the people would ask, and Samuel Mather could reply, "As Your *Conviction* is, such your faith is: as is the preparation work, such is the closing with Christ. It is a *sure rule;* and this is the reason why we so much, and so often press for *preparation* work. . . . And there is more *preparation* needful, than many think for."[92]

The culmination of this development, the enlargement of preparation to a point beyond which it could not be extended without bursting the bonds of orthodoxy, is to be seen in the writings of Cotton Mather. Even at the beginning of his career he was so far heedless of first principles as to represent his brother

[89] *A Compleat Body of Divinity* (Boston, 1726), 435.
[90] *Ibid.*, 434–36.
[91] Allen, Moody, Willard and Cotton Mather, *The Principles of the Protestant Religion Maintained* (Boston, 1690) 110.
[92] Samuel Mather, *A Dead Faith Anatomized* (Boston, 1697), 87.

Nathaniel entering into a covenant with God *before* being converted, which then became "an influence into his *Conversion* afterwards."[93] Cotton Mather never had any other conception of grace than as a process that could be "cherished and promoted"; though he paid the usual lip service to total depravity, he always heartily exhorted depraved men to set their house in order, and their provisions, according to his instructions, would have included almost every action of the religious life. "You may make a *Tryal;*" there can be no harm in trying, for "Never, I am perswaded, never any Soul miscarried, that made such Applications."[94] True, God has not promised to give grace to those who seek it, nevertheless—there is always a "nevertheless" in Cotton Mather's discourse—"'Tis many ways Advantageous, for an *Vnregenerate* Man, to Do as much as he *can,*" for "there is a probability that God intends to help him, so that he shall *do* more than he *can.*" Certainly, if a man makes his *"Impotency* a Cloak for his *Obstinacy,* it will Aggravate his Condemnation at the Last." The way to be recovered—"the way of the *New-Covenant"*—is very simple: "*Try* whether you can't give that Consent; if you *can,* 'tis done!"[95] By the beginning of the eighteenth century, preparation had come to mean for all practical purposes, that every man was able to predispose himself for grace, that his fate was in his own hands, even though grace was given of God. The memory of John Cotton's dissent remained a monitor of caution, but the preachers were no longer capable of comprehending why he had dissented.

The premise of clerical thinking in the new century remained ostensibly what it had been in the old, the inherent nature of a covenant, whether among men or between man and God. But in the later treatment, the fact that a covenant not only permits but requires a preliminary negotiation and that the terms of salvation must therefore be known to every sinner, became not a condescending mercy of God but a utilitarian convenience. The federal theology began by permitting what strict Calvinism would not, some sort of anticipatory behavior among those who desired redemption, but successive theologians steadily enlarged the field of such behavior by shifting the focus of attention from the awful majesty of God to the concrete and manageable propositions of a business

---

[93] Cotton Mather, *Early Piety, Exemplified in the Life and Death of Mr. Nathanael Mather* (London, 1689), 20.

[94] *Batteries upon the Kingdom of the Devil* (London, 1695), 108.

[95] *The Seriovs Christian* (London, 1699), 21–4.

transaction. "For this reason," Willard put it in 1700, "the *Gospel Promises* are exhibited on terms; and these terms therein proposed, do not only tell us what it is that God requires of Sinners in the treaty of Peace which he opens and manageth with them . . . but they do also give us to understand after what manner God will by his Grace convey a pardon to Sinners."[96] Puritans of the seventeenth century always assumed that God alone could fully enable men or nations to take up a covenant, but from the beginning the federalists had insisted that there is "an order in which he brings them to a participation;"[97] hence the rationalizing, secularizing tendencies of the age did not need to appear in New England as a frontal attack upon the terrible decrees of election and reprobation, but could be satisfied by a cautious translation of the initial action in the order of grace into the language of a commercial parley. The infusion of grace itself, said Cotton Mather, is immediately done by God's almighty arm, "But then, the Spirit of God, because He will deal with us as *Rational Creatures,* He also puts forth a *Moral Efficiency* for our *Conversion;* We are capable of *Treaties,* of *Proposals,* of *Overtures;* and He therefore *Exhorts* us, and Uses a variety of *Arguments* to perswade us."[98]

Once more, we must remark that the first federal theologians set forth the idea that conversion is a logical process following a discernible "order," beginning with a period of preparation, not for social but for evangelical reasons. They wished to incite men to preparedness, not in order that laws might be obeyed, but that souls might be saved. Yet they did dignify certain motions, admittedly within the attainment of the unregenerate, as the prologues to conversion. Thereupon they made the national covenant a logical possibility, for not only God but all the people could bear their part: "As in a Covenant there are Articles of agreement betweene party and party; so betweene God and his people."[99] To become a holy society, a people must know the terms of holiness and be able to observe them; the doctrine of preparation secured both conditions, and so Massachusetts and Connecticut could conceive of themselves as societies in which all men, saints or not, were pledged to observe the externals of religion. But once these societies began to decline, the inhabitants to grow remiss and be duly

[96] Willard, *A Remedy against Despair* (Boston, 1700), 42–3.
[97] *Ibid.,* 44.
[98] Cotton Mather, *A Letter to Ungospellized Plantations* (Boston, 1702), 12–3.
[99] Hooker, *The Faithful Covenanter* (London, 1644), 12.

punished by plagues and financial losses, they could all be informed; "they shall seek to him for a pardon, and upon their so doing, they shall find it."[100] Within a few decades the preparation that was first urged upon all men for the salvation of their souls was being pressed upon them for the preservation of the state. They could do what was required, and though they might miss their redemption they could reform their manners. There were still limits to what men could do merely in a way of preparation, but by staying away from the ale-houses and putting off their luxurious clothes they could make the difference between social prosperity and ruin.

But at this point a new question intruded itself upon the leaders: would men bestir themselves in order to save the society when they had no hope of escaping Hell? Might not the unregenerate understandably object that there was no reason why they should strive for a goal they could not attain merely in order that the saints might grow rich? That this question, in some form, could not be avoided is abundantly testified by the sophistries of Cotton Mather, and in him the worst forebodings of Anne Hutchinson were finally vindicated, for he began, though in the most tentative fashion, to suggest that whoever would prepare himself would almost certainly go to Heaven! First of all, he was concerned that men keep up the outward observances. "Men have a *Natural Power,* as to the *External part of Religion*"—there was no longer any qualification in his mind. Therefore it followed, "If men do not in Religion, what they have a *Natural Power* to do, they cannot with any modesty complain of the Righteous God, that He does not grant them the *Higher Power,* to Exert those Acts of Religion, which are Internal."[101] By the same token it followed that those who did exercise the lower power were practically assured of receiving the higher: "If men did in Religion, more than they do, & *All* that they could by a *Natural Power* do, there would be a greater Likelihood, (I say not, a *Certainty,* but a *Likelihood,*) that God would grant them that *Higher Power.*"[102] The founders had taken for granted that a holy society could force the proper manners upon the unregenerate; Cotton Mather could not persuade the unregenerate to mend their manners without luring them with the promise of an

[100] Willard, *A Remedy against Despair,* 44.

[101] Cotton Mather, *A Conquest over the Grand Excuse of Sinfulness and Slothfulness* (Boston, 1706), 28.

[102] *Ibid.,* 29.

almost sure chance of salvation, even though they still were deficient in grace and faith.

It was but a short step from such thinking to an open reliance upon human exertions and to a belief that conversion is worked entirely by rational argument and moral persuasion. The seeds of what Jonathan Edwards was to denounce as "Arminianism" in the mid-eighteenth century were sown in New England by Hooker and Shepard, who, ironically enough, were the two most evangelical among the founders and the most opposed to seventeenth-century forms of Arminianism. The subsequent development of their doctrine is not a mere episode in the history of a technical jargon. It is nothing less than a revelation of the direction in which Puritanism was travelling, of the fashion in which the religious world of the seventeenth century was gradually transformed into the world of the eighteenth. A teleological universe, wherein men were expected to labor for the glory of God, wherein they were to seek not their own ends but solely those appointed by Him, was imperceptibly made over into a universe in which men could trust themselves even to the extent of commencing their own conversions, for the sake of their own well-being, and God could be expected to reward them with eternal life. Even while professing the most abject fealty to the Puritan Jehovah, the Puritan divines in effect dethroned Him. The fate of New England, in the original philosophy, depended upon God's providence; the federal theology circumscribed providence by tying it to the behavior of the saints; then with the extension of the field of behavior through the elaboration of the work of preparation, the destiny of New England was taken out of the hands of God and put squarely into the keeping of the citizens. Even while invoking the concept in an effort to stem the tide of worldliness, the ministers contributed to augmenting the worldly psychology: if the natural man was now admittedly able to practice the external rules of religion without divine assistance, and if such observance would infallibly insure the prosperity of society and most probably the redemption of souls, if honesty would prove the best policy and if morality would pay dividends, then the natural man was well on his way to a freedom that would no longer need to be controlled by the strenuous ideals of supernatural sanctification and gracious enlightenment, but would find adequate regulation in the ethics of reason and the code of civic virtues.

Lotze's Influence on the Pragmatism and Practical Philosophy of William James[1]

by OTTO F. KRAUSHAAR

Reprinted from the *Journal of the History of Ideas*—Vol. I, No. 4, pp. 439–458

The genius of William James lay not only in his unusual fertility and inventiveness, but also in a degree of open-mindedness rare among philosophers. Whether dealing with experience first-hand or as mediated by the psychologies and philosophies of other thinkers, he approached his material with a mind singularly unfettered and free from bias. While he himself possessed a remarkable talent for sensing the vitality and significance of immediate experience, he was none the less eager to examine and applaud ideas from any quarter, just so long as they held promise of illuminating and enriching the stream of living experience. But he invariably transformed everything he assimilated; and the vigor and pungency of his style and phrasing lent to many neglected and forgotten ideas a vitality and popularity such as they had not enjoyed before. By means of the energetic exercise of these talents James became a ferment in philosophical thinking the world over and completely reoriented philosophy in America.

When James appeared on the scene, American philosophy was still tied securely to the intellectual apron-strings of Europe. With the debatable exception of the literary philosophers of the Concord School, there was no truly indigenous American philosophy before 1890. The publication in that year of James's *Principles of Psychology* was the opening gun in the intellectual war of American philosophical independence. But like other revolutions, this one did not come off without being well scarred by the old order. From William James, the Socrates of the intellectual revolution, to John Dewey, its Aristotle, certain elements of the idealistic philosophies, dominant during the student days of James and Dewey, persist within the framework of their new thought.

But in the new setting the old ideas readily escape detection. The way in which the mind of James was fructified by the British

[1] This is the last in a series of four studies of Lotze's influence on William James. The first, "Lotze's Influence on the Psychology of William James," appeared in the *Psych. Rev.*, XLIII (1936), 235–257. The second, "What James's Philosophical Orientation Owed to Lotze," and third, "Lotze as a Factor in the Development of James's Radical Empiricism and Pluralism," were published in the *Phil. Rev.*; the former in XLVII (1938), 517–526; the latter in XLVIII (1939), 455–471.

empirical tradition from Hume through John Mill, and also by certain strands of French thought, notably present in Renouvier and Bergson, has received ample recognition.[2] The influence, however, of that phase of post-Hegelian German idealism represented by Rudolph Hermann Lotze (1817–1881) is far less familiar, though scarcely less important. The intellectual milieu in which James grew to maturity and from which he emancipated himself eventually was heavily charged with the idealism of the "German Movement." Most of the best minds in England and America, among them such figures as the two Cairds, T. H. Green, Bosanquet, Bradley, W. T. Harris and Josiah Royce, were under the spell of Hegel's absolute idealism. It had been introduced to the English-speaking world by J. H. Stirling[3] and others in the fifties and sixties of the last century, some twenty-five years after Hegel's death. In the meantime Hegelianism in Germany had splintered into schisms and run afoul of a strong current of scientific positivism and metaphysical materialism. Lotze was one of the few, in the Germany of that day, who, trained both in the German idealistic movement and in the methodology of the new natural sciences, sought to effect a fusion of these sharply diverging currents. It so happened that his works came to the attention of the English-speaking philosophical world just as Hegelianism was at full tide there.[4] He was promptly and enthusiastically received as the one on whom the mantle of Hegel had fallen, and was the more welcome to many because he freed idealism of many of the abstractions and rigid dogmas which Hegel had fixed upon it. Moreover, it was far easier and more satisfying to fish for philosophic truth in the clear, still waters of Lotze's style than in the turgid, muddy waters of Kant or Hegel. These circumstances account for the remarkable vogue

[2] The most comprehensive treatment of the many and varied sources upon which James drew is Professor R. B. Perry's monumental work, *The Thought and Character of William James*, 2 vols., Boston, 1935.

[3] J. H. Stirling's, *The Secret of Hegel*, published in 1865, though not the first to bring Hegelianism to England, was the most potent single factor in promoting its spread and enthusiastic acceptance there. See Rudolf Metz, *A Hundred Years of British Philosophy*, translation edited by J. H. Muirhead, London and New York, 1938, Pt. II, chs. 1, 2.

[4] Lotze's "System der Philosophie," comprising a separate *Logik* and *Metaphysik*, appeared in English translation, under the editorship of B. Bosanquet, in 1884. A year later the English translation of the *Mikrokosmus* appeared. It was long used as textbook in English and American universities.

of Lotze's teaching and writing, which lasted well into the first decade of the present century. During this period the thoughts of this unassuming sage of Göttingen were the rallying point for moderate idealists all over the western hemisphere.

James, like so many of his contemporaries, was swept into the orbit of Lotze's ideas also. And even long after he had denounced the "bloodless categories" and the creaking, thumping machinery of the all-engulfing Hegelian Absolute, he continued to find nourishment in Lotze's philosophy. For though Lotze was most acceptable to the post-Hegelians, his system was many-sided and reflected the remarkable versatility of its author. His philosophy is not unlike an intellectual bazaar; in essence it is a continuous dialectic which explores every relevant hypothesis, theory, or doctrine, and ends, not infrequently, in compromise. Because of these qualities, Lotze's philosophy left the stamp of its influence on diverse systems of thought.

There were, in fact, elements in Lotze's thought which could feed the fires of James's antipathy to absolute idealism of the Hegelian type. Lotze had tried, in the first place, to disentangle certain basic ideals of the German idealistic movement from Hegel's logic and speculative method; and secondly, he aimed to establish the validity of these ideals by appeal to the concrete facts of human experience, so far as possible. In the Absolute of Hegel and the post-Hegelians, the rich variety of immediate experience fuses into an eternal noon of pure being, at the expense of the multiplicity, uniqueness and value of the concrete, empirical world. In Lotze's eyes, Hegel's aims were sound to this extent: he looked for the One in the Many, the end among the means, the universal in the particulars. But the method by which he sought the solution was illegitimate. For he translated real relations into rational relations, things into concepts, living purposes into a reified Idea. For Lotze, however, things are not identical with thoughts, individuals are not simply "moments" in the inexorable development of the Absolute, and the Many are not simply grist for the One. His system is like an empiricist counterpoise to the excesses of Hegelian rationalism. Because of this fact, "tender-minded" idealists of various persuasions, as well as "tough-minded" realists of one sort or another, found Lotze's philosophy provocative and instructive. This was particularly true of William James who also sought to reconcile moral idealism with a conception of knowledge and truth which accepted the Here and Now at its face value.

James's interest in psychology led him to begin the study of Lotze's works before Hegelianism had captured the attention of philosophers in England and America. This fact is significant. For James approached Lotze's thought in relative innocence, philosophically speaking, and looked upon it, not as a kind of attenuated Hegelian idealism, but as a promising new philosophy. The latter recommended itself to James especially because its author had undergone the same evolution of interests—from medicine through psychology to philosophy—which he was then himself undergoing. The ferment which the doctrines of Lotze provoked in his thinking came in two waves. The first extended through James's writings of the nineties, devoted largely to psychology, ethics and religion. By 1879 he had made an initial study of Lotze's basic works: *Medicinische Psychologie, Mikrokosmus, Logik,* and *Metaphysik*.[5] These books exerted a considerable and, for the most part, a positive influence in the formative stages of his thought. This is most evident in the *Principles of Psychology,* wherein James, after acknowledging his heavy indebtedness to Lotze,[6] invokes his support for a number of special theories, notably those of emotion, attention, and will.[7] Moreover, certain of Lotze's doctrines proved to be of consequence also in the framing of James's tentative metaphysics of this period. He drew support especially from Lotze's defense of indeterminism, his championing of the Many against the One and of persons against an impersonal macrocosm. While he never explicitly accepted Lotze's metaphysical view that reality consists of persons or free, person-like entities, it remained implicit in his thought; for he was temperamentally attracted to this idea. Furthermore, he attached great weight to Lotze's defense of the power of faith and of ideals; the significant rôle which Lotze attributed to these in the shaping of events found a ready

[5] See the first article listed in footnote 1, especially pp. 237–239, where evidence supporting these statements is given.

[6] ". . . I cannot resist the temptation at the end of my first literary venture to record my gratitude for the inspiration I have got from the writings of J. S. Mill, Lotze, Renouvier, Hodgson, and Wundt. . . ." (Preface, I, vii).

[7] In 1879, eleven years before the publication of his *Principles,* James wrote his friend G. Stanley Hall, ". . . it gratified and at the same time disgusted me to see how many choice pages of my everlasting psychology had been anticipated by Lotze." Quoted in R. B. Perry, *op. cit.,* II, 16.

echo in his thought. These elements were well suited to the native inclinations of James. But at the same time, he had to be on his guard against Lotze's tendency to conciliate and compromise. For in the end Lotze sought somehow to bring the Many into coincidence with the One; to consolidate the realm of persons within a personal, universal Absolute; and to identify free human initiative with the march of cosmic purpose. Then, too, Lotze had left a yawning dualism between "thoughts" and "things," which he had not succeeded in bridging to James's satisfaction. Yet in spite of these incongruent elements, the first wave of Lotze's influence is more significant in what it gave James positively than in the provocation it gave to seek a solution in other terms.

The second wave, rather less significant than the first, extended from the turn of the century to James's death in 1910. In the late nineties and again after the completion of his *Varieties of Religious Experience,* James re-examined several theses basic to Lotze's thought. But this time he broke completely with the traditional logic of idealism. True, he continued to speak with respect of that form of personalistic idealism known as pan-psychism, although he could not bring himself to embrace it openly. Gradually, as he becomes more confident of his philosophy of "pure experience," the references to Lotze become less frequent. Moreover, he now selected for special refutation certain of Lotze's favorite arguments, notably his attempt to establish metaphysical monism by proving it a necessary assumption to account for the observed fact of interaction.[8] Nevertheless, because of the amorphous character of Lotze's system it was possible for James to cling to separate doctrines while repudiating the rest. The rejection of basic theses of Lotze's metaphysics did not prevent James from seeking the support of his arguments and reputation for the special doctrines of pragmatism and in the field of ethics.

Pragmatism is a many-faceted doctrine, now commonly associated with James's name, which maintains that the meaning of ideas lies in their "working" or consequences. From this ambiguous mother-stem have branched many special forms of the doctrine, some of them methods, some of them theories of truth. In one form or another, pragmatism was an integral feature of James's thought from the outset. It was a natural corollary of his deference to immediate, concrete experience, the "show me" experi-

---

[8] *Pluralistic Universe* (1909), 55–62.

mentalist attitude which characterized his mental outlook. Though he did not give a systematic account of pragmatism until 1907, he admitted then that his essay, "On the Function of Cognition," published in 1885, was the *"fons et origo"* of the doctrine. Since pragmatism is entailed so definitely by the tenor of James's thought, it may well seem fruitless to search for "sources" elsewhere than in James himself. But though his practicalism was, so to speak, congenital and not acquired, the general form, bearings, and application of the doctrine owe a great deal to the philosophical literature of that day.

The rôle that Lotze's philosophy played in this connection has never been sifted out from the total complex of ideas which formed James's early philosophical milieu. While it is doubtless true that English and American philosophers, such as Locke, Hume, Mill and Peirce, as well as the general tradition of which their ideas were a part, furnished James the chief stimulus and support of pragmatism, it is no less true that certain elements in the German idealistic tradition from Kant to Lotze were also congenial to the doctrine. On this question we have James's own word. In enumerating the currents of thought which prepared the way for pragmatism, he gave first place to ". . . the philosophic criticisms like those of Mill, Lotze, and Sigwart, [which] have emphasized the incongruence of the forms of our thinking with the 'things' which the thinking nevertheless successfully handles.'"[9]

In Lotze's philosophy three separate doctrines, whose convergence he seeks to effect, contain distinctly pragmatic implications. The first of these may be said to be epistemological, the second is a doctrine of logic, the last is predominantly a question of ethics or moral philosophy.

The first of these is a simple and forthright doctrine, although like many other Lotzean ideas it is difficult to see how it can be squared with other elements of his system. Lotze's deference to concrete experience—the same motive which prompted his sharp attacks upon the austerity and abstractness of Hegel's logic—led him to pronounce again and again a general dictum to the effect that "things are what they are known as." In the *Medicinische Psychologie,* the soul, the self, the will, as well as lesser existents and processes are all interpreted in the light of this doctrine. The soul is simply the effects it can produce; the self is a unity if it can

[9] *Collected Essays and Reviews* (1920), 448–449.

appear, act and impress as such; the will is free and undetermined if it can effectually act as free. Similarly, in the *Mikrokosmus* and the *Metaphysik* he treats substance in an identical way. To be a substance means nothing more than to be experienced, felt, acted on as such. In short, things are not to be evaluated and judged in terms of some abstract definition of reality, but in terms of the effects they can produce in the actual world and on the living consciousness. To be sure, Lotze's predilection for teleological idealism throws an unexpected light over this seemingly radical empiricism; for to his eyes Nature stood revealed in her effects as an organic whole, determined by purposes and values. James accepted Lotze's general dictum or principle that things are what they are known as, but he knew them as something different from Lotze's description of them. Either Lotze was reading something in, or James was blind to some of the evidence. We shall see below, however, that James employed Lotze's principle in more than one connection.

A second doctrine of Lotze's, also rich with implications of pragmatism, arose out of the difference between the logical structure of thought and the actual or "real" structure of those things which are said to be known or understood by thought. Lotze begins, in characteristic fashion, by developing this difference into a sharp dialectical antithesis. He reasoned as follows: "Thought" (*das Denken*), with its formal and necessary principles and laws, introduces among "things" a good deal of conceptual apparatus to which nothing real in things corresponds. Thought may make many and various skirmishes in pursuit of the same truth, just as several trails may lead to the same mountain-top. Yet it is evident that thought does somehow conduct us to some truth about things and enables us to identify and handle them. He compared the structural apparatus of thought to a scaffolding, the product of thought to the completed edifice. Thus the process of thinking has instrumental value only.[10] To think consistently about a thing is not to copy that thing or to follow minutely its structure and articulation. Nevertheless, if the process of thought is to have any value, it must lead to a fruitful conception, with the help of which things can be ordered, understood and manipulated.

Lotze found great difficulty in squaring this sharp dualism of

[10] See especially *Logic*, Introduction, § ix; *Microcosmus*, trans. by Hamilton and Jones, Bk. VIII, ch. 1, §§ 4–8.

thing and thought with his metaphysical doctrine according to which there is a real world made up, not of concepts, but of monads organically related. He wished to show that while thought is not constitutive of reality, the product of thought (*Denkleistung*) has "real validity" (*sachliche Geltung*) nevertheless. He seeks an answer to the question, "Can the product of thought, constructed in obedience to the laws not of reality but of logic, be true of reality?" This problem occasions an exhaustive and tortuous examination, in Lotze's *Logik*, of the forms of judgment, the upshot of which is the broad conclusion that the logical laws and principles, which effect the syntheses and order of ideas in judgment, are at bottom not logical at all, but aesthetic and moral instead. In other words, the demand for logical consistency in thinking is not a bare logical demand, but arises from certain insistent aesthetic and moral demands. "The real validity of our cognition consists in the fact that it is not a meaningless show of appearances, but sets before us, instead, a world whose coherence is determined in accordance with the injunctions of the sole reality in the world, namely, the Good. In this our cognition possesses more of truth than if it copied an intrinsically valueless world of objects."[11] In this way Lotze essays the validation of knowledge of Nature by reference to the same moral and aesthetic values which constitute the ultimate ground of Nature herself.

Closely related is a third point in Lotze's philosophy which contains another germ of pragmatic doctrine. We have just seen how Lotze sought to overcome the dualism of things and thoughts by pressing to the limits of logic, thus exposing the ground on which logically valid thought, real being, and moral values can meet. This ground Lotze calls "the Good." He conceives it as the formative energy in thing and in thought, which is directly experienced in "practical" intuitions, that is, in the realization and enjoyment of values. This doctrine is nothing other than a defence of "the primacy of the practical (that is, moral or axiological) reason." Under the same designation, Kant had maintained that the "pure rational will" can rightfully postulate certain "practical" principles, such as freedom, which theoretical or scientific reason cannot "know" or prove. Lotze goes even further than Kant in the defense of practical reason; for he claims priority not only for formal principles but for values as well.

[11] *Grundzüge der Metaphysik* (1883), 92.

To these he attached both epistemological and metaphysical import. The perception of values, he claimed, not only reveals human good, but contains an insight into the nature of reality.

Consistently with this position, Lotze framed a new conception of the nature of reason. "Intellectual life," he holds, is much more than "thought." "After thought has done its work, we have yet to give ear to the pronouncements that the whole mind makes by virtue of its aesthetic and ethical criteria; . . . the whole mind rejects not only what is contradictory, that is, the unthinkable, but also the *absurd,* that is, whatever may be thought without logical contradiction, but cannot satisfy our aesthetic and moral presuppositions."[12] Our comprehension of reality comes not only from pure ratiocination obedient to the rigorous laws of logic; it has its source also in those broader and, to Lotze, more fundamental perceptions of value and purpose. Bare rational cognition is, in his phrase, *"cognitio circa rem";* while reason appreciative of worth (*"wertempfindende Vernunft"*) he calls *"cognitio rei."*[13] Moral imperatives, aesthetic intuitions and religious convictions should not be dismissed as capricious and irrelevant subjective attitudes; they are genuine insights into a reality which is intrinsically a process of purposes and values. Meaning (in the sense of the reason "why") is primary to fact (the "how"). "Being" is a process of value.

In the defense and elaboration of this position a pervasive non-rational strain comes to light in Lotze's philosophy. He is not, however, to be classed with those shallow sentimentalists who proclaim feeling and will to be the true criteria of truth only to mask the natural indolence of the intellect. The non-rational insights in Lotze's system had always to square accounts with a stubbornly rational dialectic. Thus, for example, in his *Logik* he undertakes a labyrinthine and exhaustive analysis of the forms of logical judgment; and only after eliminating every other possible interpretation of the logical synthesis effected in judgment is he willing to grant primacy to ethical and aesthetic criteria.

These, in meager sketch, are elements of Lotze's teleological

[12] *Kleine Schriften* (1885–1891), III, 63. See also I, 272, and III, 305–312. Similar statements are to be found also in the *Logic,* while the *Mikrokosmus* abounds in them.

[13] *Kleine Schriften,* III, 305–312; see also *Mikrokosmus,* Bk. II, ch. 5; Bk. IX ch. 1.

idealism which occupied James's mind while it was incubating the doctrine of pragmatism. He sifted Lotze's arguments with care. From first to last he was predisposed to follow Lotze into both non-rationalism and the assertion of the primacy of practical reason—but with important differences. Lotze, by temperament and tradition a speculative metaphysician, looked to non-rational postulates for the validation and extension of our rational knowledge of reality. James, on the other hand, was more concerned about the way in which rational and non-rational elements are interlarded in the experience of the conscious subject and in "the sentiment of rationality." While he could not follow Lotze into the devious paths of teleological monism, neither could he wholly reject this course. In the *Principles* he maintained, tentatively, a teleological conception of Nature, and asserted it to be more satisfactory than out-and-out metaphysical materialism. "That theory," he urges, "will be most generally believed which, besides offering us objects able to account satisfactorily for our sensible experience, also offers those which are most interesting, those which appeal most urgently to our aesthetic, emotional, and active needs."[14] This psychological reformulation of Lotze's doctrine of the primacy of the "practical," discloses a significant root of James's pragmatism. In the numerous intimations of pragmatism contained in James's writings up to 1900, the moral and aesthetic motivation of the doctrine clearly predominates. The results of thought are to be interpreted in the light of the ends and purposes which direct and motivate thought. Ideas are true if they lead to better adjustment. The quest of reason is dedicated, in the last analysis, to making man feel more at home in the world—biologically, psychologically, spiritually. That James recognized his kinship with Lotze in this phase of his pragmatism is indubitable. In the margins of passages in which Lotze had asserted the "primacy of the practical," James wrote, in his copies of Lotze's works, "pragmatism," or sometimes "practicalism."[15]

Although James never abandoned the "practical" motive of his pragmatism, in the period after 1900, when he was excogitating the

[14] *Principles*, II, 312. Also *ibid.*, 317; I, 401; also, "Rationality, Activity, Faith," *Princeton Rev.*, II (1882), 59; *Will to Believe* (1897), 75–76.

[15] Through the courtesy of Professor R. B. Perry, Mr. Henry James, and the officials of Widener Library, Harvard University, the author has had access to the unpublished letters, literary remains, and the library of William James.

philosophy of "pure experience," he concentrated his attention on the theoretical, logical, and scientific aspects of pragmatism. He now gave certain aspects of Lotze's dualism of "thing" and "thought" special attention, largely because he was intent on avoiding this dualism which he had tentatively adopted in the *Principles of Psychology*.[16] Once James had arrived at his new interpretation of consciousness, it was not difficult to bridge this dualism, so far as percepts are concerned. But what of concepts? Lotze, it will be remembered, had stressed the instrumental instead of the representative function of thought; concepts, he maintained, are not copies of things, but a kind of intellectual shorthand for arriving at some needful adjustment. James frequently invoked the support of this reasoning, and in the later polemical development of his doctrine gradually placed more and more emphasis on the functional character of concepts. But having gone so far with Lotze, James saw that his path was beset with difficulties. For Lotze's functional interpretation of concepts entailed the presupposition of a dualism which to James's way of thinking violated the observable continuity of nature and experience.

Lotze, too, had grappled with this problem and propounded two solutions, both of which, in James's eyes, served to reënforce the functional interpretation of "thought." The earlier of these is to be found in Lotze's little *Metaphysik* of 1841. He posed the question in the following terms: If "thought" is not identical or coincident with reality, just what is the ontological status of thought? James defines Lotze's answer approvingly in his *Pragmatism*: "May not our descriptions, Lotze asks, be themselves important additions to reality? And may not previous reality itself be there, far less for the purpose of reappearing unaltered in our knowledge, than for the very purpose of stimulating our minds to such additions as shall enhance the universe's total value? 'Die Erhöhung des vorgefundenen Daseins' is a phrase used by Prof. Eucken somewhere, which reminds one of this suggestion by the great Lotze."[17] On this view, "thought" is conceived as a later and higher development of reality, literally created in the act of thinking.

While this reasoning suited the radically futuristic aspect of James's pragmatism, Lotze, seeking a final conception of reality,

[16] See the third article listed in footnote 1, especially pp. 459–465.

[17] *Pragmatism* (1907), 256. See also *Meaning of Truth* (1909), 80.

advanced dialectically to a second position, expounded in the *Logik* of his final "System." He was one of those, James once remarked regretfully, who "spoil" their "sincere empirical evolutionism ... by the arbitrary way in which they clap on to it an absolute monism with which it has nothing to do."[18] Be this as it may, Lotze developed a new and highly influential interpretation of the kind of being which may be attributed to "thought." The being of "things" is denoted by the word "existence"; the being of "thought," however, is described as *Geltung* or "validity." The principles of logic, the forms of thought and concepts are essences or subsistents, whose reality consists not in existing but simply in "being valid."[19] The revival of Platonic realism in recent German philosophy rests in large measure on this doctrine.

James appropriated even this last stage in the development of Lotze's doctrine of thought. But the use he made of it leads one to suspect that he confused it with Lotze's far more casual notion that "things are what they are known as"; for he attributed to Lotze's *Geltung* pragmatic implications of which it was quite innocent. He asserted, for example: "For a thing to be valid, says Lotze, is the same as to make itself valid"; and he uses this statement in corroboration of the need for pragmatic verification of ideas.[20] But on Lotze's views, the synthetic bonds established in thought are valid not because of cumulative verification by experience, but by reason of the inherent self-evidence of the principles upon which the whole structure of knowledge rests. Lotze is aligned at this point with the intuitionists, not with the pragmatists. The pragmatic moment in Lotze's philosophy appears only when the question of the application or correspondence of the conceptual order to Nature is at issue.

In the light of the significant congruences in the doctrines of James and Lotze, it is not surprising that James availed himself of Lotze's pragmatic attacks upon a number of metaphysical problems, to which reference was made above. Always shrewd and circumspect, Lotze was inclined to disparage *a priori* arguments for the necessary existence of pure, inscrutable, noumenal being. Realities or processes such as substance, self, or activity, he reiterated, are nothing more than can be accounted for in the experience

[18] *Collected Essays and Reviews*, 444.
[19] See especially *Logik*, §§ 317–321, 339–341.
[20] *Essays in Radical Empiricism* (1912), 75. See also p. 167.

of them. Things are what they are worth; their natures are made manifest by the way in which they make themselves felt and effective. "Substance," he explained, "signifies everything which possesses the power of producing and experiencing effects, in so far as it possesses that power."[21] In other connections he applied the same reasoning to the definitions of the self and of activity.

Echoes of these pragmatic definitions resound all through the writings of James. "Is it not time," he inquired, "to repeat what Lotze said of substances, that to *act like* one is to *be one*?"[22] And again, "So long as our self, on the whole, makes itself good and practically maintains itself as a closed individual, why, as Lotze says, is not that enough?"[23] Similarly, respecting the problem of activity: "Lotze says somewhere that to be an entity all that is necessary is to *gelten* as an entity, to operate, or to be felt, experienced, recognized, or in any way realized, as such. In our activity-experiences the activity assuredly fulfills Lotze's demand."[24] With the help of these arguments James aimed to show that entities or powers must be defined in terms of their capability to perform the phenomena they are evoked to explain.

In sum, these instances of Lotze's influence on James show how deeply his ideas penetrated and how stoutly they fortified important aspects of James's pragmatism. But it is easy to conclude too much. Though James employs Lotze's arguments, he usually goes beyond him to a more decisive and radical position. In Lotze's conciliatory system, pragmatism, empiricism, dualism, pluralism and related positions, are significant "moments" or constituent factors of one all-inclusive organic whole of reality. Lotze's severance from the old rationalism was at best partial only. He scrutinized experience in the hope of finding within Nature the essential threads wherewith the mind would be led to the absolute whole which his idealistic predecessors had envisaged. All the original elements in Lotze—the ones that attracted James—arose from his conviction that the only Absolute worth knowing is one which is in

[21] *Metaphysic*, trans. by Bosanquet and others (1884), § 243.

[22] *Meaning of Truth*, 108; repeated in *Radical Empiricism*, 59.

[23] *Principles*, I, 350. James's account of the self and the unity of consciousness in this work is heavily indebted to Lotze. Compare, e.g., *Medicinische Psychologie*, paragraphs 418 and 422, with *Principles of Psychology*, I, pp. 292 and 330 ff. See also Lotze's *Microcosmus*, I, pp. 157 and 249; and *Metaphysic*, §§ 242–244.

[24] *Radical Empiricism*, 167. Compare with Lotze's *Microcosmus*, II, p. 636. In the margin of this passage James wrote in his copy, "Pragmatism."

the process of realizing values; and the only Absolute worth living in is one which real men and women help to make in their day-to-day activity. Whenever the logic of actual experience failed to measure up to Lotze's expectations, he fell back on practical assurances which guaranteed the ultimate unity of phenomena. James asked less of experience than Lotze. He tried to think and live with the "neutrals, indifferents, and undecideds" of experience, unresolved and at loose ends. When he speculated on a possible principle of unity, he looked for it where Lotze did—in practical reason. But in the end James could find no warrant for asserting the actuality of this unity. Unlike Lotze, he rested his case with piece-meal, pragmatic syntheses of experience, guided only by the evidence at hand and by the changing urgencies of life and thought.

Since James always acknowledged the supreme urgency of "practical" or moral claims, the center of gravity of his ideas lay quite naturally in ethics and religion. But the sincere employment of the pragmatic method, coupled with his allegiance to the pluralistic outlook, prevented James from treating either moral or religious philosophy in systematic fashion. His conclusions in these fields do not constitute an explicit doctrine but a point of view; one which does, however, entail a definite metaphysics of human nature and destiny.

The central problems of James's moral philosophy arose from his desire to combine moral idealism, which consorted traditionally with absolute monism, and empiricism, which has definite pluralistic implications. Empiricism is "tough-minded" in James's own classification; it is not naturally "on the side of the angels," where James really preferred to be. The "tender-minded" absolute idealists, on the other hand, enjoyed ready access to the realm of values, but over a route that James considered illegitimate. Lotze was confronted with a similar dilemma. This fact, coupled with the remarkable concurrences in the psychological doctrines of the two, made it possible for Lotze to furnish James in this field also with provocative ideas and supporting arguments.

A central feature of James's moral philosophy is the stout defense of absolute contingency. The principle of indeterminism is consistent with both the "strung-along universe" and the activism and meliorism of his psychology and ethics. But while he defended the prevalence of chance in the universe as a whole, he, like Lotze, insisted upon explanation of particular events in mechanistic terms wherever possible. Lotze, for his part, had impressed the concepts of psychical and psycho-physical mechanism upon modern psychology.[25] James, in his more radical way, urged psychologists to proceed on the working hypothesis "that mental action may be uniformly and absolutely a function of brain action."[26] But the moral idealism which was native to James and Lotze alike, caused them to reinterpret mechanism in such a way as to make it perfectly consistent with a teleological interpretation of reality.[27] Furthermore, they both excluded volition and associated mental phenomena from the mechanical realm. "Conditioned in all else," declared Lotze, "... we will be free at least in willing and acting."[28] And James likewise credited the effects of "interested attention and volition" to the "non-mechanical spiritual realm."[29]

The manner in which Lotze and James explain how it is possible for purposes to be efficacious in a mechanically conditioned cosmos is markedly similar. Lotze rested his case for the teleological interpretation of mechanism on the hypothesis that new monads from a noumenal realm may, from time to time, be interpolated into the mechanical realm. Once there, they are subject to the mechanical laws which condition all processes, physical as well as mental. All action, says Lotze, is the *reaction* of the entities entering into a given situation. A given event cannot, therefore, be explained solely by the presence of such and such laws; the number, position and character of the entities entering into the reactive relationship must also be taken into account. In other words, outside the realm of mechanism proper lies the realm of infinite possibility, which may be realized only in so far as it is possible to initiate new causal series in the mechanical realm. This possibility is all Lotze and James needed, the former to account for relevance of cosmic purpose to the actual course of events, the latter to account for

[25] See the first article listed in footnote 1, especially pp. 240–244.

[26] *Psychology: Briefer Course* (1892), Introduction.

[27] The reconciliation of mechanism and teleology is one of the basic motives of Lotze's philosophy. James wrestled with the same problem no less earnestly. He writes: "... A thoroughgoing interpretation of the world in terms of mechanical sequence is compatible with its being interpreted teleologically. Teleology presupposes, in fact, mechanical sequence." ["Rationality, Activity, Faith," *Princeton Rev.*, II (1882), 59.] This is repeated with slight verbal changes in *Will to Believe*, 76. James's way of posing and answering the problem is identical with Lotze's.

[28] *Microcosmus*, I, 254. See also *ibid.*, 144–150.

[29] *Principles of Psychology*, I, 594; also 454.

"chance" as well as for the power of ideals in human conduct. The degree to which they saw eye to eye on the practical aspects of the question has already been remarked upon by James's friend and Lotze's student, Carl Stumpf.[30] But in the metaphysical elaboration of the idea of contingency, Lotze's dialectic carries him to a position which James, committed to radical empiricism, cannot accept. Lotze, unwilling to leave to pure chance the noumenal intrusions into the phenomenal realm, explained them finally as the *Wirkungsweise* of God's creative intelligence. James, however, simply pointed to the brute fact of contingency. His decisive indeterminism is entirely independent of the logic of a system, while Lotze's position hinges on the acceptance of speculative dogmas common to metaphysical idealism.

The study of Lotze's works also sustained James's innate moral and political individualism. Lotze envisaged the real world as a society of personal spirits, constituting an all-embracing but personal world-spirit. Yet the component microcosms maintain their identity and personality unimpaired. Each self is a unity, not of substance, but of consciousness and action; for, Lotze avers, "the soul is a unity if it can appear to itself as such, or if it can appear to itself at all." Individual souls are the real centers of all action, enjoyment, aspiration and realization. "There is no superior region of a so-called objective spirit the forms and articulation of which are in their mere existence more worthy than the subjective soul."[31] Moreover, "there is no real subject, no substance, no place in which anything worthy or sacred can be realized except the individual Ego, the personal soul. . . ."[32] Just so for James also the concrete, personal being is the true and only locus of the experience of values. "The facts and worths of life," he declared, "need many cognizers to take them in. There is no point of view absolutely public or universal. . . ."[33] James paid his respects often to the personalistic elements in Bowne, Lotze's most devoted American disciple. And with justice he credits Lotze,

[30] "Seit dieser Zeit lehrt James mit aller Entschiedenheit Willensfreiheit im absoluten Sinne des Wortes, als ursachlose Entscheidung, als unbedingter Anfang einer neuen Kausalkette, ganz so, wie Lotze sie faszte." *William James, nach seinen Briefen* (1928), 31.

[31] *Microcosmus,* II, 540. In his copy of this work, James wrote in the margin of this passage "NB NB," ("note well" or "take notice").

[32] *Ibid.,* 539–540.

[33] *Talks to Teachers* (1899), p. v.

along with Renouvier and Sigwart, with having paved the way for a "re-anthropomorphized universe"[34]—a universe, that is, in which human individuals are important, not as the pawns of an absolute spirit, but in their own right.

The kinship of the moral philosophies of Lotze and James extends also to their philosophies of history. In accounting for the dynamics of history, Lotze championed the rôle of living, active individuals. "All which happens in history," he explains, "is only brought to pass by the thoughts, feelings, passions, and efforts of individuals, and . . . the ends towards which all these powers with their living activities are striving, do not by any means necessarily coincide with those towards which the development of the universal Idea tends."[35] History is not simply a process of natural evolution, nor can it be reduced to an inexorable phenomenology of the absolute Idea. James, too, in his own way, sought to expose the inadequacies of the evolutionary interpretation of history and its accompanying disregard of individual differences and endeavors. If James needed any corroboration of the philosophical respectability of his inherent individualism, Lotze, among others, was there to furnish this. His influence heightened James's confidence in the conviction that the motive power of history lies in "accumulated influences of individuals, of their examples, their initiatives, and their decisions."[36]

Finally, there are two aspects of James's philosophy of religion, if one may call his unsystematic reflections on this subject by that name, in which he is not averse to invoking the support of Lotze. The first of these is his attempt to formulate a conception of God. James, to be sure, was much more vitally interested in establishing and defending the legitimacy of belief, than with framing definitions or enunciating dogmas about the objects of belief. But he was always sympathetic and receptive to the testimony of sincere or orthodox believers. Like many contemporaries, he sought light on religious questions in Lotze's *Microcosmus* and *Philosophy of Religion*. In the latter volume, widely influential in its day, Lotze

[34] Review of *Personal Idealism, Mind,* n.s. XII (1903), 94.

[35] *Microcosmus*, II, 155. In the margin of this passage James wrote, "Lotze's own view—remember." A similar comment is to be found alongside a passage (*ibid.*, p. 165) in which Lotze asserts a similar point.

[36] "Great Men and Their Environment," in *Will to Believe,* 218. See also, "The Importance of Individuals," *ibid.,* 255-262.

conceived God as the convergence of fact, law and value, a personal being who is at one and the same time the source of existence, of order and of aspiration. The relationship of man to God is that of a personal microcosm to the personal macrocosm. The human experience of God is the consciousness of the universal counterpart of our own struggles for perfection and righteousness. James found this humanized and practical conception of God admirably suited to his pragmatic interpretation of religious verities. In some unpublished notes entitled "The Progress of Philosophy,"[37] James speaks of God as "the not ourselves which makes for righteousness, and which helps us when we make appeal." And he adds, "This is the practical and verifiable view of God, like Lotze."

There are echoes, also, of Lotze's doctrine in James's reflections on immortality. ". . . What Lotze says of immortality is about all that human wisdom can say," he declared, and quotes Lotze to the effect that only created things whose existence is an indispensable part of the world's meaning will endure eternally.[38] Later, in the Ingersoll Lectures of 1897–1898, James based his argument for immortality on the thesis that the brain is an organ of restriction, not of production, of mental and spiritual life. This thought, too, James had encountered in his study of Lotze's philosophy. In a marginal note in the *Microcosmus*[39] James acknowledged Lotze's clear anticipation of this idea. Other references to Lotze's conception of immortality occur, but they are as inconclusive as James's own gropings about this baffling problem.

One curious fact may be noted in closing this section. Lotze sought the absolute teleological unity of phenomena in order to reconcile the conflicting interests of different spheres of experience, of which the strife between the materialistic implications of natural science and the idealistic insistence on the reality of higher "spiritual" values provided the most crucial issue in Lotze's day. James, however, resisted the inclination to absorb the Many in the One, both because he saw no warrant in the facts and because it would disparage the moral energy, independence and dignity of man.

[37] Probably written between 1901 and 1903.

[38] *Principles*, I, 349. Lotze wrote (*Microcosmus*, I, 389), "That will last forever which on account of its excellence and its spirit must be an abiding part of the order of the universe; what lacks that preserving worth will perish."

[39] I, 642. Lotze treats of this subject in Bk. III, ch. 1, and in several connections in *Medicinische Psychologie*.

The pathways of Lotze and James crossed when Lotze prepared to draw the fangs of Hegel's all-devouring Absolute by giving renewed emphasis to pluralism and personalism, and when James searched immediate experience for the final assurance of "the not ourselves which makes for righteousness."

The reader may perhaps condone some general observations.

To the present generation of philosophers, obedient to the current intellectual gods of scientific positivism, naturalism and "realism," even the degree of rationalization which Lotze undertook is extreme and untenable. We are inclined to look upon Lotze as someone who has been "overcome," and who may therefore be neglected with impunity. How could James, radical and realist that he was, have taken him so seriously? A scrutiny of the history of ideas is the best antidote for that provincialism in time to which everyone, philosophers not excepted, is prone. James, let us not forget, knew Lotze as one of the ablest teachers and writers of his day, who first had to be in part assimilated, in part overcome, if the revolt against metaphysical idealism was to be anything more than a shallow repudiation of the past. But the systems with reference to which revolutionaries define a new position are regarded with supercilious contempt by the children of the revolt. This is the irony of history, in the face of which Lotze has suffered an unjust neglect in recent decades.

Lotze is again worthy of attention today because through his influence on James he was instrumental in shaping the liberal tradition in America on its intellectual side. The influence of such German philosophers as Fichte and Hegel tended largely to confirm and enhance many conservative tendencies in American social and political thought. On the other hand, the influence in America of figures like Schopenhauer and Nietzsche, whatever their true intentions may have been, has been on the whole inimical to the liberal conception of life. Since the occasion and the temptation to paint a black picture of German philosophical influence is again upon us, it is well to reflect on Lotze's influence, which was steadily and forcibly on the side of liberal humanitarian ideals.

American philosophy in James's day was a strange medley of hard-headed empiricism and lofty moral idealism. Even politics reflected this condition; it turned from dollar diplomacy to humanitarian idealism and back again, to the complete bewilderment of those unfamiliar with our intellectual history. In James the empiricistic and idealistic strains converge. On the one side he bore uncompromising allegiance to fact, on the other he affirmed values to the point of mysticism. Lotze's influence on James was not typical of the influence of German idealism on British and American thought. His absolutism was more in the nature of a tendency than a dogmatic idea. Like James he was skilled in observation of fact, deft in psychological introspection—a literary psychologist in the best sense of the word. To the degree in which Lotze supported James's disposition to defend the Many against the One, the free against the determined, the process against the substance, his influence as a German philosopher was unique.

But the tradition in which Lotze stood would not let him stop short of fitting the materials of experience into some framework which would endow them with meaning and significance beyond the ephemeral moment. James shared this inclination, but lacked the tradition. At the same time, his immersion in the immediate was so profound that he could not be content with any single frame of interpretation, imported or otherwise. There remained for him the difficult task of supporting the spirit with "piece-meal supernaturalism," according as the spiritual need became vivid and insistent and demanded at least a tentative synthesis. Here he was moving boldly on ground that was strictly his own, hitherto unexplored by Lotze or any other philosopher.

Timelessness and Romanticism

by GEORGES POULET

I

Romanticism is first of all a rediscovery of the mysteries of the world, a more vivid sentiment of the wonders of nature, a more acute consciousness of the enigmas of the self. Now there is nothing so mysterious, so enigmatic, so wonderful as Time. It is not only that it is the most difficult of all problems; it is also the most urgent, the one which most frequently confronts us and reminds us of its actual importance, the one which is perpetually experienced not only as a *thought*, but as the very essence of our being. We are not only living *in* time; we are living time; we *are* time.

In their efforts to express themselves it was therefore natural that the Romantic Poets should be especially attracted by the immense variety of distinct temporal experiences which they could feel and observe in themselves, and particularly by those which were more exceptional, which stood out more vividly in their consciousness.

The first of these curious temporal experiences which we may consider is paramnesia. It is well defined by Coleridge in a letter to Thelwall (1796): "Ofttimes, for a second or two, it flashed upon my mind that the then company, conversation and everything had occurred before with all the precise circumstances; so as to make reality appear as a semblance and the present like a dream in a sleep." Coleridge described it also in the first lines of a sonnet:

> Oft o'er my brain does that strange rapture roll
> Which makes the present (while its brief fit last)
> Seem a mere semblance of some unknown past . . . . [1]

One of the most impressive examples of paramnesia may be found in Shelley. In one of his prose writings, he relates that once walking with a friend in the neighbourhood of Oxford, he turned the corner of a lane. "The scene was," Shelley said, "a tame uninteresting assemblage of objects . . . . The effect which it produced on me was not such as could have been expected. I suddenly remembered to have seen that exact scene in some dream of long . . . . " And there he stops suddenly, adding in a footnote some time afterwards: "Here I was obliged to leave off, overcome by thrilling horror." "I remember well," adds Mary Shelley, "his coming to me from writing it, pale and agitated, to seek refuge in conversation from the fearful emotions it excited."[2] Paramnesia, therefore, is a very potent emotion which combines the conviction of having already seen some spectacle or event, with the certainty that we have never seen it before. Its origin

---

[1] *To John Thelwall*, Dec. 17, 1796.   [2] Shelley, *Speculations on Metaphysics, Prose Works* II, 193.

is not clear and has been widely discussed by the psychologists; but what to our point of view is significant is its effect on the mind. As we have seen in Shelley, it produces an emotion sometimes pleasant, sometimes unpleasant in the extreme, whose nature seems to be a feeling of sudden change in the relative positions of past and present, as if both, which are normally separated in our minds, suddenly, and yet without losing anything of their distinctness, were superposed or coalesced: " To find *no contradiction in the union of the old and new, to contemplate the Ancient of Days with feelings as fresh as if they then sprang forth at His own Fiat, this characterizes the minds that feel the riddle of the world,*" Coleridge said.[3] We may add, " that feel also the riddle of *time.*" Ordinarily the past for us is past, *i.e.*, perpetually pushed into unreality by an ever-new present which means for us the only reality. Paramnesia seems to bring forth before our eyes a past which is still real, still alive. It is as if, abruptly, we were projected into a timeless world or into a world where time does not flow but stands still. The incredible idea that all the past we thought we had left for ever, continues to stay here, at our very feet, invisible but intact, and in all its forgotten freshness, shoots forth in our minds. The time, indeed, is out of joint. We perceive, to use an expression of Hoffmann, who—like all the Germans of the Romantic School—experienced and described frequently this sort of feeling—we perceive " a long removed self, which lay far back in time."

Of course, paramnesia is merely an illusion. It does not bring back the past. It just makes a perception look like a recollection. Now as regards proper memory, we may find also in the Romantic poets numerous examples of a break in the dividing line between past and present. Generally our memory grows gradually fainter; it tends to disappear. But sometimes some association may revivify the past sufficiently to make it flash after a long oblivion into our consciousness; and if those associations are very potent, the flashing may be so intense that it has the vividness of the present. It occurs especially when we come back to a place we have left for a long time, whose aspect is bound in our mind with long-forgotten but at the time very familiar emotions. It is then not only as if the images of the past were suddenly brought to our inner eye with a singular force, but as if our own feelings, habits, ideas of long ago were instantaneously repossessing themselves of our soul, and substituting our past self for our present one. An earlier example of this phenomenon is in the *Nouvelle Héloïse:* " En les revoyant moi-même après si longtemps, j'éprouvai combien la présence des objets peut ranimer puissamment les sentiments violents dont on fut agité près d'eux." [4]

[3] *The Friend*, XV. [4] *Nouvelle Héloïse*, IVe part., l. 17.

But of all our senses, those of which the associative power is strongest seem to be taste, smell and, above all, hearing. In the *Task* Cowper remarks:

> There is in souls a sympathy with sounds;
> And, as the mind is pitch'd, the ear is pleased
> With melting airs, or martial, brisk or grave;
> Some chord in unison with what we hear
> Is touch'd within us, and the heart replies.
> How soft the music of those village bells
> Falling at intervals upon the ear
> In cadence sweet, now dying all away,
> Now pealing loud again and louder still,
> Clear and sonorous, as the gale comes on!
> With easy force *it opens all the cells*
> *Where mem'ry slept. Wherever I have heard*
> *A kindred melody, the scene recurs,*
> *And with it all its pleasures and its pains.*
> Such COMPREHENSIVE VIEWS the spirit takes,
> That in a few short moments I retrace
> (As in a map the voyager his course)
> The windings of my way through many years.

Mme. de Staël, at very nearly the same time, made exactly similar observations: "L'aspect des lieux, des objets qui nous entouraient, aucune circonstance accessoire, ne se lie aux événements de la vie comme la musique ... Elle rend un moment les plaisirs qu'elle retrace. C'est plutôt ressentir que se rappeler." And, speaking about a famous episode in Jean-Jacques Rousseau's *Confessions* where Jean-Jacques at the sight of a modest periwinkle in a wood experienced an indescribable emotion, because many years before the smell of this flower had been associated with all the happy feelings of his youth, and of his love for Madame de Warens, Mme. de Staël adds: " Une seule circonstance semblable lui rendait présents tous ses souvenirs. Sa maîtresse, sa patrie, sa jeunesse, ses amours, il retrouvait tout, il ressentait *tout à la fois.*" Both these passages draw our attention to two very significant aspects of this phenomenon. First, as Mme. de Staël said, " tout est ressenti à la fois," or, as Cowper said, " it opens *all* the cells." All these recollections, therefore, are perceived by the mind in such a number and in such a short time that they appear quasi-simultaneous, in a sort of altogetherness, not one after the other with the ordinary successiveness of time, but as if forming a widely spread panorama: " I retrace," Cowper said, " the winding of my way through many years, as in a *map* the voyager his course."

The other point is that the recollection does not appear to be "recollected": "C'est plutôt ressentir que se rappeler," it is a question of feeling again, of re-living the experience. The recurrence is so complete that the mind is, as it were, and to employ two Wordsworthian expressions, "for a brief moment caught from fleeting time" by a "spontaneous overflow of powerful feelings." Once again and in a very different phenomenon from paramnesia, we discover this strange experience of timelessness, which so deeply impressed the poets of that period.

The third and last of these experiences is of a slightly different nature. It is not provoked by an apparent or real recurrence of the past in the present, but, on the contrary, by a total exclusion of the past from the present, by a perfect absorption in the present. The present moment, then, is so intensely experienced that it seems as if its transience gives way to everlastingness, as if time stands still and becomes eternity. This feeling is quite current in all Romantic poetry, especially in Keats, who professed that "nothing startled him beyond the Moment."[5] Its fullest implications are expressed with great clarity by Rousseau in his famous *Rêverie* on the Lac de Bienne: "Il est un état où l'âme trouve une assiette assez solide pours *s'y reposer tout entière et rassembler là tout son être, sans avoir besoin de rappeler le passé ni d'enjamber sur l'avenir;* où le temps ne soit rien pour elle, où *le présent dure toujours, sans néanmoins marquer sa durée et sans aucune trace de succession.*" A present disconnected from the past, perpetually lasting, without any trace of succession! Here again we find the same feeling of living in another time-world, in which duration is not successive but permanent, and where our consciousness grasps at once in an all-inclusive glance an infinity of details which in normal circumstances it could only perceive one after the other in the process of change.

Is it surprising therefore if the Romantics, at a time when the prevalent sensationalism insisted on the successive character of duration, were tempted to see in the weird feelings we have described a way of escape from a time consisting of what Coleridge called "an aggregate of successive single sensations"?[6] They turned naturally towards the doctrine most opposed to mere sensationalism, the doctrine which could best explain and admit those living experiences which were for them so precious. I mean the philosophy of eternity, as it had been stated from Parmenides to the Schoolmen by all religious thinkers. Eternity is not endlessness. It is "a simultaneous full and perfect possession of interminable life." It is simultaneously

[5] *To B. Bailey,* Nov. 22, 1817. [6] *Anima Poetæ* (London, 1895), 102.

possessed, TOTA SIMUL. In it there is neither present, nor past, nor future. As Boethius expresses it: "*Nunc fluens facit tempus, nunc stans facit aeternitatem.*"

This famous theory, foreshadowed by Parmenides and Plato, first stated by the Neoplatonists, christianised by St. Augustine, elaborated by the Scholastics of the Middle Ages, adorned with every subtlety by the philosophers of the Renaissance and particularly by the divines of the Cambridge School, had also been throughout the ages adopted by the poets as the means for expressing their conception of God, or of the Future Life, or of the Ideal World. Jean de Meun, Dante, Petrarch, Chaucer, Spenser, Ronsard, Vaughan, Traherne, Crashaw, Drummond had in turn sung this "everlasting sabbath that shall run—Without succession and without a sun" (Vaughan), where "All ages and all worlds together stand" (Traherne).

But this poetry was not the poetry of the Romantics. They did not want to describe in their poems an ideal world or the abstract existence of God. They wanted to express their own concrete experiences, their own immediate realities, and to reflect in their poetry not the fixed splendor of God's eternity but their own personal confused apprehension, in the here and now, of a human timelessness. They took hold of the idea of eternity; but they removed it from its empyrean world into their own. In brief, paradoxically, they brought Eternity into Time.

II

This romantic paradox appears strikingly expressed in Coleridge. All his life he was painfully aware that the continuous association of ideas in his mind perpetually threatened to become a mere chain of logically disconnected parts: "A streaming continuum of passive association," [7] "an endless fleeting abstraction," [8] "an immense heap of little things," [9] are some of the expressions characterizing this state of mind that we may find scattered in his writings. More striking still is the following passage: "What a swarm of thoughts and feelings, endlessly minute fragments lie compact in any one moment! What if our existence was but that moment? What an unintelligible affrightful riddle, what a chaos of limbs and trunk, tailless, headless, nothing begun, nothing ended, would it not be!" [10]

No doubt, this feeling of anguish and fear when confronted with the disquieting idea that the world is a shapeless continuum of dreams succeeding one another in an arbitrary fashion, or flowing together in

---

[7] *Note in Tenneman's Geschichte der Philosophie.*   [8] *Table Talk* (Bell), 199.
[9] *To Thelwall,* Autumn 1797.   [10] *Anima Poetæ,* 245.

each moment of time in chaotic and multitudinous visions, was due in part to the opium which Coleridge started to use early in his life. But on the 16th of October, 1797, long before he became a drug-addict, he wrote to John Thelwall, " I can contemplate nothing but *parts, and parts are all little!* My mind feels as if it ached to behold and know something *great,* something *one* and *indivisible.*" Therefore, by a natural revulsion from what he called a " scudding cloudage of shapes," [11] he tried, first in his verse, later in his philosophy, to evolve the idea of a world conceived not as a plurality but as a totality: a world " one " and " indivisible," whose elements would be not merely added and following one another in the endless succession of time, but perceived altogether at once in a simultaneous whole. The very same day that he wrote to Thelwall the letter in which he complained of his inability to contemplate the outside world except as an immense heap of little things, he wrote also to another friend, Thomas Poole: " There are people who contemplate *nothing but parts, and all parts are necessary little.* And the universe to them is but *a mass of little things.*"

Here he is attributing to other people the very defect which, on the same day, in another letter, he was attributing to himself! This apparent contradiction is easily explained by the duality of his feelings and intellectual tendencies. Sometimes, when abandoned to the continuous process of his perceptions, he is dominated by them and passively submits to the discursiveness and succession of Time. Sometimes he has an inkling that it may be possible by his own action, that is, either by the imaginative flight of his poetical powers or by the intervention of speculative reasoning, to *shape* all those little things into a whole.

We know that during the first period of his career Coleridge was much under the influence of Hartley's philosophy. Of course, Hartley was an associationist of Locke's school, and it has therefore been presumed that the young Coleridge's first system was pure associationism, that is, precisely the very system which considers the world and the representations we form of it as a train of ideas, as an aggregation of little things succeeding one another in time. But we must not forget that beside Hartley the associationist there is another Hartley who appears in a rather disconcerting fashion in the second part of his *Observations on Man.* " Since God," Hartley says, " is the cause of all things, infinitely many associations will *unite* in the idea of Him, and this idea will become so predominant that, in comparison with it, ideas of all else, even of ourselves, are as nothing." [12] In other words,

---

[11] *Aids to Reflection* (Bell), 346.   [12] *Observations on Man* (London, 1801), II, 330.

all the infinite associated little things may become, as it were, absorbed in the total vision of the world, and the world itself disappear in the vision of God: "The love of the world and fear, being both annihilated, we shall receive pure happiness, of a finite degree, from the love of God .... We will be indefinitely happy in the love of God, by the previous annihilation of self and the world." [13]

In this curious development of a system that begins as mere sensationalism and ends in pure mysticism, is it surprising that the young Coleridge paid more attention to the latter part, so different from the dry matter-of-factness of the dominant philosophy of the time, and so near, not only to the great idealist conceptions of Berkeley, Spinoza, Plotinus and Bruno which will be the favorite philosophies of Coleridge's later years, but also to the great Platonist tradition of the Cambridge School and the English divines which he was about to continue and prolong in the nineteenth century? One may perhaps tentatively suggest that it was the associationist Hartley who taught Coleridge that behind the reality of the *many* there is the reality of the *one,* behind the reality of successive time there exists, not only for God but even in exceptional moments for man himself, the privilege of living in a non-successive time. In his *Religious Musings,* written during this period, it was these mystical possibilities that Coleridge had in view:

> 'Tis the sublime of man,
> Our noontide majesty to know ourselves
> Parts and proportions of one wondrous whole!

And, more significantly, in another passage of the same poem:

> From hope and firmer faith, to perfect love
> Attracted and absorb'd; and centred there
> God only to behold and know and feel,
> Till by exclusive consciousness of God
> All self-annihilated it shall make
> God its identity: God all in all!
> We and Our Father One!

To these last lines Coleridge himself affixed the following footnote: "See this demonstrated by Hartley, vol. I, p. 114 and vol. V, p. 329." Hartley's passage referred to is in the *Observations on Man:* "Since God is the source of all good, and consequently must at last appear to be so, i.e. be associated with all our pleasures, it seems to follow ... that the idea of God, and of the ways by which his goodness and happiness are made manifest, must, at least, take place and absorb all other ideas, and He himself become ... *all in all.*"

This Scriptural expression employed by Hartley, *all in all,* was to become for Coleridge not an end as for Hartley but a starting-point. The infinite interdependence of things, and still more, the intuitive faculty by which all those related but distinct things differently situated along the infinite line of time may be comprehended *at once,* in a single moment, in the altogetherness of a whole, was to become for Coleridge the cardinal principle of his philosophy.

First, of his philosophy of life. " I should define life absolutely," Coleridge said, " as the principle of unity in multeity .... I define life as the principle of individuation, or the power which unites a given *all* into a *whole* .... " [14]

His philosophy of art: " What is beauty? It is, in the abstract, the unity of the manifold, the coalescence of the diverse," [15] and, more subjectively: " The Sense of Beauty subsists in simultaneous intuitions of the relation of parts each to each and of all to a whole." [16]

Consequently Coleridge's famous theory of literary criticism must appear as a rigorous application of this imaginative power of the creative artist to absorb the parts into a whole: " The poet ... diffuses a tone and spirit of unity that blends, and, as it were, fuses, each to each, by that synthetic and magical power, imagination." [17]

We may therefore understand very clearly the immense importance accorded in Coleridge's thought to the imagination, and the full meaning of the epithets by which he carefully and repeatedly enlarges and defines this quality in man, to his eyes directly and fully divine. Imagination is for him *creative, generating, modifying, shaping.* But, above all, there are two epithets which Coleridge coined himself and never tired of repeating, " *esemplastic* " or " *esenoplastic,*" which he got from the German of Schelling, *In-eins-bildung,* and *coadunative,* both of which mean the faculty that forms the many into one, and which he opposed to the mere *aggregating* power, an epithet reserved for the inferior power of " fancy."

It seems clear that in Coleridge's opinion this " coadunative " faculty of imagination endows the artist, the poet, and man in general with the power of eluding some of the effects of time, and especially its patchiness and fleetingness. It enables man not only to reduce " multitude to unity " but also " succession to an instant," or, to use another Coleridgean expression, " It combines many circumstances into one moment of consciousness."

The Coleridgean imagination, therefore, by its creative activity, but above all by its faculty of combining different moments of time

[13] *Ibid.* [14] *Theory of Life,* 385.
[15] *Miscellanies,* 51. [16] *Ibid.,* 20. [17] *Biographia Literaria,* ch. XIV.

into one moment of consciousness, recalls irresistibly the definition of the Deity as formulated by the Schoolmen. This resemblance is not fortuitous. In a letter written to Thomas Clarkson on October 13, 1806, that is, in the more fruitful period of his maturity, after having defined Eternity in the very terms of the Schoolmen, as " the incommunicable attribute, and may we not say, the Synonime of God, simultaneous possession of all equally," Coleridge proceeds to discern in the human soul a " reflex consciousness " which " seems the first approach to, and a shadow of, the divine *Permanency* "; and he adds: " The first effect of the divine working in us [is] to find [bind?] the past and the future with the present, and thereby to let in upon us some faint glimmering of the state in which past, present and future are coadunated in the adorable I AM " of God. It seems therefore that for Coleridge there exists between the endless succession of moments, which is the ordinary lot of man, and the simultaneous apprehension of those moments in the perpetually present consciousness of God, an intermediary state of consciousness, a quasi-simultaneity not unlike the concept of *aevum* in Aquinas's philosophy, in which by the power of imagination the human mind is able to fuse at least part of its past and its present, with some premonition of its future, into a simultaneous whole. Precisely in this manner does the poetic faculty proceed. And it may even be possible that after our death this visionary activity would enlarge its scope to the point of embracing the totality of existence: " The very idea of such a consciousness," Coleridge wrote, " implies a recollection after the sleep of death of all material circumstances that were at least immediately previous to it."

We come here to the essential belief of Coleridge, and moreover of nearly all the Romanticists, the belief in the continued existence of the past, in the wonderful possibilities of its revival. Nothing is lost. All our life, and especially all our childhood, with all our perceptions, images and feelings, and whatever ideas we have had, persists in our mind; but as we are living in duration, it is not permitted to us to have anything but rare glimpses, disconnected reminiscences, of this immense treasure stored in a remote place in our soul. Should our imagination now be confronted at once with such an infinity of detail, it could not but perceive them as details, that is, one after another, without possibility of taking in the whole; or, stunned as it were by the vastness of this expanse, it would be unable to perceive the order which binds the different aspects of our Past; it would be a chaos, a delirium. And delirium, for Coleridge, is nothing else than uncontrolled memory and time gone mad.

The last passage of Coleridge I intend to consider comes from the *Biographia Literaria*. After having criticised in the first chapters the theory of association as set forth by Locke and Hartley, on the grounds that if it were true, the span of our lifetime would be divided in little bits by the despotic succession of our inward and outward impressions or recollections, he proceeds to retell the case of an illiterate young woman who, being seized with a nervous fever, recited during her fits full passages in Latin, Greek and Hebrew. After some investigation it was ascertained that many years before she had been kitchen-maid to an old Protestant pastor, and that it was the old man's custom to walk up and down a passage of his house into which the kitchen-door opened, and to read to himself with a loud voice out of his favourite books.

"This fact," Coleridge said, "contributes to make it even probable, that all thoughts are in themselves imperishable; and that if the intelligent faculty should be rendered more comprehensive, it would require only a different and apportioned organization, the *body celestial* instead of the *body terrestrial,* to bring before every human soul the collective experience of its whole past existence. And this, perchance, is the Dread Book of Judgment, in whose mysterious hieroglyphics every idle word is recorded! Yea, in the very nature of a living spirit, it may be more possible that heaven and earth should pass away, than that a single act, a single thought, should be loosened or lost from that living chain of causes, to all whose links, conscious or unconscious, the free-will, our absolute self, is co-extensive and co-present."

This passage is of some importance, first, because it gives a particularly complete statement of Coleridge's most profound beliefs, but also because it offers us an opportunity to trace the sources from which they are derived. Of course there is no doubt that they were based, first of all, on personal experience. For Coleridge, the Past was never dead. In his tragedy *Remorse,* he spoke of "the imperishable memory of the deed," and indeed the whole tragedy was nothing else but the development of that thought. The two poems that symbolically reflect his most intimate feelings express the same idea: in the *Ancient Mariner* we find:

> The pang, the curse, with which they died,
> Had *never passed away,*

and in *Christabel:*

> But neither heat, nor frost, nor thunder
> Shall wholly *do away,* I ween,
> The marks of that which once hath been.

On the other hand, Coleridge considerably elaborated these personal certitudes by means of philosophical and mystical doctrines. He got the idea of the *Totum Simul* from the Cambridge philosophers or Bishop Berkeley. He found the idea of the ideality of time in Kant, and Schelling taught him that it is imagination which endows man with the power of escaping the limitations of time. But these were purely philosophical theories, and by their very nature quite different from the deep, spontaneous feelings he experienced in himself and put into his poetry. I think that the link between those philosophical convictions and these living experiences is to be found in the writings of Swedenborg. Coleridge was deeply impressed by the Swedish mystic, whom he declared to be " above praise " and " a man of philosophic genius, indicative and involvent," endowed with " a madness indeed celestial and flowing from a divine mind." [18]

It will be remembered that in the passage from the *Biographia Literaria* just quoted, Coleridge suggests that it would require only a *body celestial* instead of a *body terrestrial* to bring before every human soul the collective experience, the *totum simul,* of its whole past existence. The distinction between body celestial and terrestrial, current among the mystics, is elaborated at great length by Swedenborg. But what is especially Swedenborgian is the idea of an " interior memory " specially allocated to *celestial bodies*. In *Arcana Coelestia* Swedenborg says: " The interior memory . . . is such that there are inscribed in it all the particular things, yea, the most particular, which man hath at any time thought, spoken and done . . . with the most minute circumstances, from his earliest infancy to extreme old age. Man hath with him the memory of all these things when he comes into another life."

These are the very words employed by Coleridge in the passage quoted from the *Biographia Literaria*. But there is more. Immediately after the passage quoted Coleridge adds: " And this is perchance the Dread Book of Judgment, in whose mysterious hieroglyphics every idle word is recorded." In the similar passage from Swedenborg, writen half a century before, we find: " This is the Book of Life which is opened in another life, and according to which he is judged." [19] Obviously, Coleridge's Dread Book of Judgment is a direct reminiscence from Swedenborg's Book of Life.

[18] Note in Swedenborg's *De Cultu et Amore Dei*. [19] *Arcana Coelestia* (London, 1803), 2474.

III

Coleridge is not the only English poet in whom we can find this theory. It is very easy to trace it in all the Romanticists. Blake is an obvious starting-point. Not only was he a mystic, but, despite some late recantations, a follower of Swedenborg, haunted with the idea of evading the process of time, and possessing in the same manner as God in one's own consciousness the totality of the universe to its most "minute particular." "His unremitting effort," Middleton Murry says, was to see his own life as the revelation of Eternity."[20] And this Eternity again is no other than a *Totum Simul:*

> Hear the voice of the Bard
> Who Present, Past, and Future sees,

we read in his Introduction to the *Songs of Experience*. And he conceives in his poem of *Jerusalem* an ethereal city, Golgonooza, where he viewed

> . . . all that has existed in the space of six thousand years
> Permanent and not lost, not lost nor vanish'd, and every little act,
> Word, work and wish that has existed, all remaining still . . .
> For every thing exists and not one sigh, nor smile nor tear
> One hair nor particle of dust, not one can pass away.

And in another poem, *Milton:*

> Not one moment
> Of Time is lost, nor one event of Space unpermanent,
> But all remain . . .
> They vanish not from me and mine, we guard them first and last.
> The generations of men run on in the tide of Time
> But leave their destin'd lineaments permanent for ever and ever.

It may seem a little singular to pass without transition from Blake to Byron. No two poets are so unlike. But if we open the latter's *Hebrew Melodies,* written not long after Blake's greatest poems, we find with some surprise a note not dissimilar. Speaking of the soul in the Hereafter, Byron says:

> Eternal, boundless, undecay'd,
>   A thought unseen but seeing all,
> All, all in earth or skies display'd
>   Shall it survey; shall it recall:
> Each fainter trace that memory holds
>   So darkly of departed years,
> *In one broad glance* the soul beholds
>   And all that was *at once appears.*

[20] *William Blake* (London, 1933), 107.

In Byron, however, as one would expect, the note is defiant; it manifests a sort of nostalgic impatience: " Let me," says Cain to Lucifer, " let me, or happy or unhappy, learn / To *anticipate* my immortality." For him eternity is an "intoxication." Nevertheless the resemblances to some of Coleridge's and Blake's passages are so obvious that we may be tempted to say that Byron found his inspiration either in them or in their common source, Swedenborg. But the idea of Byron reading Swedenborg doesn't somehow appear very likely. On the other hand, he did not even know of the existence of Blake; and as for Coleridge, whom he admired as a poet, he prudently avoided studying him as a philosopher. But there is another channel through which the poetical possibilities of the *Totum Simul* may have been presented to Byron. In 1793 Samuel Rogers had published a poem entitled *The Pleasures of Memory*, which pleased Byron so much that he wrote expressly for Rogers a short piece *"Written in a blank leaf of the Pleasures of Memory."* There he played with the idea that Rogers was dead and that the Goddess of Memory repayed

>The homage offer'd at her shrine,
>And blend, while ages roll away,
>Her name immortally with [Rogers's!].

We may doubt that this highly fanciful but slightly funereal prospect appeared altogether satisfactory to his friend, but anyhow it proves that this particular poem of Rogers had arrested Byron's imagination. Now, in these *Pleasures of Memory* the central episode tells about the dead souls who in their new quality become angels and are able to recollect all their past life:[21]

>All that till now their rapt researches knew,
>*Not call'd in slow succession to review*
>But, as a landscape meets the eye of day,
>*At once* presented to their glad survey.

Compare this last line with Byron's " In one broad glance the soul beholds / And all that was at once appears," and you will conclude that it is highly probable that Byron got his *Totum Simul* idea from Rogers. But from whom, in his turn, did Rogers get his? We might indulge in fanciful suppositions if Rogers had not been good enough to give us most clearly this source in a footnote. It is a quotation: " The several degrees of angels may probably have larger views [than ours] and some of them be endowed with capacities able to *retain*

[21] *The Pleasures of Memory* (1793), 62–64. See also note, p. 90.

together, and constantly set before them, *as in one picture,* all their past knowledge *at once.*" And the author of this very Thomistic *Totum Simul* can hardly be called a Schoolman or a mystic, since he is no other than Locke himself in his *Essay on the Human Understanding* (b. 2, ch. 10).

Neither did Shelley feel obliged, in order to provide himself with the same theme, to read the fearful folios of *Arcana Coelestia.* He borrowed it from the most obvious source of all Shelleyan thoughts, Godwin. In his quality of professed atheist Shelley evidently could not accept the idea of God and therefore of God's eternity. On the other hand he had a vivid apprehension of the deficiencies of time. "Time is evanescent, but poetry," Shelley says, " *arrests* the vanishing apparitions which haunt the interlunations of life." "A poet participates in the eternal, the infinite, and the one; as far as relates to his conceptions, time and place and number are not." But of what kind is this poetical eternity if it is not akin to God—since God does not exist? The answer is rather obscure: "Poetry awakens and enlarges the mind itself by rendering it the receptacle of a thousand unapprehended combinations of thought . . . . It enlarges the circumference of the imagination . . . . " Those are Shelley's words in his *Defense of Poetry.* At first, perhaps, we do not see very clearly the relation between eternity and the enlargement of the circumference of the mind. But if we put this passage, written in 1820, by the side of another from *Queen Mab,* written in 1813 (the seven years which separate them make up nearly all Shelley's adult life), we may be able to see what he is aiming at. The *Queen Mab* passage is unfortunately rather involved. Here it is:

> Him, still from hope to hope the bliss pursuing
> Which from the exhaustless lore of human weal
> Dawns on the virtuous mind, the thoughts that rise
> In time-destroying infiniteness, gift
> With self-enshrined eternity, that mocks
> The unprevailing hoariness of age,
> And man, once fleeting o'er the transient scene
> Swift as an unremembered vision, *stands*
> Immortal upon earth.[22]

Out of this rather intricate sentence, it is possible to extract some definite ideas: 1) Eternity may be apprehended in time by the "virtuous mind." 2) It will prevail over the transience of time, and in some way substitute for its fleetingness a sort of immobility: Man once fleeting over the transient scene, is now *standing. To stand!*

[22] *Queen Mab,* ll. 203-211.

These very words remind us of one of the familiar expressions used by Boethius for the *Totum Simul*: "*Nunc Stans*," a standing now. It is the Totum Simul conceived not under its aspect of altogetherness, or union of past, present and future, but under the aspect of non-successive duration. The present moment may be, to a particularly quick consciousness (that is, to the *virtuous mind* of Shelley), so rich in particulars, so full in details ordinarily unperceived, that it may be equivalent to a far wider span of time in the common mind. Eternity, therefore, is merely an infinite intensity of attention concentrated on a single point of time; or, as Shelley puts it himself in a footnote to the lines quoted before: "If the human mind, by any future improvement of his sensibility, should become conscious of an infinite number of ideas in a minute, that minute would be eternity." And he adds: "See Godwin, *Political Justice,* vol. I, p. 411, and Condorcet, *époque IX.*" Following his directions, we find in Godwin this remark: "We have a multitude of different successive perceptions in every moment of our existence." No doubt Shelley got there the idea of an infinite number of ideas in one moment of consciousness, but, as we may perceive, for Godwin these perceptions are successive and therefore not in timelessness or eternity. So Shelley, in repeating Godwin, leaves out the essential idea of succession; more than that, he replaces it by the *Nunc Stans, i.e.,* its very opposite.

Besides, Godwin concerns himself only, as Locke did, with the fluctuations of ideas in the common mind, in common duration: Shelley dreams of a super-humanity, attaining in the future such a degree of super-awareness that the conditions of time would be changed altogether for each and every man. This implies the idea of progressive education of the mind, the source of which may be found in the second reference of the *Queen Mab* passage. In his *Esquisse d'un tableau historique des progrès de l'esprit humain,* Condorcet foresees that man by the progress of scientific methods will be more and more able to combine in a very little space of time the proofs of a greater number of truths: "Ce qu'avec une même force d'attention on peut apprendre dans le même espace de temps, s'accroîtra nécessairement." It is a purely rational belief, associated with the pedagogical preoccupations familiar to the eighteenth century; just as Godwin's passage was a mere development of the eighteenth-century's no less familiar sensationalism. It is therefore significant that by the combination of two so unmystical systems Shelley evolved boldly a doctrine of earthly eternity very similar to those which Coleridge or Blake arrived at by an entirely different process.

It would be also of great interest to study the different processes followed by the other great writers of the Romantic or Victorian eras, Wordsworth, Keats, Tennyson, Browning, Carlyle, and, in America, Poe, Hawthorne, Melville, Emerson, Thoreau, Whitman. In all of them, the idea of Eternity possessed by man in time appears in one form or another again and again. But we must turn to the last writers we have selected as objects of our inquiries, De Quincey and Baudelaire.

IV

In De Quincey and Baudelaire this mysterious feeling of eternity in time receives its most modern expression. Without losing anything of its mysteriousness, it seems in these writers so intimately related to their dominant emotions and spiritual life, and on the other hand so aptly and spontaneously put into the medium of their own particular mode of expression, that it appears completely natural and as it were the very essence of their genius. As regards some of the poets we have just reviewed, Byron for instance, we cannot entirely get rid of the idea that this feeling was no more for them than a deep but accidental experience; in others—I mean Shelley especially—an experience that was indeed essential but perhaps realized only in part. In Coleridge, on the other hand, there is no doubt that the sentiment of eternity was not only felt but thought; but the two activities are not always fused into one. Blake, of course, is different; in him the fusion is complete; both the emotional experience and the rational idea manifest themselves at once; they are one. But Blake is very exceptional; he has the abnormality of the pure mystic. It is only in De Quincey or Baudelaire that this blending of feeling and thought appears as a natural achievement.

This does not mean, however, that De Quincey or Baudelaire stands alone, independent of any intellectual influence. In both of them it is possible to discern the mark of their predecessors. But the *Totum Simul* was not for them a ready-made system which they blindly accepted or submissively repeated. First of all, it was a tremendous experience whose consequences they were ineluctably forced to accept on the sheer weight of an inner personal evidence. To understand this fully, we have to remember that both were opium-eaters. Now, one important effect of opium-eating is that which it has upon the senses of space and time: " The sense of space and, in the end, the sense of time," De Quincey said, " were powerfully affected.... Space swelled and was amplified to an extent of unutterable infinity. This, however, did not disturb me so much as the vast expansion of time! I sometimes seemed to have lived for seventy or a hundred years in one night." As Baudelaire will say in *Les Fleurs du mal* (*Les Poisons*): " L'opium agrandit ce qui n'a pas de bornes,—Allonge l'illimité,—Approfondit le temps, creuse la volupté."

If time therefore in these exceptional circumstances seems infinitely lengthened, it will appear intolerably shortened in ordinary life: " The narrow track of time," deplores DeQuincey, " How incalculably narrow is the true and actual present," and again: " All is finite in the present," " The time contracts into a mathematical point." And Baudelaire insists on the psychological contrast which exists between the two times, in a prose poem, *La Chambre double:* " Il n'est plus de minutes, il n'est plus de secondes! Le temps a disparu: c'est l'éternité qui règne, une éternité de délices.—Mais un coup terrible, lourd, a retenti à la porte. . . . Toute cette magie a disparu au coup brutal frappé par le Spectre."

It was therefore natural that both De Quincey and Baudelaire were inclined to escape from the narrow track of ordinary time, and to try to create for themselves, and maintain as long as possible, the illusion of an artificial eternity. And they proceeded to realize this infinite amplification of time by swelling the " narrow track " with as many memories as they could. Time for them tended to approach eternity in so far as the present was more and more extended by the recollections of the past. This process of evocation became an art: " Je sais l'art d'évoquer les minutes heureuses,—Et revis mon passé blotti dans tes genoux." Compare with these disconnected notes jotted down by Baudelaire in his diary: " Un *culte* (magisme, sorcellerie évocatoire) . . . intensité, sonorité, limpidité, vibrativité, profondeur et retentissement dans l'espace et dans le temps. Il y a des moments de l'existence où le temps et l'étendue sont plus profonds et le sentiment de l'existence immensément augmenté." An infinite increase of the sentiment of existence, is a very apt definition of the modern, preëminently psychological apprehension of the *Totum Simul*. We find, described at some length, in the *Confessions of an Opium-Eater,* one of those culminating points of existence: " I was told once by a near relative of mine, that having in her childhood fallen into a river, and being on the very verge of death . . . she saw *in a moment* her whole life, in its minutest incidents, arrayed before her *simultaneously* as in a mirror." This instance of inward illumination in case of approaching death is well-known; it has been many times discussed by the psychologists; but De Quincey was the first to give it its full emphasis; and what is even more important is the fact that De Quincey insists on the non-successiveness to be found in this phenomenon. In *Suspiria de Profundis,* written twenty-four years after the *Confessions,* he insists again on this point: " *In a moment, in the twinkling of an eye,* every act, every design of her past life, lived again, arraying themselves *not as a succession, but as parts of a coexistence.*" Why insist so much on this point if De Quincey's idea was not that it may be possible to evade the successiveness of time, and replace it by the simultaneity of another state, eternity?

That he was aware of the metaphysical consequences implied by such a conviction is proved by the fact that to write these passages De Quincey made use of at least two authors in whom these metaphysical implications are clearly set forth. In the passage of the *Confessions* already quoted, after having stated the idea of simultaneity, he adds: " This, from some opium experience of mine, I can believe: I have indeed seen the same thing asserted twice in modern books, and accompanied by a remark which, I am convinced, is true, viz., that the dread book of account, which the Scriptures speak of, is, in fact, the mind itself of each individual . . . . There is no such thing as forgetting possible."

This Book of account which is the mind itself, is already familiar to us. We have still in mind Coleridge's sentence in *Biographia Literaria:* " This is perchance the Dread book of Judgment in whose mysterious hieroglyphics every idle word is recorded," and Swedenborg's " This is the Book of Life . . . according to which he is judged." There seems to be no doubt that the two books in which De Quincey found asserted the double idea of the imperishability of the past and the simultaneity of all our recollections in a supreme moment of consciousness, were *Biographia Literaria* and *Arcana Coelestia.* We know that De Quincey's relations to Coleridge were those of a disciple to a master; and on the other hand we know also that De Quincey was initiated at a very early date into Swedenborgianism by a clergyman, Mr. Clowes. He tells us in his reminiscences that " more than once on casually turning over a volume of Swedenborg, he has certainly found most curious and felicitous passages." In 1824, less than three years after the publication of the *Confessions of an Opium-Eater,* De Quincey published in the *London Magazine* a partial translation of Kant's *Dreams of a Ghost-Seer* (1763), under the title of *Abstract of Swedenborgianism by Immanuel Kant.* Kant's essay was in fact an attack against Swedenborg, but it was also, as duly translated by De Quincey, a very adequate summary of the system of the spiritual world exhibited by Swedenborg, and we can find there in particular this passage: " [For Swedenborg] in the inner memory is retained whatsoever has vanished from the outer . . . . And, after death, the remembrance of all which ever entered the soul of man and even all that had perished to himself, constitutes the *entire book of his life.*" De Quincey, of course, published this translation three years after his *Confessions,* but in consideration of the identity of the two passages, we may fairly suppose that he knew Kant's essay before writing his *Confessions,* and made use of it in them.

Just as De Quincey made use of Coleridge and Swedenborg, Baudelaire made use of De Quincey. De Quincey's *Confessions* had already been translated into French in 1828 by Musset, and this translation was not without influence on the development of French romanticism, as has been demonstrated in the *Mercure de France* in a very able essay.[23] The author of this essay, Professor Randolph Hughes, failed however to see the importance of the factor of *time* in both De Quincey and his French followers, especially in Balzac, Gautier and Nerval: " Ces hommes," Balzac wrote in *La Peau de Chagrin,* " ont-ils le pouvoir de faire venir l'univers dans leur cerveau, ou leur cerveau est-il un talisman avec lequel ils abolissent les lois du temps et de l'espace? " And in the same book, again: " Vous êtes-vous jamais lancé dans l'immensité de l'espace et du temps? " Gautier also: " Rien ne meurt. Tout existe toujours," or " Les esprits pour qui le temps n'existe plus n'ont pas d'heure puisqu'ils plongent dans l'éternité." And Gérard de Nerval: " Rien ne meurt de ce qui a frappé l'intelligence. L'éternité conserve dans son sein une sorte d'histoire universelle visible par les yeux de l'âme, synchronisme divin qui nous ferait participer un jour à la science de Celui qui voit d'un seul coup d'oeil tout l'avenir et tout le passé."

But among the followers of De Quincey Baudelaire stands first. He did not content himself with reading Musset's translation. He read De Quincey in the English text, and he endeavoured to give a French version of the *Confessions.* This version is the *Paradis artificiels.* It is not a mere translation. It is less and it is more. It is a continuous commentary, interpretation, development of the English text; and, above all, it is a personal appropriation of De Quincey's masterpiece, the substitution of Baudelaire's own experiences to those of his English master; so that, in what is apparently a free translation of a foreign author, Baudelaire betrays his innermost feelings.

Now, in the *Paradis artificiels* we find the following passage directly inspired by De Quincey: " Souvent des êtres, surpris par un accident subit . . . ont vu s'allumer dans leur cerveau tout le théâtre de leur vie passée. Le temps a été annihilé . . . . Et ce qu'il y a de plus singulier dans cette expérience . . . ce n'est pas la simultanéité de tant

---

[23] *Merc. de France* (1er août 1939).

d'éléments qui furent successifs, c'est la réapparition de tout ce que l'être ne connaissait plus mais qu'il est cependant forcé de reconnaître comme lui étant propre. L'oubli n'est donc que momentané." This is pure De Quincey, of course, but immediately after Baudelaire adds, speaking this time in his own name: " Si dans cette croyance il y a quelque chose d'infiniment consolant dans le cas où notre esprit se tourne vers cette partie de nous-même que nous pouvons considérer avec complaisance, n'y a-t-il pas aussi quelque chose d'infiniment terrible, dans le cas . . .où notre esprit se tournera vers cette partie de nous-même que nous ne pouvons affronter qu'avec horreur. Dans le spirituel aussi bien que dans le matériel rien ne se perd." Here Baudelaire is speaking for himself and betraying his most secret fear. The promise of integral resurrection is not for him a matter of hope but of terror. Unlike De Quincey, he is not so much haunted by regrets as by remorse. He is the poet of irreparability.

But, as we have seen, he is also of all poets the one who has given to the faculty of total resurrection the status of a conscious art. Therefore it is not without reason that the greatest master of the art of reminiscence in our time, Marcel Proust, declared that Baudelaire was the most important of his predecessors. Indeed, in Proust we may find the culmination of those untiring efforts to bring eternity down to the level of man. His enormous novel is literally an infinite quest to bring back the past into the present, the past not as past, not as a series of points of time, but as a simultaneous whole possessed in its entirety. For, those resurrections, Proust said, " dans la seconde qu'elles durent, sont *si totales* qu'elles . . . forcent nos narines à respirer l'air de lieux pourtant si lointains." And elsewhere: " L'être qui goûtait en moi cette impression . . . (était) un être qui n'apparaissait que, quand par une de ces identités entre le passé et le présent, il pouvait se trouver dans le seul milieu où il pût vivre . . . en dehors du temps."

The only medium in which he could live, out of time! This timelessness, this mystical and yet real experience of eternity, on which Proust gives the fullest and most elaborate testimony in our time, would it have been possible to experience this, as Proust did, and as indeed all our generation does still, had it not been for the long chain of philosophers and poets who expressed their thoughts or their feelings on this essential problem of humanity—and divinity—from Parmenides to Baudelaire? Each poet, each religion, each philosophy, each time has collaborated in man's attempts to escape out of time.

James Marsh and American Philosophy*

by JOHN DEWEY

Reprinted from the *Journal of the History of Ideas*—Vol. II, No. 2, pp. 131-150

In the years 1829, 1831, and 1832, an event of considerable intellectual importance took place in this University town. For in these years Chauncey Goodrich published in Burlington, Vermont, editions of three of the more important writings of Samuel Taylor Coleridge, namely, *Aids to Reflection*, *The Friend* and *The Statesman's Manual*. The first of these contains the well-known Introduction by James Marsh, and it is the Centenary of its publication that brings us together to-day.

In associating the name of romantic philosophy with the work of James Marsh, it is important that we should appreciate the sense in which the word "romantic" is employed. Words change their meaning, and to-day such a title may seem to imply a certain disparagement, since realism in some form is the now prevailing mode. In the sense in which the word was earlier used, a somewhat technical one, the opposite of romantic was not realistic, but rather classic. The word was used to denote what was taken to be the modern spirit in distinction from that of antiquity, and more particularly the spirit of the Teutonic and Protestant North in distinction from the Latin and Catholic South.

Fortunately an essay written during Dr. Marsh's last year in Andover Seminary and published in the *North American Review* for July, 1822, enables us to seize, independently of labels, what Marsh himself thought the difference in question to consist of. "The modern mind," he says, "removes the centre of its thought and feelings from the 'world without' to the 'world within'." More in detail he says, in speaking of the Greeks, that "they had no conception of a boundless and invisible world in the bosom of which all that is visible sinks into the littleness of a microcosm."[1]

* Lecture delivered at the University of Vermont, November 26, 1929, in commemoration of the centenary of the publication of James Marsh's "Introduction" to Coleridge's *Aids to Reflection*.

[1] *North American Review.* Vol. XV, p. 107.

In contrast with this attitude he says: "In the mind of a modern all this is changed. His more serious thoughts are withdrawn from the world around him and turned in upon himself. All the phenomena of external nature, with all the materials which history and science have treasured up for the use of the past, are but the mere instruments to shadow forth the fervors of a restless spirit at last conscious of its own powers and expanding with conceptions of the boundless and the infinite." The change is definitely connected with the influence of Christianity in general and of the Protestant and earlier Barbarian North in particular.

I am concerned with the ideas and principles of the philosophical work of Marsh rather than with its historical origin, development, and influence.[2] But it would be unfitting to pass the occasion by without noting the broad and deep scholarship of Marsh as it is made evident even in this the earliest of his published writings. He had mastered Italian, Spanish, and German, as well as Latin, Greek, and Hebrew, at that early date. This was no attainment since he had never been abroad, and since there were few facilities for study at the time. His writings show that he not only knew the languages, but had an extensive and familiar acquaintance with their literatures. I may not go into detail, but it is not too much to say that he was probably the first American scholar to have an intimate first-hand acquaintance with the writings of Immanuel Kant, including not only the *Critiques of Pure* and *Practical Reason,* but his *Anthropology,* and especially his writings on the philosophic basis of natural science. In the latter connection it is worthy of note that Marsh's readings in the scientific literature of his day were wide and influenced his speculations; Oersted with his principle of polarity influenced him chiefly along with Kant. His interpretation of Kant was affected, of course, by his admiration for Coleridge, but also by his reading of Fries.

While his indebtedness to Coleridge was great, it was somewhat less than his distrust of his own powers would intimate. He came to Coleridge with a preparation both in reading and in his thinking, which fitted him to appreciate the latter, but which also absolves him from any charge of being a mere disciple. The

[2] A careful and thoroughly trustworthy account of the latter has already been given by Professor Marjorie Nicolson. See the article entitled "James Marsh and the Vermont Transcendentalists," in the *Philosophical Review* for Jan. 1925.

interest that Marsh had in Coleridge sprang primarily from a common interest in religion and a common desire to arouse among believers in Christianity a vital realization of its spiritual truth. There is much in Coleridge's *Aids to Reflection* that is far outside the main currents of present-day thought even in religious circles. Aside from penetrating flashes of insight, a reader to-day is likely to be left indifferent to its substance and repelled by its form. He may easily find it of only antiquarian interest. To employ a juster statement, it is mainly of historical interest. To say this is to say that to grasp its meaning and its influence in its own time we must place it in its own context in the intellectual and moral atmosphere of the early nineteenth century. We must recall that it was a period before Darwin and the evolutionists; before, indeed, modern science had itself left any great impress on the popular mind; a period when the peculiar problems forced upon modern society by the industrial revolution were only beginning faintly to show themselves. It was a time when, outside of a few radicals, there was nominal acceptance of established institutions and doctrines but little concern for their inner meaning. It was, on the whole, a period of intellectual apathy and indifference.

The two essays of John Stuart Mill upon Bentham and Coleridge respectively give a clear picture of the general temper of the day. Among other things Mill says, "The existing institutions in Church and State were to be preserved inviolate, in outward semblance at least, but were required to be, practically, as much of a nullity as possible." More specifically in speaking of the Church he says, "On condition of not making too much noise about religion, or taking it too much in earnest, the church was supported, even by philosophers, as a 'bulwark against fanaticism,' a sedative to the religious spirit, to prevent it from disturbing the harmony of society or the tranquility of states." He sums it up by saying that "on the whole, England had neither the benefits, such as they were, of the new ideas, nor of the old. We had a government which we respected too much to attempt to change it, but not enough to trust it with any power, or look to it for any services that were not compelled. We had a Church which had ceased to fulfill the honest purposes of a Church but which we made a great point of keeping up as the pretence or simulacrum of one. We had a highly spiritual religion (which we were instructed to obey from selfish motives) and the most mechanical and worldly notions on every other subject." As he says, "An age like this, an age without earnestness, was the natural era of compromises and half-convictions."

In this situation, Bentham was the innovator, the critic, and destroyer of the old. Coleridge was the unusual type of conservative, the thinker who demanded that the *meaning* of the old be comprehended and acted upon. As Mill says, "Bentham asked of every custom and institution 'Is it true?' while Coleridge asked, 'What is its meaning?'" The latter question, in the existing state of things, was as disturbing as the other; its import was as radical, for it was a challenge to the existing state of belief and action. The more obvious phase of the radicalism of Coleridge in religion is found in his attack on what he called its bibliolatry. He condemned the doctrine of literal inspiration as a superstition; he urged the acceptance of the teachings of Scripture on the ground that they "find" one in the deepest and most spiritual part of one's nature. Faith was a state of the will and the affections, not a merely intellectual assent to doctrinal and historical propositions. As Mill says, he was more truly liberal than many liberals.

But while he disconnected faith from the Understanding, he connected it with a higher faculty, the Reason, which is one with the true Will of man. Coleridge said: "He who begins by loving Christianity better than truth will proceed by loving his own sect or church better than Christianity and end in loving himself better than all." But he held with equal firmness that Christianity is itself a system of truth which, when rightly appropriated in the rational will and affection of men, is identical with the truth of philosophy itself. This assertion of the inherent rationality of Christian truth was the animating purpose of his *Aids to Reflection,* and it was this which appealed to James Marsh; and it is in this sense that he may be described as a disciple of Coleridge. It was in a combination of the teaching of the great English divines of the seventeenth century, themselves under the spell of Plato, and the German transcendental philosophy of the late eighteenth and early nineteenth century, that Coleridge found the especial philosophical framework by which to support his contention of the intrinsic philosophical truth of the Christian faith. Since Marsh himself was already a student of the same sources, all the circumstances conspired to attach his exposition to Coleridge.

If I dwell upon the inherent liberalism of Coleridge's teaching under the circumstances of his own day, as described by Mill, a member of the opposite school, it is because without allusion to that fact we are without the historic key to the work of Marsh also. In our own idea, and under present conditions, the philosophy of Marsh seems conservative. There is comparatively little interest, even in theological circles, in the doctrines to whose clarification, in the light of reason, he devoted himself. One sees his thought in its proper perspective only as one places it against the background of the prevailing interests of his own day. By temperament, Marsh shrank from controversy; he deprecated becoming involved in it. But the most casual reader of the Introduction prefaced to the republication of Coleridge's *Aids to Reflection* will see that its undercurrent is the feeling that what Coleridge says and what he himself says goes contrary to the doctrines that possess the mind of contemporary religious circles, while conjoined with this is the sense that he is under a religious as well as a philosophical obligation to combat the tendency of these beliefs. It was not just the fate or the spread of a particular philosophical system that he was concerned with, but the re-awakening of a truly spiritual religion which had been obscured and depressed under the influence of the prevalent philosophies of John Locke and the Scottish school. It was as an ally of spiritual and personal religion that he turned to the German philosophy, actuated by the conviction that the same evils which Coleridge found in England were found also in his own country.

It is worth while to quote from the Introduction at some length what he has to say upon this subject. "It is our peculiar misfortune in this country that, while the philosophy of Locke and the Scottish writers has been received in full faith as the only rational system and its leading principles especially passed off as unquestionable, the strong attachment to religion and the fondness for speculation, by both of which we are strongly characterized, have led us to combine and associate these principles, such as they are, with our religious interests and opinions, so variously and so intimately, that by most persons they are considered as necessary parts of the same system." He himself held that the philosophical principles thus popularly read into the Christian faith were, in fact, profoundly discordant with the latter. As he says, "A system of philosophy which excludes the very idea of all spiritual power and agency cannot possibly co-exist with a religion essentially spiritual." Like Coleridge, he anticipates being regarded as a heretic in religion because he is desirous of searching out a philosophy that is consistent instead of inconsistent with the spiritual truths of Christianity which are to him its essence.

In the attempt, to which I now turn, to expound the positive philosophy of Marsh, one may appropriately return to the essay of 1822, to which allusion has already been made. Christianity presented itself to him not only as the great cause of the intellectual and emotional change from the world of classic to that of modern mind, as expressed in literature, politics, and social life, as well as in religion, but as inherently a revelation of philosophic truth. Revelation from without was required because of the fallen state of man. But the revelation was not external, much less arbitrary in *content*. It was rather a recovery of the essential ultimate truths about nature, man, and ultimate reality. It is for that reason that I said that Christianity was to him a truly philosophic revelation. Were I to attempt to select a single passage that might serve as an illuminating text of what he thought and taught, it would be, I think, the following: A thinking man "has and can have but one system in which his philosophy becomes religious and his religion philosophical."

As I have already indicated, the full meaning of this position can hardly be recovered at the present time. It must be considered in relation to the time in which Dr. Marsh lived. It had nothing in common with the views upon philosophy which prevailed in the academic audiences and popular thought of the time. These, as we have also noted, were based upon Locke as modified by the ruling Scotch school, and upon Paley. The orthodox conceived of Christianity as a merely external revelation; the dissenters from orthodoxy relied upon proof from design in nature of the existence of God and upon what Marsh, following Kant and Coleridge, called "Understanding" in distinction from "Reason." There is much evidence that Dr. Marsh felt himself between two dangers. One was that he should be thought to reduce Christianity to a mere body of doctrines, a speculative intellectual scheme. The other was that he should be thought faithless to the living power of Christianity in re-making life and thus be classed with unbelieving critics. The situation in which he thus found himself accounts, I think, for the air of apologetic timidity which surrounds the expression of his deepest thoughts. In part it was due, undoubtedly, to his modest distrust of himself, but in larger part, to the situation with which his period confronted him. He was quite right, no one who reads him can doubt that fact, in thinking of himself as a deeply devoted man in his own personality. Indeed, for inner and humble piety and spirituality he had few peers among his contemporaries. But he had, in addition, the distinctively philosophic instinct. He wanted to see the universe and all phases of life as a whole. When he gave rein to his instinct in this direction, he found himself at once conscious that he was coming into conflict with the ideas which dominated not only American society but the churches themselves. He neither mitigated his own Christian sense nor ceased to philosophize. But his activity in the latter field was, it seems to me, restricted. He never developed the independence in thought which matched his philosophic powers. It is probable, as Dr. Nicolson has made clear, that he, as the means of directing Emerson to Coleridge, and indirectly at least, made a profound impress upon the American "transcendental" movement. But he never had the detached position which marked Emerson, for example, and accordingly did not reach an unimpeded development of his own powers.

It is, however, time to turn more directly to his basic thought in which for him the religious truth of Christianity was found to be one with the truth of philosophy as a theory of God, the universe, and man. Formulas are somewhat dangerous. But for the sake of brevity, if for no other reason, a formula or label seems necessary. I shall, accordingly, venture to say that his philosophy is an Aristotelian version of Kant made under the influence of a profound conviction of the inherent *moral* truths of the teachings of Christianity. The formula involves, unfortunately, considerable technical reference to historic systems. The external evidence shows that he was more of a student of Plato and of the great divines of the seventeenth century who are more influenced by Plato, than of Aristotle. But we know also by external testimony that the *Metaphysics* and the *De Anima* of Aristotle were always by him. And it seems fairly evident that his objective interpretation of Kant, his disregard for the phenomenalism and subjective imagination. But they are also necessary principles of the existence of all physical things and events, since the latter are and occur in space and time. Thus mathematics forms the basis of physical science.

He was probably influenced by Fries in this objective interpretation. But there is the deeper influence which I have called Aristotelian. This influence appears in his treatment of the relations of sense to Understanding and of both to Reason, and also in his entire philosophy of nature, in its relation to mind. Instead of making a separation between sense, Understanding, and Reason, they present themselves in Marsh's account as three successive stages in a progressive realization of the nature of ultimate reality. Each of the two earlier, namely, sense and Understanding, forms the conditions under which the third manifests itself and leads up to it. For each contains in itself principles which point beyond itself and which create the necessity of a fuller and deeper apprehension of the nature of the real.

What I have called the Aristotelianism of his position is seen in the fact that he did not isolate this ascending series of sense, Understanding, and rational will from the natural universe as did Kant, but rather saw in it a progressive realization of the conditions and potentialities found in nature itself. I have not run across in him any allusion to Hegel, although he seems to have known Fichte. But like Hegel, instead of putting the subject in opposition to the object or the world, he regarded the subject, who comes most completely to himself in the rational will, as the culmination, the consummation, of the energies constituting the sensible and physical world. While not a scientist, in any technical sense, Marsh was widely read in the science of his day, and thought he found in it the evidence for the truth of the conception that nature presents to us an ascending scale of energies in which the lower are both the condition and the premonitions of the higher until we arrive at self-conscious mind itself.

His conception of sense is, in the epistemological language of to-day, realistic. He holds that in sense we can distinguish the received material, the seen, heard, and touched qualities from the acts of mind that form seeing, hearing, touching, and that we refer the material of sensed qualities to a ground of reality outside ourselves, just as we refer the acts of sensing to the self as the abiding view of nature found in Kant, came to him ultimately, whether directly or through Coleridge, from Aristotle.

To explain what meaning this statement has in connection with Marsh's own metaphysical system, it is necessary to digress into a technical field which I would otherwise gladly avoid. In Kant, as all students know of him, there is a definite separation made between sense, Understanding, and Reason. In consequence, the affections of the mind called sensations are regarded by him as "mental" in character, and as organized by forms of space and time which are themselves ultimately mental in character. The categories of the Understanding, while they provide universality and constancy for these sense impressions, do not, therefore, get beyond knowledge of phenomena. While Reason furnished ideals of unity and complete totality, which go beyond the scope of the Understanding, they are for us unrealizable ideals. When we suppose that Reason gives us knowledge of the real nature of things, we are led into illusions. Knowledge must remain within the bounds of phenomena, that is, of the logical organization of the materials of sense.

Now it is a striking fact that, while Dr. Marsh freely employs the Kantian terminology, and while he uses constantly not only the general distinctions of sense, Understanding, and Reason, but also special conclusions reached by Kant in treating them, he never even refers to the Kantian limitation of knowledge to phenomena—what is usually termed the "subjectivism" of Kant.

For example, while he treats, like Kant, mathematics as a science of space and time as necessary and hence *a priori* forms of perceptual experience, he also has in mind the absolute space and time of Newtonian physics and not just mental forms. They are forms of actual and external things of nature, not merely forms of mind. Thus our geometry and other mathematics is a rational science of the conditions under which all physical things exist, not merely a science of our conditions of experiencing them. In and of themselves as conditions of the possibility of physical things and their changes, they "constitute" in his own words, "the sphere of possibility and of those possible determinations of quantity and form which are the objects of pure mathematical science." The free development of these possibilities, independent of the restrictions imposed by actual existence, is the work of the productive ground of their reality. We perceive qualities of sense as qualities of an object existing outwardly and independently. Sense, however, does not give knowledge, even of the physical world, but only material for knowledge. The Understanding is necessary to judge the sensory material and to know *what* is presented in them. We have to interpret the material of sense. The Understanding operates by acts of distinguishing, comparing, and thus brings out the relations implicit in sensuous material. Without these connective and organizing relations, we do not know an object but merely have a number of qualities before us. We have the power to become self-conscious of the relating activities of the mind. We note that they proceed by certain necessary laws in as far as they result in knowledge. The Understanding is not free to judge in any arbitrary sense of freedom. To attain knowledge we must judge or understand in necessary ways, or else we do not attain knowledge of objects but only personal fancies. This law of understanding or knowing objects proceeds from the mind itself, and it, when we recognize it and take note of it, forms what is termed Reason. In the Understanding (that is, in scientific knowledge of nature) this agency operates spontaneously; but when it notes its own operation and becomes self-conscious, we recognize it as rational will, which is the animating principle, one and the same in character, or universal in all knowing minds; and hence identical with the divine intellect which is the light that lighteth every man that cometh into the world. It is reason because it operates by necessary principles; it is will when it is viewed as an agency complete and self-sufficient in itself.

This technical excursion into what Marsh calls rational psychology may help express the sense of what has been called the Aristotelian element in him. He insists that the powers of the mind or self are called forth only by objects correlative to them. The sensibility remains a mere potentiality until it is called into action by nature. We cannot hear or see or touch except as the mind is affected by things having color, sound, and solidity. There is no difference between this and the action and reaction of iron and a magnet upon each other. In the same way, the powers of the Understanding remain mere possibilities until they are called into action by the actual relations which subsist among objects. The orderly, logical structure is both the condition that calls the powers into action and realizes their potentialities, and the object upon which they expend themselves, just as much as the qualities of things are both the actualizing conditions and the objects upon which the capacities of the mind terminate in exercise or sensibility. Similarly, the objective of self-conscious, rational will is both the condition and the object of the exercise of our Reason.

The essentially Aristotelian nature of this conception of each lower stage forming the conditions of the actualizing of some potentiality of mind and then supplying the material upon which a higher expression of the same mind exercises itself will be obvious, I think, to every philosophic student. It is through the use of this conception that Marsh escapes from the charmed circle of limitation within the self that holds the Kantian philosophy spell-bound. The world in its status as a manifold of qualities, as a logically interconnected whole, and as summed up in universal self-conscious will, has to be there independently of our minds in order that the capacities of our minds may be stimulated into real existence and have material upon which to work.

It was said, however, that this Aristotelian interpretation of Kant is made under the influence of ideas derived from Christian faith. Marsh separates himself from Greek thought, whether that of Plato or Aristotle, in two ways. First, he conceives of mind as identical with the self, the "I" or personality, an identification that is like nothing found in ancient thought, and one which he associates with the influence of Christianity. It is another way of saying the same thing to point out that he introduces into the classic conception of reason an element foreign to it in its original statement—namely, the conception of reason as *will*—that is, of a power to institute and seek to realize ends that are universal and necessary, that are supplied by nature but which flow from its own nature as a personal rational self. It is the very nature of these ends that they cannot be realized by themselves or by any merely intellectual process. Their nature demands that they be embodied in the material of sense and of the natural world as an object of knowledge, or that all the material of appetite connected with the senses or of desire directed upon natural objects be subdued and transformed into agencies of expressing the true ultimate nature of the rational will. To put it a little more concretely, Aristotle held that reason could be actualized in contemplative knowledge apart from any effort to change the world of nature and social institutions into its own likeness and embodiment. Following the spirit of Christian teaching, Marsh denied any such possibility. He held that Reason can realize itself and be truly aware or conscious of its own intrinsic nature only as it operates to make over the world, whether physical or social, into an embodiment of its own principles. Marsh constantly condemns what he calls speculation and the speculative tendency, by which he means a separation of knowledge and the intellect from action and the will. By its own nature, reason terminates in action and that action is the transformation of the spiritual potentialities found in the natural world, physical and institutional, into spiritual realities.

The other point of connection of Marsh's philosophy with the Christian faith is more specific, less general. Accepting the idea that man is a fallen creature, he accepted also the idea of Coleridge that original sin is not a mere historic fact, going back to a historic progenitor, but is the act of the will itself by which it takes as the principle and moving spring of its own action something derived not from its own inherent nature but from some source outside itself—the appetites of sense, or the desires that are used by the thought of ends derived from the world about us. I shall not extend my excursion into technicalities to trouble you with his philosophic rendering of the theological doctrines of sin, conscience, and freedom of the will, but no exposition of his basic idea of the equation of philosophy with religion would be complete without reference to the particular way in which he applies his conception of the necessity of a correlative object in order to awaken the potentialities of the self into reality. The correlative object of the conscience and will, through which they, as they exist in man, can be aroused into actuality of operation and being, is no abstract law. As will and conscience are personal, belonging to a self, so their correlative object must also be personal. At this point, the religious character of his philosophy most clearly reveals and expresses itself. This correlative personal object is the manifestation of the divine in Christ. In his own words: "The true end of our being presented by the spiritual law is the realization, practically, in our own being, of that perfect idea which the law itself presupposes, and of which Christ is the glorious manifestation."

And again, "the spiritual principle may be said to have only a potential reality, or, as it enters into the life of nature, a false and delusive show of reality, until, awakened from above by its own spiritual correlatives, it receives the engrafted word, and is empowered to rise above the thralldom of nature."

The discussion will now turn to a consideration of somewhat more concrete matters (although not, according to the view of Marsh, more genuinely human interests and concerns)—to what Marsh has to say upon society in general and education in particular. Unfortunately, what is left to us in the published record is all too scanty. But there are suggestions adequate to a reconstruction of his fundamental philosophy. Here, too, we may fittingly begin by recourse to Coleridge, in spite of the fact that there is less direct evidence of his connection with Coleridge in this matter than in that of the identification of the Christian religion with true philosophy. Coleridge, in common with the German school which he represented, conceived social institutions as essentially educative in nature and function. They were the outward manifestation of law and reason by means of which the intelligence and conscience of individuals are awakened and by which they are nourished till they become capable of independent activity, and then express themselves in loyalty to social institutions and devotion to improving them until these institutions are still better fitted to perform their educative task for humanity.

Coleridge with considerable courage applied this conception to the Church as an institution in distinction from the inward and spiritual communion of the faithful—an application that took its point, of course, from the fact that there was an established Church allied with the political order in England. With rather surprising daring, he proclaimed that the Church, in this institutional sense, is not inherently a religious corporation. In his own words, "Religion may be an indispensable ally but is not the essential constitutive end of that national institute which is unfortunately, at least improperly, styled the church; a name, which in its best sense, is exclusively appropriate to the Church of Christ." Then with an obvious etymological reference to the original meaning of clergy as connected with clerks or writers, he goes on to say "the clerisy of the nation, or national church in its primary acceptation and original intention, comprehended the learned of all denominations, the sages and professors of law and jurisprudence, of medicine and physiology, of music and civil and military architecture, with the mathematical as their common organ; in short, all the arts and sciences, the possession and application of which constitute the civilization of a nation, as well as the theological." The latter, he goes on to say, rightfully claimed the precedence but only because "theology was the root and trunk of the knowledge of civilized man; because it gave unity and the circulating sap of life to all other sciences, by virtue of which alone they could be contemplated as forming the living tree of knowledge." It is primarily as educators that those especially called clergy of the established church are to be regarded, and it was even well, according to Coleridge, that they should serve an apprenticeship as village schoolmasters before becoming pastors.

It is evident that, owing to the non-existence of an established church in the United States, this portion of Coleridge's teaching could not directly influence the thought of Marsh. Indeed, he naturally thought that the condition in which the institutional church was but the outward expression or body of the inner and spiritual church represented a higher principle than could be expressed by any politically established church. But indirectly, Marsh's ideas move in a like direction, although with such differences as the difference between the political organization of Great Britain and of our country would naturally suggest.

It is interesting to note that Marsh makes, in a sermon at the dedication of the chapel of the University, a distinction between civilization and culture similar to that drawn by Kant and other German thinkers. Civilization, he says, in effect, is concerned with the adaptation of the acts and services of the individual to the needs and conditions of existing society. It is a discipline of the faculties with reference to the occupations of civil society. Culture is the development of the powers of individuals with reference to the ends that make them truly human; it transcends any existing social order and régime because it elevates them into the possession of the spiritual law of reason, of universal will, and the end of humanity as such. It aims at control by this inner law of rational will instead of by the ordinances and customs of a given society. From the obligations imposed by the interests of higher and common humanity, no state policy can absolve us. The peoples of the East, he says, are, perhaps, more civilized than those of the West, for their institutions and the discipline they provide fit the individual to some definite place and work in the social order. But we, he says, are not destined to be the working instruments for attaining the lower ends imposed by the state of civilization. And he adds these very significant words: "We can hardly, indeed, be said to be subjects of any state, considered in its ordinary sense, as body politic with a fixed constitution and a determinate organization of its several powers. But we are constituent members of a community in which the highest worth and perfection and happiness of the individual free persons composing it constitute the highest aim and the perfection of the community as a whole. With us there is nothing so fixed by the forms of political and civil organization as to obstruct our efforts for promoting the full and free development of all our powers, both individual and social. Indeed, where the principle of self-government is admitted to such an extent as it is in this state, there is, in fact, nothing fixed or permanent, but as it is made so by that which is permanent and abiding in the intelligence and fixed rational principles of action in the self-governed. The self-preserving principle of our government is to be found only in the continuing determination and unchanging aims of its subjects." From this Dr. Marsh draws the inevitable conclusion that the function of an educational institution is a cultivation of the community, which is identical with the full development of all the powers of its individual persons.

It is to be regretted that Dr. Marsh never achieved a complete exposition of his social and political philosophy. While changes in vocabulary might be needed to adapt the principles he here expresses to present conditions, he has stated, it seems to me, a principle which is fundamental to the distinctive American social system, if we have any such system, and one which stands in need of enforcement at the present time. When Dr. Marsh wrote, the idea of nationalism, in its modern sense, had hardly made its appearance in this country. There was little if any worship of the state as a political organization. Individuals were still conscious of their power organized as a free community to make and unmake states—that is, special forms of political organization. There was, indeed, great admiration for the American form of government and much patriotism in loyalty to it. But it was devotion to its underlying principle as an expression of a free and self-governing community, not to its form. It was regarded as a symbol and as a means, not as an end fixed in itself to which the will and conscience of individuals must be subordinated.

In my judgment, this subordination of the state to the community is the great contribution of American life to the world's history, and it is clearly expressed in the utterances of Dr. Marsh. But recent events have tended to obscure it. Forces have been at work to assimilate the original idea of the state and its organization to older European notions and traditions. The state is now held up as an end in itself; self-styled patriotic organizations make it their business to proclaim the identity of the loyalty and patriotism of individuals with devotion to the state as a fixed institution. The constitution of the state is treated not as a means and instrument to the well-being of the community of free self-governing individuals, but as something having value and sanctity in and of itself. We have, unconsciously in large measure but yet pervadingly, come to doubt the validity of our original American ideal. We tend to submit individuality to the state instead of acting upon the belief that the state in its constitution, laws, and administration, can be made the means of furthering the ends of a community of free individuals.

Dr. Marsh wrote in the full if insensible consciousness of the pioneer period of American life. The true individualism of that era has been eclipsed because it has been misunderstood. It is now often treated as if it were an exaltation of individuals free from social relations and responsibilities. Marsh expresses its genuine spirit when he refers, as he does constantly, to the *community* of individuals. The essence of our earlier pioneer individualism was not non-social, much less anti-social; it involved no indifference to the claims of society. Its working ideal was neighborliness and mutual service. It did not deny the claims of government and law, but it held them in subordination to the needs of a changing and developing society of individuals. Community relationships were to enable an individual to reach a fuller manifestation of his own powers, and this development was in turn to be a factor in modifying the organized and stated civil and political order so that more individuals would be capable of genuine participation in the self-government and self-movement of society—so that, in short, more individuals might come into the possession of that freedom which was their birth-right. Depreciation of the value of our earlier pioneer individualism is but the negative sense of our surrender of the native idea of the subordination of state and government to the social community and our approximation to the older European idea of the state as an end in itself. If I may be allowed a personal word, I would say that I shall never cease to be grateful that I was born at a time and a place where the earlier ideal of liberty and the self-governing community of citizens still sufficiently prevailed, so that I unconsciously imbibed a sense of its meaning. In Vermont, perhaps even more than elsewhere, there was embodied in the spirit of the people the conviction that governments were like the houses we live in, made to contribute to human welfare, and that those who lived in them were as free to change and extend the one as they were the other, when developing needs of the human family called for such alterations and modifications. So deeply bred in Vermonters was this conviction that I still think that one is more loyally patriotic to the ideal of America when one maintains this view than when one conceives of patriotism as rigid attachment to a form of the state alleged to be fixed forever, and recognizes the claims of a common human society as superior to those of any particular political form.

Dr. Marsh's views of education were a reflection of his general social philosophy. It goes without saying that he conceived of education in a deeply religious spirit and that to him religion was, in words reminiscent of a passage already quoted from Coleridge, "the sap of life to the growing tree of knowledge." But we have also in interpreting his words to recall that to him religious truth was one with rational truth about the universe itself and about man's nature in relation to it. In his own words again, religious truth "is not so much a distinct and separate part of what should be taught in a system of instruction, to be learned and stored up in the mind for future use, as a pervading and life-giving principle and power that should act upon the mind in every stage and process of its development, and bring all the powers of the soul, as they are unfolded, under its holy and humanizing influence." The conception of what religion and religious truth are may change; they have undergone change since Marsh taught and wrote. But some organizing, pervading, and life-giving principle to bind together all the specialisms and details which so abound is still as greatly needed in education to-day as it was when Marsh spoke.

The ideas of Dr. Marsh upon more specific matters of the organization and conduct of university education reflect his fundamental conceptions. In stating them I depend chiefly upon the record of his successor in the chair of philosophy, Professor Joseph Torrey in the Memoir he prefixed to the collection of Marsh's writings. It was the latter's opinion "that the rules for the admission of students are too limited and inflexible." There is no reason why those unfortunately prevented from taking advantage of the whole of the course should not have the privilege of taking the part that lies within their means. "He was also for allowing more latitude to the native inclinations and tendencies of different minds. It was absurd to expect every young mind to develop in just the same way; and equally absurd to confine each one to the same kind and quantity of study." Again, "he thought the methods of instruction in use too formal and inefficient. There was not enough of actual teaching, and too much importance was attached to text-books. He wanted to see more constant and familiar intercourse between the mind of teacher and learner." It was more important to invigorate and sharpen the student's powers of independent thought and judgment than to bend them to apprehending the ideas of others. As to college discipline and morals, he also distrusted the system of minute external regulation and conformity. He was also opposed to the then prevailing methods of classification and promotion of students. Merely formal examinations he thought of little value.

These points sound strangely like the criticisms and proposals of educational reformers from his day to this. They were not, however, with him concessions to practical expediency. They were reflections of his fundamental faith in individuality and in the spirit as opposed to the letter and mechanical form. But this emphasis upon the value of individuality was accompanied, in his views on education as elsewhere, with an equal sense that the ultimate end was a community of cultivated individuals. The ultimate purpose of education is "to elevate the condition and character of the great body of the people." Nowhere as much as in the United States were schools "made, as they are here, an important and leading object in the policy of government," and nowhere else was the experiment given a fair trial of "placing all classes and all individuals upon the same level providing for all the same system of free, public instruction."[3]

I have chosen to try to get some idea of the relation of Dr. Marsh's thought to that of his own time rather than to engage in general eulogy of him. But the record discloses a mind at once deeply sensitive and deeply rational. The period was not favorable to far-reaching thought, which always demands a certain audacity lacking both to the period and to Dr. Marsh's temperament. He did not carry his questionings beyond the received order of beliefs in religion. He depended upon others, notably Coleridge and the German idealists, for the language in which to clothe his philosophic speculations. But, none the less, because of his sensitivity one feels that, even when he speaks of things that do not make the appeal now that they did in a time when men were more engrossed in theology, there is nothing second-hand in his thought. There were realities of which he had an intimate personal sense behind his most transcendental speculations. It is characteristic of him that he holds that knowledge of spiritual truth is always more than theoretical and intellectual. It was the product of activity as well as its cause. It had to be lived in order to be known. The low rating which he gave sense as compared with Understanding was not, for example, a merely cognitive matter. The "thralldom of sense" was a moral and personal affair. And so his depreciation of Understanding in comparison with Reason was not technical. In what he called Understanding he saw the root of the skills and the conventions which enable men to make a shrewd adjustment of means to ends, in dealing with nature and with fellowmen. It was the key to what is termed success. But the ends which it prescribed were just those of worldly success, and so Reason was to him the symbol of the ability of man to live on a higher and more inclusive plane which he called that of spirit, and in which he found the distinctive dignity of man. Religion was to him the supreme worth, and yet his conception of what constitutes religion was a virtual condemnation of a large part of that which passed in his time and still passes for religion, as being merely an attempt to include God and the next world in a scheme of personal advance-

[3] These words were spoken, be it noted, before the great public school revival of the eighteen-forties occurred in this country.

ment and success. Underneath the somewhat outmoded form of his philosophy one feels a rare personality, gifted in scholarship, ever eager for more knowledge, who wished to use scholarship and philosophy to awaken his fellowmen to a sense of the possibilities that were theirs by right as men, and to quicken them to realize these possibilities in themselves. His transcendentalism is the outer form congenial in his day to that purpose. The underlying substance is a wistful aspiration for full and ordered living.

Existential Philosophy

by PAUL TILLICH

Reprinted from the *Journal of the History of Ideas*—Vol. V, No. 1, pp. 44–70

The distinctive way of philosophizing which today calls itself "*Existenzphilosophie*" or "Existential" philosophy emerged as one of the major currents of German thought under the Weimar Republic, counting among its leaders such men as Heidegger and Jaspers. But its history goes back at least a century, to the decade of the 1840's, when its main contentions were formulated by thinkers like Schelling, Kierkegaard, and Marx, in sharp criticism of the reigning "rationalism" or panlogism of the Hegelians; and in the next generation Nietzsche and Dilthey were among its protagonists. Its roots are still more ancient, deeply embedded in the pre-Cartesian German tradition of supra-rationalism and "*Innerlichkeit*" represented by Böhme.

"Existential" Philosophy thus seems a specifically German creation. It sprang originally from the tensions of the German intellectual situation in the early nineteenth century. It has been strongly influenced by the political and spiritual catastrophes of the Germans in our own generation. Its terminology has been largely determined by the genius and often by the demon of the German language—a fact which makes the translation of Heidegger's *Sein und Zeit* practically impossible.

But when we come to understand the import of the name and the basic critical drive of the "Existential" philosophy, we realize that it is part of a more general philosophical movement which counts its representatives in France, England, and America as well as in Germany. For in calling men back to "Existence," these German thinkers are criticising the identification of Reality or Being with Reality-as-known, with the object of Reason or thought. Starting from the traditional distinction between "essence" and "existence," they insist that Reality or Being in its concreteness and fullness is not "essence," is not the object of cognitive experience, but is rather "existence," is Reality as immediately experienced, with the accent on the inner and personal character of man's immediate experience. Like Bergson, Bradley, James, and Dewey, the "Existential" philosophers are appealing from the conclusions of "rationalistic" thinking, which equates Reality with the object of thought, with relations or "essence," to Reality as men experience it immediately in their actual living. They consequently take their place with all those who have regarded man's "immediate experience" as revealing more completely the nature and traits of Reality than man's cognitive experience. The philosophy of "Existence" is hence one version of that widespread appeal to immediate experience which has been so marked a feature of recent thought. In its influence not only on ideas but also on historical events, the international character of the movement is obvious—as witness the names of Marx, Nietzsche, and Bergson.

This appeal to "Existence" emerged just a hundred years ago, in the decade from 1840 to 1850. During the winter of 1841–42 Schelling delivered his lectures on *Die Philosophie der Mythologie und der Offenbarung* in the University of Berlin, before a distinguished audience including Engels, Kierkegaard, Bakunin, and Burckhardt. In 1840 Trendelenburg's *Logische Untersuchungen* had appeared. In 1843 Ludwig Feuerbach's *Grundsätze der Philosophie der Zukunft* came out. In 1844 Marx wrote his manuscript *Nationalökonomie und Philosophie,* not published till a few years ago. The same year brought Max Stirner's *Der Einzige und sein Eigentum* and Kierkegaard's recently translated *Philosophical Fragments;* it also brought the second edition of Schopenhauer's *The World as Will and Idea,* which subsequently came to have a tremendous influence on "Existential" philosophy. In 1845–46 Marx wrote the manuscript of *Die Deutsche Ideologie,* including the *Thesen über Feuerbach,* and in 1846 Kierkegaard brought out the classic work of "Existential" philosophy in the narrower sense of the term, *Concluding Unscientific Postscript.* Schelling's Berlin lectures are based on his development of the position achieved in the *Philosophy of Freedom* in 1809, and the *Weltalter* in 1811. In his Munich lectures in the later twenties he had tried to show that the "positive philosophy," as he calls his type of Existential philosophy, had predecessors in men like Pascal, Jacobi, and Hamann, and in the theosophic tradition stemming from Böhme. Kant contributed to it through his Copernican revolution. Even in Plato "Existential" elements are obvious, especially in the non-dialectical method of the *Timaeus.* For Schelling takes the problem of the "positive philosophy" to be as old as philosophy itself. And in this Kierkegaard and Heidegger fully agree, as appears in Kierkegaard's use of the authority of Socrates, in Heidegger's close relation to Aristotle and Kant, and in the praise Lessing receives from all the Existential philosophers.

After this striking emergence of Existential philosophy in the fifth decade of the nineteenth century, the impulse of the movement subsided; it was replaced by Neokantian idealism or naturalistic empiricism. Feuerbach and Marx were interpreted as dogmatic materialists, Kierkegaard remained completely unknown, Schelling's latest period was buried with a few contemptuous sentences in the textbooks on the history of philosophy. But a new impulse to "Existential" thinking came from the "*Lebensphilosophie*" or "Philosophy of Life" of the eighteen-eighties. During this decade appeared Nietzsche's most important works. In 1883 Dilthey published his *Einleitung in die Geisteswissenschaften;* Bergson's *Essai sur les Données Immédiates de la Conscience* came out in 1889. The "Philosophy of Life" is not identical with Existential philosophy. But if we understand the latter in a larger sense—as for historical and systematic reasons we must—then the "Philosophy of Life" includes most of the distinctive motives of Existential philosophy. Accordingly I should also assign certain features of pragmatism, especially of William James' thought, to this philosophy of Existence as immediately experienced.

The third and contemporary form of Existential philosophy has resulted from a combination of this "Philosophy of Life" with Husserl's shift of emphasis from existent objects to the mind that makes them its objects, and with the rediscovery of Kierkegaard and of the early developments of Marx. On the one hand Heidegger[1] and Jaspers,[2] on the other the Existential interpretation of history found in German "Religious Socialism,"[3] are the main representatives of this third period of the philosophy of experienced Existence.

I do *not* propose to give here a history of Existential philosophy. This has been done, in rather fragmentary and implicit fashion, by Karl Löwith,[4] Herbert Marcuse,[5] and others of the younger genera-

[1] Martin Heidegger, *Sein und Zeit* (Halle, 1927); *Kant und das Problem der Metaphysik* (Bonn, 1929).

[2] Karl Jaspers, *Philosophie,* 3 vols. (Berlin, 1938; 1st ed., 1932); *Vernunft und Existenz* (Groningen, 1935).

[3] Paul Tillich, *The Interpretation of History* (New York, 1936).

[4] Karl Löwith, *Von Hegel bis Nietzsche* (Zürich, 1941).

[5] Herbert Marcuse, *Reason and Revolution* (New York and Oxford, 1941). See also Werner Brock, *Contemporary German Philosophy* (Cambridge, 1935).

tion who have felt the actual impact on their lives of the problems emphasized by Existential philosophy. But I shall offer a comparative study of those ideas which are characteristic for most of the Existential philosophers, disregarding the distinctive features of their individual systems. My own evaluation and interpretation of the significance of these ideas will remain implicit in my exposition. I shall state them explicitly only in a short conclusion.

I. THE METHODOLOGICAL FOUNDATIONS OF THE EXISTENTIAL PHILOSOPHY

1. The distinction between *essentia* and *existentia* in the philosophical tradition

The philosophy of "Existence" derives its name, and its way of formulating its critical opposition to rationalistic views of Reality, from the traditional distinction between "essence" and "existence." "Existence"—which comes from *existere,* meaning *heraustreten* or "emerge"—designates in its root meaning "being" within the totality of Being, in distinction from "not being." *Dasein,* a word which has received a pregnant meaning in Heidegger's *Sein und Zeit,* adds the concrete element of "being in a special place," being *da* or "there." The scholastic distinction between *essentia* and *existentia* was the first step toward giving a more significant meaning to the word "existence." In that distinction, "essence" signifies the What, the τi $\dot{\epsilon}\sigma\tau\iota\nu$ or *quid est* of a thing; "existence" signifies the That, the $\ddot{o}\tau\iota$ $\dot{\epsilon}\sigma\tau\iota\nu$ or *quod est*. *Essentia* thus designates what a thing is *known* to be, the non-temporal object of knowledge in a temporal and changing thing, the $o\dot{v}\sigma\iota a$ of that thing which makes it possible. But whether a thing is real or not is not implied in its essence: we do not know whether there is such a thing by knowing its "essence" alone. This must be decided by an existential proposition.

The assertion of the scholastics that in God essence and existence are identical is the second step in the development of the meaning of "existence." The Unconditioned cannot be conditioned by a difference between its essence and its existence. In absolute Being there is no possibility which is not an actuality: it is pure

The introduction to *Schelling, The Ages of the World,* translated with introduction and notes by Frederick de Wolfe Bolman, Jr. (New York, 1942), gives an excellent description of Schelling's development from an Essential to an Existential philosophy.

actuality. In all finite beings, on the other hand, this difference is present; in them existence as something separated from essence is the mark of finitude.

The third step in the enrichment of the term "existence" came from the discussion of the ontological argument, from its criticism by Kant and its re-establishment in a changed and broadened form by Hegel. This discussion brought out the fundamental fallacy involved. The ontological argument relies on the sound principle of the identity of Being and thinking, which all thinking presupposes: this identity is the *"Unvordenkliche"* (that principle prior to which thought cannot take place, the *Prius* of all thinking), as Schelling called it. But the argument surreptitiously transforms this principle into a highest Being, for the existence or non-existence of which demonstrations can be advanced. Kant's criticism of this interpretation is valid; but it does not touch the principle itself. On the contrary, Kant himself, in a powerful passage, describes the *Unvordenklichkeit* of Being-as-such from the point of view of an imagined highest Being who asks himself: Whence do I come? Hegel not only re-establishes the ontological argument in a purified form, he extends the principle of the identity of Being and thought to the whole of Being in so far as it is the "self-actualization of the Absolute." In this way he tries to overcome the separation of existence from essence in finite beings: for him, the finite is infinite both in its essence *and* in its existence.

2. Hegel's doctrine of essence and existence

The post-Hegelian attack on Hegel's dialectical system is directed against his attempt to absorb the whole of reality, not only in its essential but also in its existential and especially in its historical aspect, into the dialectical movement of "pure thought." The logical expression of this attempt is found in statements like these concerning essence and existence: "Essence *necessarily* appears." It transforms itself into existence. Existence is the being of essence, and therefore existence can be called "essential being." Essence *is* existence, it is not distinguished from its existence.[6]

It is in the light of these definitions that certain familiar propositions of Hegel's *Philosophy of Right* must be understood. If existence is essential being, reason is real and reality is rational.

[6] Hegel, *Logik,* ed. Lasson, II, 103, 105.

And therefore: "It is the task of philosophy to understand what is; for what is, is Reason. . . . If philosophy builds a world as it ought to be, such a world can indeed be realized, but only in imagination, a plastic material on which anything can be impressed."⁷ The task of philosophy is not to sketch an ideal world; on the contrary, we must say: the task of philosophy is "the reconciliation with reality." In contrast to this statement it can be said: the task of Existential philosophy was first of all to destroy this Hegelian "reconciliation"—which was merely conceptual, and left existence itself unreconciled.

3. Dialectical and temporal movement

Trendelenburg's *Logische Untersuchungen* seem to have made an impression on the post-Hegelian philosophers very similar to that made by Husserl's *Logische Untersuchungen* on the post-Neokantians. He expresses his criticism of the dialectical movement in Hegel's *Logic* as follows: "Out of pure Being, which is explicitly an abstraction, and of Nothing—also an explicit abstraction—Becoming cannot suddenly emerge, this concrete intuition which controls life and death."⁸ Two things are required—and implicitly supposed by Hegel—in order to "think" movement: a thinking subject, and an intuition of time and space. The principle of negation, moreover, the driving force of the dialectical process, cannot lead to anything new without presupposing the experience of the thinking subject. It is motion that distinguishes the realm of existence from the realm of essence.

Kierkegaard, who occasionally refers to Trendelenburg, expresses his insight as to the difference between merely dialectical and real Becoming in a more vivid way: "Pure thought is a recent invention and a 'lunatic postulate.' The negation of a preceding synthesis requires time. But time cannot find a place in pure thought."⁹

Schelling calls the claim of Hegel's rational system to embrace not only the real, the What, but also its reality, the That, a "deception." No "merely logical process is also a process of real becoming."¹⁰ When Hegel uses phrases such as: "the Idea decides to

---

⁷ Hegel, *Philosophie des Rechts,* ed. Lasson, 14, 15.
⁸ Trendelenburg, *Logische Untersuchungen* (Berlin, 1840), 25.
⁹ Kierkegaard, *Concluding Unscientific Postscript* (tr. Lowrie, Princeton, 1941), 278.

become Nature," or, "Nature is the fall of the Idea," he is either describing a real, non-dialectical event, or his terminology is meaningless.

Marx attacks in similar fashion the Hegelian transition from logic to Nature. He calls it "the fantastically described transition from the abstract thinker to sense experience."[11] But his criticism is more fundamental. It is directed against Hegel's category of *"Aufheben"* (which means both negating and preserving in a higher synthesis). "Because thinking is taken to imply at the same time its 'opposite,' sensible existence, and since it therefore claims that its motion is a real and sensed action, it believes that the process of *'Aufheben'* in thought, which in fact leaves the object as it is, has actually overcome the object."[12] This confusion between dialectical negation, which removes nothing but merely labels things as having been *"aufgehoben,"* and real revolutionary "negation" through practical activity, is responsible for the reactionary character of Hegel's dialectical system—in spite of its principle of negation. It is obvious that this criticism strikes not only Hegel, but every rational theory of progressive evolution, idealistic as well as naturalistic, including the later so-called "scientific Marxism."

4. Possibility and actuality

The impotence of the "philosophy of essence" to explain existence is manifest in the fact that reason can deal only with possibilities: *Essentia est possibilitas.* Schelling writes: "Reason reaches what can be or will be—but only as an idea, and therefore, in comparison with real Being, only as a possibility."[13] Kierkegaard may have learned this from Schelling; he writes: "Abstract thought can grasp reality only by destroying it, and this destruction of reality consists in transforming it into mere possibility."[14] This is especially true of history: we cannot know an historical reality until we have resolved it into a mere possibility. "The only reality to which an existing individual may have a relation that is

---

[10] Schelling, *Sämtliche Werke*, Cotta ed. (Stuttgart, 1856–61), II, 3, 65.

[11] Marx, *Der Historische Materialismus*, ed. Alfred Kröner (Leipzig, 1932), I, 343.

[12] *Ibid.*, 338.

[13] Schelling, *Werke*, II, 3, 66.

[14] Kierkegaard, *Concluding Unscientific Postscript*, 279.

more than merely cognitive is his own reality, the fact that he exists."[15] Only in the aesthetic attitude—in Kierkegaard's psychology, the attitude of detachment—can we be related to "essence," the realm of possibility. In the aesthetic attitude, which includes the merely cognitive, there are always many possibilities, and in it no "decision" is demanded; in the ethical attitude a personal decision must always be made.

Very interesting is a statement of Marx making exactly the same point. He notes that according to Hegel "my real human existence is my philosophical existence." Hence if our existential being comes to perfect realization only in the medium of thought, my real natural "existence" is my existence as a philosopher of nature, my real religious "existence" is my existence as a philosopher of religion. But this is the negation of religion as well as of humanity. This criticism touches not only Hegel but also those who are today replacing religion with the philosophy of religion, and those who are trying to dissolve human existence into a mere scientific "possibility."

5. The immediate and personal experience of Existence

Since Existence cannot be approached rationally—since it is "external" to all thought, as Feuerbach and Schelling emphasize—it must be approached empirically. Schelling discusses empiricism at great length. He is so much in sympathy with it that he declares he would prefer English empiricism to the dialectical system of Hegel. He wrote the often-quoted and misquoted sentence that the true philosophers among the English and French are their great scientists. On the other hand, he differentiates between the various forms of "empiricism." He denies what he calls "sense empiricism," but he accepts what he calls "a priori empiricism." Of the latter he says, "Rational philosophy is likewise empirical with respect to its material."[16] But its truth does not depend on any existence. "It would be true even if nothing existed."[17] For its object is the realm of intelligible relations—of the *Sachverhalte*, as Husserl later called it.

As distinguished from such an "a priori empiricism," the approach of Existential philosophy to "Existence" is completely a

[15] *Ibid.*, 280.
[16] Schelling, *Werke*, II, 3, 102.
[17] *Ibid.*, 128.

posteriori. We experience "Existence" in the same way we experience a person through his actions. We do not draw conclusions from observed effects to their causes, but we encounter a person immediately in his utterances. In the same way, Schelling suggests, we should look at the world-process as the continuous self-revelation of the *Unvordenkliche* (that which all thinking must presuppose). This *Unvordenkliche* is not God, but it reveals itself as God to those who receive the revelation in some immediate crisis of experience. This revelation involves freedom on both sides; it is not a necessity of thought, like the idea of the "Absolute" taken as the highest concept of rational philosophy. In this fashion Schelling returns to Kant's critical position: God as God is an object of faith, and there is no rational realization of the idea of God. For pure thought God remains a mere possibility; on this Kant and Schelling agree. But then Schelling goes on to try to approach the God of revelation in terms of a third type of empiricism, "metaphysical empiricism"—a procedure that leads him to a speculative reinterpretation of the history of religion. The speculative urge in his mind conquered the Existential restriction and humility he had himself postulated.

Although the philosophers of "Existence" denied Schelling's "metaphysical empiricism"—many of them were greatly disappointed by his Berlin lectures—they all demanded with him an "empirical" or experiential approach to Existence. And since they assumed that Existence is given immediately in the inner personal experience or concrete "Existence" of men, they all started with the immediate personal experience of the existing experiencer. They turned, not to the *thinking subject*, like Descartes, but to the *existing subject*—to the "*sum*" in *cogito ergo sum*, as Heidegger puts it. The description of this *sum*, of the character of immediate personal experience, is different for each representative of Existential philosophy. But on the basis of this personal experience each of them develops a theory in rational terms, a philosophy. They all try to "think Existence," to develop its implications, not only to live in "Existential" immediate experience.

Thus for Schelling the approach to Existence is the immediate personal experience of the Christian, traditional faith—although rationally interpreted. For Kierkegaard it is the immediate personal experience of the individual in the face of eternity, his personal faith—although interpreted by a most refined dialectical reasoning. For Feuerbach it is the immediate personal experience of man as man in his sense-existence—although developed into a doctrine of Man. For Marx it is the immediate personal experience of the socially determined man, his Existence as a member of a social class—though interpreted in terms of a universal socio-economic theory. For Nietzsche it is the immediate personal experience of a biologically determined being, his Existence as an embodiment of the Will to Power—although expressed in a metaphysics of Life. For Bergson it is the immediate personal experience of dynamic vitality, man's Existence as duration and creativity—although expressed in words taken from the realm of non-existential space. For Dilthey it is the immediate personal experience of the intellectual life, man's Existence in a special cultural situation—although explained in a universal *Geistesphilosophie*. For Jaspers it is the immediate personal experience of the inner activity of the Self, man's Existence as "self-transcendence"—although described in terms of an immanent psychology. For Heidegger it is the immediate personal experience of that kind of being who is "concerned" with Being, his Existence as care, anxiety, and resoluteness—although claiming to describe the structure of Being itself. For the Religious Socialist it is the immediate personal experience of man's historical Existence, the pregnant historical moment—although expressed in a general interpretation of history.

6. The Existential thinker

The approach to Existence or Reality through immediate personal experience leads to the idea of the "Existential thinker," a term coined by Kierkegaard but applicable to all Existential philosophers. "The way of objective reflexion makes the subject accidental and thereby transforms his Existence into something impersonal—truth also becomes impersonal, and this impersonal character is precisely its objective validity; for all interest, like all decision, is rooted in personal experience."[18]

The Existential thinker is the interested or passionate thinker. Although Hegel applies the words "interest" and "passion" to those driving forces in history which the "cunning Idea" uses for its purposes, there is for him no problem of Existential think-

[18] Kierkegaard, *Concluding Unscientific Postscript*, 173.

ing, because individuals are but the agents of the objective dialectical process. It is chiefly Marx who uses the term "interest" in this connection, though it is not lacking in Kierkegaard also. According to Marx, the Idea always fails when it is divorced from interest.[19] When united with interest, it can be either ideology or truth. It is "ideology" if, while claiming to represent society as a whole, it expresses merely the interest of a partial group. It is "true" if the partial group whose interest it expresses represents by its very nature the interest of the entire society. For Marx, in the period of capitalism this group is the proletariat. In this way he tries to unite universal validity with the concrete situation of the Existential thinker.

Feuerbach and Kierkegaard prefer the term "passion" for the attitude of the Existential thinker. In his beautifully written *Grundsätze der Philosophie der Zukunft* Feuerbach says: "Do not wish to be a philosopher in contrast to being a man . . . do not think as a thinker . . . think as a living, real being . . . think in Existence."[20] "Love is passion, and only passion is the mark of Existence."[21] In order to unite this attitude with the demand for objectivity, he says: "Only what is as an object of passion—really is."[22] The passionately living man knows the true nature of man and life.

Kierkegaard's famous definition of truth reads, "An objective uncertainty held fast in the most passionate personal experience is the truth, the highest truth attainable for an Existing individual."[23] This, he continues, is the definition of faith. Such a view seems to exclude any objective validity, and can hardly be considered the basis for an Existential philosophy. But Kierkegaard tries to show through the example of Socrates that the Existential thinker can be a philosopher. "The Socratic ignorance which Socrates held fast with the entire passion of his personal experience, was thus an expression of the principle that the eternal truth is related to an Existing individual." The validity of the truth which appears in a passionate personal experience is based on the relation of the Eternal to the Existing individual.

[19] Marx, *Der Historische Materialismus*, I, 379.
[20] Feuerbach, *Grundsätze der Philosophie der Zukunft* (Zürich, 1843), 78.
[21] *Ibid.*, 60.
[22] *Ibid.*, 60.
[23] Kierkegaard, *Postscript*, 182.

The Existential thinker cannot have pupils in the ordinary sense. He cannot communicate any ideas, because *they* are just *not* the truth he wants to teach. He can only create in his pupil by indirect communication that "Existential state" or personal experience out of which the pupil may think and act. Kierkegaard carries out this interpretation for Socrates. But all Existential philosophers have made similar statements—naturally, for if the approach to Existence is through personal experience, the only possibility of educating is to bring the pupil by indirect methods to a personal experience of his own Existence.

Interest, passion, indirect communication—all these qualities of the Existential thinker are forcefully expressed in Nietzsche. In no respect is he more obviously a philosopher of experienced Existence than in his description of Existential thinking. None of the later Existential philosophers has approached him in this, though they all hold the same attitude. While in Marx objective validity is united with "Existential" personal experience because of the special situation of the proletariat, in Nietzsche it is the Master-man in general and his prophet in particular who stand in the favored place where validity and Existence coincide.

The Existential thinker needs special forms of expression, because personal Existence cannot be expressed in terms of objective experience. So Schelling uses the traditional religious symbols, Kierkegaard paradox, irony, and the pseudonym, Nietzsche the oracle, Bergson images and fluid concepts, Heidegger a mixture of psychological and ontological terms, Jaspers what he calls "ciphers," the Religious Socialist concepts oscillating between immanence and transcendence. They all wrestle with the problem of personal or "non-objective" thinking and its expression—this is the calamity of the Existential thinker.

II. ONTOLOGICAL PROBLEMS OF THE EXISTENTIAL PHILOSOPHY

1. Existential immediacy and the subject-object distinction

The thinking of the Existential thinker is based on his immediate personal and inner experience. It is rooted in an interpretation of Being or Reality which does *not* identify Reality with "objective being." But it would be equally misleading to say that it identifies Reality with "subjective being," with "consciousness" or feeling. Such a view would still leave the meaning of "subjective" determined by its contrast with that of "objective"; and this is just the contrary of what the Existential philosophy is aiming at. Like many other appeals to immediate experience, it is trying to find a level on which the contrast between "subject" and "object" has not arisen. It aims to cut under the "subject-object distinction" and to reach that stratum of Being which Jaspers, for instance, calls the *"Ursprung"* or "Source." But in order to penetrate to this stratum we must leave the sphere of "objective" things and pass through the corresponding "subjective" inner experience, until we arrive at the immediate creative experience or "Source." " 'Existence' is something that can never become a mere object; it is the 'Source' whence springs my thinking and acting.''[24] Schelling follows Hegel in emphasizing the "subject" and its freedom against Substance and its necessity. But while in Hegel the "subject" is immediately identified with the *thinking* subject, in Schelling it becomes rather the "Existing" or immediately experiencing subject.

All the Existential philosophers reject any identification of Being or Reality with the objects of thought, which they feel is the great threat to personal human Existence in our period. Nietzsche writes in the third book of the *Will to Power:* "Knowledge and Becoming exclude each other. Consequently knowledge must signify something different. A 'will to make recognizable' must precede it; a special kind of becoming, man, must have created the deception of Being''[25]—that is, of objective Being. All the categories establishing the objective world are useful deceptions necessary for the preservation of the human race. But the "Source," Life itself, cannot be made into an object of thought by these categories.

For Bergson we lose our genuine Existence, our real nature, if we think of ourselves in the "spatialized" terms appropriate to objective things. "The moments in which we grasp ourselves are rare, and consequently we are seldom free. Our existence is more in space than in time."[26] Real Existence, our true nature, is the life in self-possession and duration.

According to Marx, *"Verdinglichung,"* for men to become "ob-

[24] Jaspers, *Philosophie*, I, 15.

[25] Nietzsche, *Wille zur Macht* (1884–88); *Werke* (Taschenausgabe, Leipzig, 1906), IX, 387.

[26] Bergson, *Essai sur les Données Immédiates de la Conscience* (German tr., Jena, 1911), 182.

jects," things or commodities, is characteristic of the present world. But to be essentially human is just the opposite. Natural forces and their transformation through technology are really *man's* natural forces, they are man's objects, confirming *his* individuality. Industry is the secret revelation of the powers of human nature.[27]

Jaspers declares that personal Existence ("Existential Subjectivity") is the center and aim of Reality. No being who lacks such a personal experience can ever understand Existence. But those beings who do possess it can themselves understand such defective and sub-human creatures to be the result of a tragic loss of personal Existence. Heidegger denies that it is possible to approach Being through objective reality, and insists that "Existential Being," *Dasein,* self-relatedness, is the only door to Being itself. The objective world (*"Das Vorhandene"*) is a late product of immediate personal experience.

The meaning of this desperate refusal to identify Reality with the world of objects is clearly brought out by Nietzsche when he says: "When we have reached the inevitable universal economic administration of the earth, then mankind as a machine can find its meaning in the service of this monstrous mechanism of smaller and smaller cogs adapted to the whole."[28] No one any longer knows the significance of this huge process. Mankind demands a new aim, a new meaning for life. In these words anxiety about the social character of the "objective world" is clearly revealed as the motive for the fight of the philosophers of personal Existence against "objectivation," against the transformation of men into impersonal "objects."

2. Psychological and ontological concepts

The principle of personal Existence or "Existential Subjectivity" demands a special type of concept in which to describe this immediate personal experience. These concepts must be "non-objectivating," they must not transform men into things; but at the same time they must not be merely "subjective." In the light of this double demand we can understand the choice of psychological notions with a non-psychological connotation.

If the philosophy of personal Existence is right in maintaining

[27] Marx, *Der Historische Materialismus,* I, 301, 304.
[28] Nietzsche, *Wille zur Macht, Werke,* X, 114.

that immediate experience is the door to the creative "Source" of Being, it is necessary for the concepts describing immediate experience to be at the same time descriptive of the structure of Being itself. The so-called "affects" are then not mere subjective emotions with no ontological significance; they are half-symbolic, half-realistic indications of the structure of Reality itself. It is in this way that Heidegger and many other philosophers of personal Existence are to be understood. Heidegger fills his book *Sein und Zeit* not with definitions of *Sein*-as-such or *Zeit*-as-such, but with descriptions of what he calls *Dasein* and *Zeitlichkeit,* temporal or finite Existence. In these descriptions he speaks of *Sorge* (care) as the general character of Existence, or of *Angst* (anxiety) as the relation of man to nothingness, or of fear of death, conscience, guilt, despair, daily life, loneliness, etc. But he insists again and again that these characterizations are not "ontic," describing merely a particular being, Man, but are rather "ontological," describing the very structure of Being itself. He denies that their negative character, their seemingly pessimistic connotations, have anything to do with actual pessimism. They all point to human finitude, the real theme of the philosophy of personal Existence. It remains, of course, an open question how the psychological meaning of these concepts can be distinguished from their ontological meaning. Most of the criticism directed against Heidegger deals with this problem; and it appears that Heidegger implicitly admitted that he was unable to explain the difference clearly, and that he himself has increasingly emphasized human nature as the starting-point of the Existential ontology.

But this does not solve the problem. It is obvious that all the Existential philosophers and their predecessors have developed ontology in psychological terms. In Böhme, in Baader, in Schelling's *Human Freedom,* and in many other places, we find the belief in an essential relationship between human nature and Being, the belief that the innermost center of Nature lies in the heart of man. An especially important example of this ontological use of a psychological term is the conception of "Will" as the ultimate principle of Being. We find this in Böhme and in all those influenced by him, and before Böhme in Augustine, Duns Scotus, and Luther. Schelling's early view of the Will as *"Ur-Sein"* and his whole later voluntarism developed in his doctrine of Freedom, Nietzsche's symbol of the Will to Power, Bergson's *élan vital,* Schopenhauer's ontology of Will, the "Unconscious" of Hartmann and Freud—all these concepts of the non-rational are psychological notions with an ontological significance. The philosophers of Existence have used them, as well as other psychological concepts, to protect us from the annihilation of the "creative Source" by an "objective world" created out of that "Source" which is now swallowing it like a monstrous mechanism.

3. The principle of Finitude

In Hegel the whole world-process is explained in terms of the dialectical identity of the finite with the infinite. The Existential divorce of the finite from the infinite is entirely denied, not merely, as in mysticism, overcome in occasional ecstatic experiences. Kant's critical warning against such undue transgression of the limits of the finite mind is quite ignored.

The philosophy of experienced Existence re-establishes the consciousness of the divorce of the finite from the infinite. All the Existential philosophers strongly emphasize this point. Schelling, himself more responsible than anyone else for the victory of the Principle of Identity, and of intellectual intuition as the means of achieving it, later asserts that it is valid only in the realm of essence, not in that of existence. Kierkegaard follows Schelling: "The rationalistic Idea is the Identity of subject and object, the unity of thought and Being. Existence, on the other hand, is their separation."[29] With respect to finitude he says: "Existence is a synthesis of the infinite and the finite."[30] But this synthesis is just the opposite of Identity. It is the basis of Existential despair, of the will to get rid of oneself. Despair is the expression of the relation of separation in this synthesis; it reveals the dynamic insecurity of the spirit. Jaspers' description of the "boundary-situations," our historical relativity, death, suffering, struggle, guilt, points in the same direction. Especially strong is the idea of finitude expressed in his doctrine of the necessary *Scheitern* (shipwreck) of the finite in its relation to the infinite. "Since Personal Existence tries in the process of becoming to transcend the measure of its finitude, the finite being—is finally ruined."[31]

Feuerbach says: "The subject which has nothing outside itself,

[29] Kierkegaard, *Concluding Unscientific Postscript*, 112.
[30] *Ibid.*, 350.
[31] Jaspers, *Philosophie*, III, 229.

and therefore no limits within itself, has ceased to be a finite subject."[32] Marx describes man as a being related to objects through want, sensuality, activity, suffering, and passion. Nietzsche's pragmatic view of knowledge as well as his longing for eternity shows his consciousness of our finitude in thinking and being.

But most important in this connection is Heidegger's attempt to interpret Kant's critical philosophy in terms of Existential philosophy, primarily in terms of human finitude. In his *Kant and the Problem of Metaphysics* (1929) he introduces the subject of his inquiry as Kant's attempt to found metaphysics on the human, that is, the finite, character of reason.[33] Finitude is the very structure of the human mind, to be distinguished from mere shortcomings, error, or accidental limitations. While for Kant God—as a mere ideal—has an infinite "intuition," man has a finite intuition, and therefore needs to employ discursive thinking. "The character of the finitude of intuition is its receptivity."[34] Therefore finite knowledge has "objects"—the definition of finitude in Feuerbach and Marx, with which Dilthey's interpretation of reality as resistance may be compared. For Heidegger, Kant's epistemological problem is: "How must that finite being we call man be equipped in order to be aware of a kind of Being which is not the same as he himself?"[35] The several chapters of the *Kritik* answer this question step by step. "The revelation of the structure of the 'pure synthesis' reveals the very nature of the finitude of reason."[36] While an ontology which claims to have knowledge of Being a priori is arrogant, an ontology which restricts itself to the structure of finitude is possible.[37] Such an ontology can be called a doctrine of human nature, but not in the sense of giving any special knowledge of the human race. An ontological doctrine of man develops the structure of finitude as man finds it in himself as the center of his own personal Existence. He alone of all finite beings is aware of his own finitude; therefore the way to ontology passes through the doctrine of man. But of course, in traveling this way he cannot escape his finitude. The way to finitude is itself finite and cannot

[32] Feuerbach, *Grundsätze*, 39.
[33] P. 19.
[34] *Ibid.*, 23.
[35] *Ibid.*, 39.
[36] *Ibid.*, 66.
[37] *Ibid.*, 118.

claim finality: such is the limit set upon the Existential thinker. Heidegger concludes his analysis with the statement that the fight against Kant's doctrine of the *Ding-an-sich* was a fight against the acknowledgement of the finitude of our human experience in knowing.

4. Time as "Existential" or immediately experienced, and Time as measured

For the whole Existential philosophy the analysis of finitude culminates in the analysis of Time. The insight that existence is distinguished from essence by its temporal character is as old as the philosophy of Existence. An essay on the doctrine of Time in the different philosophers of Existence, their agreements and their differences, would be a worth-while task. I must confine myself to a few suggestions.

The general tendency is to distinguish "Existential" or immediately experienced Time from dialectical timelessness on the one hand, and from the infinite, quantitative, measured Time of the objective world, on the other. That qualitative Time is characteristic of Personal Experience is the general theme of the Existential philosophy. In his *Weltalter* Schelling distinguishes three qualitatively different kinds of Time: the pre-temporal, the temporal, and the post-temporal; he tries to escape from infinite progress and regress by assuming a beginning and an end. Kierkegaard seeks to escape from measured and objective Time through his doctrine of the *Augenblick,* the pregnant moment in which Eternity touches Time and demands a personal decision. Secondly, he tries to avoid the objectivity of the Past through his idea of *"Gleichzeitgkeit,"* which takes all history to be contemporaneous with the pregnant moment, and claims a repetition of the Past is a present possibility. Nietzsche escapes from infinite, quantitative Time through his doctrine of "eternal recurrence," which gives to every moment the weight of eternity, and through his eschatological division of Time through the symbol of the "Great Noon."

Marx's distinction between pre-history and history tries to introduce a definite qualitative element into the course of quantitative Time. Religious Socialism, through its doctrine of the "center of history" which determines the beginning and the end of "historical Time," and through its idea of "time fulfilled" or the *Kairos,* has tried to go in the same direction of transcending quantitative through qualitative Time. Bergson's fight against quantitative and objective Time, in which Time is subjected to Space, belongs to the same line of development.

Most radical is Heidegger's distinction between "Existential" and objective Time. No one has emphasized so strongly as he the identity between experienced Existence and temporality: "Temporality is the genuine meaning of Care,"[38] and Care is finite Existence. Heidegger carries through this idea with respect to the whole structure of experienced Existence, especially in connection with the anticipation of our own death, which generates the way in which we can grasp ourselves as a whole. In his analysis of Kant he indicates that for himself Time is defined by "self-affection," grasping oneself or one's Personal Existence. Temporality is Existentiality. In distinction from this qualitative Time, objective Time is the Time of the flight from our own Personal Existence into the universal "one," the "everyone," the average human Existence, in which quantitative measurement is necessary and justified. But this universal Time is not *eigentlich* or proper; it is Time objectified, and it must be interpreted in the light of Existential Time, Time as immediately experienced, and not *vice versa*.

III. THE ETHICAL ATTITUDE OF THE EXISTENTIAL PHILOSOPHY

1. History viewed in the light of the future

All the Existential philosophers agree on the historical character of immediate personal experience. But this fact that man has a fundamentally "historical Existence" does not mean merely that he has a theoretical interest in the past; his Existence is not directed toward the past at all. It is the attitude not of the detached spectator, but of the actor who must face the future and make personal decisions.

Schelling calls his positive philosophy "historical philosophy," because being "historical" means for him being open for the future. Since the revelation of *das Unvordenkliche* is never completed, the positive philosophy is never finished. We have already touched on Kierkegaard's doctrines of the "pregnant moment," of contemporaneity and repetition, as well as on the use made of these ideas by German Religious Socialism to interpret history.

---

[38] Heidegger, *Sein und Zeit* (Halle, 1927), 326.

For Marx man's experience is fundamentally conditioned by the historical and cultural setting of his life. Human nature is itself historical, and cannot be understood without an understanding of its present stage of dehumanization, and of the demand for a "real humanism" in the future. Philosophical doctrines of human nature and of ontology are dependent on the revolutionary achievement in the future of what man has the power to make of himself.

In his second *Unzeitgemässe Betrachtung* Nietzsche states emphatically the historical character of human experience. "The word of the past is always an oracle uttered. Only as builders of the future, as knowing the present, will you understand it."[39] In this Heidegger follows Nietzsche: The historical character of human experience lies in its orientation toward the future. Mere historical knowledge is not man's real rôle as an historical being. Absorption in the past is an estrangement from our task as the makers of history.[40]

2. Finitude and estrangement

The description of man's "Existential situation" or present estate as finitude is usually connected with the contrast between man's present estate and what he is "essentially," and therefore ought to be. Ever since Schelling's *On Human Freedom*, the world we are living in, including Nature, has been described as a disrupted unity, as fragments and ruins. In accord with Kant's half-mythological and genuinely "Existential" doctrine of radical evil, Schelling speaks of the transcendent Fall of Man as the "presupposition of the tragic nature of Existence." Kierkegaard's famous work on *Angst*, in which he interprets the transition from essence to existence, is his psychological masterpiece: the *Angst* of finitude drives man to action and at the same time to an alienation from his essential being and to the profounder *Angst* of guilt and despair.

Both Schelling and Kierkegaard aim to distinguish "finitude" from "alienation" or "estrangement." But neither really succeeds; the finite character of immediate personal experience makes the "Fall" practically inescapable. Nietzsche, Heidegger, Jaspers, and Bergson do not even try to make a distinction. They describe immediate experience in terms of both finitude *and* guilt— that is, in tragic terms. *Verfallenheit*, being lost and a prey to the

[39] Nietzsche, *Unzeitgemässe Betrachtungen, Werke*, II, 161.
[40] Heidegger, *Sein und Zeit*, 396.

necessity of existing, constitutes guilt. As Heidegger says, "Being guilty is not the result of a guilty act, but conversely, the act is possible only because of an original 'being guilty.' "[41] The tragic interpretation of life which has prevailed among the European intelligentsia during the last decades is not unrelated to the Existential philosophy.

Marx described the situation of dehumanization and self-estrangement in innumerable fragments. One of the most precious pieces is his description of the function of money as the main symbol of self-estrangement or alienation in present society. But estrangement is not for him an inevitable tragic necessity. It is the product of a special historical situation, and can be overcome through human action. It is in this attitude that the Utopian elements of the later Marxist movements are rooted. But the subsequent history of these movements has shown that Marx's description of man as a passionate and suffering being holds true even after a victorious revolution. The relation between finitude and estrangement is fundamental for Existential philosophy.

3. Finitude and loneliness

Every personal Existence is unique, says Jaspers: "We are completely irreplaceable. We are not merely cases of universal Being."[42] Heidegger speaks of the *Jemeinigkeit* of personal Existence, its belonging to me and nobody else.[43] Men usually live in the common experiences of daily life, covering over with talk and action their real inner personal experience. But conscience, guilt, having to die, come home to the individual only in his inner loneliness. The death of another as an objective event has nothing to do with our personal attitude toward our own death. Nietzsche praises the higher type of man who is lonely and cut off not only from the masses but also from others like himself. Nietzsche's estimate of the average man is exactly that of Heidegger and Jaspers. Kierkegaard goes even beyond them in emphasizing man's inner experience of loneliness before God. Anything objective and universal has no other meaning for him than an escape from the ethical decision each individual has to make.

Feuerbach and Marx seem to diverge on this point from the

[41] Heidegger, *Sein und Zeit*, 284.
[42] Jaspers, *Vernunft und Existenz* (Groningen, 1935), 19.
[43] Heidegger, *Sein und Zeit*, 42.

other philosophers of Human Existence. Feuerbach makes a very profound comment on the problem of loneliness: "True dialectic is not a monologue of the lonely thinker with himself. It is a dialogue between the Ego and the Thou."[44] This Ego-Thou philosophy has had great influence on present-day German theology since Buber and Griesebach. But the question is, what can we substitute for this inner loneliness? Without such an alternative the Ego-Thou relation remains a mere form. This is implied in Marx's criticism of Feuerbach, that he knows man in the abstract, and man the individual, but not man the social being. Marx himself sees only this social man. But he there discovers man's estrangement, which is not only man's estrangement from himself but also from every other man. For him, this loneliness arises from present historical conditions which must be transformed. But the struggle to create true humanity in the proletariat has led in actual fact not to "community," but only to "solidarity," a relation which is still external and remains a symbol of man's estrangement.

In all the Existential philosophers it is this loss of community that has provoked the flight from the objective world. Only in that world—in what Herakleitos called "the common world in which we live our waking lives"—is genuine community between man and man possible. If this common world has disappeared or grown intolerable, the individual turns to his lonely inner experience, where he is forced to spin out dreams which isolate him still further from this world, even though his objective knowledge of it may be very extensive. Here is suggested much of the social background of the philosophy of Human Existence.

CONCLUSION—THE SIGNIFICANCE OF THE EXISTENTIAL PHILOSOPHY

We have considered a large group of Existential philosophers, covering a period of about a hundred years. They represent many different and even contradictory tendencies in philosophic thought, and they had many different and even contradictory effects on religion and politics. Do they all exhibit some common trait which justifies calling them all "Existential philosophers?" If the above analysis is correct, there can be no doubt that they display a very fundamental unity. This unity can be described in both negative and positive terms: all the philosophers of Existence share a com-

[44] Feuerbach, *Grundsätze*, 83.

mon opposition to a common foe, and all have a common aim, though they try to attain it in very different ways.

What all philosophers of Existence oppose is the "rational" system of thought and life developed by Western industrial society and its philosophic representatives. During the last hundred years the implications of this system have become increasingly clear: a logical or naturalistic mechanism which seemed to destroy individual freedom, personal decision and organic community; an analytic rationalism which saps the vital forces of life and transforms everything, including man himself, into an object of calculation and control; a secularized humanism which cuts man and the world off from the creative Source and the ultimate mystery of existence. The Existential philosophers, supported by poets and artists in every European country, were consciously or subconsciously aware of the approach of this self-estranged form of life. They tried to resist it in a desperate struggle which drove them often to mental self-destruction and made their utterances extremely aggressive, passionate, paradoxical, fragmentary, revolutionary, prophetic and ecstatic. But this did not prevent them from achieving fundamental insights into the sociological structure of modern society and the psychological dynamics of modern man, into the originality and spontaneity of life, into the paradoxical character of religion and the Existential roots of knowledge. They immensely enriched philosophy, if it be taken as man's interpretation of his own existence; and they worked out intellectual tools and spiritual symbols for the European revolution of the twentieth century.

To understand the fundamental drive and function of Existential philosophy, it is necessary to view it against the background of what was happening in the nineteenth-century religious situation, especially in Germany. For all the groups that appeared after 1830 had to face a common problem, the problem created by the breakdown of the religious tradition under the impact of enlightenment, social revolution, and bourgeois liberalism. First among the educated classes, then increasingly in the mass of industrial workers, religion lost its "immediacy," it ceased to offer an unquestioned sense of direction and relevance to human living. What was lost in immediacy Hegel tried to restore by conscious reinterpretation. But this mediating reinterpretation was attacked and dissolved from both sides, by a revived theology on the one hand and by philosophical positivism on the other. The Existential philosophers were trying to discover an ultimate meaning of life beyond the reach of reinterpretation, revived theologies, or positivism. In their search they passionately rejected the "estranged" objective world with its religious radicals, reactionaries, and mediators. They turned toward man's immediate experience, toward "subjectivity," not as something opposed to "objectivity," but as that living experience in which both objectivity and subjectivity are rooted. They turned toward Reality as men experience it immediately in their actual living, to *Innerlichkeit* or inward experience. They tried to discover the creative realm of being which is prior to and beyond the distinction between objectivity and subjectivity.

If the experience of this level of living is "mystical," Existential philosophy can be called the attempt to reconquer the meaning of life in "mystical" terms after it had been lost in ecclesiastical as well as in positivistic terms. It is however necessary to redefine "mystical" if we are to apply it to Existential philosophy. In this context the term does not indicate a mystical union with the transcendent Absolute; it signifies rather a venture of faith toward union with the depths of life, whether made by an individual or a group. There is more of the Protestant than the Catholic heritage in this kind of "mysticism"; but it *is* mysticism in trying to transcend the estranged "objectivity" as well as the empty "subjectivity" of the present epoch. Historically speaking, the Existential philosophy attempts to return to a pre-Cartesian attitude, to an attitude in which the sharp gulf between the subjective and the objective "realms" had not yet been created, and the essence of objectivity could be found in the depth of subjectivity—in which God could be best approached through the soul.

This problem and this solution are in some respects peculiar to the German situation, in others common to all European culture: analogies to the Existential philosophy can be found all over Europe from France to Russia, from Italy to Norway. It is the desperate struggle to find a new meaning of life in a reality from which men have been estranged, in a cultural situation in which two great traditions, the Christian and the humanistic, have lost their comprehensive character and their convincing power. The turning towards *Innerlichkeit,* or more precisely towards the creative sources of life in the depth of man's experience, occurred throughout Europe. For sociological reasons it was in Germany both more philosophical and more radical than in other lands. There it became that quasi-religious power that transformed society, first in Russia and then in other parts of Europe, during the first half of the twentieth century.

In understanding Existential philosophy a comparison with the situation in England may be helpful. England is the only European country in which the Existential problem of finding a new meaning for life had no significance, because there positivism and the religious tradition lived on side by side, united by a social conformism which prevented radical questions about the meaning of human "Existence." It is important to note that the one country without an Existential philosophy is that in which during the period from 1830 to 1930 the religious tradition remained strongest. This illustrates once more the dependence of the Existential philosophy on the problems created by the breakdown of the religious tradition on the European continent.

In their struggle against the meaninglessness of modern technological civilization, the several philosophers of Existence used very different methods and had very different aims. In all of them the Existential emphasis was only one factor among others, more or less controlling. Schelling shared the belief of German Romanticism that a new philosophy, and in particular a new interpretation of religion, could produce a new reality. But this assumption was wrong; and his immediate influence remained very limited, restricted to the theology of the restoration period. Feuerbach's significance for Existential thinking lies more in his destruction of Hegel's reconciliation of Christianity with modern philosophy than in his metaphysical materialism, which indeed considerably strengthened the bourgeois-mechanistic interpretation of nature and man.

Kierkegaard represents the religious wing of Existential philosophy. He himself claimed not to be a philosopher, and those who consider him the classic type of Existential thinking often assert that a genuinely Existential thinker cannot be one. But Kierkegaard's actual work reveals a much more intimate connection. As a religious thinker he encountered the obstacle of a church which had become "bourgeois" in both theory and practice, and he was able to maintain his own radical Christianity only in terms of an absolute paradox and of a passionately personal devotion. As a philosophical thinker, however, he produced a "dialectical" psychology which has contributed greatly to an anti-rationalistic and anti-mechanistic interpretation of human nature.

If we call Marx an Existential thinker, this can obviously apply only to certain particular strains of his thought: to his struggle against the self-estrangement of man under capitalism, against any theory that merely interprets the world without changing it, against the assumption that knowledge is quite independent of the social situation in which it is sought. Like Kierkegaard, Marx wanted to be no philosopher: he pronounced the end of all philosophy and its transformation into a revolutionary sociology. But the impulse he gave to the interpretation of history, his doctrine of "ideology," his introduction of sociological analysis into economics, made him a powerful force in the philosophic discussion of the end of the nineteenth and the beginning of the twentieth centuries, long before he became the greatest political force in the fight of the twentieth century against the traditions of the nineteenth.

Like Marx, Nietzsche and the *"Lebensphilosophen"* are Existential philosophers only in certain of their views. Nietzsche's attack on "European nihilism," his biological interpretation of the categories of knowledge, his fragmentary and prophetic style, his eschatological passion; Dilthey's problem of the Existential roots of the different interpretations of life; Bergson's attack on spatial rationality in the name of creative vitality; the primacy of life as over against its products in Simmel and Scheler—all these ideas reveal their Existential character. But just as Marx never called into question natural science, economic theory, and dialectical reason, so Nietzsche and the *Lebensphilosophen* always presupposed the scientific method and an ontology of life. Heidegger, and less emphatically Jaspers, returned to the Kierkegaardian type of Existential philosophy, and in particular to the dialectical psychology of Kierkegaard. They reintroduced the term "Existential" to designate a philosophy that appealed to immediate personal experience, and they coöperated with a theology that was profoundly influenced by Kierkegaard, especially by his attack on the secularized bourgeois churches. But with the help of Aristotle and the *"Lebensphilosophie"* Heidegger transformed the dialectical psychology into a new ontology, radically rejecting the religious implications of the Existential attitude, and replacing it with the unchecked resoluteness of the tragic and heroic individual.

It is a dramatic picture that Existential philosophy presents: the polarity between the Existential attitude and its philosophic expression dominates the whole movement. At times the Existential element prevails, at times the philosophical—even in the same thinker. In them all the critical interest is predominant. All of them are reacting—in theory and practice—against an historical destiny the fulfilment of which they are furthering by their very reaction against it. They are the expression of the great revolution within and against Western industrial society which was prepared in the nineteenth century and is being carried out in the twentieth.

Reflections on Religion and Modern Individualism*

by HERBERT BUTTERFIELD

I. INTRODUCTION

The relationship between religion and individualism involves a whole aspect of the history of mankind, and compels us to envisage the past in terms of long periods. It has wider bearings still; for, here, the past is not merely passed and done with—we are entangled in the question of the relationship between history and life. The very title that covers our proceedings this week—'Individualism since the Renaissance: Growth or Decline?'—almost betrays an anxiety, almost gives a wink to our prepossessions.

Loopholes for prejudice certainly still exist; for some of the problems are perhaps not even to be solved by intensive research. Possibly they call for a more comprehensive type of scientific treatment. In a sense we are ultimately concerned with the question why Western civilization proved so much more dynamic than other civilizations—why, for example, it developed so greatly after the age of scholasticism, while the Islamic world so soon came to a halt. Perhaps we can never construct a history of individualism, or understand the profoundest things in our own past, until the comparative study of both religions and civilizations has been raised to a higher power.

It is interesting that the International Society for the History of Ideas should inaugurate its career with a conference on Individualism, a subject which can hardly be kept within the conventional realm of the History of Ideas. Here, at any rate, ideas do not simply breed themselves out of the logic of previous ideas, as though their genealogy could be tracked down in a succession of books. I once heard Heisenberg put forward the suggestion that the Scientific Revolution might be traceable ultimately to a subtle change in man's feeling for 'matter.' I remember being struck by what seemed to be an unconscious change of feeling in early XVIth-century England when you began to regard it as too anomalous that a section of the people (the clergy) were not subject to 'the law of the land.' There are profound changes which are not explicitly recorded, or accounted for, in the formal literature; and ideas may be born out of despairs and frustrations, battles and predicaments, and man's perpetual wrestling with experience. The History of Ideas constantly has to sink back into the ocean of General History.

* This paper was presented before the First Meeting of the International Society for the History of Ideas, held at Peterhouse, Cambridge University, Sept. 3, 1960.

I suspect that when Lord Acton talked about 'the History of Liberty' he did not mean something abstracted from general history in the way that we can abstract the history of music or the growth of the idea of progress. In a sense the whole of world-history seems to have been to him the history of liberty; here was the real theme of the epic of mankind. On this view, the advance of civilization is the progress to greater differentiation of personality, greater moral autonomy, and, at the same time, greater responsibility, for the individual.

I am not sure that Acton's thinking can be understood unless it is realized that he was interested in what I might call questions of the last resort. He was concerned ultimately with the crucial kind of freedom which allows a man to choose the God whom he will worship and the moral end for which he shall live. At this high point, freedom is a right to be asserted not merely against governments but against society itself, not merely against kings but also against the democracy. The individual must be able to confront the tyranny of majorities, the prejudices of the prevailing culture, and the dominating spirit of the age itself. If a man has ratified the Christian Gospel in his heart he must be in a position to follow his faith though he live in Xth-century China or in XXth-century Russia. Acton's whole angle of approach to the problem of liberty had been decided in his youthful Munich days, when his outlook and his obsessions were much more 'Catholic' than they afterwards became. He had to grapple with the problem at the point of crucial test, therefore; he had to find the basis from which a mere individual could confront not only the power but also the moral claims of mundane society as such, each man deciding to what purpose he would conduct his own life.

Acton's whole line of approach led him to behave as though he assumed that the monolithic state was the primary enemy of liberty. This may have led him to do less than justice to classical antiquity, a field in which his knowledge may have been less masterly than he imagined. Even if there had been no slavery in ancient Athens, he would have regarded classical Greece as hostile to his idea of liberty, because it held duty to be a thing prescribed by the state; the individual had no ground from which to resist the claims of secular society, the tyranny of majorities.

I do not know whether Acton did less than justice to something rather different: the influence of modern appreciations, even modern misinterpretations, of ancient Athens. We ourselves, however, may be in danger of arguing in a circle here, if it is true that the modern world has tended to run its own current prejudices and obsessions into its picture of antiquity. There may have been a XIXth-century 'Whig interpretation' of Athenian history which was the result rather than the cause of the predominance that Whiggism acquired in that century. In a world of different conditions the teaching of ancient Greece may have operated in favor of what are really autocratic doctrines. I wonder whether Acton did sufficient justice to the influence of ancient teaching as it manifested itself in the Renaissance doctrine of Man. But, again, I do not know whether the Renaissance doctrine of Man would have been quite the same if there had never been an anterior Christian Humanism.

Given his angle of approach, Acton was almost bound to reach the view that in reality it was religion which provided the basis for the assertion of the individual within society, or against society. Only an inner, compelling sense of duty, only a summons in the heart which was felt to be the voice of God, gave the individual any standing against society or his fellow-men. And the expansion of liberty throughout the centuries has been the expansion of the scope which the world has been prepared to allow to the individual conscience. Acton asserted that it is the individual (and not society) which has the 'soul,' the direct contact with God, and the eternal destiny. He appalled even Protestants by his bitter attacks on persecution, and it was said in Cambridge that he had the Inquisition 'on the brain.' But he saw religion as an important factor in the history of liberty, and he thought that the danger to liberty in the XXth century would come from the monolithic state.

His view has received a certain reinforcement from events which have taken place since his death. It seems that the happenings of the present day may remedy our lack of experience (or our deficiency in imagination) and alter our appreciation of the past. When I was young, we tended to assume that only a Church would desire the persecution of heresy, the coercion of conscience. The existence of an allegedly supernatural religion seemed to be the sole reason for the appearance of such an evil in the world. Since the First World War we have come to realize that the desire to establish an orthodoxy may be a secular as well as a religious danger. The desire to eliminate heresy (if necessary by persecution) seems to be a human, and not merely a Christian, failing, after all. It now becomes more plausible to argue (with Acton) that persecution came, not from Christianity as such, but from the human element that was intermixed with it—that the Church or its agents might have been at fault but that the principles of the religion itself had been the seeds of liberty.

This leaves us with no guarantee against the return of religious (as well as secular) persecution. It overlooks the fact that a religion claiming to be supernatural may have its pitfalls, since those who feel themselves the agents of God may think that they must use power when power is within their reach. If Acton became frantic, and came near to screaming, when he remembered persecution, it was because churchmen did not realize the profundity of the problem and too easily shrugged it off as a thing of the past.

II. THE PROBLEM OF THE 'CHRISTIAN SOCIETY'

Under more primitive conditions it is the whole people that seems to be solid in a corporate faith, and religion serves the body politic as a bond of union. It is Jeremiah who has been described as 'the father of all individualism in religion,' and 'the first, whether in Israel or elsewhere, to stand face to face with his God, apart from and even opposed to the people to whom he belonged.' A significant new stage is recorded or typified in Jeremiah, XXXI, 33, which seems to mark a change in the consciousness of men, a change that one is surprised to find so clearly registered in an historical document. God, whose Promise to the Children of Israel is one which developed with the passage of time, is described as saying (under what is called the New Covenant): "I will put my law in their inward parts and write it in their hearts." In a neighboring passage (ver. 29–30) Jeremiah modifies the view that the children shall suffer for the sins of their fathers, and says that "every one shall die for his own iniquity." Ezekiel is associated with a similar kind of individualism; and perhaps such teaching would have special meaning in the period of the Exile, when the body politic no longer existed, and religion was no longer tied so definitely to a locality, or even to the Temple in Jerusalem. The corporate faith was not superseded in reality, but Jeremiah's thesis tended to the interiorizing of religion, and the prophet seems conscious that religion is now being carried to a higher level. Within revealed religion itself, the ground was being prepared for the establishment of an internal sanction or authority capable of confronting first the State, and then the Church, and, in the last resort, the Revelation itself.

This is only one side of the picture, however. If we look at the other side, the evidence is equally portentous. Even after the promulgation of the New Covenant there seems to be a relapse, and Judaism, re-established in its own land, appears to have hardened and 'caked' into a rigid corporate system. More significant still, Christianity (though in various respects it was calculated to carry the 'interiorizing' of religion to a greater depth) took to persecution at just about the earliest moment that the idea of such a thing became feasible at all. The alliance with power and the resort to force occurred in a period not greatly remote from the days of the New Testament itself. At only a slightly earlier date, it had been Christian martyrs who had vindicated the notion of a divine summons within the consciences of men. The Church began its persecuting policy, moreover, not in a comparatively primitive society in which the group naturally prevails over the individual and religion assumes corporate, superstitious forms, but in a highly civilized world where men were sufficiently advanced to realize the issues at stake, to question and resent the policy.

It seems, then, that the state may become particularly dangerous when allied with a militant creed. The greatest menace to liberty (or the one which aims its threat at the highest point) is what we call 'Caesaropapism.' There is (or there was historically) something in the nature of a supernational religion which makes it easy to regard the dissident as not merely wrong but also diabolical. Even in the XVIth and XVIIth centuries men who were themselves under persecution might complain that wrong religion was persecuting right religion. But the same men might refuse to concede that the right religion, if ever it acquired the power, should withhold from persecution.

After the Barbarian Invasions, a considerable section of Europe was made Christian by external pressure—by military conquest and by royal decree, for example. The story is sometimes a cruel one, but less surprising and disquieting than the emergence of persecution in the ancient Roman Empire. More primitive societies tend to have corporate beliefs, and these particular societies were perhaps due to be captured violently by one new creed or another. Christianity may have given to the populations concerned a better basis for a life of reason than the superstitions it replaced. In any case, the Church gave the lead in education and in the recovery of the learning of classical antiquity.

But if the rôle of the medieval, authoritarian Church is understandable and defensible, this can only be on an argument that justifies it as a temporary system, suited to more primitive conditions, appropriate to an interim stage in the history of a civilization. If religion adopts this particular relationship to society, it becomes, itself, all the more subject to the influence of historical conditioning circumstances. Christianity was not unique in the way in which it presided over a civilization in its formative period. It was assuming the rôle which other religions have performed, whether in pagan antiquity or in the case of medieval Islam. In this respect it was choosing (or circumstances compelled it to choose) to be like the rest, to hanker after the Old Covenant.

For well over a thousand years, then, we see Christianity as the established faith in Europe, but a great part of Asia and Africa is similarly under the sway of Islam. By methods of a curiously parallel kind, a large section of the globe in the XXth century has been captured by communism. These systems establish themselves through revolution or military conquest, and they secure mass-conversion through governmental pressure. It was in Christian history that there was to emerge the technique of reducing dissident individuals to the status of what we call second-class citizens. Once safely established, however, all the systems in question can prolong themselves for a thousand years; and for this they will not need the continuous use of force, or the unremitting resort to persecution. The creed can be transmitted from parent to child, or through an educational system, or by general contagion, or by the organization of vested interests. The rising generation may accept the faith partly because it is not allowed to know the nature of the alternatives, not allowed to know that a choice is open to it. Partly, acceptance may even be the effect of prevailing custom, social convention, and a certain indolence of mind. When things are on this footing you can have a Europe in which, for many centuries, the Bible is accepted as a sacred book, while the people who accept it, if they had been born in Asia or in Africa, would have found it equally natural to believe in the Koran. Religion comes to stand as a regional affair—a hard, hereditary slab of Christianity on one part of the map, and a similar slab of hereditary Islam on another part.

The conflict, the evil and the tragedy—if they do not appear at the beginning—are bound to emerge in the fullness of time, when the interim period has come to an end. The Church seems unable to envisage its presidency as a temporary one, and dreads the loss of what it regards as 'a Christian society,' its establishment of the City of God on earth. Christian Messianism suffered like ancient Jewish Messianism from having been too worldly in its dreams; and nothing appeared to be more disastrous, more blasphemous, than the return of Christianity to something more like the conditions of New Testament times. In any case the coming of individualism always looks like a disintegration of society, and the XXth century itself no sooner entered into the inheritance of its liberal predecessors than it became frightened of the very liberalism, frightened of what it called 'intellectual anarchy.' In the XVIth century not only Roman Catholicism but the emergent Protestantism tried to maintain 'the Christian society' by force. And what they persecuted now were awakened consciences.

Yet, if consciences were awake by this time, if men were willing to accept persecution rather than forsake those beliefs that they had ratified in their hearts, this itself would seem to have been due to the fact that the medieval Church had done its work so well. It would seem that a faithful Church, collaborating with a rising civilization, deepens interior religion and leads to the more personal appropriation of religious experience. By that very fact, it works to the undoing of the solid, unanimous 'Christian Commonwealth.' If religion produced the authoritarian system, it also produced the rebellion against the system, as though the internal aspect of the faith were at war with the external. The total result over the long medieval period may have been a deepening of personality, a training of conscience, and a heightening of the sense of individual responsibility, particularly in the matter of religion itself.

Acton, fearing the unbridled State, held that the medieval system had contributed to liberty in one important respect. In the case of a revealed religion the fusion of Church and State may not be quite complete—the result may not really be monolithic. The conflict between the spiritual and secular arms tempered the tyranny of both, and reduced both to the necessity of persuading human beings— appealing to an internal arbiter. In the competition between rival authorities, the individual was bound to gain something, and political theory (even if it was politico-ecclesiastical theory) became for the West a dynamic thing. I am not clear, however, that anything quite parallel to this favored the individual, or produced the same dynamism, in the lands under the Eastern Orthodox Church. The 'Christian Society' is never guaranteed against the dangers which Western Europe then managed to avoid. The Pope might not have been in a condition to maintain the exhilarating conflict with the Emperor in the West if he had not been favored by the situation after the Barbarian Invasions. The Church had already shown in the ancient Roman Empire some of the tendencies that lead to Caesaropapism. If it had succeeded in crushing Protestantism in the XVIth century, Europe might have been more orderly, more unanimous in the faith, but the history of Spain suggests that it might have been less dynamic—enduring with the stillness that we associate (perhaps wrongly) with the Orient.

III. THE TRANSITION TO MODERN WESTERN IDEALS

In Renaissance cities that were under the rule of tyrants, life (at least in many quarters) seemed to have an extraordinary exuberance, finding great varieties of expression, and sprouting into remarkable personalities. The Spain of Philip II, in spite of the Inquisition and the heavy hand of orthodoxy, blossomed into a wonderful literature, whose chief characteristic was its riotous individualism. In both cases human beings had to work within certain limiting terms, but there always seems to be great room for variety and mental agility within the limiting terms. The limits are not always even felt to be a constriction; the artist may be happy to work for tyrant or pope, while Catholicism may operate in literature as an inspiration rather than a check.

It might be asked what more was needed for the fulfilment of personality. For, at this time, the famous modern campaigns for 'the rights of the individual' were still to come.

One of the features of our modern history is a sort of heightening of the notion of individual responsibility, and the dissemination of this amongst wider sections of the population. It gives Western man the appearance of being adult and self-standing; and I am not sure that it is quite paralleled in the other civilizations of the globe. The individual, fighting for 'freedom of conscience,' is asserting (perhaps against authority and custom) his responsibility for his own religion. Before the Reformation, before there was the stimulus of doctrinal conflict, the laymen in various regions seem to have begun to take more of a hand in the life of the Church. But in the subsequent controversies considerable numbers of people were involved (through their religion) in wider national issues, and the great feature of the West is the growing sense of responsibility for public affairs. What is remarkable today is the way in which an undergraduate or an artisan is liable to feel a responsibility when he thinks of the nuclear weapon, the treatment of African natives, or the future of the food-problem in India. If earlier ages had a parallel to this feeling of responsibility and this oecumenical solicitude, it was perhaps in the spirit which moved those missionaries who travelled to the ends of the earth for the saving of souls. A Russian aristocrat, who had returned to her homeland some time after the Revolution, was quoted to me as having reported that, though the atrocities had been great, she had been surprised to find the peasants (whom in the old days they had regarded as rather like cows) straightening their backs and holding up their heads. Whether this was true or not, it points to a recognizable aspect of our modern development—a Western 'progress' that had a 'moral' significance.

In the early modern centuries the movement is part of our religious history. It tends to be hostile to whatever may be the presiding Church; and it works to the undoing of the state as a 'religious society.'

At first it seemed that the Reformation might result in the hardening of the notion of a 'Christian Commonwealth.' Martin Luther did not intend its relaxation; he was concerned rather to establish right religion in the world. The Reformation, especially since it led to the principle of *cujus regio ejus religio,* encouraged Caesaropapism on the scale of the nation-state. Authority was tightened, or was felt as more oppressive; and now it was a case of a tyranny more close at hand. We ought to be surprised at the firmness of those dissident consciences which checked the rise of this imposing power. Yet the dissidents themselves were often seeking to establish their own equally authoritarian system.

We today find it curious that men who insisted on the voice of conscience within themselves, and were willing enough to suffer for their own consciences, were so unable to see the case for the other man's conscience. In a way, the interior nature of religion—and the internal sanction for it—were genuinely recognized; but, while faith was so militant and authoritarian, it could not be admitted that more than one choice was really open to the individual. Since religion was an absolute, and there could be only one absolute, the religious dissident could not be regarded as really representing a case of conscience at all. It would seem that, from a mundane point of view, a religion claiming to be supernatural can be a dangerous thing for the world, unless it has as its over-ruling principle the kind of 'charity' which presses towards imaginative understanding.

The modern centuries achieved a reconciliation between the absolutism of revealed religion and the relativity which the recognition of the individual conscience seemed to entail. The transition appears to be an easy one in retrospect, for we today are not imprisoned in dreams of a 'Christian society,' or in notions of celestial and diabolical systems, semi-materialist in character. We can take our start from a clearer recognition of the interior and voluntarist nature of religion. In the XVIIth century the process required a higher exercise of sympathetic understanding, and I wonder whether I am right in feeling that in the XVIIth century the principle of 'charity' was gaining ground, or developing in a more imaginative way. I remember seeing the principle adduced in Cromwellian England in order to persuade people to put themselves in the other man's place, and to realize that the other man was following his conscience too. It was more easy for a time to adopt this attitude towards other kinds of Protestants than towards Roman Catholics. The duty of dealing with others in the way in which one would want them to deal with oneself is seen by Thomas Hobbes as the fundamental law of nature, the thing that was really self-evident.

Concerning the rôle of religion in the history of liberty we can say that the claim for 'freedom of conscience' arose out of Christianity, and that the dream of a 'Christian society' was first shattered by pious men. These did not intend freedom for the people who differed from them, however; and, far from meaning to break 'the Christian Commonwealth,' they were often conducting a crusade for the purpose of re-shaping it to their heart's desire. It was the situation—the rise of competing versions of Christianity, and the failure of any one of these to drive out the rest—which impelled the world to ideas of religious liberty far removed from the original intention. Some may feel that the very pressures of the predicament compelled Christianity, in its organized form, to revert to its original nature, or to become more faithful to its essential principles. Before the end of the story, a religious ideal of 'freedom of conscience' had distinctly emerged; and this was not without significance. But the process was too slow, and it looks as if the tragedy worked itself out to the bitter end, toleration being imposed to a great degree by mundane interests, almost as a gift from the World to the Church. It must have owed much to war-weariness, the coming of religious indifference, the rise of a rationalism associated with the scientific movement, and the development of a relativist attitude, partly encouraged by the co-existence of multiple forms of Christianity, partly produced by the dawning realization that, in global history, Christianity looked like a regional affair. Historical conjunctures, political calculations, economic motives, even at moments the desperate state of governmental finances, induced kings now to make compromises in the wars of religion, now to abandon the ideal of uniformity in their own lands. At times the case against continued persecution seems to have been presented as the protest of a terrestrial morality against a morality supposed to be supra-terrestrial. One would think that religious liberty might have been achieved in Europe in ways less painful, ways perhaps less harmful to the cause of religion itself. Churchmen, however, had understandably gone on clinging to the beautiful dream of the uniform 'religious society,' existing to the glory of God. There are mixtures of the spiritual and the mundane that seem like poetry at first, but then become more sinister than mere self-regarding politics, and have to be rectified, if necessary, by some clean worldly-mindedness.

The existence of religious dissent within the Church-State systems of the post-Reformation period had important effects on the wider history of freedom. It was the nonconformists who were in the best position for continuing the conflict which the spiritual authority had waged against the temporal in the Middle Ages. Since they were unable to adduce either the *fiat* of the king or the verdict of society in their support, they had to place entire reliance on a higher authority outside the state. In relation to the whole existing order, they were fixed at an angle of permanent hostility, a body absolutely predisposed for criticism, the precursors of the whole system of a standing opposition within the state. They not only brought to the criticism of the existing order criteria from entirely outside that order, but in one sense they transcended the rôle which the medieval church had fulfilled in relation to the secular authorities. They had recently emerged from what might be called 'insurrectionary' forms of Christianity, ready with radical criticisms of the religious society as it had hitherto existed, and more eager than official Christianity to refer everything back to first principles or scriptural teaching. The compound nature of the politico-ecclesiastical systems then existing, and their own grievances against the government of the day, made it almost inevitable that religious dissidents should become the apostles of political and social revolution or reform.

In the early modern centuries the egalitarian principle reappears —and now, perhaps, to greater effect than before—still basing itself on the idea of the equality of all men in the sight of God. There are fallacies in the argument, but where the spiritual and the mundane are so entangled—where society is supposed to be a 'Christian society' —it must have seemed natural to claim rights for the lowliest classes on the ground that Christ had made all men free. Already in the XVIth century, religious radicalism was associated with communistic experiments, and here the practices of the early Church had an understandable influence. Apart from the political and social speculations in Cromwellian England, John Bellers, before the end of the XVIIth century, was producing the socialistic design which influenced Robert Owen.

Nonconformity performed its famous function as a result of the predicament in which it stood. Men who held the same doctrinal principles were soon working to a different purpose when they had captured the government and achieved settled authority over the body politic. Nor could it be said that nonconformity performs its historic function at the present day, when it is no longer set at an angle of predisposed hostility. Perhaps it tends rather to be part of the Establishment, seeing the preservation of the existing régime as essential to religion itself. It would almost be true to say that the rôle of standing opposition and the function of radical criticism which had belonged to nonconformity in England, passed (particularly in France) to what might be called the 'lapsed Christians,' who had a good deal of the same outlook, so far as mundane affairs were concerned, but separated it entirely from religious dogma. Some of them claimed to be better followers of Christ than the Christians, because they put the principle of charity before rites and ceremonies; and it seemed that their breach with the Church enabled them to emancipate themselves from conventionalities and work more freely for objects which the Churches themselves count as good at the present day. At a later stage again, there were still more militant enemies of religion who stood out in the same way as the boldest and most radical critics of the existing order. It sometimes happened that the criticisms which these people had to make were a repetition or extension of ones which religious dissidents had been the first to put forward. Sometimes the reforms which had been first demanded by religious minorities were put into execution through the efforts of non-Christians, and against the bitter resistance of churchmen. Sometimes the enemies of religion have brought out criticisms of society which one is surprised that Christians themselves had not been the first to make. In all this there may be a criticism of historical Christianity, so far as concerns its relations with society, at least in modern times.

It seems clear, however, that in the XVIth and XVIIth centuries it would have been dangerous—dangerous even to liberty and individualism—if the religious dissidents had been left in command of the field. Where they secured local predominance for a moment the sects produced their own tyranny and then generally provoked a reaction. The churches which worked rather in the defense of the existing régime would seem therefore to have had their own important function to perform; and the radicalism of the religious dissidents perhaps helps to explain the intensified conservatism of the other party.

When a civilization, which has been developing for a thousand years under a presiding religion, breaks away from such tutelage, it becomes interesting to know how far anything of that religion lingers on in modes of thought, unconscious assumptions, and the basic structure of the human outlook. If a number of religious civilizations have been through this process independently, the result may be superficially the same in each case, but a closer examination may show that profounder divergencies exist. In each case, the character of the prevailing religion may have influenced mental habits and human attitudes, or branded its patterns on the basic material of the culture that has undergone the secularization. I remember hearing a citizen of Pakistan described as a secular liberal, and being told that his mind had been considerably 'westernized'; yet I gather that, on the last analysis, his thought still revealed subtle preconceptions or inclinations only to be explained through Mohammedan legal ideas that go back for many centuries.

A general secularization of thought is visible in Western Europe from about 1700, and, in a very real sense, from about that time, the Church loses its former leadership in society. Many of the mundane values of the previous generations still persisted, however, though separated from Christian dogma; and, indeed, the influence of religion over the masses and over much of the intelligentsia itself remains remarkable until almost the present century. Mazzini said that the French Revolution did not herald a new age (for Italy herself was about to do that) but merely wound up the old one, the era of Christianity, the era of Individualism. In the XVIIIth century, as religion declined, the secular writers seemed to talk more than ever of 'conscience' and the 'rights of conscience,' taking over from their religious predecessors an idea eminently capable of laicization. The political radicals in England picked up not only the ideals but also the techniques and the machinery of the nonconformist; and, for example, the new types of radical club, which terrified Pitt and the aristocracy in 1792, took over the organization and the penny-a-week payments of the Methodist 'class-meeting,' with occasionally a prayer and a democratic hymn, as well as readings from Tom Paine instead of the Bible. It would be difficult to measure to what a degree there lurks (below the level of our conscious intellectual systems) a residue of assumptions about life on the earth, or the dim shape of a view about the nature of man, which go back to religious ages more remote.

Just as American humor differs from English humor (and I imagine that the differences would be delicate matters to explain) it would seem that American notions of liberty may differ subtly from British notions, diverging somewhat, for example, in respect of freedom of the press. It is possible to imagine intellectual contexts in which Acton's principle of 'freedom of conscience' would seem either implausible or unimportant or devoid of any foothold for effective defense. An idea which seems as clear and clean as that of liberty may rest on unseen foundations—Acton thought, for example, that liberty was impossible except amongst peoples who were conscious of living under an invisible system of over-ruling law. Events in the XXth century suggest that a particular kind of respect for personality, which has become second nature to us, must not be merely taken for granted, as though it would exist amongst people who were traditionless. It must be regarded as the product of a complicated process. The historian is wrong if he tries to trace things back to a single cause, which is the source of all the other causes. Modern individualism perhaps requires for its explanation nothing less than the narrative of all our preceding history.

It is difficult to see how individualism could have developed as it did, or how Western civilization could have become so dynamic, without the remarkable economic expansion of Western Europe. When we see how the spirit of enterprise could spread from industry and commerce to other fields, or how exhilarating the life of cities could become, we might feel that economic progress is not merely the condition but the actual cause of modern individualism. The main seats of the Renaissance in Italy, South Germany, and the Netherlands were on the old line of Eastern trade, and in city-states that had flourished on industry and commerce. Holland and England played a leading part in the history of liberty at a time when they, in turn, had come into the path of economic advance.

All the same, it is not so clear, now, as once it seemed to be, that economic opportunity and economic development must necessarily bring freer play for the individual (rather than more elaborate slave-systems or tyrannical trading kings) unless there is a prior bias towards individualism in the form of the existing order. It is possible that tendencies to individualism were partly the cause and not merely the result of the dynamic character of the European economy in later medieval and early modern times. I am not sure that absolutely inescapable economic necessities (independent of any constricting effects of Catholicism) provide us with the complete and sufficient explanation of the decline of Spain, after the glories of its Golden Age.

If by 'individualism' we mean vigorous and luxuriant life, and the sheer multiplicity of human types, it would seem that nature can be prodigal in personalities, eccentric figures and varieties of style, even where there is tyrannical government—even, indeed, in a Dickensian slum. (At the same time the XVIIIth century, even where it made almost a religion of 'individualism,' can surprise us by its uniformities and conventionalities in matters of taste.) But if by 'individualism' we have in mind the autonomy of men who are determined to decide the main purpose of their lives and feel a similar responsibility for public affairs (so that they move to a greater command of their destiny, and may decide to have democratic government even if they believe it militarily less efficient)—here is something which depends on the existence and transmission of a complicated body of inherited assumptions and ideas.

INDEX

Abbildung eines Kunstrichters, Die, G. F. Meier, 193, 195, 197, 199
Abegg, Lily, 375
Absolutism, Prussian, and Hegel, 426n
Académie des Beaux Arts, 184
Académie des Inscriptions et Médailles, 172, 178, 193
Académie des Sciences, 172, 174
Académie Française, 171, 305
Académie Royale de Peinture et de Sculpture, 171, 172
Accademia del Disegno, 163
Accademia della Crusca, 171
Accademia de S. Luca, 171
Acton, Lord: on Rousseau, 427; on liberty, 726–728, 737—*Letters to Mary Gladstone*, 427
Adams, Henry: 84; on history, 40
Addams, Jane: on human nature, 468–481 *passim*; and Emerson, 471; and positivism, 471, 472; and Dewey, 472; and James, 472; and Darwinism, 472–473, 476; and Tolstoy, 474; on human solidarity, 473–474; and socialism, 475; on the sexual instinct, 477–480; and Freud, 479; on deviant behavior, 480–481—*Twenty Years at Hull House*, 469; *Newer Ideals of Peace*, 474; *Democracy and Social Ethics*, 476
Addison, Joseph: 179; and 18th-century aesthetics, 188, 192n
Adversus Haereses Panarium, Epiphanius, 500
Aeschylus, 65
Aesthetica, A. G. Baumgarten, 193–205 *passim*
Aesthetics: 9–16 *passim*, 38, 127–144 *passim*, 193; and intellectual history, 87; theory of, 145–206; and symbolic systems, 556
Alberti, L. B., 162, 217
Albertus Magnus, on Peter Lombard, 507
Alberuni, 37
Alembert, Jean d': and Francis Bacon, 182; on philosophy, 182; on history, 182; and Batteux, 183 —*Discours*, 182–183, 200
Alienation: in modern society, 436–437; in existential philosophy, 717–719
Ambrose, Saint: 101, 532; on Symmachus, 534—*Roma*, 535–536; *On Faith*, 536
American Historical Association, 69
Ammonius Saccas, 498–499
Anabaptists, 239, 388
Anatomy, in Renaissance art academies, 163
Anaxagoras, 28
André, Père: and Descartes, 180—*L'Essai sur le Beau*, 180, 182
Andrews, Charles M., on historiography, 69
Angel, Philips, on Rembrandt, 217–218, 223
Angoulême, Marguerite d', 133
Anne, Saint, 93–138 *passim*
Annus Mirabilis, J. Dryden, 387
Ansai Zuihitsu, I Sadatake, 361
Antidotarie Chyrurgucall, An, J. Banister, 585
Anti-Semitism, in the Middle Ages, 565
Apelles, 214
Apologists, the, and Philo of Alexandria, 494–496
Apology, Bishop Melito of Sardis, 526–527

Aquinas, Saint Thomas: 425, 427, 448, 559, 666; on the doctrine of the Immaculate Conception, 107; and Hugo of St. Victor, 156; on art, 157–158; on beauty, 158; on Peter Lombard, 507; on divine attributes, 508–512 passim; on time and eternity, 551; on Aristotle's politics, 561–562—*Summa Theologica*, 496, 509, 510; *Summa contra Gentiles*, 509

Archaeology, 94

Archimedes, 32

Architecture: 20, 151; and the theory of the fine arts, 153–206 passim

Argenson, d', 414

Arians, 499, 536

Aristarchus, 39

Aristophanes, 65

Aristotle: 26, 30, 33, 38, 154, 156, 164, 180, 189, 334, 352, 427, 487, 491, 582, 686, 688, 689, 700, 724; on the syllogism, 27; on material substance, 28; his doctrine of the four causes, 52–53; on history, 66; on art, 148; on education, 153; on music, 161; and Herder, 201; and Aquinas, 561–562; on medicine, 577; and Dewey compared, 638—*Metaphysica*, 26–27, 202, 492, 496, 684; *Historia Animalium*, 51; *Politicia*, 67, 153, 350, 352; *Rhetorica*, 149, 150, 160; *Organon*, 150; *De Poetica*, 150, 151, 153, 160; *Physica*, 152, 490; *De Anima*, 490–491, 684

Aristotelianism, 26–27

Arithmetic, 154, 156, 158, 334

Arminianism, 611–637 passim

Arnold, Matthew, and Goethe, 275

Art: 109, 113, 114; and psychoanalysis, 93–126 passim; in the Renaissance, 93–126 passim, 127–144; criticism of, 145–206 passim; in 17th-century Holland, 207–224; Taine's theory of, 283–309 passim

Arte de' Cenni, L', G. Bonifacio, 169

Arte graphica, De, C. A. du Fresnoy, 173

Associationism, in Coleridge, 663

Astronomy, 65, 154, 155, 156, 334, 553

Augustine, Saint: 38, 149, 158, 427, 494, 518, 662, 712; and Occam, 507; on progress, 519–543 passim; and Origen, 524–525; on the Incarnation, 546—*Confessions*, 31; *De Ordine*, 448; *De Consensu Evangelistarum*, 488; *Contra Maximinum Arianum*, 496; *The City of God*, 515–543 passim; *Retractions*, 521, 522, 540; *Enarrations on the Psalms*, 532–534, 538–539; *Sermon on the Fall of the City*, 537

Aulard, Alphonse, 431

Authoritarianism, 371, 393

Avicenna, 588

Baader, Franz Xavier von, 512

Babeuf, François E., 410, 430

Bach, Johann Sebastian: 28: early life, 225–226; his sacred music, 227–228; at Eisenach and Ohrdruf, 228–230; at Luneburg, 231–233; as an organist, 234, 237, 250; and Buxtehude, 235–237; and the development of the cantata, 237–239, 243–245; and Pietism, 239–242, 245, 265, 267; and Vivaldi, 247; his keyboard music, 253–255; his growing isolation, 259–263; Dilthey on, 264, 266; his historical significance, 264–268

Bacon, Francis: 34, 65, 385; on history, 35; on poetry, 169; and D'Alembert, 182, 183; and the Tudor Renaissance, 382–383—*Advancement of Learning*, 383; *Novum Organum*, 383

Bacon, Roger, 574—*Opera Inedita*, 572

Bakunin, Michael, 699

Balzac, Honoré de, 290—*La Peau de Chagrin*, 676

Bandelli, Vincenzo, 107

Barrès, Maurice, and the French Revolution, 405
Bassano, Giacomo da, 220
Batteux, Charles, 180–181, 182, 183, 190, 192, 193, 195
Baudelaire, Charles: paramnesia in, 673–677 *passim;* and Proust, 677 —*Les Fleurs du Mal,* 674
Bayle, Pierre, 407, 412
Beard, Charles, on history, 70
Beaumarchais, 415
Beauty, in Medieval philosophy, 158–159; in Renaissance thought, 167; and goodness, 177. *See also* Aesthetics
Becker, Carl, on history, 70
Beethoven, Ludwig von, 282
Being, the great chain of, 25, 31
Bellers, John, 735
Bellini, Jacopo, 131
Bentham, Jeremy, 680, 681
Bereckheyde, Gerrit, 208
Bergson, Henri: 639, 707–717 *passim,* 723; and existentialism, 699; on time, 716—*L'Essai sur les Données Immédiates de la Conscience,* 700, 710
Berkeley, George: 28, 53, 513, 664; his philosophy, 21–22; and Coleridge, 668
Bernard of Clairvaux, Saint: 567, 574; on the Immaculate Conception, 107
Berr, Henri, 43
Besant, Annie, 467
Bibliotheca Universalis, C. Gesner, 168
Biology, 45, 57, 64, 65, 97, 319, 553
Birth of Mankynde, The, E. Roesslin, 584
Black Death, 50
Blake, William: 672; and Swedenborg, 669–670
Blanc, Charles, 137
Blanc, Louis, 430
Blanqui, Auguste, 430, 439
Boethius, 662, 672
Böhme, Jakob, 698, 712

Boke against the Disease Commonly Called the Sweate, J. Caius, 585
Bonald, Louis de, 405
Boogaard, J., 221
Borghini, Raffaelo, 129
Bosanquet, Bernard, 639
Bossuet, Jacques Bénigne, 408—*Le Discours sur l'histoire universelle,* 38
Botticelli, 124
Boulainvilliers, Henri de, 414
Bourget, Paul: and Taine, 307; and the French Revolution, 405—*Le Disciple,* 307
Bowels of Tender Mercy, The, O. Sedgwick, 611
Bradlaugh, Charles, 467
Bradley, Francis Herbert, 639, 698
Braque, Georges, 129
Breast-Plate of Faith and Love, The, J. Preston, 611
Brentano, Clemens, 277
Brescianino, Girolamo, 116
Breton, André, 403
Breviary of Healthe, The, A. Boorde, 581
Briefe Declaration of the Worthy Arte of Medicine, A, T. Gale, 579
Brinton, Crane, 83
Brissot, Jacques, 416
Britannia, sive Florentissimorum Regnorum Angliae ..., W. Camden, 380
Browning, Robert, 673
Brunetière, Ferdinand, on Taine, 306–307
Bruno, Giordano, 551, 664
Buckle, Henry Thomas, 40, 51
Buddha, 39, 65
Buddhism, and Christianity, 555–556
Burckhardt, Jacob, 131, 699
Burke, Edmund; 419, 427; and Kant, 202; and Taine, 293—*Reflections on the Revolution in France,* 293
Bury, John Bagnell, 44, 46, 409—*Selected Essays,* 46; *The Idea of Progress,* 525

Butler, Josephine, 450
Butterfield, Herbert, on history, 38–39
Byron, Lord: 673; and Taine, 292–295 *passim;* and Swedenborg, 670

Calvin, John, 307, 612, 619, 633
Calvinism: and capitalism, 328; theocratic radicalism in, 388; in New England, 604–637
Capella, Martianus, 154
Capitalism: and Calvinism, 328; and the double standard, 461–463
Caravaggio, Michelangelo da, 210, 213
Carlyle, Thomas: 673; and Goethe, 275
Cassirer, Ernst: 73; on history, 71 —*Rousseau, Kant and Goethe,* 426
Castell of Health, The, T. Elyot, 589–590
Catechetical Lectures, Cyril of Jerusalem, 518
Catholicism, Roman, and Renan, 559. *See also* Christianity, Roman Catholic Church
Censorship, in the Middle Ages, 569–571 *passim*
Chamberlain, Houston Stewart, 277
Chamfort, Sébastien Roch Nicolas, 414
Chaucer, 377, 569, 574, 662
Chavannes, Edouard, 367, 368
Chevalerie, La, L. Gautier, 567–568
China: and the Enlightenment, 354; antiquity of, 367; civilization of, 354–376 *passim*
Chirurgia, Lanfranc, 577
Christ. *See* Jesus Christ
Christ in the Universe, A. Meynell, 552–553
Christianity: 41n, 288, 404, 454, 499; Coleridge on, 80; idea of progress in, 515–543 *passim;* internal crisis in, 544–557 *passim;* and Buddhism, 555–556; and Hinduism, 555–556; Marsh on, 683–684, 688, 691, 696; and society, 728–731; and freedom of conscience, 733–735; and the French Revolution, 737
Christs Teares Over Jerusalem, T. Nashe, 592
Chrysostom, John, Saint, 518, 532
Cicero, 148, 149, 154, 187, 317, 427, 506—*On Divination,* 100, 101; *Orator,* 152; *Pro Archia poeta,* 154
Cimabue, Giovanni, 162, 214
Clark, Sir Kenneth, 93
Classicism, 21, 25, 170, 191
Clément, Charles, 137, 138
Clement of Alexandria, 495, 489
Cohen, Morris R., 33
Cohortatio ad Graecos, Pseudo-Justin Martyr, 486
Coke, Sir Edward, 65
Colbert, Jean Baptiste, 171, 172
Coleridge, Samuel: 12, 14; and Kant, 191, 668; and German romanticism, 191; and Goethe, 275; paramnesia in, 658–668 *passim;* Hartley's influence on, 663–664; and Schelling, 665–666; and Biship Berkeley, 668; and Swedenborg, 668–670; and De Quincey, 675; and Marsh, 678–696 *passim;* on Christianity, 681—*Anima Poetae,* 661, 662; *Table Talk,* 662; *Aids to Reflection,* 663, 678–682 *passim; Religious Musings,* 664; *Miscellanies,* 665; *Theory of Life,* 665; *Biographia Literaria,* 665, 667, 668, 675; *The Statesman's Manuel,* 678; *The Friend,* 678
Collectaneae, Praefationes, Epistolae, Orationes, Petrus Ramus, 168
Collectivism, 420
Collège de France, 361, 363, 367
Collier, Jeremy, 447, 455–456
Collingwood, R. G.: 32, 73, 74, 76; on history, 71

Comenius, John Amos, 34
Communism, 554. *See also* Marx, Marxism
Compendiosa totius Anatomiae delineatio, T. Gemini, 578
Compendious Declaration . . . , T. Rainold, 588
Compleat Body of Divinity, A, S. Willard, 632–634
Comte, Auguste: 418; and the sociology of knowledge, 33; on history, 40, 313; and the French Revolution, 405
Condillac, Etienne Bonnot de, 287, 302, 414
Condorcet, Antoine-Nicolas de, 425, 672
Confucius, 39, 358, 360, 363, 365
Confucianists, 355, 360
Consulate of Stilicho, On the, Claudianus, 516
Copernicus, 33, 39, 46, 269, 544
Copernican revolution, the: in ideas, 16; and Christian thought, 551–552
Coppenol, and Rembrandt, 221
Cornwell, Francis, 620–623 *passim*
Cosmology, 26
Cotton, John; and Hooker, 617–619; and Hutchinson, 619–621; and Increase Mather, 632—*The Way of Life*, 618; *The New Covenant*, 618, 624; *Gospel Conversion*, 619; *Exposition upon the Thirteenth Chapter of the Revelation*, 622; *A Reply to Mr. Williams*, 623; *Christ the Fountaine of Life*, 624; *A Treatise of the Covenant of Grace*, 624; *The Way of Congregational Churches Cleared*, 624, 625
Courtier, The, Castiglione, 166
Cousin, Victor: 189, 301; and Kant, 184; and the Roman Catholic Church, 285, 287—*Du Vrai, du Beau et du Bien*, 184
Cowper, William, paramnesia in, 660

Cranach, Lukas, 111
Criticism, literary, Coleridge's theory of, 665
Critische Betrachtungen über die Poetischen Gemälde der Dichter, J. Bodmer, 192
Critische Dichtkunst, J. Breitinger, 192
Croce, Benedetto: 32, 130; on philosophy, 52; on history, 59, 71–74 *passim;* on Vico, 169
Cromwell, Oliver: 381, 390; Milton on, 394–395; and the Puritan Revolution, 395–399
Cyclopaedia, E. Chambers, 169
Cyril of Alexandria, 532
Cyrurgia, Guido de Cauliaco, 577

Dance, the: 153, 155, 161, 181, 196; in ancient Greece, 150
Daniel, Samuel, 379
Dante, 12, 157, 273, 566, 662
Danton, Georges Jacques, 306, 415, 423
Darwin, Charles: 37, 269, 544, 680; influence on Taine, 291
Darwinism, 37, 40, 471–476 *passim*
Da Vinci, Leonardo, 93–144 *passim*, 163, 166, 165, 303
Dead Faith Anatomized, A, S. Mather, 633
Death of the Persecutors, On the, Lactantius, 528
Decker, Jeremias de, on Rembrandt, 220–221
Deism, 25, 405
Delisle de Sales, 411
Delvaille, J., 409
Democritus, 31, 216
Demos, Raphael, 486
Dennis, John, on poetry, painting, and music, 186–187
De Quincey, Thomas: paramnesia in, 673–677; and Coleridge, 675–*The Confessions of an Opium-Eater*, 674, 675, 676
Descartes, René: 28, 174, 203, 266, 415, 425, 485, 570, 706; and André,

180; on divine attributes, 512–514 passim; and Mersenne, 513—*Discours de la Méthode*, 31; *Meditatio*, 512; *Sextae Responsiones*, 512; *Principia Philosophiae*, 513
Descriptiones, Callistratus, 150, 152
Description of Greece. Pausanias, 101
Desmoulins, Camille, 413, 416
Determinism, psychological, in Taine, 305
Dewey, John: 698; on history, 71; and Addams, 472; and Aristotle compared, 638—*Art as Experience*, 38
Diacceto, Francesco da, 167
Dialogue against the feuer Pestilence, W. Bulletin, 582
Dialogue between Sorenes and Chyrurgi, W. Bulletin, 596–597
Dialogue philosophicall, A, T. Tymme, 579
Dictionnaire portatif des Beaux-Arts . . . , J. Lacombe, 183
Diderot, Denis: 188, 403, 414, 415; and Shaftesbury, Addison, and Hutcheson, 181; on the liberal and mechanical arts, 182—*Lettre sur les Sourds et Muets*, 181
Diece Libri de Pensieri Diversi, A. Tassoni, 169
Digression sur les Anciens et les Modernes, Fontenelle, 175
Dilthey, Wilhelm: 73, 707; on Bach, 264, 266; and existentialism, 698, 723; his interpretation of reality, 714—*Die Einleitung in die Geisteswissenschaften*, 700
Dionysius the Areopagite, 110, 158
Discourse of the Preservation of the Sight, A, A. Laurentius, 595
Discourse of the Suffocation of the Mother, E. Jorden, 595
Dissertation on the Rise . . . of Poetry and Musick, J. Brown, 190–191
Doctrine of Faith, The, J. Rogers, 616

Doctrines économiques en France depuis 1870, G. Pirou, 430
Domesticall Duties, Of, W. Gouge, 454–455
Dominic, Saint, 567
Donatello, 114
Donne, John, 384
Dostoevsky, Fyodor, 445
Double standard, the, in England, 446–467
Drummond, William, 662
Dryden, John, 186
Dubois, Pierre, 573
Dubos, Abbé, 178–179, 190, 192
Duhem, Pierre, 36, 37
Duns Scotus: 712; on divine attributes, 510–511—*Opera Oxoniensis*, 510
Dürer, Albrecht, 111, 139n
Durkheim, Emile, 325–332 passim—*The Elementary Forms of the Religious Life*, 325; *De La Division du Travail*, 327; *Le Suicide*, 327
Dury, John, 34
Dutie of a Faithfull Magistrate, Of the, J. Ewich, 593

Eckermann, Johann Peter, 278, 280, 282
Ecole des Beaux-Arts, 298, 299
Ecole Normale Superiéure, 284, 285, 286, 430
Economics, and religion, 68
Education: 53, 154; in the Middle Ages, 70, 156; Aristotle on, 153; in the Renaissance, 159; and socialism, 285, 442; Marsh on, 694–695
Edwards, Jonathan, 637
Einstein, Albert, 61, 269
Einzige und sein Eigentum, Der, M. Stirner, 699
Electricity, 61
Elements, Euclid, 31, 58
Elements of Criticism, Henry Home, Lord Kames, 190–191
Eliot, George: and Emerson, 426; and Rousseau, 426–427

Ellis, Havelock, 126n
Emerson, Ralph Waldo: 673, 684; and Goethe, 275; and Eliot, 426; influence on Addams, 471
Empedocles, 28
Empiricism, in James, 651
Encyclopédie ou Dictionnaire Raisonné des Sciences, des Arts et des Métiers, L', 181, 182, 183, 184, 199, 410, 413, 418
Encyclopedists, French, 33, 195
Engels, Friedrich, 699—*Anti-Dühring: Herr Eugen Dühring's Revolution in Science*, 444
England: nationalism in, 377–402; feudal law in, 462
English Mans Treasure, The, T. Vicary, 581
Enlightenment, the: 261, 262, 263, 425, 544; French, and the Italian Renaissance, 170; rationalism in, 335; and Romantic Sinophilia, 354, 361; and the French Revolution, 403–427 *passim*
Entretiens sur . . . des plus excellens Peintres anciens et modernes, A. Félibien, 133–134
Entusiasmo delle Belle Arti, Dell', S. Bettinelli, 170
Epistle Concerning the Excellencies of the English Tongue, An, R. Carew, 380
Epistle upon the Present Pestilence, An, H. Clapham, 692
Erasmus, 568
Erigena, John Scotus, 507—*De Divisione Naturae*, 502, 505; *De Praedestinatione*, 505
Eros di Leonardo, G. Fumagalli, 126n
Essay on Taste, An, A. Gerard, 190–191
Este, Isabella d', 116
Ethics: 202, 387, 414; in Medieval education, 156; in Addams' thought, 468–481 *passim*
Ethnology, 373

Euphues and His England, J. Lyly, 381
Euripides, 65
Eusebius: 518, 536, 538; on progress in history, 529–532, 534, 542–543 —*Historia Ecclesiastica*, 498, 526, 528; *Demonstratio Evangelica*, 528; *Life of Constantine*, 528–529; *Praeparatio Evangelica*, 530, 531; *Theophania*, 530–531
Evelyn, John, 185
Evolution, doctrine of, 472. *See also* Darwin, Darwinism
Existentialism: 74; and James, 700. *See also* Philosophy

Fall of Man, The, G. Goodman, 384
Familiares, Petrarch, 522
Farewell to Physicke, W. Cary, 589
Félibien, André, 173
Fénelon, Francois, 573
Feudalism: 288; in England, 462–463
Feuerbach, Ludwig: 700, 705, 707, 708; on alienation, 718–719; and Hegel, 722—*Grundsätze der Philosophie der Zukunft*, 699, 708, 713–714
Fichte, Johann Gottlieb: 65, 277, 281, 685; and Rousseau, 426; influence on American philosophers, 656
Ficino, Marsilio, 167
Fide Orthodoxa, De, John of Damascus, 503
Fioravanti, 588
Flaubert, Gustave, 295
Flinck, Govaert, 220, 222
Folklore, 94, 102, 373
Fons Vitae, Avicebrol, 506
Fouillée, Alfred, 419
Fourier, Charles, 430
Fournière, Eugène, 430
Fox, George, and Anne Hutchinson, 625
Francis of Assisi, Saint, 566, 567, 574
Franck, Salomo, 243

Fréart de Chambray, 173
Frederick the Great, 279
Freemasons, and the French Revolution, 406, 408
French Academy in Rome, 171
French Revolution, the: 293, 307, 388, 399; Taine on, 308; influence of 18th-century ideas on, 403–427; and the Freemasons, 405, 407
Freud, Sigmund: 127, 140, 458, 459, 713; on Da Vinci, 93–126 *passim*; on sexual morality, 459–460; and Addams, 479—*Eine Kindheitserinnerung des Leonardo da Vinci*, 93, 104, 141–142
Freudianism, 143, 473
Fries, Jakob Friedrich, and Marsh, 679, 685
Fromm, Erich, 86
Fruits of Philosophy, Knowlton, 467

Galen, 152, 163, 577, 580, 588
Galileo, 29, 33, 174
Gautier, Théophile: 138, 139n, 140, 143, 676; on Da Vinci, 135–136
Geology, 45, 64
Geometry: 154, 155, 156, 334, 686; in Renaissance art academies, 163
Geschichte des Chinesischen Reiches ..., Die, O. Francke, 367
Ghandi, 39
Ghiberti, Lorenzo, 214
Gibbon, Edward, 29
Gilbert de la Porrée, 505, 506, 507, 508
Ginsberg, Morris, 71n
Giocondo, Francesco del, 128
Giono, Jean, 403
Giotto, 162, 214
Giovio, Paolo, 129
Gladstone, William, 458
Godwin, William, and Shelley, 671–672
Goethe, Johann Wolfgang von: 148, 204; his aesthetic theory, 200–201; his debt to Spinoza, 272; and Leibniz, 273; and Christianity, 275; influence on Arnold, 275; influence on Carlyle, 275; influence on Coleridge, 275; influence on Emerson, 275; influence on Schiller, 275, 281; and romanticism, 276–278, 281; influence on Hegel, 280–281; and Nietzsche, 281; and Rousseau, 426—*Wilhelm Meisters Wanderjahre*, 201, 280, 281; *Faust*, 269–279 *passim; Dichtung und Wahrheit*, 282
Golden Bough, The J. Frazer, 324
Golden Legend, The, J. Voragine, 101, 110
Gospel-Covenant, The, P. Bulkeley, 614–615
Gottschalk, Louis, on history, 78
Government of Health, The, W. Bulletin, 596
Grammar, in the liberal arts, 154–159 *passim*, 182
Granet, Marcel: 368, 373; on Chinese antiquity, 367
Gravitation, laws of, 61
Gray, Alexander, on socialism, 429
Green, Thomas Hill, 639
Greenlaw, Edwin, 14
Grosseteste, Robert, 574

Hakluyt, Richard, 382
Hall, G. Stanley, 471
Hals, Frans, 208, 222
Hamann, Johann Georg, 699
Handel, George Frederick, 191, 226, 228, 231, 234, 251, 253, 256, 259, 264
Hannibal, 537
Harris, William Torrey, 639
Hartley, David: 667; and Locke, 663; influence on Coleridge, 663–664—*Observations on Man ...*, 663–665
Hartmann, Nicolai, 713
Harvard University, 376
Harvey, William, 603
Haydn, Franz Joseph, 28
Heaton, Mrs. Charles W., 135
Hegel, G. W. F.: 31, 53, 62, 65, 279, 304, 305, 335, 685, 702, 707, 720; and the sociology of knowledge, 33; on history, 40, 44, 66, 142, 272,

313; his determinism, 63; Goethe's influence on, 280, 281; on Asian civilizations, 366; and Prussian absolutism, 426n; on the French Revolution, 426n; influence on American philosophers, 639–641, 656; and Lotze, 643; his doctrine of essences, 702–703; and Schelling, 703–704, 710; and Marx, 704, 705; and Feuerbach, 722—*The Phenomenology of the Mind*, 351, 426n; *The Philosophy of Right*, 702, 703; *The Science of Logic*, 703

Hegelian Idealists, on history, 51

Hegelianism: and metaphysical materialism, 638; and positivism, 639

Heidegger, Martin: 698–724 *passim*; on time, 716—*Sein und Zeit*, 698, 701, 712, 716, 718; *Kant and the Problem of Metaphysics*, 714

Heine, Heinrich, 279

Heisenberg, Werner, 51

Held, Julius, on Rembrandt, 211

Helvétius, Claude Adrien, 407

Heraclitus of Ephesus, 44–45, 216, 489, 719

Hérault de Séchelles, 416

Herder, Johann Gottfried von: 200; and Aristotle, 201; and Lessing, 201; on aesthetics, 201–202 *passim*

Heresis, Against, Irenaeus of Lyons, 517, 530

Hermann, K. F., 486

Hermiae, Ammonius. *See* Ammonius Hermiae

Herodotus, 52

Hesiod, 149

Hesse, Hermann, 281

Hieroglyphica, P. Valeriano, 94, 100

'Higher Criticism', and Spinoza, 36

Hinduism, and Christianity, 555–556

Hippocrates, 148, 577, 580

Hippolytus, 517

Histoire des Peintres de Toutes les Ecoles, P. Mantz, 135, 137

Historicism, and political philosophy, 333–353 *passim*

Historiography: 32, 81–89 *passim*; of ideas, 25; in the 17th century, 35; scientific, 39–40; theory of, 69–80; and political philosophy, 333–353 *passim*

Historische Taschenbuch, F. von Raumer, 224

History: 35, 169, 183, 373, 704; and allied disciplines, 3–9 *passim*, 73–89 *passim*; causation in, 4–5, 42–68; of ideas, reflections on, 9–23 *passim*; of ideas, problems and methods in 24–41; objectivity in the study of, 69–73 *passim*; and the liberal arts, 155–206 *passim*; philosophy of, 313–317 *passim*; and the humanities, 313–317 *passim*; and political philosophy, 333–353; progress in, 343–349 *passim*; justice in, 438; Hellenistic theory of, 517; Christian interpretation of, 544–557 *passim*; and myth, 547–557 *passim*; and freedom of thought, 558–559; and medieval scholasticism, 559; James on, 654; Lotze on, 654; Schelling on, 716. *See also* Historicism, Historiography

History of European Morals, W. E. H. Lecky, 448

History of Painting in Italy, The, L. Lanzi, 134

History of the Royal Society of London . . ., T. Sprat, 386–387

History of the War of the Ancients and Moderns, F. de Callière, 186

Hitler, Adolf, 38, 42, 279

Hobbes, Thomas, 35, 733

Holbach, Baron d', 414

Homer, 65, 149

Hoogstraeten, Samuel van, on Rembrandt, 224

Hooker, Thomas, 609–637 *passim*

Horace, 49, 149, 180, 217, 567—*De arte poetica*, 151, 164, 173

Horapollo, 94

Houbraken, Arnold, 208

Houssaye, Arsène, 134, 137

Hubbard, Elbert, 135, 139

Hughes, Randolph, 676
Hugo, Victor, 404
Hugo of St. Victor: and Thomas Aquinas, 156; and Vincent of Beauvais, 156
Huizinga, Johan, 207
Humanism: 14, 317, 371, 387; in the Middle Ages, 159; Christian, 472, 727; and Neo-Thomism, 558–576 passim
Hume, David: 21, 28, 639, 643; his scepticism, 22; on history, 40, 313, 350; on causation, 53–54; on the double standard, 467—*Essays Moral and Political*, 53–54; *A Treatise of Human Nature*, 54; *An Enquiry Concerning the Principles of Morals*, 188; *Theory of Politics*, 467
Husserl, Edmund, 700, 703, 705
Hutcheson, Francis: 182; and Shaftesbury, 188; and Reid, 189 —*An Inquiry into the Original of our Ideas of Beauty and Virtue*, 188
Hutchinson, Anne: 636; and Cotton, 619–621; and Wheelwright, 621–622; and Fox, 625
Huygens, Christian, on Rembrandt, 218–219, 223
Huygens, Constantin, on Rembrandt, 212–215, 218, 221

Iconology, 36
Idea of Progress, The, G. H. Hildebrand, 532
Idealism: in American philosophy, 21; in Berkeley's thought, 21–22; moral, in Lotze, 652; moral, in James, 652
Iggers, Georg, on the Saint-Simonians, 429
Imagines, Philostratus, 152
Immaculate Conception, the doctrine of, 107, 108, 112, 116
Incertitudine et vanitate scientiarum, Agrippa of Nettesheim, 168
Individualism: 25, 33, 41, 77, 333, 390, 399, 400, 401, 693, 694; and universal qualities, 27; in history, 43, 434; and Pietism, 265; and socialism, 428–445; in James' thought, 653–654; modern, and religion, 725–738
Industrial Revolution, and working-class morality, 457
Institutio Oratoria, Quintilian, 151
Irenaeus, Saint, 518, 525
Isidore of Seville, 156
Islam, theology of, 501–506 passim

James, William: 474, 698; and Addams, 472; and Socrates, 638; and Lotze, 638–657 passim; and Hegel, 640; interest in psychology, 641; his practicalism, 643; and Kant, 643; on nature, 647; his empiricism, 651; on human nature, 651; his moral idealism, 652; individualism in, 653–654; on history, 654; on religion, 654–655; and existentialism, 700— *Principles of Psychology*, 638, 641, 647, 648, 649, 652; *Collected Essays and Reviews*, 642; *A Pluralistic Universe*, 642; *The Varieties of Religious Experience*, 642; *The Meaning of Truth*, 648, 650; *Pragmatism*, 648; *Essays in Radical Empiricism*, 649, 650; *Talks to Teachers on Psychology*, 653; *The Will to Believe*, 654
Jansenism, 565
Jaspers, Karl, 698–723 passim
Jaurès, Jean: career, 430–431; on individualism, 431–445 passim— *De la Réalité du Monde Sensible*, 430
Jean de Meun, 662
Jefferson, Thomas, 65
Jerome, Saint, 515–516, 518, 524, 532, 534
Jesus Christ, 39, 65, 93–122 passim, 221, 268, 414, 444, 445, 493, 494, 517, 526–538 passim, 549, 587, 619–631 passim, 689

Jinsai, Ito, 360
Johnson, Andrew, 60
Johnson, Samuel. *See Life of Samuel Johnson*
Jones, Ernest, 102, 126n, 459
Jowett, Benjamin, 36
Julien, Stanislas, 363, 364
Julius Caesar, 40n, 43, 271, 272
Jung, Carl, 126n
Jurisprudence, 156, 165, 335

Kangakusha, schools of, 360–361, 369
Kant, Immanuel: 65, 140, 147, 189, 196, 198, 639, 645, 691, 700, 702, 713, 714, 715, 717; and Cousin, 184; and Coleridge, 191; on aesthetics, 202–205; and Rousseau, 426; and James, 643; and Coleridge, 668; influence on Marsh, 679–688 *passim*; his 'Copernican revolution,' 699; and Schelling, 706—*Beobachtungen über das Gefühl des Schönen und Erhabenen*, 202; *Kritik der reinen Vernunft*, 202, 315; *Kritik der Urtheilskraft*, 202–203; *Träume eines Geistersehers*, 675, 676
Keats, John, 661, 673
Keiser, Reinhard, 233, 234
Keller, Gottfried, 281
Key of Philosophie, The, J. Hester, 588
Kierkegaard, Sören: 698–723 *passim*; on alienation, 718—*Philosophical Fragments*, 699; *Concluding Unscientific Postscript*, 699, 703, 704, 705, 713
Kiesewetter, Christoph, 230
Kinsey, A. C., 466
Kleist, Heinrich von, 278
Koch, Robert, 26
Kolloff, Eduard, 224
Krieger, Leonard, 35
Kropotkin, Peter, 473

Lactantius, Firmianus, 518, 525, 530
La Fontaine, 286, 288

Lamb, Charles, 12
Lamprecht, S. P., 46
Langlois, François, 216, 217
Lanson, Gustave, 406
Lao-Tze, 39
Law: natural, in Roman jurisprudence, 340; positive, in Roman jurisprudence, 340, 388; common, in England, 388; feudal, in England, 462
Lawrence, D. H., Rousseau's influence on, 426
Legge, James, 364
Leibniz, G. W. von: 28, 203; his monadology, 32; on history, 35; influence on Goethe, 273
Lemonnier, P. C., 132
Lenin, Nikolai, 407
Leninism, 373
Léonard de Vinci, Delecluze, 134
Leonardo da Vinci, P. Valéry, 143
Leonardo da Vinci and His Works, C. W. Heaton, 139
Leonardo the Florentine, R. Taylor, 142
Le Play, Frédéric, and the French Revolution, 405
Lerner, Max, 16
Leroux, Pierre, 428
Lessing, Gotthold Ephraim: 65, 201n, 558, 700; and Herder, 201 —*Laokoon*, 196, 197, 201
Lewis, C. S., 10, 11, 13n
Liberal Arts, the: in Antiquity, 147–155 *passim*; in the Middle Ages, 156–159
Liberalism: the crisis in, 35; Taine on, 307–308
Lievens, Jan, 212, 213, 214
Life of Samuel Johnson, The, J. Boswell, 460, 465
Lincoln, Abraham, 39, 60, 272, 471
Linguistics, 373, 556
Literary Criticism, 170–176 *passim*
Literature: 171, 185–206 *passim*; and aesthetics, 9–16 *passim*; and humanism, 14; Christian, 110; in the Middle Ages, 159; Latin, in

the Renaissance, 160, 162–164, 166; in 17th-century England, 185. *See also* Poetry, Romanticism
Loci e Libro Veritatum, T. Gascoigne, 572
Locke, John: 21, 22, 28, 33, 53, 415, 417, 418, 643, 667, 672, 682, 683; his theory of ideas, 26; and empirical psychology, 305; his political philosophy, 339; and the French Revolution, 405, 406; and Hartley, 663—*An Essay Concerning Human Understanding,* 456, 671
Logic: 150; and the sociology of knowledge, 17; and the history of ideas, 19–23 *passim;* and the liberal arts, 154, 156, 157, 182
Logische Untersuchungen, F. A. Trendelenburg, 699, 703
Lombard, Peter. *See* Peter Lombard
Lopez, Alphonso, and Rembrandt, 207
Lotze, Rudolf Hermann: influence on James, 638–657 *passim;* on nature, 644–645, 650; moral idealism in, 652; on history, 654; on religion, 654–655; and Hegel, 656—*Die Medicinische Psychologie,* 641, 643; *Die Metaphysik,* 641, 644, 648, 650; *Mikrokosmus,* 644, 650–655 *passim; Die Logik,* 645, 646
Louvre, 97, 98, 111–120 *passim*
Lovejoy, Arthur O.: 86, 131; on the history of ideas, 3–23—*The Great Chain of Being,* 3n; *Essays in the History of Ideas,* 25
Löwith, Karl, 700
Lucas, E. V., 135
Luchaire, Achille, on religion in the Middle Ages, 570
Lugt, Frits, 207
Lukaciewicz, on Aristotle, 27
Lulli, G. B., 171, 191
Luther, Martin: 712; on the cult of Saint Anne, 106; on the Christian commonwealth, 732–733

Lytell Pratyce in Medycyne, Johannes de Vigo, 585

Mably, G. B. de, 405, 411, 415
McCurdy, Edward, 135—*Leonardo da Vinci,* 139–140
Mach, Ernst, 29
Machiavelli, Niccolò, 35
MacIver, A. M., 71n
Maclagan, Eric, 98-99, 126n
Magnus, Albertus. *See* Albertus Magnus
Maimonides, 506, 508
Maistre, Joseph de, and the French Revolution, 405
Malinowski, B. K., his sociology, 323–332 *passim*
Malon, Benoît, 430
Malthusianism, 40
Mann, Thomas, 280, 281
Mannheim, Karl, 17, 33
Manufacturing Population of England, The, P. Gaskell, 457
Marat, J. P., 306, 415
Marcus Agrippa, 216
Maritain, Jacques, and humanism, 558–576 *passim*
Marmontel, J. F., 415
Marrow of Sacred Divinity, The, W. Ames, 608
Marsh, James: and Coleridge, 678–696 *passim;* on modern philosophy, 678–679; and Kant, 679–688 *passim;* and Fries, 679, 685; on Christianity, 683–684, 688–691, 696; his rational psychology, 686–688; and Greek philosophy, 687–688; his social philosophy, 691–692; on education, 694–695
Marshall, John, 65
Marsilius of Padua, 573
Marvell, Andrew, 390
Marx, Karl: 304, 305, 407, 408, 410, 430, 437; on history, 33, 66, 313, 431, 434; on Hegel, 272, 704, 705; on Asian civilizations, 366; and existentialism, 698–723 *passim;* on human nature and alienation, 710–723 *passim*

Marxism, 40, 143, 373, 403, 413, 473
Mary, Saint, 93–122 *passim,* 221, 568
Masaccio, 111, 119
Maspero, Henri, 367, 368, 373
Materialism, historical; influence on Japanese scholarship, 370, 371; and the French Revolution, 412
Mathematics: 151, 155, 686; in physics, 57; and painting, 163; and symbolic systems, 556
Mather, Cotton, 634–636 *passim*
Mather, Increase, 632
Matrimonial Honour, D. Rogers, 454
Maurras, Charles, 405, 419
Mazzini, Giuseppe, 471, 737
Mechanics, 65, 176
Medicina, De, C. Celsus, 577
Medicine: 57, 165; and the liberal arts, 154; in the Middle Ages, 156; and theology, 577–603 *passim.* See also Koch, Pasteur
Medieval People, E. Power, 568
Melville, Herman, 673
Mendeleyev, D. I., 29
Mendelssohn, Moses: 201; and 18th-century aesthetics, 196–199
Mersenne, Marin: 30, 266; and Descartes, 512
Metaphysics: 83, 432; scholastic, Voltaire on, 38
Method of Phisick, The, P. Barrough, 585, 590
Methodology, in the history of ideas, 3–41 *passim*
Meun, Jean de. *See* Jean de Meun
Meyer, Ludovicus, 513
Michelangelo, 119, 221, 282
Michelet, Jules, 404, 422
Middle Ages, the: 379; liberal arts in, 156; serfdom in, 561–564; Jews in, 565; censorship in, 569–571; education in, 571
Midsummer of Italian Art, The, F. P. Stearns, 139
Mill, John Stuart: 63, 430, 639, 643, 682; on Bentham, 80; on religion, 680–681
Milton, John, on liberty, 390–394
Mirabeau, Comte de, 415, 423
Miscellanies . . . , Marquis of Halifax, 447
Mises, Ludwig von, 429
Modest Defence of Publick Stews, A, B. Mandeville, 448
Modo Generalis Concilii Habendi, De, G. Durand, 573
Mohammed, 216
Molière, 566
Montaigne: 133, 408, 414, 418, 425; on Socrates, 270
Montesquieu: 33, 405–414 *passim,* 425; and the French Revolution, 416–417
Monteverdi, Claudio, 248, 266
Moralium Exemplorum libri novem, V. Maximus, 101
More, Henry, and Newton, 32
More, Sir Thomas, 383, 563, 564
Morellet, André, 411
Morelly, N., 414
Mornet, Daniel, 406, 407, 412—*Les Origines intellectuelles de la Révolution française,* 410–411, 419
Morris, William, and Taine, 300
Most Excellent Worckes of Chirurgery, The, J. Vigo, 578
Mozart, Wolfgang Amadeus, 28, 547
Müller, Max, 326
Munzer, Thomas, 239
Music: in ancient Greece, 150, 151; and poetry, 153–161 *passim,* 170–206 *passim;* theory of, in the Renaissance, 161–162, 166; theory of, in ancient Greece, 173; and painting, 173; in the 18th century, 225–268
Musophilus, S. Daniel, 380, 382
Mysticism, 28

Napoleon, 43, 45, 59, 272, 305, 416, 424, 425, 450
Nationalism: 692; English, genesis of, 377–402; and socialism, 440

National Socialism, 554
Nature: 25, 131, 132, 337, 423; and art, 148; Lotze on, 644–645; James on, 647; and romanticism, 658
Nature, human: problem of, 8–9; Taine on, 296; Milton on, 391; Addams on, 468–481 *passim*; James on, 651; Marx on, 710–723 *passim*
Naudé, Gabriel, 407
Needefull Treatise of Chyrurgerie, J. Banister, 584
Neo-Platonism and Neo-Platonists, 32, 123, 132, 499, 501, 662
Neo-Thomism and Neo-Thomists, 158–159, 558–576 *passim*
Nerval, Gérard de, 676
Neumeister, Erdmann, 243, 244, 257
Nevv Convenant, J. Preston, 610
Newton, Isaac: 61; and Galileo, 30; and Kepler, 30; indebtedness to More, 32; and the Cambridge Neo-Platonists, 32
Nietzsche, Friedrich: 279, 280, 410, 418, 420, 706–723 *passim*; and Goethe, 280, 281; influence on American Philosophers, 656; and existentialism, 698, 699; on alienation, 718
Nominalism, 26, 34, 64
Norton, John, 630–633 *passim*
Novellara, Pietro da, 116

Occam (Ockham), William of: 560; and Augustine, 508; on divine attributes, 508–511 *passim*
Opera: 176, 204; in the Renaissance, 162; in 18th-century Germany, 233
Opitz, Martin, 192
Oratio, Dio Chrysostom, 152
Oratio Contra Arianos, Athanasius, 500
Oriential Despotism, K. Wittfogel, 375
Origen: 494, 497, 498, 523, 527, 528; and Ammonius Saccas, 499; and Augustine, 524, 525; on the Incarnation, 546—*In Joannem*, 494, *Against Celsus*, 527, 530
Ortega y Gasset, José, 315, 409
Ostade, Adriaen van, 208
Owen, Robert, 735

Paganism, in the Italian Renaissance, 300
Paine, Thomas, 84, 737
Painting: 151–161 *passim*, 179–206 *passim*; and poetry, 164–178 *passim*; and sculpture, 165; as a science, 166; and the liberal arts, 167; and music, 173
Panaetius, 149, 152
Paracelsus, 588
Paré, Ambroise, 580, 590, 561, 603
Pareto, Vilfredo, his sociology, 321–332 *passim*
Parmenides, 661, 662
Parrhasius, 214
Parrington, Vernon L., 86
Parthenon, 127, 299
Pascal, Blaise, 31, 425, 558, 699
Pasteur, Louis, 26
Pater, Walter, 97, 139
Paul, Saint, 517, 518, 519, 537
Peacham, Henry, 185
Pearle of Practice, J. Hester, 588
Pearson, Karl, on scientific method, 48, 54
Peirce, Charles S., 33, 36, 41, 61, 643
Pelagianism, 627, 631
Pels, Andries, on Rembrandt, 223, 224
Pemble, William, 616, 617, 618
Perfetta poesia italiana, Della, L. A. Muratori, 169
Perfume against the Noysome Pestilence, A, R. Fenton, 591
Perrault, Charles: 179; and Wotton, 185–186—*Parallèle des Anciens et des Modernes*, 175; *Le Cabinet des Beaux Arts*, 176
Peter, Saint, 537
Peter Lombard: 508; and Albertus Magnus, 507; and Aquinas, 507

Petrarch, 661
Philo of Alexandria (Philo Judaeus): 216; on Platonic ideas, 487–496 *passim;* and Plotinus, 498—*De Opificio Mundi,* 488; *De Fuga et Inventione,* 492; *Quis Rerum Divinarum Heres,* 492
Philology, 94
Philosophes, the: 430; and the French Revolution, 403–427 *passim,* 435
Philosophie au Moyen Age, La, E. Gilson, 560
Philosophy: 86, 87, 110, 154, 183, 503; history of, 21; ancient, 152, 270–271, 687–688; and the liberal arts, 154, 157, 158, 182–206 *passim;* in Medieval education, 156, 159; in the Renaissance, 159; political, and history, 333–353; and theology, 485–514; symbolic systems in, 556; American, and Marsh, 678–697; existential 698–724. *See also* Cosmology, Empiricism, Enlightenment, Ethics, Humanism, Idealism, Individualism, Logic, Metaphysics, Positivism, Pragmatism, Realism, Relativism, Scholasticism, Utilitarianism
Philostratus, 163
Phonetics, 373
Physics: 64, 65, 66; in antiquity, 32; laws of, 51; mathematical formulations in, 57; in the Middle Ages, 156. *See also* Einstein, Galileo, Gravitation, Mach
Pico Della Mirandola, 573
Pietism, 230, 239–241
Piles, R. de, 173
Placitis Philosophorum, De, Aëtius, 486
Planctu Ecclesiae, A. Pelagius, 572
Plato: 26, 27, 31, 36, 65, 80, 101, 149, 154, 164, 184, 187, 217, 270, 337, 417, 418, 472, 485–514 *passim,* 662, 694, 688; his theory of ideas, 25, 30, 484–513 *passim;* his cosmology, 38, 488; on history, 66; on art, 148, 152; on politics, 339; Whitehead on, 484—*Parmenides,* 26, 490, 491; *Apology,* 31, 149, 270, 271; *Crito,* 31, 271; *Phaedo,* 31, 271; *Timaeus,* 38, 152, 488, 489, 490, 491, 698; *Phaedrus,* 148, 149, 150, 490; *Symposium,* 148, 271, 490; *Ion,* 149; *Republic,* 150, 151, 152, 153, 334, 490; *Cratylus,* 153; *Sophist,* 153, 491
Platonism: 26; in the Renaissance, 160, 177
Pleasures of Memory, The, S. Rogers, 670
Pleasures of the Imagination, The, M. Akenside, 190
Pliny, the Elder, 130, 163
—*Natural History,* 100, 101, 152
Plotinus: 187, 497, 664; on beauty, 149, 166, 167; on art, 152; his theory of ideas, 487; and Philo, 498; and Ammonius Saccas, 499 —*Enneades,* 487
Plutarch, 31, 32, 52, 164
Poe, Edgar Allan, 673
Poeticarum Institutionum, Jacobus Pontanus, 166, 170
Poetices libri septem, C. Scaliger 168
Poetics, La Mesnardière, 170
Poetry: 149, 150, 151, 152, 153, 160, 180, 181; and the liberal arts, 154, 155, 157, 159, 161, 178, 182–206 *passim;* baroque, 162; theory of, in French classicism, 170–176; in 17th-century England, 185. *See also* Literature, Romanticism
Poincaré, Henri, 61
Polybius, 20, 52
Popper, Karl, 33
Porphyry: 500; on Ammonius Saccas, 498—*De Abstinentia ab Esu Animalium,* 103, 123; *Isagoge,* 500
Positivism: 51, 577; in social theory, 319–332 *passim;* influence on Addams, 471, 472; and Hegelianism, 639

Poussin, Nicolas, 171, 173, 210
Pragmatism: 25, 371, 700; and Addams, 472; origins of, 642–643
Price, Derek, 29
Proclus, 31, 148, 184
Profitable and Necessarie Booke of Obseruations, A, W. Clowes, 584, 596
Progress: 41, 56, 362, 410, 726; in history, 343–349 *passim;* and science, 29, 382–383, 385; the Christian idea of, 515–543 *passim;* idea of, in contemporary thought, 546–547; in Western civilization, 732
Prooued Practice for all young Chirurgians, A, W. Clowes, 584
Protestantism: and capitalism, 328; preparation for salvation in, 604–636 *passim*
Protogenes, 214
Proudhon, Pierre-Joseph, 410, 428, 430, 442
Proust, Marcel, and Baudelaire, 677
Psychoanalytic Explorations in Art, E. Kris, 108, 118
Psychoanalysis: and art, 93–126 *passim,* 140–143 *passim;* dissociation in, 458–459
Psychologism, 33
Psychology: 53, 75, 140, 288, 296, 319, 320, 459; and 18th-century aesthetics, 191; empirical, and Locke, 305; and symbolic systems, 556. *See also* Addams, Freud, Hall, Hartley, James, Jung, Lotze, Marsh, Psychologism
Ptolemy, 33, 39
Pufendorf, Samuel von, and 17th-century historiography, 35
Pulchro, De, Augustinus Niphus, 167
Puritans, the: 307, 402, 455, 565; and English nationalism, 387–395 *passim;* on adultery, 463–464; in New England, 604–637

Quakers and Quakerism, 471, 625
Quetelet, L. A. J., 51

Rabaut de Saint-Etienne, Jean-Paul, 415–416
Rabelais, 133
Racialism, 40
Rainow, T. I., on Alberuni's alleged Darwinism, 37
Raleigh, Sir Walter, and English nationalism, 382
Ranke, Leopold von, 366, 369
Raphael, 115, 119, 129, 133, 217, 221, 223, 299
Raynal, G. T. F., 405, 412, 416
Real Christian, The G. Firmin, 617
Realism, Platonic, in German Philosophy, 649
Reason and Revolution, H. Marcuse, 700
Redon, Odilon, 129
Reformation, the: 387, 391, 452, 565, 567, 732; and English nationalism, 379–380; individualism in, 434; slavery in, 562. *See also* Anabaptists, Arminianism, Calvin, Luther, Pietism, Protestantism, Puritans, Quakers, Roman Catholic Church, Theology
Refutation of Three Opposers of Truth, A, G. Keith, 625
Reid, Thomas, and Hutcheson, 189
Relativism, historical, in Taine, 288–309 *passim*
Religion: 67, 106, 147, 178, 414; and economics, 68; in the Renaissance, 162; sociology of, 318–332; in James's thought, 654–655; Lotze on, 654–655; and modern individualism, 725–738. *See also* Catholicism, Christianity, Islam, Pietism, Protestantism, Puritans, Reformation, Quakers, Roman Catholic Church, Theology
Remaines, J. Preston, 611n
Rembrandt, 209–224 *passim*
Remedy against Despair, A., S. Willard, 635–636
Rémusat, Abel, and Sinology in France, 361–364—*Les Nouveaux Mélanges Asiatique,* 362

Renaissance, the: 150, 177, 185, 298, 379, 380, 391, 522, 738; aesthetic theory in, 157–170; music theory in, 161–162; literature in, 162, 166; religion in, 162, 576–602 *passim;* painting in, 162, 163, 166; Italian, and the French Enlightenment, 170; Italian, and French classicism, 170; paganism in, 300; Taine on, 300–313; Tudor, and Francis Bacon, 382; English patriotism in, 388–389; individualism in, 434; and the idea of progress, 546; medicine in, 577–603 *passim;* philosophers in, 662; tyrants in, 731

Renan, Ernest: 404; and the French Revolution, 405; and Catholicism, 559

Renouvier, Charles, 639, 653

Repplier, Anges, 468

Republica Anglorum, De, T. Smith, 380

Restif de La Bretonne, 415

Reynolds, Sir Joshua, 186

Rhetoric, 150, 154, 156, 157, 159

Richelieu, and the Académie Française, 171

Rickert, Heinrich, 71n, 73, 74

Riess, Ludwig, 369

Rijksmuseum, 220

Robespierre: 306, 407, 410; and Catholicism, 422; and Rousseau, 422–423—*Mémoires,* 422; *Observations sur le Projet d'Instruction Publique,* 422–423

Rolland, Madame, 422

Roman Catholic Church, 107, 110, 285, 414, 550–551, 730–731. See also Catholicism, Christianity, Religion, Theology

Roman empire: barbarian invasions of, 46–49, 55; and China, 55–56

Romanticism: 25, 135, 137, 191; in literature, 21; German, and Coleridge, 191; and Taine, 288–292 *passim;* and Rousseau, 424; and timelessness, 658–677 *passim;* and Schelling, 722. *See also* Poetry

Rome and China, F. J. Teggart, 47

Ronsard, Pierre de, 662

Roosevelt, Theodore, 468

Rousseau, Jean-Jacques: 31, 403–427 *passim,* 445; and the French Revolution, 417–427; on wealth, 420; influence on Robespierre, 422–423; cult of, 424; and romanticism, 424; and Fichte, 426; and Goethe, 426; influence on Kant, 426; influence on Lawrence, 426; influence on Thoreau, 426; influence on Eliot, 426–427; and Tolstoi, 426; paramnesia in, 661—*Le Contrat Social,* 408–424 *passim; Discours sur l'Inégalité,* 417, 418, 421; *La Nouvelle Heloïse,* 418, 659; *Emile,* 421; *Les Confessions,* 426, 660

Rousseau et la Révolution Française, E. Champion, 408

Rousseau et Tolstoi, M. Markovitch, 426

Royal Academy, 97

Royal Society, 174, 185, 385–386

Royce, Josiah, 639

Rubens, 122, 210, 220

Ruisdael, Jacob, 208, 222

Ruskin, John, 300

Sabellianism, 501, 502, 503

Saccas, Ammonius. *See* Ammonius Saccas

Sade, Marquis de, 414

Saint-Evremond, 407

Saint-Just, Louis-Antoine de: 410, 420, 423; and Rousseau, 421–422 —*Discours Concernant le Jugement de Louis XVI,* 420; *L'Esprit de la Révolution et de la Constitution de la France,* 422

Saint-Simon, Henri de, and individualism, 429

Sallustius, 547

Sandrart, Joachim von, on Rembrandt, 222–224

Sarto, Andrea del, 129

Sartre, Jean-Paul, 403

Savonarola, 168
Schapiro, J. Salwyn, on Proudhon, 428
Scheler, Max, 354, 723
Schelling, F. W. J. von: 65, 277, 698, 700, 702, 709, 713; and Coleridge, 665–668; on Hegel, 703–704, 710; and Kant, 706; on history, 716; and German romanticism, 722— *Die Philosophie der Mythologie und der Offenbarung*, 699; *Philosophy of Freedom*, 699; *Weltalter*, 699, 715; *On Human Freedom*, 712, 717
Schlegel, J. A., 193
Schiller, J. C. F. von: 148; and Goethe, 275, 281; on poetry, 273
Schinz, Albert, on Rousseau, 421
Scholasticism, medieval, and history, 559
Schopenhauer, Arthur: 65, 140, 281, 712; and Goethe, 277n; influence on American philosophers, 656— *The World as Will and Idea*, 699
Schutz, Heinrich, 229, 230, 231, 232, 248
Science: history of, 29; progress in, 29; humanistic, Tatarkiewicz on, 39; physical, causation in, 68. See also Astronomy, Biology, Electricity, Evolution, Geology, Mechanics, Medicine, Physics
Scientific method, Person on, 48, 54
Scientific thought, continuity in, 30
Sculpture: 150–173 *passim*, 179–206 *passim*; in the Renaissance, 162–163; and painting, 165
Séailles, Gabriel, 135
Secret of Hegel, The, J. Stirling, 639
Seilliére, Ernest, 419
Seneca, 152, 414
Serfdom, in the Middle Ages, 561–564
Settignano, Desiderio da, 114
Seven Books of Histories against the Pagans, Orosius, 521–522
Sextus Empiricus, 154
Shaftesbury, Anthony, Earl of: 192; influence on 18th-century aesthetics, 187–188; and Hutcheson, 188
Shakespeare: 12, 36, 65, 128, 219; and Goethe, 273, 282; and Taine, 294
Shelley, Percy Bysshe: 673; paramnesia in, 658–659; and Godwin, 671–672
Shepard, Thomas, 614, 619, 621; 627–628, 637
Short Dialogue Concerning the Plagues Infection, A, J. Balmford, 593
Short Discoverie of Ignorant Practisers of Phisicke, J. Cotta, 580
Shorte Treatize of the Plague, A, T. Beza, 593
Siéyès, Abbé, 415
Siéyès et sa pensée, P. Bastid, 415
Simmel, Georg, 723
Simonides, 151, 164
Simons, Walter M., 35
Sinology, development of, in Europe, 361–364
Sistine Chapel, 108
Smith, Adam, 82
Socialism: and education, 285; English, 401; myths of, 425; in the French Revolution, 434–436; and nationalism, 440; and Addams, 476. See also Babeuf, L. Blanc, Blanqui, Engels, Jaurès, Leroux, Marx, Marxism, Proudhon, Saint-Simon
Social theory: positivism in, 319–332 *passim*. See also Durkheim, Malinowski, Marx, Pareto, Weber
Sociétés de Pensée, Les, A. Cochin, 405
Sociologism: M. R. Cohen's critique of, 33; Popper on, 33
Sociology: 53, 73, 75, 373; of knowledge, 17–19, 33–34; of religion, 318–332
Socrates: 25, 39, 65, 270–281 *passim*, 448, 490, 558, 699, 708, 709; and James compared, 637
Sophists, 150

Sophocles, 65
Southey, Robert, 294
Spectator, The, and 18th-century aesthetics, 188
Spencer, Herbert: 320, 331; on history, 66, 313—*Principles of Sociology,* 319
Spengler, Oswald: 296, 309; on history, 40, 66
Spenser, Edmund, 662
Spinoza: 28, 53, 62, 203, 286, 307, 485, 513, 664; on history, 35; and 'higher criticism' of the Bible, 36; his determinism, 63; and Goethe, 272; on divine attributes, 513–514 —*De emendatione intellectu,* 31; *Short Treatise,* 513
Staël, Madame de, 660
Steele, Richard, 455
Steen, Jan, 208, 220, 222
Sterry, Peter, 15
Stoics: 307, 523, 524; on art, 148; Zenonian, theory of ideas, 487
Stumpf, Carl, 653
Sulzer, Johann Georg, 184
Supreme Being, the, cult of, 422
Swedenborg, Emmanuel: 671, 676; and Coleridge, 667–669; and Blake, 669–670; and Byron, 670
Sweetser, Moses, 134
Swinburne, Algernon Charles, 139n
Syllogism, the, Aristotle on, 27
Symmachus: and Ambrose, 535; and Prudentius, 536–537
Symposium on Ancient Chinese History, Ku Chieh-kang, 372–373

Tacitus, 52
Taine, Hippolyte Adolphe: 136, 404; on art, 283–309 *passim;* education of, 284–286 *passim;* and Catholicism, 286; and romanticism, 288–292 *passim,* 301; on history, 288–309 *passim;* and Darwin, 291; on Byron, 292–295 *passim;* on Burke, 293; on Shakespeare, 294; on human nature, 296; and Ruskin, 300; and Morris, 300; on the Renaissance, 300–303 *passim;* and Brunetière, 306–307 *passim;* and Bourget, 307; on liberalism, 307–308 *passim;* on the French Revolution, 308, 405, 406, 407—*De l'Intelligence,* 286; *Les Philosophes Français du XIXe Siècle,* 287; *Les Origines de la France Contemporaine,* 306, 308, 309
Tatarkiewicz W., on the humanistic sciences, 39
Tawney, R. H., 88
Taylor, A. E., on history, 50
Telemann, Georg Philipp, 258, 259
Tennyson, Alfred, 63, 673
Tertullian, 495, 517, 518, 521, 527, 530
Tess of the d'Urbervilles, T. Hardy, 461
Tetens, Johann Nicolas, 198
Thales, 28, 46
Theodoret of Cyprus, 532
Theology: natural, 25; and art, 93–126 *passim;* medieval, 156, 158; and philosophy, 485–514 *passim;* and Elizabethan medicine, 577–603 *passim;* in New England, 604–637. *See also* Anabaptists, Arminianism, Calvin, Catholicism, Christianity, Islam, Luther, Pietism, Protestantism, Puritans, Quakers, Reformation, Roman Catholic Church
Theophrastus, 27, 51–52
Theorie der Schönen Künste und Wissenschaften, F. Riedel, 200
Theory of Painting, The, J. Richardson, 186
Thomas Aquinas, Saint. *See* Aquinas, Thomas
Thoreau, Henry David: 673; and Rousseau, 426
Three Treatises . . . , J. Harris, 189, 192n
Thucydides, 65
Tiberius, 49
Tillyard, E. M. W., 13n
Titian, 217, 220

Tocqueville, Alexis de: 404; and the French Revolution, 405
Tolstoy, Leo: and Rousseau, 426; and Addams, 474
Tomé, Luca di, 112
Toussaint, 411
Toynbee, Arnold, 40
Tractatus de Laudibus Sanctissimae Annae, J. Tritenheim, 108, 109
Traherne, Thomas, 662
Traité du Beau, J. de Crousaz, 177, 182
Trajan, 49
Trattato dell' arte della pittura, G. Lomazzo, 129
Treasure of Euonymus, The, K. Gesner, 594–595
Treatise for the Artificiall Cure of Struma, W. Clowes, 584, 596, 597
Treatise of the Covenant of Grace, A, J. Ball, 608, 609
Treatise of the Disease Called Morbus Gallicus, W. Clowes, 583–584, 589
Treatise of the Pestilence, A, T. Phayre, 581
Trésor des Merveilles de Fontainbleau, Père Dan, 133
Trevor-Roper, H. R., 34
Trosman, Harry, 126n
Turner, J. M. W., 576
Tychonius, 525
Tylor, Edward, 319, 320, 331

Uffizi Gallery, 219
'Unit-ideas,' in Lovejoy's methodology, 24–25
Universities: medieval, 156–157, 165; in the Renaissance, 159
Universities of Europe in the Middle Ages, The, H. Rashdall, 573
Urinall of Physick, The, R. Recorde, 585
Utilitarianism, 297
Utopianism, 297

Van den Bos, Lambert, 220
Van den Vondel, Joost, on Rembrandt, 221–222

Van der Helst, Bartholomeus, 220
Van der Heyden, Jan, 208
Van Dyck, Anthony, 216
Van Gogh, Vincent, 211
Van Mander, Karel, 220
Varro, Marcus Terentius, 151, 154
Vasari, Giorgio: 122–142 *passim*, 163, 220, 303; on Da Vinci, 98
Vaughan, C. E., 421
Vaughan, Henry, 102, 103, 661
Vergil (Virgil), 127, 516, 536, 576
Vermeer, Jan, 208, 222
Vermische Philosophische Schriften, J. Sulzer, 198–200
Verrocchio, Andrea del, 113, 114, 122
Versuch einer Critischen Dichtkunst, J. Gottsched, 192
Vesalius, Andreas, 603
Veteribus Scriptoribus, De, Dionysius of Halicarnassus, 151
Vicissitude ou Variété des Choses de l'Univers, De la, L. Leroy, 133
Vico, Giovanni Battista: on history, 66; on poetry, 169
Vignon, Claude, 216
Villani, Filippo, 162
Vincent of Beauvais, 156
Vivaldi, Antonio, 247
Vives, Juan Luis, 168, 460, 464, 465
Voltaire: 33, 43, 179, 403, 404, 405, 414, 415, 425; on scholastic metaphysics, 38; on history, 313; on the French Revolution, 426
Vos, Jan, 220, 221
Vossius, G. J., 168–169

Wagner, Richard, 277, 279
Waller, Edmund, 390
Walsh, W. H., 71n
Walter, Gérard, 415
Webb, Daniel, 190
Weber, Max: 88; on religion, 328–332 *passim*; on China, 368; on India, 368—*The Protestant Ethic and the Spirit of Capitalism*, 328
Wheelwright, John, 621–622
Whitehead, Alfred North, on Plato, 485—*Science and the Modern World*, 559

Whitman, Walt, 673
Wilczynski, Jan Z., on Alberuni's alleged Darwinism, 37
William Blake, Middleton Murry, 669
Williams, Roger, 622
Winckelmann, Johann Joachim, 196
Windelband, Wilhelm, 71n, 73
Winthrop, John, 605, 606, 607, 620, 622, 623
Witte, Emanuel de, 208
Wohl, R. R., 126n

Wordsworth, William, 661, 673
Works, William Perkins, 608, 611
World's Leading Painters, The, G. B. Rose, 139
Wotton, William: 179; and Perrault, 185–186
Wyclif (Wycliffe), John, 562

Zeno, the Eleatic, 53, 270
Zola, Emile, 295
Zuccolo, 170

DATE DUE

OCT 15 '64			
NOV 12 '64			
OCT 6 1975			
GAYLORD			PRINTED IN U.S.A.